Dominic
Dos Santos

Mathematics *for*

3D Game Programming

and Computer Graphics

Second Edition

Mathematics *for*

3D Game Programming

and Computer Graphics

Second Edition

Eric Lengyel

CHARLES RIVER MEDIA, INC.
Hingham, Massachusetts

Editor: David Pallai
Production: Eric Lengyel
Cover Design: The Printed Image

CHARLES RIVER MEDIA, INC.
10 Downer Avenue
Hingham, Massachusetts 02043
781-740-0400
781-740-8816 (FAX)
info@charlesriver.com
www.charlesriver.com

This book is printed on acid-free paper.

Eric Lengyel. *Mathematics for 3D Game Programming and Computer Graphics, Second Edition.*
ISBN: 1-58450-277-0

Library of Congress Cataloging-in-Publication Data

Lengyel, Eric.
    Mathematics for 3D game programming & computer graphics / Eric Lengyel.—2nd ed.
      p. cm.
    ISBN 1-58450-277-0 (alk. paper)
    1. Computer games—Programming. 2. Three-dimensional display systems—Mathematics.
  3. Computer graphics—Mathematics. I. Title.
  QA76.76.C672 L46 2003
  794.8'16693—dc22

                              2003019938

Printed in the United States of America
03 7 6 5 4 3 2 First Edition

CHARLES RIVER MEDIA titles are available for site license or bulk purchase by institutions, user groups, corporations, etc. For additional information, please contact the Special Sales Department at 781-740-0400.

Contents

Preface

This book illustrates mathematical techniques that a software engineer would need to develop a professional-quality 3D graphics engine. Particular attention is paid to the derivation of key results in order to provide a complete exposition of the subject and to encourage a deep understanding of the mechanics behind the mathematical tools used by game programmers.

Most of the material in this book is presented in a manner that is independent of the underlying 3D graphics system used to render images. We assume that the reader is familiar with the basic concepts needed to use a 3D graphics library and understands how models are constructed out of vertices and polygons. However, the book begins with a short review of the rendering pipeline as it is implemented in the OpenGL library. When it becomes necessary to discuss a topic in the context of a 3D graphics library, OpenGL is the one that we choose due to its availability across multiple platforms.

Code examples in this book are presented in standard C++. In various places, we also demonstrate certain techniques using vertex programs and fragment programs. These programs use the assembly-like vector instruction sets exposed by the `GL_ARB_vertex_program` and `GL_ARB_fragment_program` extensions to OpenGL.

Each chapter ends with a summary of the important equations and formulas derived within the text. The summary is intended to serve as a reference tool so that the reader is not required to wade through long discussions of the subject matter in order to find a single result. There are also several exercises at the end of each chapter. Answers to exercises requiring a calculation are given in Appendix E.

What's New in the Second Edition

In the second edition, four new chapters have been added, and original chapters have been updated to reflect advances in 3D rendering technology. First, a preliminary chapter about the rendering pipeline provides a review of the tasks performed by modern graphics hardware and establishes the context in which later rendering discussions occur. Next, the presentation of the stencil shadow technique appearing in the first edition has been greatly expanded and now occupies its own chapter. Finally, two chapters covering entirely new material have been appended to the book. The first of these chapters discusses numerical methods useful for solving problems that arise in the course of 3D graphics engine development. The second chapter describes several classes of parametric curves and surfaces.

Many discussions have been updated to reflect advances in graphics technology. In Chapter 6, the original implementation of the Cook-Torrance illumination model has been replaced with vertex and fragment programs that make use of newer hardware capabilities. As already mentioned, the discussion of the stencil shadow algorithm has been updated, and its implementation also takes advantage of recently created OpenGL extensions. Other more minor updates have been made throughout the book.

Contents Overview

Chapter 0: The Rendering Pipeline. This is a preliminary chapter that provides an overview of the rendering pipeline in the context of the OpenGL library. Many of the topics mentioned in this chapter are examined in higher detail elsewhere in the book, so mathematical discussions are intentionally avoided here.

Chapter 1: Vectors. This chapter begins the mathematical portion of the book with a thorough review of vector quantities and their properties. Vectors are of fundamental importance in the study of 3D computer graphics, and we make extensive use of operations such as the dot product and cross product throughout the book.

Chapter 2: Matrices. An understanding of matrices is another basic necessity of 3D game programming. This chapter discusses elementary concepts such as matrix representation of linear systems as well as more advanced topics, including eigenvectors and diagonalization, which are required later in the book.

Chapter 3: Transforms. In Chapter 3, we investigate matrices as a tool for performing transformations such as translations, rotations, and scales. We introduce the concept of four-dimensional homogeneous coordinates, which are widely used in 3D graphics systems to move between different coordinate spaces. We also study the properties of quaternions and their usefulness as a transformation tool.

Chapter 4: 3D Engine Geometry. It is at this point that we begin to see material presented in the first three chapters applied to practical applications in 3D game programming and computer graphics. After analyzing lines and planes in 3D space, we introduce the view frustum and its relationship to the virtual camera. This chapter includes topics such as field of view, perspective-correct interpolation, and projection matrices.

Chapter 5: Ray Tracing. Ray tracing methods are useful in many areas of game programming, including light map generation, line-of-sight determination, and collision detection. This chapter begins with analytical and numerical root-finding techniques, and then presents methods for intersecting rays with common geometrical objects. Finally, calculation of reflection and refraction vectors is discussed.

Chapter 6: Illumination. Chapter 6 discusses a wide range of topics related to illumination and shading methods. We begin with an enumeration of the different types of light sources and then proceed to simple reflection models. Later, we inspect methods for adding detail to rendered surfaces using texture maps, gloss maps, and bump maps. The chapter closes with a detailed explanation of the Cook-Torrance physical illumination model.

Chapter 7: Visibility Determination. The performance of a 3D engine is heavily dependent on its ability to determine what parts of a scene are visible. This chapter presents methods for constructing various types of bounding volumes and subsequently testing their visibility against the view frustum. Large-scale visibility determination enabled through spatial partitioning and the use of portal systems is also examined.

Chapter 8: Collision Detection. Collision detection is necessary for interaction between different objects in a game universe. This chapter presents general methods for determining whether moving objects collide with the static environment and whether they collide with each other.

Chapter 9: Polygonal Techniques. Chapter 9 presents several techniques involving the manipulation of polygonal models. The first topic covered is decal application to arbitrary surfaces and includes a related method for performing vertex depth offset. Other topics include billboarding techniques used for various special effects, a polygon reduction technique, T-junction elimination, and polygon triangulation.

Chapter 10: Shadows. This chapter contains an extensive investigation of the stencil shadow algorithm. The theoretical basis of the algorithm is examined, and details of the engineering techniques necessary for a robust implementation are presented in detail.

Chapter 11: Linear Physics. At this point in the book, we begin a two-chapter survey of various topics in classical physics that pertain to the motion that objects are likely to exhibit in a 3D game. Chapter 11 begins with a discussion of position functions as solutions to second-order differential equations. We then investigate projectile motion both through empty space and through a resistive medium, and close with a look at frictional forces.

Chapter 12: Rotational Physics. Chapter 12 continues the treatment of physics with a rather advanced exposition on rotation. We first study the forces experienced by an object in a rotating environment. Next, we examine rigid body motion and derive the relationship between angular velocity and angular momentum through the inertia tensor. Also included is a discussion of the oscillatory motion exhibited by springs and pendulums.

Chapter 13: Fluid Simulation. We continue with the theme of physical simulation by presenting a physical model for fluid motion based on the two-dimensional wave equation. We develop a method for evaluating the positions of the vertices on a regular grid representing the surface of a fluid and discuss the conditions necessary for stability.

Chapter 14: Numerical Methods. In this chapter, we examine numerical techniques for solving three particular types of problems. We first discuss effective methods for finding the solutions to linear systems of any size. Next, we present an iterative technique for determining the eigenvalues and eigenvectors of a 3×3 symmetric matrix. Finally, we study methods for approximating the solutions to ordinary differential equations.

Chapter 15: Curves and Surfaces. The book finishes with an examination of a broad variety of cubic curves, include Bézier curves and B-splines. We also discuss how concepts pertaining to two-dimensional curves are extended to three-dimensional surfaces.

Appendix A: Complex Numbers. Although not used extensively, complex numbers do appear in a few places in the text. Appendix A reviews the concept of complex numbers and discusses the properties that are used elsewhere in the book.

Appendix B: Trigonometry Reference. Appendix B reviews the trigonometric functions and quickly derives many formulas and identities that are used throughout this book.

Appendix C: Coordinate Systems. Appendix C provides a brief overview of Cartesian coordinates, cylindrical coordinates, and spherical coordinates. These coordinate systems appear in several places throughout the book, but are used most extensively in Chapter 11.

Appendix D: Taylor Series. The Taylor series of various functions are employed in a number of places throughout the book. Appendix D derives the Taylor series and reviews power series representations for many common functions.

Appendix E: Answers to Exercises. This appendix contains the answer to every exercise in the book whose solution can represented by a mathematical expression.

Notational Conventions

We have been careful to use consistent notations throughout this book. Scalar quantities are always represented by italic Roman or Greek letters. Vectors, matrices, and quaternions are always represented by boldface letters. A single component of a vector, matrix, or quaternion is a scalar quantity, so it is italic. For example, the x component of the vector $\mathbf{v}$ is written v_x. These conventions and other notational standards used throughout the book are summarized in the following table.

Quantity/Operation	Notation/Examples
Scalars	Italic letters: x, t, A, α, ω
Angles	Italic Greek letters: θ, φ, α
Vectors	Boldface letters: $\mathbf{V}, \mathbf{P}, \mathbf{x}, \boldsymbol{\omega}$
Quaternions	Boldface letters: $\mathbf{q}, \mathbf{q}_1, \mathbf{q}_2$
Matrices	Boldface letters: $\mathbf{M}, \mathbf{P}$
RGB Colors	Script letters: $\mathcal{A}, \mathcal{B}, \mathcal{C}, \varrho$
Magnitude of a vector	Double bar: $\|\mathbf{P}\|$
Conjugate of a complex number z or a quaternion $\mathbf{q}$	Overbar: $\bar{z}, \bar{\mathbf{q}}$
Transpose of a matrix	Superscript T: $\mathbf{M}^{\mathrm{T}}$
Determinant of a matrix	$\det \mathbf{M}$ or single bars: $|\mathbf{M}|$
Time derivative	Dot notation: $\dfrac{d}{dt}\mathbf{x}(t) = \dot{\mathbf{x}}(t)$
Binomial coefficient	$\dbinom{n}{k} = \dfrac{n!}{k!(n-k)!}$
Floor of x	$\lfloor x \rfloor$
Ceiling of x	$\lceil x \rceil$
Fractional part of x	$\mathrm{frac}(x)$
Sign of x	$\mathrm{sgn}(x) = \begin{cases} 1, & \text{if } x > 0 \\ 0, & \text{if } x = 0 \\ -1, & \text{if } x < 0 \end{cases}$
Closed interval	$[a,b] = \{x \mid a \le x \le b\}$
Open interval	$(a,b) = \{x \mid a < x < b\}$
Interval closed at one end and open at the other end	$[a,b) = \{x \mid a \le x < b\}$ $(a,b] = \{x \mid a < x \le b\}$
Set of real numbers	$\mathbb{R}$
Set of complex numbers	$\mathbb{C}$
Set of quaternions	$\mathbb{H}$

Chapter **0**

The Rendering Pipeline

This chapter provides a preliminary review of the rendering pipeline. It covers general functions, such as vertex transformation and primitive rasterization, which are performed by modern 3D graphics hardware. Readers who are familiar with these concepts may safely skip ahead. We intentionally avoid mathematical discussions in this chapter and instead provide pointers to other parts of the book where each particular portion of the rendering pipeline is examined in greater detail.

0.1 Graphics Processors

A typical scene that is to be rendered as 3D graphics is composed of many separate objects. The geometrical forms of these objects are each represented by a set of vertices and a particular type of *graphics primitive* that indicates how the vertices are connected to produce a shape. Figure 0.1 illustrates the ten types of graphics primitive defined by the OpenGL library. Graphics hardware is capable of rendering a set of individual points, a series of line segments, or a group of filled polygons. Most of the time, the surface of a 3D model is represented by a list of triangles, each of which references three points in a list of vertices.

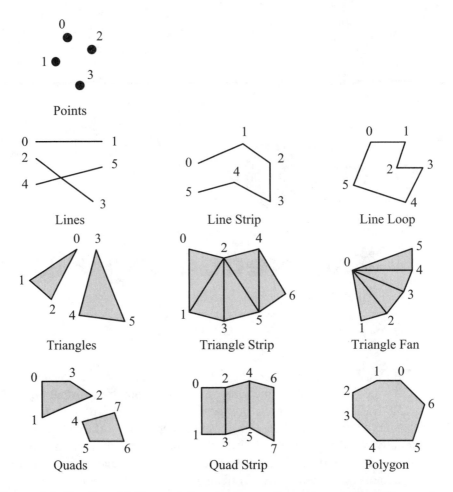

Figure 0.1 The OpenGL library defines ten types of graphics primitive. The numbers indicate the order in which the vertices are specified for each primitive type.

The usual modern 3D graphics board possesses a dedicated Graphics Processing Unit (GPU) that executes instructions independently of the Central Processing Unit (CPU). The CPU sends rendering commands to the GPU, which then performs the rendering operations while the CPU continues with other tasks. This is called *asynchronous operation*. When geometrical information is submitted to a rendering library such as OpenGL, the function calls used to request the rendering operations typically return a significant amount of time before the GPU has finished rendering the graphics. The lag time between the submission of a rendering command and the completion of the rendering operation does not normally cause problems, but there are cases when the time at which drawing completes needs to be known. There exist OpenGL extensions that allow the program run-ning on the CPU to determine when a particular set of rendering commands have finished executing on the GPU. Such synchronization has the tendency to slow down a 3D graphics application, so it is usually avoided whenever possible if performance is important.

An application communicates with the GPU by sending commands to a ren-dering library, such as OpenGL, which in turn sends commands to a *driver* that knows how to speak to the GPU in its native language. The interface to OpenGL is called a *Hardware Abstraction Layer* (HAL) because it exposes a common set of functions that can be used to render a scene on any graphics hardware that supports the OpenGL architecture. The driver translates the OpenGL function calls into code that the GPU can understand. A 3D graphics driver usually im-plements OpenGL functions directly to minimize the overhead of issuing render-ing commands. The block diagram shown in Figure 0.2 illustrates the communications that take place between the CPU and GPU.

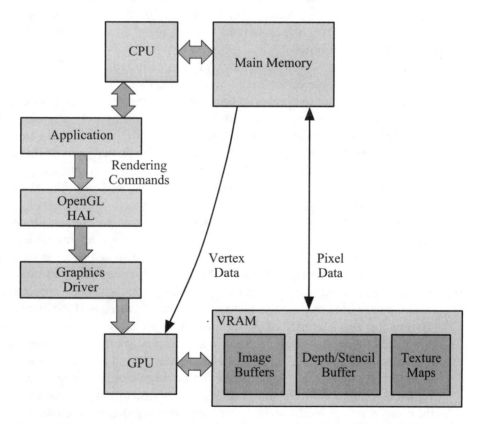

Figure 0.2 The communications that take place between the CPU and GPU.

A 3D graphics board has its own memory core, which is commonly called VRAM (*Video Random Access Memory*). The GPU may store any information in VRAM, but there are several types of data that can almost always be found in the graphics board's memory when a 3D graphics application is running. Most importantly, VRAM contains the front and back *image buffers*. The front image buffer contains the exact pixel data that is visible in the viewport. The *viewport* is the area of the display containing the rendered image and may be a subregion of a window, the entire contents of a window, or the full area of the display. The back image buffer is the location to which the GPU actually renders a scene. The back image buffer is not visible and exists so that a scene can be rendered in its entirety before being shown to the user. Once an image has been completely rendered, the front and back image buffers are exchanged. This operation is called a *buffer swap* and can be performed either by changing the memory address that represents the base of the visible image buffer or by copying the contents of the back image buffer to the front image buffer. The buffer swap is often synchronized with the refresh frequency of the display to avoid an artifact known as *tearing*. Tearing occurs when a buffer swap is performed during the display refresh interval, causing the upper and lower parts of a viewport to show data from different image buffers.

Also stored in VRAM is a block of data called the *depth buffer* or *z-buffer*. The depth buffer stores, for every pixel in the image buffer, a value that represents how far away the pixel is or how deep the pixel lies in the image. The depth buffer is used to perform hidden surface elimination by only allowing a pixel to be drawn if its depth is less than the depth of the pixel already in the image buffer. Depth is measured as the distance from the virtual camera through which we observe the scene being rendered. The name *z*-buffer comes from the convention that the *z*-axis points directly out of the display screen in the camera's local coordinate system. (See Section 4.3.)

An application may request that a *stencil buffer* be created along with the image buffers and the depth buffer. The stencil buffer contains an integer mask for each pixel in the image buffer that can be used to enable or disable drawing on a per-pixel basis. The operations that can be performed in the stencil buffer are described in Section 0.3, later in this chapter. An advanced application of the stencil buffer used to generate real-time shadows is discussed in Chapter 10.

For the vast majority of 3D rendering applications, the usage of VRAM is dominated by *texture maps*. Texture maps are images that are applied to the surface of an object to give it greater visual detail. In advanced rendering applications, texture maps may contain information other than a simple pixel image. For instance, a *bump map* contains vectors that represent varying slopes at different locations on an object's surface. Texture mapping details, including the process of bump mapping, are discussed in detail in Chapter 6.

0.2 Vertex Transformation

Geometrical data is passed to the graphics hardware in the context of a three-dimensional space. One of the jobs performed by the graphics hardware is to transform this data into geometry that can be drawn into a two-dimensional viewport. There are several different coordinate systems associated with the rendering pipeline—their relationships are shown in Figure 0.3. The vertices of a model are typically stored in *object space*, a coordinate system that is local to the particular model and used only by that model. The position and orientation of each model are often stored in *world space*, a global coordinate system that ties all of the object spaces together. Before an object can be rendered, its vertices must be transformed into *camera space* (also called *eye space*), the space in which the *x* and *y* axes are aligned to the display and the *z*-axis is parallel to the viewing direction. (See Section 4.3.) It is possible to transform vertices from object space directly into camera space by concatenating the matrices representing the transformations from object space to world space and from world space to camera space. The product of these transformations is called the *model-view* transformation.

   Once a model's vertices have been transformed into camera space, they undergo a *projection* transformation that has the effect of applying perspective so that geometry becomes smaller as the distance from the camera increases. (Projections are discussed in Section 4.5.) The projection is performed in four-dimensional *homogeneous coordinates*, described in Section 3.4, and the space in which the vertices exist after projection is called *homogeneous clip space*. Homogeneous clip space is so named because it is in this space that graphics primitives are clipped to the boundaries of the visible region of the scene, ensuring that no attempt is made to render any part of a primitive that falls outside the viewport.

   In homogeneous clip space, vertices have *normalized device coordinates*. The term *normalized* pertains to the fact that the *x*-, *y*-, and *z*-coordinates of each vertex fall in the range $[-1,1]$, but reflect the final positions in which they will appear in the viewport. The vertices must undergo one more transformation, called the *viewport transformation*, that maps the normalized coordinates to the actual range of pixel coordinates covered by the viewport. The *z*-coordinate is usually mapped to the floating-point range $[0,1]$, but this is subsequently scaled to the integer range corresponding to the number of bits per pixel utilized by the depth buffer. After the viewport transformation, vertex positions are said to lie in *window space*.

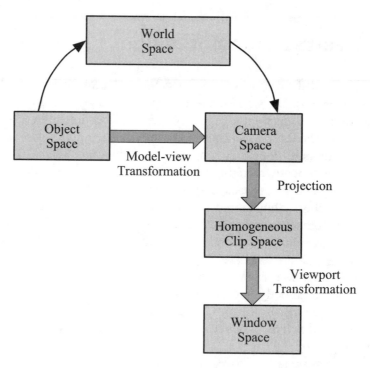

Figure 0.3 The coordinate spaces appearing in the rendering pipeline. Vertex positions are submitted to the graphics library in object space and are eventually transformed into window space for primitive rasterization.

A graphics processor usually performs several per-vertex calculations in addition to the transformation from object space to window space. For instance, the OpenGL lighting model determines the color and intensity of light reaching each vertex and then calculates how much of that is reflected toward the camera. The reflected color assigned to each vertex is interpolated over the area of a graphics primitive in the manner described in Section 4.4.2. This process is called *per-vertex lighting*. More-advanced graphics applications may perform *per-pixel lighting* to achieve highly detailed lighting interactions at every pixel covered by a graphics primitive. Per-vertex and per-pixel lighting are discussed in Sections 6.7 and 6.8.

Each vertex may also carry with it one or more sets of *texture coordinates*. Texture coordinates may be explicitly specified by an application or automatically generated by the GPU. When a graphics primitive is rendered, the texture coordinates are interpolated over the area of the primitive and used to look up colors in a texture map. These colors are then combined with other interpolated data at each pixel to determine the final color that appears in the viewport.

0.3 Rasterization and Fragment Operations

Once a model's vertices have been clipped and transformed into window space, the GPU must determine what pixels in the viewport are covered by each graphics primitive. The process of filling in the horizontal spans of pixels belonging to a primitive is called *rasterization*. The GPU calculates the depth, interpolated vertex colors, and interpolated texture coordinates for each pixel. This information, combined with the location of the pixel itself, is called a *fragment*.

The process through which a graphics primitive is converted to a set of fragments is illustrated in Figure 0.4. An application may specify that *face culling* be performed as the first stage of this process. Face culling applies only to polygonal graphics primitives and removes either the polygons that are facing away from the camera or those that are facing toward the camera. Ordinarily, face culling is employed as an optimization that skips polygons facing away from the camera (*backfacing* polygons) since they correspond to the unseen far side of a model.

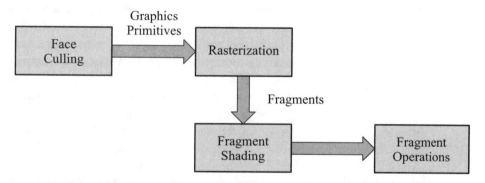

Figure 0.4 A graphics primitive is converted to a set of fragments during rasterization. After shading, fragments undergo the operations shown in Figure 0.5.

A graphics application specifies how the fragment data is used to determine the final color and final depth of each pixel during rasterization. This process is called *fragment shading* or *pixel shading*. The final color may simply be given by the product of an interpolated vertex color and a value fetched from a texture map, or it may be the result of a complex per-pixel lighting calculation. The final depth is ordinarily just the unaltered interpolated depth, but advanced 3D graphics hardware allows an application to replace the depth with the result of an arbitrary calculation.

Figure 0.5 illustrates the operations performed for each fragment generated during rasterization. Most of these operations determine whether a fragment should be drawn to the viewport or discarded altogether. Although these operations occur logically after fragment shading, most GPUs perform as many tests as possible before performing fragment shading calculations to avoid spending time figuring out the colors of fragments that will ultimately be discarded.

The first fragment operation performed, and the only one that cannot be disabled, is the *pixel ownership test*. The pixel ownership test simply determines whether a fragment lies in the region of the viewport that is currently visible on the display. A possible reason that the pixel ownership test fails is that another window is obscuring a portion of the viewport. In this case, fragments falling behind the obscuring window are not drawn.

Next, the *scissor test* is performed. An application may specify a rectangle in the viewport, called the *scissor rectangle*, to which rendering should be restricted. Any fragments falling outside the scissor rectangle are discarded. A particular application of the scissor rectangle in the context of the stencil shadow algorithm is discussed in Section 10.7.

If the scissor test passes, a fragment undergoes the *alpha test*. When the final color of a fragment is calculated, an application may also calculate an *alpha* value that usually represents the degree of transparency associated with the fragment. The alpha test compares the final alpha value of a fragment to a constant value that is preset by the application. The application specifies what relationship between the two values (such as less than, greater than, or equal to) causes the test to pass. If the relationship is not satisfied, then the fragment is discarded.

After the alpha test passes, a fragment moves on to the *stencil test*. The stencil test reads the value stored in the stencil buffer at a fragment's location and compares it to a value previously specified by the application. The stencil test passes only if a specific relationship is satisfied (e.g., the stencil value is equal to a particular value); otherwise, the stencil test fails, and the fragment is discarded. An application is able to specify actions to be taken in the stencil buffer when the stencil test passes or fails. Additionally, if the stencil test passes, the value in the stencil buffer may be affected in a way that depends on the result of the depth test (described next). For instance, an application may choose to increment the value in the stencil buffer if the stencil test passes and the depth test fails. This functionality is used extensively by the shadow-rendering technique described in Chapter 10.

The final test undergone by a fragment is the *depth test*. The depth test compares the final depth associated with a fragment to the value currently residing in the depth buffer. If the fragment's depth does not satisfy an application-specified relationship with the value in the depth buffer, then the fragment is discarded. Normally, the depth test is configured so that a fragment passes the depth test only if its depth is less than or equal to the value in the depth buffer. When the depth test passes, the depth buffer is updated with the depth of the fragment to facilitate hidden surface removal for subsequently rendered primitives.

Once the pixel ownership test, scissor test, alpha test, stencil test, and depth test have all passed, a fragment's final color is blended into the image buffer. The *blending* operation calculates a new color by combining the fragment's final color and the color already stored in the image buffer at the fragment's location. The fragment's alpha value and the alpha value stored in the image buffer may also be used to determine the color that ultimately appears in the viewport. The blending operation may be configured to simply replace the previous color in the image buffer, or it may produce special visual effects such as transparency.

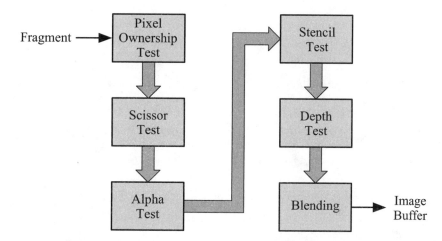

Figure 0.5 Operations performed before a fragment is written to the image buffer.

Chapter **1**

Vectors

Vectors are of fundamental importance in any 3D game engine. They are used to represent points in space, such as the locations of objects in a game or the vertices of a triangle mesh. They are also used to represent spatial directions, such as the orientation of the camera or the surface normals of a triangle mesh. Understanding how to manipulate vectors is an essential skill of the successful 3D programmer.

Throughout this book, we encounter vectors of various types, usually representing two-dimensional, three-dimensional, or four-dimensional quantities. For now, we make no distinction between vectors representing points and vectors representing directions, nor do we concern ourselves with how vectors are transformed from one coordinate system to another. These topics are extremely important in 3D engine development, however, and are addressed in Chapter 3.

1.1 Vector Properties

We assume that the reader possesses a basic understanding of vectors, but it is beneficial to provide a quick review of properties that are used extensively throughout this book. Although more abstract definitions are possible, we usually restrict ourselves to vectors defined by n-tuples of real numbers, where n is typically 2, 3, or 4. An n-dimensional vector $\mathbf{V}$ can be written as

$$\mathbf{V} = \langle V_1, V_2, \ldots, V_n \rangle, \tag{1.1}$$

where the numbers V_i are called the *components* of the vector $\mathbf{V}$. We have used numbered subscripts here, but the components will usually be labeled with the name of the axis to which they correspond. For instance, the components of a three-dimensional point $\mathbf{P}$ could be written as P_x, P_y, and P_z.

The vector $\mathbf{V}$ in Equation (1.1) may also be represented by a matrix having a single column and n rows:

$$\mathbf{V} = \begin{bmatrix} V_1 \\ V_2 \\ \vdots \\ V_n \end{bmatrix}. \tag{1.2}$$

We treat this column vector as having a meaning identical to that of the comma-separated list of components written in Equation (1.1). Vectors are normally expressed in these forms, but we sometimes need to express vectors as a matrix consisting of a single row and n columns. We write row vectors as the transpose of their corresponding column vectors:

$$\mathbf{V}^{\mathrm{T}} = \begin{bmatrix} V_1 & V_2 & \cdots & V_n \end{bmatrix}. \tag{1.3}$$

A vector may be multiplied by a scalar to produce a new vector whose components retain the same relative proportions. The product of a scalar a and a vector $\mathbf{V}$ is defined as

$$a\mathbf{V} = \mathbf{V}a = \langle aV_1, aV_2, \ldots, aV_n \rangle. \tag{1.4}$$

In the case that $a = -1$, we use the slightly simplified notation $-\mathbf{V}$ to represent the negation of the vector $\mathbf{V}$.

Vectors add and subtract componentwise. Thus, given two vectors $\mathbf{P}$ and $\mathbf{Q}$, we define the sum $\mathbf{P} + \mathbf{Q}$ as

$$\mathbf{P} + \mathbf{Q} = \langle P_1 + Q_1, P_2 + Q_2, \ldots, P_n + Q_n \rangle. \tag{1.5}$$

The difference between two vectors, written $\mathbf{P} - \mathbf{Q}$, is really just a notational simplification of the sum $\mathbf{P} + (-\mathbf{Q})$.

With the above definitions in hand, we are now ready to examine some fundamental properties of vector arithmetic.

Theorem 1.1. Given any two scalars a and b, and any three vectors $\mathbf{P}$, $\mathbf{Q}$, and $\mathbf{R}$, the following properties hold.

(a) $\mathbf{P} + \mathbf{Q} = \mathbf{Q} + \mathbf{P}$

(b) $(\mathbf{P} + \mathbf{Q}) + \mathbf{R} = \mathbf{P} + (\mathbf{Q} + \mathbf{R})$

(c) $(ab)\mathbf{P} = a(b\mathbf{P})$

(d) $a(\mathbf{P} + \mathbf{Q}) = a\mathbf{P} + a\mathbf{Q}$

(e) $(a + b)\mathbf{P} = a\mathbf{P} + b\mathbf{P}$

Using the associative and commutative properties of the real numbers, these properties are easily verified through direct computation.

The *magnitude* of an n-dimensional vector $\mathbf{V}$ is a scalar denoted by $\|\mathbf{V}\|$ and is given by the formula

$$\|\mathbf{V}\| = \sqrt{\sum_{i=1}^{n} V_i^2} \,. \tag{1.6}$$

The magnitude of a vector is also sometimes called the *norm* or the *length* of a vector. A vector having a magnitude of exactly one is said to have *unit length*, or may simply be called a *unit vector*. When $\mathbf{V}$ represents a three-dimensional point or direction, Equation (1.6) can be written as

$$\|\mathbf{V}\| = \sqrt{V_x^2 + V_y^2 + V_z^2} \,. \tag{1.7}$$

A vector $\mathbf{V}$ having at least one nonzero component can be resized to unit length through multiplication by $1/\|\mathbf{V}\|$. This operation is called *normalization* and is used often in 3D graphics. It should be noted that the term *to normalize* is in no way related to the term *normal vector*, which refers to a vector that is perpendicular to a surface at a particular point.

The magnitude function given in Equation (1.6) obeys the following rules.

Theorem 1.2. Given any scalar a and any two vectors $\mathbf{P}$ and $\mathbf{Q}$, the following properties hold.

(a) $\|\mathbf{P}\| \geq 0$

(b) $\|\mathbf{P}\| = 0$ if and only if $\mathbf{P} = \langle 0, 0, \ldots, 0 \rangle$

(c) $\|a\mathbf{P}\| = |a|\|\mathbf{P}\|$

(d) $\|\mathbf{P} + \mathbf{Q}\| \leq \|\mathbf{P}\| + \|\mathbf{Q}\|$

Proof.

(a) This follows from the fact that the radicand in Equation (1.6) is a sum of squares, which cannot be less than zero.

(b) Suppose that $\mathbf{P} = \langle 0, 0, \ldots, 0 \rangle$. Then the radicand in Equation (1.6) evaluates to zero, so $\|\mathbf{P}\| = 0$. Conversely, if we assume $\|\mathbf{P}\| = 0$, then each component of $\mathbf{P}$ must be zero, since otherwise the sum in Equation (1.6) would be a positive number.

(c) Evaluating Equation (1.6), we have the following.

$$\|a\mathbf{P}\| = \sqrt{\sum_{i=1}^{n} a^2 P_i^2}$$

$$= \sqrt{a^2 \sum_{i=1}^{n} P_i^2}$$

$$= |a| \sqrt{\sum_{i=1}^{n} P_i^2}$$

$$= |a| \|\mathbf{P}\| \tag{1.8}$$

(d) This is known as the *triangle inequality* since a geometric proof can be given if we treat $\mathbf{P}$ and $\mathbf{Q}$ as two sides of a triangle. As shown in Figure 1.1, $\mathbf{P} + \mathbf{Q}$ forms the third side of the triangle, which cannot have a length greater than the sum of the other two sides. ∎

We will be able to give an algebraic proof of the triangle inequality after introducing the dot product in the next section.

1.2 Dot Products

The *dot product* of two vectors, also known as the *scalar product* or *inner product*, is one of the most heavily used operations in 3D graphics because it supplies a measure of the difference between the directions in which the two vectors point.

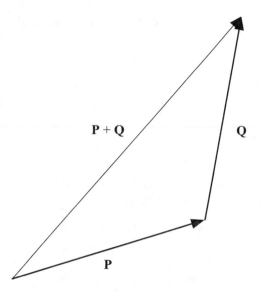

Figure 1.1 The triangle inequality states that $\|\mathbf{P} + \mathbf{Q}\| \leq \|\mathbf{P}\| + \|\mathbf{Q}\|$. Geometrically, this follows from the fact that the length of one side of a triangle can be no longer than the sum of the lengths of the other two sides.

Definition 1.3. The dot product of two n-dimensional vectors $\mathbf{P}$ and $\mathbf{Q}$, written as $\mathbf{P} \cdot \mathbf{Q}$, is the scalar quantity given by the formula

$$\mathbf{P} \cdot \mathbf{Q} = \sum_{i=1}^{n} P_i Q_i. \tag{1.9}$$

This definition states that the dot product of two vectors is given by the sum of the products of each component. In three dimensions, we have

$$\mathbf{P} \cdot \mathbf{Q} = P_x Q_x + P_y Q_y + P_z Q_z. \tag{1.10}$$

The dot product $\mathbf{P} \cdot \mathbf{Q}$ may also be expressed as the matrix product

$$\mathbf{P}^{\mathrm{T}} \mathbf{Q} = \begin{bmatrix} P_1 & P_2 & \cdots & P_n \end{bmatrix} \begin{bmatrix} Q_1 \\ Q_2 \\ \vdots \\ Q_n \end{bmatrix}, \tag{1.11}$$

which yields a 1×1 matrix (i.e., a scalar) whose single entry is equal to the sum in Equation (1.9).

Now for an important theorem that reveals the ubiquitous utility of the dot product.

> **Theorem 1.4.** Given two n-dimensional vectors $\mathbf{P}$ and $\mathbf{Q}$, the dot product $\mathbf{P} \cdot \mathbf{Q}$ satisfies the equation
>
> $$\mathbf{P} \cdot \mathbf{Q} = \|\mathbf{P}\| \|\mathbf{Q}\| \cos \alpha, \tag{1.12}$$
>
> where α is the planar angle between the lines connecting the origin to the points represented by $\mathbf{P}$ and $\mathbf{Q}$.
>
> **Proof.** Let α be the angle between the vectors $\mathbf{P}$ and $\mathbf{Q}$, as shown in Figure 1.2. By the law of cosines (see Appendix B, Section B.6), we know
>
> $$\|\mathbf{P} - \mathbf{Q}\|^2 = \|\mathbf{P}\|^2 + \|\mathbf{Q}\|^2 - 2\|\mathbf{P}\| \|\mathbf{Q}\| \cos \alpha. \tag{1.13}$$
>
> This expands to
>
> $$\sum_{i=1}^{n} (P_i - Q_i)^2 = \sum_{i=1}^{n} P_i^2 + \sum_{i=1}^{n} Q_i^2 - 2\|\mathbf{P}\| \|\mathbf{Q}\| \cos \alpha. \tag{1.14}$$
>
> All the P_i^2 and Q_i^2 terms cancel, and we are left with
>
> $$\sum_{i=1}^{n} -2P_i Q_i = -2\|\mathbf{P}\| \|\mathbf{Q}\| \cos \alpha. \tag{1.15}$$
>
> Dividing both sides by -2 gives us the desired result. ∎

A couple of important facts follow immediately from Theorem 1.4. The first is that two vectors $\mathbf{P}$ and $\mathbf{Q}$ are perpendicular if and only if $\mathbf{P} \cdot \mathbf{Q} = 0$. This follows from the fact that the cosine function is zero at an angle of 90 degrees. Vectors whose dot product yields zero are called *orthogonal*. We define the *zero vector*, $\mathbf{0} \equiv \langle 0, 0, \ldots, 0 \rangle$, to be orthogonal to every vector $\mathbf{P}$, since $\mathbf{0} \cdot \mathbf{P}$ always equals zero.

The second fact is that the sign of the dot product tells us how close two vectors are to pointing in the same direction. Referring to Figure 1.3, we can consider the plane passing through the origin and perpendicular to a vector $\mathbf{P}$. Any vector lying on the same side of the plane as $\mathbf{P}$ yields a positive dot product with $\mathbf{P}$, and any vector lying on the opposite side of the plane from $\mathbf{P}$ yields a negative dot product with $\mathbf{P}$.

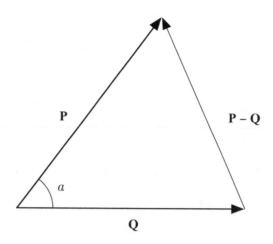

Figure 1.2 The dot product is related to the angle between two vectors by the equation $\mathbf{P}\cdot\mathbf{Q} = \|\mathbf{P}\|\|\mathbf{Q}\|\cos\alpha$.

Several additional properties of the dot product are presented by the following theorem.

Theorem 1.5. Given any scalar a and any three vectors $\mathbf{P}$, $\mathbf{Q}$, and $\mathbf{R}$, the following properties hold.

(a) $\mathbf{P}\cdot\mathbf{Q} = \mathbf{Q}\cdot\mathbf{P}$

(b) $(a\mathbf{P})\cdot\mathbf{Q} = a(\mathbf{P}\cdot\mathbf{Q})$

(c) $\mathbf{P}\cdot(\mathbf{Q}+\mathbf{R}) = \mathbf{P}\cdot\mathbf{Q}+\mathbf{P}\cdot\mathbf{R}$

(d) $\mathbf{P}\cdot\mathbf{P} = \|\mathbf{P}\|^2$

(e) $|\mathbf{P}\cdot\mathbf{Q}| \leq \|\mathbf{P}\|\|\mathbf{Q}\|$

Proof. Parts (a), (b), and (c) are easily verified using the associative and commutative properties of the real numbers. Part (d) follows directly from the definition of $\|\mathbf{P}\|$ given in Equation (1.6) and the definition of the dot product given in Equation (1.9). Part (e) is implied by Theorem 1.4 since $|\cos\alpha|\leq 1$. ∎

We use the notation P^2 when we take the dot product of a vector $\mathbf{P}$ with itself. Thus, by part (d) of Theorem 1.5, we can say that $\mathbf{P}\cdot\mathbf{P}$, P^2, and $\|\mathbf{P}\|^2$ all have identical meanings. We use italics instead of boldface in the expression P^2 because it is a scalar quantity.

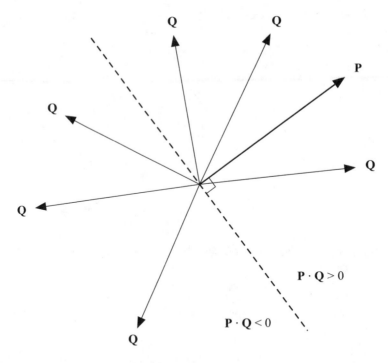

Figure 1.3 The sign of the dot product tells us whether two vectors lie on the same side or on opposite sides of a plane.

Part (e) of Theorem 1.5 is known as the *Cauchy-Schwarz inequality* and gives us a tool that we can use to provide the following algebraic proof of the triangle inequality.

Proof of Theorem 1.2(d). (Triangle Inequality) Beginning with $\|\mathbf{P}+\mathbf{Q}\|^2$, we can calculate

$$
\begin{aligned}
\|\mathbf{P}+\mathbf{Q}\|^2 &= (\mathbf{P}+\mathbf{Q})\cdot(\mathbf{P}+\mathbf{Q}) \\
&= \mathbf{P}^2 + \mathbf{Q}^2 + 2\mathbf{P}\cdot\mathbf{Q} \\
&\le \mathbf{P}^2 + \mathbf{Q}^2 + 2\|\mathbf{P}\|\|\mathbf{Q}\| \\
&= (\|\mathbf{P}\|+\|\mathbf{Q}\|)^2 ,
\end{aligned}
\tag{1.16}
$$

where Theorem 1.5(e) has been used to attain the inequality. Taking square roots, we arrive at the desired result. ■

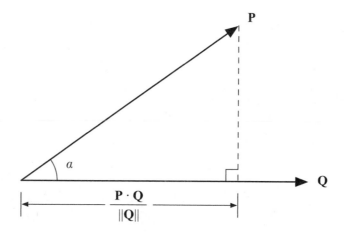

Figure 1.4 The length of the projection of the vector **P** onto the vector **Q** is given by **P**·**Q**/‖**Q**‖ because **P**·**Q** = ‖**P**‖‖**Q**‖cos α.

The situation often arises in which we need to decompose a vector **P** into components that are parallel and perpendicular to another vector **Q**. As shown in Figure 1.4, if we think of the vector **P** as the hypotenuse of a right triangle, then the perpendicular projection of **P** onto the vector **Q** produces the side adjacent to the angle α between **P** and **Q**.

Basic trigonometry tells us that the length of the side adjacent to α is given by ‖**P**‖cos α. Theorem 1.4 gives us a way to calculate the same quantity without knowing the angle α:

$$\|\mathbf{P}\|\cos\alpha = \frac{\mathbf{P}\cdot\mathbf{Q}}{\|\mathbf{Q}\|}. \tag{1.17}$$

To obtain a vector that has this length and is parallel to **Q**, we simply multiply by the unit vector **Q**/‖**Q**‖. We now have the following formula for the projection of **P** onto **Q**, which we denote by $\text{proj}_{\mathbf{Q}}\,\mathbf{P}$.

$$\text{proj}_{\mathbf{Q}}\,\mathbf{P} = \frac{\mathbf{P}\cdot\mathbf{Q}}{\|\mathbf{Q}\|^2}\mathbf{Q} \tag{1.18}$$

The perpendicular component of **P** with respect to **Q**, denoted by $\text{perp}_{\mathbf{Q}}\,\mathbf{P}$, is simply the vector left over when we subtract away the parallel component given by Equation (1.18) from the original vector **P**:

$$\text{perp}_Q \mathbf{P} = \mathbf{P} - \text{proj}_Q \mathbf{P}$$

$$= \mathbf{P} - \frac{\mathbf{P} \cdot \mathbf{Q}}{\|\mathbf{Q}\|^2} \mathbf{Q}. \tag{1.19}$$

The projection of $\mathbf{P}$ onto $\mathbf{Q}$ is a linear transformation of $\mathbf{P}$ and can thus be expressed as a matrix-vector product. In three dimensions, $\text{proj}_Q \mathbf{P}$ can be computed using the alternative formula

$$\text{proj}_Q \mathbf{P} = \frac{1}{\|\mathbf{Q}\|^2} \begin{bmatrix} Q_x^2 & Q_x Q_y & Q_x Q_z \\ Q_x Q_y & Q_y^2 & Q_y Q_z \\ Q_x Q_z & Q_y Q_z & Q_z^2 \end{bmatrix} \begin{bmatrix} P_x \\ P_y \\ P_z \end{bmatrix}. \tag{1.20}$$

1.3 Cross Products

The *cross product* of two three-dimensional vectors, also known as the *vector product*, returns a new vector that is perpendicular to both of the vectors being multiplied together. This property has many uses in computer graphics, one of which is a method for calculating a surface normal at a particular point given two distinct tangent vectors.

Definition 1.6. The cross product of two 3D vectors $\mathbf{P}$ and $\mathbf{Q}$, written as $\mathbf{P} \times \mathbf{Q}$, is a vector quantity given by the formula

$$\mathbf{P} \times \mathbf{Q} = \langle P_y Q_z - P_z Q_y, P_z Q_x - P_x Q_z, P_x Q_y - P_y Q_x \rangle. \tag{1.21}$$

A commonly used tool for remembering this formula is to calculate cross products by evaluating the pseudodeterminant

$$\mathbf{P} \times \mathbf{Q} = \begin{vmatrix} \mathbf{i} & \mathbf{j} & \mathbf{k} \\ P_x & P_y & P_z \\ Q_x & Q_y & Q_z \end{vmatrix}. \tag{1.22}$$

where $\mathbf{i}$, $\mathbf{j}$, and $\mathbf{k}$ are unit vectors parallel to the x-, y-, and z-axes:

$$\mathbf{i} = \langle 1,0,0 \rangle$$
$$\mathbf{j} = \langle 0,1,0 \rangle$$
$$\mathbf{k} = \langle 0,0,1 \rangle. \tag{1.23}$$

We call the right side of Equation (1.22) a pseudodeterminant because the top row of the matrix consists of vectors, whereas the remaining entries are scalars. Nevertheless, the usual method for evaluating a determinant does produce the correct value for the cross product, as shown below.

$$\begin{vmatrix} \mathbf{i} & \mathbf{j} & \mathbf{k} \\ P_x & P_y & P_z \\ Q_x & Q_y & Q_z \end{vmatrix} = \mathbf{i}\left(P_y Q_z - P_z Q_y\right) - \mathbf{j}\left(P_x Q_z - P_z Q_x\right) + \mathbf{k}\left(P_x Q_y - P_y Q_x\right) \tag{1.24}$$

The cross product $\mathbf{P} \times \mathbf{Q}$ can also be expressed as a linear transformation derived from $\mathbf{P}$ that operates on $\mathbf{Q}$ as follows.

$$\mathbf{P} \times \mathbf{Q} = \begin{bmatrix} 0 & -P_z & P_y \\ P_z & 0 & -P_x \\ -P_y & P_x & 0 \end{bmatrix} \begin{bmatrix} Q_x \\ Q_y \\ Q_z \end{bmatrix} \tag{1.25}$$

As mentioned previously, the cross product $\mathbf{P} \times \mathbf{Q}$ produces a vector that is perpendicular to both of the vectors $\mathbf{P}$ and $\mathbf{Q}$. This fact is summarized by the following theorem.

Theorem 1.7. Let $\mathbf{P}$ and $\mathbf{Q}$ be any two 3D vectors. Then $(\mathbf{P} \times \mathbf{Q}) \cdot \mathbf{P} = 0$ and $(\mathbf{P} \times \mathbf{Q}) \cdot \mathbf{Q} = 0$.

Proof. Applying the definitions of the cross product and the dot product, we have the following for $(\mathbf{P} \times \mathbf{Q}) \cdot \mathbf{P}$:

$$\begin{aligned} (\mathbf{P} \times \mathbf{Q}) \cdot \mathbf{P} &= \langle P_y Q_z - P_z Q_y, P_z Q_x - P_x Q_z, P_x Q_y - P_y Q_x \rangle \cdot \mathbf{P} \\ &= P_x P_y Q_z - P_x P_z Q_y + P_y P_z Q_x - P_x P_y Q_z + P_x P_z Q_y - P_y P_z Q_x \\ &= 0. \end{aligned} \tag{1.26}$$

The fact that $(\mathbf{P} \times \mathbf{Q}) \cdot \mathbf{Q} = 0$ is proven in a similar manner. ∎

The same result arises when we consider the fact that given any three 3D vectors **P**, **Q**, and **R**, the expression $(\mathbf{P} \times \mathbf{Q}) \cdot \mathbf{R}$ may be evaluated by calculating the determinant

$$(\mathbf{P} \times \mathbf{Q}) \cdot \mathbf{R} = \begin{vmatrix} P_x & P_y & P_z \\ Q_x & Q_y & Q_z \\ R_x & R_y & R_z \end{vmatrix}. \tag{1.27}$$

If any one of the vectors **P**, **Q**, or **R** can be expressed as a linear combination of the other two vectors, then this determinant evaluates to zero. This includes the cases in which $\mathbf{R} = \mathbf{P}$ or $\mathbf{R} = \mathbf{Q}$.

Like the dot product, the cross product has trigonometric significance.

Theorem 1.8. Given two 3D vectors **P** and **Q**, the cross product $\mathbf{P} \times \mathbf{Q}$ satisfies the equation

$$\|\mathbf{P} \times \mathbf{Q}\| = \|\mathbf{P}\|\|\mathbf{Q}\|\sin\alpha, \tag{1.28}$$

where α is the planar angle between the lines connecting the origin to the points represented by **P** and **Q**.

Proof. Squaring $\|\mathbf{P} \times \mathbf{Q}\|$, we have

$$\begin{aligned}
\|\mathbf{P} \times \mathbf{Q}\|^2 &= \|\langle P_y Q_z - P_z Q_y, P_z Q_x - P_x Q_z, P_x Q_y - P_y Q_x \rangle\|^2 \\
&= (P_y Q_z - P_z Q_y)^2 + (P_z Q_x - P_x Q_z)^2 + (P_x Q_y - P_y Q_x)^2 \\
&= (P_y^2 + P_z^2)Q_x^2 + (P_x^2 + P_z^2)Q_y^2 + (P_x^2 + P_y^2)Q_z^2 \\
&\quad - 2P_x Q_x P_y Q_y - 2P_x Q_x P_z Q_z - 2P_y Q_y P_z Q_z.
\end{aligned} \tag{1.29}$$

By adding and subtracting $P_x^2 Q_x^2 + P_y^2 Q_y^2 + P_z^2 Q_z^2$ on the right side of this equation, we can write

$$\begin{aligned}
\|\mathbf{P} \times \mathbf{Q}\|^2 &= (P_x^2 + P_y^2 + P_z^2)(Q_x^2 + Q_y^2 + Q_z^2) \\
&\quad - (P_x Q_x + P_y Q_y + P_z Q_z)^2 \\
&= \|\mathbf{P}\|^2\|\mathbf{Q}\|^2 - (\mathbf{P} \cdot \mathbf{Q})^2.
\end{aligned} \tag{1.30}$$

Replacing the dot product with the right side of Equation (1.12), we have

$$\|\mathbf{P} \times \mathbf{Q}\|^2 = \|\mathbf{P}\|^2 \|\mathbf{Q}\|^2 - \|\mathbf{P}\|^2 \|\mathbf{Q}\|^2 \cos^2 \alpha$$
$$= \|\mathbf{P}\|^2 \|\mathbf{Q}\|^2 (1 - \cos^2 \alpha)$$
$$= \|\mathbf{P}\|^2 \|\mathbf{Q}\|^2 \sin^2 \alpha. \tag{1.31}$$

Taking square roots proves the theorem. ∎

As shown in Figure 1.5, Theorem 1.8 demonstrates that the magnitude of the cross product $\mathbf{P} \times \mathbf{Q}$ is equal to the area of the parallelogram whose sides are formed by the vectors $\mathbf{P}$ and $\mathbf{Q}$. As a consequence, the area A of an arbitrary triangle whose vertices are given by the points $\mathbf{V}_1$, $\mathbf{V}_2$, and $\mathbf{V}_3$ can be calculated using the formula

$$A = \frac{1}{2} \|(\mathbf{V}_2 - \mathbf{V}_1) \times (\mathbf{V}_3 - \mathbf{V}_1)\|. \tag{1.32}$$

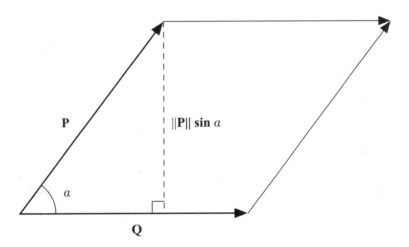

Figure 1.5 This parallelogram has base width $\|\mathbf{Q}\|$ and height $\|\mathbf{P}\| \sin \alpha$. The product of these two lengths is equal to $\|\mathbf{P} \times \mathbf{Q}\|$ and gives the area of the parallelogram.

We know that any nonzero result of the cross product must be perpendicular to the two vectors being multiplied together, but there are two possible directions that satisfy this requirement. It turns out that the cross product follows a pattern called the *right hand rule*. As shown in Figure 1.6, if the fingers of the right hand are aligned with a vector $\mathbf{P}$, and the palm is facing in the direction of a vector $\mathbf{Q}$, then the thumb points along the direction of the cross product $\mathbf{P} \times \mathbf{Q}$.

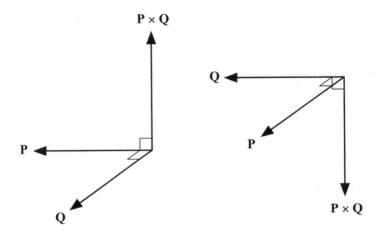

Figure 1.6 The right hand rule provides a way for determining in which direction the cross product points. When the vectors **P** and **Q** are interchanged, their cross product is negated.

The unit vectors **i**, **j**, and **k**, which point in the directions of the positive x-, y-, and z-axes, respectively, behave as follows. If we order the axes in a circular fashion so that **i** precedes **j**, **j** precedes **k**, and **k** precedes **i**, then the cross product of two of these vectors *in order* yields the third vector as follows.

$$\begin{aligned}
\mathbf{i} \times \mathbf{j} &= \mathbf{k} \\
\mathbf{j} \times \mathbf{k} &= \mathbf{i} \\
\mathbf{k} \times \mathbf{i} &= \mathbf{j}
\end{aligned} \tag{1.33}$$

The cross product of two of the vectors *in reverse order* yields the negation of the third vector as follows.

$$\begin{aligned}
\mathbf{j} \times \mathbf{i} &= -\mathbf{k} \\
\mathbf{k} \times \mathbf{j} &= -\mathbf{i} \\
\mathbf{i} \times \mathbf{k} &= -\mathbf{j}
\end{aligned} \tag{1.34}$$

Several additional properties of the cross product are presented by the following theorem.

Theorem 1.9. Given any two scalars a and b, and any three 3D vectors **P**, **Q**, and **R**, the following properties hold.

(a) $\mathbf{Q} \times \mathbf{P} = -(\mathbf{P} \times \mathbf{Q})$

(b) $(a\mathbf{P}) \times \mathbf{Q} = a(\mathbf{P} \times \mathbf{Q})$

(c) $\mathbf{P} \times (\mathbf{Q} + \mathbf{R}) = \mathbf{P} \times \mathbf{Q} + \mathbf{P} \times \mathbf{R}$

(d) $\mathbf{P} \times \mathbf{P} = \mathbf{0} = \langle 0,0,0 \rangle$

(e) $(\mathbf{P} \times \mathbf{Q}) \cdot \mathbf{R} = (\mathbf{R} \times \mathbf{P}) \cdot \mathbf{Q} = (\mathbf{Q} \times \mathbf{R}) \cdot \mathbf{P}$

(f) $\mathbf{P} \times (\mathbf{Q} \times \mathbf{P}) = \mathbf{P} \times \mathbf{Q} \times \mathbf{P} = P^2 \mathbf{Q} - (\mathbf{P} \cdot \mathbf{Q}) \mathbf{P}$

Proof. Parts (a) through (d) follow immediately from the definition of the cross product and the associative and commutative properties of the real numbers. Part (e) can be directly verified using Equation (1.27). For part (f), we first observe that

$$\begin{aligned}
\mathbf{P} \times (\mathbf{Q} \times \mathbf{P}) &= \mathbf{P} \times -(\mathbf{P} \times \mathbf{Q}) \\
&= -[-(\mathbf{P} \times \mathbf{Q}) \times \mathbf{P}] \\
&= \mathbf{P} \times \mathbf{Q} \times \mathbf{P}.
\end{aligned} \tag{1.35}$$

Direct computation of the x-component gives us

$$\begin{aligned}
(\mathbf{P} \times \mathbf{Q} \times \mathbf{P})_x &= (\langle P_y Q_z - P_z Q_y, P_z Q_x - P_x Q_z, P_x Q_y - P_y Q_x \rangle \times \mathbf{P})_x \\
&= (P_z Q_x - P_x Q_z) P_z - (P_x Q_y - P_y Q_x) P_y \\
&= (P_y^2 + P_z^2) Q_x - (P_y Q_y + P_z Q_z) P_x,
\end{aligned} \tag{1.36}$$

which isn't quite what we need, but we can add and subtract a $P_x^2 Q_x$ term to achieve our desired result, as follows:

$$\begin{aligned}
(P_y^2 + P_z^2) & Q_x - (P_y Q_y + P_z Q_z) P_x \\
&= (P_y^2 + P_z^2) Q_x + P_x^2 Q_x - (P_y Q_y + P_z Q_z) P_x - P_x^2 Q_x \\
&= (P_x^2 + P_y^2 + P_z^2) Q_x - (P_x Q_x + P_y Q_y + P_z Q_z) P_x \\
&= P^2 Q_x - (\mathbf{P} \cdot \mathbf{Q}) P_x.
\end{aligned} \tag{1.37}$$

The y- and z-components can be checked in a similar manner. ∎

By part (a) of Theorem 1.9, the cross product is not a commutative operation. Because reversing the order of the vectors has the effect of negating the product, the cross product is labeled *anticommutative*. Additionally, it is worth noting that the cross product is not an associative operation. That is, given any three 3D vectors **P**, **Q**, and **R**, it may be true that $(\mathbf{P}\times\mathbf{Q})\times\mathbf{R} \neq \mathbf{P}\times(\mathbf{Q}\times\mathbf{R})$. As an example, let $\mathbf{P} = \langle 1,1,0 \rangle$, $\mathbf{Q} = \langle 0,1,1 \rangle$, and $\mathbf{R} = \langle 1,0,1 \rangle$. First calculating $(\mathbf{P}\times\mathbf{Q})\times\mathbf{R}$, we have

$$\mathbf{P}\times\mathbf{Q} = \begin{vmatrix} \mathbf{i} & \mathbf{j} & \mathbf{k} \\ 1 & 1 & 0 \\ 0 & 1 & 1 \end{vmatrix} = \langle 1,-1,1 \rangle$$

$$(\mathbf{P}\times\mathbf{Q})\times\mathbf{R} = \begin{vmatrix} \mathbf{i} & \mathbf{j} & \mathbf{k} \\ 1 & -1 & 1 \\ 1 & 0 & 1 \end{vmatrix} = \langle -1,0,1 \rangle. \tag{1.38}$$

Now calculating $\mathbf{P}\times(\mathbf{Q}\times\mathbf{R})$, we have

$$\mathbf{Q}\times\mathbf{R} = \begin{vmatrix} \mathbf{i} & \mathbf{j} & \mathbf{k} \\ 0 & 1 & 1 \\ 1 & 0 & 1 \end{vmatrix} = \langle 1,1,-1 \rangle$$

$$\mathbf{P}\times(\mathbf{Q}\times\mathbf{R}) = \begin{vmatrix} \mathbf{i} & \mathbf{j} & \mathbf{k} \\ 1 & 1 & 0 \\ 1 & 1 & -1 \end{vmatrix} = \langle -1,1,0 \rangle, \tag{1.39}$$

which yields a different result.

1.4 Vector Spaces

The vectors we have dealt with so far belong to sets called *vector spaces*. An examination of vector spaces allows us to introduce concepts that are important for our study of matrices in Chapter 2.

Definition 1.10. A vector space is a set V, whose elements are called vectors, for which addition and scalar multiplication are defined, and the following properties hold.

(a) V is closed under addition. That is, for any elements **P** and **Q** in V, the sum $\mathbf{P}+\mathbf{Q}$ is an element of V.

(b) V is closed under scalar multiplication. That is, for any real number a and any element $\mathbf{P}$ in V, the product $a\mathbf{P}$ is an element of V.

(c) There exists an element in V called $\mathbf{0}$ such that for any element $\mathbf{P}$ in V, $\mathbf{P} + \mathbf{0} = \mathbf{0} + \mathbf{P} = \mathbf{P}$.

(d) For every element $\mathbf{P}$ in V, there exists an element $\mathbf{Q}$ in V such that $\mathbf{P} + \mathbf{Q} = \mathbf{0}$.

(e) Addition is associative. That is, for any elements $\mathbf{P}$, $\mathbf{Q}$, and $\mathbf{R}$ in V, $(\mathbf{P} + \mathbf{Q}) + \mathbf{R} = \mathbf{P} + (\mathbf{Q} + \mathbf{R})$.

(f) Scalar multiplication is associative. That is, for any real numbers a and b, and any element $\mathbf{P}$ in V, $(ab)\mathbf{P} = a(b\mathbf{P})$.

(g) Scalar multiplication distributes over vector addition. That is, for any real number a, and any elements $\mathbf{P}$ and $\mathbf{Q}$ in V, $a(\mathbf{P} + \mathbf{Q}) = a\mathbf{P} + a\mathbf{Q}$.

(h) Addition of scalars distributes over scalar multiplication. That is, for any real numbers a and b, and any element $\mathbf{P}$ in V, $(a+b)\mathbf{P} = a\mathbf{P} + b\mathbf{P}$.

Many of the properties required of vector spaces are mentioned in Section 1.1 and are easily shown to be satisfied for vectors having the form of n-tuples of real numbers. We denote the vector space consisting of all such n-tuples by $\mathbb{R}^n$. For instance, the vector space consisting of all 3D vectors is denoted by $\mathbb{R}^3$.

Every vector space can be generated by linear combinations of a subset of vectors called a *basis* for the vector space. Before we can define exactly what a basis is, we need to know what it means for a set of vectors to be linearly independent.

Definition 1.11. A set of n vectors $\{\mathbf{e}_1, \mathbf{e}_2, \ldots, \mathbf{e}_n\}$ is *linearly independent* if there do not exist real numbers $a_1, a_2, \ldots, a_n$, where at least one of the a_i is not zero, such that

$$a_1\mathbf{e}_1 + a_2\mathbf{e}_2 + \cdots + a_n\mathbf{e}_n = \mathbf{0}. \tag{1.40}$$

Otherwise, the set $\{\mathbf{e}_1, \mathbf{e}_2, \ldots, \mathbf{e}_n\}$ is called *linearly dependent*.

An n-dimensional vector space is one that can be generated by a set of n linearly independent vectors. Such a generating set is called a basis, whose formal definition follows.

Definition 1.12. A basis $\mathcal{B}$ for a vector space V is a set of n linearly independent vectors $\mathcal{B} = \{\mathbf{e}_1, \mathbf{e}_2, \ldots, \mathbf{e}_n\}$ for which, given any element $\mathbf{P}$ in V, there exist real numbers $a_1, a_2, \ldots, a_n$ such that

$$\mathbf{P} = a_1\mathbf{e}_1 + a_2\mathbf{e}_2 + \cdots + a_n\mathbf{e}_n. \tag{1.41}$$

Every basis of an *n*-dimensional vector space has exactly *n* vectors in it. For instance, it is impossible to find a set of four linearly independent vectors in $\mathbb{R}^3$, and a set of two linearly independent vectors is insufficient to generate the entire vector space.

There are an infinite number of choices for a basis of any of the vector spaces $\mathbb{R}^n$. We assign special terms to those that have certain properties.

Definition 1.13. A basis $\mathcal{B} = \{\mathbf{e}_1, \mathbf{e}_2, \ldots, \mathbf{e}_n\}$ for a vector space is called *orthogonal* if for every pair (i, j) with $i \neq j$, we have $\mathbf{e}_i \cdot \mathbf{e}_j = 0$.

The fact that the dot product between two vectors is zero actually implies that the vectors are linearly independent, as the following theorem demonstrates.

Theorem 1.14. Given two nonzero vectors $\mathbf{e}_1$ and $\mathbf{e}_2$, if $\mathbf{e}_1 \cdot \mathbf{e}_2 = 0$, then $\mathbf{e}_1$ and $\mathbf{e}_2$ are linearly independent.

Proof. We suppose that $\mathbf{e}_1$ and $\mathbf{e}_2$ are not linearly independent and arrive at a contradiction. If $\mathbf{e}_1$ and $\mathbf{e}_2$ are linearly dependent, then there exist scalars a_1 and a_2 such that $a_1\mathbf{e}_1 + a_2\mathbf{e}_2 = \mathbf{0}$. Note that a_2 cannot be zero since it would require that a_1 also be zero. Thus, we can write $\mathbf{e}_2 = -(a_1/a_2)\mathbf{e}_1$. But then $\mathbf{e}_1 \cdot \mathbf{e}_2 = -(a_1/a_2)e_1^2 \neq 0$, a contradiction. ∎

This theorem shows that if we can find any *n* orthogonal vectors in a vector space V, then they form a basis for V.

A more specific term is given to a basis whose elements all have unit length. For convenience, we introduce the *Kronecker delta* symbol δ_{ij}, which is defined as

$$\delta_{ij} \equiv \begin{cases} 1, & \text{if } i = j; \\ 0, & \text{if } i \neq j. \end{cases} \tag{1.42}$$

Definition 1.15. A basis $\mathcal{B} = \{\mathbf{e}_1, \mathbf{e}_2, \ldots, \mathbf{e}_n\}$ for a vector space is called *orthonormal* if for every pair (i, j) we have $\mathbf{e}_i \cdot \mathbf{e}_j = \delta_{ij}$.

The set $\{\mathbf{i}, \mathbf{j}, \mathbf{k}\}$ is obviously an orthonormal basis for $\mathbb{R}^3$. A slightly less trivial example of an orthonormal basis for $\mathbb{R}^3$ is given by the three vectors $\langle \frac{\sqrt{2}}{2}, \frac{\sqrt{2}}{2}, 0 \rangle$, $\langle -\frac{\sqrt{2}}{2}, \frac{\sqrt{2}}{2}, 0 \rangle$, and $\langle 0, 0, 1 \rangle$.

There is a simple method by which a linearly independent set of *n* vectors can be transformed into an orthogonal basis for $\mathbb{R}^n$. The basic idea is to subtract away the projection of each vector onto the vectors preceding it in the set. Whatever vector is left over must then be orthogonal to its predecessors. The exact procedure is as follows.

> **Algorithm 1.16. Gram-Schmidt Orthogonalization.** Given a set of n linearly independent vectors $\mathcal{B} = \{\mathbf{e}_1, \mathbf{e}_2, \ldots, \mathbf{e}_n\}$, this algorithm produces a set $\mathcal{B}' = \{\mathbf{e}'_1, \mathbf{e}'_2, \ldots, \mathbf{e}'_n\}$ such that $\mathbf{e}'_i \cdot \mathbf{e}'_j = 0$ whenever $i \neq j$.
>
> **A.** Set $\mathbf{e}'_1 = \mathbf{e}_1$.
>
> **B.** Begin with the index $i = 2$.
>
> **C.** Subtract the projection of $\mathbf{e}_i$ onto the vectors $\mathbf{e}'_1, \mathbf{e}'_2, \ldots, \mathbf{e}'_{i-1}$ from $\mathbf{e}_i$ and store the result in $\mathbf{e}'_i$. That is,
>
> $$\mathbf{e}'_i = \mathbf{e}_i - \sum_{k=1}^{i-1} \frac{\mathbf{e}_i \cdot \mathbf{e}'_k}{\mathbf{e}'^2_k} \mathbf{e}'_k. \tag{1.43}$$
>
> **D.** If $i < n$, increment i and loop to step **C**.

Chapter 1 Summary

Dot Products

The dot product between two n-dimensional vectors $\mathbf{P}$ and $\mathbf{Q}$ is a scalar defined by

$$\mathbf{P} \cdot \mathbf{Q} = \sum_{i=1}^{n} P_i Q_i = P_1 Q_1 + P_2 Q_2 + \cdots + P_n Q_n.$$

The dot product is related to the angle α between the vectors $\mathbf{P}$ and $\mathbf{Q}$ by the formula

$$\mathbf{P} \cdot \mathbf{Q} = \|\mathbf{P}\| \|\mathbf{Q}\| \cos \alpha.$$

Vector Projections

The projection of a vector $\mathbf{P}$ onto a vector $\mathbf{Q}$ is given by

$$\text{proj}_{\mathbf{Q}} \mathbf{P} = \frac{\mathbf{P} \cdot \mathbf{Q}}{\|\mathbf{Q}\|^2} \mathbf{Q},$$

and the component of $\mathbf{P}$ that is perpendicular to $\mathbf{Q}$ is given by

$$\operatorname{perp}_{\mathbf{Q}} \mathbf{P} = \mathbf{P} - \operatorname{proj}_{\mathbf{Q}} \mathbf{P}$$
$$= \mathbf{P} - \frac{\mathbf{P} \cdot \mathbf{Q}}{\|\mathbf{Q}\|^2} \mathbf{Q}.$$

Cross Products

The cross product between two 3D vectors $\mathbf{P}$ and $\mathbf{Q}$ is a 3D vector defined by

$$\mathbf{P} \times \mathbf{Q} = \langle P_y Q_z - P_z Q_y, P_z Q_x - P_x Q_z, P_x Q_y - P_y Q_x \rangle.$$

This can also be written as the matrix-vector product

$$\mathbf{P} \times \mathbf{Q} = \begin{bmatrix} 0 & -P_z & P_y \\ P_z & 0 & -P_x \\ -P_y & P_x & 0 \end{bmatrix} \begin{bmatrix} Q_x \\ Q_y \\ Q_z \end{bmatrix}.$$

The magnitude of the cross product is related to the angle α between the vectors $\mathbf{P}$ and $\mathbf{Q}$ by the formula

$$\|\mathbf{P} \times \mathbf{Q}\| = \|\mathbf{P}\| \|\mathbf{Q}\| \sin \alpha.$$

Gram-Schmidt Orthogonalization

A basis $\mathcal{B} = \{\mathbf{e}_1, \mathbf{e}_2, \ldots, \mathbf{e}_n\}$ for an n-dimensional vector space can be orthogonalized by constructing a new set of vectors $\mathcal{B}' = \{\mathbf{e}_1', \mathbf{e}_2', \ldots, \mathbf{e}_n'\}$ using the formula

$$\mathbf{e}_i' = \mathbf{e}_i - \sum_{k=1}^{i-1} \frac{\mathbf{e}_i \cdot \mathbf{e}_k'}{\mathbf{e}_k'^2} \mathbf{e}_k'.$$

Exercises for Chapter 1

1. Let $\mathbf{P} = \langle 2, 2, 1 \rangle$ and $\mathbf{Q} = \langle 1, -2, 0 \rangle$. Calculate the following.

    (a) $\mathbf{P} \cdot \mathbf{Q}$

    (b) $\mathbf{P} \times \mathbf{Q}$

    (c) $\operatorname{proj}_{\mathbf{P}} \mathbf{Q}$

2. Orthogonalize the following set of vectors.

$$\mathbf{e}_1 = \left\langle \frac{\sqrt{2}}{2}, \frac{\sqrt{2}}{2}, 0 \right\rangle$$
$$\mathbf{e}_2 = \left\langle -1, 1, -1 \right\rangle$$
$$\mathbf{e}_3 = \left\langle 0, -2, -2 \right\rangle$$

3. Calculate the area of the triangle whose vertices lie at the points $\langle 1, 2, 3 \rangle$, $\langle -2, 2, 4 \rangle$, and $\langle 7, -8, 0 \rangle$.

4. Prove that for any three 3D vectors **P**, **Q**, and **R**,

$$\mathbf{P} \times \mathbf{Q} \times \mathbf{R} = (\mathbf{P} \cdot \mathbf{R}) \mathbf{Q} - (\mathbf{Q} \cdot \mathbf{R}) \mathbf{P}.$$

5. Prove that for any two vectors **P** and **Q**,

$$\|\mathbf{P} - \mathbf{Q}\| \geq \|\mathbf{P}\| - \|\mathbf{Q}\|,$$

and show that this implies the extended triangle inequality,

$$\|\mathbf{P}\| - \|\mathbf{Q}\| \leq \|\mathbf{P} + \mathbf{Q}\| \leq \|\mathbf{P}\| + \|\mathbf{Q}\|.$$

6. Implement a C++ class that encapsulates a 3D vector. The class should possess floating-point data members for the vector's x-, y-, and z-components. In addition to a default constructor, which should not perform any initialization, the class should have a constructor that takes three floating-point numbers as arguments and initializes the vector's components to those values. The class should also include overloaded operators for vector addition and subtraction, multiplication and division by scalars, the dot product, and the cross product. Finally, write a function that calculates the magnitude of a 3D vector object.

Chapter **2**

Matrices

In a 3D graphics engine, calculations can be performed in a multitude of different Cartesian coordinate spaces. Moving from one coordinate space to another requires the use of transformation matrices. We casually referred to matrices at various places in Chapter 1; and in this chapter, we acknowledge the importance of matrices in 3D graphics programming by presenting a more formal exposition of their properties. The process of transforming points and direction vectors from one coordinate space to another is described in Chapter 3.

2.1 Matrix Properties

An $n \times m$ matrix $\mathbf{M}$ is an array of numbers having n rows and m columns. If $n = m$, then we say that the matrix $\mathbf{M}$ is *square*. We write M_{ij} to refer to the entry of $\mathbf{M}$ that resides at the i-th row of the j-th column. As an example, suppose that $\mathbf{F}$ is a 3×4 matrix. Then we could write

$$
\mathbf{F} = \begin{bmatrix} F_{11} & F_{12} & F_{13} & F_{14} \\ F_{21} & F_{22} & F_{23} & F_{24} \\ F_{31} & F_{32} & F_{33} & F_{34} \end{bmatrix}. \tag{2.1}
$$

The entries for which $i = j$ are called the *main diagonal* entries of the matrix. A square matrix whose only nonzero entries appear on the main diagonal is called a *diagonal* matrix.

The *transpose* of an $n \times m$ matrix $\mathbf{M}$, which we denote by $\mathbf{M}^T$, is an $m \times n$ matrix for which the (i, j) entry is equal to M_{ji} (i.e., $M_{ij}^T = M_{ji}$). The transpose of the matrix $\mathbf{F}$ in Equation (2.1) is

$$\mathbf{F}^T = \begin{bmatrix} F_{11} & F_{21} & F_{31} \\ F_{12} & F_{22} & F_{32} \\ F_{13} & F_{23} & F_{33} \\ F_{14} & F_{24} & F_{34} \end{bmatrix}. \tag{2.2}$$

As with vectors (which can be thought of as $n \times 1$ matrices), scalar multiplication is defined for matrices. Given a scalar a and an $n \times m$ matrix $\mathbf{M}$, the product $a\mathbf{M}$ is given by

$$a\mathbf{M} = \mathbf{M}a = \begin{bmatrix} aM_{11} & aM_{12} & \cdots & aM_{1m} \\ aM_{21} & aM_{22} & \cdots & aM_{2m} \\ \vdots & \vdots & \ddots & \vdots \\ aM_{n1} & aM_{n2} & \cdots & aM_{nm} \end{bmatrix}. \tag{2.3}$$

Also in a manner similar to vectors, matrices add entrywise. Given two $n \times m$ matrices $\mathbf{F}$ and $\mathbf{G}$, the sum $\mathbf{F} + \mathbf{G}$ is given by

$$\mathbf{F} + \mathbf{G} = \begin{bmatrix} F_{11} + G_{11} & F_{12} + G_{12} & \cdots & F_{1m} + G_{1m} \\ F_{21} + G_{21} & F_{22} + G_{22} & \cdots & F_{2m} + G_{2m} \\ \vdots & \vdots & \ddots & \vdots \\ F_{n1} + G_{n1} & F_{n2} + G_{n2} & \cdots & F_{nm} + G_{nm} \end{bmatrix}. \tag{2.4}$$

Two matrices $\mathbf{F}$ and $\mathbf{G}$ can be multiplied together, provided that the number of columns in $\mathbf{F}$ is equal to the number of rows in $\mathbf{G}$. If $\mathbf{F}$ is an $n \times m$ matrix and $\mathbf{G}$ is an $m \times p$ matrix, then the product $\mathbf{FG}$ is an $n \times p$ matrix whose (i, j) entry is given by

$$(\mathbf{FG})_{ij} = \sum_{k=1}^{m} F_{ik} G_{kj}. \tag{2.5}$$

Another way of looking at this is that the (i, j) entry of $\mathbf{FG}$ is equal to the dot product of the i-th row of $\mathbf{F}$ and the j-th column of $\mathbf{G}$.

There is an $n \times n$ matrix called the *identity* matrix, denoted by $\mathbf{I}_n$, for which $\mathbf{MI}_n = \mathbf{I}_n \mathbf{M} = \mathbf{M}$ for any $n \times n$ matrix $\mathbf{M}$. The identity matrix has the form

$$\mathbf{I}_n = \begin{bmatrix} 1 & 0 & \cdots & 0 \\ 0 & 1 & \cdots & 0 \\ \vdots & \vdots & \ddots & \vdots \\ 0 & 0 & \cdots & 1 \end{bmatrix}. \tag{2.6}$$

We usually drop the subscript n and denote the identity matrix simply by $\mathbf{I}$, since the size of the matrix can be inferred from the context.

Several additional properties of matrices are given by the two theorems that follow.

Theorem 2.1. Given any two scalars a and b and any three $n \times m$ matrices $\mathbf{F}$, $\mathbf{G}$, and $\mathbf{H}$, the following properties hold.

(a) $\mathbf{F} + \mathbf{G} = \mathbf{G} + \mathbf{F}$

(b) $(\mathbf{F} + \mathbf{G}) + \mathbf{H} = \mathbf{F} + (\mathbf{G} + \mathbf{H})$

(c) $a(b\mathbf{F}) = (ab)\mathbf{F}$

(d) $a(\mathbf{F} + \mathbf{G}) = a\mathbf{F} + a\mathbf{G}$

(e) $(a + b)\mathbf{F} = a\mathbf{F} + b\mathbf{F}$

As with vectors, these properties are easily verified through direct computation using the associative and commutative properties of the real numbers.

Theorem 2.2. Given any scalar a, an $n \times m$ matrix $\mathbf{F}$, an $m \times p$ matrix $\mathbf{G}$, and a $p \times q$ matrix $\mathbf{H}$, the following properties hold.

(a) $(a\mathbf{F})\mathbf{G} = a(\mathbf{FG})$

(b) $(\mathbf{FG})\mathbf{H} = \mathbf{F}(\mathbf{GH})$

(c) $(\mathbf{FG})^{\mathrm{T}} = \mathbf{G}^{\mathrm{T}}\mathbf{F}^{\mathrm{T}}$

Proof.

(a) Using the definition for matrix multiplication given by Equation (2.5), the (i, j) entry of $(a\mathbf{F})\mathbf{G}$ is

$$\begin{aligned}
[(a\mathbf{F})\mathbf{G}]_{ij} &= \sum_{k=1}^{m} (a\mathbf{F})_{ik} G_{kj} \\
&= \sum_{k=1}^{m} a\left(F_{ik} G_{kj}\right) \\
&= a\sum_{k=1}^{m} F_{ik} G_{kj} \\
&= a(\mathbf{FG})_{ij}.
\end{aligned} \tag{2.7}$$

(b) Again using Equation (2.5), the (i, j) entry of $(\mathbf{FG})\mathbf{H}$ is

$$\begin{aligned}
[(\mathbf{FG})\mathbf{H}]_{ij} &= \sum_{k=1}^{p} (\mathbf{FG})_{ik} H_{kj} \\
&= \sum_{k=1}^{p} \left(\sum_{l=1}^{m} F_{il} G_{lk} \right) H_{kj} \\
&= \sum_{l=1}^{m} F_{il} \left(\sum_{k=1}^{p} G_{lk} H_{kj} \right) \\
&= \sum_{l=1}^{m} F_{il} (\mathbf{GH})_{lj} \\
&= [\mathbf{F}(\mathbf{GH})]_{ij}.
\end{aligned} \tag{2.8}$$

(c) Applying Equation (2.5), and reversing the indexes whenever a transpose operation is added or removed, we have for the (i, j) entry of $(\mathbf{FG})^{\mathrm{T}}$

$$\begin{aligned}
(\mathbf{FG})_{ij}^{\mathrm{T}} &= (\mathbf{FG})_{ji} \\
&= \sum_{k=1}^{m} F_{jk} G_{ki} \\
&= \sum_{k=1}^{m} F_{kj}^{\mathrm{T}} G_{ik}^{\mathrm{T}} \\
&= \left(\mathbf{G}^{\mathrm{T}} \mathbf{F}^{\mathrm{T}}\right)_{ij}. \quad \blacksquare
\end{aligned} \tag{2.9}$$

2.2 Linear Systems

Matrices provide a compact and convenient way to represent systems of linear equations. For instance, the linear system given by the equations

$$3x + 2y - 3z = -13$$
$$4x - 3y + 6z = 7$$
$$x - z = -5 \qquad (2.10)$$

can be represented in matrix form as

$$\begin{bmatrix} 3 & 2 & -3 \\ 4 & -3 & 6 \\ 1 & 0 & -1 \end{bmatrix} \begin{bmatrix} x \\ y \\ z \end{bmatrix} = \begin{bmatrix} -13 \\ 7 \\ -5 \end{bmatrix}. \qquad (2.11)$$

The matrix preceding the vector $\langle x, y, z \rangle$ of unknowns is called the *coefficient matrix*, and the column vector on the right side of the equals sign is called the *constant vector*. Linear systems for which the constant vector is nonzero (like the example above) are called *nonhomogeneous*. Linear systems for which every entry of the constant vector is zero are called *homogeneous*.

Finding solutions to a system of linear equations can be achieved by performing *elementary row operations* on the matrix formed by concatenating the coefficient matrix and the constant vector.

Definition 2.3. An *elementary row operation* is one of the following three operations that can be performed on a matrix.

(a) Exchange two rows.

(b) Multiply a row by a nonzero scalar.

(c) Add a multiple of one row to another row.

For the example given by Equation (2.11), the augmented matrix formed by concatenating the coefficient matrix and constant vector is

$$\begin{bmatrix} 3 & 2 & -3 & \vdots & -13 \\ 4 & -3 & 6 & \vdots & 7 \\ 1 & 0 & -1 & \vdots & -5 \end{bmatrix}. \tag{2.12}$$

Elementary row operations modify the augmented matrix representation of a linear system in such a way that the solution to the system is not affected, but it becomes much easier to calculate. When solving a linear system using elementary row operations, our goal is to transform the coefficient matrix into its *reduced form*, defined as follows.

Definition 2.4. A matrix is in *reduced form* if and only if it satisfies the following conditions.

(a) For every nonzero row, the leftmost nonzero entry, called the *leading entry*, is 1.

(b) Every nonzero row precedes every row of zeros. That is, all rows of zeros reside at the bottom of the matrix.

(c) If a row's leading entry resides in column j, then no other row has a nonzero entry in column j.

(d) For every pair of nonzero rows i_1 and i_2 such that $i_2 > i_1$, the columns j_1 and j_2 containing those rows' leading entries must satisfy $j_2 > j_1$.

This definition tells us that the leading entries of a matrix in reduced form move to the right as we move downward through its rows. Furthermore, any column containing a leading entry of a row has a 1 at that location and zeros everywhere else.

Example 2.5. The following matrix is in reduced form.

$$\begin{bmatrix} 1 & 0 & -3 & 0 \\ 0 & 1 & 2 & 0 \\ 0 & 0 & 0 & 1 \\ 0 & 0 & 0 & 0 \end{bmatrix} \tag{2.13}$$

However, the matrix

$$\begin{bmatrix} 1 & 0 & 0 & 3 \\ 0 & 0 & 1 & 0 \\ 0 & 2 & 0 & 0 \\ 0 & 0 & 0 & 1 \end{bmatrix} \tag{2.14}$$

is *not* in reduced form because the leading entry of the third row does not fall to the right of the leading entry of the second row. Furthermore, the fourth column, which contains the leading entry of the fourth row, is not zero every-where else. ∎

Algorithm 2.6 describes which elementary row operations to apply to the augmented matrix representation of a linear system in order to transform its coefficient matrix into its reduced form.

Algorithm 2.6. This algorithm transforms an $n \times (n+1)$ augmented matrix $\mathbf{M}$ representing a linear system into its reduced form. At each step, $\mathbf{M}$ refers to the *current* state of the matrix, not the original state.

A. Set the row i equal to 1.

B. Set the column j equal to 1. We will loop through columns 1 to n.

C. Find the row k with $k \geq i$ for which M_{kj} has the largest absolute value. If no such row exists for which $M_{kj} \neq 0$, then skip to step H.

D. If $k \neq i$, then exchange rows k and i using elementary row operation (a) under Definition 2.3.

E. Multiply row i by $1/M_{ij}$. This sets the (i, j) entry of $\mathbf{M}$ to 1 using elementary row operation (b).

F. For each row r, where $1 \leq r \leq n$ and $r \neq i$, add $-M_{rj}$ times row i to row r. This step clears each entry above and below row i in column j to 0 using elementary row operation (c).

G. Increment i.

H. If $j < n$, increment j and loop to step C.

The procedure performed by steps C and D is known as *pivoting*. In addition to its ability to remove zeros from the main diagonal, pivoting is absolutely essential for numerical stability. The following example demonstrates the application of Algorithm 2.6 to the nonhomogeneous linear system given by Equation (2.11).

After the augmented coefficient matrix is reduced, the solution to the system becomes obvious.

Example 2.7. Solve the nonhomogeneous linear system

$$\begin{bmatrix} 3 & 2 & -3 \\ 4 & -3 & 6 \\ 1 & 0 & -1 \end{bmatrix} \begin{bmatrix} x \\ y \\ z \end{bmatrix} = \begin{bmatrix} -13 \\ 7 \\ -5 \end{bmatrix}. \tag{2.15}$$

Solution. We first form the augmented matrix

$$\left[\begin{array}{ccc|c} 3 & 2 & -3 & -13 \\ 4 & -3 & 6 & 7 \\ 1 & 0 & -1 & -5 \end{array}\right]. \tag{2.16}$$

We must now pivot (using steps C and D) so that the row containing the largest entry in the first column appears in the first row. We therefore exchange the first two rows. To produce a leading entry of 1, we then multiply the first row by $\frac{1}{4}$, as follows.

$$\xrightarrow[\text{Multiply new row 1 by } \frac{1}{4}]{\text{Exchange rows 1 and 2}} \left[\begin{array}{ccc|c} 1 & -\frac{3}{4} & \frac{3}{2} & \frac{7}{4} \\ 3 & 2 & -3 & -13 \\ 1 & 0 & -1 & -5 \end{array}\right] \tag{2.17}$$

Applying step G of Algorithm 2.6, we now eliminate the other nonzero entries in the first column.

$$\xrightarrow[\text{Add } -1 \times \text{row 1 to row 3}]{\text{Add } -3 \times \text{row 1 to row 2}} \left[\begin{array}{ccc|c} 1 & -\frac{3}{4} & \frac{3}{2} & \frac{7}{4} \\ 0 & \frac{17}{4} & -\frac{15}{2} & -\frac{73}{4} \\ 0 & \frac{3}{4} & -\frac{5}{2} & -\frac{27}{4} \end{array}\right] \tag{2.18}$$

Moving to the second row, we multiply by $\frac{4}{17}$ to obtain a leading entry of 1.

$$\xrightarrow{\text{Multiply row 2 by } -\frac{4}{3}} \begin{bmatrix} 1 & \frac{2}{3} & -1 & \vline & \frac{7}{4} \\ 0 & 1 & -\frac{30}{17} & \vline & -\frac{73}{17} \\ 0 & \frac{3}{4} & -\frac{5}{2} & \vline & -\frac{27}{4} \end{bmatrix} \tag{2.19}$$

Again applying step G, we eliminate the other nonzero entries in the second column.

$$\xrightarrow[\text{Add } -\frac{3}{4} \times \text{row 2 to row 3}]{\text{Add } -\frac{2}{3} \times \text{row 2 to row 1}} \begin{bmatrix} 1 & 0 & \frac{3}{17} & \vline & -\frac{25}{17} \\ 0 & 1 & -\frac{30}{17} & \vline & \frac{73}{17} \\ 0 & 0 & -\frac{20}{17} & \vline & -\frac{60}{17} \end{bmatrix} \tag{2.20}$$

Finally, we apply the same steps to the third row, as follows.

$$\xrightarrow{\text{Multiply row 3 by } -\frac{17}{20}} \begin{bmatrix} 1 & 0 & \frac{3}{17} & \vline & -\frac{25}{17} \\ 0 & 1 & -\frac{30}{17} & \vline & -\frac{73}{17} \\ 0 & 0 & 1 & \vline & 3 \end{bmatrix}$$

$$\xrightarrow[\text{Add } \frac{30}{17} \times \text{row 3 to row 2}]{\text{Add } -\frac{3}{17} \times \text{row 3 to row 1}} \begin{bmatrix} 1 & 0 & 0 & \vline & -2 \\ 0 & 1 & 0 & \vline & 1 \\ 0 & 0 & 1 & \vline & 3 \end{bmatrix} \tag{2.21}$$

The coefficient matrix has now been completely transformed into its reduced form. The reduced augmented matrix represents the equation

$$\begin{bmatrix} 1 & 0 & 0 \\ 0 & 1 & 0 \\ 0 & 0 & 1 \end{bmatrix} \begin{bmatrix} x \\ y \\ z \end{bmatrix} = \begin{bmatrix} -2 \\ 1 \\ 3 \end{bmatrix}, \tag{2.22}$$

from which the solution to the original system is immediate:

$$\begin{aligned} x &= -2 \\ y &= 1 \\ z &= 3. \ \blacksquare \end{aligned} \tag{2.23}$$

In the previous example, we found that the reduced form of the coefficient matrix was equal to the identity matrix. In such a case, the corresponding linear system has exactly one solution. When the reduced coefficient matrix has one or more rows of zeros, however, the corresponding system may have no solution at all, or may have infinitely many solutions. If the entry in the constant vector corresponding to a row of zeros in the coefficient matrix is *not* zero, then the system has no solution because that row equates zero to a nonzero number. In the remaining case that the entry in the constant vector is zero, there are infinitely many solutions to the linear system that must be expressed in terms of arbitrary constants. The number of arbitrary constants is equal to the number of rows of zeros, and arbitrary constants are assigned to variables corresponding to columns of the reduced coefficient matrix that do not contain a leading entry.

Example 2.8. Solve the following homogeneous linear system.

$$2x + y + 3z = 0$$
$$y - z = 0$$
$$x + 3y - z = 0 \tag{2.24}$$

Solution. The augmented matrix representation of this system is given by

$$\left[\begin{array}{ccc|c} 2 & 1 & 3 & 0 \\ 0 & 1 & -1 & 0 \\ 1 & 3 & -1 & 0 \end{array}\right]. \tag{2.25}$$

Using Algorithm 2.6 to calculate the reduced form gives us the matrix

$$\left[\begin{array}{ccc|c} 1 & 0 & 2 & 0 \\ 0 & 1 & -1 & 0 \\ 0 & 0 & 0 & 0 \end{array}\right]. \tag{2.26}$$

Since this matrix has a row of zeros, we can assign an arbitrary value to the variable corresponding to the third column since it does not contain a leading entry; in this case we set $z = a$. The first two rows then represent the equations

$$x + 2a = 0$$
$$y - a = 0, \tag{2.27}$$

so the solution to the system can be written as

$$\begin{bmatrix} x \\ y \\ z \end{bmatrix} = a \begin{bmatrix} -2 \\ 1 \\ 1 \end{bmatrix}. \quad \blacksquare \tag{2.28}$$

Homogeneous linear systems always have at least one solution—the zero vector. Nontrivial solutions exist only when the reduced form of the coefficient matrix possesses at least one row of zeros.

2.3 Matrix Inverses

An $n \times n$ matrix $\mathbf{M}$ is *invertible* if there exists a matrix, which we denote by $\mathbf{M}^{-1}$, such that $\mathbf{MM}^{-1} = \mathbf{M}^{-1}\mathbf{M} = \mathbf{I}$. The matrix $\mathbf{M}^{-1}$ is called the *inverse* of $\mathbf{M}$. Not every matrix has an inverse, and those that do not are called *singular*. An example of a singular matrix is any one that has a row or column consisting of all zeros.

Theorem 2.9. A matrix possessing a row or column consisting entirely of zeros is not invertible.

Proof. Suppose every entry in row r of an $n \times n$ matrix $\mathbf{F}$ is 0. For any $n \times n$ matrix $\mathbf{G}$, the (r,r) entry of the product $\mathbf{FG}$ is given by $\sum_{k=1}^{n} F_{rk} G_{kr}$. Since each of the F_{rk} is 0, the (r,r) entry of $\mathbf{FG}$ is 0. Since the inverse of $\mathbf{F}$ would need to produce a 1 in the (r,r) entry, $\mathbf{F}$ cannot have an inverse. A similar argument proves the theorem for a matrix possessing a column of zeros. $\blacksquare$

Using this theorem, we will be able to show later in this section that any matrix possessing a row that is a linear combination of the other rows of the matrix is singular. The same is true for the columns of a matrix due to the following fact.

Theorem 2.10. A matrix $\mathbf{M}$ is invertible if and only if $\mathbf{M}^{\mathrm{T}}$ is invertible.

Proof. Assume $\mathbf{M}$ is invertible. Then $\mathbf{M}^{-1}$ exists, so we can write

$$\mathbf{M}^{\mathrm{T}}\left(\mathbf{M}^{-1}\right)^{\mathrm{T}} = \left(\mathbf{M}^{-1}\mathbf{M}\right)^{\mathrm{T}} = \mathbf{I}^{\mathrm{T}} = \mathbf{I} \tag{2.29}$$

and

$$\left(\mathbf{M}^{-1}\right)^{\mathrm{T}}\mathbf{M}^{\mathrm{T}} = \left(\mathbf{M}\mathbf{M}^{-1}\right)^{\mathrm{T}} = \mathbf{I}^{\mathrm{T}} = \mathbf{I}. \tag{2.30}$$

Therefore, $\left(\mathbf{M}^{-1}\right)^{\mathrm{T}}$ is the inverse of $\mathbf{M}^{\mathrm{T}}$. Similarly, if we assume that $\mathbf{M}^{\mathrm{T}}$ is invertible, then $\left(\mathbf{M}^{\mathrm{T}}\right)^{-1}$ exists, so we can write

$$\mathbf{M}\left[\left(\mathbf{M}^{\mathrm{T}}\right)^{-1}\right]^{\mathrm{T}} = \left[\left(\mathbf{M}^{\mathrm{T}}\right)^{-1}\mathbf{M}^{\mathrm{T}}\right]^{\mathrm{T}} = \mathbf{I}^{\mathrm{T}} = \mathbf{I} \tag{2.31}$$

and

$$\left[\left(\mathbf{M}^{\mathrm{T}}\right)^{-1}\right]^{\mathrm{T}}\mathbf{M} = \left[\mathbf{M}^{\mathrm{T}}\left(\mathbf{M}^{\mathrm{T}}\right)^{-1}\right]^{\mathrm{T}} = \mathbf{I}^{\mathrm{T}} = \mathbf{I}. \tag{2.32}$$

Therefore, $\left[\left(\mathbf{M}^{\mathrm{T}}\right)^{-1}\right]^{\mathrm{T}}$ is the inverse of $\mathbf{M}$. ∎

Before proceeding to a method for calculating inverses, we make one more observation.

Theorem 2.11. If $\mathbf{F}$ and $\mathbf{G}$ are $n \times n$ invertible matrices, then the product $\mathbf{FG}$ is invertible, and $\left(\mathbf{FG}\right)^{-1} = \mathbf{G}^{-1}\mathbf{F}^{-1}$.

Proof. We can verify this theorem through direct computation using the fact that matrix multiplication is associative:

$$\mathbf{G}^{-1}\mathbf{F}^{-1}\left(\mathbf{FG}\right) = \mathbf{G}^{-1}\left(\mathbf{F}^{-1}\mathbf{F}\right)\mathbf{G} = \mathbf{G}^{-1}\mathbf{G} = \mathbf{I}. \ \blacksquare \tag{2.33}$$

A method similar to that used to transform a matrix into its reduced form (see Algorithm 2.6) can also be used to calculate the inverse of a matrix. To find the inverse of an $n \times n$ matrix $\mathbf{M}$, we first construct an $n \times 2n$ matrix $\tilde{\mathbf{M}}$ by concatenating the identity matrix to the right of $\mathbf{M}$, as shown below.

$$\tilde{\mathbf{M}} = \begin{bmatrix} M_{11} & M_{12} & \cdots & M_{1n} & 1 & 0 & \cdots & 0 \\ M_{21} & M_{22} & \cdots & M_{2n} & 0 & 1 & \cdots & 0 \\ \vdots & \vdots & \ddots & \vdots & \vdots & \vdots & \ddots & \vdots \\ M_{n1} & M_{n2} & \cdots & M_{nn} & 0 & 0 & \cdots & 1 \end{bmatrix} \tag{2.34}$$

Performing elementary row operations on the entire matrix $\tilde{\mathbf{M}}$ until the left side $n \times n$ matrix becomes the identity matrix $\mathbf{I}_n$ yields the inverse of $\mathbf{M}$ in the right side $n \times n$ matrix. This process is known as *Gauss-Jordan elimination* and is illustrated in Algorithm 2.12.

Algorithm 2.12. Gauss-Jordan Elimination. This algorithm calculates the inverse of an $n \times n$ matrix $\mathbf{M}$.

A. Construct the augmented matrix $\tilde{\mathbf{M}}$ given in Equation (2.34). Throughout this algorithm, $\tilde{\mathbf{M}}$ refers to the *current* state of the augmented matrix, not the original state.

B. Set the column j equal to 1. We will loop through columns 1 to n.

C. Find the row i with $i \geq j$ such that $\tilde{M}_{ij}$ has the largest absolute value. If no such row exists for which $\tilde{M}_{ij} \neq 0$, then $\mathbf{M}$ is not invertible.

D. If $i \neq j$, then exchange rows i and j using elementary row operation (a) under Definition 2.3. This is the pivot operation necessary to remove zeros from the main diagonal and to provide numerical stability.

E. Multiply row j by $1/\tilde{M}_{jj}$. This sets the (j, j) entry of $\tilde{\mathbf{M}}$ to 1 using elementary row operation (b).

F. For each row r where $1 \leq r \leq n$ and $r \neq j$, add $-\tilde{M}_{rj}$ times row j to row r. This step clears each entry above and below row j in column j to 0 using elementary row operation (c).

G. If $j < n$, increment j and loop to step C.

The implementation of Algorithm 2.12 is straightforward and has the benefit that it can determine whether a matrix is invertible. The following example demonstrates the inner workings of the algorithm.

Example 2.13. Calculate the inverse of the 3×3 matrix $\mathbf{M}$ given by

$$\mathbf{M} = \begin{bmatrix} 2 & 3 & 8 \\ 6 & 0 & -3 \\ -1 & 3 & 2 \end{bmatrix}. \tag{2.35}$$

Solution. Concatenating the identity matrix to $\mathbf{M}$, we have

$$\tilde{\mathbf{M}} = \left[\begin{array}{ccc|ccc} 2 & 3 & 8 & 1 & 0 & 0 \\ 6 & 0 & -3 & 0 & 1 & 0 \\ -1 & 3 & 2 & 0 & 0 & 1 \end{array} \right]. \tag{2.36}$$

We now apply steps C through F of the algorithm for $j = 1$.

$$\xrightarrow[\text{Multiply new row 1 by } \frac{1}{6}]{\text{Exchange rows 1 and 2}} \begin{bmatrix} 1 & 0 & -\frac{1}{2} & 0 & \frac{1}{6} & 0 \\ 2 & 3 & 8 & 1 & 0 & 0 \\ -1 & 3 & 2 & 0 & 0 & 1 \end{bmatrix}$$

$$\xrightarrow[\text{Add row 1 to row 3}]{\text{Add } -2 \times \text{row 1 to row 2}} \begin{bmatrix} 1 & 0 & -\frac{1}{2} & 0 & \frac{1}{6} & 0 \\ 0 & 3 & 9 & 1 & -\frac{1}{3} & 0 \\ 0 & 3 & \frac{3}{2} & 0 & \frac{1}{6} & 1 \end{bmatrix} \tag{2.37}$$

Applying the same steps for $j = 2$ gives us the following.

$$\xrightarrow[]{\text{Multiply row 2 by } \frac{1}{3}} \begin{bmatrix} 1 & 0 & -\frac{1}{2} & 0 & \frac{1}{6} & 0 \\ 0 & 1 & 3 & \frac{1}{3} & -\frac{1}{9} & 0 \\ 0 & 3 & \frac{3}{2} & 0 & \frac{1}{6} & 1 \end{bmatrix}$$

$$\xrightarrow[]{\text{Add } -3 \times \text{row 2 to row 3}} \begin{bmatrix} 1 & 0 & -\frac{1}{2} & 0 & \frac{1}{6} & 0 \\ 0 & 1 & 3 & \frac{1}{3} & -\frac{1}{9} & 0 \\ 0 & 0 & -\frac{15}{2} & -1 & \frac{1}{2} & 1 \end{bmatrix} \tag{2.38}$$

Finally, we apply the algorithm for $j = 3$.

$$\xrightarrow[]{\text{Multiply row 3 by } -\frac{2}{15}} \begin{bmatrix} 1 & 0 & -\frac{1}{2} & 0 & \frac{1}{6} & 0 \\ 0 & 1 & 3 & \frac{1}{3} & -\frac{1}{9} & 0 \\ 0 & 0 & 1 & \frac{2}{15} & -\frac{1}{15} & -\frac{2}{15} \end{bmatrix}$$

$$\xrightarrow[\text{Add } -3 \times \text{row 3 to row 2}]{\text{Add } \frac{1}{2} \times \text{row 3 to row 1}} \begin{bmatrix} 1 & 0 & 0 & \frac{1}{15} & \frac{2}{15} & -\frac{1}{15} \\ 0 & 1 & 0 & -\frac{1}{15} & \frac{4}{45} & \frac{2}{5} \\ 0 & 0 & 1 & \frac{2}{15} & -\frac{1}{15} & -\frac{2}{15} \end{bmatrix} \tag{2.39}$$

The right side 3×3 matrix is now equal to the inverse of $\mathbf{M}$:

$$\mathbf{M}^{-1} = \frac{1}{45} \begin{bmatrix} 3 & 6 & -3 \\ -3 & 4 & 18 \\ 6 & -3 & -6 \end{bmatrix}. \quad \blacksquare \tag{2.40}$$

To understand why Algorithm 2.12 supplies the inverse of a matrix, we need the following theorem.

Theorem 2.14. Let $\mathbf{M}'$ be the $n \times n$ matrix resulting from the performance of an elementary row operation on the $n \times n$ matrix $\mathbf{M}$. Then $\mathbf{M}' = \mathbf{EM}$, where $\mathbf{E}$ is the $n \times n$ matrix resulting from the same elementary row operation performed on the identity matrix.

Proof. We shall give separate proofs for each of the three elementary row operations listed in Definition 2.3.

(a) Let $\mathbf{E}$ be equal to the identity matrix after rows r and s have been exchanged. Then the entries of $\mathbf{E}$ are given by

$$E_{ij} = \begin{cases} \delta_{ij}, & \text{if } i \neq r \text{ and } i \neq s; \\ \delta_{sj}, & \text{if } i = r; \\ \delta_{rj}, & \text{if } i = s, \end{cases} \tag{2.41}$$

where δ_{ij} is the Kronecker delta symbol defined by Equation (1.42). The entries of the product $\mathbf{EM}$ are then given by

$$(\mathbf{EM})_{ij} = \sum_{k=1}^{n} E_{ik} M_{kj} = \begin{cases} M_{ij}, & \text{if } i \neq r \text{ and } i \neq s; \\ M_{sj}, & \text{if } i = r; \\ M_{rj}, & \text{if } i = s. \end{cases} \tag{2.42}$$

Thus, rows r and s of the matrix $\mathbf{M}$ have been exchanged.

(b) Let $\mathbf{E}$ be equal to the identity matrix after row r has been multiplied by a scalar a. Then the entries of $\mathbf{E}$ are given by

$$E_{ij} = \begin{cases} \delta_{ij}, & \text{if } i \neq r; \\ a\delta_{ij}, & \text{if } i = r. \end{cases} \tag{2.43}$$

The entries of the product $\mathbf{EM}$ are then given by

$$(\mathbf{EM})_{ij} = \sum_{k=1}^{n} E_{ik} M_{kj} = \begin{cases} M_{ij}, & \text{if } i \neq r; \\ aM_{ij}, & \text{if } i = r. \end{cases} \tag{2.44}$$

Thus, row r of the matrix $\mathbf{M}$ has been multiplied by a.

(c) Let $\mathbf{E}$ be equal to the identity matrix after row r has been multiplied by a scalar a and added to row s. Then the entries of $\mathbf{E}$ are given by

$$E_{ij} = \begin{cases} \delta_{ij}, & \text{if } i \neq s; \\ \delta_{ij} + a\delta_{rj}, & \text{if } i = s. \end{cases} \tag{2.45}$$

The entries of the product $\mathbf{EM}$ are then given by

$$(\mathbf{EM})_{ij} = \sum_{k=1}^{n} E_{ik} M_{kj} = \begin{cases} M_{ij}, & \text{if } i \neq s; \\ M_{ij} + aM_{rj}, & \text{if } i = s. \end{cases} \tag{2.46}$$

Thus, row r of the matrix $\mathbf{M}$ has been multiplied by a and added to row s. ∎

The matrix $\mathbf{E}$ that represents the result of an elementary row operation performed on the identity matrix is called an *elementary* matrix. If we have to apply k elementary row operations to transform a matrix $\mathbf{M}$ into the identity matrix, then

$$\mathbf{I} = \mathbf{E}_k \mathbf{E}_{k-1} \cdots \mathbf{E}_1 \mathbf{M}, \tag{2.47}$$

where the matrices $\mathbf{E}_1, \mathbf{E}_2, \ldots, \mathbf{E}_k$ are the elementary matrices corresponding to the same k row operations applied to the identity matrix. This actually shows that the product $\mathbf{E}_k \mathbf{E}_{k-1} \cdots \mathbf{E}_1$ is equal to the inverse of $\mathbf{M}$, and it is exactly what we get when we apply the k row operations to the identity matrix concatenated to the matrix $\mathbf{M}$ in Equation (2.34).

If a matrix $\mathbf{M}$ is singular, then finding elementary matrices $\mathbf{E}_1, \mathbf{E}_2, \ldots, \mathbf{E}_k$ that satisfy Equation (2.47) is impossible. This is true because singular matrices are exactly those whose rows form a linearly dependent set, as the following theorem states.

Theorem 2.15. An $n \times n$ matrix $\mathbf{M}$ is invertible if and only if the rows of $\mathbf{M}$ form a linearly independent set of vectors.

Proof. Let the rows of $\mathbf{M}$ be denoted by $\mathbf{R}_1^{\mathrm{T}}, \mathbf{R}_2^{\mathrm{T}}, \ldots, \mathbf{R}_n^{\mathrm{T}}$. We prove this theorem in two parts.

(a) We prove that if $\mathbf{M}$ is invertible, then the rows of $\mathbf{M}$ form a linearly independent set of vectors by proving the contrapositive, which states that if the rows of $\mathbf{M}$ form a linearly dependent set of vectors, then $\mathbf{M}$ must be singular. So assume that the rows of $\mathbf{M}$ are linearly dependent. Then there exists a row r that can be written as a linear combination of k other rows of the matrix as follows.

$$\mathbf{R}_r^{\mathrm{T}} = a_1\mathbf{R}_{s_1}^{\mathrm{T}} + a_2\mathbf{R}_{s_2}^{\mathrm{T}} + \cdots + a_k\mathbf{R}_{s_k}^{\mathrm{T}} \qquad (2.48)$$

The values of a_i are scalars, and the values of s_i index k rows in the matrix $\mathbf{M}$ other than row r. Let the $n \times n$ matrix $\mathbf{E}_i$ be equal to the elementary matrix representing the addition of a_i times row s_i to row r. Then we can write

$$\mathbf{M} = \mathbf{E}_k\mathbf{E}_{k-1}\cdots\mathbf{E}_1\mathbf{M}', \qquad (2.49)$$

where $\mathbf{M}'$ is equal to $\mathbf{M}$, except that row r has been replaced by all zeros. By Theorem 2.9, the matrix $\mathbf{M}'$ is singular, and thus $\mathbf{M}$ is singular.

(b) Now assume that the rows of $\mathbf{M}$ form a linearly independent set of vectors. We first observe that performing elementary row operations on a matrix does not alter the property of linear independence within the rows. Running through Algorithm 2.12, if step C fails, then rows j through n of the matrix at that point form a linearly dependent set since the number of columns for which the rows $\mathbf{R}_j^{\mathrm{T}}$ through $\mathbf{R}_n^{\mathrm{T}}$ have at least one nonzero entry is less than the number of rows itself. This is a contradiction, so step C of the algorithm cannot fail, and $\mathbf{M}$ must be invertible. ∎

This theorem tells us that *every* singular matrix can be written as a product of elementary matrices and a matrix that has a row of zeros. With the introduction of determinants in the next section, this fact allows us to devise a test for singularity.

2.4 Determinants

The determinant of a square matrix is a scalar quantity derived from the entries of the matrix. The determinant of a matrix $\mathbf{M}$ is denoted by $\det\mathbf{M}$. When displaying the entries of a matrix, we replace the brackets on the left and right of the matrix with vertical bars to indicate that we are evaluating the determinant. For example, the determinant of a 3×3 matrix $\mathbf{M}$ is written as

$$\det \mathbf{M} = \begin{vmatrix} M_{11} & M_{12} & M_{13} \\ M_{21} & M_{22} & M_{23} \\ M_{31} & M_{32} & M_{33} \end{vmatrix}. \tag{2.50}$$

The value of the determinant of an $n \times n$ matrix is given by a recursive formula. For notational convenience, let the symbol $\mathbf{M}^{\{i,j\}}$ denote the $(n-1) \times (n-1)$ matrix whose entries consist of the original entries of $\mathbf{M}$ after deleting the i-th row and the j-th column. For example, suppose that $\mathbf{M}$ is the following 3×3 matrix.

$$\mathbf{M} = \begin{bmatrix} 1 & 2 & 3 \\ 4 & 5 & 6 \\ 7 & 8 & 9 \end{bmatrix} \tag{2.51}$$

Then $\mathbf{M}^{\{2,3\}}$ is the following 2×2 matrix.

$$\mathbf{M}^{\{2,3\}} = \begin{bmatrix} 1 & 2 \\ 7 & 8 \end{bmatrix} \tag{2.52}$$

The formula for the determinant is recursive and can be expressed in terms of the following definition.

Definition 2.16. Let $\mathbf{M}$ be an $n \times n$ matrix. We define the *cofactor* $C_{ij}(\mathbf{M})$ of the matrix entry M_{ij} as follows.

$$C_{ij}(\mathbf{M}) \equiv (-1)^{i+j} \det \mathbf{M}^{\{i,j\}}. \tag{2.53}$$

Using cofactors, a method for calculating the determinant of an $n \times n$ matrix can be expressed as follows. First, define the determinant of a 1×1 matrix to be the entry of the matrix itself. Then the determinant of an $n \times n$ matrix $\mathbf{M}$ is given by both the formula

$$\det \mathbf{M} = \sum_{i=1}^{n} M_{ik} C_{ik}(\mathbf{M}) \tag{2.54}$$

and the formula

$$\det \mathbf{M} = \sum_{j=1}^{n} M_{kj} C_{kj}(\mathbf{M}),\qquad(2.55)$$

where k is an arbitrarily chosen constant such that $1 \le k \le n$. Remarkably, both formulas give the same value for the determinant regardless of the choice of k. The determinant of $\mathbf{M}$ is given by the sum along any row or column of products of entries of $\mathbf{M}$ and their cofactors.

An explicit formula for the determinant of a 2×2 matrix is easy to extract from Equations (2.54) and (2.55):

$$\begin{vmatrix} a & b \\ c & d \end{vmatrix} = ad - bc.\qquad(2.56)$$

We also give an explicit formula for the determinant of a 3×3 matrix. The following is written as one would evaluate Equation (2.55) with $k = 1$.

$$\begin{vmatrix} a_{11} & a_{12} & a_{13} \\ a_{21} & a_{22} & a_{23} \\ a_{31} & a_{32} & a_{33} \end{vmatrix} = a_{11} \begin{vmatrix} a_{22} & a_{23} \\ a_{32} & a_{33} \end{vmatrix} - a_{12} \begin{vmatrix} a_{21} & a_{23} \\ a_{31} & a_{33} \end{vmatrix} + a_{13} \begin{vmatrix} a_{21} & a_{22} \\ a_{31} & a_{32} \end{vmatrix}$$

$$= a_{11}\left(a_{22}a_{33} - a_{23}a_{32} \right) - a_{12}\left(a_{21}a_{33} - a_{23}a_{31} \right)$$
$$+ a_{13}\left(a_{21}a_{32} - a_{22}a_{31} \right)\qquad(2.57)$$

Clearly, the determinant of the identity matrix $\mathbf{I}_n$ is 1 for any n since choosing $k = 1$ reduces Equation (2.55) to $\det \mathbf{I}_n = I_{11} \det \mathbf{I}_{n-1}$.

We can derive some useful information from studying how elementary row operations (see Definition 2.3) affect the determinant of a matrix. This provides a way of evaluating determinants that is usually more efficient than direct application of Equations (2.54) and (2.55).

Theorem 2.17. Performing elementary row operations on a matrix has the following effects on the determinant of that matrix.

(a) Exchanging two rows negates the determinant.

(b) Multiplying a row by a scalar a multiplies the determinant by a.

(c) Adding a multiple of one row to another row has no effect on the determinant.

Proof.

(a) We prove this by induction. The operation does not apply to 1×1 matrices, but for a 2×2 matrix, we can observe the result through direct computation.

$$\begin{vmatrix} c & d \\ a & b \end{vmatrix} = cb - ad = -(ad - cb) = -\begin{vmatrix} a & b \\ c & d \end{vmatrix} \quad (2.58)$$

Now, for an $n \times n$ matrix, we can assume that the result is true for all matrices up to size $(n-1) \times (n-1)$. Let $\mathbf{G}$ represent the result of exchanging rows r and s of a matrix $\mathbf{F}$. Choosing another row k such that $k \neq r$ and $k \neq s$, evaluation of Equation (2.55) gives us

$$\det \mathbf{G} = \sum_{j=1}^{n} G_{kj} C_{kj}(\mathbf{G}) = \sum_{j=1}^{n} (-1)^{k+j} G_{kj} \det \mathbf{G}^{\{k,j\}}. \quad (2.59)$$

Since $\mathbf{G}^{\{k,j\}}$ is an $(n-1) \times (n-1)$ matrix, we know by induction that $\det \mathbf{G}^{\{k,j\}} = -\det \mathbf{F}^{\{k,j\}}$ for each j. Thus, $\det \mathbf{G} = -\det \mathbf{F}$.

(b) Let $\mathbf{G}$ represent the result of multiplying row k of a matrix $\mathbf{F}$ by the scalar a. Then evaluation of Equation (2.55) gives us

$$\det \mathbf{G} = \sum_{j=1}^{n} G_{kj} C_{kj}(\mathbf{G})$$

$$= \sum_{j=1}^{n} a F_{kj} C_{kj}(\mathbf{F}). \quad (2.60)$$

Thus, $\det \mathbf{G} = a \det \mathbf{F}$. ∎

Before we can prove part (c), we need the following corollary to part (a).

Corollary 2.18. The determinant of a matrix having two identical rows is zero.

Proof. Suppose the matrix $\mathbf{M}$ has two identical rows. If we exchange these rows, then no change has been made to the matrix, but the determinant has been negated. So $\det \mathbf{M} = -\det \mathbf{M}$, and we must therefore have $\det \mathbf{M} = 0$. ∎

Proof of Theorem 2.17(c). Let $\mathbf{G}$ represent the result of adding the scalar a times row r of a matrix $\mathbf{F}$ to row k of $\mathbf{F}$. Then evaluating Equation (2.55) gives us

$$\det \mathbf{G} = \sum_{j=1}^{n} G_{kj} C_{kj}(\mathbf{G})$$

$$= \sum_{j=1}^{n} \left(F_{kj} + a F_{rj} \right) C_{kj}(\mathbf{F})$$

$$= \det \mathbf{F} + a \sum_{j=1}^{n} F_{rj} C_{kj}(\mathbf{F}). \tag{2.61}$$

The sum $\sum_{j=1}^{k} F_{rj} C_{kj}(\mathbf{F})$ is equivalent to the determinant of the matrix $\mathbf{F}$ with the entries in row k replaced by the entries from row r. Since this matrix has two identical rows, its determinant is zero by Corollary 2.18. Therefore, $\det \mathbf{G} = \det \mathbf{F}$. ■

Since elementary matrices are representative of elementary row operations performed on the identity matrix, we can deduce their determinants from Theorem 2.17. An elementary matrix that represents an exchange of rows has a determinant of -1, an elementary matrix that represents a row multiplied by a scalar a has a determinant of a, and an elementary matrix that represents a multiple of one row added to another row has a determinant of 1. These are the exact numbers by which the determinant of any matrix is multiplied when the corresponding elementary row operations are performed on them. We can therefore conclude that if $\mathbf{E}$ is an $n \times n$ elementary matrix, then $\det \mathbf{EM} = \det \mathbf{E} \det \mathbf{M}$ for any $n \times n$ matrix $\mathbf{M}$ since multiplication by $\mathbf{E}$ performs the elementary row operation on $\mathbf{M}$. This result leads us to the following two important theorems.

Theorem 2.19. An $n \times n$ matrix $\mathbf{M}$ is invertible if and only if $\det \mathbf{M} \neq 0$.

Proof. Suppose that $\mathbf{M}$ is invertible. Then $\mathbf{M}$ can be written as a product of elementary matrices, each having a nonzero determinant. Since the determinant of a product of elementary matrices is equal to the product of the determinants of those matrices, the determinant of $\mathbf{M}$ cannot be zero. Now suppose that $\mathbf{M}$ is singular. Then $\mathbf{M}$ can be written as a product of elementary matrices and a matrix having a row of zeros because the rows of $\mathbf{M}$ must be linearly dependent. Since the determinant of a matrix possessing a row of zeros is zero, the determinant of the product is also zero. ■

Theorem 2.20. For any two $n \times n$ matrices $\mathbf{F}$ and $\mathbf{G}$, $\det \mathbf{FG} = \det \mathbf{F} \det \mathbf{G}$.

Proof. If either $\mathbf{F}$ or $\mathbf{G}$ is singular, then $\mathbf{FG}$ is singular and the equation holds since both sides are zero. Otherwise, both $\mathbf{F}$ and $\mathbf{G}$ can be factored completely into elementary matrices. Since the determinant of a product of elementary matrices is the product of the determinants, the equation holds. ■

Theorem 2.19 gives us a test for singularity. Once we know that the determinant of an $n \times n$ matrix $\mathbf{M}$ is not zero, we can use the following formula to calculate the entries of $\mathbf{M}^{-1}$.

Theorem 2.21. Let $\mathbf{F}$ be an $n \times n$ matrix and define the entries of an $n \times n$ matrix $\mathbf{G}$ using the formula

$$\mathbf{G}_{ij} = \frac{C_{ji}(\mathbf{F})}{\det \mathbf{F}}, \tag{2.62}$$

where $C_{ji}(\mathbf{F})$ is the cofactor of $\left(\mathbf{F}^{\mathrm{T}}\right)_{ij}$. Then $\mathbf{G} = \mathbf{F}^{-1}$.

Proof. Using the multiplication formula for $\mathbf{FG}$, we have

$$\left(\mathbf{FG}\right)_{ij} = \sum_{k=1}^{n} F_{ik} G_{kj}$$

$$= \sum_{k=1}^{n} F_{ik} \frac{C_{jk}(\mathbf{F})}{\det \mathbf{F}}$$

$$= \frac{1}{\det \mathbf{F}} \sum_{k=1}^{n} F_{ik} C_{jk}(\mathbf{F}). \tag{2.63}$$

If $i = j$, then the summation gives the determinant of $\mathbf{F}$ equivalently to Equation (2.54), so multiplying by $1/\det \mathbf{F}$ gives us $\left(\mathbf{FG}\right)_{ij} = 1$. If $i \neq j$, then the summation gives the determinant of a matrix equal to $\mathbf{F}$ except that row j has been replaced by the entries in row i. Since the matrix has two identical rows, its determinant is zero, and thus $\left(\mathbf{FG}\right)_{ij} = 0$. Since the main diagonal entries of $\mathbf{FG}$ are 1 and all the remaining entries are 0, $\mathbf{FG}$ is the identity matrix. A similar argument proves that $\mathbf{GF}$ is the identity matrix, so $\mathbf{G} = \mathbf{F}^{-1}$. ∎

Using Equation (2.62), we can derive explicit formulas for the inverses of matrices having sizes that are commonly used in computer graphics. The inverse of a 2×2 matrix $\mathbf{A}$ is given by

$$\mathbf{A}^{-1} = \frac{1}{\det \mathbf{A}} \begin{bmatrix} A_{22} & -A_{12} \\ -A_{21} & A_{11} \end{bmatrix}. \tag{2.64}$$

The inverse of a 3×3 matrix $\mathbf{B}$ is given by

$$\mathbf{B}^{-1} = \frac{1}{\det \mathbf{B}} \begin{bmatrix} B_{22}B_{33} - B_{23}B_{32} & B_{13}B_{32} - B_{12}B_{33} & B_{12}B_{23} - B_{13}B_{22} \\ B_{23}B_{31} - B_{21}B_{33} & B_{11}B_{33} - B_{13}B_{31} & B_{13}B_{21} - B_{11}B_{23} \\ B_{21}B_{32} - B_{22}B_{31} & B_{12}B_{31} - B_{11}B_{32} & B_{11}B_{22} - B_{12}B_{21} \end{bmatrix}. \quad (2.65)$$

The inverse of a matrix $\mathbf{M}$ can be expressed as $\mathbf{M}^C/\det \mathbf{M}$, where the notation $\mathbf{M}^C$ is used to denote the matrix of cofactors of the entries of $\mathbf{M}^T$. That is, $(\mathbf{M}^C)_{ij} = C_{ij}(\mathbf{M}^T)$. Since calculating $\det \mathbf{M}$ also requires that we calculate the cofactor of every entry of $\mathbf{M}$, we can use the entries of the matrix $\mathbf{M}^C$ to evaluate the determinant of $\mathbf{M}$ more efficiently. Equation (2.55) can be written as

$$\det \mathbf{M} = \sum_{j=1}^{n} M_{kj} C_{kj}(\mathbf{M})$$

$$= \sum_{j=1}^{n} M_{kj} C_{jk}(\mathbf{M}^T)$$

$$= \sum_{j=1}^{n} M_{kj} (\mathbf{M}^C)_{jk}. \quad (2.66)$$

Thus, the determinant can be evaluated by choosing any row k of the matrix $\mathbf{M}$ and summing the products with the entries of the k-th column of the matrix $\mathbf{M}^C$. For the 3×3 matrix $\mathbf{B}$, we have the following expression for $\mathbf{B}^{-1}$ in which we have chosen $k = 1$.

$$\mathbf{B}^C = \begin{bmatrix} B_{22}B_{33} - B_{23}B_{32} & B_{13}B_{32} - B_{12}B_{33} & B_{12}B_{23} - B_{13}B_{22} \\ B_{23}B_{31} - B_{21}B_{33} & B_{11}B_{33} - B_{13}B_{31} & B_{13}B_{21} - B_{11}B_{23} \\ B_{21}B_{32} - B_{22}B_{31} & B_{12}B_{31} - B_{11}B_{32} & B_{11}B_{22} - B_{12}B_{21} \end{bmatrix}$$

$$\mathbf{B}^{-1} = \frac{\mathbf{B}^C}{\displaystyle\sum_{j=1}^{n} B_{1j} (\mathbf{B}^C)_{j1}} \quad (2.67)$$

One final observation that we make in this section concerns linear systems of the form $\mathbf{Mx} = \mathbf{r}$, where $\mathbf{x}$ is a vector of n unknowns and $\mathbf{r}$ is a vector of n constants. If the matrix $\mathbf{M}$ is invertible, then the solution to this system is given by $\mathbf{x} = \mathbf{M}^{-1}\mathbf{r}$. Again using the notation $\mathbf{M}^C$ to denote the matrix of cofactors of the entries of $\mathbf{M}^T$, we can write

$$\mathbf{x} = \frac{\mathbf{M}^{\mathrm{C}}}{\det \mathbf{M}} \mathbf{r}. \qquad (2.68)$$

The k-th component of $\mathbf{x}$ is thus given by the formula

$$\begin{aligned}
x_k &= \frac{1}{\det \mathbf{M}} \sum_{i=1}^{n} \left(\mathbf{M}^{\mathrm{C}} \right)_{ki} r_i \\
&= \frac{1}{\det \mathbf{M}} \sum_{i=1}^{n} C_{ik}(\mathbf{M}) r_i.
\end{aligned} \qquad (2.69)$$

By the definition given in Equation (2.53), the quantity $C_{ik}(\mathbf{M})$ does not depend on any entries in the k-th column of the matrix $\mathbf{M}$. Comparing the summation $\sum_{i=1}^{n} C_{ik}(\mathbf{M}) r_i$ to Equation (2.54), we see that it is equal to the determinant of the matrix whose k-th column is equal to the vector $\mathbf{r}$ and whose other columns are equal to those of the matrix $\mathbf{M}$. Defining the notation

$$\mathbf{M}_k(\mathbf{r}) \equiv [\mathbf{M}_1 \quad \cdots \quad \mathbf{M}_{k-1} \quad \mathbf{r} \quad \mathbf{M}_{k+1} \quad \cdots \quad \mathbf{M}_n], \qquad (2.70)$$

where $\mathbf{M}_j$ represents the j-th column of $\mathbf{M}$, we can write Equation (2.69) as

$$x_k = \frac{\det \mathbf{M}_k(\mathbf{r})}{\det \mathbf{M}}. \qquad (2.71)$$

Equation (2.71) is known as *Cramer's rule*. Since it requires a determinant calculation for each unknown in a linear system, using Cramer's rule is far less efficient than simply inverting the coefficient matrix and multiplying it by the constant vector. Cramer's rule does, however, tell us that if the coefficients and constants in a linear system are all integers and $\det \mathbf{M} = \pm 1$, then the unknowns must all be integers.

2.5 Eigenvalues and Eigenvectors

For every invertible square matrix, there exist vectors that, when multiplied by the matrix, are changed only in magnitude and not in direction. That is, for an $n \times n$ matrix $\mathbf{M}$, there exist nonzero n-dimensional vectors $\mathbf{V}_1, \mathbf{V}_2, \ldots, \mathbf{V}_n$ such that

$$\mathbf{M} \mathbf{V}_i = \lambda_i \mathbf{V}_i. \qquad (2.72)$$

The scalars λ_i are called the *eigenvalues* of the matrix $\mathbf{M}$, and the vectors $\mathbf{V}_i$ are called the *eigenvectors* that correspond to those eigenvalues.

The eigenvalues of a matrix can be determined by first rearranging Equation (2.72) to read

$$(\mathbf{M} - \lambda_i \mathbf{I})\mathbf{V}_i = \mathbf{0}, \tag{2.73}$$

where $\mathbf{I}$ is the $n \times n$ identity matrix. For this equation to be true for nonzero vectors $\mathbf{V}_i$, the matrix $\mathbf{M} - \lambda_i \mathbf{I}$ must be singular. This is necessary because otherwise we could invert $\mathbf{M} - \lambda_i \mathbf{I}$ and write

$$\mathbf{V}_i = (\mathbf{M} - \lambda_i \mathbf{I})^{-1}\mathbf{0} = \mathbf{0}, \tag{2.74}$$

contradicting the assumption that $\mathbf{V}_i \neq \mathbf{0}$. Since $\mathbf{M} - \lambda_i \mathbf{I}$ is singular, its determinant must be zero, so we can calculate the eigenvalues λ_i by solving the equation

$$\det(\mathbf{M} - \lambda \mathbf{I}) = 0. \tag{2.75}$$

The degree n polynomial in λ given by Equation (2.75) is called the *characteristic polynomial* of the matrix $\mathbf{M}$. The roots of this polynomial yield the eigenvalues of the matrix $\mathbf{M}$.

Example 2.22. Calculate the eigenvalues of the matrix

$$\mathbf{M} = \begin{bmatrix} 1 & 1 \\ 3 & -1 \end{bmatrix}. \tag{2.76}$$

Solution. The matrix $\mathbf{M} - \lambda \mathbf{I}$ is given by

$$\mathbf{M} - \lambda \mathbf{I} = \begin{bmatrix} 1-\lambda & 1 \\ 3 & -1-\lambda \end{bmatrix}.$$

Evaluating the determinant of $\mathbf{M} - \lambda \mathbf{I}$ produces the characteristic polynomial

$$(1-\lambda)(-1-\lambda) - 3. \tag{2.77}$$

Simplifying this polynomial and setting it equal to zero gives us

$$\lambda^2 - 4 = 0, \tag{2.78}$$

from which it follows that the eigenvalues of $\mathbf{M}$ are $\lambda_1 = 2$ and $\lambda_2 = -2$. ∎

Once the eigenvalues have been determined, the corresponding eigenvectors are calculated by solving the homogeneous system given by Equation (2.73). Since the matrix $\mathbf{M} - \lambda_i \mathbf{I}$ is singular, its reduced form has at least one row of zeros, so there are infinitely many solutions. An obvious property of Equation (2.72) is that if $\mathbf{V}_i$ is an eigenvector corresponding to the eigenvalue λ_i, then any scalar multiple $a\mathbf{V}_i$ is also an eigenvector. Thus, eigenvectors are always written in terms of an arbitrary constant, which if desired, may be chosen so that the eigenvector has unit length.

Example 2.23. Calculate the eigenvectors of the matrix

$$\mathbf{M} = \begin{bmatrix} 1 & 1 \\ 3 & -1 \end{bmatrix}. \tag{2.79}$$

Solution. In Example 2.22, we found that the matrix $\mathbf{M}$ has the eigenvalues $\lambda_1 = 2$ and $\lambda_2 = -2$. Corresponding eigenvectors are found by solving the linear system $(\mathbf{M} - \lambda_i \mathbf{I})\mathbf{V}_i = \mathbf{0}$. For the eigenvalue $\lambda_1 = 2$ we have

$$\begin{bmatrix} -1 & 1 \\ 3 & -3 \end{bmatrix} \mathbf{V}_1 = \begin{bmatrix} 0 \\ 0 \end{bmatrix}, \tag{2.80}$$

and for the eigenvalue $\lambda_2 = -2$ we have

$$\begin{bmatrix} 3 & 1 \\ 3 & 1 \end{bmatrix} \mathbf{V}_2 = \begin{bmatrix} 0 \\ 0 \end{bmatrix}. \tag{2.81}$$

These systems yield the solutions

$$\mathbf{V}_1 = a \begin{bmatrix} 1 \\ 1 \end{bmatrix}$$

$$\mathbf{V}_2 = b \begin{bmatrix} 1 \\ -3 \end{bmatrix}, \tag{2.82}$$

where the scalars a and b are arbitrary nonzero constants. ∎

In general, the eigenvalues of a matrix, given by the roots of its characteristic polynomial, are complex numbers. This means that the corresponding eigenvectors can also have complex entries. A type of matrix that is guaranteed to have real eigenvalues and therefore real eigenvectors, however, is the symmetric matrix.

Definition 2.24. An $n \times n$ matrix $\mathbf{M}$ is *symmetric* if and only if $M_{ij} = M_{ji}$ for all i and j. That is, a matrix whose entries are symmetric about the main diagonal is called symmetric.

The eigenvalues and eigenvectors of symmetric matrices possess the properties given by the following two theorems.

Theorem 2.25. The eigenvalues of a symmetric matrix $\mathbf{M}$ having real entries are real numbers.

Proof. Let λ be an eigenvalue of the matrix $\mathbf{M}$, and let $\mathbf{V}$ be a corresponding eigenvector such that $\mathbf{MV} = \lambda \mathbf{V}$. Multiplying both sides of this equation on the left by the row vector $\bar{\mathbf{V}}^{\mathrm{T}}$ gives us

$$\bar{\mathbf{V}}^{\mathrm{T}}\mathbf{MV} = \bar{\mathbf{V}}^{\mathrm{T}}\lambda \mathbf{V} = \lambda \bar{\mathbf{V}}^{\mathrm{T}}\mathbf{V}, \tag{2.83}$$

where the overbar denotes complex conjugation, which for vectors and matrices is performed componentwise. Since the product of a complex number $a + bi$ and its conjugate $a - bi$ is equal to the real number $a^2 + b^2$, the product $\bar{\mathbf{V}}^{\mathrm{T}}\mathbf{V}$ is a real number. By showing that the product $\bar{\mathbf{V}}^{\mathrm{T}}\mathbf{MV}$ is also a real number, we can conclude that λ is real. We can examine the conjugate of $\bar{\mathbf{V}}^{\mathrm{T}}\mathbf{MV}$ to get

$$\overline{\bar{\mathbf{V}}^{\mathrm{T}}\mathbf{MV}} = \mathbf{V}^{\mathrm{T}}\mathbf{M}\bar{\mathbf{V}}, \tag{2.84}$$

where we have used the fact that $\bar{\mathbf{M}} = \mathbf{M}$ because the matrix $\mathbf{M}$ has real entries. Since the quantity $\mathbf{V}^{\mathrm{T}}\mathbf{M}\bar{\mathbf{V}}$ is a 1×1 matrix, it is equal to its own transpose. We may thus write

$$\mathbf{V}^{\mathrm{T}}\mathbf{M}\bar{\mathbf{V}} = \left(\mathbf{V}^{\mathrm{T}}\mathbf{M}\bar{\mathbf{V}}\right)^{\mathrm{T}} = \bar{\mathbf{V}}^{\mathrm{T}}\mathbf{M}^{\mathrm{T}}\mathbf{V}. \tag{2.85}$$

Because the matrix $\mathbf{M}$ is symmetric, $\mathbf{M}^{\mathrm{T}} = \mathbf{M}$, so we now have

$$\overline{\bar{\mathbf{V}}^{\mathrm{T}}\mathbf{MV}} = \bar{\mathbf{V}}^{\mathrm{T}}\mathbf{MV}, \tag{2.86}$$

showing that the quantity $\bar{\mathbf{V}}^{\mathrm{T}}\mathbf{MV}$ is equal to its own conjugate and is therefore a real number. This proves that the eigenvalue λ must be real. ∎

Theorem 2.26. Any two eigenvectors associated with distinct eigenvalues of a symmetric matrix $\mathbf{M}$ are orthogonal.

Proof. Let λ_1 and λ_2 be distinct eigenvalues of the matrix $\mathbf{M}$, and let $\mathbf{V}_1$ and $\mathbf{V}_2$ be the associated eigenvectors. Then we have the equations $\mathbf{M}\mathbf{V}_1 = \lambda_1 \mathbf{V}_1$ and $\mathbf{M}\mathbf{V}_2 = \lambda_2 \mathbf{V}_2$. We can show that $\lambda_1 \mathbf{V}_1^T \mathbf{V}_2 = \lambda_2 \mathbf{V}_1^T \mathbf{V}_2$ by writing

$$
\begin{aligned}
\lambda_1 \mathbf{V}_1^T \mathbf{V}_2 &= (\lambda_1 \mathbf{V}_1)^T \mathbf{V}_2 \\
&= (\mathbf{M}\mathbf{V}_1)^T \mathbf{V}_2 \\
&= \mathbf{V}_1^T \mathbf{M} \mathbf{V}_2 \\
&= \lambda_2 \mathbf{V}_1^T \mathbf{V}_2,
\end{aligned}
\tag{2.87}
$$

where we have used the fact that $\mathbf{M}^T = \mathbf{M}$. This tells us that

$$
(\lambda_1 - \lambda_2)\mathbf{V}_1^T \mathbf{V}_2 = 0,
\tag{2.88}
$$

but the eigenvalues λ_1 and λ_2 are distinct, so we must have $\mathbf{V}_1^T \mathbf{V}_2 = 0$. Since this quantity is simply the dot product $\mathbf{V}_1 \cdot \mathbf{V}_2$, the eigenvectors are orthogonal. ∎

2.6 Diagonalization

Recall that a diagonal matrix is one that has nonzero entries only along the main diagonal. That is, an $n \times n$ matrix $\mathbf{M}$ is a diagonal matrix if $M_{ij} = 0$ whenever $i \neq j$. Given a square matrix $\mathbf{M}$, if we can find a matrix $\mathbf{A}$ such that $\mathbf{A}^{-1}\mathbf{M}\mathbf{A}$ is a diagonal matrix, then we say that $\mathbf{A}$ *diagonalizes* $\mathbf{M}$. Although not true in general, the following theorem states that any $n \times n$ matrix for which we can find n linearly independent eigenvectors can be diagonalized.

Theorem 2.27. Let $\mathbf{M}$ be an $n \times n$ matrix having eigenvalues $\lambda_1, \lambda_2, \ldots, \lambda_n$, and suppose that there exist corresponding eigenvectors $\mathbf{V}_1, \mathbf{V}_2, \ldots, \mathbf{V}_n$ that form a linearly independent set. Then the matrix $\mathbf{A}$ given by

$$
\mathbf{A} = \begin{bmatrix} \mathbf{V}_1 & \mathbf{V}_2 & \cdots & \mathbf{V}_n \end{bmatrix}
\tag{2.89}
$$

(i.e., the columns of the matrix $\mathbf{A}$ are the eigenvectors $\mathbf{V}_1, \mathbf{V}_2, \ldots, \mathbf{V}_n$) diagonalizes $\mathbf{M}$, and the main diagonal entries of the product $\mathbf{A}^{-1}\mathbf{M}\mathbf{A}$ are the eigenvalues of $\mathbf{M}$:

$$A^{-1}MA = \begin{bmatrix} \lambda_1 & 0 & \cdots & 0 \\ 0 & \lambda_2 & \cdots & 0 \\ \vdots & \vdots & \ddots & \vdots \\ 0 & 0 & \cdots & \lambda_n \end{bmatrix}. \qquad (2.90)$$

Conversely, if there exists an invertible matrix A such that $A^{-1}MA$ is a diagonal matrix, then the columns of A must be eigenvectors of M, and the main diagonal entries of $A^{-1}MA$ are the corresponding eigenvalues of M.

Proof. We first examine the product MA. Since the j-th column of A is the eigenvector V_j, the j-th column of MA is equal to MV_j. Since V_j is an eigenvector, we have $MV_j = \lambda_j V_j$, so the product MA can be written as

$$MA = \begin{bmatrix} \lambda_1 V_1 & \lambda_2 V_2 & \cdots & \lambda_n V_n \end{bmatrix}$$

$$= \begin{bmatrix} V_1 & V_2 & \cdots & V_n \end{bmatrix} \begin{bmatrix} \lambda_1 & 0 & \cdots & 0 \\ 0 & \lambda_2 & \cdots & 0 \\ \vdots & \vdots & \ddots & \vdots \\ 0 & 0 & \cdots & \lambda_n \end{bmatrix}$$

$$= A \begin{bmatrix} \lambda_1 & 0 & \cdots & 0 \\ 0 & \lambda_2 & \cdots & 0 \\ \vdots & \vdots & \ddots & \vdots \\ 0 & 0 & \cdots & \lambda_n \end{bmatrix}. \qquad (2.91)$$

Since the eigenvectors V_j are linearly independent, the matrix A is invertible, and the product $A^{-1}MA$ can be written as

$$A^{-1}MA = A^{-1}A \begin{bmatrix} \lambda_1 & 0 & \cdots & 0 \\ 0 & \lambda_2 & \cdots & 0 \\ \vdots & \vdots & \ddots & \vdots \\ 0 & 0 & \cdots & \lambda_n \end{bmatrix} = \begin{bmatrix} \lambda_1 & 0 & \cdots & 0 \\ 0 & \lambda_2 & \cdots & 0 \\ \vdots & \vdots & \ddots & \vdots \\ 0 & 0 & \cdots & \lambda_n \end{bmatrix}. \qquad (2.92)$$

Now we prove the converse assertion that any invertible matrix A that diagonalizes M must be composed of the eigenvectors of M. Suppose that D is an

$n \times n$ diagonal matrix such that $\mathbf{D} = \mathbf{A}^{-1}\mathbf{MA}$ for some $n \times n$ matrix $\mathbf{A}$. Then we may write

$$\mathbf{AD} = \mathbf{MA}. \tag{2.93}$$

Let $\mathbf{V}_j$ denote the j-th column of $\mathbf{A}$, and let $d_1, d_2, \ldots, d_n$ be the main diagonal entries of $\mathbf{D}$. The product $\mathbf{AD}$ is given by

$$\mathbf{AD} = \begin{bmatrix} \mathbf{V}_1 & \mathbf{V}_2 & \cdots & \mathbf{V}_n \end{bmatrix} \begin{bmatrix} d_1 & 0 & \cdots & 0 \\ 0 & d_2 & \cdots & 0 \\ \vdots & \vdots & \ddots & \vdots \\ 0 & 0 & \cdots & d_n \end{bmatrix}$$

$$= \begin{bmatrix} d_1 \mathbf{V}_1 & d_2 \mathbf{V}_2 & \cdots & d_n \mathbf{V}_n \end{bmatrix}, \tag{2.94}$$

and the product $\mathbf{MA}$ is given by

$$\mathbf{MA} = \begin{bmatrix} \mathbf{MV}_1 & \mathbf{MV}_2 & \cdots & \mathbf{MV}_n \end{bmatrix}. \tag{2.95}$$

Equating the j-th column of $\mathbf{AD}$ with the j-th column of $\mathbf{MA}$ demonstrates that $\mathbf{MV}_j = d_j \mathbf{V}_j$, and thus each $\mathbf{V}_j$ is an eigenvector of $\mathbf{M}$ corresponding to the eigenvalue d_j. ∎

Since the eigenvectors of a symmetric matrix $\mathbf{M}$ are orthogonal, the matrix $\mathbf{A}$ whose columns are composed of unit-length eigenvectors of $\mathbf{M}$ is an orthogonal matrix and therefore satisfies $\mathbf{A}^{-1} = \mathbf{A}^{\mathrm{T}}$. The diagonal matrix $\mathbf{D}$ consisting of the eigenvalues of a symmetric matrix $\mathbf{M}$ can thus be expressed as

$$\mathbf{D} = \mathbf{A}^{\mathrm{T}}\mathbf{MA}. \tag{2.96}$$

Example 2.28. Find a matrix that diagonalizes the matrix

$$\mathbf{M} = \begin{bmatrix} 2 & 1 & 0 \\ 1 & 1 & 0 \\ 0 & 0 & -1 \end{bmatrix}. \tag{2.97}$$

Solution. The characteristic polynomial for $\mathbf{M}$ is

$$\det(\mathbf{M} - \lambda\mathbf{I}) = -\lambda^3 + 2\lambda^2 + 2\lambda - 1$$
$$= -(\lambda + 1)(\lambda^2 - 3\lambda + 1). \tag{2.98}$$

The roots of this polynomial give us the eigenvalues

$$\lambda_1 = -1$$
$$\lambda_2 = \frac{3 + \sqrt{5}}{2}$$
$$\lambda_3 = \frac{3 - \sqrt{5}}{2}. \tag{2.99}$$

The eigenvector $\mathbf{V}_1$ corresponding to the eigenvalue λ_1 is given by the solution to the homogeneous linear system

$$\begin{bmatrix} 3 & 1 & 0 \\ 1 & 2 & 0 \\ 0 & 0 & 0 \end{bmatrix} \mathbf{V}_1 = \begin{bmatrix} 0 \\ 0 \\ 0 \end{bmatrix}. \tag{2.100}$$

Reducing the coefficient matrix gives us

$$\begin{bmatrix} 1 & 0 & 0 \\ 0 & 1 & 0 \\ 0 & 0 & 0 \end{bmatrix} \mathbf{V}_1 = \begin{bmatrix} 0 \\ 0 \\ 0 \end{bmatrix}, \tag{2.101}$$

and the solution is thus given by

$$\mathbf{V}_1 = a \begin{bmatrix} 0 \\ 0 \\ 1 \end{bmatrix}. \tag{2.102}$$

For the eigenvalue λ_2, we need to solve the system

$$\begin{bmatrix} \dfrac{1-\sqrt{5}}{2} & 1 & 0 \\[2ex] 1 & \dfrac{-1-\sqrt{5}}{2} & 0 \\[2ex] 0 & 0 & \dfrac{-5-\sqrt{5}}{2} \end{bmatrix} V_2 = \begin{bmatrix} 0 \\ 0 \\ 0 \end{bmatrix}. \tag{2.103}$$

This reduces to

$$\begin{bmatrix} 1 & \dfrac{-1-\sqrt{5}}{2} & 0 \\[2ex] 0 & 0 & 1 \\[2ex] 0 & 0 & 0 \end{bmatrix} V_2 = \begin{bmatrix} 0 \\ 0 \\ 0 \end{bmatrix}, \tag{2.104}$$

and our second eigenvector is given by

$$V_2 = b \begin{bmatrix} \dfrac{1+\sqrt{5}}{2} \\[2ex] 1 \\[1ex] 0 \end{bmatrix}. \tag{2.105}$$

Similarly, the eigenvector V_3 is equal to

$$V_3 = c \begin{bmatrix} \dfrac{1-\sqrt{5}}{2} \\[2ex] 1 \\[1ex] 0 \end{bmatrix}. \tag{2.106}$$

We choose the constants a, b, and c so that the eigenvectors have unit length. A quick test verifies that the eigenvectors are orthogonal as expected since the matrix M is symmetric. Define the matrix A as

$$A = \begin{bmatrix} \dfrac{\mathbf{V}_1}{\|\mathbf{V}_1\|} & \dfrac{\mathbf{V}_2}{\|\mathbf{V}_2\|} & \dfrac{\mathbf{V}_3}{\|\mathbf{V}_3\|} \end{bmatrix}$$

$$\approx \begin{bmatrix} 0 & 0.851 & -0.526 \\ 0 & 0.526 & 0.851 \\ 1 & 0 & 0 \end{bmatrix}. \tag{2.107}$$

A is an orthogonal matrix that diagonalizes $\mathbf{M}$:

$$\mathbf{A}^{-1}\mathbf{M}\mathbf{A} = \mathbf{A}^{\mathrm{T}}\mathbf{M}\mathbf{A} = \begin{bmatrix} -1 & 0 & 0 \\ 0 & \dfrac{3+\sqrt{5}}{2} & 0 \\ 0 & 0 & \dfrac{3-\sqrt{5}}{2} \end{bmatrix}. \ \blacksquare \tag{2.108}$$

Chapter 2 Summary

Matrix Products

If $\mathbf{F}$ is an $n \times m$ matrix and $\mathbf{G}$ is an $m \times p$ matrix, then the product $\mathbf{FG}$ is an $n \times p$ matrix whose (i, j) entry is given by

$$(\mathbf{FG})_{ij} = \sum_{k=1}^{m} F_{ik} G_{kj}.$$

Determinants

The determinant of an $n \times n$ matrix $\mathbf{M}$ is given by the formulas

$$\det \mathbf{M} = \sum_{i=1}^{n} M_{ik} C_{ik}(\mathbf{M})$$

and

$$\det \mathbf{M} = \sum_{j=1}^{n} M_{kj} C_{kj}(\mathbf{M}),$$

where $C_{ij}(\mathbf{M})$ is the cofactor of M_{ij} defined by $C_{ij}(\mathbf{M}) = (-1)^{i+j} \det \mathbf{M}^{\{i,j\}}$.

The determinant of a 2×2 matrix is given by

$$\begin{vmatrix} a & b \\ c & d \end{vmatrix} = ad - bc,$$

and the determinant of a 3×3 matrix is given by

$$\begin{vmatrix} a_{11} & a_{12} & a_{13} \\ a_{21} & a_{22} & a_{23} \\ a_{31} & a_{32} & a_{33} \end{vmatrix} = a_{11}(a_{22}a_{33} - a_{23}a_{32}) - a_{12}(a_{21}a_{33} - a_{23}a_{31}) + a_{13}(a_{21}a_{32} - a_{22}a_{31}).$$

Matrix Inverses

An $n \times n$ matrix $\mathbf{M}$ is invertible if and only if the columns of $\mathbf{M}$ form a linearly independent set. Equivalently, $\mathbf{M}$ is invertible if and only if $\det \mathbf{M} \neq 0$.

The entries of the inverse $\mathbf{G}$ of an $n \times n$ matrix $\mathbf{F}$ can be calculated by using the explicit formula

$$G_{ij} = \frac{C_{ji}(\mathbf{F})}{\det \mathbf{F}}.$$

Using this formula, the inverse of a 2×2 matrix $\mathbf{A}$ is given by

$$\mathbf{A}^{-1} = \frac{1}{\det \mathbf{A}} \begin{bmatrix} A_{22} & -A_{12} \\ -A_{21} & A_{11} \end{bmatrix},$$

and the inverse of a 3×3 matrix $\mathbf{B}$ is given by

$$\mathbf{B}^{-1} = \frac{1}{\det \mathbf{B}} \begin{bmatrix} B_{22}B_{33} - B_{23}B_{32} & B_{13}B_{32} - B_{12}B_{33} & B_{12}B_{23} - B_{13}B_{22} \\ B_{23}B_{31} - B_{21}B_{33} & B_{11}B_{33} - B_{13}B_{31} & B_{13}B_{21} - B_{11}B_{23} \\ B_{21}B_{32} - B_{22}B_{31} & B_{12}B_{31} - B_{11}B_{32} & B_{11}B_{22} - B_{12}B_{21} \end{bmatrix}.$$

Eigenvalues and Eigenvectors

The eigenvalues of an $n \times n$ matrix $\mathbf{M}$ are equal to the roots of the characteristic polynomial given by

$$\det(\mathbf{M} - \lambda\mathbf{I}).$$

An eigenvector $\mathbf{V}$ associated with the eigenvalue λ of the matrix $\mathbf{M}$ is given by the solution to the homogeneous linear system

$$(\mathbf{M} - \lambda\mathbf{I})\mathbf{V} = \mathbf{0}.$$

The eigenvalues of a real symmetric matrix are real, and the eigenvectors corresponding to distinct eigenvalues of a real symmetric matrix are orthogonal.

Diagonalization

If $\mathbf{V}_1, \mathbf{V}_2, \ldots, \mathbf{V}_n$ are linearly independent eigenvectors of an $n \times n$ matrix $\mathbf{M}$, then the matrix $\mathbf{A}$ given by

$$\mathbf{A} = \begin{bmatrix} \mathbf{V}_1 & \mathbf{V}_2 & \cdots & \mathbf{V}_n \end{bmatrix}$$

diagonalizes $\mathbf{M}$, meaning that

$$\mathbf{A}^{-1}\mathbf{M}\mathbf{A} = \begin{bmatrix} \lambda_1 & 0 & \cdots & 0 \\ 0 & \lambda_2 & \cdots & 0 \\ \vdots & \vdots & \ddots & \vdots \\ 0 & 0 & \cdots & \lambda_n \end{bmatrix},$$

where $\lambda_1, \lambda_2, \ldots, \lambda_n$ are the eigenvalues of $\mathbf{M}$.

Exercises for Chapter 2

1. Calculate the determinants of the following matrices.

(a) $\begin{bmatrix} 2 & 7 \\ -3 & \frac{1}{2} \end{bmatrix}$

(b) $\begin{bmatrix} 0 & 0 & 1 \\ 0 & 1 & 0 \\ 1 & 0 & 0 \end{bmatrix}$

(c) $\begin{bmatrix} \frac{1}{2} & \frac{\sqrt{3}}{2} & 0 \\ -\frac{\sqrt{3}}{2} & \frac{1}{2} & 0 \\ 0 & 0 & 1 \end{bmatrix}$
(d) $\begin{bmatrix} 5 & 7 & 1 \\ 17 & 2 & 64 \\ 10 & 14 & 2 \end{bmatrix}$

2. Calculate the inverses of the following matrices.

(a) $\begin{bmatrix} 2 & 0 & 0 \\ 0 & 3 & 0 \\ 0 & 0 & 4 \end{bmatrix}$
(b) $\begin{bmatrix} 1 & 0 & 0 \\ 0 & 2 & 2 \\ 3 & 0 & 8 \end{bmatrix}$

(c) $\begin{bmatrix} \cos\theta & 0 & -\sin\theta \\ 0 & 1 & 0 \\ \sin\theta & 0 & \cos\theta \end{bmatrix}$
(d) $\begin{bmatrix} 1 & 0 & 0 & 4 \\ 0 & 1 & 0 & 3 \\ 0 & 0 & 1 & 7 \\ 0 & 0 & 0 & 1 \end{bmatrix}$

3. Solve the following homogeneous linear system.

$$4x + 3y + 2z = 0$$
$$x - y - 3z = 0$$
$$2x + 3y + 4z = 0$$

4. Calculate the eigenvalues of the following matrix.

$$\begin{bmatrix} 2 & 0 & 0 \\ 5 & 2 & 3 \\ -4 & 3 & 2 \end{bmatrix}$$

5. Let $\mathbf{M}$ be an $n \times n$ matrix whose rows are given by the vectors $\mathbf{R}_1^T, \mathbf{R}_2^T, \ldots, \mathbf{R}_n^T$. Prove that if the rows of $\mathbf{M}$ form a linearly independent set, then the rows of the matrix $\mathbf{EM}$, where $\mathbf{E}$ is an elementary matrix, also form a linearly independent set.

6. An *upper triangular* matrix $\mathbf{M}$ is one for which $M_{ij} = 0$ whenever $i > j$. That is, all the entries below the main diagonal are zero. Prove that the determi-

nant of an upper triangular matrix is equal to the product of the entries on the main diagonal.

7. Let **D** be an $n \times n$ diagonal matrix whose main diagonal entries are $d_1, d_2, \ldots, d_n$:

$$\mathbf{D} = \begin{bmatrix} d_1 & 0 & \cdots & 0 \\ 0 & d_2 & \cdots & 0 \\ \vdots & \vdots & \ddots & \vdots \\ 0 & 0 & \cdots & d_n \end{bmatrix}.$$

Show that the inverse of **D** is also a diagonal matrix, and that its main diagonal entries are given by $1/d_1, 1/d_2, \ldots, 1/d_n$.

8. Implement a C++ class that encapsulates a 3×3 matrix. The class should possess storage for the nine entries of the matrix. In addition to the default constructor, which should not perform any initialization, the class should have a constructor that takes nine floating-point numbers as arguments and initializes the matrix's entries to those values. The class should also include overloaded operators for addition, subtraction, multiplication, and division by scalars, multiplication by another 3×3 matrix, and multiplication by a 3D vector object (see Chapter 1, Exercise 6). Provide a function that initializes a matrix to the identity. Finally, write functions that calculate the determinant of a 3×3 matrix and calculate the inverse of a 3×3 matrix.

Chapter **3**

Transforms

Throughout any 3D graphics engine architecture, it is often necessary to transform a set of vectors from one coordinate space to another. For instance, vertex coordinates for a model may be stored in object space, but need to be transformed to camera space before the model can be rendered. In this chapter, we concern ourselves with linear transformations among different Cartesian coordinate frames. Such transformations include simple scales and translations, as well as arbitrary rotations.

3.1 Linear Transformations

Suppose that we have established a 3D coordinate system C consisting of an origin and three coordinate axes, in which a point $\mathbf{P}$ has the coordinates $\langle x, y, z \rangle$. The values x, y, and z can be thought of as the distances that one must travel along each of the coordinate axes from the origin in order to reach the point $\mathbf{P}$. Suppose now that we introduce a second coordinate system C' in which coordinates $\langle x', y', z' \rangle$ can be expressed as linear functions of coordinates $\langle x, y, z \rangle$ in C. That is, suppose we can write

$$x'(x, y, z) = U_1 x + V_1 y + W_1 z + T_1$$
$$y'(x, y, z) = U_2 x + V_2 y + W_2 z + T_2$$
$$z'(x, y, z) = U_3 x + V_3 y + W_3 z + T_3.$$ (3.1)

This constitutes a *linear transformation* from C to C' and can be written in matrix form as follows.

$$\begin{bmatrix} x' \\ y' \\ z' \end{bmatrix} = \begin{bmatrix} U_1 & V_1 & W_1 \\ U_2 & V_2 & W_2 \\ U_3 & V_3 & W_3 \end{bmatrix} \begin{bmatrix} x \\ y \\ z \end{bmatrix} + \begin{bmatrix} T_1 \\ T_2 \\ T_3 \end{bmatrix}$$ (3.2)

The coordinates x', y', and z' can be thought of as the distances that one must travel along the axes in C' to reach the point **P**. The vector **T** represents the translation from the origin of C to the origin of C', and the matrix whose columns are the vectors **U**, **V**, and **W** represents how the orientation of the coordinate axes is changed when transforming from C to C'. Assuming the transformation is invertible, the linear transformation from C' to C is given by

$$\begin{bmatrix} x \\ y \\ z \end{bmatrix} = \begin{bmatrix} U_1 & V_1 & W_1 \\ U_2 & V_2 & W_2 \\ U_3 & V_3 & W_3 \end{bmatrix}^{-1} \left(\begin{bmatrix} x' \\ y' \\ z' \end{bmatrix} - \begin{bmatrix} T_1 \\ T_2 \\ T_3 \end{bmatrix} \right).$$ (3.3)

In Section 3.4, we will combine the 3×3 matrix and translation vector **T** into a single 4×4 transformation matrix. Before we reach that point, we will focus solely on linear transformations for which $\mathbf{T} \equiv \mathbf{0}$, in which case the vectors **U**, **V**, and **W** represent the images in C' of the basis vectors $\langle 1,0,0 \rangle$, $\langle 0,1,0 \rangle$, and $\langle 0,0,1 \rangle$ in C.

Multiple linear transformations can be concatenated and represented by a single matrix and translation. For example, vertex coordinates may need to be transformed from object space to world space and then from world space to camera space. The two transformations are combined into a single transformation that maps object-space coordinates directly to camera-space coordinates.

3.1.1 Orthogonal Matrices

Most 3×3 matrices arising in computer graphics applications are orthogonal. An orthogonal matrix is simply one whose inverse is equal to its transpose.

> **Definition 3.1.** An invertible $n \times n$ matrix $\mathbf{M}$ is called *orthogonal* if and only if $\mathbf{M}^{-1} = \mathbf{M}^{\mathrm{T}}$.

As the following theorem demonstrates, any matrix whose columns form an orthonormal set of vectors is orthogonal.

> **Theorem 3.2.** If the vectors $\mathbf{V}_1, \mathbf{V}_2, \ldots, \mathbf{V}_n$ form an orthonormal set, then the $n \times n$ matrix constructed by setting the j-th column equal to $\mathbf{V}_j$ for all $1 \leq j \leq n$ is orthogonal.
>
> **Proof.** Suppose that the vectors $\mathbf{V}_1, \mathbf{V}_2, \ldots, \mathbf{V}_n$ form an orthonormal set, and let $\mathbf{M}$ be the $n \times n$ matrix whose columns are given by the $\mathbf{V}_j$'s. Since the $\mathbf{V}_j$'s are orthonormal, $\mathbf{V}_i \cdot \mathbf{V}_j = \delta_{ij}$ where δ_{ij} is the Kronecker delta symbol. Since the (i, j) entry of the matrix product $\mathbf{M}^{\mathrm{T}}\mathbf{M}$ is equal to the dot product $\mathbf{V}_i \cdot \mathbf{V}_j$, we have $\mathbf{M}^{\mathrm{T}}\mathbf{M} = \mathbf{I}$. Therefore, $\mathbf{M}^{\mathrm{T}} = \mathbf{M}^{-1}$. ∎

Orthogonal matrices also possess the property that they preserve lengths and angles when they are used to transform vectors. A matrix $\mathbf{M}$ preserves length if for any vector $\mathbf{P}$ we have

$$\|\mathbf{MP}\| = \|\mathbf{P}\|. \tag{3.4}$$

A matrix that preserves lengths also preserves angles if for any two vectors $\mathbf{P}_1$ and $\mathbf{P}_2$ we have

$$(\mathbf{MP}_1) \cdot (\mathbf{MP}_2) = \mathbf{P}_1 \cdot \mathbf{P}_2. \tag{3.5}$$

The following theorem proves that an orthogonal matrix satisfies Equations (3.4) and (3.5).

> **Theorem 3.3.** If the $n \times n$ matrix $\mathbf{M}$ is orthogonal, then $\mathbf{M}$ preserves lengths and angles.
>
> **Proof.** Let $\mathbf{M}$ be orthogonal. We will first show that the dot product between two vectors $\mathbf{P}_1$ and $\mathbf{P}_2$ is preserved by a transformation by $\mathbf{M}$, and then use that result to show that $\mathbf{M}$ preserves lengths. Examining the dot product between the transformed vectors gives us

$$(\mathbf{MP_1}) \cdot (\mathbf{MP_2}) = (\mathbf{MP_1})^{\mathrm{T}} \mathbf{MP_2} = \mathbf{P_1^T M^T M P_2}. \tag{3.6}$$

Since $\mathbf{M}$ is orthogonal, $\mathbf{M}^{-1} = \mathbf{M}^{\mathrm{T}}$, so

$$\mathbf{P_1^T M^T M P_2} = \mathbf{P_1^T P_2} = \mathbf{P_1} \cdot \mathbf{P_2}. \tag{3.7}$$

This also implies that the length of a vector $\mathbf{P}$ is preserved when transformed by the matrix $\mathbf{M}$ since $\|\mathbf{P}\|^2 = \mathbf{P} \cdot \mathbf{P}$. ∎

Since orthogonal matrices preserve lengths and angles, they preserve the overall structure of a coordinate system. Orthogonal matrices can thus represent only combinations of rotations and reflections. Rotations are discussed in detail in Section 3.3. A *reflection transform* (also called an *inversion transformation*) refers to the operation performed when points are mirrored in a certain direction. For example, the matrix

$$\begin{bmatrix} 1 & 0 & 0 \\ 0 & 1 & 0 \\ 0 & 0 & -1 \end{bmatrix} \tag{3.8}$$

reflects the z-coordinate of a point across the x-y plane.

3.1.2 Handedness

In three dimensions, a basis $\mathcal{B}$ for a coordinate system given by the 3D vectors $\mathbf{V_1}$, $\mathbf{V_2}$, and $\mathbf{V_3}$ possesses a property called *handedness*. A right-handed basis is one for which $(\mathbf{V_1} \times \mathbf{V_2}) \cdot \mathbf{V_3} > 0$. That is, in a right-handed coordinate system, the direction in which the cross product between $\mathbf{V_1}$ and $\mathbf{V_2}$ points (which follows the right hand rule) forms an acute angle with the direction in which $\mathbf{V_3}$ points. If $\mathcal{B}$ is an orthonormal right-handed basis, we have $\mathbf{V_1} \times \mathbf{V_2} = \mathbf{V_3}$. If $(\mathbf{V_1} \times \mathbf{V_2}) \cdot \mathbf{V_3} < 0$, then the basis $\mathcal{B}$ is left-handed.

Performing an odd number of reflections reverses handedness. An even number of reflections is always equivalent to a rotation, so any series of reflections can always be regarded as a single rotation followed by at most one reflection. The existence of a reflection within a 3×3 matrix can be detected by examining the determinant. If the determinant of a 3×3 matrix $\mathbf{M}$ is negative, then a reflection is present, and $\mathbf{M}$ reverses the handedness of any set of basis vectors transformed by it. If the determinant is positive, then $\mathbf{M}$ preserves handedness.

An orthogonal matrix **M** can only have a determinant of 1 or −1. If det **M** = 1, the matrix **M** represents a pure rotation. If det **M** = −1, then the matrix **M** represents a rotation followed by a reflection.

3.2 Scaling Transforms

To scale a vector **P** by a factor of a, we simply calculate $\mathbf{P}' = a\mathbf{P}$. In three dimensions, this operation can also be expressed as the matrix product

$$\mathbf{P}' = \begin{bmatrix} a & 0 & 0 \\ 0 & a & 0 \\ 0 & 0 & a \end{bmatrix}\begin{bmatrix} P_x \\ P_y \\ P_z \end{bmatrix}. \tag{3.9}$$

This is called a *uniform* scale. If we wish to scale a vector by different amounts along the x-, y-, and z-axes, as shown in Figure 3.1, then we can use a matrix that is similar to the uniform scale matrix, but whose diagonal entries are not necessarily all equal. This is called a *nonuniform* scale and can be expressed as the matrix product

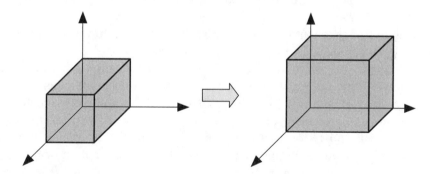

Figure 3.1 Nonuniform scaling.

$$\mathbf{P}' = \begin{bmatrix} a & 0 & 0 \\ 0 & b & 0 \\ 0 & 0 & c \end{bmatrix} \begin{bmatrix} P_x \\ P_y \\ P_z \end{bmatrix}. \tag{3.10}$$

A slightly more complex scaling operation that one may wish to perform is a nonuniform scale that is applied along three arbitrary axes. Suppose that we want to scale by a factor a along the axis $\mathbf{U}$, by a factor b along the axis $\mathbf{V}$, and by a factor c along the axis $\mathbf{W}$. Then we can transform from the $(\mathbf{U}, \mathbf{V}, \mathbf{W})$ coordinate system to the $(\mathbf{i}, \mathbf{j}, \mathbf{k})$ coordinate system, apply the scaling operation in this system using Equation (3.10), and then transform back into the $(\mathbf{U}, \mathbf{V}, \mathbf{W})$ coordinate system. This gives us the following matrix product.

$$\mathbf{P}' = \begin{bmatrix} U_x & V_x & W_x \\ U_y & V_y & W_y \\ U_z & V_z & W_z \end{bmatrix} \begin{bmatrix} a & 0 & 0 \\ 0 & b & 0 \\ 0 & 0 & c \end{bmatrix} \begin{bmatrix} U_x & V_x & W_x \\ U_y & V_y & W_y \\ U_z & V_z & W_z \end{bmatrix}^{-1} \begin{bmatrix} P_x \\ P_y \\ P_z \end{bmatrix} \tag{3.11}$$

3.3 Rotation Transforms

We can find 3×3 matrices that rotate a coordinate system through an angle θ about the x-, y-, or z-axis without much difficulty. We consider a rotation by a positive angle about the axis $\mathbf{A}$ to be that which performs a counterclockwise rotation when the axis $\mathbf{A}$ is pointing toward us.

First, we will find a general formula for rotations in two dimensions. As shown in Figure 3.2, we can perform a 90-degree counterclockwise rotation of a 2D vector $\mathbf{P}$ in the x-y plane by exchanging the x- and y-coordinates and negating the new x-coordinate. Calling the rotated vector $\mathbf{Q}$, we have $\mathbf{Q} = \langle -P_y, P_x \rangle$. The vectors $\mathbf{P}$ and $\mathbf{Q}$ form an orthogonal basis for the x-y plane. We can therefore express any vector in the x-y plane as a linear combination of these two vectors. In particular, as shown in Figure 3.3, any 2D vector $\mathbf{P}'$ that results from the rotation of the vector $\mathbf{P}$ through an angle θ can be expressed in terms of its components that are parallel to $\mathbf{P}$ and $\mathbf{Q}$. Basic trigonometry lets us write

$$\mathbf{P}' = \mathbf{P}\cos\theta + \mathbf{Q}\sin\theta. \tag{3.12}$$

This gives us the following expressions for the components of $\mathbf{P}'$.

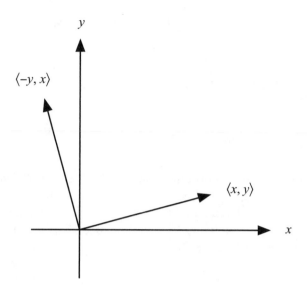

Figure 3.2 Rotation by 90 degrees in the *x-y* plane.

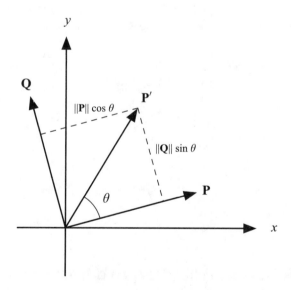

Figure 3.3. A rotated vector can be expressed as the linear combination of the original vector and the 90-degree counterclockwise rotation of the original vector.

$$P'_x = P_x \cos\theta - P_y \sin\theta$$
$$P'_y = P_y \cos\theta + P_x \sin\theta \qquad (3.13)$$

We can rewrite this in matrix form as follows.

$$\mathbf{P}' = \begin{bmatrix} \cos\theta & -\sin\theta \\ \sin\theta & \cos\theta \end{bmatrix} \mathbf{P} \qquad (3.14)$$

The 2D rotation matrix in Equation (3.14) can be extended to a rotation about the z-axis in three dimensions by taking the third row and column from the identity matrix. This ensures that the z-coordinate of a vector remains fixed during a rotation about the z-axis, as we would expect. The matrix $\mathbf{R}_z(\theta)$ that performs a rotation through the angle θ about the z-axis is thus given by

$$\mathbf{R}_z(\theta) = \begin{bmatrix} \cos\theta & -\sin\theta & 0 \\ \sin\theta & \cos\theta & 0 \\ 0 & 0 & 1 \end{bmatrix}. \qquad (3.15)$$

Similarly, we can derive the following 3×3 matrices $\mathbf{R}_x(\theta)$ and $\mathbf{R}_y(\theta)$ that perform rotations through an angle θ about the x- and y-axes, respectively.

$$\mathbf{R}_x(\theta) = \begin{bmatrix} 1 & 0 & 0 \\ 0 & \cos\theta & -\sin\theta \\ 0 & \sin\theta & \cos\theta \end{bmatrix}$$

$$\mathbf{R}_y(\theta) = \begin{bmatrix} \cos\theta & 0 & \sin\theta \\ 0 & 1 & 0 \\ -\sin\theta & 0 & \cos\theta \end{bmatrix} \qquad (3.16)$$

3.3.1 Rotation About an Arbitrary Axis

Suppose that we wish to rotate a vector $\mathbf{P}$ through an angle θ about an arbitrary axis whose direction is represented by a unit vector $\mathbf{A}$. We can decompose the vector $\mathbf{P}$ into components that are parallel to $\mathbf{A}$ and perpendicular to $\mathbf{A}$ as shown in Figure 3.4. Since the parallel component (the projection of $\mathbf{P}$ onto $\mathbf{A}$) remains unchanged during the rotation, we can reduce the problem to that of rotating the perpendicular component of **P** about **A**.

Since **A** is a unit vector, we have the following simplified formula for the projection of **P** onto **A**.

$$\text{proj}_A \, \mathbf{P} = (\mathbf{A} \cdot \mathbf{P})\mathbf{A} \tag{3.17}$$

The component of **P** that is perpendicular to **A** is then given by

$$\text{perp}_A \, \mathbf{P} = \mathbf{P} - (\mathbf{A} \cdot \mathbf{P})\mathbf{A}. \tag{3.18}$$

Once we rotate this perpendicular component about **A**, we will add the constant parallel component given by Equation (3.17) to arrive at our final answer.

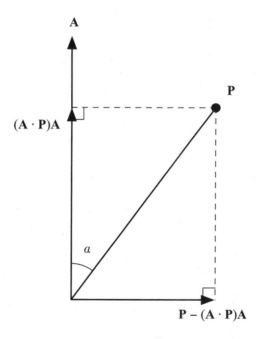

Figure 3.4 Rotation about an arbitrary axis.

The rotation of the perpendicular component takes place in the plane perpendicular to the axis **A**. As before, we express the rotated vector as a linear combination of $\text{perp}_A \, \mathbf{P}$ and the vector that results from a 90-degree counterclockwise rotation of $\text{perp}_A \, \mathbf{P}$ about **A**. Fortunately, such an expression is easy to find. Let α be the angle between the original vector **P** and the axis **A**. Note that the length of $\text{perp}_\mathbf{A}\,\mathbf{P}$ is equal to $\|\mathbf{P}\|\sin\alpha$ because it forms the side opposite the angle α shown in Figure 3.4. A vector of the same length that points in the direction that we want is given by $\mathbf{A}\times\mathbf{P}$.

We can now express the rotation of $\text{perp}_\mathbf{A}\,\mathbf{P}$ through an angle θ as

$$[\mathbf{P}-(\mathbf{A}\cdot\mathbf{P})\mathbf{A}]\cos\theta+(\mathbf{A}\times\mathbf{P})\sin\theta. \tag{3.19}$$

Adding $\text{proj}_\mathbf{A}\,\mathbf{P}$ to this gives us the following expression for the rotation of the original vector $\mathbf{P}$ about the axis $\mathbf{A}$.

$$\mathbf{P}'=\mathbf{P}\cos\theta+(\mathbf{A}\times\mathbf{P})\sin\theta+\mathbf{A}(\mathbf{A}\cdot\mathbf{P})(1-\cos\theta) \tag{3.20}$$

Replacing $\mathbf{A}\times\mathbf{P}$ and $\mathbf{A}(\mathbf{A}\cdot\mathbf{P})$ in Equation (3.20) with their matrix equivalents given by Equations (1.25) and (1.20) respectively, we have

$$\mathbf{P}'=\begin{bmatrix}1&0&0\\0&1&0\\0&0&1\end{bmatrix}\mathbf{P}\cos\theta+\begin{bmatrix}0&-A_z&A_y\\A_z&0&-A_x\\-A_y&A_x&0\end{bmatrix}\mathbf{P}\sin\theta$$
$$+\begin{bmatrix}A_x^2&A_xA_y&A_xA_z\\A_xA_y&A_y^2&A_yA_z\\A_xA_z&A_yA_z&A_z^2\end{bmatrix}\mathbf{P}(1-\cos\theta). \tag{3.21}$$

Combining these terms and setting $c=\cos\theta$ and $s=\sin\theta$ gives us the following formula for the matrix $\mathbf{R}_\mathbf{A}(\theta)$ that rotates a vector through an angle θ about the axis $\mathbf{A}$.

$$\mathbf{R}_\mathbf{A}(\theta)=\begin{bmatrix}c+(1-c)A_x^2&(1-c)A_xA_y-sA_z&(1-c)A_xA_z+sA_y\\(1-c)A_xA_y+sA_z&c+(1-c)A_y^2&(1-c)A_yA_z-sA_x\\(1-c)A_xA_z-sA_y&(1-c)A_yA_z+sA_x&c+(1-c)A_z^2\end{bmatrix} \tag{3.22}$$

3.4 Homogeneous Coordinates

Up to this point, we have dealt only with transforms that can be expressed as the operation of a 3×3 matrix on a three-dimensional vector. A series of such transforms could be represented by a single 3×3 matrix equal to the product of the matrices corresponding to the individual transforms. An important transform that has been left out is the translation operation. A coordinate system is translated in space without otherwise affecting the orientation or scale of the axes by simply adding an offset vector. This operation cannot be expressed in terms of a 3×3 matrix. Thus, to transform a point $\mathbf{P}$ from one coordinate system to another, we usually find ourselves performing the operation

$$\mathbf{P}' = \mathbf{MP} + \mathbf{T}, \tag{3.23}$$

where $\mathbf{M}$ is some invertible 3×3 matrix and $\mathbf{T}$ is a 3D translation vector. Performing two operations of the type shown in Equation (3.23) results in the rather messy equation

$$\begin{aligned}
\mathbf{P}' &= \mathbf{M}_2 \left(\mathbf{M}_1 \mathbf{P} + \mathbf{T}_1 \right) + \mathbf{T}_2 \\
&= \left(\mathbf{M}_2 \mathbf{M}_1 \right) \mathbf{P} + \mathbf{M}_2 \mathbf{T}_1 + \mathbf{T}_2,
\end{aligned} \tag{3.24}$$

requiring that we keep track of the matrix component $\mathbf{M}_n \mathbf{M}_{n-1}$ as well as the translation component $\mathbf{M}_n \mathbf{T}_{n-1} + \mathbf{T}_n$ at each stage when concatenating n transforms.

3.4.1 Four-Dimensional Transforms

Fortunately, there is a compact and elegant way to represent these transforms within a single mathematical entity. We can do this by extending our vectors to four-dimensional *homogeneous coordinates* and using 4×4 matrices to transform them. A 3D point $\mathbf{P}$ is extended to four dimensions by setting its fourth coordinate, which we call the *w*-coordinate, equal to 1. We construct a 4×4 transformation matrix $\mathbf{F}$ corresponding to the 3×3 matrix $\mathbf{M}$ and the 3D translation $\mathbf{T}$ as follows.

$$\mathbf{F} = \left[\begin{array}{c:c} \mathbf{M} & \mathbf{T} \\ \hdashline \mathbf{0} & 1 \end{array}\right] = \left[\begin{array}{ccc:c} M_{11} & M_{12} & M_{13} & T_x \\ M_{21} & M_{22} & M_{23} & T_y \\ M_{31} & M_{32} & M_{33} & T_z \\ \hdashline 0 & 0 & 0 & 1 \end{array}\right] \tag{3.25}$$

Multiplying this matrix by the vector $\langle P_x, P_y, P_z, 1 \rangle$ transforms the x-, y-, and z-coordinates of the vector in exactly the same way as Equation (3.23) and leaves a 1 in the w-coordinate. Furthermore, multiplying two transformation matrices of the form shown in Equation (3.25) yields another matrix of the same form that is equivalent to the pair of transforms performed in Equation (3.24).

If we solve Equation (3.23) for $\mathbf{P}$, we have

$$\mathbf{P} = \mathbf{M}^{-1}\mathbf{P}' - \mathbf{M}^{-1}\mathbf{T}. \tag{3.26}$$

We would therefore expect the inverse of the 4×4 matrix $\mathbf{F}$ from Equation (3.25) to be

$$\mathbf{F}^{-1} = \left[\begin{array}{c:c} \mathbf{M}^{-1} & -\mathbf{M}^{-1}\mathbf{T} \\ \hdashline \mathbf{0} & 1 \end{array}\right] = \left[\begin{array}{ccc:c} M_{11}^{-1} & M_{12}^{-1} & M_{13}^{-1} & -(\mathbf{M}^{-1}\mathbf{T})_x \\ M_{21}^{-1} & M_{22}^{-1} & M_{23}^{-1} & -(\mathbf{M}^{-1}\mathbf{T})_y \\ M_{31}^{-1} & M_{32}^{-1} & M_{33}^{-1} & -(\mathbf{M}^{-1}\mathbf{T})_z \\ \hdashline 0 & 0 & 0 & 1 \end{array}\right], \tag{3.27}$$

and the following computation verifies that this is true.

$$\mathbf{F}\mathbf{F}^{-1} = \left[\begin{array}{c:c} \mathbf{M} & \mathbf{T} \\ \hdashline \mathbf{0} & 1 \end{array}\right]\left[\begin{array}{c:c} \mathbf{M}^{-1} & -\mathbf{M}^{-1}\mathbf{T} \\ \hdashline \mathbf{0} & 1 \end{array}\right]$$

$$
= \left[
\begin{array}{c|c}
\mathbf{M}\mathbf{M}^{-1} & \mathbf{M}\left(-\mathbf{M}^{-1}\mathbf{T}\right)+\mathbf{T} \\
\hline
\mathbf{0} & 1
\end{array}
\right]
$$

$$
= \left[
\begin{array}{c|c}
\mathbf{I}_3 & \mathbf{0} \\
\hline
\mathbf{0} & 1
\end{array}
\right] = \mathbf{I}_4 \tag{3.28}
$$

3.4.2 Points and Directions

We have now come to a point where it is necessary to make a distinction between vectors that represent points in three-dimensional space and vectors that represent directions in three-dimensional space. Unlike points, direction vectors should remain invariant under translation.

To transform direction vectors using the same 4×4 transformation matrices that we use to transform points, we extend direction vectors to four dimensions by setting the w-coordinate to 0. This nullifies the fourth column of the matrix $\mathbf{F}$ in Equation (3.25), leaving only the upper left 3×3 portion of the matrix to affect the direction vector.

The difference between two points $\mathbf{P}$ and $\mathbf{Q}$ having a w-coordinate of 1 results in a direction vector $\mathbf{Q}-\mathbf{P}$ having a w-coordinate of 0. This makes sense because $\mathbf{Q}-\mathbf{P}$ represents the direction pointing from $\mathbf{P}$ to $\mathbf{Q}$, which we would expect not to be affected by a translation.

3.4.3 Geometrical Interpretation of the *w*-Coordinate

The w-coordinates of the four-dimensional vectors with which we have been working so far have a meaning that goes beyond their utility during transformations using 4×4 matrices. Before, we extended a three-dimensional point to four-dimensional space by adding a 1 in the w-coordinate position. Now, we define a mapping that works in the reverse direction. Suppose we have a 4D point $\mathbf{P}=\langle x,y,z,w \rangle$ whose w-coordinate is not 0. Then we define the image of $\mathbf{P}$ in three-dimensional space, which we denote by $\tilde{\mathbf{P}}$, as the projection of $\mathbf{P}$ into the three-dimensional space in which $w = 1$ using the formula

$$\tilde{\mathbf{P}} = \left\langle \frac{x}{w}, \frac{y}{w}, \frac{z}{w} \right\rangle. \tag{3.29}$$

As shown in Figure 3.5 (but without the z-axis to make visualization easier), the 3D point $\tilde{\mathbf{P}}$ corresponds to the point where the line connecting the point $\mathbf{P}$ to the origin intersects the space where $w = 1$. Thus, any scalar multiple of the 4D vector $\mathbf{P}$ represents the same point in three-dimensional space. The importance of this projection in 3D graphics is discussed in detail in Section 4.5.

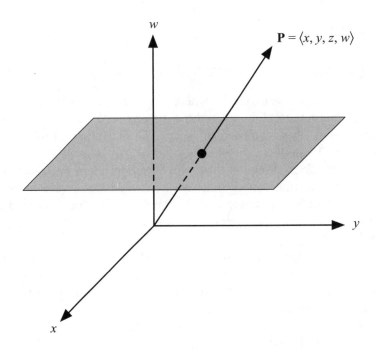

Figure 3.5 A 4D point $\mathbf{P}$ is projected into three-dimensional space by calculating the point where the line connecting the point to the origin intersects the space where $w = 1$.

3.5 Transforming Normal Vectors

In addition to its position in space, a vertex belonging to a polygonal model usually carries additional information about how it fits into the surrounding surface. In particular, a vertex may have a tangent vector and a normal vector associated with it. When we transform a model, we need to transform not only the vertex positions, but these vectors as well.

Tangent vectors can often be calculated by taking the difference between one vertex and another, and thus we would expect that a transformed tangent vector could be expressed as the difference between two transformed points. If $\mathbf{M}$ is a 3×3 matrix with which we transform a vertex position, then the same matrix $\mathbf{M}$ can be used to correctly transform the tangent vector at that vertex. (We limit ourselves to 3×3 matrices in this section since tangent and normal directions are unaffected by translations.) Some care must be taken when transforming normal vectors, however. Figure 3.6 shows what can happen when a nonorthogonal matrix $\mathbf{M}$ is used to transform a normal vector. The transformed normal can often end up pointing in a direction that is not perpendicular to the transformed surface.

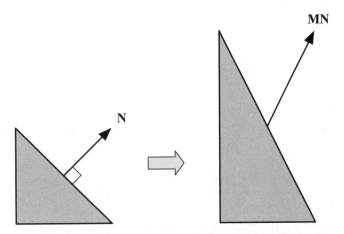

Figure 3.6 Transforming a normal vector **N** with a nonorthogonal matrix **M**.

Since tangents and normals are perpendicular, the tangent vector $\mathbf{T}$ and the normal vector $\mathbf{N}$ associated with a vertex must satisfy the equation $\mathbf{N} \cdot \mathbf{T} = 0$. We must also require that this equation be satisfied by the transformed tangent vector $\mathbf{T}'$ and the transformed normal vector $\mathbf{N}'$. Given a transformation matrix $\mathbf{M}$, we know that $\mathbf{T}' = \mathbf{MT}$. We would like to find the transformation matrix $\mathbf{G}$ with which the vector $\mathbf{N}$ should be transformed so that

$$\mathbf{N}' \cdot \mathbf{T}' = (\mathbf{GN}) \cdot (\mathbf{MT}) = 0. \tag{3.30}$$

A little algebraic manipulation gives us

$$
\begin{aligned}
(\mathbf{GN}) \cdot (\mathbf{MT}) &= (\mathbf{GN})^{\mathrm{T}} (\mathbf{MT}) \\
&= \mathbf{N}^{\mathrm{T}} \mathbf{G}^{\mathrm{T}} \mathbf{MT}.
\end{aligned} \tag{3.31}
$$

Since $\mathbf{N}^{\mathrm{T}}\mathbf{T} = 0$, the equation $\mathbf{N}^{\mathrm{T}}\mathbf{G}^{\mathrm{T}}\mathbf{MT} = 0$ is satisfied if $\mathbf{G}^{\mathrm{T}}\mathbf{M} = \mathbf{I}$. We therefore conclude that $\mathbf{G} = \left(\mathbf{M}^{-1}\right)^{\mathrm{T}}$. This tells us that a normal vector is correctly transformed using the *inverse transpose* of the matrix used to transform points. Vectors that must be transformed in this way are called *covariant* vectors, and vectors that are transformed in the ordinary fashion using the matrix $\mathbf{M}$ (such as points and tangent vectors) are called *contravariant* vectors.

If the matrix $\mathbf{M}$ is orthogonal, then $\mathbf{M}^{-1} = \mathbf{M}^{\mathrm{T}}$, and thus $\left(\mathbf{M}^{-1}\right)^{\mathrm{T}} = \mathbf{M}$. Therefore, the inverse transpose operation required to transform normal vectors can be avoided when $\mathbf{M}$ is known to be orthogonal, as is the case when $\mathbf{M}$ is equal to one of the rotation matrices $\mathbf{R}_x$, $\mathbf{R}_y$, $\mathbf{R}_z$, or $\mathbf{R}_A$ presented earlier in this chapter.

3.6 Quaternions

A *quaternion* is an alternative mathematical entity that 3D graphics programmers use to represent rotations. The use of quaternions has advantages over the use of rotation matrices in many situations because quaternions require less storage space, concatenation of quaternions requires fewer arithmetic operations, and quaternions are more easily interpolated for producing smooth animation.

3.6.1 Quaternion Mathematics

The set of quaternions, known by mathematicians as the ring of Hamiltonian quaternions and denoted by $\mathbb{H}$, can be thought of as a four-dimensional vector space for which an element $\mathbf{q}$ has the form

$$\mathbf{q} = \langle w, x, y, z \rangle = w + xi + yj + zk. \tag{3.32}$$

A quaternion is often written as $\mathbf{q} = s + \mathbf{v}$, where s represents the scalar part corresponding to the w-component of $\mathbf{q}$, and $\mathbf{v}$ represents the vector part corresponding to the x-, y-, and z-components of $\mathbf{q}$.

The set of quaternions is a natural extension of the set of complex numbers. Multiplication of quaternions is defined using the ordinary distributive law and adhering to the following rules when multiplying the "imaginary" components i, j, and k.

$$
\begin{aligned}
i^2 &= j^2 = k^2 = -1 \\
ij &= -ji = k \\
jk &= -kj = i \\
ki &= -ik = j
\end{aligned}
\tag{3.33}
$$

Multiplication of quaternions is not commutative, and so we must be careful to multiply terms in the correct order. For two quaternions $\mathbf{q}_1 = w_1 + x_1 i + y_1 j + z_1 k$ and $\mathbf{q}_2 = w_2 + x_2 i + y_2 j + z_2 k$, the product $\mathbf{q}_1 \mathbf{q}_2$ is given by

$$
\begin{aligned}
\mathbf{q}_1 \mathbf{q}_2 = {} & \left(w_1 w_2 - x_1 x_2 - y_1 y_2 - z_1 z_2 \right) \\
& + \left(w_1 x_2 + x_1 w_2 + y_1 z_2 - z_1 y_2 \right) i \\
& + \left(w_1 y_2 - x_1 z_2 + y_1 w_2 + z_1 x_2 \right) j \\
& + \left(w_1 z_2 + x_1 y_2 - y_1 x_2 + z_1 w_2 \right) k.
\end{aligned}
\tag{3.34}
$$

When written in scalar-vector form, the product of two quaternions $\mathbf{q}_1 = s_1 + \mathbf{v}_1$ and $\mathbf{q}_2 = s_2 + \mathbf{v}_2$ can be written as

$$
\mathbf{q}_1 \mathbf{q}_2 = s_1 s_2 - \mathbf{v}_1 \cdot \mathbf{v}_2 + s_1 \mathbf{v}_2 + s_2 \mathbf{v}_1 + \mathbf{v}_1 \times \mathbf{v}_2.
\tag{3.35}
$$

Like complex numbers (see Appendix A), quaternions have conjugates, and they are defined as follows.

Definition 3.4. The *conjugate* of a quaternion $\mathbf{q} = s + \mathbf{v}$, denoted by $\overline{\mathbf{q}}$, is given by $\overline{\mathbf{q}} = s - \mathbf{v}$.

A short calculation reveals that the product of a quaternion $\mathbf{q}$ and its conjugate $\overline{\mathbf{q}}$ is equal to the dot product of $\mathbf{q}$ with itself, which is also equal to the square of the magnitude of $\mathbf{q}$. That is,

$$
\mathbf{q}\overline{\mathbf{q}} = \overline{\mathbf{q}}\mathbf{q} = \mathbf{q} \cdot \mathbf{q} = \|\mathbf{q}\|^2 = q^2.
\tag{3.36}
$$

This leads us to a formula for the multiplicative inverse of a quaternion.

Theorem 3.5. The *inverse* of a nonzero quaternion $\mathbf{q}$, denoted by $\mathbf{q}^{-1}$, is given by

$$\mathbf{q}^{-1} = \frac{\overline{\mathbf{q}}}{q^2}. \tag{3.37}$$

Proof. Applying Equation (3.36), we have

$$\mathbf{q}\mathbf{q}^{-1} = \frac{\mathbf{q}\overline{\mathbf{q}}}{q^2} = \frac{q^2}{q^2} = 1 \tag{3.38}$$

and

$$\mathbf{q}^{-1}\mathbf{q} = \frac{\overline{\mathbf{q}}\mathbf{q}}{q^2} = \frac{q^2}{q^2} = 1, \tag{3.39}$$

thus proving the theorem. ∎

3.6.2 Rotations with Quaternions

A rotation in three dimensions can be thought of as a function φ that maps $\mathbb{R}^3$ onto itself. For φ to represent a rotation, it must preserve lengths, angles, and handedness. Length preservation is satisfied if

$$\|\varphi(\mathbf{P})\| = \|\mathbf{P}\|. \tag{3.40}$$

The angle between the line segments connecting the origin to any two points $\mathbf{P}_1$ and $\mathbf{P}_2$ is preserved if

$$\varphi(\mathbf{P}_1) \cdot \varphi(\mathbf{P}_2) = \mathbf{P}_1 \cdot \mathbf{P}_2. \tag{3.41}$$

Finally, handedness is preserved if

$$\varphi(\mathbf{P}_1) \times \varphi(\mathbf{P}_2) = \varphi(\mathbf{P}_1 \times \mathbf{P}_2). \tag{3.42}$$

Extending the function φ to a mapping from $\mathbb{H}$ onto itself by requiring that $\varphi(s + \mathbf{v}) = s + \varphi(\mathbf{v})$ allows us to rewrite Equation (3.41) as

$$\varphi(\mathbf{P}_1) \cdot \varphi(\mathbf{P}_2) = \varphi(\mathbf{P}_1 \cdot \mathbf{P}_2). \tag{3.43}$$

Treating $\mathbf{P}_1$ and $\mathbf{P}_2$ as quaternions with zero scalar part enables us to combine Equations (3.42) and (3.43) since $\mathbf{P}_1\mathbf{P}_2 = -\mathbf{P}_1 \cdot \mathbf{P}_2 + \mathbf{P}_1 \times \mathbf{P}_2$. We can therefore write the angle preservation and handedness preservation requirements as the single equation

$$\varphi(\mathbf{P}_1)\varphi(\mathbf{P}_2) = \varphi(\mathbf{P}_1\mathbf{P}_2). \tag{3.44}$$

A function φ that satisfies this equation is called a *homomorphism*.

The class of functions given by

$$\varphi_{\mathbf{q}}(\mathbf{P}) = \mathbf{q}\mathbf{P}\mathbf{q}^{-1}, \tag{3.45}$$

where $\mathbf{q}$ is a nonzero quaternion, satisfies the requirements stated in Equations (3.40) and (3.44), and thus represents a set of rotations. This fact can be proven by first observing that the function $\varphi_{\mathbf{q}}$ preserves lengths because

$$\left\|\varphi_{\mathbf{q}}(\mathbf{P})\right\| = \left\|\mathbf{q}\mathbf{P}\mathbf{q}^{-1}\right\| = \left\|\mathbf{q}\right\|\left\|\mathbf{P}\right\|\left\|\mathbf{q}^{-1}\right\| = \left\|\mathbf{P}\right\|\frac{\left\|\mathbf{q}\right\|\left\|\overline{\mathbf{q}}\right\|}{q^2} = \left\|\mathbf{P}\right\|. \tag{3.46}$$

Furthermore, $\varphi_{\mathbf{q}}$ is a homomorphism since

$$\varphi_{\mathbf{q}}(\mathbf{P}_1)\varphi_{\mathbf{q}}(\mathbf{P}_2) = \mathbf{q}\mathbf{P}_1\mathbf{q}^{-1}\mathbf{q}\mathbf{P}_2\mathbf{q}^{-1} = \mathbf{q}\mathbf{P}_1\mathbf{P}_2\mathbf{q}^{-1} = \varphi_{\mathbf{q}}(\mathbf{P}_1\mathbf{P}_2). \tag{3.47}$$

We now need to find a formula for the quaternion $\mathbf{q}$ corresponding to a rotation through the angle θ about the axis $\mathbf{A}$. A quick calculation shows that $\varphi_{a\mathbf{q}} = \varphi_{\mathbf{q}}$ for any nonzero scalar a, so to keep things as simple as possible, we will concern ourselves only with unit quaternions.

Let $\mathbf{q} = s + \mathbf{v}$ be a unit quaternion. Then $\mathbf{q}^{-1} = s - \mathbf{v}$, and given a point $\mathbf{P}$, we have

$$\begin{aligned}
\mathbf{q}\mathbf{P}\mathbf{q}^{-1} &= (s + \mathbf{v})\mathbf{P}(s - \mathbf{v}) \\
&= (-\mathbf{v} \cdot \mathbf{P} + s\mathbf{P} + \mathbf{v} \times \mathbf{P})(s - \mathbf{v}) \\
&= -s\mathbf{v} \cdot \mathbf{P} + s^2\mathbf{P} + s\mathbf{v} \times \mathbf{P} + (\mathbf{v} \cdot \mathbf{P})\mathbf{v} - s\mathbf{P}\mathbf{v} - (\mathbf{v} \times \mathbf{P})\mathbf{v} \\
&= s^2\mathbf{P} + 2s\mathbf{v} \times \mathbf{P} + (\mathbf{v} \cdot \mathbf{P})\mathbf{v} - \mathbf{v} \times \mathbf{P} \times \mathbf{v}.
\end{aligned} \tag{3.48}$$

After applying Theorem 1.9(f) to the cross product $\mathbf{v} \times \mathbf{P} \times \mathbf{v}$, this becomes

$$\mathbf{q}\mathbf{P}\mathbf{q}^{-1} = (s^2 - \mathbf{v}^2)\mathbf{P} + 2s\mathbf{v} \times \mathbf{P} + 2(\mathbf{v} \cdot \mathbf{P})\mathbf{v}. \tag{3.49}$$

Setting $\mathbf{v} = t\mathbf{A}$, where $\mathbf{A}$ is a unit vector, lets us rewrite this equation as

$$\mathbf{q}\mathbf{P}\mathbf{q}^{-1} = \left(s^2 - t^2\right)\mathbf{P} + 2st\mathbf{A}\times\mathbf{P} + 2t^2\left(\mathbf{A}\cdot\mathbf{P}\right)\mathbf{A}. \qquad (3.50)$$

When we compare this to the formula for rotation about an arbitrary axis given in Equation (3.20), we can infer the following equalities.

$$s^2 - t^2 = \cos\theta$$
$$2st = \sin\theta$$
$$2t^2 = 1 - \cos\theta \qquad (3.51)$$

The third equality gives us

$$t = \sqrt{\frac{1 - \cos\theta}{2}} = \sin\frac{\theta}{2}. \qquad (3.52)$$

The first and third equalities together tell us that $s^2 + t^2 = 1$, so we must have $s = \cos(\theta/2)$. (The fact that $\sin 2\theta = 2\sin\theta\cos\theta$ verifies that the second equality is satisfied by these values for s and t.)

We have now determined that the unit quaternion $\mathbf{q}$ corresponding to a rotation through the angle θ about the axis $\mathbf{A}$ is given by

$$\mathbf{q} = \cos\frac{\theta}{2} + \mathbf{A}\sin\frac{\theta}{2}. \qquad (3.53)$$

It should be noted that any scalar multiple of the quaternion $\mathbf{q}$ (in particular, $-\mathbf{q}$) also represents the same rotation since

$$\left(a\mathbf{q}\right)\mathbf{P}\left(a\mathbf{q}\right)^{-1} = a\mathbf{q}\mathbf{P}\frac{\mathbf{q}^{-1}}{a} = \mathbf{q}\mathbf{P}\mathbf{q}^{-1}. \qquad (3.54)$$

The product of two quaternions $\mathbf{q}_1$ and $\mathbf{q}_2$ also represents a rotation. Specifically, the product $\mathbf{q}_1\mathbf{q}_2$ represents the rotation resulting from first rotating by $\mathbf{q}_2$ and then by $\mathbf{q}_1$. Since

$$\mathbf{q}_1\left(\mathbf{q}_2\mathbf{P}\mathbf{q}_2^{-1}\right)\mathbf{q}_1^{-1} = \left(\mathbf{q}_1\mathbf{q}_2\right)\mathbf{P}\left(\mathbf{q}_1\mathbf{q}_2\right)^{-1}, \qquad (3.55)$$

we can concatenate as many quaternions as we want to produce a single quaternion representing the entire series of rotations. Multiplying two quaternions together requires 16 multiply-add operations, whereas multiplying two 3×3 matrices together requires 27. Thus, some computational efficiency can be gained by using quaternions in situations in which many rotations may be applied to an object.

It is often necessary to convert a quaternion into the equivalent 3×3 rotation matrix, for instance, to pass the transform for an object to a 3D graphics library. We can determine the formula for the matrix corresponding to the quaternion $\mathbf{q} = s + t\mathbf{A}$ by using Equations (1.25) and (1.20) to write Equation (3.50) in matrix form. (This is nearly identical to the technique used in Section 3.3.1.) This gives us

$$\mathbf{qPq}^{-1} = \begin{bmatrix} s^2 - t^2 & 0 & 0 \\ 0 & s^2 - t^2 & 0 \\ 0 & 0 & s^2 - t^2 \end{bmatrix} \mathbf{P} + \begin{bmatrix} 0 & -2stA_z & 2stA_y \\ 2stA_z & 0 & -2stA_x \\ -2stA_y & 2stA_x & 0 \end{bmatrix} \mathbf{P}$$

$$+ \begin{bmatrix} 2t^2 A_x^2 & 2t^2 A_x A_y & 2t^2 A_x A_z \\ 2t^2 A_x A_y & 2t^2 A_y^2 & 2t^2 A_y A_z \\ 2t^2 A_x A_z & 2t^2 A_y A_z & 2t^2 A_z^2 \end{bmatrix} \mathbf{P}. \tag{3.56}$$

Writing the quaternion $\mathbf{q}$ as the four-dimensional vector $\mathbf{q} = \langle w, x, y, z \rangle$, we have $w = s$, $x = tA_x$, $y = tA_y$, and $z = tA_z$. Since $\mathbf{A}$ is a unit vector,

$$x^2 + y^2 + z^2 = t^2 A^2 = t^2. \tag{3.57}$$

Rewriting Equation (3.56) in terms of the components w, x, y, and z gives us

$$\mathbf{qPq}^{-1} = \begin{bmatrix} w^2 - x^2 - y^2 - z^2 & 0 & 0 \\ 0 & w^2 - x^2 - y^2 - z^2 & 0 \\ 0 & 0 & w^2 - x^2 - y^2 - z^2 \end{bmatrix} \mathbf{P}$$

$$+ \begin{bmatrix} 0 & -2wz & 2wy \\ 2wz & 0 & -2wx \\ -2wy & 2wx & 0 \end{bmatrix} \mathbf{P} + \begin{bmatrix} 2x^2 & 2xy & 2xz \\ 2xy & 2y^2 & 2yz \\ 2xz & 2yz & 2z^2 \end{bmatrix} \mathbf{P}. \tag{3.58}$$

Since $\mathbf{q}$ is a unit quaternion, we know that $w^2 + x^2 + y^2 + z^2 = 1$, so we can write

$$w^2 - x^2 - y^2 - z^2 = 1 - 2x^2 - 2y^2 - 2z^2. \tag{3.59}$$

Using this equation and combining the three matrices gives us the following formula for the matrix $\mathbf{R_q}$, the rotation matrix corresponding to the quaternion $\mathbf{q}$.

$$\mathbf{R_q} = \begin{bmatrix} 1-2y^2-2z^2 & 2xy-2wz & 2xz+2wy \\ 2xy+2wz & 1-2x^2-2z^2 & 2yz-2wx \\ 2xz-2wy & 2yz+2wx & 1-2x^2-2y^2 \end{bmatrix} \tag{3.60}$$

3.6.3 Spherical Linear Interpolation

Because quaternions are represented by vectors, they are well suited for interpolation. When an object is being animated, interpolation is useful for generating intermediate orientations that fall between precalculated key frames.

The simplest type of interpolation is *linear interpolation*. For two unit quaternions $\mathbf{q}_1$ and $\mathbf{q}_2$, the linearly interpolated quaternion $\mathbf{q}(t)$ is given by

$$\mathbf{q}(t) = (1-t)\mathbf{q}_1 + t\mathbf{q}_2. \tag{3.61}$$

The function $\mathbf{q}(t)$ changes smoothly along the line segment connecting $\mathbf{q}_1$ and $\mathbf{q}_2$ as t varies from 0 to 1. As shown in Figure 3.7, $\mathbf{q}(t)$ does not maintain the unit length of $\mathbf{q}_1$ and $\mathbf{q}_2$, but we can renormalize at each point by instead using the function

$$\mathbf{q}(t) = \frac{(1-t)\mathbf{q}_1 + t\mathbf{q}_2}{\|(1-t)\mathbf{q}_1 + t\mathbf{q}_2\|}. \tag{3.62}$$

Now we have a function that traces out the arc between $\mathbf{q}_1$ and $\mathbf{q}_2$, shown in Figure 3.7 as a two-dimensional cross-section of what is actually occurring on the surface of the four-dimensional unit hypersphere.

Although linear interpolation is efficient, it has the drawback that the function $\mathbf{q}(t)$ given by Equation (3.62) does not trace out the arc between $\mathbf{q}_1$ and $\mathbf{q}_2$ at a constant rate. The graph of $\cos^{-1}(\mathbf{q}(t) \cdot \mathbf{q}_1)$ shown in Figure 3.8 demonstrates that the rate at which the angle between $\mathbf{q}(t)$ and $\mathbf{q}_1$ changes is relatively slow at the endpoints where $t = 0$ and $t = 1$, and is the fastest where $t = \frac{1}{2}$.

We would like to find a function $\mathbf{q}(t)$ that interpolates the quaternions $\mathbf{q}_1$ and $\mathbf{q}_2$, preserves unit length, and sweeps through the angle between $\mathbf{q}_1$ and $\mathbf{q}_2$ at a constant rate. If $\mathbf{q}_1$ and $\mathbf{q}_2$ are separated by an angle θ, then such a function would generate quaternions forming the angle θt between $\mathbf{q}(t)$ and $\mathbf{q}_1$ as t varies from 0 to 1.

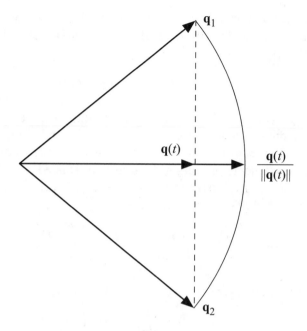

Figure 3.7 Linear interpolation of quaternions.

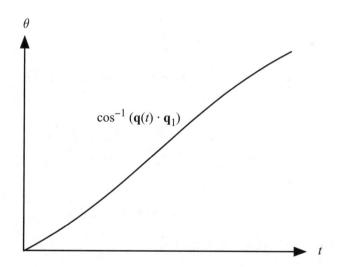

Figure 3.8 Graph of $\cos^{-1}(\mathbf{q}(t) \cdot \mathbf{q}_1)$, where $\mathbf{q}(t)$ is the normalized linear interpolation function given by Equation (3.62).

Figure 3.9 shows the quaternion $\mathbf{q}(t)$ lying on the arc connecting $\mathbf{q}_1$ and $\mathbf{q}_2$, forming the angle θt with $\mathbf{q}_1$, and forming the angle $\theta(1-t)$ with $\mathbf{q}_2$. We can write $\mathbf{q}(t)$ as

$$\mathbf{q}(t) = a(t)\mathbf{q}_1 + b(t)\mathbf{q}_2 \qquad (3.63)$$

by letting $a(t)$ and $b(t)$ represent the lengths of the components of $\mathbf{q}(t)$ lying along the directions $\mathbf{q}_1$ and $\mathbf{q}_2$. As shown in Figure 3.9(a), we can determine the length $a(t)$ by constructing similar triangles. The perpendicular distance from $\mathbf{q}_1$ to the line segment connecting the origin to $\mathbf{q}_2$ is equal to $\|\mathbf{q}_1\|\sin\theta$. The perpendicular distance from $\mathbf{q}(t)$ to this line segment is equal to $\|\mathbf{q}(t)\|\sin\theta(1-t)$. Using similar triangles, we have the relation

$$\frac{a(t)}{\|\mathbf{q}_1\|} = \frac{\|\mathbf{q}(t)\|\sin\theta(1-t)}{\|\mathbf{q}_1\|\sin\theta}. \qquad (3.64)$$

Since $\|\mathbf{q}_1\| = 1$ and $\|\mathbf{q}(t)\| = 1$, we can simplify this to

$$a(t) = \frac{\sin\theta(1-t)}{\sin\theta}. \qquad (3.65)$$

Figure 3.9(b) shows the same procedure used to find the length $b(t)$, which is given by

$$b(t) = \frac{\sin\theta t}{\sin\theta}. \qquad (3.66)$$

We can now define the *spherical linear interpolation* function $\mathbf{q}(t)$ as follows.

$$\mathbf{q}(t) = \frac{\sin\theta(1-t)}{\sin\theta}\mathbf{q}_1 + \frac{\sin\theta t}{\sin\theta}\mathbf{q}_2 \qquad (3.67)$$

The angle θ is given by

$$\theta = \cos^{-1}(\mathbf{q}_1 \cdot \mathbf{q}_2), \qquad (3.68)$$

and thus, $\sin\theta$ can be replaced by

$$\sin\theta = \sqrt{1 - (\mathbf{q}_1 \cdot \mathbf{q}_2)^2} \qquad (3.69)$$

if desired. Since the quaternions $\mathbf{q}$ and $-\mathbf{q}$ represent the same rotation, the signs of the quaternions $\mathbf{q}_1$ and $\mathbf{q}_2$ are usually chosen such that $\mathbf{q}_1 \cdot \mathbf{q}_2 \geq 0$. This also ensures that the interpolation takes place over the shortest path.

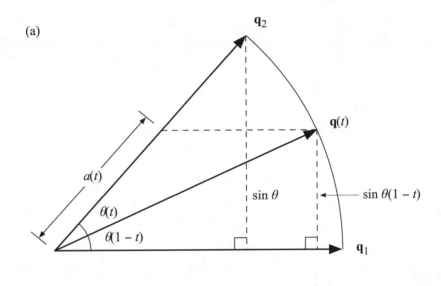

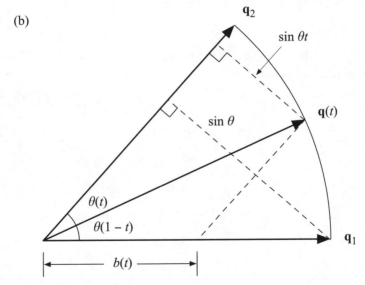

Figure 3.9 Similar triangles can be used to determine the length of (a) the component of $\mathbf{q}(t)$ that lies along the direction of $\mathbf{q}_1$ and (b) the component of $\mathbf{q}(t)$ that lies along the direction of $\mathbf{q}_2$.

Chapter 3 Summary

Orthogonal Matrices

An invertible $n \times n$ matrix $\mathbf{M}$ is called *orthogonal* if and only if $\mathbf{M}^{-1} = \mathbf{M}^{\mathrm{T}}$. A matrix whose columns form an orthonormal set of vectors is orthogonal. Orthogonal matrices preserve lengths and angles, and thus perform only rotations and reflections.

Scaling Transforms

A scaling operation in three dimensions is performed using the transformation matrix

$$\begin{bmatrix} a & 0 & 0 \\ 0 & b & 0 \\ 0 & 0 & c \end{bmatrix}.$$

If $a = b = c$, then this matrix represents a uniform scale, which can also be performed using scalar multiplication.

Rotation Transforms

Rotations through an angle θ about the x-, y-, and z-axes are performed using the following transformation matrices.

$$\mathbf{R}_x(\theta) = \begin{bmatrix} 1 & 0 & 0 \\ 0 & \cos\theta & -\sin\theta \\ 0 & \sin\theta & \cos\theta \end{bmatrix}$$

$$\mathbf{R}_y(\theta) = \begin{bmatrix} \cos\theta & 0 & \sin\theta \\ 0 & 1 & 0 \\ -\sin\theta & 0 & \cos\theta \end{bmatrix}$$

$$\mathbf{R}_z(\theta) = \begin{bmatrix} \cos\theta & -\sin\theta & 0 \\ \sin\theta & \cos\theta & 0 \\ 0 & 0 & 1 \end{bmatrix}$$

A rotation through an angle θ about an arbitrary axis $\mathbf{A}$ is performed using the transformation matrix

$$\mathbf{R}_\mathbf{A}(\theta) = \begin{bmatrix} c+(1-c)A_x^2 & (1-c)A_xA_y - sA_z & (1-c)A_xA_z + sA_y \\ (1-c)A_xA_y + sA_z & c+(1-c)A_y^2 & (1-c)A_yA_z - sA_x \\ (1-c)A_xA_z - sA_y & (1-c)A_yA_z + sA_x & c+(1-c)A_z^2 \end{bmatrix},$$

where $c = \cos\theta$ and $s = \sin\theta$.

Homogeneous Coordinates

A vector $\mathbf{P}$ representing a three-dimensional point is extended to four-dimensional homogeneous coordinates by setting the w-coordinate to 1. A vector $\mathbf{D}$ representing a three-dimensional direction is extended to homogeneous coordinates by setting the w-coordinate to 0.

A 3×3 transformation matrix $\mathbf{M}$ and a 3D translation vector $\mathbf{T}$ can be combined using the 4×4 transformation matrix

$$\mathbf{F} = \left[\begin{array}{ccc:c} M_{11} & M_{12} & M_{13} & T_x \\ M_{21} & M_{22} & M_{23} & T_y \\ M_{31} & M_{32} & M_{33} & T_z \\ \hdashline 0 & 0 & 0 & 1 \end{array} \right].$$

Normal vectors must be transformed using the inverse transpose of the matrix used to transform points.

Quaternions

The unit quaternion corresponding to a rotation through an angle θ about the unit axis $\mathbf{A}$ is given by

$$\mathbf{q} = \cos\frac{\theta}{2} + \mathbf{A}\sin\frac{\theta}{2}.$$

A quaternion $\mathbf{q}$ applies a rotation transformation to a point $\mathbf{P}$ using the homomorphism $\mathbf{P}' = \mathbf{q}\mathbf{P}\mathbf{q}^{-1}$. The transformation performed by the quaternion $\mathbf{q} = \langle w, x, y, z \rangle$ is equivalent to the transformation performed by the 3×3 matrix

$$\mathbf{R_q} = \begin{bmatrix} 1-2y^2-2z^2 & 2xy-2wz & 2xz+2wy \\ 2xy+2wz & 1-2x^2-2z^2 & 2yz-2wx \\ 2xz-2wy & 2yz+2wx & 1-2x^2-2y^2 \end{bmatrix}.$$

Spherical Linear Interpolation

Two quaternions $\mathbf{q}_1$ and $\mathbf{q}_2$ are spherically interpolated using the formula

$$\mathbf{q}(t) = \frac{\sin\theta(1-t)}{\sin\theta}\mathbf{q}_1 + \frac{\sin\theta t}{\sin\theta}\mathbf{q}_2,$$

where $0 \le t \le 1$.

Exercises for Chapter 3

1. Calculate the 3×3 rotation matrices that perform a rotation of 30 degrees about the x-, y-, and z-axes.

2. Exhibit a unit quaternion that performs a rotation of 60 degrees about the axis $\langle 0,3,4 \rangle$.

3. Prove Equation (3.35).

4. Let $\mathbf{N}$ be the normal vector to a surface at a point $\mathbf{P}$, and let $\mathbf{S}$ and $\mathbf{T}$ be tangent vectors at the point $\mathbf{P}$ such that $\mathbf{S}\times\mathbf{T}=\mathbf{N}$. Given an invertible 3×3 matrix $\mathbf{M}$, show that $(\mathbf{MS})\times(\mathbf{MT})=(\det\mathbf{M})(\mathbf{M}^{-1})^{\mathrm{T}}(\mathbf{S}\times\mathbf{T})$, supporting the fact that normals are correctly transformed by the inverse transpose of the matrix $\mathbf{M}$. [*Hint.* Use Equation (1.25) to write the cross product $(\mathbf{MS})\times(\mathbf{MT})$ as

$$(\mathbf{MS})\times(\mathbf{MT}) = \begin{bmatrix} 0 & -(\mathbf{MS})_z & (\mathbf{MS})_y \\ (\mathbf{MS})_z & 0 & -(\mathbf{MS})_x \\ -(\mathbf{MS})_y & (\mathbf{MS})_x & 0 \end{bmatrix}\mathbf{MT}.$$

Then find a matrix $\mathbf{G}$ such that

$$\mathbf{G}\begin{bmatrix} 0 & -S_z & S_y \\ S_z & 0 & -S_x \\ -S_y & S_x & 0 \end{bmatrix} = \begin{bmatrix} 0 & -(\mathbf{MS})_z & (\mathbf{MS})_y \\ (\mathbf{MS})_z & 0 & -(\mathbf{MS})_x \\ -(\mathbf{MS})_y & (\mathbf{MS})_x & 0 \end{bmatrix}\mathbf{M},$$

and finally use Equation (2.65) to show that $\mathbf{G} = (\det\mathbf{M})(\mathbf{M}^{-1})^{\mathrm{T}}$.]

5. Implement a C++ class that encapsulates a quaternion. The class should possess data members for the quaternion's w-, x-, y-, and z-components. In addition to a default constructor, which should not perform any initialization, the class should have a constructor that takes four floating-point numbers as arguments and initializes the quaternion's components to those values. The class should also include overloaded operators for addition, subtraction, multiplication, and division by scalars, and the quaternion product defined by Equation (3.34). Include a function that takes an angle θ and an axis $\mathbf{A}$ as parameters and returns the unit quaternion representing the rotation through the angle θ about the axis $\mathbf{A}$. Also include a function that converts a quaternion into a 3×3 rotation matrix using Equation (3.60). Finally, write functions that calculate the magnitude of a quaternion and the inverse of a quaternion.

Chapter 4

3D Engine Geometry

In this chapter, we draw upon the material presented in the first three chapters to begin our study of its practical applications to the art and science of 3D game programming. After a treatment of the nature of lines and planes in three-dimensional space, we introduce the view frustum and examine some of the important mathematics governing the virtual camera through which we see our game universe.

4.1 Lines in 3D Space

Given two 3D points $\mathbf{P}_1$ and $\mathbf{P}_2$, we can define the line that passes through these points parametrically as

$$\mathbf{P}(t) = (1-t)\mathbf{P}_1 + t\mathbf{P}_2, \tag{4.1}$$

where the parameter t ranges over all real numbers. The line segment connecting $\mathbf{P}_1$ and $\mathbf{P}_2$ corresponds to values of t between 0 and 1.

A *ray* is a line having a single endpoint $\mathbf{S}$ and extending to infinity in a given direction $\mathbf{V}$. Rays are typically expressed by the parametric equation

$$\mathbf{P}(t) = \mathbf{S} + t\mathbf{V},\tag{4.2}$$

where t is allowed to be greater than or equal to zero. This equation is often used to represent lines as well. Note that this equation is equivalent to Equation (4.1) if we let $\mathbf{S} = \mathbf{P}_1$ and $\mathbf{V} = \mathbf{P}_2 - \mathbf{P}_1$.

4.1.1 Distance between a Point and a Line

The distance d from a point $\mathbf{Q}$ to a line defined by the endpoint $\mathbf{S}$ and the direction $\mathbf{V}$ can be found by calculating the magnitude of the component of $\mathbf{Q} - \mathbf{S}$ that is perpendicular to the line, as shown in Figure 4.1.

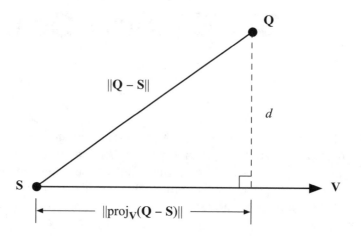

Figure 4.1 The distance d from a point $\mathbf{Q}$ to the line $\mathbf{S} + t\mathbf{V}$ is found by calculating the length of the perpendicular component of $\mathbf{Q} - \mathbf{S}$ with respect to the line.

Using the Pythagorean theorem, the squared distance between the point $\mathbf{Q}$ and the line can be obtained by subtracting the square of the projection of $\mathbf{Q} - \mathbf{S}$ onto the direction $\mathbf{V}$ from the square of $\mathbf{Q} - \mathbf{S}$. This gives us

$$d^2 = (\mathbf{Q} - \mathbf{S})^2 - [\mathrm{proj}_{\mathbf{V}}(\mathbf{Q} - \mathbf{S})]^2$$
$$= (\mathbf{Q} - \mathbf{S})^2 - \left[\frac{(\mathbf{Q} - \mathbf{S}) \cdot \mathbf{V}}{V^2}\mathbf{V}\right]^2.\tag{4.3}$$

Simplifying a bit and taking the square root gives us the distance d that we desire:

$$d = \sqrt{(\mathbf{Q}-\mathbf{S})^2 - \frac{[(\mathbf{Q}-\mathbf{S})\cdot\mathbf{V}]^2}{V^2}}. \tag{4.4}$$

4.1.2 Distance between Two Lines

In two dimensions, two lines are either parallel or they intersect at a single point. In three dimensions, there are more possibilities. Two lines that are not parallel and do not intersect are called *skew*. A formula giving the minimum distance between points on skew lines can be found by using a little calculus.

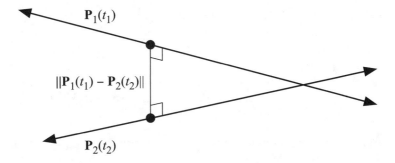

Figure 4.2 The distance between skew lines $\mathbf{P}_1(t_1)$ and $\mathbf{P}_2(t_2)$ is calculated by finding the parameters t_1 and t_2 minimizing $\|\mathbf{P}_1(t_1) - \mathbf{P}_2(t_2)\|$.

Suppose that we have two lines, as shown in Figure 4.2, defined by the parametric functions

$$\mathbf{P}_1(t_1) = \mathbf{S}_1 + t_1 \mathbf{V}_1$$
$$\mathbf{P}_2(t_2) = \mathbf{S}_2 + t_2 \mathbf{V}_2, \tag{4.5}$$

where t_1 and t_2 range over all real numbers. Then the squared distance between a point on the line $\mathbf{P}_1(t_1)$ and a point on the line $\mathbf{P}_2(t_2)$ can be written as the following function of the parameters t_1 and t_2.

$$f(t_1, t_2) = \|\mathbf{P}_1(t_1) - \mathbf{P}_2(t_2)\|^2 \tag{4.6}$$

Expanding the square and substituting the definitions of the functions $\mathbf{P}_1(t_1)$ and $\mathbf{P}_2(t_2)$ gives us

$$f(t_1, t_2) = \mathbf{P}_1(t_1)^2 + \mathbf{P}_2(t_2)^2 - 2\mathbf{P}_1(t_1) \cdot \mathbf{P}_2(t_2)$$
$$= (\mathbf{S}_1 + t_1\mathbf{V}_1)^2 + (\mathbf{S}_2 + t_2\mathbf{V}_2)^2$$
$$- 2(\mathbf{S}_1 \cdot \mathbf{S}_2 + t_1\mathbf{V}_1 \cdot \mathbf{S}_2 + t_2\mathbf{V}_2 \cdot \mathbf{S}_1 + t_1t_2\mathbf{V}_1 \cdot \mathbf{V}_2)$$
$$= S_1^2 + t_1^2V_1^2 + 2t_1\mathbf{S}_1 \cdot \mathbf{V}_1 + S_2^2 + t_2^2V_2^2 + 2t_2\mathbf{S}_2 \cdot \mathbf{V}_2$$
$$- 2(\mathbf{S}_1 \cdot \mathbf{S}_2 + t_1\mathbf{V}_1 \cdot \mathbf{S}_2 + t_2\mathbf{V}_2 \cdot \mathbf{S}_1 + t_1t_2\mathbf{V}_1 \cdot \mathbf{V}_2). \tag{4.7}$$

The minimum value attained by the function f can be found by setting partial derivatives with respect to t_1 and t_2 equal to zero. This provides us with the equations

$$\frac{\partial f}{\partial t_1} = 2t_1V_1^2 + 2\mathbf{S}_1 \cdot \mathbf{V}_1 - 2\mathbf{V}_1 \cdot \mathbf{S}_2 - 2t_2\mathbf{V}_1 \cdot \mathbf{V}_2 = 0 \tag{4.8}$$

and

$$\frac{\partial f}{\partial t_2} = 2t_2V_2^2 + 2\mathbf{S}_2 \cdot \mathbf{V}_2 - 2\mathbf{V}_2 \cdot \mathbf{S}_1 - 2t_1\mathbf{V}_1 \cdot \mathbf{V}_2 = 0. \tag{4.9}$$

After removing a factor of two, we can write these equations in matrix form as follows.

$$\begin{bmatrix} V_1^2 & -\mathbf{V}_1 \cdot \mathbf{V}_2 \\ \mathbf{V}_1 \cdot \mathbf{V}_2 & -V_2^2 \end{bmatrix} \begin{bmatrix} t_1 \\ t_2 \end{bmatrix} = \begin{bmatrix} (\mathbf{S}_2 - \mathbf{S}_1) \cdot \mathbf{V}_1 \\ (\mathbf{S}_2 - \mathbf{S}_1) \cdot \mathbf{V}_2 \end{bmatrix} \tag{4.10}$$

Solving this equation for t_1 and t_2 gives us

$$\begin{bmatrix} t_1 \\ t_2 \end{bmatrix} = \begin{bmatrix} V_1^2 & -\mathbf{V}_1 \cdot \mathbf{V}_2 \\ \mathbf{V}_1 \cdot \mathbf{V}_2 & -V_2^2 \end{bmatrix}^{-1} \begin{bmatrix} (\mathbf{S}_2 - \mathbf{S}_1) \cdot \mathbf{V}_1 \\ (\mathbf{S}_2 - \mathbf{S}_1) \cdot \mathbf{V}_2 \end{bmatrix}$$
$$= \frac{1}{(\mathbf{V}_1 \cdot \mathbf{V}_2)^2 - V_1^2V_2^2} \begin{bmatrix} -V_2^2 & \mathbf{V}_1 \cdot \mathbf{V}_2 \\ -\mathbf{V}_1 \cdot \mathbf{V}_2 & V_1^2 \end{bmatrix} \begin{bmatrix} (\mathbf{S}_2 - \mathbf{S}_1) \cdot \mathbf{V}_1 \\ (\mathbf{S}_2 - \mathbf{S}_1) \cdot \mathbf{V}_2 \end{bmatrix}. \tag{4.11}$$

Plugging these values of t_1 and t_2 back into the function f gives us the minimum squared distance between the two lines. Taking a square root gives us the actual distance that we want. If the direction vectors $\mathbf{V}_1$ and $\mathbf{V}_2$ have unit length, then Equation (4.11) simplifies a bit since $V_1^2 = 1$ and $V_2^2 = 1$.

If the quantity $(\mathbf{V}_1 \cdot \mathbf{V}_2)^2 - V_1^2V_2^2$ is zero, then the lines are parallel, in which case the distance between the two lines is equal to the distance between any point on one of the lines and the other line. This is illustrated in Figure 4.3. In particular, we can use Equation (4.3) to measure the distance from the point $\mathbf{S}_1$ to the line $\mathbf{P}_2(t_2)$ or the distance from the point $\mathbf{S}_2$ to the line $\mathbf{P}_1(t_1)$.

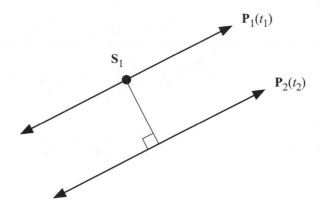

Figure 4.3 The distance between parallel lines is given by the distance from a point on one line to the other line.

4.2 Planes in 3D Space

Given a 3D point $\mathbf{P}$ and a normal vector $\mathbf{N}$, the plane passing through the point $\mathbf{P}$ and perpendicular to the direction $\mathbf{N}$ can be defined as the set of points $\mathbf{Q}$ such that $\mathbf{N} \cdot (\mathbf{Q} - \mathbf{P}) = 0$. As shown in Figure 4.4, this is the set of points whose difference with $\mathbf{P}$ is perpendicular to the normal direction $\mathbf{N}$. The equation for a plane is commonly written as

$$Ax + By + Cz + D = 0, \tag{4.12}$$

where A, B, and C are the x-, y-, and z-components of the normal vector $\mathbf{N}$, and $D = -\mathbf{N} \cdot \mathbf{P}$. As shown in Figure 4.5, the value $|D|/\|\mathbf{N}\|$ is the distance by which the plane is offset from a parallel plane that passes through the origin.

The normal vector $\mathbf{N}$ is often normalized to unit length because in that case the equation

$$d = \mathbf{N} \cdot \mathbf{Q} + D \tag{4.13}$$

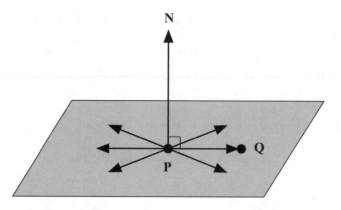

Figure 4.4 A plane is defined by the set of points **Q** whose difference with a point **P**, known to lie in the plane, is perpendicular to the normal direction **N**.

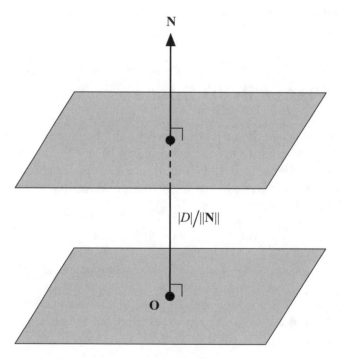

Figure 4.5 The value of D in Equation (4.12) is proportional to the perpendicular distance from the origin to the plane.

gives the signed distance from the plane to an arbitrary point $\mathbf{Q}$. If $d = 0$, then the point $\mathbf{Q}$ lies in the plane. If $d > 0$, we say that the point $\mathbf{Q}$ lies on the positive side of the plane since $\mathbf{Q}$ would be on the side in which the normal vector points. Otherwise, if $d < 0$, we say that the point $\mathbf{Q}$ lies on the negative side of the plane.

It is convenient to represent a plane using a four-dimensional vector. The shorthand notation $\langle \mathbf{N}, D \rangle$ is used to denote the plane consisting of points $\mathbf{Q}$ satisfying $\mathbf{N} \cdot \mathbf{Q} + D = 0$. If we treat our three-dimensional points instead as four-dimensional homogeneous points having a w-coordinate of 1, then Equation (4.13) can be rewritten as $d = \mathbf{L} \cdot \mathbf{Q}$, where $\mathbf{L} = \langle \mathbf{N}, D \rangle$. A point $\mathbf{Q}$ lies in the plane if $\mathbf{L} \cdot \mathbf{Q} = 0$.

4.2.1 Intersection of a Line and a Plane

Finding the point where a line intersects a plane is a common calculation performed by 3D engines. In particular, it is used extensively during polygon clipping, which is discussed in detail in Sections 7.4.1 and 9.2.2.

Let $\mathbf{P}(t) = \mathbf{S} + t\mathbf{V}$ represent a line containing the point $\mathbf{S}$ and running parallel to the direction $\mathbf{V}$. For a plane defined by the normal direction $\mathbf{N}$ and the signed distance D from the origin, we can find the point where the line intersects the plane by solving the equation

$$\mathbf{N} \cdot \mathbf{P}(t) + D = 0 \qquad (4.14)$$

for t. Substituting $\mathbf{S} + t\mathbf{V}$ for $\mathbf{P}(t)$ gives us

$$\mathbf{N} \cdot \mathbf{S} + (\mathbf{N} \cdot \mathbf{V})t + D = 0, \qquad (4.15)$$

and after solving this for t, we arrive at

$$t = \frac{-(\mathbf{N} \cdot \mathbf{S} + D)}{\mathbf{N} \cdot \mathbf{V}}. \qquad (4.16)$$

Plugging this value of t back into the line equation $\mathbf{P}(t) = \mathbf{S} + t\mathbf{V}$ produces the point of intersection. If $\mathbf{N} \cdot \mathbf{V} = 0$, then the line is parallel to the plane (the plane normal $\mathbf{N}$ is perpendicular to the line direction $\mathbf{V}$). In this case, the line lies in the plane itself if $\mathbf{N} \cdot \mathbf{S} + D = 0$; otherwise, there is no intersection.

We may also express the value of t given in Equation (4.16) in terms of the four-dimensional representation of a plane. Given a plane $\mathbf{L} = \langle \mathbf{N}, D \rangle$, we have

$$t = -\frac{\mathbf{L} \cdot \mathbf{S}}{\mathbf{L} \cdot \mathbf{V}}. \qquad (4.17)$$

Since $\mathbf{S}$ is a point, its w-coordinate is 1. However, since $\mathbf{V}$ is a direction vector, its extension to homogeneous coordinates requires that we assign it a w-coordinate of 0 (as discussed in Section 3.4.2). This confirms that Equation (4.17) is equivalent to Equation (4.16).

4.2.2 Intersection of Three Planes

Regions of space are often defined by a list of planes that form the boundary of a convex polyhedron. The edges and vertices belonging to this polyhedron can be found by performing a series of calculations that determine the points at which sets of three planes intersect.

Let $\mathbf{L}_1 = \langle \mathbf{N}_1, D_1 \rangle$, $\mathbf{L}_2 = \langle \mathbf{N}_2, D_2 \rangle$, and $\mathbf{L}_3 = \langle \mathbf{N}_3, D_3 \rangle$ be three arbitrary planes. We can find a point $\mathbf{Q}$ that lies in all three planes by solving the following system.

$$
\begin{aligned}
\mathbf{L}_1 \cdot \mathbf{Q} &= 0 \\
\mathbf{L}_2 \cdot \mathbf{Q} &= 0 \\
\mathbf{L}_3 \cdot \mathbf{Q} &= 0
\end{aligned}
\tag{4.18}
$$

This can be written in matrix form as

$$
\mathbf{M}\mathbf{Q} = \begin{bmatrix} -D_1 \\ -D_2 \\ -D_3 \end{bmatrix},
\tag{4.19}
$$

where the matrix $\mathbf{M}$ is given by

$$
\mathbf{M} = \begin{bmatrix}
(\mathbf{N}_1)_x & (\mathbf{N}_1)_y & (\mathbf{N}_1)_z \\
(\mathbf{N}_2)_x & (\mathbf{N}_2)_y & (\mathbf{N}_2)_z \\
(\mathbf{N}_3)_x & (\mathbf{N}_3)_y & (\mathbf{N}_3)_z
\end{bmatrix}.
\tag{4.20}
$$

Assuming that the matrix $\mathbf{M}$ is invertible, solving for the point $\mathbf{Q}$ as follows produces the unique point where the three planes intersect.

$$\mathbf{Q} = \mathbf{M}^{-1} \begin{bmatrix} -D_1 \\ -D_2 \\ -D_3 \end{bmatrix} \tag{4.21}$$

If $\mathbf{M}$ is singular (i.e., $\det \mathbf{M} = 0$), then the three planes do not intersect at a point. This happens when the three normal vectors all lie in the same plane, an example of which is shown in Figure 4.6.

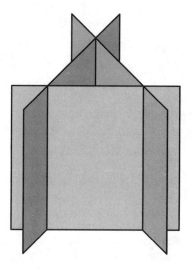

Figure 4.6 Three planes do not necessarily intersect at a point.

When two nonparallel planes $\mathbf{L}_1 = \langle \mathbf{N}_1, D_1 \rangle$ and $\mathbf{L}_2 = \langle \mathbf{N}_2, D_2 \rangle$ intersect, they do so at a line. As shown in Figure 4.7, the direction $\mathbf{V}$ in which the line of intersection runs is perpendicular to the normals of both planes and can thus be expressed by $\mathbf{V} = \mathbf{N}_1 \times \mathbf{N}_2$. To form a complete description of a line, we also need to provide a point that lies on the line. This can be accomplished by constructing a third plane $\mathbf{L}_3 = \langle \mathbf{V}, 0 \rangle$ that passes through the origin and whose normal direction is $\mathbf{V}$. We can then solve for the point where all three planes intersect, which is guaranteed to exist in this situation.

Using Equation (4.21), we can compute a point $\mathbf{Q}$ that lies on the line of intersection as follows.

$$\mathbf{Q} = \begin{bmatrix} (\mathbf{N}_1)_x & (\mathbf{N}_1)_y & (\mathbf{N}_1)_z \\ (\mathbf{N}_2)_x & (\mathbf{N}_2)_y & (\mathbf{N}_2)_z \\ V_x & V_y & V_z \end{bmatrix}^{-1} \begin{bmatrix} -D_1 \\ -D_2 \\ 0 \end{bmatrix} \tag{4.22}$$

The line where the two planes $\mathbf{L}_1$ and $\mathbf{L}_2$ intersect is given by $\mathbf{P}(t) = \mathbf{Q} + t\mathbf{V}$.

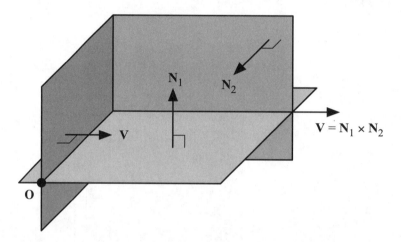

Figure 4.7 Two planes having normal vectors $\mathbf{N}_1$ and $\mathbf{N}_2$ intersect at a line running in the direction $\mathbf{V}$. A point on this line can be found by finding the intersection point with a third plane passing through the origin and having normal $\mathbf{V}$.

4.2.3 Transforming Planes

Suppose that we wish to transform a plane using a 3×3 matrix $\mathbf{M}$ and a 3D translation vector $\mathbf{T}$. We know that we can transform the normal direction $\mathbf{N}$ using the inverse transpose of $\mathbf{M}$, but we also have the signed distance from the origin D to worry about. If we know that a point $\mathbf{P}$ lies in the original plane, then we can calculate the signed distance D' from the transformed plane to the origin using the equation

$$\begin{aligned} D' &= -\left((\mathbf{M}^{-1})^\mathrm{T}\mathbf{N}\right) \cdot (\mathbf{MP} + \mathbf{T}) \\ &= -\left((\mathbf{M}^{-1})^\mathrm{T}\mathbf{N}\right)^\mathrm{T}\mathbf{MP} - \left((\mathbf{M}^{-1})^\mathrm{T}\mathbf{N}\right)^\mathrm{T}\mathbf{T} \\ &= -\mathbf{N}^\mathrm{T}\mathbf{M}^{-1}\mathbf{MP} - \mathbf{N}^\mathrm{T}\mathbf{M}^{-1}\mathbf{T} \\ &= D - \mathbf{N} \cdot \mathbf{M}^{-1}\mathbf{T}. \end{aligned} \tag{4.23}$$

Recall from Equation (3.27) that the inverse of the 4×4 matrix $\mathbf{F}$ constructed from the 3×3 matrix $\mathbf{M}$ and the 3D translation vector $\mathbf{T}$ is given by

$$\mathbf{F}^{-1} = \left[\begin{array}{c|c} \mathbf{M}^{-1} & -\mathbf{M}^{-1}\mathbf{T} \\ \hline \mathbf{0} & 1 \end{array} \right]. \tag{4.24}$$

We therefore have for the transpose of $\mathbf{F}^{-1}$

$$\left(\mathbf{F}^{-1}\right)^{\mathrm{T}} = \left[\begin{array}{c|c} \left(\mathbf{M}^{-1}\right)^{\mathrm{T}} & \mathbf{0} \\ \hline -\mathbf{M}^{-1}\mathbf{T} & 1 \end{array} \right]. \tag{4.25}$$

The quantity $D - \mathbf{N} \cdot \mathbf{M}^{-1}\mathbf{T}$ is exactly the dot product between the fourth row of $\left(\mathbf{F}^{-1}\right)^{\mathrm{T}}$ and the 4D vector $\langle \mathbf{N}_x, \mathbf{N}_y, \mathbf{N}_z, D \rangle$. This shows that we may treat planes as four-dimensional vectors that transform in the same manner as three-dimensional normal vectors, except that we use the inverse transpose of the 4×4 transformation matrix. Thus, the plane $\mathbf{L} = \langle \mathbf{N}, D \rangle$ transforms using the 4×4 matrix $\mathbf{F}$ as

$$\mathbf{L}' = \left(\mathbf{F}^{-1}\right)^{\mathrm{T}}\mathbf{L}. \tag{4.26}$$

4.3 The View Frustum

Figure 4.8 shows the *view frustum*, the volume of space containing everything that is visible in a three-dimensional scene. The view frustum is shaped like a pyramid whose apex lies at the camera position. It has this shape because it represents the exact volume that would be visible to a camera that is looking through a rectangular window—the computer screen. The view frustum is bounded by six planes, four of which correspond to the edges of the screen and are called the *left*, *right*, *bottom*, and *top* frustum planes. The remaining two planes are called the *near* and *far* frustum planes, and define the minimum and maximum distances at which objects in a scene are visible to the camera.

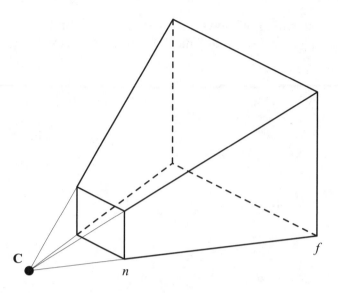

Figure 4.8 The view frustum encloses the space bounded by the near plane lying at a distance *n* from the camera, the far plane lying at a distance *f* from the camera, and four side planes that pass through the camera position **C**.

The view frustum is aligned to *camera space*. Camera space, also called *eye space*, is the coordinate system in which the camera lies at the origin, the *x*-axis points to the right, and the *y*-axis points upward. The direction in which the *z*-axis points depends on the 3D graphics library being used. Within the OpenGL library, the *z*-axis points in the direction opposite that in which the camera points. This forms a right-handed coordinate system and is shown in Figure 4.9. (Under Direct3D, the *z*-axis points in the same direction that the camera points and forms a left-handed coordinate system.)

4.3.1 Field of View

The projection plane, shown in Figure 4.10, is a plane that is perpendicular to the camera's viewing direction and lies at the distance *e* from the camera where the left and right frustum planes intersect it at $x = -1$ and $x = 1$. The distance *e*, which is sometimes called the *focal length* of the camera, depends on the angle α formed between the left and right frustum plane. The angle α is called the *horizontal field of view* angle.

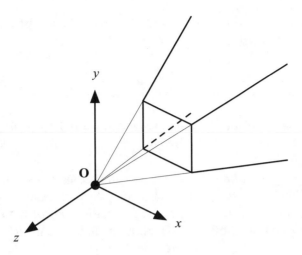

Figure 4.9 Camera space in OpenGL.

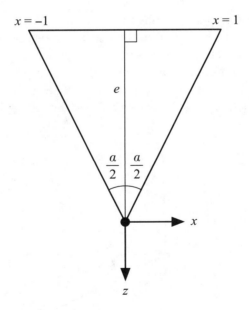

Figure 4.10 The distance *e* from the camera to the projection plane depends on the horizontal field of view angle *α*.

For a desired horizontal field of view α, the distance e to the projection plane is given by the trigonometric relation

$$e = \frac{1}{\tan(\alpha/2)}. \tag{4.27}$$

Larger fields of view are equivalent to shorter focal lengths. A camera can be made to "zoom in" by diminishing the field of view angle, thus causing a longer focal length.

The *aspect ratio* of a display screen is equal to its height divided by its width. For example, a 640×480 pixel display has an aspect ratio of 0.75. Since most displays are not square, but rectangular, the *vertical* field of view is not equal to the horizontal field of view. The bottom and top frustum planes intersect the projection plane at $y = \pm a$, where a is the aspect ratio of the display. This forms the triangle shown in Figure 4.11, and thus the vertical field of view angle β is given by

$$\beta = 2\tan^{-1}(a/e). \tag{4.28}$$

The four side planes of the view frustum carve a rectangle out of the projection plane at a distance e from the camera whose edges lie at $x = \pm 1$ and $y = \pm a$. The OpenGL function `glFrustum()` requires that we specify a rectangle at the distance n from the camera, where n is the near plane distance. Scaling our rectangle by a factor of n/e, we place the left edge at $x = -n/e$, the right edge at $x = n/e$, the bottom edge at $y = -an/e$, and the top edge at $y = an/e$.

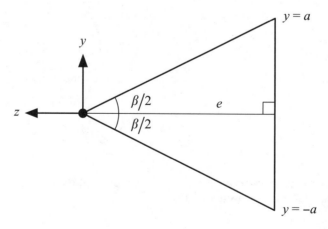

Figure 4.11 The vertical field of view angle β depends on the aspect ratio a.

4.3.2 Frustum Planes

The camera-space normal directions for the six view frustum planes are shown in Figure 4.12. The inward-pointing normal directions for the four side planes are found by rotating the directions along which the sides point 90 degrees toward the center of the frustum. The four side planes each pass through the origin, so they each have $D = 0$. The near plane lies at a distance n from the origin in the same direction in which its normal points, so it has $D = -n$. The far plane lies at a distance f from the origin in the opposite direction in which its normal points, so it has $D = f$. The four-dimensional plane vectors corresponding to the six sides of the view frustum are summarized in Table 4.1. In this table, the normal directions for the four side planes have been normalized to unit length.

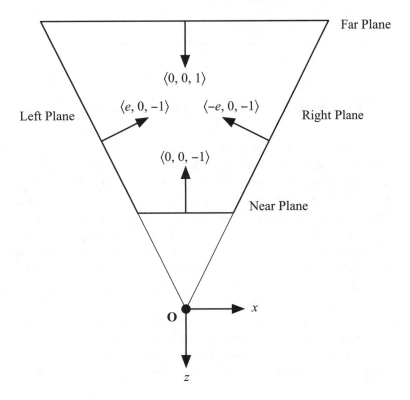

Figure 4.12 View frustum plane normal directions in OpenGL camera space.

Table 4.1 View frustum plane vectors in OpenGL camera space in terms of the focal length e, the aspect ratio a, the near plane distance n, and the far plane distance f.

Plane	$\langle \mathbf{N}, D \rangle$
Near	$\langle 0, 0, -1, -n \rangle$
Far	$\langle 0, 0, 1, f \rangle$
Left	$\left\langle \dfrac{e}{\sqrt{e^2+1}}, 0, -\dfrac{1}{\sqrt{e^2+1}}, 0 \right\rangle$
Right	$\left\langle -\dfrac{e}{\sqrt{e^2+1}}, 0, -\dfrac{1}{\sqrt{e^2+1}}, 0 \right\rangle$
Bottom	$\left\langle 0, \dfrac{e}{\sqrt{e^2+a^2}}, -\dfrac{a}{\sqrt{e^2+a^2}}, 0 \right\rangle$
Top	$\left\langle 0, -\dfrac{e}{\sqrt{e^2+a^2}}, -\dfrac{a}{\sqrt{e^2+a^2}}, 0 \right\rangle$

4.4 Perspective-Correct Interpolation

When a 3D graphics processor renders a triangle on the screen, it rasterizes it one scanline at a time. The vertices of a triangle, in addition to their positions in camera space, carry information such as lighting colors and texture mapping coordinates, which must be interpolated across the face of the triangle. When a single scanline of a triangle is drawn, the information at each pixel is an interpolated value derived from the values known at the left and right endpoints.

As shown in Figure 4.13, correct interpolation across the face of a triangle is not linear since equally spaced steps taken on the projection plane correspond to larger steps taken on the face of a triangle as the distance from the camera increases. Graphics processors must use a nonlinear method of interpolation for texture-mapping coordinates to avoid distortion of the texture map. Although modern hardware now interpolates other types of information associated with a vertex, such as lighting colors, older graphics cards simply use linear interpolation since the difference is not as noticeable as it is with texture maps.

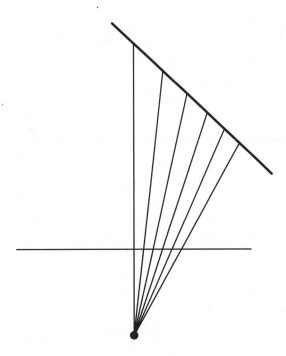

Figure 4.13 Equally spaced steps taken on the projection plane correspond to larger steps taken on the face of a triangle as the distance from the camera increases. Thus, correct interpolation across the face of a triangle is not linear.

4.4.1 Depth Interpolation

It is important to note that the z-coordinates (representing the depth) of points on the face of a triangle are interpolated linearly by 3D graphics hardware, contrary to the perspective-correct method presented in this section. An explanation for this follows in Section 4.5.1, which discusses the perspective projection matrix.

Figure 4.14 shows a line segment lying in the x-z plane that corresponds to a single scanline of a triangle. During rasterization, points on this line segment are sampled by casting rays through equally spaced points on the projection plane, which represent pixels on the display screen.

Assuming that the segment does not belong to a line that passes through the origin (in which case the triangle would be viewed edge-on and would thus not be visible), we can describe the line with the equation

$$ax + bz = c, \tag{4.29}$$

where $c \neq 0$.

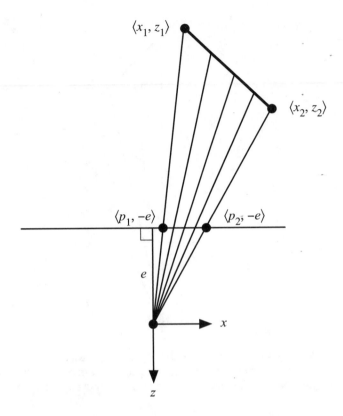

Figure 4.14 The line segment corresponding to a single scanline of a triangle is sampled by casting rays through equally spaced points on the projection plane.

Given a point $\langle x, z \rangle$ that lies on the line, we can cast a ray from the origin (the camera position) to the point $\langle x, z \rangle$ and determine where it intersects the projection plane. The z-coordinate at the projection plane is always equal to $-e$. We can find the x-coordinate p on the projection plane corresponding to the point $\langle x, z \rangle$ by using the following relationship derived from the similar triangles shown in Figure 4.14.

$$\frac{p}{x} = \frac{-e}{z} \tag{4.30}$$

Solving this for x and it plugging back into Equation (4.29) lets us rewrite our line equation as follows.

$$\left(-\frac{ap}{e}+b\right)z=c \cdot$$

(4.31)

It is convenient for us to manipulate this equation further by writing it in such a way that $1/z$ appears on one side:

$$\frac{1}{z}=-\frac{ap}{ce}+\frac{b}{c}.$$

(4.32)

Let us call the endpoints of the line segment $\langle x_1, z_1 \rangle$ and $\langle x_2, z_2 \rangle$, and their images on the projection plane $\langle p_1, -e \rangle$ and $\langle p_2, -e \rangle$. Let $p_3 = (1-t)p_1 + tp_2$, for some t satisfying $0 \le t \le 1$, be the x-coordinate of an interpolated point on the projection plane. We would like to find the z-coordinate of the point $\langle x_3, z_3 \rangle$ where the ray cast through the point $\langle p_3, -e \rangle$ intersects the face of the triangle. Plugging $p_3 = (1-t)p_1 + tp_2$ and z_3 into Equation (4.32) gives us

$$\begin{aligned}
\frac{1}{z_3} &= -\frac{ap_3}{ce} + \frac{b}{c} \\
&= -\frac{ap_1}{ce}(1-t) - \frac{ap_2}{ce}t + \frac{b}{c} \\
&= \left(-\frac{ap_1}{ce} + \frac{b}{c}\right)(1-t) + \left(-\frac{ap_2}{ce} + \frac{b}{c}\right)t \\
&= \frac{1}{z_1}(1-t) + \frac{1}{z_2}t.
\end{aligned}$$

(4.33)

This result demonstrates that the *reciprocal* of the z-coordinate is correctly interpolated in a linear manner across the face of a triangle.

4.4.2 Vertex Attribute Interpolation

Vertices carry information such as lighting colors and texture mapping coordinates that from here on are collectively referred to as vertex attributes. Each vertex attribute must be interpolated across the face of a triangle when it is rasterized. Suppose that the endpoints of a scanline have depth values of z_1 and z_2, and possess scalar attributes b_1 and b_2, respectively. We would expect the interpolated attribute value b_3 to form the same proportion with the total difference along the line segment as does the interpolated depth value z_3. That is, the equation

$$\frac{b_3 - b_1}{b_2 - b_1} = \frac{z_3 - z_1}{z_2 - z_1} \tag{4.34}$$

should be satisfied. Substituting the value

$$z_3 = \frac{1}{\dfrac{1}{z_1}(1-t) + \dfrac{1}{z_2}t} \tag{4.35}$$

given by Equation (4.33) and solving for b_3 gives us

$$b_3 = \frac{b_1 z_2 (1-t) + b_2 z_1 t}{z_2 (1-t) + z_1 t}. \tag{4.36}$$

Multiplying the numerator and denominator by $1/z_1 z_2$ allows us to extract a factor of z_3 from the right-hand side of the equation as follows.

$$\begin{aligned}
b_3 &= \frac{\dfrac{b_1}{z_1}(1-t) + \dfrac{b_2}{z_2}t}{\dfrac{1}{z_1}(1-t) + \dfrac{1}{z_2}t} \\
&= z_3 \left[\frac{b_1}{z_1}(1-t) + \frac{b_2}{z_2}t \right].
\end{aligned} \tag{4.37}$$

This demonstrates that the value b/z can be linearly interpolated across the face of a triangle. Graphics processors first calculate the linearly interpolated value of $1/z$ when rasterizing a scanline. The reciprocal is then calculated and multiplied by the linearly interpolated value of b/z to obtain the perspective-correct interpolated value of any vertex attribute b.

4.5 Projections

To render a three-dimensional scene on a two-dimensional display screen, we need to determine where on the screen each vertex in the scene should be drawn. As we have already seen, we can determine where a vertex located at a position $\mathbf{P}$ falls on the projection plane by calculating where the ray cast from the origin toward the point $\mathbf{P}$ intersects it. The x- and y-coordinates of the projected point are given by the formulas

$$x = -\frac{e}{P_z}P_x \text{ and } y = -\frac{e}{P_z}P_y. \tag{4.38}$$

(Remember that the value of P_z is negative since the camera points in the negative z direction.)

Applying the above formula to the z-coordinate would always result in a projected depth of $-e$. Useful depth information is needed, however, to perform hidden surface removal, so 3D graphics systems instead use homogeneous coordinates to project vertices in four-dimensional space.

4.5.1 Perspective Projections

A perspective projection that maps x- and y-coordinates to the correct place on the projection plane while maintaining depth information is achieved by mapping the view frustum to a cube, as shown in Figure 4.15. This cube is the projection into 3D space of what is called *homogeneous clip space*. It is centered at the origin in OpenGL and extends from negative one to positive one on each of the x-, y-, and z-axes. The mapping to homogenous clip space is performed by first using a 4×4 projection matrix that, among other actions, places the negative z-coordinate of a camera-space point into the w-coordinate of the transformed point. Subsequent division by the w-coordinate produces a three-dimensional point having *normalized device coordinates*.

Let $\mathbf{P} = \langle P_x, P_y, P_z, 1 \rangle$ be a homogeneous point in camera space that lies inside the view frustum. The OpenGL function `glFrustum()` takes as parameters the left edge $x = l$, the right edge $x = r$, the bottom edge $y = b$, and the top edge $y = t$ of the rectangle carved out of the near plane by the four side planes of the view frustum. The near plane lies at $z = -n$, so we can calculate the projected x- and y-coordinates of the point $\mathbf{P}$ on the near plane using the equations

$$x = -\frac{n}{P_z}P_x \text{ and } y = -\frac{n}{P_z}P_y. \tag{4.39}$$

Any point in lying in the view frustum satisfies $l \le x \le r$ and $b \le y \le t$ on the near plane. We want to map these ranges to the $[-1,1]$ range needed to fit the view frustum into homogeneous clip space. This can be accomplished using the simple linear functions

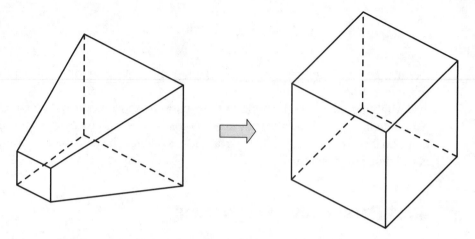

Figure 4.15 The perspective projection maps the view frustum to the cube representing homogeneous clip space.

$$x' = (x - l)\frac{2}{r - l} - 1 \qquad (4.40)$$

and

$$y' = (y - b)\frac{2}{t - b} - 1. \qquad (4.41)$$

Substituting the values of x and y given in Equation (4.39) and simplifying yields

$$x' = \frac{2n}{r - l}\left(-\frac{P_x}{P_z}\right) - \frac{r + l}{r - l} \qquad (4.42)$$

and

$$y' = \frac{2n}{t - b}\left(-\frac{P_y}{P_z}\right) - \frac{t + b}{t - b}. \qquad (4.43)$$

Mapping the projected z-coordinate to the range $[-1,1]$ involves somewhat more complex computation. Since the point **P** lies inside the view frustum, its z-coordinate must satisfy $-f \leq P_z \leq -n$, where n and f are the distances from the camera to the near and far planes, respectively. We wish to find a function that maps $-n \rightarrow -1$ and $-f \rightarrow 1$. (Note that such a mapping reflects the z-axis; therefore, homogeneous clip space is left-handed.) Since z-coordinates must have their reciprocals interpolated during rasterization, we construct this mapping function so that it is a function of $1/z$, consequently allowing projected depth values to be interpolated linearly. Our mapping function thus has the form

$$z' = \frac{A}{z} + B. \tag{4.44}$$

We can solve for the unknowns A and B by plugging in the known mappings $-n \rightarrow -1$ and $-f \rightarrow 1$ to get

$$-1 = \frac{A}{-n} + B \quad \text{and} \quad 1 = \frac{A}{-f} + B. \tag{4.45}$$

A little algebra yields the following values for A and B:

$$A = \frac{2nf}{f-n} \quad \text{and} \quad B = \frac{f+n}{f-n}. \tag{4.46}$$

The z-coordinate is thus mapped to the range $[-1,1]$ by the function

$$z' = -\frac{2nf}{f-n}\left(-\frac{1}{P_z}\right) + \frac{f+n}{f-n}. \tag{4.47}$$

Equations (4.42), (4.43), and (4.47) each contain a division by $-P_z$. The 3D point $\tilde{\mathbf{P}}' = \langle x', y', z' \rangle$ is equivalent to the 4D homogeneous point

$$\mathbf{P}' = \langle -x'P_z, -y'P_z, -z'P_z, -P_z \rangle \tag{4.48}$$

after division by the w-coordinate. Since the values of $-x'P_z$, $-y'P_z$, and $-z'P_z$ given by the equations

$$-x'P_z = \frac{2n}{r-l}P_x + \frac{r+l}{r-l}P_z, \tag{4.49}$$

$$-y'P_z = \frac{2n}{t-b}P_y + \frac{t+b}{t-b}P_z, \tag{4.50}$$

and

$$-z'P_z = -\frac{f+n}{f-n}P_z - \frac{2nf}{f-n} \tag{4.51}$$

are linear functions of the coordinates of the point **P**, we can use a 4×4 matrix $\mathbf{M}_{frustum}$ to calculate the point **P**′ as follows.

$$\mathbf{P}' = \mathbf{M}_{frustum}\mathbf{P} = \begin{bmatrix} \dfrac{2n}{r-l} & 0 & \dfrac{r+l}{r-l} & 0 \\[2ex] 0 & \dfrac{2n}{t-b} & \dfrac{t+b}{t-b} & 0 \\[2ex] 0 & 0 & -\dfrac{f+n}{f-n} & -\dfrac{2nf}{f-n} \\[2ex] 0 & 0 & -1 & 0 \end{bmatrix} \begin{bmatrix} P_x \\ P_y \\ P_z \\ 1 \end{bmatrix} \tag{4.52}$$

The matrix $\mathbf{M}_{frustum}$ in Equation (4.52) is the OpenGL perspective projection matrix generated by the glFrustum() function. Camera-space points are transformed by this matrix into homogeneous clip space in such a way that the w-coordinate holds the negation of the original camera-space z-coordinate. When interpolating vertex attributes (see Section 4.4.2), it is actually this w-coordinate whose reciprocal is interpolated, serving as the value of z in Equation (4.37).

It is possible to construct a view frustum that is not bounded in depth by allowing the far plane distance f to tend to infinity. The resulting projection matrix $\mathbf{M}_{infinite}$ is given by

$$\mathbf{M}_{infinite} = \lim_{f \to \infty} \mathbf{M}_{frustum} = \begin{bmatrix} \dfrac{2n}{r-l} & 0 & \dfrac{r+l}{r-l} & 0 \\[2ex] 0 & \dfrac{2n}{t-b} & \dfrac{t+b}{t-b} & 0 \\[2ex] 0 & 0 & -1 & -2n \\[2ex] 0 & 0 & -1 & 0 \end{bmatrix}. \tag{4.52}$$

This is a perfectly valid projection matrix that allows objects to be rendered at any depth greater than or equal to n. Furthermore, it allows vertices having a w-coordinate of 0 to be rendered correctly. The interpretation of a camera-space point $\mathbf{Q} = \langle Q_x, Q_y, Q_z, 0 \rangle$ is that of a point that lies infinitely far from the camera in the direction $\langle Q_x, Q_y, Q_z \rangle$. Transforming $\mathbf{Q}$ with the matrix $\mathbf{M}_{\text{infinite}}$ gives us

$$
\mathbf{M}_{\text{infinite}}\mathbf{Q} =
\begin{bmatrix}
\dfrac{2n}{r-l} & 0 & \dfrac{r+l}{r-l} & 0 \\[2mm]
0 & \dfrac{2n}{t-b} & \dfrac{t+b}{t-b} & 0 \\[2mm]
0 & 0 & -1 & -2n \\[2mm]
0 & 0 & -1 & 0
\end{bmatrix}
\begin{bmatrix}
Q_x \\[1mm] Q_y \\[1mm] Q_z \\[1mm] 0
\end{bmatrix}
=
\begin{bmatrix}
\dfrac{2n}{r-l}Q_x + \dfrac{r+l}{r-l}Q_z \\[2mm]
\dfrac{2n}{t-b}Q_y + \dfrac{t+b}{t-b}Q_z \\[2mm]
-Q_z \\[2mm]
-Q_z
\end{bmatrix},
\qquad (4.53)
$$

which produces a projected point having the maximum z-coordinate of 1 after division by its w-coordinate. This ability to project points lying at infinity is required by the shadow-rendering technique described in Chapter 10.

4.5.2 Orthographic Projections

An orthographic projection, also known as a parallel projection, is one in which no perspective distortion occurs. As shown in Figure 4.16, camera-space points are always mapped to the projection plane by casting rays that are parallel to the camera's viewing direction.

The view volume for an orthographic projection is defined by a rectangle lying in the x-y plane and near and far plane distances. Since there is no perspective distortion, depth values for a triangle in an orthographic projection can be interpolated linearly. Thus, our mapping to normalized device coordinates can be performed linearly on all three axes. The functions mapping the x- and y-coordinates from the ranges $[l,r]$ and $[b,t]$ to the range $[-1,1]$ are given by

$$
x' = \frac{2}{r-l}x - \frac{r+l}{r-l} \qquad (4.54)
$$

and

$$
y' = \frac{2}{t-b}y - \frac{t+b}{t-b}. \qquad (4.55)
$$

In a similar manner, but negating z so that $-n \rightarrow -1$ and $-f \rightarrow 1$, we can map the z-coordinate from the range $[-f,-n]$ to the range $[-1,1]$ using the function

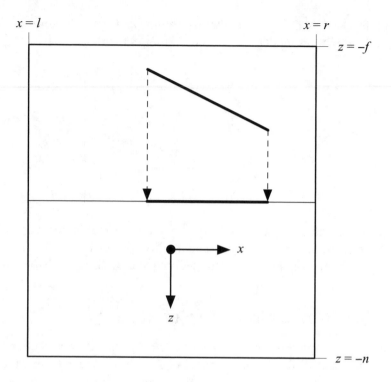

Figure 4.16 An orthographic projection.

$$z' = \frac{-2}{f-n}z - \frac{f+n}{f-n}.$$

(4.56)

Writing these three functions in matrix form gives us

$$\mathbf{P}' = \mathbf{M}_{ortho}\mathbf{P} = \begin{bmatrix} \dfrac{2}{r-l} & 0 & 0 & -\dfrac{r+l}{r-l} \\ 0 & \dfrac{2}{t-b} & 0 & -\dfrac{t+b}{t-b} \\ 0 & 0 & \dfrac{-2}{f-n} & -\dfrac{f+n}{f-n} \\ 0 & 0 & 0 & 1 \end{bmatrix} \begin{bmatrix} P_x \\ P_y \\ P_z \\ 1 \end{bmatrix}.$$

(4.57)

The matrix $\mathbf{M}_{ortho}$ in Equation (4.57) is the OpenGL orthographic projection matrix generated by the glOrtho() function. Note that the w-coordinate remains 1 after the transformation, and thus no perspective projection takes place.

4.5.3 Extracting Frustum Planes

It is remarkably simple to extract the four-dimensional vectors corresponding to the six camera-space view frustum planes from an arbitrary projection matrix $\mathbf{M}$. The technique presented here derives from the fact that the planes are always the same in clip space. They are actually rather trivial since, as shown in Figure 4.17, each plane's normal is parallel to one of the principal axes.

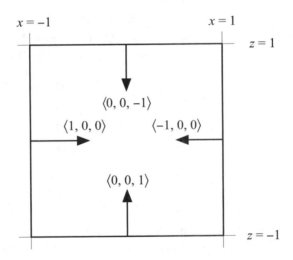

Figure 4.17 The four-dimensional plane vectors bounding the cube-shaped homogeneous clip space.

Let $\mathbf{L}'$ be one of the six planes that bound clip space. The inverse of the matrix $\mathbf{M}$ transforms from clip space into camera space. Since planes are transformed by the inverse transpose of a matrix, the camera-space plane $\mathbf{L}$ corresponding to the clip space plane $\mathbf{L}'$ is given by

$$\mathbf{L} = \left[\left(\mathbf{M}^{-1} \right)^{-1} \right]^{\mathrm{T}} \mathbf{L}' = \mathbf{M}^{\mathrm{T}} \mathbf{L}'. \tag{4.58}$$

The clip-space plane vectors are listed in Table 4.2. Since each plane vector contains two nonzero entries, and these entries are all ± 1, we can write each camera-space view frustum plane as a sum or difference of two columns of the matrix $\mathbf{M}^{\mathrm{T}}$, which is equivalent to the sum or difference of two rows of the matrix $\mathbf{M}$.

Table 4.2 Clip-space plane vectors.

Plane	$\langle \mathbf{N}, D \rangle$
Near	$\langle 0,0,1,1 \rangle$
Far	$\langle 0,0,-1,1 \rangle$
Left	$\langle 1,0,0,1 \rangle$
Right	$\langle -1,0,0,1 \rangle$
Bottom	$\langle 0,1,0,1 \rangle$
Top	$\langle 0,-1,0,1 \rangle$

Using the notation $\mathbf{M}_i$ to represent row i of the matrix $\mathbf{M}$, we have the following formulas for the camera-space view frustum planes. These do not produce plane vectors having unit normals, so they need to be rescaled.

$$near = \mathbf{M}_4 + \mathbf{M}_3$$
$$far = \mathbf{M}_4 - \mathbf{M}_3$$
$$left = \mathbf{M}_4 + \mathbf{M}_1$$
$$right = \mathbf{M}_4 - \mathbf{M}_1$$
$$bottom = \mathbf{M}_4 + \mathbf{M}_2$$
$$top = \mathbf{M}_4 - \mathbf{M}_2 \tag{4.59}$$

These equations are valid for *any* projection matrix, with the exception of the far plane for the infinite projection matrix given by Equation (4.52). It should be noted, however, that if the focal length and aspect ratio are known for a particular view frustum, then the formulas in Table 4.1 provide a significantly more efficient way of calculating the frustum planes.

Chapter 4 Summary

Lines

A line passing through the point $\mathbf{P}_0$ and running parallel to the direction $\mathbf{V}$ is expressed as

$$\mathbf{P}(t) = \mathbf{P}_0 + t\mathbf{V}.$$

The distance from a point $\mathbf{Q}$ to the line $\mathbf{P}(t)$ is given by

$$d = \sqrt{(\mathbf{Q} - \mathbf{P}_0)^2 - \frac{[(\mathbf{Q} - \mathbf{P}_0) \cdot \mathbf{V}]^2}{V^2}}.$$

Planes

A plane having normal direction $\mathbf{N}$ and containing the point $\mathbf{P}_0$ is expressed as

$$\mathbf{N} \cdot \mathbf{P} + D = 0,$$

where $D = -\mathbf{N} \cdot \mathbf{P}_0$. This can also be expressed as $\mathbf{L} \cdot \mathbf{P} = 0$, where $\mathbf{L}$ is the 4D vector $\langle \mathbf{N}, D \rangle$ and $\mathbf{P}$ is a homogeneous point with a w-coordinate of 1. The distance from a point $\mathbf{Q}$ to a plane $\mathbf{L}$ is simply $\mathbf{L} \cdot \mathbf{Q}$.

Planes must be transformed using the inverse transpose of a matrix used to transform points.

Intersection of a Line and a Plane

The parameter t where a line $\mathbf{P}(t) = \mathbf{Q} + t\mathbf{V}$ intersects a plane $\mathbf{L}$ is given by

$$t = -\frac{\mathbf{L} \cdot \mathbf{Q}}{\mathbf{L} \cdot \mathbf{V}}.$$

The View Frustum

The focal length e of a view frustum having a horizontal field of view angle α is given by

$$e = \frac{1}{\tan(\alpha/2)}.$$

For a display having an aspect ratio a, the rectangle carved out of the near plane at a distance n from the camera is bounded by $x = \pm n/e$ and $y = \pm an/e$.

Perspective-Correct Interpolation

In a perspective projection, depth values z_1 and z_2 are correctly interpolated by linearly interpolating their reciprocals:

$$\frac{1}{z_3} = \frac{1}{z_1}(1 - t) + \frac{1}{z_2}t.$$

Perspective-correct vertex attribute interpolation uses the similar formula

$$\frac{b_3}{z_3} = \left[\frac{b_1}{z_1}(1-t) + \frac{b_2}{z_2}t\right],$$

where b_1 and b_2 are vertex attribute values.

Perspective Projections

The perspective projection matrix $\mathbf{M}_{frustum}$ that transforms points from camera space into clip space is given by

$$\mathbf{M}_{frustum} = \begin{bmatrix} \dfrac{2n}{r-l} & 0 & \dfrac{r+l}{r-l} & 0 \\[2ex] 0 & \dfrac{2n}{t-b} & \dfrac{t+b}{t-b} & 0 \\[2ex] 0 & 0 & -\dfrac{f+n}{f-n} & -\dfrac{2nf}{f-n} \\[2ex] 0 & 0 & -1 & 0 \end{bmatrix},$$

where n and f are the distances from the camera to the near and far planes, and l, r, b, and t are the left, right, bottom, and top edges of the viewing rectangle carved out of the near plane.

An infinite view frustum can be constructed by allowing the far plane distance f to tend to infinity. The corresponding projection matrix $\mathbf{M}_{infinite}$ is given by

$$\mathbf{M}_{infinite} = \lim_{f \to \infty} \mathbf{M}_{frustum} = \begin{bmatrix} \dfrac{2n}{r-l} & 0 & \dfrac{r+l}{r-l} & 0 \\[2ex] 0 & \dfrac{2n}{t-b} & \dfrac{t+b}{t-b} & 0 \\[2ex] 0 & 0 & -1 & -2n \\[2ex] 0 & 0 & -1 & 0 \end{bmatrix}.$$

Exercises for Chapter 4

1. Determine a 4D vector $\langle \mathbf{N}, D \rangle$ corresponding to the plane that passes through the three points $\langle 1,2,0 \rangle$, $\langle 2,0,-1 \rangle$, and $\langle 3,-2,1 \rangle$.

2. Find an expression for the parameter t representing the point on the line $\mathbf{P}(t) = \mathbf{S} + t\mathbf{V}$ that is closest to another point $\mathbf{Q}$.

3. Show that the distance d from a point $\mathbf{Q}$ to the line $\mathbf{P}(t) = \mathbf{S} + t\mathbf{V}$ can be expressed as

$$d = \frac{\|(\mathbf{Q} - \mathbf{S}) \times \mathbf{V}\|}{\|\mathbf{V}\|}.$$

4. The horizontal field of view angle for a particular view frustum is 75 degrees. Calculate the corresponding vertical field of view angle for a 1280×1024 pixel display.

5. Calculate the left, right, bottom, and top planes for a view frustum having a horizontal field of view of 90 degrees and an aspect ratio of 0.75.

6. Suppose that z-coordinates in homogeneous clip space occupied the range $[0,1]$ instead of $[-1,1]$. In a manner similar to that used to derive the matrix in Equation (4.52), derive a perspective projection matrix that maps $-n \rightarrow 0$ and $-f \rightarrow 1$.

Chapter **5**

Ray Tracing

T he term *ray tracing* refers to any algorithm that follows beams of light to determine with which objects they interact in the world. Applications include light map generation, visibility determination, collision detection, and line-of-sight testing. This chapter describes how the points of intersection where a ray strikes an object can be found and how to alter the path of a ray when it strikes a reflective or refractive surface.

5.1 Root Finding

The problem of finding the points at which a line defined by the equation

$$\mathbf{P}(t) = \mathbf{S} + t\mathbf{V} \tag{5.1}$$

intersects a surface generally requires finding the roots of a degree n polynomial in t. For planar surfaces, the degree of the polynomial is one, and a solution is easily found. For quadric surfaces, such as a sphere or cylinder, the degree of the polynomial is two, and a solution can be found using the quadratic equation. For more complex surfaces, such as splines and tori, the degree of the polynomial is three or four, in which case we can still find solutions analytically, but at much greater computational expense.

Analytic solutions to polynomials of degrees two, three, and four are presented in this section. Complete derivations of the solutions to cubic and quartic equations are beyond the scope of this book, however. We also examine a numerical root-finding technique known as Newton's method.

5.1.1 Quadratic Polynomials

The roots of a quadratic polynomial in t can be found by using a little algebraic manipulation to solve the equation

$$at^2 + bt + c = 0. \tag{5.2}$$

Subtracting c from both sides and then dividing by a gives us

$$t^2 + \frac{b}{a}t = -\frac{c}{a}. \tag{5.3}$$

We can complete the square on the left side of the equation by adding $b^2/4a^2$ to both sides as follows.

$$t^2 + \frac{b}{a}t + \frac{b^2}{4a^2} = -\frac{c}{a} + \frac{b^2}{4a^2} \tag{5.4}$$

Writing the left side of the equation as a square and using a common denominator on the right side gives us

$$\left(t + \frac{b}{2a}\right)^2 = \frac{b^2 - 4ac}{4a^2}. \tag{5.5}$$

Taking square roots and then subtracting $b/2a$ from both sides yields

$$t = \frac{-b \pm \sqrt{b^2 - 4ac}}{2a}. \tag{5.6}$$

This is the well-known quadratic equation. The quantity $D = b^2 - 4ac$ is called the *discriminant* of the polynomial and reveals how many real roots it has. If $D > 0$, then there are two real roots. If $D = 0$, then there is one real root, and it is given by $t = -b/2a$. For the remaining case in which $D < 0$, there are no real roots. Evaluating the discriminant allows us to determine whether a ray intersects an object without actually calculating the points of intersection.

5.1.2 Cubic Polynomials

A cubic equation having the form

$$t^3 + at^2 + bt + c = 0 \tag{5.7}$$

(where we have performed any necessary division to produce a leading coefficient of 1) can be shifted to eliminate the quadratic term by making the substitution

$$t = x - \frac{a}{3}. \tag{5.8}$$

This gives us the equation

$$x^3 + px + q = 0, \tag{5.9}$$

where

$$p = -\frac{1}{3}a^2 + b$$

$$q = \frac{2}{27}a^3 - \frac{1}{3}ab + c. \tag{5.10}$$

Once a solution x to Equation (5.9) is found, we subtract $a/3$ to obtain the solution t to Equation (5.7).

The discriminant D of a cubic polynomial is given by

$$D = -4p^3 - 27q^2. \tag{5.11}$$

By setting

$$r = \sqrt[3]{-\frac{1}{2}q + \sqrt{-\frac{1}{108}D}}$$

$$s = \sqrt[3]{-\frac{1}{2}q - \sqrt{-\frac{1}{108}D}}, \tag{5.12}$$

we can express the three complex roots of Equation (5.9) as

$$x_1 = r + s$$
$$x_2 = \rho r + \rho^2 s$$
$$x_3 = \rho^2 r + \rho s, \tag{5.13}$$

where ρ is the primitive cube root of unity given by $\rho = -\frac{1}{2} + i\frac{\sqrt{3}}{2}$. (Note that $\rho^2 = -\frac{1}{2} - i\frac{\sqrt{3}}{2}$.)

We can simplify our arithmetic significantly by making the substitutions

$$p' = \frac{p}{3} = -\frac{1}{9}a^2 + \frac{1}{3}b$$
$$q' = \frac{q}{2} = \frac{1}{27}a^3 - \frac{1}{6}ab + \frac{1}{2}c. \tag{5.14}$$

The discriminant is then given by

$$D = -108\left(p'^3 + q'^2\right). \tag{5.15}$$

Setting

$$D' = \frac{D}{108} = -\left(p'^3 + q'^2\right) \tag{5.16}$$

lets us express r and s as

$$r = \sqrt[3]{-q' + \sqrt{-D'}}$$
$$s = \sqrt[3]{-q' - \sqrt{-D'}}. \tag{5.17}$$

As with quadratic equations, the discriminant gives us information about how many real roots exist. In the case that $D' < 0$, the value of x_1 given in Equation (5.13) represents the only real solution of Equation (5.9).

In the case that $D' = 0$, we have $r = s$, so there are two real solutions, one of which is a double root:

$$x_1 = 2r$$
$$x_2, x_3 = \left(\rho + \rho^2\right)r = -r. \tag{5.18}$$

In the remaining case that $D' > 0$, Equation (5.13) yields three distinct real solutions. Unfortunately, we still have to use complex numbers to calculate these solutions. An alternative method can be applied in this case that does not require complex arithmetic. The method relies on the trigonometric identity

$$4\cos^3\theta - 3\cos\theta = \cos 3\theta, \tag{5.19}$$

which can be verified using the Euler formula (see Exercise 1 at the end of this chapter). Making the substitution $x = 2m\cos\theta$ in Equation (5.9) with $m = \sqrt{-p/3}$, gives us

$$8m^3\cos^3\theta + 2pm\cos\theta + q = 0. \tag{5.20}$$

(Note that p must be negative in order for D' to be positive.) Replacing p with $-3m^2$ and factoring $2m^3$ out of the first two terms yields

$$2m^3\left(4\cos^3\theta - 3\cos\theta\right) + q = 0. \tag{5.21}$$

Applying Equation (5.19) and solving for $\cos 3\theta$ gives us

$$\cos 3\theta = \frac{-q}{2m^3} = \frac{-q/2}{\sqrt{-p^3/27}} = \frac{-q'}{\sqrt{-p'^3}}. \tag{5.22}$$

Since $D' > 0$, Equation (5.16) implies that $q'^2 < -p'^3$, thereby guaranteeing that the right side of Equation (5.22) is always less than 1 in absolute value. The inverse cosine is thus defined, and we can solve for θ to arrive at

$$\theta = \frac{1}{3}\cos^{-1}\left(\frac{-q'}{\sqrt{-p'^3}}\right). \tag{5.23}$$

Therefore, one solution to Equation (5.9) is given by

$$x_1 = 2m\cos\theta = 2\sqrt{-p'}\cos\theta. \tag{5.24}$$

Since $\cos(3\theta + 2\pi k) = \cos(3\theta)$ for any integer k, we can write

$$\theta_k = \frac{1}{3}\cos^{-1}\left(\frac{-q'}{\sqrt{-p'^3}}\right) - \frac{2\pi}{3}k. \tag{5.25}$$

Distinct values of $\cos\theta_k$ are generated by choosing three values for k that are congruent to 0, 1, and 2 modulo 3. Using $k = \pm 1$, we can express the remaining two solutions to Equation (5.9) as

$$x_2 = 2\sqrt{-p'} \cos\left(\theta + \frac{2\pi}{3}\right)$$

$$x_3 = 2\sqrt{-p'} \cos\left(\theta - \frac{2\pi}{3}\right). \tag{5.26}$$

5.1.3 Quartic Polynomials

A quartic equation having the form

$$t^4 + at^3 + bt^2 + ct + d = 0 \tag{5.27}$$

(where again we have performed any necessary division to produce a leading coefficient of 1) can be shifted to eliminate the cubic term by making the substitution

$$t = x - \frac{a}{4}. \tag{5.28}$$

This gives us the equation

$$x^4 + px^2 + qx + r = 0, \tag{5.29}$$

where

$$p = -\frac{3}{8}a^2 + b$$

$$q = \frac{1}{8}a^3 - \frac{1}{2}ab + c$$

$$r = -\frac{3}{256}a^4 + \frac{1}{16}a^2b - \frac{1}{4}ac + d. \tag{5.30}$$

Once a solution x to Equation (5.29) is found, we subtract $a/4$ to obtain the solution t to Equation (5.27).

The roots of the quartic equation are found by first finding a solution to the cubic equation

$$y^3 - \frac{p}{2}y^2 - ry + \frac{4rp - q^2}{8} = 0. \tag{5.31}$$

Let y be any real solution to this equation. If $q \geq 0$, then the solutions to the quartic equation are equal to the solutions to the two quadratic equations

$$x^2 + x\sqrt{2y - p} + y - \sqrt{y^2 - r} = 0$$
$$x^2 - x\sqrt{2y - p} + y + \sqrt{y^2 - r} = 0. \qquad (5.32)$$

If $q < 0$, then the solutions to the quartic equation are equal to the solutions to the two quadratic equations

$$x^2 + x\sqrt{2y - p} + y + \sqrt{y^2 - r} = 0$$
$$x^2 - x\sqrt{2y - p} + y - \sqrt{y^2 - r} = 0. \qquad (5.33)$$

5.1.4 Newton's Method

The Newton-Raphson iteration method, usually just called Newton's method, is a numerical technique that can find roots of an arbitrary continuous function by iterating a formula that depends on the function and its derivative.

Suppose that we wish to find the root of the function f graphed in Figure 5.1. For now, let us assume that we have an initial guess x_0 for the root of the function (more is said about how to choose this value shortly). The slope of the tangent line to the curve at the point $(x_0, f(x_0))$ is given by the derivative $f'(x_0)$. We can write the equation for this tangent line as follows.

$$y - f(x_0) = f'(x_0)(x - x_0) \qquad (5.34)$$

Notice that this line intersects the x-axis at a point that is much closer to the actual root of f than our initial guess x_0. Solving Equation (5.34) for x when $y = 0$ gives us the refinement formula

$$x_{i+1} = x_i - \frac{f(x_i)}{f'(x_i)}, \qquad (5.35)$$

where we have relabeled x with x_{i+1} and x_0 with x_i. Applying this formula multiple times produces a sequence $x_0, x_1, x_2, \ldots$ whose values, under the right conditions, approach the root of f.

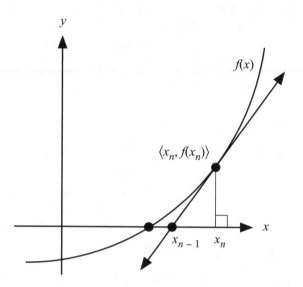

Figure 5.1 The tangent to a function tends to intersect the x-axis closer to a root of the function.

Newton's method converges extremely quickly and thus requires very few iterations to exceed any desired precision. We can in fact show that Newton's method converges quadratically, which means that with each iteration, the number of significant digits in an approximated root roughly doubles. We prove this claim by first setting

$$g(x) = \frac{f(x)}{f'(x)}. \tag{5.36}$$

Let r be the actual root of the function f to which we are converging. We define ε_i to be the error between the i-th approximation x_i and the root r:

$$\varepsilon_i = x_i - r. \tag{5.37}$$

Using this in Equation (5.35) allows us to write

$$\varepsilon_{i+1} = \varepsilon_i - g(x_i). \tag{5.38}$$

We can approximate the function $g(x_i)$ with the first three terms of its Taylor series (see Appendix D) as follows.

$$g(x_i) = g(r + \varepsilon_i) \approx g(r) + \varepsilon_i g'(r) + \frac{\varepsilon_i^2}{2} g''(r) \tag{5.39}$$

The first and second derivatives of $g(x)$ are given by

$$g'(x) = 1 - \frac{f(x) f''(x)}{[f'(x)]^2}$$

$$g''(x) = \frac{2 f(x) f'(x) [f''(x)]^2 - [f'(x)]^2 [f(x) f'''(x) + f'(x) f''(x)]}{[f'(x)]^4}. \tag{5.40}$$

Since $f(r) = 0$, these expressions simplify greatly when evaluated at r. The function g and its first two derivatives produce the following values at r.

$$g(r) = 0$$
$$g'(r) = 1$$
$$g''(r) = -\frac{f''(r)}{f'(r)} \tag{5.41}$$

Plugging these into Equation (5.39) gives us

$$g(x_i) \approx \varepsilon_i - \frac{\varepsilon_i^2}{2} \frac{f''(r)}{f'(r)}. \tag{5.42}$$

Finally, substituting this into Equation (5.38) yields

$$\varepsilon_{i+1} \approx \frac{\varepsilon_i^2}{2} \frac{f''(r)}{f'(r)}. \tag{5.43}$$

Newton's method is not guaranteed to converge to a solution. In particular, if the initial guess is chosen at a point where the derivative of the function is zero, then the tangent line is horizontal and does not intersect the x-axis, preventing us from proceeding any further. The initial guess has to be somewhat close to the actual root to guarantee a convergence. When searching for the intersection of a ray with a complex object, we can usually find a good initial guess by first intersecting the ray with the surface of a relatively simple bounding volume. For example, to find where a ray defined by $\mathbf{P}(t) = \mathbf{S} + t\mathbf{V}$ intersects a torus, we can first find a value of t where the ray intersects a box bounding the torus, and then use this value of t as our initial guess for the torus intersection.

5.1.5 Refinement of Reciprocals and Square Roots

Most modern graphics hardware can approximate the reciprocal of a number as well as the reciprocal square root of a number to at least a few bits of precision. For instance, the GL_ARB_vertex_program extension to OpenGL exposes the vertex program instructions RCP and RSQ. These instructions produce an approximation to a reciprocal and reciprocal square root, respectively, that can be refined to greater precision using Newton's method.

The reciprocal of a number r can be found by calculating the root of the function

$$f(x) = x^{-1} - r \tag{5.44}$$

since $f(1/r) = 0$. Plugging this function into Equation (5.35) gives us

$$x_{n+1} = x_n - \frac{x_n^{-1} - r}{-x_n^{-2}}$$
$$= x_n(2 - rx_n). \tag{5.45}$$

This formula can be iterated to produce a high-precision reciprocal of the number r, provided that each $x_i > 0$. This is due to the fact that the function $f(x)$ attains a singularity at $x = 0$. Enforcing this condition on the first refinement x_1 allows us to determine the interval inside which our initial approximation x_0 must fall. Since x_1 must be greater than zero, we have

$$x_0(2 - rx_0) > 0, \tag{5.46}$$

which yields the following restriction on x_0.

$$0 < x_0 < \frac{2}{r} \tag{5.47}$$

Thus, the initial approximation cannot be worse than double the reciprocal of r.

The reciprocal of the square root of a number r can be found by calculating the positive root of the function

$$f(x) = x^{-2} - r. \tag{5.48}$$

Plugging this function into Equation (5.35) gives us

$$x_{n+1} = x_n - \frac{x_n^{-2} - r}{-2x_n^{-3}}$$

$$= \frac{1}{2} x_n \left(3 - rx_n^2\right). \tag{5.49}$$

This sequence converges as long as each $x_i > 0$, so our initial approximation x_0 must satisfy

$$0 < x_0 < \sqrt{\frac{3}{r}}. \tag{5.50}$$

Once the reciprocal square root has been calculated to acceptable precision, the square root of r can be calculated using a single multiplication because $\sqrt{r} = r \cdot \left(1/\sqrt{r}\right)$.

5.2 Surface Intersections

Computing the point at which a ray intersects a surface is central to ray tracing. We define a ray $\mathbf{P}(t)$ using the equation

$$\mathbf{P}(t) = \mathbf{S} + t\mathbf{V}, \tag{5.51}$$

where $\mathbf{S}$ represents the ray's starting position and $\mathbf{V}$ represents the direction in which the ray points. In this section, we present specific solutions for the intersection of a ray with a few common types of objects (additional objects are left as exercises). With the exception of the triangle, intersections are computed in *object space*, the space in which the natural center of an object coincides with the origin and the object's natural axes are aligned to the coordinate axes. Intersections with arbitrarily oriented objects are performed by first transforming the ray into object space. Once an intersection is detected, information such as the point of intersection and the normal vector at that point can be transformed back into world space.

5.2.1 Intersection of a Ray and a Triangle

A triangle is described by the position in space of its three vertices $\mathbf{P}_0$, $\mathbf{P}_1$, and $\mathbf{P}_2$. We determine the plane in which the triangle lies by first calculating the normal vector $\mathbf{N}$ as follows.

$$\mathbf{N} = (\mathbf{P}_1 - \mathbf{P}_0) \times (\mathbf{P}_2 - \mathbf{P}_0) \tag{5.52}$$

The signed distance d to the origin is given by the negative dot product of $\mathbf{N}$ with any point in the plane, so we choose the vertex $\mathbf{P}_0$ to construct the 4D plane vector $\mathbf{L} = \langle \mathbf{N}, -\mathbf{N} \cdot \mathbf{P}_0 \rangle$. As discussed in Section 4.2.1, the value of t corresponding to the point where the ray in Equation (5.51) intersects the plane $\mathbf{L}$ is given by

$$t = -\frac{\mathbf{L} \cdot \mathbf{S}}{\mathbf{L} \cdot \mathbf{V}}. \tag{5.53}$$

If $\mathbf{L} \cdot \mathbf{V} = 0$, then no intersection occurs. Otherwise, plugging this value of t back into Equation (5.51) produces the point $\mathbf{P}$ where the ray intersects the plane of the triangle.

We now have the problem of determining whether the point $\mathbf{P}$ lies inside the triangle's edges. We do so by calculating the *barycentric coordinates* of $\mathbf{P}$ with respect to the triangle's vertices $\mathbf{P}_0$, $\mathbf{P}_1$, and $\mathbf{P}_2$. The barycentric coordinates represent a weighted average of the triangle's vertices and are expressed as the scalars w_0, w_1, and w_2 such that

$$\mathbf{P} = w_0 \mathbf{P}_0 + w_1 \mathbf{P}_1 + w_2 \mathbf{P}_2, \tag{5.54}$$

where $w_0 + w_1 + w_2 = 1$. Replacing w_0 with $1 - w_1 - w_2$, we can write

$$\begin{aligned} \mathbf{P} &= (1 - w_1 - w_2) \mathbf{P}_0 + w_1 \mathbf{P}_1 + w_2 \mathbf{P}_2 \\ &= \mathbf{P}_0 + w_1 (\mathbf{P}_1 - \mathbf{P}_0) + w_2 (\mathbf{P}_2 - \mathbf{P}_1). \end{aligned} \tag{5.55}$$

We perform the remainder of our calculations relative to the point $\mathbf{P}_0$ by defining

$$\begin{aligned} \mathbf{R} &= \mathbf{P} - \mathbf{P}_0 \\ \mathbf{Q}_1 &= \mathbf{P}_1 - \mathbf{P}_0 \\ \mathbf{Q}_2 &= \mathbf{P}_2 - \mathbf{P}_0. \end{aligned} \tag{5.56}$$

Equation (5.55) now becomes

$$\mathbf{R} = w_1 \mathbf{Q}_1 + w_2 \mathbf{Q}_2. \tag{5.57}$$

Taking the dot product of both sides of Equation (5.57) first with $\mathbf{Q}_1$ and then with $\mathbf{Q}_2$ gives us the two equations

$$\begin{aligned} \mathbf{R} \cdot \mathbf{Q}_1 &= w_1 Q_1^2 + w_2 (\mathbf{Q}_1 \cdot \mathbf{Q}_2) \\ \mathbf{R} \cdot \mathbf{Q}_2 &= w_1 (\mathbf{Q}_1 \cdot \mathbf{Q}_2) + w_2 Q_2^2, \end{aligned} \tag{5.58}$$

which are written in matrix form as

$$\begin{bmatrix} Q_1^2 & \mathbf{Q}_1 \cdot \mathbf{Q}_2 \\ \mathbf{Q}_1 \cdot \mathbf{Q}_2 & Q_2^2 \end{bmatrix} \begin{bmatrix} w_1 \\ w_2 \end{bmatrix} = \begin{bmatrix} \mathbf{R} \cdot \mathbf{Q}_1 \\ \mathbf{R} \cdot \mathbf{Q}_2 \end{bmatrix}. \tag{5.59}$$

We can now easily solve for w_1 and w_2 as follows.

$$\begin{aligned} \begin{bmatrix} w_1 \\ w_2 \end{bmatrix} &= \begin{bmatrix} Q_1^2 & \mathbf{Q}_1 \cdot \mathbf{Q}_2 \\ \mathbf{Q}_1 \cdot \mathbf{Q}_2 & Q_2^2 \end{bmatrix}^{-1} \begin{bmatrix} \mathbf{R} \cdot \mathbf{Q}_1 \\ \mathbf{R} \cdot \mathbf{Q}_2 \end{bmatrix} \\ &= \frac{1}{Q_1^2 Q_2^2 - (\mathbf{Q}_1 \cdot \mathbf{Q}_2)^2} \begin{bmatrix} Q_2^2 & -\mathbf{Q}_1 \cdot \mathbf{Q}_2 \\ -\mathbf{Q}_1 \cdot \mathbf{Q}_2 & Q_1^2 \end{bmatrix} \begin{bmatrix} \mathbf{R} \cdot \mathbf{Q}_1 \\ \mathbf{R} \cdot \mathbf{Q}_2 \end{bmatrix} \end{aligned} \tag{5.60}$$

The point $\mathbf{R}$ lies inside the triangle if and only if all three weights w_0, w_1, and w_2 are nonnegative. Since $w_0 = 1 - w_1 - w_2$, this implies that $w_1 + w_2 \leq 1$.

If the vertices $\mathbf{P}_0$, $\mathbf{P}_1$, and $\mathbf{P}_2$ have any associated attributes, such as a color or texture coordinate set, then the interpolated value of those attributes at the point $\mathbf{R}$ can be calculated using the weights w_0, w_1, and w_2. For instance, if the texture coordinates $\langle s_0, t_0 \rangle$, $\langle s_1, t_1 \rangle$, and $\langle s_2, t_2 \rangle$ are associated with the vertices $\mathbf{P}_0$, $\mathbf{P}_1$, and $\mathbf{P}_2$, then the texture coordinates $\langle s, t \rangle$ at the point $\mathbf{R}$ are given by

$$\begin{aligned} s &= w_0 s_0 + w_1 s_1 + w_2 s_2 \\ t &= w_0 t_0 + w_1 t_1 + w_2 t_2. \end{aligned} \tag{5.61}$$

5.2.2 Intersection of a Ray and a Box

A box is described by the six plane equations

$$\begin{aligned} x &= 0 & x &= r_x \\ y &= 0 & y &= r_y \\ z &= 0 & z &= r_z, \end{aligned} \tag{5.62}$$

where r_x, r_y, and r_z represent the dimensions of the box. At most three of these planes need to be considered for intersection by the ray since at least three planes must face away from the ray's direction $\mathbf{V}$. We can determine which planes need to be tested by examining the components of $\mathbf{V}$ one at a time. For instance, if $V_x = 0$, then we know that the ray cannot intersect either of the planes $x = 0$ or $x = r_x$ because $\mathbf{V}$ is parallel to them. If $V_x > 0$, then we do not need to test for an intersection with the plane $x = r_x$ since it represents a back side of the box from the ray's perspective. Similarly, if $V_x < 0$, then we do not need to test for an intersection with the plane $x = 0$. The same principle applies to the y- and z-components of $\mathbf{V}$.

Once we have found the point where a ray intersects a plane, we must check that the point falls within the face of the box by examining the two coordinates corresponding to the directions parallel to the plane. For instance, the value of t corresponding to the point where the ray given by Equation (5.51) intersects the plane $x = r_x$ is given by

$$t = \frac{r_x - S_x}{V_x}. \tag{5.63}$$

To lie within the corresponding face of the box, the y- and z-coordinates of the point $\mathbf{P}(t)$ must satisfy

$$0 \le [\mathbf{P}(t)]_y \le r_y$$
$$0 \le [\mathbf{P}(t)]_z \le r_z. \tag{5.64}$$

If either of these conditions fails, then no intersection takes place within the face. If both conditions pass, then an intersection has been found, in which case there is no need to test any other planes since no closer intersection can occur.

5.2.3 Intersection of a Ray and a Sphere

A sphere of radius r centered at the origin is described by the equation

$$x^2 + y^2 + z^2 = r^2. \tag{5.65}$$

Substituting the components of the ray $\mathbf{P}(t)$ in Equation (5.51) for x, y, and z gives us

$$(S_x + tV_x)^2 + (S_y + tV_y)^2 + (S_z + tV_z)^2 = r^2. \tag{5.66}$$

Expanding the squares and collecting on t yields the following quadratic equation.

$$\left(V_x^2 + V_y^2 + V_z^2\right)t^2 + 2\left(S_xV_x + S_yV_y + S_zV_z\right)t + S_x^2 + S_y^2 + S_z^2 - r^2 = 0 \tag{5.67}$$

The coefficients a, b, and c used in Equation (5.2) can be expressed in terms of the vectors $\mathbf{S}$ and $\mathbf{V}$ as follows.

$$a = V^2$$
$$b = 2(\mathbf{S} \cdot \mathbf{V})$$
$$c = S^2 - r^2 \tag{5.68}$$

Calculating the discriminant $D = b^2 - 4ac$ tells us whether the ray intersects the sphere. As illustrated in Figure 5.2, if $D < 0$, then no intersection occurs; if $D = 0$, then the ray is tangent to the sphere; and if $D > 0$, then there are two distinct points of intersection. If the ray intersects the sphere at two points, then the point closer to the ray's origin $\mathbf{S}$, which corresponds to the smaller value of t, is always given by

$$t = \frac{-b - \sqrt{D}}{2a} \tag{5.69}$$

because a is guaranteed to be positive.

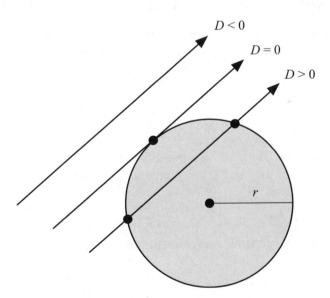

Figure 5.2 The discriminant D indicates whether a ray intersects a sphere. If $D < 0$, then no intersection occurs. If $D = 0$, then the ray is tangent to the sphere at a single point. If $D > 0$, then the ray intersects the sphere at two distinct points.

The intersection of a ray and an ellipsoid can be determined by replacing Equation (5.65) with the equation

$$x^2 + m^2 y^2 + n^2 z^2 = r^2, \tag{5.70}$$

where m is the ratio of the x semi-axis length to the y semi-axis length, and n is the ratio of the x semi-axis length to the z semi-axis length. Plugging the components of the ray into this equation yields another quadratic polynomial whose coefficients are given by

$$
\begin{aligned}
a &= V_x^2 + m^2 V_y^2 + n^2 V_z^2 \\
b &= 2\left(S_x V_x + m^2 S_y V_y + n^2 S_z V_z\right) \\
c &= S_x^2 + m^2 S_y^2 + n^2 S_z^2 - r^2.
\end{aligned}
\tag{5.71}
$$

Again, the discriminant indicates whether an intersection occurs. If so, the intersection parameter t is given by Equation (5.69).

5.2.4 Intersection of a Ray and a Cylinder

The lateral surface of an elliptical cylinder whose radius on the x-axis is r, whose radius on the y-axis is s, whose height is h, and whose base is centered on the origin of the x-y plane (see Figure 5.3) is described by the equation

$$
\begin{aligned}
x^2 + m^2 y^2 &= r^2 \\
0 &\leq z \leq h,
\end{aligned}
\tag{5.72}
$$

where $m = r/s$. If $r = s$, then the cylinder is circular and $m = 1$. Substituting the components of the ray $\mathbf{P}(t)$ in Equation (5.51) for x and y gives us

$$\left(S_x + tV_x\right)^2 + m^2 \left(S_y + tV_y\right)^2 = r^2. \tag{5.73}$$

Expanding the squares and collecting on t yields the following quadratic equation.

$$\left(V_x^2 + m^2 V_y^2\right)t^2 + 2\left(S_x V_x + m^2 S_y V_y\right)t + S_x^2 + m^2 S_y^2 - r^2 = 0 \tag{5.74}$$

As with the sphere, the discriminant indicates whether an intersection occurs. Solutions to this equation give the values of t where the ray intersects the infinite cylinder centered on the z-axis. The z-coordinates of the points of intersection must be tested so that they satisfy $0 \leq z \leq h$.

In the context of collision detection, the problem arises in which we need to know whether a moving sphere intersects a line segment representing an edge of a polygonal model. The problem is transformed into determining whether a ray intersects a cylinder with a given radius and arbitrary endpoints. This situation is discussed in Section 8.2.

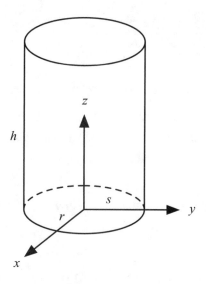

Figure 5.3 Object space for an elliptical cylinder.

5.2.5 Intersection of a Ray and a Torus

A cross section of the surface of a circular torus having primary radius r_1 and secondary radius r_2 is shown in Figure 5.4. The circle of radius r_1 lying in the x-y plane represents the center of another circle of radius r_2 perpendicular to the first, which is revolved about the z-axis. The equation describing the revolved circle is

$$s^2 + z^2 = r_2^2, \tag{5.75}$$

where the value of s is the distance to the primary circle in the x-y plane:

$$s = \sqrt{x^2 + y^2} - r_1. \tag{5.76}$$

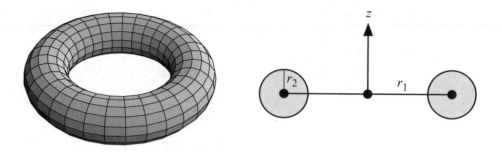

Figure 5.4 A torus and its cross section.

Substituting this into Equation (5.75) and expanding the square gives us

$$x^2 + y^2 + z^2 + r_1^2 - r_2^2 - 2r_1\sqrt{x^2 + y^2} = 0. \qquad (5.77)$$

Isolating the radical and squaring again yields the following equation for a torus.

$$\left(x^2 + y^2 + z^2 + r_1^2 - r_2^2\right)^2 = 4r_1^2\left(x^2 + y^2\right) \qquad (5.78)$$

Substituting the components of the ray $\mathbf{P}(t)$ in Equation (5.51) for x, y, and z gives us

$$\left[\left(S_x + tV_x\right)^2 + \left(S_y + tV_y\right)^2 + \left(S_z + tV_z\right)^2 + r_1^2 - r_2^2\right]^2$$
$$= 4r_1^2\left[\left(S_x + tV_x\right)^2 + \left(S_y + tV_y\right)^2\right]. \qquad (5.79)$$

After considerable algebraic simplification, this can be expressed as the quartic equation

$$at^4 + bt^3 + ct^2 + dt + e = 0, \qquad (5.80)$$

where

$$a = V^4$$
$$b = 4V^2(\mathbf{S} \cdot \mathbf{V})$$
$$c = 2V^2\left(S^2 + r_1^2 - r_2^2\right) - 4r_1^2\left(V_x^2 + V_y^2\right) + 4(\mathbf{S} \cdot \mathbf{V})^2$$

$$d = 8r_1^2 S_z V_z + 4(\mathbf{S} \cdot \mathbf{V})(S^2 - r_1^2 - r_2^2)$$

$$e = S_x^4 + S_y^4 + S_z^4 + (r_1^2 - r_2^2)^2$$

$$+ 2\left[S_x^2 S_y^2 + S_z^2 (r_1^2 - r_2^2) + (S_x^2 + S_y^2)(S_z^2 - r_1^2 - r_2^2) \right]. \tag{5.81}$$

After dividing by a to obtain a leading coefficient of 1, this equation can be solved using the method presented in Section 5.1.3. If the vector $\mathbf{V}$ is normalized, then the division by a is unnecessary, and the calculations for b and c simplify to

$$b = 4(\mathbf{S} \cdot \mathbf{V})$$

$$c = 2(S^2 + r_1^2 - r_2^2) - 4r_1^2(1 - V_z^2) + 4(\mathbf{S} \cdot \mathbf{V})^2. \tag{5.82}$$

5.3 Normal Vector Calculation

It is sometimes convenient to represent a surface using an implicit function $f(x, y, z)$ whose value is zero at any point $\langle x, y, z \rangle$ on the surface and whose value is nonzero elsewhere. An example of such a function is that of an ellipsoid:

$$f(x, y, z) = \frac{x^2}{a^2} + \frac{y^2}{b^2} + \frac{z^2}{c^2} - 1. \tag{5.83}$$

Using the implicit function representation, it is possible for us to derive a general formula for the normal direction at any point on a surface.

Suppose that $f(x, y, z)$ represents a surface S, so that $f(x, y, z) = 0$ for any point on S. Let C be a curve defined by differentiable parametric functions $x(t)$, $y(t)$, and $z(t)$ which lies on the surface S. Then the tangent vector $\mathbf{T}$ to the curve C at the point $\langle x(t), y(t), z(t) \rangle$ is given by

$$\mathbf{T} = \left\langle \frac{d}{dt} x(t), \frac{d}{dt} y(t), \frac{d}{dt} z(t) \right\rangle. \tag{5.84}$$

Since the curve C lies on the surface S, $\mathbf{T}$ is also tangent to the surface S. Also, since $f(x(t), y(t), z(t)) = 0$ for any value of t, we know that $df/dt = 0$ everywhere on the curve C. Using the chain rule, we can write

$$0 = \frac{df}{dt} = \frac{\partial f}{\partial x} \frac{dx}{dt} + \frac{\partial f}{\partial y} \frac{dy}{dt} + \frac{\partial f}{\partial z} \frac{dz}{dt} = \left\langle \frac{\partial f}{\partial x}, \frac{\partial f}{\partial y}, \frac{\partial f}{\partial z} \right\rangle \cdot \mathbf{T}. \tag{5.85}$$

Because its dot product with **T** is always zero, the vector $\langle \partial f / \partial x, \partial f / \partial y, \partial f / \partial z \rangle$ must be normal to the surface S. This vector is called the *gradient* of f at the point $\langle x, y, z \rangle$ and is usually written $\nabla f(x, y, z)$, where the symbol ∇ is the *del* operator defined by

$$\nabla = \mathbf{i} \frac{\partial}{\partial x} + \mathbf{j} \frac{\partial}{\partial y} + \mathbf{k} \frac{\partial}{\partial z}. \tag{5.86}$$

We can now express the formula for the normal vector **N** to a surface defined by the equation $f(x, y, z) = 0$ as

$$\mathbf{N} = \nabla f(x, y, z). \tag{5.87}$$

Continuing the example given in Equation (5.83), we have the following expression for the normal to the surface of an ellipsoid.

$$\mathbf{N} = \left\langle \frac{2x}{a^2}, \frac{2y}{b^2}, \frac{2z}{c^2} \right\rangle \tag{5.88}$$

5.4 Reflection and Refraction Vectors

When a beam of light strikes the surface of an object, part of its energy is absorbed by the surface, part of its energy is reflected away from the surface, and part of its energy may be transmitted through the object itself. Chapter 6 discusses this interaction in detail. This section explains how the direction of reflection and refraction can be calculated for a ray that intersects a shiny or transparent surface.

5.4.1 Reflection Vector Calculation

The direction of the reflection of light on a shiny surface (such as a mirror) follows the simple rule that the angle of incidence is equal to the angle of reflection. As shown in Figure 5.5, this is the same as saying that the angle between the normal vector **N** and the direction **L** pointing toward the incoming light is equal to the angle between the normal vector and the direction **R** of the reflected light.

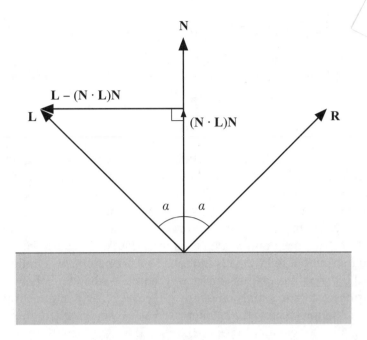

Figure 5.5 The direction of reflection **R** forms the same angle with the normal vector **N** as the direction **L** pointing toward the incoming light. It is found by subtracting twice the component of **L** that is perpendicular to **N** from **L** itself.

We assume that the vectors **N** and **L** have been normalized to unit length. To derive a formula that gives us the reflection direction **R** in terms of the light direction **L** and the normal vector **N**, we first calculate the component of **L** that is perpendicular to the normal direction:

$$\mathrm{perp}_N \, \mathbf{L} = \mathbf{L} - (\mathbf{N} \cdot \mathbf{L})\mathbf{N}. \tag{5.89}$$

The vector **R** lies at twice the distance from **L** as does its projection onto the normal vector **N**. We can thus express **R** as

$$\begin{aligned} \mathbf{R} &= \mathbf{L} - 2\,\mathrm{perp}_N \, \mathbf{L} \\ &= \mathbf{L} - 2\big[\mathbf{L} - (\mathbf{N}\cdot\mathbf{L})\mathbf{N}\big] \\ &= 2(\mathbf{N}\cdot\mathbf{L})\mathbf{N} - \mathbf{L}. \end{aligned} \tag{5.90}$$

5.4.2 Refraction Vector Calculation

Transparent surfaces possess a property called the index of refraction. According to Snell's law, the angle of incidence θ_L and the angle of transmission θ_T (shown in Figure 5.6) are related by the equation

$$\eta_L \sin\theta_L = \eta_T \sin\theta_T, \tag{5.91}$$

where η_L is the index of refraction of the material that the light is leaving, and η_T is the index of refraction of the material that the light is entering. The index of refraction of air is usually taken to be 1.00. Higher indexes of refraction create a greater bending effect at the interface between two materials.

We assume that the normal vector $\mathbf{N}$ and the direction toward the incoming light $\mathbf{L}$ have been normalized to unit length. We express the direction $\mathbf{T}$ in which the transmitted light travels in terms of its components parallel and perpendicular to the normal vector. As shown in Figure 5.6, the component of $\mathbf{T}$ parallel to the normal vector is simply given by $-\mathbf{N}\cos\theta_T$. The component of $\mathbf{T}$ perpendicular to the normal vector can be expressed as $-\mathbf{G}\sin\theta_T$, where the vector $\mathbf{G}$ is the unit length vector parallel to $\operatorname{perp}_{\mathbf{N}}\mathbf{L}$. Since $\mathbf{L}$ has unit length, $\|\operatorname{perp}_{\mathbf{N}}\mathbf{L}\| = \sin\theta_L$, so

$$\mathbf{G} = \frac{\operatorname{perp}_{\mathbf{N}}\mathbf{L}}{\sin\theta_L} = \frac{\mathbf{L}-(\mathbf{N}\cdot\mathbf{L})\mathbf{N}}{\sin\theta_L}. \tag{5.92}$$

We can now express the refraction vector $\mathbf{T}$ as

$$\begin{aligned}
\mathbf{T} &= -\mathbf{N}\cos\theta_T - \mathbf{G}\sin\theta_T \\
&= -\mathbf{N}\cos\theta_T - \frac{\sin\theta_T}{\sin\theta_L}[\mathbf{L}-(\mathbf{N}\cdot\mathbf{L})\mathbf{N}].
\end{aligned} \tag{5.93}$$

Using Equation (5.91), we can replace the quotient of sines with η_L/η_T:

$$\mathbf{T} = -\mathbf{N}\cos\theta_T - \frac{\eta_L}{\eta_T}[\mathbf{L}-(\mathbf{N}\cdot\mathbf{L})\mathbf{N}]. \tag{5.94}$$

Replacing $\cos\theta_T$ with $\sqrt{1-\sin^2\theta_T}$ and then using Equation (5.91) again to replace $\sin\theta_T$ with $(\eta_L/\eta_T)\sin\theta_L$ gives us

$$\mathbf{T} = -\mathbf{N}\sqrt{1-\frac{\eta_L^2}{\eta_T^2}\sin^2\theta_L} - \frac{\eta_L}{\eta_T}[\mathbf{L}-(\mathbf{N}\cdot\mathbf{L})\mathbf{N}]. \tag{5.95}$$

Replacing $\sin^2\theta_L$ with $1-\cos^2\theta_L = 1-(\mathbf{N}\cdot\mathbf{L})^2$ finally yields

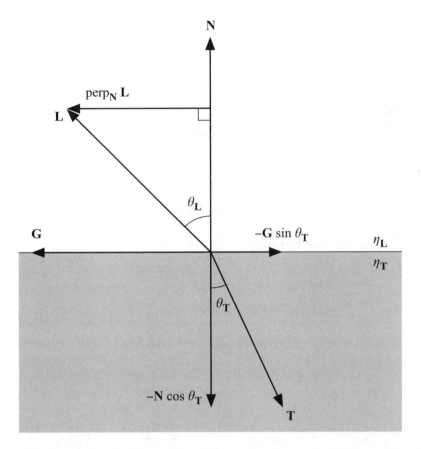

Figure 5.6 The angle of incidence θ_L and the angle of transmission θ_T are related by Snell's law, given in Equation (5.91). The refraction vector **T** is expressed in terms of its components parallel and perpendicular to the normal vector **N**.

$$\mathbf{T} = \left(\frac{\eta_L}{\eta_T} \mathbf{N} \cdot \mathbf{L} - \sqrt{1 - \frac{\eta_L^2}{\eta_T^2} \left[1 - (\mathbf{N} \cdot \mathbf{L})^2 \right]} \right) \mathbf{N} - \frac{\eta_L}{\eta_T} \mathbf{L}. \qquad (5.96)$$

If $\eta_L > \eta_T$, then it is possible for the quantity inside the radical in Equation (5.96) to be negative. This happens when light inside a medium having a higher index of refraction makes a wide angle of incidence with the surface leading to a medium having a lower index of refraction. Specifically, Equation (5.96) is only valid when $\sin \theta_L \leq \eta_T / \eta_L$. If the quantity inside the radical is negative, a phenomenon known as *total internal reflection* occurs. This means that light is not refracted, but is actually reflected inside the medium using Equation (5.90).

Chapter 5 Summary

Analytic Root Finding

Solutions to the quadratic equation $at^2 + bt + c = 0$ are given by the quadratic equation:

$$t = \frac{-b \pm \sqrt{b^2 - 4ac}}{2a}.$$

Cubic and quartic equations can also be solved analytically.

Numerical Root Finding

Roots of a function $f(x)$ can be found numerically using Newton's method, which refines an approximate solution x_n using the formula

$$x_{n+1} = x_n - \frac{f(x_n)}{f'(x_n)}.$$

The refinement formula for the reciprocal x_n of a number r is

$$x_{n+1} = x_n(2 - rx_n),$$

and the refinement formula for the reciprocal square root x_n of a number r is

$$x_{n+1} = \frac{1}{2} x_n (3 - rx_n^2).$$

Intersection of a Ray and a Sphere

The points where a ray $\mathbf{P}(t) = \mathbf{S} + t\mathbf{V}$ intersect a sphere of radius r are given by the solutions of the quadratic equation

$$V^2 t^2 + 2(\mathbf{S} \cdot \mathbf{V})t + S^2 - r^2 = 0.$$

Normal Vector Calculation

The normal vector at a point $\langle x, y, z \rangle$ on a surface defined by the function $f(x, y, z) = 0$ is given by $\mathbf{N} = \nabla f(x, y, z)$.

Reflection Vector Calculation

The reflection $\mathbf{R}$ of a vector $\mathbf{L}$ across the normal vector $\mathbf{N}$ is given by

$$\mathbf{R} = 2(\mathbf{N} \cdot \mathbf{L})\mathbf{N} - \mathbf{L}.$$

Transmission Vector Calculation

The direction $\mathbf{T}$ in which light is transmitted when leaving a medium having index of refraction η_L and entering a medium having index of refraction η_T is given by

$$\mathbf{T} = \left(\frac{\eta_L}{\eta_T} \mathbf{N} \cdot \mathbf{L} - \sqrt{1 - \frac{\eta_L^2}{\eta_T^2} \left[1 - (\mathbf{N} \cdot \mathbf{L})^2 \right]} \right) \mathbf{N} - \frac{\eta_L}{\eta_T} \mathbf{L},$$

where $\mathbf{L}$ is the direction pointing toward the incident light, and $\mathbf{N}$ is the surface normal.

Exercises for Chapter 5

1. Use the Euler formula (which states that $e^{\alpha i} = \cos\alpha + i\sin\alpha$) to verify the trigonometric identity

    $$4\cos^3\theta - 3\cos\theta = \cos 3\theta.$$

    [*Hint.* Equate the real components of the equation $\left(e^{\theta i} \right)^3 = e^{(3\theta)i}$.]

2. Use Newton's method to approximate the root of the function $f(x) = \ln x + x - 7$.

3. Find a general formula that can be used to refine an approximation x_n of the p-th root of a number r using Newton's method.

4. Let $\mathbf{P}_0$, $\mathbf{P}_1$, and $\mathbf{P}_2$ be the three vertices of the triangle T shown in Figure 5.7. Show that each of the barycentric coordinates w_i of a point $\mathbf{P}$ lying inside the triangle is given by the ratio of the area of the subtriangle U_i formed using $\mathbf{P}$ and the two vertices $\mathbf{P}_{i+1\,(\mathrm{mod}\,3)}$ and $\mathbf{P}_{i+2\,(\mathrm{mod}\,3)}$ to the area of the triangle T.

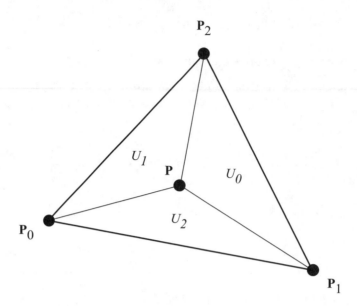

Figure 5.7 The triangle used in Exercise 4.

5. Let w_1, w_2, and w_3 be the barycentric coordinates of a point $\mathbf{P}$ with respect to a triangle whose vertices are $\mathbf{P}_0$, $\mathbf{P}_1$, and $\mathbf{P}_2$. Let $\mathbf{N}$ be the direction normal to the triangle. Show that the barycentric coordinates of the point $\mathbf{P} + r\mathbf{N}$ are the same as those of the point $\mathbf{P}$ for any scalar r.

6. Calculate the unit length surface normal to the paraboloid defined by $f(x, y, z) = 2x^2 + 3y^2 - z = 0$ at the point $\langle -1, 2, 14 \rangle$.

7. Derive the polynomial whose roots give the values of t at which the ray $\mathbf{P}(t) = \mathbf{S} + t\mathbf{V}$ intersects a cone whose radius (at the base) is r, whose height is h, and whose base is centered on the origin of the x-y plane as shown in Figure 5.8.

8. The *critical angle* at the interface between two media is the smallest angle of incidence at which total internal reflection occurs. Determine the critical angle for a beam of light traveling upward through water toward the surface where it meets the air. The index of refraction of water is 1.33, and the index of refraction of air is 1.00.

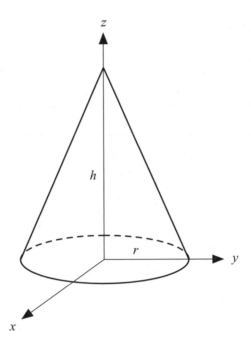

Figure 5.8 The cone used in Exercise 7.

9.   Suppose that a coordinate transformation is defined by

$$\begin{bmatrix} x' \\ y' \\ z' \end{bmatrix} = \mathbf{M} \begin{bmatrix} x \\ y \\ z \end{bmatrix},$$

where $\mathbf{M}$ is an invertible 3×3 matrix. The del operator ∇' in the primed coordinate system is defined as

$$\nabla' = \left\langle \frac{\partial}{\partial x'}, \frac{\partial}{\partial y'}, \frac{\partial}{\partial z'} \right\rangle.$$

Show that $\nabla' = \left(\mathbf{M}^{-1} \right)^{\mathrm{T}} \nabla$. [*Hint.* Treat each unprimed coordinate as a function of all three primed coordinates by writing

$$x = x(x', y', z')$$
$$y = y(x', y', z')$$
$$z = z(x', y', z')$$

and apply the chain rule for partial differentiation, which for the x-coordinate gives us

$$\frac{\partial}{\partial x'} = \frac{\partial x}{\partial x'} \frac{\partial}{\partial x} + \frac{\partial y}{\partial x'} \frac{\partial}{\partial y} + \frac{\partial z}{\partial x'} \frac{\partial}{\partial z}.]$$

Chapter **6**

Illumination

This chapter describes the mathematics used to illuminate a surface. The term *illumination* is often used to describe the process by which the amount of light reaching a surface is determined. The term *shading* normally describes the methods used to determine the color and intensity of light reflected toward the viewer for each pixel representing a surface. This color depends on the properties of the light sources illuminating the surface as well as the reflective characteristics of the surface itself.

The interaction between light and a surface is a complex physical process. Photons can be absorbed, reflected, or transmitted when they strike the surface of a material. To model this interaction using the whole of today's knowledge of physics would be far too computationally time-consuming. Instead, we must settle for models that approximate the expected appearance of a surface. We begin with simple models that are widely used because they are computationally efficient and produce acceptable results, but really are not physically accurate. Later, we examine more costly techniques that more closely model the true physical interaction of light with a surface.

6.1 RGB Color

A precise model describing the reflection of light by a surface would account for every wavelength of light in the visible spectrum. Most computer monitors, however, display color information using a combination of only three wavelengths of light: red, green, and blue. This system is commonly referred to as *RGB color*. Intermediate wavelengths are simulated by blending these three primary colors together in appropriate ratios. For instance, yellow is produced by blending equal parts red and green. Colors that are made up of more than one wavelength of light, such as brown, can also be simulated using RGB color.

The lighting models presented in this chapter utilize the RGB color system. The intensity of reflected light at a point on a surface is calculated for red, green, and blue wavelengths simultaneously. Since the same operations are performed for each of these components, we express our mathematical formulas using a three-component entity that we simply call a *color*.

Colors are expressed as triplets of red, green, and blue components whose values range from 0 to 1. These colors represent both the spectral composition of light, which determines what color the eye perceives, as well as the intensity of light. We denote colors by script letters to distinguish them from vectors. A single red, green, or blue component of a color C is denoted by using a subscript r, g, or b (hence, we can write $C = (C_r, C_g, C_b)$).

A color C can be multiplied by a scalar s to produce a new color:

$$sC = (sC_r, sC_g, sC_b). \tag{6.1}$$

Addition and multiplication of colors are performed componentwise. That is, for two colors C and D, we have

$$C + D = (C_r + D_r, C_g + D_g, C_b + D_b)$$
$$CD = (C_r D_r, C_g D_g, C_b D_b). \tag{6.2}$$

Color multiplication, either by another color or by a scalar, is also called *modulation*. The color of a pixel belonging to a rendered triangle is usually determined through some combination of colors from multiple sources. The color of a pixel on the face of a triangle is commonly derived from the product of a color looked up in a texture map and another color that is interpolated among the triangle's vertices. In this case, we say that the texture color is *modulated* by the vertex color.

6.2 Light Sources

The color that we calculate for any point on a surface is the sum of contributions from all the light sources that illuminate the surface. The standard types of light sources supported by 3D graphics systems come in four varieties: ambient, directional, point, and spot. This section describes each of these types of light sources and how they contribute to the radiation present at a point in space.

6.2.1 Ambient Light

The *ambient* light present at a certain location is the low-intensity light that arises from the many reflections of light on all nearby surfaces in an environment. Using ambient light provides a rough approximation of the general brightness of an area and replaces the complexities of calculating all the interobject reflections in a scene.

Ambient light appears to come from every direction with equal intensity, and thus illuminates every part of an object uniformly. The color $\mathcal{A}$ of the ambient light is usually a constant in a scene, but it may also be a function of spatial position. For instance, one can use a three-dimensional texture map to store samples of the ambient light on a regular grid that permeates a region of the world.

6.2.2 Directional Light Sources

A *directional* light source, also known as an *infinite* light source, is one that radiates light in a single direction from infinitely far away. Directional lights are typically used to model light sources such as the sun, whose rays can be considered parallel. Since they have no position in space, directional lights have infinite range, and the intensity of the light they radiate does not diminish over distance, as does the intensity of point lights and spot lights.

6.2.3 Point Light Sources

A *point* light source is one that radiates light equally in every direction from a single point in space. The intensity of light naturally decreases with distance according to the inverse square law. OpenGL and Direct3D both implement a generalization of this concept that allows us to control the intensity of light radiated by a point light source using the reciprocal of a quadratic polynomial.

Suppose that a point light source has been placed at a point $\mathbf{P}$. The intensity C of light reaching a point in space $\mathbf{Q}$ is given by

$$C = \frac{1}{k_c + k_l d + k_q d^2} C_0,$$ (6.3)

where C_0 is the color of the light, d is the distance between the light source and $\mathbf{Q}$ (i.e., $d = \|\mathbf{P} - \mathbf{Q}\|$), and the constants k_c, k_l, and k_q are called the constant, linear, and quadratic attenuation constants.

6.2.4 Spot Light Sources

A *spot* light is similar to a point light but has a preferred direction of radiation. The intensity of a spot light is attenuated over distance in the same way that it is for a point light and is also attenuated by another factor called the spot light effect.

Suppose that a spot light source has been placed at a point $\mathbf{P}$ and has a spot direction $\mathbf{R}$. The intensity C of light reaching a point in space $\mathbf{Q}$ is given by

$$C = \frac{\max\{-\mathbf{R} \cdot \mathbf{L}, 0\}^p}{k_c + k_l d + k_q d^2} C_0,$$ (6.4)

where C_0 is the color of the light; d is the distance between the light source and $\mathbf{Q}$; k_c, k_l, and k_q are the attenuation constants; and $\mathbf{L}$ is the unit length direction pointing from $\mathbf{Q}$ toward the light source:

$$\mathbf{L} = \frac{\mathbf{P} - \mathbf{Q}}{\|\mathbf{P} - \mathbf{Q}\|}.$$ (6.5)

The exponent p controls how concentrated the spot light is. As shown in Figure 6.1, a large value of p corresponds to a highly focused spot light having a sharp falloff, whereas a smaller value of p corresponds to a less concentrated beam. The spot light is most intense when $\mathbf{R} = -\mathbf{L}$ and gradually falls off as the angle between $\mathbf{R}$ and $-\mathbf{L}$ increases. No radiation from a spot light reaches a point for which the angle between $\mathbf{R}$ and $-\mathbf{L}$ is greater than 90 degrees.

Figure 6.1 The spot light exponent p controls how concentrated the beam of a spot light is. From left to right, the spot light exponents used to illuminate the ground are 2, 10, 50, and 100.

6.3 Diffuse Lighting

A diffuse surface is one for which part of the light incident on a point on the surface is scattered in random directions. The average effect is that a certain color of light, the surface's diffuse reflection color, is reflected uniformly in every direction. This is called the *Lambertian* reflection, and because light is reflected equally in every direction, the appearance of the Lambertian reflection does not depend on the position of the observer.

As shown in Figure 6.2, a beam of light having a cross-sectional area A illuminates the same area A on a surface only if the surface is perpendicular to the direction in which the light is traveling. As the angle between the normal vector and the light direction increases, so does the surface area illuminated by the beam of light. If the angle between the normal vector and light direction is θ, then the surface area illuminated by the beam of light is equal to $A/\cos\theta$. This results in a *decrease* in the intensity of the light per unit surface area by a factor of $\cos\theta$.

The value of $\cos\theta$ is given by the dot product between the normal vector $\mathbf{N}$ and the unit direction to the light source $\mathbf{L}$. A negative dot product means that the surface is facing away from the light source and should not be illuminated at all. Thus, we clamp the dot product to zero in our illumination calculations.

We can now begin to construct a formula that calculates the color of light $\mathcal{K}$ that is reflected toward the viewer from a given point $\mathbf{Q}$ on a surface. This formula is written in terms of the intensity $\mathcal{C}_i$ of each of n lights illuminating the point $\mathbf{Q}$, which is constant for directional light sources and is given by Equations (6.3) and (6.4) for point and spot light sources. The reflected light is modulated by the surface's diffuse reflection color $\mathcal{D}$. Adding the contributions from n light sources and considering the ambient intensity $\mathcal{A}$, we can express the diffuse component of our lighting formula as

$$\mathcal{K}_{\text{diffuse}} = \mathcal{D}\mathcal{A} + \mathcal{D}\sum_{i=1}^{n} \mathcal{C}_i \max\{\mathbf{N}\cdot\mathbf{L}_i, 0\}, \tag{6.6}$$

where the unit vector $\mathbf{L}_i$ points from $\mathbf{Q}$ toward the i-th light source.

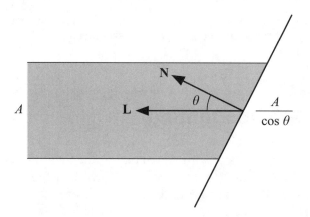

Figure 6.2 The surface area illuminated by a beam of light increases as the angle θ between the surface normal and direction to the light increases, decreasing the intensity of incident light per unit area.

6.4 Texture Mapping

One or more *texture maps* may be applied to a surface to achieve greater detail, as shown in Figure 6.3. At each point on a surface, a *texel* (texture pixel) is looked up in each texture map and combined in some way with the lighting formula. In the simplest case, a sample from a diffuse texture map is looked up and used to modulate the diffuse reflection color. More advanced applications are discussed later in this chapter.

Let the color $\mathcal{T}$ represent a filtered sample from a texture map at a point on a surface. Using this color to modulate the diffuse reflection color produces the following augmented version of Equation (6.6).

$$\mathcal{K}_{\text{diffuse}} = \mathcal{D}\mathcal{T}\mathcal{A} + \mathcal{D}\mathcal{T}\sum_{i=1}^{n} \mathcal{C}_i \max\{\mathbf{N}\cdot\mathbf{L}_i, 0\} \tag{6.7}$$

The actual color sampled from the texture map is determined by texture coordinates applied to an object. Texture coordinates are either precomputed and stored with each vertex of a triangle mesh or calculated at runtime to produce some special effect. The texture coordinates are then interpolated using Equation (4.37) across the face of a triangle when it is rendered. There may be from one to four coordinates at each vertex, and they are labeled s, t, r, and q. The next few sections describe the different varieties of texture maps and how texture coordinates are used to look up a texel in each type.

Figure 6.3 Applying a texture map adds detail to a surface.

6.4.1 Standard Texture Maps

One, two, or three texture coordinates may be used to look up texels in one-, two-, or three-dimensional texture maps. As shown in Figure 6.4, the entire width, height, and depth of a texture map corresponds to coordinate values lying between 0 and 1 in the s, t, and r directions, respectively.

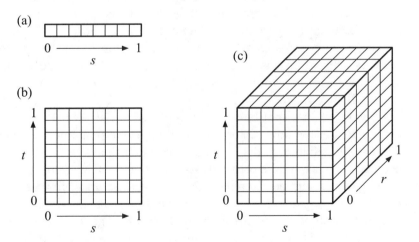

Figure 6.4   Texture space for (a) 1D texture maps, (b) 2D texture maps, and (c) 3D texture maps.

A one-dimensional texture map can be thought of as a two-dimensional texture map that is only a single pixel in height. Likewise, a two-dimensional texture map can be thought of as a three-dimensional texture map that is only a single pixel in depth. When t- and r-coordinates are not specified, they are assumed to be zero.

6.4.2 Projective Texture Maps

The fourth texture coordinate is used for projective texture mapping, an application of which is described later in this section. The q-coordinate behaves in much the same way the w-coordinate does for homogeneous points and is assumed to be one when not specified. The interpolated s-, t-, and r-coordinates are divided by the interpolated q-coordinate. For a scanline whose endpoints have texture coordinates $\langle s_1,t_1,r_1,q_1 \rangle$ and $\langle s_2,t_2,r_2,q_2 \rangle$, we can use Equation (4.37) to calculate interpolated values s_3 and q_3 at some intermediate parameter $u \in [0,1]$. The quotient of these two values gives the following expression for the s-coordinate used to sample the texture map.

$$s = \frac{s_3}{q_3} = \frac{(1-u)\dfrac{s_1}{z_1} + u\dfrac{s_2}{z_2}}{(1-u)\dfrac{q_1}{z_1} + u\dfrac{q_2}{z_2}} \tag{6.8}$$

Similar expressions give the projected t and r texture coordinates.

One application of projective texture maps is the simulation of a spot light that projects an image onto the environment. As shown in Figure 6.5, the projected image becomes larger as the distance from the spot light increases. The effect is achieved by using a 4×4 texture matrix to map the vertex positions of an object to texture coordinates $\langle s,t,0,q \rangle$ such that division by q produces the correct 2D texture coordinates $\langle s,t \rangle$ used to sample the projected image.

Suppose that a spot light has been placed at the point $\mathbf{P}$ and points in the direction $\mathbf{R}$. Let the unit vectors $\mathbf{S}$ and $\mathbf{T}$ lie in the plane perpendicular to $\mathbf{R}$ such that they are aligned to the directions in which the s- and t-axes of the projected texture image should be oriented (see Figure 6.5). Each vertex position $\langle x,y,z,1 \rangle$ belonging to a surface illuminated by the spot light must first be transformed into the coordinate system in which the spot light lies at the origin, and the x-, y-, and z-axes correspond to the directions $\mathbf{S}$, $\mathbf{T}$, and $\mathbf{R}$. This can be accomplished using the inverse of the matrix whose columns are the vectors $\mathbf{S}$, $\mathbf{T}$, $\mathbf{R}$, and $\mathbf{P}$. If $\mathbf{S}$ and $\mathbf{T}$ are orthogonal (i.e., the projected image is not skewed), the transformation is given by

$$\mathbf{M}_1 = \begin{bmatrix} S_x & S_y & S_z & -\mathbf{S}\cdot\mathbf{P} \\ T_x & T_y & T_z & -\mathbf{T}\cdot\mathbf{P} \\ R_x & R_y & R_z & -\mathbf{R}\cdot\mathbf{P} \\ 0 & 0 & 0 & 1 \end{bmatrix}. \tag{6.9}$$

(Note that this matrix transforms into a left-handed coordinate system since $\mathbf{S}\times\mathbf{T}=-\mathbf{R}$.)

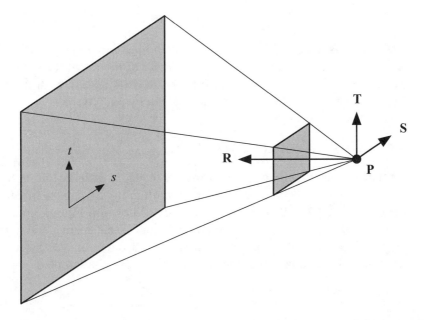

Figure 6.5 A projective texture map can be used to simulate a spot light that projects an image onto the environment.

Now we need to multiply the matrix in Equation (6.9) by a second matrix that performs the projection. Just as we define the focal length of the view frustum, we can define the focal length of the spot light projection in terms of an apex angle α. The focal length e is given by

$$e = \frac{1}{\tan(\alpha/2)}. \tag{6.10}$$

Let a be the aspect ratio of the texture map, equal to its height divided by its width. Every vertex position should be projected onto the plane lying at a distance e from the spot light, where we want to map the interval $[-1,1]$ in the x direction to $[0,1]$, and we want to map the interval $[-a,a]$ in the y direction to $[0,1]$. The matrix

$$\mathbf{M}_2 = \begin{bmatrix} e/2 & 0 & 1/2 & 0 \\ 0 & e/2a & 1/2 & 0 \\ 0 & 0 & 0 & 0 \\ 0 & 0 & 1 & 0 \end{bmatrix}$$

(6.11)

performs this mapping and causes the projection to occur when the s- and t-coordinates are divided by the q-coordinate of the result. Combining the matrices given in Equations (6.9) and (6.11), the 4×4 texture matrix $\mathbf{M}$ used to implement a projected spot light image is given by $\mathbf{M} = \mathbf{M}_2 \mathbf{M}_1$.

6.4.3 Cube Texture Maps

A relatively new method of texturing an object is enabled through the use of a *cube texture map*. Cube texture maps are often used to approximate an environmental reflection on the surface of a model. Shown in Figure 6.6, a cube texture map consists of six two-dimensional components that correspond to the faces of a cube. The s-, t-, and r-coordinates represent a direction vector emanating from the center of the cube that points toward the texel to be sampled.

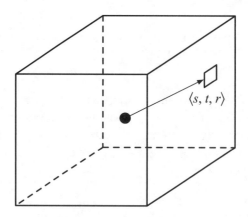

Figure 6.6 A cube texture map consists of six components that correspond to the faces of a cube.

Which face to sample is determined by the sign of the coordinate having the largest absolute value. The other two coordinates are divided by the largest coordinate and remapped to the range $[0,1]$ using the formulas listed in Table 6.1 to produce 2D texture coordinates $\langle s', t' \rangle$. These coordinates are then used to sample the two-dimensional texture map for the corresponding face of the cube texture map. Figure 6.7 shows the orientation of the cube map axes relative to each of the six faces.

Table 6.1 Formulas used to calculate the 2D coordinates $\langle s', t' \rangle$ used to sample a texel in one of the six faces of a cube texture map.

Face	s'	t'
Positive x	$\dfrac{1}{2} - \dfrac{r}{2s}$	$\dfrac{1}{2} - \dfrac{t}{2s}$
Negative x	$\dfrac{1}{2} - \dfrac{r}{2s}$	$\dfrac{1}{2} + \dfrac{t}{2s}$
Positive y	$\dfrac{1}{2} + \dfrac{s}{2t}$	$\dfrac{1}{2} + \dfrac{r}{2t}$
Negative y	$\dfrac{1}{2} - \dfrac{s}{2t}$	$\dfrac{1}{2} + \dfrac{r}{2t}$
Positive z	$\dfrac{1}{2} + \dfrac{s}{2r}$	$\dfrac{1}{2} - \dfrac{t}{2r}$
Negative z	$\dfrac{1}{2} + \dfrac{s}{2r}$	$\dfrac{1}{2} + \dfrac{t}{2r}$

Texture coordinates used in conjunction with cube texture maps are typically generated at runtime. For instance, environment mapping can be performed by calculating the reflection of the direction to the camera and storing it in the $\langle s, t, r \rangle$ coordinates at each vertex of a triangle mesh. The reflection direction calculation is normally implemented in hardware, so this can be done very efficiently.

An invaluable application of cube texture maps is that of normalizing vectors. A *normalization cube map* is a cube texture map that, instead of storing color images in each of its six faces, stores an array of vectors that are encoded as RGB colors using the following formulas.

$$\text{red} = \frac{x+1}{2}$$

$$\text{green} = \frac{y+1}{2}$$

$$\text{blue} = \frac{z+1}{2} \tag{6.12}$$

The vector stored at each pixel of a face of the cube map is the unit length vector $\langle s,t,r \rangle$ that causes that pixel to be sampled. The use of a normalization cube map becomes desirable when performing per-pixel lighting because interpolation of surface normals across the face of a triangle inexorably produces normal vectors whose length is less than unity.

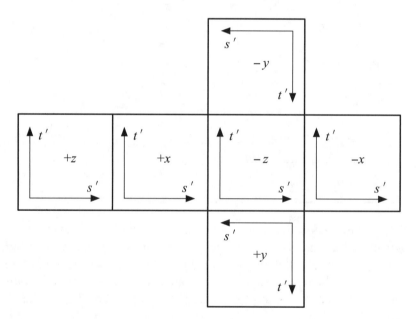

Figure 6.7 Orientation of the cube map axes relative to each of the six faces.

6.4.4 Filtering and Mipmaps

When a model is rendered with a texture map applied to its surface, it is almost never the case that the resolution of a texture map matches the resolution of the viewport in which it is displayed. As a model moves closer to the camera, the relative resolution of the viewport increases compared to that of the texture map.

Using only one sample from the texture map at each pixel results in a blocky appearance, so rendering hardware normally fetches four samples from the texture map at each pixel and blends them together. In a process called *bilinear filtering*, the four samples are blended using a weighted average that depends on the exact texture coordinates corresponding to the pixel being rendered.

Suppose a two-dimensional texture map having width w and height h is being sampled using the texture coordinates $\langle s,t \rangle$ and make the following definitions.

$$i = \left\lfloor ws - \tfrac{1}{2} \right\rfloor$$
$$j = \left\lfloor ht - \tfrac{1}{2} \right\rfloor$$
$$\alpha = \mathrm{frac}\left(ws - \tfrac{1}{2}\right)$$
$$\beta = \mathrm{frac}\left(ht - \tfrac{1}{2}\right) \tag{6.13}$$

The bilinearly filtered texture value $\mathcal{T}$ is given by

$$\mathcal{T} = (1-\alpha)(1-\beta)\mathcal{T}_{\langle i,j \rangle} + \alpha(1-\beta)\mathcal{T}_{\langle i+1,j \rangle}$$
$$+ (1-\alpha)\beta\mathcal{T}_{\langle i,j+1 \rangle} + \alpha\beta\mathcal{T}_{\langle i+1,j+1 \rangle}, \tag{6.14}$$

where $\mathcal{T}_{\langle i,j \rangle}$ represents the value stored in the texture map at the integral texel coordinates $\langle i, j \rangle$.

As a model moves away from the camera and the relative resolution of the viewport decreases compared to that of the texture map, the area of a single pixel can cover a region enclosing many texels in the texture map. Even if bilinear filtering is applied, the low sampling resolution often leads to severe aliasing artifacts. The solution to this problem is to generate prefiltered versions of a texture map at lower resolutions. As shown in Figure 6.8, each smaller image is exactly half the width and half the height of the image that is one size larger. The array of texture images is called a *mipmap* (derived from the phrase *multum in parvo*, meaning many in a small place). Since the sum of the infinite series

$$1 + \frac{1}{4} + \frac{1}{16} + \frac{1}{64} + \cdots \tag{6.15}$$

is $\tfrac{4}{3}$, adding mipmap images to a texture map increases the storage requirements by only one-third of the texture map's original size.

When using mipmaps and bilinear filtering, rendering hardware chooses a mipmap image at each pixel by examining the derivatives $\partial \mathbf{S}/\partial x$ and $\partial \mathbf{S}/\partial y$, where x and y are the viewport coordinates of the pixel, and $\mathbf{S}$ represents the interpolated components of the texture coordinate set at the pixel. The largest image in a mipmap is called level 0, and smaller images are numbered sequentially.

Larger texture coordinate derivatives cause higher-numbered mipmap images being used. Let n and m be the base-2 logarithms of the width and height of a two-dimensional texture map (whose width and height are thus 2^n and 2^m). Let $s(x,y)$ and $t(x,y)$ be functions that map viewport coordinates x and y to texture coordinates s and t, and define $u(x,y) = 2^n s(x,y)$ and $v(x,y) = 2^m t(x,y)$. The level-of-detail parameter λ is determined by calculating

$$\rho_x = \sqrt{\left(\frac{\partial u}{\partial x}\right)^2 + \left(\frac{\partial v}{\partial x}\right)^2}$$

$$\rho_y = \sqrt{\left(\frac{\partial u}{\partial y}\right)^2 + \left(\frac{\partial v}{\partial y}\right)^2}$$

$$\lambda = \log_2\left[\max\left(\rho_x, \rho_y\right)\right]. \tag{6.16}$$

When using bilinear filtering (or no filtering), the value of λ is rounded to the nearest integer and clamped to the range $[0, \max(n,m)]$. Four texture samples are then fetched from the corresponding mipmap image level and blended using Equation (6.14).

As a model moves toward or away from the camera, abrupt changes in the mipmap level may be unsightly, so rendering hardware provides a mode called *trilinear filtering* in which two mipmap levels are sampled (using bilinear filtering) and blended together. Texture values $\mathcal{T}_1$ and $\mathcal{T}_2$ are sampled from mipmap levels $\lfloor \lambda \rfloor$ and $\lfloor \lambda \rfloor + 1$, respectively, and blended using the formula

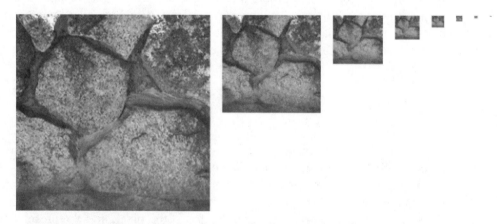

Figure 6.8 Mipmap images for a particular texture map. Each smaller image is exactly half the width and half the height of the preceding image.

$$\mathcal{T} = (1 - \text{frac}(\lambda))\mathcal{T}_1 + \text{frac}(\lambda)\mathcal{T}_2 \qquad (6.17)$$

to arrive at the final texture value $\mathcal{T}$.

Mipmapping for one-dimensional and three-dimensional texture maps operates by considering one or three texture coordinates in Equation (6.16). For cube texture maps, mipmapping operates independently for each of the six two-dimensional faces.

6.5 Specular Lighting

In addition to the uniform diffuse reflection, surfaces tend to reflect light strongly along the path given by the reflection of the incident direction across the surface normal. This results in the appearance of a shiny highlight on a surface called a *specularity*. Unlike the diffuse reflection, the specular reflection visible on a surface depends on the position of the viewer.

Figure 6.9 shows the normal vector $\mathbf{N}$ at a point $\mathbf{Q}$ on a surface, the unit direction to viewer vector $\mathbf{V}$, the unit direction to light vector $\mathbf{L}$, and the direct reflection vector $\mathbf{R}$ calculated using Equation (5.90). Specular highlights are the most intense when the reflection direction $\mathbf{R}$ points toward the viewer and decrease in intensity as the angle between $\mathbf{R}$ and the direction to the viewer $\mathbf{V}$ increases.

A model that produces a believable (but having almost no real physical basis) rendition of specular highlights uses the expression

$$\mathcal{S}\mathcal{C} \max\{\mathbf{R} \cdot \mathbf{V}, 0\}^m (\mathbf{N} \cdot \mathbf{L} > 0) \qquad (6.18)$$

to calculate the specular contribution from a single light source, where $\mathcal{S}$ is the surface's specular reflection color, $\mathcal{C}$ is the intensity of the incident light, and m is called the *specular exponent*. The expression $(\mathbf{N} \cdot \mathbf{L} > 0)$ is a boolean expression that evaluates to 1 if true and 0 otherwise. This prevents specular highlights from showing up at points on a surface that face away from the light source.

The specular exponent m controls the sharpness of the specular highlight. As shown in Figure 6.10, a small value of m produces a dull highlight that fades out over a relatively large distance, and a large value of m produces a sharp highlight that fades out quickly as the vectors $\mathbf{V}$ and $\mathbf{R}$ diverge.

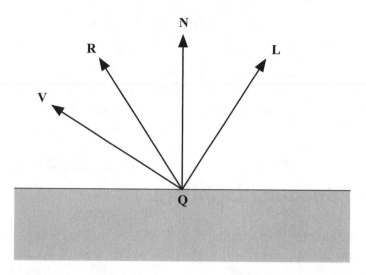

Figure 6.9 The intensity of the specular reflection is related to the angle between the direction to viewer vector **V** and the direct reflection vector **R** corresponding to the direction to light vector **L**.

Figure 6.10 The specular exponent m controls the sharpness of the specular highlight seen on a surface. From left to right, the specular exponents used to illuminate the tori are 2, 10, 50, and 100.

An alternative formulation of specular highlights that requires less calculation in some cases makes use of a direction called the *halfway vector*. Shown in Figure 6.11, the halfway vector **H** is the vector lying exactly halfway between the direction to viewer vector **V** and the direction light vector **L**. Specular highlights are the most intense when **H** points in the direction of the normal vector **N**. Using this model, we replace the dot product **R · V** in Equation (6.18) with the dot product **N · H**. This produces different results in terms of the rate at which the specular highlights diminish, but still retains the general characteristics of our original model.

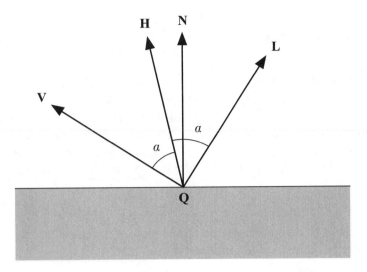

Figure 6.11 The angle between the normal vector **N** and the halfway vector **H** can also be used to determine specular intensity.

Adding the contributions from n light sources, we can express the specular component of our lighting formula as

$$\mathcal{K}_{\text{specular}} = \mathcal{S} \sum_{i=1}^{n} \mathcal{C}_i \max\{\mathbf{N} \cdot \mathbf{H}_i, 0\}^m \, (\mathbf{N} \cdot \mathbf{L}_i > 0), \qquad (6.19)$$

where $\mathbf{H}_i$ is the halfway vector for the i-th light source given by

$$\mathbf{H}_i = \frac{\mathbf{L}_i + \mathbf{V}}{\|\mathbf{L}_i + \mathbf{V}\|}. \qquad (6.20)$$

Just as a texture map can be used to modulate the diffuse component of the lighting formula, we can also use a map to modulate the specular component. Such a map is called a *gloss map* and determines the intensity of the specularity at each point on a surface. Using the color $\mathcal{G}$ to represent a filtered sample from the gloss map, we can augment the formula for the specular contribution as follows.

$$\mathcal{K}_{\text{specular}} = \mathcal{S}\mathcal{G} \sum_{i=1}^{n} \mathcal{C}_i \max\{\mathbf{N} \cdot \mathbf{H}_i, 0\}^m \, (\mathbf{N} \cdot \mathbf{L}_i > 0) \qquad (6.21)$$

6.6 Emission

Some objects may emit light in addition to reflecting it. To give an object the appearance of emitting a uniform glow, we add an emission color $\mathcal{E}$ to our lighting formula. This emission color can also be modulated by an *emission map* that determines the color and intensity of the glow at each point on a surface. Using the color $\mathcal{M}$ to represent a filtered sample from the emission map, the emission component of the lighting formula is given by the simple expression

$$\mathcal{K}_{\text{emission}} = \mathcal{E}\mathcal{M}. \tag{6.22}$$

Figure 6.12 demonstrates the application of an emission map to the surface of a model in addition to an ordinary texture map.

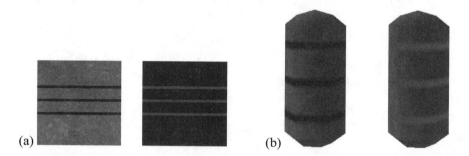

(a)   (b)

Figure 6.12 (a) An ordinary texture map and an emission map. (b) The model on the left has only the ordinary texture map applied to it. The model on the right includes the emission map. Unlike the ordinary texture map, the emission map is unaffected by the direction of the surface normal, and it determines which parts of the surface appear to give off a glow.

6.7 Shading

Information about the surface of a model, such as the positions of points on the surface and the normal vectors at those points, are stored only for each vertex of a triangle mesh. When a single triangle is rendered, information known at each vertex is interpolated across the face of the triangle, as discussed in Section 4.4.2. Conventional lighting pipelines calculate diffuse and specular illumination only at the vertices of a mesh. More modern graphics hardware enables the calculation of the entire illumination formula at every individual pixel drawn to the display. The manner in which lighting is determined for the surface of a triangle, combined with any number of texture maps, is called *shading*.

6.7.1 Calculating Normal Vectors

To apply the lighting formula to a triangle mesh, we need to have a representation of the surface normal at each vertex. We can calculate the normal vector for a single triangle by using the cross product. The unit-length normal vector $\mathbf{N}$ of a triangle whose vertices lie at the points $\mathbf{P}_0$, $\mathbf{P}_1$, and $\mathbf{P}_2$ is given by

$$\mathbf{N} = \frac{(\mathbf{P}_1 - \mathbf{P}_0) \times (\mathbf{P}_2 - \mathbf{P}_0)}{\left\| (\mathbf{P}_1 - \mathbf{P}_0) \times (\mathbf{P}_2 - \mathbf{P}_0) \right\|}. \tag{6.23}$$

This assumes that the vertices are oriented in a counterclockwise fashion when the normal points toward the viewer, as shown in Figure 6.13.

The normal vector at a single vertex is typically calculated by averaging the normal vectors of all triangles that share that vertex. Using the formula

$$\mathbf{N}_{\text{vertex}} = \frac{\displaystyle\sum_{i=1}^{k} \mathbf{N}_i}{\left\| \displaystyle\sum_{i=1}^{k} \mathbf{N}_i \right\|} \tag{6.24}$$

to calculate the normal vector $\mathbf{N}_{\text{vertex}}$ for a vertex shared by k triangles results in a vertex normal that is influenced equally by the normal vector $\mathbf{N}_i$ of each of the triangles surrounding it.

An alternative formulation, illustrated in Figure 6.14, makes use of the fact that the cross product of two vectors is proportional to the area of the triangle that they form. By using the unnormalized triangle normals calculated with the equation

$$\mathbf{N} = (\mathbf{P}_1 - \mathbf{P}_0) \times (\mathbf{P}_2 - \mathbf{P}_0) \tag{6.25}$$

instead of Equation (6.23) and then averaging using Equation (6.24), we can calculate a vertex normal that is more strongly influenced by triangles with greater area. This method produces more appealing vertex normals for some models.

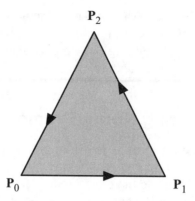

Figure 6.13 The vertices of a triangle should be oriented in a counterclockwise fashion when the normal vector points toward the viewer.

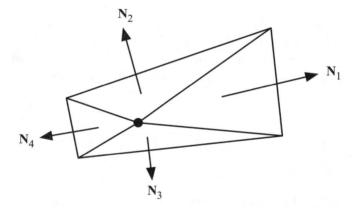

Figure 6.14 By averaging the unnormalized normal vectors of each triangle sharing a vertex, a vertex normal can be calculated that is influenced more strongly by triangles with greater area.

6.7.2 Gouraud Shading

The interpolation of lighting values calculated at each vertex across the face of a triangle is known as *Gouraud shading*. Before the advent of graphics hardware capable of performing per-pixel lighting calculations, diffuse and specular colors were calculated only at each vertex of a triangle mesh. This method calculates the colors

$$\mathcal{K}_{\text{primary}} = \mathcal{E} + \mathcal{D}\mathcal{A} + \mathcal{D}\sum_{i=1}^{n} \mathcal{C}_i \max\{\mathbf{N}\cdot\mathbf{L}_i, 0\}$$

$$\mathcal{K}_{\text{secondary}} = \mathcal{S}\sum_{i=1}^{n} \mathcal{C}_i \max\{\mathbf{N}\cdot\mathbf{H}_i, 0\}^m\,(\mathbf{N}\cdot\mathbf{L}_i > 0) \qquad (6.26)$$

at each vertex and interpolates them across the face of a triangle. The color $\mathcal{K}$ of a pixel is then calculated using the equation

$$\mathcal{K} = \mathcal{K}_{\text{primary}} \circ \mathcal{T}_1 \circ \mathcal{T}_2 \circ \cdots \circ \mathcal{T}_k + \mathcal{K}_{\text{secondary}}, \qquad (6.27)$$

where each $\mathcal{T}_i$ represents a color sampled from one of k texture maps, and the operation $\circ$ is one of several available texture combination operations, including modulation and addition.

6.7.3 Phong Shading

Instead of interpolating lighting values calculated at each vertex, a *Phong-shaded* triangle interpolates the vertex normals and evaluates the lighting formula at each pixel. Graphics hardware that can perform complex calculations on a per-pixel basis (a process called *pixel shading* or *fragment shading*) can be configured to evaluate the entire expression

$$\mathcal{K} = \mathcal{K}_{\text{emission}} + \mathcal{K}_{\text{diffuse}} + \mathcal{K}_{\text{specular}}$$

$$= \mathcal{E}\mathcal{M} + \mathcal{D}\mathcal{T}\mathcal{A} + \sum_{i=1}^{n} \mathcal{C}_i\left[\mathcal{D}\mathcal{T}\,(\mathbf{N}\cdot\mathbf{L}_i) + \mathcal{S}\mathcal{G}\,(\mathbf{N}\cdot\mathbf{H}_i)^m\,(\mathbf{N}\cdot\mathbf{L}_i > 0)\right] \quad (6.28)$$

at each pixel composing the face of a triangle. In the interests of simplicity, we have omitted the maximum functions here, but it should be noted that the diffuse and specular dot products in this equation are clamped to zero. The intensity $\mathcal{C}_i$ of each of the n light sources is still calculated at each vertex and interpolated across the face of a triangle. These values and the interpolated normal vector are used to evaluate $\mathcal{K}$ at each pixel. Of course, not every component of Equation (6.28) needs to be present.

An advantage that Phong shading possesses over Gouraud shading is that it does a far better job of modeling specularity due to the fact that the dot product $\mathbf{N}\cdot\mathbf{H}$ is evaluated at every pixel. When a sharp specular highlight falls in the interior of a triangle, Gouraud shading produces poor results because the specular component calculated at the triangle's vertices is unrepresentative of the true values existing elsewhere on the face of the triangle.

A problem that arises when using Phong shading is that interpolated normal vectors do not retain the unit length that they have at the vertices. Densely tessellated models for which the normal vectors belonging to neighboring vertices differ in direction by only a small amount may not produce visually unacceptable artifacts, but most models exhibit a noticeable darkening of the specularity in the interior of each triangle. This problem is solved by using a normalization cube map (see Section 6.4.3). Normal vectors are passed into the texture engine as $\langle s,t,r \rangle$ mapping coordinates, which results in the output of unit vectors encoded as RGB colors.

6.8 Bump Mapping

The surface detail that an observer perceives when an object is viewed from any direction other than edge-on is generally determined by the way in which its surface is illuminated. The illumination at each pixel rendered is determined by the normal vector used during the evaluation of the lighting formula. So far, we have been limited to calculating normal vectors only at the vertices of a triangle mesh and using a smoothly interpolated normal vector elsewhere. This coarse resolution prevents us from illuminating any details that are smaller in size than a typical triangle in a mesh. *Bump mapping* is a technique that presents the illusion of greater detail to the viewer by using a texture map to perturb the normal vector at each pixel.

6.8.1 Bump Map Construction

High-resolution information about how the normal vector is perturbed is stored in a two-dimensional array of three-dimensional vectors called a *bump map* or *normal map*. Each vector in the bump map represents the direction in which the normal vector should point relative to the interpolated normal vector at a point inside the face of a triangle. The vector $\langle 0,0,1 \rangle$ represents an unperturbed normal, whereas any other vector represents a modification to the normal that affects the result of the lighting formula.

A bump map is typically constructed by extracting normal vectors from a height map whose contents represent the height of a flat surface at each pixel. To derive the normal vector corresponding to a particular pixel in the height map, we first calculate tangents in the s and t directions, which are based on the difference in height between adjacent pixels. Using the notation $H(i,j)$ to represent the value stored at coordinates $\langle i,j \rangle$ in a $w \times h$ pixel height map, we can express the tangent vectors $\mathbf{S}(i,j)$ and $\mathbf{T}(i,j)$, aligned to the s and t directions, respectively, as follows.

$$\mathbf{S}(i,j) = \langle 1,0,aH(i+1,j) - aH(i-1,j) \rangle$$
$$\mathbf{T}(i,j) = \langle 0,1,aH(i,j+1) - aH(i,j-1) \rangle \qquad (6.29)$$

The constant a is scale factor that can be used to vary the range of the height values, controlling how pronounced the perturbed normals are. If we let S_z and T_z denote the z-components of $\mathbf{S}(i,j)$ and $\mathbf{T}(i,j)$, then the normal vector $\mathbf{N}(i,j)$ is calculated using the cross product

$$\mathbf{N}(i,j) = \frac{\mathbf{S}(i,j) \times \mathbf{T}(i,j)}{\|\mathbf{S}(i,j) \times \mathbf{T}(i,j)\|} = \frac{\langle -S_z, -T_z, 1 \rangle}{\sqrt{S_z^2 + T_z^2 + 1}}. \qquad (6.30)$$

The components of each normal vector are encoded as an RGB color using the relations given in Equation (6.12). Figure 6.15 shows a grayscale height map and the corresponding bump map calculated using Equation (6.30).

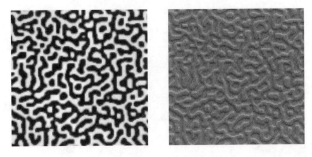

Figure 6.15 A height map and the corresponding bump map containing perturbed normal vectors. A pastel purple color is prevalent in the bump map since the unperturbed normal vector $\langle 0,0,1 \rangle$ corresponds to the RGB color $\left(\frac{1}{2},\frac{1}{2},1\right)$.

6.8.2 Tangent Space

Since the vector $\langle 0,0,1 \rangle$ in a bump map represents an unperturbed normal, we need it to correspond to the interpolated normal vector that we would ordinarily use in the lighting formula. This can be achieved by constructing a coordinate system at each vertex in which the vertex normal always points along the positive z-axis. In addition to the normal vector, we need two vectors that are tangent to the surface at each vertex in order to form an orthonormal basis. The resulting coordinate system is called *tangent space* or *vertex space* and is shown in Figure 6.16.

Once a tangent-space coordinate system has been established at each vertex of a triangle mesh, the direction to light vector **L** is calculated at each vertex and transformed into the tangent space. The tangent-space vector **L** is then interpolated across the face of a triangle. Since the vector $\langle 0,0,1 \rangle$ in tangent space corresponds to the normal vector, the dot product between the tangent-space direction to light **L** and a sample from a bump map produces a valid Lambertian reflection term.

The tangent vectors at each vertex must be chosen so that they are aligned to the texture space of the bump map. For surfaces generated by parametric functions, tangents can usually be calculated by simply taking derivatives with respect to each of the parameters. Arbitrary triangle meshes, however, can have bump maps applied to them in any orientation, which necessitates a more general method for determining the tangent directions at each vertex.

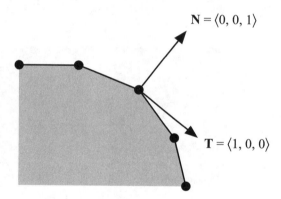

Figure 6.16 Tangent space is aligned to the tangent plane and normal vector at a vertex.

6.8.3 Calculating Tangent Vectors

Our goal is to find a 3×3 matrix at each vertex that transforms vectors from object space into tangent space. To accomplish this, we consider the more intuitive problem of transforming vectors in the reverse direction from tangent space into object space. Since the normal vector at a vertex corresponds to $\langle 0,0,1 \rangle$ in tangent space, we know that the z-axis of our tangent space always gets mapped to a vertex's normal vector.

We want our tangent space to be aligned such that the x-axis corresponds to the s direction in the bump map and the y-axis corresponds to the t direction in the bump map. That is, if $\mathbf{Q}$ represents a point inside the triangle, we would like to be able to write

$$\mathbf{Q} - \mathbf{P}_0 = (s - s_0)\mathbf{T} + (t - t_0)\mathbf{B}, \tag{6.31}$$

where $\mathbf{T}$ and $\mathbf{B}$ are tangent vectors aligned to the texture map, $\mathbf{P}_0$ is the position of one of the vertices of the triangle, and $\langle s_0, t_0 \rangle$ are the texture coordinates at that vertex. The letter $\mathbf{B}$ is commonly meant to stand for *binormal*, but this is not an intuitive term since $\mathbf{B}$ represents a direction that is tangent to the surface, not normal. As discussed in Section 15.8, the term is derived from the local coordinate system following the path of a curve in which there is a single tangent direction and two orthogonal normal directions. We shall instead use the term *bitangent* since it provides a more accurate description of the quantity that it represents.

Suppose that we have a triangle whose vertex positions are given by the points $\mathbf{P}_0$, $\mathbf{P}_1$, and $\mathbf{P}_2$, and whose corresponding texture coordinates are given by $\langle s_0, t_0 \rangle$, $\langle s_1, t_1 \rangle$, and $\langle s_2, t_2 \rangle$. Our calculations can be made much simpler by working relative to the vertex $\mathbf{P}_0$, so we let

$$\begin{aligned} \mathbf{Q}_1 &= \mathbf{P}_1 - \mathbf{P}_0 \\ \mathbf{Q}_2 &= \mathbf{P}_2 - \mathbf{P}_0 \end{aligned} \tag{6.32}$$

and

$$\begin{aligned} \langle s_1, t_1 \rangle &= \langle s_1 - s_0, t_1 - t_0 \rangle \\ \langle s_2, t_2 \rangle &= \langle s_2 - s_0, t_2 - t_0 \rangle. \end{aligned} \tag{6.33}$$

We need to solve the following equations for $\mathbf{T}$ and $\mathbf{B}$.

$$\begin{aligned} \mathbf{Q}_1 &= s_1 \mathbf{T} + t_1 \mathbf{B} \\ \mathbf{Q}_2 &= s_2 \mathbf{T} + t_2 \mathbf{B} \end{aligned} \tag{6.34}$$

This is a linear system with six unknowns (three for each $\mathbf{T}$ and $\mathbf{B}$) and six equations (the x-, y-, and z-components of the two equations). We can write this in matrix form as follows.

$$\begin{bmatrix} (\mathbf{Q}_1)_x & (\mathbf{Q}_1)_y & (\mathbf{Q}_1)_z \\ (\mathbf{Q}_2)_x & (\mathbf{Q}_2)_y & (\mathbf{Q}_2)_z \end{bmatrix} = \begin{bmatrix} s_1 & t_1 \\ s_2 & t_2 \end{bmatrix} \begin{bmatrix} T_x & T_y & T_z \\ B_x & B_y & B_z \end{bmatrix} \tag{6.35}$$

Multiplying both sides by the inverse of the $\langle s,t \rangle$ matrix, we have

$$\begin{bmatrix} T_x & T_y & T_z \\ B_x & B_y & B_z \end{bmatrix} = \frac{1}{s_1 t_2 - s_2 t_1} \begin{bmatrix} t_2 & -t_1 \\ -s_2 & s_1 \end{bmatrix} \begin{bmatrix} (\mathbf{Q}_1)_x & (\mathbf{Q}_1)_y & (\mathbf{Q}_1)_z \\ (\mathbf{Q}_2)_x & (\mathbf{Q}_2)_y & (\mathbf{Q}_2)_z \end{bmatrix}. \quad (6.36)$$

This gives us the (unnormalized) **T** and **B** tangent vectors for the triangle whose vertices are $\mathbf{P}_0$, $\mathbf{P}_1$, and $\mathbf{P}_2$. To find the tangent vectors for a single vertex, we average the tangents for all triangles sharing that vertex in a manner similar to the way in which vertex normals are commonly calculated. In the case that neighboring triangles have discontinuous texture mapping, vertices along the border are generally already duplicated since they have different mapping coordinates anyway. We do not average tangents from such triangles because the result would not accurately represent the orientation of the bump map for either triangle.

Once we have the normal vector **N** and the tangent vectors **T** and **B** for a vertex, we can transform from tangent space into object space using the matrix

$$\begin{bmatrix} T_x & B_x & N_x \\ T_y & B_y & N_y \\ T_z & B_z & N_z \end{bmatrix}. \quad (6.37)$$

To transform in the opposite direction (from object space to tangent space—what we want to do to the light direction), we can simply use the inverse of this matrix. It is not necessarily true that the tangent vectors are perpendicular to each other or to the normal vector, so the inverse of this matrix is not generally equal to its transpose. It is safe to assume, however, that the three vectors will at least be *close* to orthogonal, so using the Gram-Schmidt algorithm (see Algorithm 1.16) to orthogonalize them should not cause any unacceptable distortions. Using this process, new (still unnormalized) tangent vectors **T'** and **B'** are given by

$$\mathbf{T}' = \mathbf{T} - (\mathbf{N} \cdot \mathbf{T})\mathbf{N}$$
$$\mathbf{B}' = \mathbf{B} - (\mathbf{N} \cdot \mathbf{B})\mathbf{N} - (\mathbf{T}' \cdot \mathbf{B})\mathbf{T}'. \quad (6.38)$$

Normalizing these vectors and storing them as the tangent and bitangent for a vertex lets us use the matrix

$$\begin{bmatrix} T'_x & T'_y & T'_z \\ B'_x & B'_y & B'_z \\ N_x & N_y & N_z \end{bmatrix} \quad (6.39)$$

to transform the direction to light from object space into tangent space. Taking the dot product of the transformed light direction with a sample from the bump map then produces the correct Lambertian diffuse lighting value.

It is not necessary to store an extra array containing the per-vertex bitangent since the cross product $\mathbf{N} \times \mathbf{T}'$ can be used to obtain $m\mathbf{B}'$, where $m = \pm 1$ represents the handedness of the tangent space. The handedness value must be stored per-vertex since the bitangent $\mathbf{B}'$ obtained from $\mathbf{N} \times \mathbf{T}'$ may point in the wrong direction. The value of m is equal to the determinant of the matrix in Equation (6.39). One may find it convenient to store the per-vertex tangent vector $\mathbf{T}'$ as a four-dimensional entity whose w-coordinate holds the value of m. Then the bitangent $\mathbf{B}'$ can be computed using the formula

$$\mathbf{B}' = T'_w (\mathbf{N} \times \mathbf{T}'), \tag{6.40}$$

where the cross product ignores the w-coordinate. This works nicely for vertex programs by avoiding the need to specify an additional array containing the per-vertex m values.

6.8.4 Implementation

Bump mapping operations can be divided into those calculated for each vertex and those calculated for each pixel. At each vertex, we must calculate the direction to light $\mathbf{L}$ and the halfway vector $\mathbf{H}$, and transform them into tangent space using Equation (6.39). The vertex program shown in listing 6.1 performs these calculations for a surface illuminated by a directional light source (for which $\mathbf{L}$ is constant).

Listing 6.1 This vertex program performs the calculations necessary for bump mapping. Program environment parameter 0 contains the object-space camera position, and program environment parameter 1 contains the object-space direction to the infinite light source. The orthonormalized tangent $\mathbf{T}'$ is read from vertex attribute array 0, and the bitangent $\mathbf{B}'$ is calculated using Equation (6.40). The tangent-space direction to light $\mathbf{L}$ is stored in texture coordinate set 2, and the tangent-space halfway vector $\mathbf{H}$ is stored in texture coordinate set 3. The bump map is bound to texture unit 0, and the ordinary texture map is bound to texture unit 1.

```
!!ARBvp1.0

ATTRIB    normal  = vertex.normal;
ATTRIB    tangent = vertex.attrib[0];

PARAM     mvp[4]  = {state.matrix.mvp};
```

```
PARAM      camera  = program.env[0];
PARAM      light   = program.env[1];

TEMP       bitangent, vdir, halfway, temp;

# Transform vertex
DP4        result.position.x, mvp[0], vertex.position;
DP4        result.position.y, mvp[1], vertex.position;
DP4        result.position.z, mvp[2], vertex.position;
DP4        result.position.w, mvp[3], vertex.position;

# B = (N x T) * T.w
XPD        bitangent, normal, tangent;
MUL        bitangent, bitangent, tangent.w;

# Compute normalized V
ADD        view, camera, -vertex.position;
DP3        temp, view, view;
RSQ        temp, temp.x;
MUL        view, view, temp;

# Compute normalized H
ADD        halfway, view, light;
DP3        temp, halfway, halfway;
RSQ        temp, temp.x;
MUL        halfway, halfway, temp;

# Transform L into tangent space
DP3        result.texcoord[2].x, tangent, light;
DP3        result.texcoord[2].y, bitangent, light;
DP3        result.texcoord[2].z, normal, light;

# Transform H into tangent space
DP3        result.texcoord[3].x, tangent, halfway;
DP3        result.texcoord[3].y, bitangent, halfway;
DP3        result.texcoord[3].z, normal, halfway;

# Copy texture coords
MOV        result.texcoord[0], vertex.texcoord[0];
MOV        result.texcoord[1], vertex.texcoord[1];
END
```

The dot products $\mathbf{N} \cdot \mathbf{L}$ and $\mathbf{N} \cdot \mathbf{H}$ are calculated for every pixel, where the normal vector $\mathbf{N}$ is sampled from the bump map and the vectors $\mathbf{L}$ and $\mathbf{H}$ are interpolated among the values calculated at each vertex. Since these vectors are interpolated, their magnitudes can become slightly reduced, which may cause the interiors of triangles to appear darker than they should. This effect is often not noticeable, but models lacking sufficient tessellation may require the use of normalization cube maps.

The per-pixel dot products can be calculated using fragment programs or earlier OpenGL extensions such as `GL_NV_register_combiners`. If fragment programs are not being used, the quantity $\mathbf{N} \cdot \mathbf{H}$ can then be raised to a power by successively squaring it, but this allows only small power-of-two exponents. OpenGL implementations capable of dependent texture fetches (e.g., through the `GL_NV_texture_shader` extension) enable arbitrary specular exponents to be used by storing the values $(\mathbf{N} \cdot \mathbf{H})^m$ in a 2D texture map indexed by the s-coordinate $\mathbf{N} \cdot \mathbf{H}$ and the t-coordinate $\mathbf{H} \cdot \mathbf{H}$, removing the need to normalize the halfway vector. (See [LENG03] for details.)

6.9 A Physical Reflection Model

The manner in which we have calculated the reflection of light on a surface before this point is computationally cheap and produces visually pleasing results in many cases, but it is not an accurate model of the physically correct distribution of reflected light. Achieving greater realism requires that we use a better model of a surface's microscopic structure and that we apply a little electromagnetic theory.

6.9.1 Bidirectional Reflectance Distribution Functions

In general, our goal is to model the way in which the radiant energy contained in a beam of light is redistributed when it strikes a surface. Some of the energy is absorbed by the surface, some may be transmitted through the surface, and whatever energy remains is reflected. The reflected energy is usually scattered in every direction, but not in a uniform manner. A function that takes the direction $\mathbf{L}$ to a light source and a reflection direction $\mathbf{R}$, and returns the amount of incident light from the direction $\mathbf{L}$ that is reflected in the direction $\mathbf{R}$ is called a *Bidirectional Reflectance Distribution Function* (BRDF).

The precise definition of a BRDF requires that we first introduce some terminology from the field of *radiometry*, the study of the transfer of energy via radiation. The radiant power (energy per unit time) emitted by a light source or received by a surface is called *flux* and is measured in watts (W). The power emitted by a light source or received by a surface per unit area is called *flux density* and is measured in watts per square meter ($W \cdot m^{-2}$). The flux density emitted by a surface is called the surface's *radiosity*, and the flux density incident on a surface is called the *irradiance* of the light.

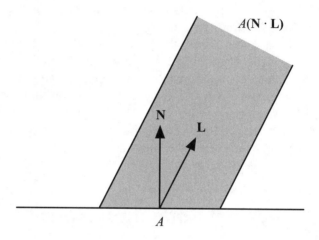

Figure 6.17 The flux density incident on an area *A* of a surface is equal to the flux density of an incident light beam scaled by a factor of $\mathbf{N} \cdot \mathbf{L}$.

Figure 6.17 illustrates a situation in which a light source is emitting P watts of power toward a surface of area A. The power received by the surface is equal to the power emitted by the light source, but the flux densities received and emitted are different because of the Lambertian effect. The area of the beam is equal to $A(\mathbf{N} \cdot \mathbf{L})$, where $\mathbf{N}$ is the unit surface normal and $\mathbf{L}$ is the unit direction-to-light vector. The flux density Φ_E emitted by the light source is thus given by

$$\Phi_E = \frac{P}{A(\mathbf{N} \cdot \mathbf{L})}. \tag{6.41}$$

Since the flux density Φ_I incident on the surface is equal to P/A, we have the relation

$$\Phi_I = \Phi_E(\mathbf{N} \cdot \mathbf{L}). \tag{6.42}$$

The direction from which light illuminates a surface is defined in terms of solid angles, the three-dimensional analog of planar angles. As Figure 6.18 illustrates, the measure of a planar angle θ in radians is given by the arc length l swept out on a circle divided by the radius r of the circle: $\theta = l/r$. Extending this to three dimensions, the measure of a solid angle ω corresponding to an area A on the surface of a sphere of radius r is defined as $\omega = A/r^2$. The unit of solid angle measure is the *steradian*, abbreviated sr. Since the surface area of a sphere of radius r is equal to $4\pi r^2$, there are 4π steradians in the solid angle representing the entire sphere.

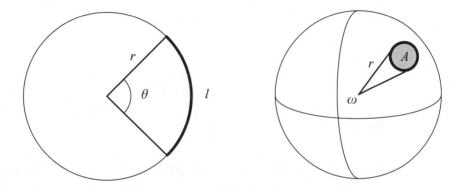

Figure 6.18 Planar angles are equal to the arc length that they sweep out divided by the radius of the circle. Similarly, solid angles are equal to the surface area that subtends them divided by the square of the radius of the sphere.

A differential solid angle $d\omega$ can be written in terms of the differential azimuthal angle $d\theta$ and the differential polar angle $d\varphi$. As shown in Figure 6.19, the circle at the polar angle φ that lies parallel to the x-y plane and passes through the point $\langle r, \theta, \varphi \rangle$ has radius $r\sin\varphi$. Thus, the differential arc length in the azimuthal direction on this circle is equal to $r\sin\varphi\,d\theta$. Multiplying this by the differential arc length $r\,d\varphi$ in the polar direction gives us the following expression for the differential surface area dA.

$$dA = r^2 \sin\varphi\,d\theta\,d\varphi \qquad (6.43)$$

Dividing by r^2 gives us the expression for the corresponding differential solid angle $d\omega$:

$$d\omega = \sin\varphi\,d\theta\,d\varphi. \qquad (6.44)$$

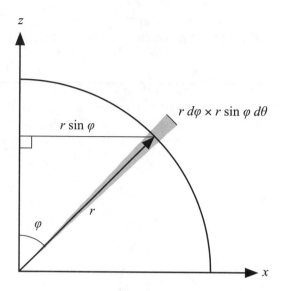

Figure 6.19 The differential surface area at the point $\langle r, \theta, \varphi \rangle$ on a sphere is equal to $r^2 \sin \varphi \, d\theta \, d\varphi$.

Radiance is the term used to describe the flux density of radiation per unit solid angle and is measured in watts per square meter per steradian ($\text{W} \cdot \text{m}^{-2} \cdot \text{sr}^{-1}$). The irradiance (flux density) Φ_I of the light received by a differential area dA on a surface is equal to the following integral of the radiance $C_I(\mathbf{L})$ received by the area, where the direction to light $\mathbf{L}$ ranges over the unit hemisphere Ω above the surface. (The angles θ and φ are the azimuthal and polar angles corresponding to the direction $\mathbf{L}$.)

$$\Phi_I = \int_{\Omega} C_I(\mathbf{L}) \, d\omega$$
$$= \int_0^{2\pi} \int_0^{\pi/2} C_I(\theta, \varphi) \sin \varphi \, d\varphi \, d\theta \tag{6.45}$$

For the same reason that the flux density received by a surface and the flux density emitted by a light source are related by Equation (6.42), the radiance C_I received by a surface and the radiance C_E emitted by a light source are related by

$$C_I = C_E(\mathbf{N} \cdot \mathbf{L}) = C_E \cos \varphi. \tag{6.46}$$

We can therefore rewrite Equation (6.45) as

$$\Phi_I = \int_\Omega C_E(\mathbf{L})(\mathbf{N} \cdot \mathbf{L}) d\omega$$

$$= \int_0^{2\pi} \int_0^{\pi/2} C_E(\theta, \varphi) \cos\varphi \sin\varphi \, d\varphi \, d\theta. \qquad (6.47)$$

The *bidirectional reflectivity* $\rho(\mathbf{V}, \mathbf{L})$ at a point on a surface is a function of the direction to viewer $\mathbf{V}$ and the direction to light $\mathbf{L}$. It is equal to the ratio of the differential reflected radiance dC_R to the differential incident irradiance $d\Phi_I$:

$$\rho(\mathbf{V}, \mathbf{L}) = \frac{dC_R}{d\Phi_I} = \frac{dC_R}{C_E(\mathbf{L})(\mathbf{N} \cdot \mathbf{L}) d\omega}. \qquad (6.48)$$

The function $\rho(\mathbf{V}, \mathbf{L})$ is the BRDF that we use to calculate the radiance of the light reflected in a specific direction from a surface using the equation

$$dC_R = \rho(\mathbf{V}, \mathbf{L}) C_E(\mathbf{L})(\mathbf{N} \cdot \mathbf{L}) d\omega. \qquad (6.49)$$

Directional, point, and spot light sources illuminate a point on a surface from a single direction. Thus, instead of integrating Equation (6.49) to determine the amount of light $C_R(\mathbf{V})$ from n sources reflected in the direction to viewer $\mathbf{V}$, we simply sum over the discrete directions to light $\mathbf{L}_i$:

$$C_R(\mathbf{V}) = \sum_{i=1}^{n} \rho(\mathbf{V}, \mathbf{L}_i) C_i(\mathbf{N} \cdot \mathbf{L}_i). \qquad (6.50)$$

Up to this point in our discussion of BRDFs, we have not said anything about color. In addition to the incoming and outgoing light directions, a BRDF should be a function of the wavelength of the light. Applications requiring accurate reflection models across the entire spectrum typically evaluate a BRDF at several wavelengths and then fit a curve to the resulting numbers. For real-time computer graphics, we find it sufficient to treat our BRDFs as functions that take the RGB color of the incident light and return the RGB color of the reflected light. From this point on, we assume that all operations involving a BRDF take place for each of the red, green, and blue components of light.

The diffuse and specular reflection formulas given in Equations (6.6) and (6.19) can be reproduced by defining the RGB-color BRDF ϱ as

$$\varrho(\mathbf{V}, \mathbf{L}) = \mathcal{D} + \mathcal{S} \frac{(\mathbf{N} \cdot \mathbf{H})^m}{\mathbf{N} \cdot \mathbf{L}}. \qquad (6.51)$$

The term *bidirectional* means that the function ϱ should be invariant when the directions **V** and **L** are exchanged. That is, ϱ should satisfy the reciprocity property

$$\varrho(\mathbf{V},\mathbf{L}) = \varrho(\mathbf{L},\mathbf{V}) \tag{6.52}$$

required by the fact that reversing the direction that light travels along a certain path should not produce different results. The function ϱ given by Equation (6.51) does not satisfy the bidirectional requirement, however, and therefore cannot be physically correct.

Another physical law violated by Equation (6.51) is conservation of energy. Any physically correct BRDF must not reflect more light from a point on a surface than is incident at that point. We can divide the reflected energy given by the BRDF ϱ into diffuse and specular components by writing

$$\varrho(\mathbf{V},\mathbf{L}) = k\mathcal{D} + (1-k)\varrho_s(\mathbf{V},\mathbf{L}), \tag{6.53}$$

where $\mathcal{D}$ is the surface's diffuse reflection color and k represents the fraction of the incident light that is diffusely reflected. The remaining fraction $1-k$ of the incident light is either absorbed or makes up a specular reflection. These effects are modeled by the function ϱ_s, which is described in the next section.

6.9.2 Cook-Torrance Illumination

The Cook-Torrance illumination model [COOK82] produces a realistic specular reflection by treating a surface as being composed of planar microscopic facets called *microfacets*. Each microfacet is treated as a perfect reflector that obeys the reflective laws of electromagnetic theory. The roughness of a surface is characterized by the slopes of the microfacets. As shown in Figure 6.20, a rough surface is composed of microfacets having greatly varying slopes, whereas the microfacets for a relatively smooth surface have only small slopes.

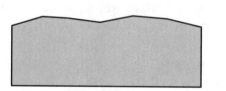 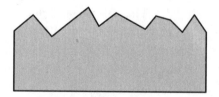

Figure 6.20 Surface roughness is characterized by how much the slopes of the microfacets vary.

Cook and Torrance use the following formula for the specular component ϱ_s of the BRDF given in Equation (6.53).

$$\varrho_s(\mathbf{V},\mathbf{L}) = \mathcal{F}(\mathbf{V},\mathbf{L}) \frac{D(\mathbf{V},\mathbf{L})G(\mathbf{V},\mathbf{L})}{\pi(\mathbf{N}\cdot\mathbf{V})(\mathbf{N}\cdot\mathbf{L})} \tag{6.54}$$

$\mathcal{F}$ is the Fresnel factor, which describes the amount and color of light reflected as a function of the angle of incidence; D is the microfacet distribution function, which returns the fraction of microfacets oriented in a given direction; and G is the geometrical attenuation factor, which accounts for self-shadowing of the microfacets. Since the microfacets are perfect reflectors, only those microfacets whose normal vectors point in the direction of the halfway vector $\mathbf{H}$ contribute to the specular reflection.

The π appearing in the denominator of Equation (6.54) is a normalization factor that accounts for the fact that the incident flux density Φ_I at a surface for a constant emitted radiance C_E is given by

$$\Phi_I = C_E \int_{\Omega}(\mathbf{N}\cdot\mathbf{L})\,d\omega = \int_0^{\pi}\int_0^{\pi/2}\cos\varphi\sin\varphi\,d\varphi\,d\theta = \pi C_E. \tag{6.55}$$

6.9.3 The Fresnel Factor

The interaction of an electromagnetic wave and a surface results in a reflected wave and a transmitted wave. The energy contained in the reflected wave is equal to the energy contained in the incident wave minus the energy contained in the transmitted wave (which is quickly absorbed by opaque materials). The electric field of the incident light can be decomposed into components that are polarized with respect to the plane containing the surface normal $\mathbf{N}$ and the direction to light $\mathbf{L}$. The component parallel to this plane is called p-polarized, and the component perpendicular to this plane is called s-polarized. The Fresnel factors giving, for a single wavelength, the fractions F_p and F_s of the amount of light reflected for these components are

$$F_p = \frac{\tan^2(\theta_1 - \theta_2)}{\tan^2(\theta_1 + \theta_2)} \tag{6.56}$$

and

$$F_s = \frac{\sin^2(\theta_1 - \theta_2)}{\sin^2(\theta_1 + \theta_2)}, \tag{6.57}$$

where θ_1 is the angle of incidence and θ_2 is the wavelength-dependent angle of transmittance. For unpolarized light, we simply average these to obtain the Fresnel factor F_λ corresponding to the wavelength λ:

$$F_\lambda = \frac{1}{2}\left[\frac{\tan^2(\theta_1 - \theta_2)}{\tan^2(\theta_1 + \theta_2)} + \frac{\sin^2(\theta_1 - \theta_2)}{\sin^2(\theta_1 + \theta_2)}\right]. \tag{6.58}$$

The angle of incidence θ_1 is equal to $\cos^{-1}(\mathbf{L} \cdot \mathbf{H})$ since every microfacet contributing to the specular reflection is oriented such that its normal vector points along the halfway vector $\mathbf{H}$. It turns out that we can write the Fresnel factor in terms of $\mathbf{L} \cdot \mathbf{H}$ and the indexes of refraction η_1 and η_2 of the two materials by applying some trigonometric identities and using Snell's law. Factoring the sine function out of Equation (6.58) gives us

$$F_\lambda = \frac{1}{2}\frac{\sin^2(\theta_1 - \theta_2)}{\sin^2(\theta_1 + \theta_2)}\left[\frac{\cos^2(\theta_1 + \theta_2)}{\cos^2(\theta_1 - \theta_2)} + 1\right]. \tag{6.59}$$

Applying the trigonometric identities for sums and differences of angles to the sine factors yields

$$\frac{\sin(\theta_1 - \theta_2)}{\sin(\theta_1 + \theta_2)} = \frac{\sin\theta_1 \cos\theta_2 - \cos\theta_1 \sin\theta_2}{\sin\theta_1 \cos\theta_2 + \cos\theta_1 \sin\theta_2}$$

$$= \frac{\eta_\lambda \cos\theta_2 - \cos\theta_1}{\eta_\lambda \cos\theta_2 + \cos\theta_1}, \tag{6.60}$$

where Snell's law has been used to obtain

$$\eta_\lambda = \frac{\eta_2}{\eta_1} = \frac{\sin\theta_1}{\sin\theta_2}. \tag{6.61}$$

We can express $\cos\theta_2$ in terms of $\cos\theta_1$ and η by writing Snell's law in the form

$$\eta_1\sqrt{1 - \cos^2\theta_1} = \eta_2\sqrt{1 - \cos^2\theta_2} \tag{6.62}$$

and solving for $\cos\theta_2$:

$$\cos\theta_2 = \sqrt{1 - \frac{1}{\eta_\lambda^2}\left(1 - \cos^2\theta_1\right)}. \tag{6.63}$$

Defining the variable g as

$$g = \eta_\lambda \cos\theta_2 = \sqrt{\eta_\lambda^2 - 1 + (\mathbf{L}\cdot\mathbf{H})^2} \qquad (6.64)$$

lets us express the quotient of the sine functions as

$$\frac{\sin(\theta_1 - \theta_2)}{\sin(\theta_1 + \theta_2)} = \frac{g - \mathbf{L}\cdot\mathbf{H}}{g + \mathbf{L}\cdot\mathbf{H}}. \qquad (6.65)$$

A similar procedure allows us to express the cosine factors in terms of g and $\mathbf{L}\cdot\mathbf{H}$. We begin by applying angle sum and difference identities:

$$\begin{aligned}
\frac{\cos(\theta_1 + \theta_2)}{\cos(\theta_1 - \theta_2)} &= \frac{\cos\theta_1\cos\theta_2 - \sin\theta_1\sin\theta_2}{\cos\theta_1\cos\theta_2 + \sin\theta_1\sin\theta_2} \\
&= \frac{\cos\theta_1\cos\theta_2 - \eta_\lambda\sin^2\theta_2}{\cos\theta_1\cos\theta_2 + \eta_\lambda\sin^2\theta_2}.
\end{aligned} \qquad (6.66)$$

Again using the variable g defined in Equation (6.64), we can write this as

$$\begin{aligned}
\frac{\cos(\theta_1 + \theta_2)}{\cos(\theta_1 - \theta_2)} &= \frac{g\cos\theta_1 - \eta_\lambda^2(1 - \cos^2\theta_2)}{g\cos\theta_1 + \eta_\lambda^2(1 - \cos^2\theta_2)} \\
&= \frac{g\cos\theta_1 - \eta_\lambda^2 + g^2}{g\cos\theta_1 + \eta_\lambda^2 - g^2} \\
&= \frac{(\mathbf{L}\cdot\mathbf{H})(g + \mathbf{L}\cdot\mathbf{H}) - 1}{(\mathbf{L}\cdot\mathbf{H})(g - \mathbf{L}\cdot\mathbf{H}) + 1}.
\end{aligned} \qquad (6.67)$$

The Fresnel factor can now be entirely expressed in terms of $\mathbf{L}\cdot\mathbf{H}$ and η_λ as follows.

$$F_\lambda(\mathbf{V},\mathbf{L}) = \frac{1}{2}\frac{(g - \mathbf{L}\cdot\mathbf{H})^2}{(g + \mathbf{L}\cdot\mathbf{H})^2}\left(\frac{[(\mathbf{L}\cdot\mathbf{H})(g + \mathbf{L}\cdot\mathbf{H}) - 1]^2}{[(\mathbf{L}\cdot\mathbf{H})(g - \mathbf{L}\cdot\mathbf{H}) + 1]^2} + 1\right) \qquad (6.68)$$

The RGB color Fresnel factor $\mathcal{F}(\mathbf{V},\mathbf{L})$ simply consists of the function $F_\lambda(\mathbf{V},\mathbf{L})$ evaluated at red, green, and blue wavelengths.

We can make a couple of observations about the behavior of the function F_λ. First, as the angle of incidence approaches 90 degrees, the value of $\mathbf{L}\cdot\mathbf{H}$ approaches 0, and thus the value of F_λ approaches 1. This means that at grazing angles, all the incident light is reflected, leaving none to be absorbed by the surface. Second, for normal incidence in which the incident angle is 0, the value of $\mathbf{L}\cdot\mathbf{H}$ is 1, and F_λ reduces to

$$(F_\lambda)_{\mathbf{L}=\mathbf{H}} = \left(\frac{\eta_\lambda - 1}{\eta_\lambda + 1}\right)^2. \tag{6.69}$$

This gives us a convenient way of deriving an approximate value for η_λ if all that is known about a material is the specular color S reflected at normal incidence. Solving Equation (6.69) for η_λ yields

$$\eta_\lambda = \frac{1 + \sqrt{(F_\lambda)_{\mathbf{L}=\mathbf{H}}}}{1 - \sqrt{(F_\lambda)_{\mathbf{L}=\mathbf{H}}}}. \tag{6.70}$$

Once a value of η_λ has been calculated with this equation by setting the value of $(F_\lambda)_{\mathbf{L}=\mathbf{H}}$ at red, green, and blue wavelengths equal to the red, green, and blue components of S, it can be used in Equation (6.68) to calculate reflectance for any other angle of incidence.

6.9.4 The Microfacet Distribution Function

Given a halfway vector $\mathbf{H}$, the microfacet distribution function returns the fraction of microfacets whose normal vectors point along the direction $\mathbf{H}$. For rough surfaces, the Beckmann distribution function [BECK63] given by

$$D_m(\mathbf{V},\mathbf{L}) = \frac{1}{4m^2(\mathbf{N}\cdot\mathbf{H})^4}\exp\left(\frac{(\mathbf{N}\cdot\mathbf{H})^2 - 1}{m^2(\mathbf{N}\cdot\mathbf{H})^2}\right) \tag{6.71}$$

describes the distribution of microfacet orientations in terms of the root mean square slope m. Large values of m correspond to rough surfaces and thus produce a wide distribution of microfacet orientations. As shown in Figure 6.21, smaller values of m correspond to smoother surfaces and produce relatively narrow distributions, which result in a sharper specularity.

The function given by Equation (6.71) is *isotropic*, meaning that it is invariant under a rotation about the normal vector $\mathbf{N}$. As long as the angle between the direction to viewer $\mathbf{V}$ and direction to light $\mathbf{L}$ remains constant, and the angle between each of these vectors and the normal vector remains constant, the distribution of microfacets also remains constant. Many surfaces, however, possess different degrees of roughness in different directions. These surfaces are called *anisotropic* reflectors and include materials such as brushed metal, hair, and certain fabrics.

(a)

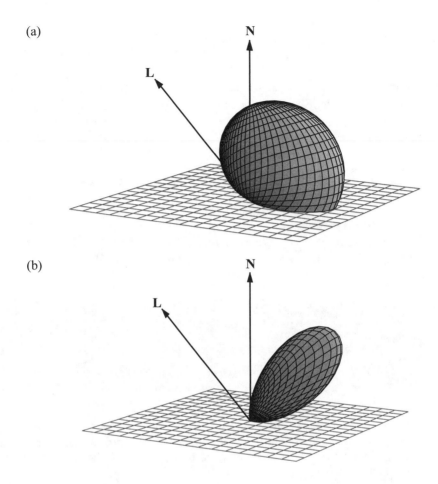

(b)

Figure 6.21 Microfacet distributions given by Equation (6.71) modeling (a) a rough surface using $m = 0.6$ and (b) a relatively smooth surface using $m = 0.25$.

We can modify the microfacet distribution function to account for anisotropic surface roughness by changing Equation (6.71) to

$$D_{\mathbf{m}}(\mathbf{V},\mathbf{L}) = \frac{1}{4m_x m_y (\mathbf{N} \cdot \mathbf{H})^4} \exp\left[\left(\frac{(\mathbf{T} \cdot \mathbf{P})^2}{m_x^2} + \frac{1-(\mathbf{T} \cdot \mathbf{P})^2}{m_y^2}\right)\frac{(\mathbf{N} \cdot \mathbf{H})^2 - 1}{(\mathbf{N} \cdot \mathbf{H})^2}\right], \quad (6.72)$$

where $\mathbf{m}$ is a two-dimensional roughness vector, $\mathbf{T}$ is the tangent to the surface aligned to the direction in which the roughness is m_x, and $\mathbf{P}$ is the normalized projection of the halfway vector $\mathbf{H}$ onto the tangent plane:

$$\mathbf{P} = \frac{\mathbf{H} - (\mathbf{N} \cdot \mathbf{H})\mathbf{N}}{\|\mathbf{H} - (\mathbf{N} \cdot \mathbf{H})\mathbf{N}\|}. \tag{6.73}$$

Figure 6.22 shows a disk rendered with both isotropic and anisotropic surface roughness values. Some surfaces exhibit roughness at multiple scales. This can be accounted for by calculating a weighted average of microfacet distribution functions

$$D(\mathbf{V}, \mathbf{L}) = \sum_{i=1}^{n} w_i D_{\mathbf{m}_i}(\mathbf{V}, \mathbf{L}), \tag{6.74}$$

where multiple roughness values $\mathbf{m}_i$ are used and the weights w_i sum to unity. Figure 6.23 shows two objects rendered with different values of $\mathbf{m}$ and another object rendered using a weighted sum of those same values.

Figure 6.22   A disk rendered using the anisotropic distribution function given by Equation (6.72). For each image $m_y = 0.1$. From left to right the values of m_x are 0.1 (isotropic), 0.12, 0.15, and 0.2. The tangent vectors are aligned to concentric rings around the center of the disk—they are perpendicular to the radial direction at every point on the surface.

6.9.5 The Geometrical Attenuation Factor

Some of the light incident on a single microfacet may be blocked by adjacent microfacets before it reaches the surface or after it has been reflected. This blocking results in a slight darkening of the specular reflection and is accounted for by the geometrical attenuation factor. Blocked light is essentially scattered in random directions and ultimately contributes to the surface's diffuse reflection.

Figure 6.23 Copper vases rendered with isotropic microfacet distributions. The first two images use a single roughness value of $m_1 = 0.1$ (left) and $m_2 = 0.25$ (center). The rightmost image combines these using the weights $w_1 = 0.4$ and $w_2 = 0.6$.

We can derive an estimate of how much light is blocked due to surface roughness by assuming that microfacets always form V-shaped grooves. Figure 6.24(a) illustrates a situation in which light reflected by a microfacet is partially blocked by an adjacent microfacet. In this case, light is blocked after being reflected. Reversing the direction in which the light travels exhibits the case in which light is blocked before reaching the microfacet, as shown in Figure 6.24(b).

The application of a little trigonometry leads us to a formula giving the fraction of light reflected by a microfacet that still reaches the viewer after being partially blocked by an adjacent microfacet. As shown in Figure 6.25, we would like to determine the portion x of the width w of a microfacet that is visible to the viewer. We first observe that

$$w = \frac{1}{\sin \alpha}, \tag{6.75}$$

and that by the law of sines (see Appendix B, Section B.6),

$$x = \frac{2 \sin \gamma}{\sin (\beta + \pi/2)}. \tag{6.76}$$

We can express each of the sine functions in Equations (6.75) and (6.76) as cosine functions that have been shifted by $\pi/2$ radians by writing

$$\sin \alpha = \cos (\pi/2 - \alpha) = \mathbf{N} \cdot \mathbf{H}$$
$$\sin (\beta + \pi/2) = \cos \beta = \mathbf{V} \cdot \mathbf{H}$$
$$\sin \gamma = \cos (\pi/2 - \gamma) = \mathbf{N} \cdot \mathbf{V}. \tag{6.77}$$

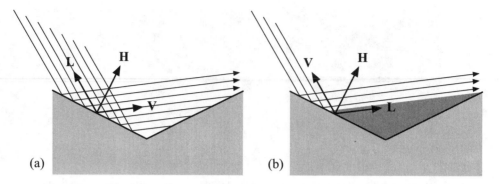

Figure 6.24 (a) Light reflected by the left microfacet is partially blocked by the right microfacet. (b) Light is blocked by the right microfacet before reaching the left microfacet.

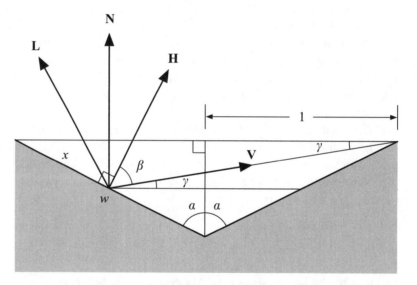

Figure 6.25 The fraction of light reflected from the left microfacet that reaches the viewer is equal to x/w. The halfway vector **H** is normal to the microfacet surface since only microfacets possessing that orientation contribute to the specular reflection.

Using the dot products corresponding to each of the cosine functions lets us express the fraction of light G_1 reaching the viewer as

$$G_1 = \frac{x}{w} = \frac{2(\mathbf{N} \cdot \mathbf{H})(\mathbf{N} \cdot \mathbf{V})}{\mathbf{V} \cdot \mathbf{H}}. \tag{6.78}$$

When light is blocked before reaching a microfacet, we can calculate the fraction G_2 that still reaches the viewer by simply exchanging the vectors $\mathbf{V}$ and $\mathbf{L}$ in Figure 6.25 to obtain

$$G_2 = \frac{x}{w} = \frac{2(\mathbf{N} \cdot \mathbf{H})(\mathbf{N} \cdot \mathbf{L})}{\mathbf{L} \cdot \mathbf{H}}. \tag{6.79}$$

The three possible cases pertaining to light reflected by a microfacet are that the light is completely unobstructed (the fraction of light reaching the viewer is one), that some of the reflected light is blocked, and that some of the incident light is blocked. We account for all three cases by defining the geometrical attenuation factor as the minimum fraction of light that reaches the viewer:

$$\begin{aligned} G(\mathbf{V}, \mathbf{L}) &= \min\left\{1, G_1, G_2\right\} \\ &= \min\left\{1, \frac{2(\mathbf{N} \cdot \mathbf{H})(\mathbf{N} \cdot \mathbf{V})}{\mathbf{L} \cdot \mathbf{H}}, \frac{2(\mathbf{N} \cdot \mathbf{H})(\mathbf{N} \cdot \mathbf{L})}{\mathbf{L} \cdot \mathbf{H}}\right\}. \end{aligned} \tag{6.80}$$

We have changed the denominator of G_1 to $\mathbf{L} \cdot \mathbf{H}$. This is allowable because, by the definition of the halfway vector, the angle between $\mathbf{L}$ and $\mathbf{H}$ is equal to the angle between $\mathbf{V}$ and $\mathbf{H}$, and thus $\mathbf{V} \cdot \mathbf{H} = \mathbf{L} \cdot \mathbf{H}$.

6.9.6 Implementation

Ray tracing applications can directly apply Equation (6.54) in its entirety whenever a ray intersects a surface. For real-time applications where greater efficiency is required, we need to sacrifice a little precision for better performance. For sufficiently tessellated surfaces, evaluating Equation (6.54) at each vertex might produce good results, but architectural geometry in games generally does not possess such tessellation. Modern GPUs can evaluate Equation (6.54) at every pixel with a fragment program. We can avoid many of the microfacet shading calculations by using texture maps to essentially store lookup tables that are indexed by quantities such as $\mathbf{N} \cdot \mathbf{H}$ and $\mathbf{L} \cdot \mathbf{H}$.

Adding a texture map factor $\mathcal{T}$ and a gloss map factor $\mathcal{G}$ to Equation (6.53) and substituting the BRDF ϱ into Equation (6.50) gives us the following formula for the color of light $\mathcal{K}$ reflected toward the viewer by a surface illuminated by a single light source, where $\mathcal{C}$ is the color of the light and k is the fraction of light that is reflected diffusely.

$$\mathcal{K} = \mathcal{C}(\mathbf{N} \cdot \mathbf{L})\left[k\mathcal{D}\mathcal{T} + (1-k)\mathcal{G}\varrho_s(\mathbf{V}, \mathbf{L})\right] \tag{6.81}$$

Substituting Equation (6.54) for $\varrho_s(\mathbf{V}, \mathbf{L})$ gives us

$$\mathcal{K} = k\mathcal{C}\mathcal{D}\mathcal{T}(\mathbf{N}\cdot\mathbf{L}) + (1-k)\mathcal{C}\mathcal{G}\mathcal{F}(\mathbf{V},\mathbf{L})\frac{D_m(\mathbf{V},\mathbf{L})G(\mathbf{V},\mathbf{L})}{\pi(\mathbf{N}\cdot\mathbf{V})}. \qquad (6.82)$$

The only quantity on which the Fresnel factor $\mathcal{F}(\mathbf{V},\mathbf{L})$ depends is $\mathbf{L}\cdot\mathbf{H}$, and the only quantity on which the isotropic microfacet distribution function $D_m(\mathbf{V},\mathbf{L})$ depends is $\mathbf{N}\cdot\mathbf{H}$. Given a normal-incidence specular reflection color $\mathcal{S}$ and a microfacet root mean square slope m, we can construct a texture map whose s and t coordinates correspond to $\mathbf{N}\cdot\mathbf{H}$ and $\mathbf{L}\cdot\mathbf{H}$, respectively, and whose color values represent the product $\mathcal{F}(\mathbf{V},\mathbf{L})D_m(\mathbf{V},\mathbf{L})/\pi$. An example of such a texture map is shown in Figure 6.26.

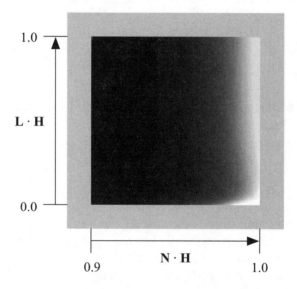

Figure 6.26 A texture map representing the product $\mathcal{F}(\mathbf{V},\mathbf{L})D_m(\mathbf{V},\mathbf{L})/\pi$. The s-coordinate corresponds to the quantity $10(\mathbf{N}\cdot\mathbf{H})-9$, and the t-coordinate corresponds to the quantity $\mathbf{L}\cdot\mathbf{H}$. This image was generated using the normal-incidence specular reflection color $\mathcal{S} = (0.8, 0.6, 0.1)$ and the microfacet root mean square slope $m = 0.2$.

For small values of m, the value of the microfacet distribution function D_m is significant only when $\mathbf{N}\cdot\mathbf{H}$ is near 1. To maximize the resolution of the useful information in the texture containing the products $\mathcal{F}(\mathbf{V},\mathbf{L})D_m(\mathbf{V},\mathbf{L})/\pi$, we map the range $[0,1]$ of s texture coordinates to the range $[x,1]$, where x is the value of $\mathbf{N}\cdot\mathbf{H}$ for which $D_m(\mathbf{V},\mathbf{L})/\pi = \varepsilon$ for some small threshold ε. We cannot find the value of x analytically, but we can apply Newton's method (see Section 5.1.4) to the function

$$f(x) = \frac{1}{4\pi m^2 x^4} \exp\left(\frac{x^2 - 1}{m^2 x^2}\right) - \varepsilon. \tag{6.83}$$

The refinement formula used to find the value of x for which $f(x) = 0$ is given by

$$\begin{aligned} x_{i+1} &= x_i - \frac{f(x_i)}{f'(x_i)} \\ &= x_i - \frac{m^2 x_i^3}{2 - 4m^2 x_i^2}\left(1 - 4\pi\varepsilon m^2 x_i^4 e^{\left(1 - x_i^2\right)/m^2 x_i^2}\right). \end{aligned} \tag{6.84}$$

Using an initial value of $x_0 = 1$ may require several iterations of this refinement formula since the slope of the function $f(x)$ may be steep at $x = 1$. Once the value of x for which $f(x) = 0$ is known, we map values of $\mathbf{N} \cdot \mathbf{H}$ from the range $[x, 1]$ to the range $[0, 1]$ using the formula

$$s = \frac{\mathbf{N} \cdot \mathbf{H} - x}{1 - x}. \tag{6.85}$$

It is convenient for us to perform the microfacet lighting calculations in tangent space since in this setting $\mathbf{N} = \langle 0, 0, 1 \rangle$ and, for calculations pertaining to anisotropic microfacet distributions, $\mathbf{T} = \langle 1, 0, 0 \rangle$. The vertex program shown in Listing 6.2 demonstrates how the tangent-space view direction $\mathbf{V}$ and direction to light $\mathbf{L}$ can be calculated at each vertex for a point light source. These vectors are then interpolated across the face of a triangle as it is rasterized and used to calculate the halfway vector $\mathbf{H}$ for each fragment.

Listing 6.2 This vertex program transforms the view direction $\mathbf{V}$ and the direction to light $\mathbf{L}$ into tangent space, and stores the results in texture coordinate sets 1 and 2. The interpolated values of $\mathbf{V}$ and $\mathbf{L}$ are then used by a fragment program to perform microfacet shading. Program environment parameter 0 contains the object-space camera position, and program environment parameter 1 contains the object-space light position. The orthonormalized tangents are read from vertex attribute array 0, and the bitangents are calculated using Equation (6.40).

```
!!ARBvp1.0

ATTRIB    normal  = vertex.normal;
ATTRIB    tangent = vertex.attrib[0];

PARAM     mvp[4]  = {state.matrix.mvp};
PARAM     camera  = program.env[0];
```

```
PARAM       light    = program.env[1];

TEMP        bitangent, vdir, ldir, temp;

# Transform vertex
DP4         result.position.x, mvp[0], vertex.position;
DP4         result.position.y, mvp[1], vertex.position;
DP4         result.position.z, mvp[2], vertex.position;
DP4         result.position.w, mvp[3], vertex.position;

# B = (N x T) * T.w
XPD         bitangent, normal, tangent;
MUL         bitangent, bitangent, tangent.w;

# Calculate normalized V and L
ADD         vdir, camera, -vertex.position;
ADD         ldir, light, -vertex.position;
DP3         temp.x, vdir, vdir;
DP3         temp.y, ldir, ldir;
RSQ         temp.x, temp.x;
RSQ         temp.y, temp.y;
MUL         vdir, vdir, temp.x;
MUL         ldir, ldir, temp.y;

# Transform into tangent space
DP3         result.texcoord[1].x, tangent, vdir;
DP3         result.texcoord[1].y, bitangent, vdir;
DP3         result.texcoord[1].z, normal, vdir;
DP3         result.texcoord[2].x, tangent, ldir;
DP3         result.texcoord[2].y, bitangent, ldir;
DP3         result.texcoord[2].z, normal, ldir;
END
```

In tangent space, $\mathbf{N} \cdot \mathbf{L} = L_z$, $\mathbf{N} \cdot \mathbf{V} = V_z$, and $\mathbf{N} \cdot \mathbf{H} = H_z$. The specular component of Equation (6.82) becomes

$$\mathcal{K}_{\text{specular}} = (1-k)\mathcal{C}\mathcal{G}\mathcal{S}(H_z, \mathbf{L} \cdot \mathbf{H})\frac{G(\mathbf{V},\mathbf{L})}{V_z}, \qquad (6.86)$$

where $\mathcal{S}(H_z, \mathbf{L} \cdot \mathbf{H})$ represents the product $\mathcal{F}(\mathbf{V},\mathbf{L})D_m(\mathbf{V},\mathbf{L})/\pi$ that is looked up in a texture map. The fragment program shown in Listing 6.3 calculates the halfway vector $\mathbf{H}$, performs a texture fetch to obtain the value of $\mathcal{S}(H_z, \mathbf{L} \cdot \mathbf{H})$, and multiplies it by the precomputed value of $(1-k)\mathcal{C}$. The geometrical attenuation factor $G(\mathbf{V}, \mathbf{L})$ sometimes makes a subtle contribution and may be omitted. When present, its value is calculated in tangent space using the formula

$$G(\mathbf{V}, \mathbf{L}) = \frac{2H_z}{\mathbf{L} \cdot \mathbf{H}} \min(V_z, L_z) \tag{6.87}$$

and using the saturation operation to clamp the result to the range $[0,1]$.

Listing 6.3 This fragment program performs the calculations necessary for isotropic microfacet shading. Texture coordinate set 1 contains the interpolated view direction **V**, and texture coordinate set 2 contains the interpolated light direction **L** generated by the vertex program in Listing 6.2. Program local parameter 0 contains the product $kC\mathcal{D}$, program local parameter 1 contains the product $(1-k)\mathcal{C}$, and program local parameter 2 contains the scale and bias used to map the values of $\mathbf{N} \cdot \mathbf{H}$ to the range $[0,1]$. The 2D texture map containing the product $\mathcal{F}(\mathbf{V}, \mathbf{L}) D_m(\mathbf{V}, \mathbf{L}) / \pi$ is bound to texture image unit 0.

```
!!ARBfp1.0

ATTRIB    view  = fragment.texcoord[1];
ATTRIB    light = fragment.texcoord[2];

PARAM     diffuse  = program.local[0];
PARAM     specular = program.local[1];
PARAM     range    = program.local[2];

TEMP      colr, vdir, ldir, hdir, geom, txtr, temp;

# Normalize V and L
DP3       temp.x, view, view;
DP3       temp.y, light, light;
RSQ       temp.x, temp.x;
RSQ       temp.y, temp.y;
MUL       vdir, view, temp.x;
MUL       ldir, light, temp.y;

# Calculate H
ADD       hdir, vdir, ldir;
DP3       temp, hdir, hdir;
RSQ       temp, temp.x;
MUL       hdir, hdir, temp;

# Scale and bias N*H
MAD       txtr.x, hdir.z, range.x, range.y;
```

```
# Calculate L*H
DP3        txtr.y, ldir, hdir;

# Look up product F(V,L)D(V,L)/pi
TEX        colr, txtr, texture[0], 2D;

# Divide by N*V
RCP        temp, vdir.z;
MUL        colr, colr, temp;

# Calculate geometrical attenuation
# (May be omitted)
RCP        temp, txtr.y;
MIN        geom, vdir.z, ldir.z;
ADD        geom, geom, geom;
MUL        geom, geom, hdir.z;
MUL_SAT    geom, geom, temp;
MUL        colr, colr, geom;

# Multiply specular by (1-k)C and add kCD(N*L)
MUL        temp, diffuse, ldir.z;
MAD        result.color, colr, specular, temp;
END
```

For anisotropic microfacet distributions, we can use a 3D texture map whose r-coordinate corresponds to the quantity $(\mathbf{T}\cdot\mathbf{P})^2$, where $\mathbf{P}$ is the projection of the halfway vector $\mathbf{H}$ onto the tangent plane. In tangent space, Equation (6.73) becomes

$$\mathbf{P} = \frac{\langle H_x, H_y, 0 \rangle}{\sqrt{H_x^2 + H_y^2}}, \tag{6.88}$$

and thus

$$(\mathbf{T}\cdot\mathbf{P})^2 = \frac{H_x^2}{H_x^2 + H_y^2}. \tag{6.89}$$

The 3D texture map contains the product $\mathcal{F}(\mathbf{V},\mathbf{L})D_m(\mathbf{V},\mathbf{L})/\pi$, where $D_m(\mathbf{V},\mathbf{L})$ is the anisotropic distribution function given by Equation (6.72). The fragment program shown in Listing 6.4 implements Equation (6.89) to perform anisotropic microfacet shading.

Listing 6.4 This fragment program performs the calculations necessary for aniso-tropic microfacet shading. Texture coordinate sets and program parameters are used in the same way as in Listing 6.3. The 3D texture map containing the product $\mathcal{F}(\mathbf{V},\mathbf{L})D_m(\mathbf{V},\mathbf{L})/\pi$ is bound to texture image unit 0.

```
!!ARBfp1.0

ATTRIB    view  = fragment.texcoord[1];
ATTRIB    light = fragment.texcoord[2];

PARAM     diffuse  = program.local[0];
PARAM     specular = program.local[1];
PARAM     range    = program.local[2];

TEMP      colr, vdir, ldir, hdir, geom, txtr, temp;

# Normalize V and L
DP3       temp.x, view, view;
DP3       temp.y, light, light;
RSQ       temp.x, temp.x;
RSQ       temp.y, temp.y;
MUL       vdir, view, temp.x;
MUL       ldir, light, temp.y;

# Calculate H
ADD       hdir, vdir, ldir;
DP3       temp, hdir, hdir;
RSQ       temp, temp.x;
MUL       hdir, hdir, temp;

# Scale and bias N*H
MAD       txtr.x, hdir.z, range.x, range.y;

# Calculate L*H
DP3       txtr.y, ldir, hdir;

# Calculate (T*P)^2 = Hx^2 / (Hx^2 + Hy^2)
MUL       temp.x, hdir.x, hdir.x;
MAD       temp.z, hdir.y, hdir.y, temp.x;
RCP       temp.z, temp.z;
MUL       txtr.z, temp.x, temp.z;

# Look up product F(V,L)D(V,L)/pi
TEX       colr, txtr, texture[0], 3D;
```

```
# Divide by N*V
RCP        temp, vdir.z;
MUL        colr, colr, temp;

# Calculate geometrical attenuation
# (May be omitted)
RCP        temp, txtr.y;
MIN        geom, vdir.z, ldir.z;
ADD        geom, geom, geom;
MUL        geom, geom, hdir.z;
MUL_SAT    geom, geom, temp;
MUL        colr, colr, geom;

# Multiply specular by (1-k)C and add kCD(N*L)
MUL        temp, diffuse, ldir.z;
MAD        result.color, colr, specular, temp;
END
```

Chapter 6 Summary

Point Light Source Attenuation

The intensity C of a point light source at a distance d from its position is given by

$$C = \frac{1}{k_c + k_l d + k_q d^2} C_0,$$

where C_0 is the color of the light, and the constants k_c, k_l, and k_q control the attenuation.

Spot Light Source Attenuation

The intensity C of a spot light source at a point $\mathbf{Q}$ lying at a distance d from the light's position is given by

$$C = \frac{\max\{-\mathbf{R} \cdot \mathbf{L}, 0\}^p}{k_c + k_l d + k_q d^2} C_0,$$

where C_0 is the color of the light; k_c, k_l, and k_q are the attenuation constants; $\mathbf{R}$ is the direction in which the spot light is pointing; $\mathbf{L}$ is the unit vector pointing from

$\mathbf{Q}$ to the light position; and the exponent p controls the rate at which the intensity falls off as the angle between $\mathbf{R}$ and $-\mathbf{L}$ increases.

Ambient and Diffuse Lighting

The ambient and diffuse contribution to the illumination color calculated at a point $\mathbf{Q}$ on a surface is given by the expression

$$\mathcal{K}_{\text{diffuse}} = \mathcal{D}\mathcal{A} + \mathcal{D}\sum_{i=1}^{n} \mathcal{C}_i \max\{\mathbf{N}\cdot\mathbf{L}_i, 0\},$$

where $\mathcal{D}$ is the surface's diffuse reflection color, $\mathbf{N}$ is the normal vector to the surface, $\mathbf{L}_i$ is the unit vector pointing from $\mathbf{Q}$ toward the i-th light, $\mathcal{C}_i$ is the intensity of the i-th light at the point $\mathbf{Q}$, and $\mathcal{A}$ represents the ambient light color.

Specular Lighting

The specular contribution to the illumination color calculated at a point $\mathbf{Q}$ on a surface is given by the expression

$$\mathcal{K}_{\text{specular}} = \mathcal{S}\sum_{i=1}^{n} \mathcal{C}_i \max\{\mathbf{N}\cdot\mathbf{H}_i, 0\}^m (\mathbf{N}\cdot\mathbf{L}_i > 0),$$

where $\mathcal{S}$ is the surface's specular reflection color; $\mathbf{H}_i$ is the unit halfway vector at the point $\mathbf{Q}$, which lies halfway between the direction to light $\mathbf{L}_i$ and the direction to the viewer; and m controls the sharpness of the specularity. The expression $(\mathbf{N}\cdot\mathbf{L}_i > 0)$ evaluates to 1 or 0, depending on whether the surface is facing the light.

Total Illumination Equation

The reflected color $\mathcal{K}$ calculated at a point $\mathbf{Q}$ on a surface illuminated by n lights is given by

$$\mathcal{K} = \mathcal{E}\mathcal{M} + \mathcal{D}\mathcal{T}\mathcal{A} + \sum_{i=1}^{n} \mathcal{C}_i \left[\mathcal{D}\mathcal{T}(\mathbf{N}\cdot\mathbf{L}_i) + \mathcal{S}\mathcal{G}(\mathbf{N}\cdot\mathbf{H}_i)^m (\mathbf{N}\cdot\mathbf{L}_i > 0)\right],$$

where the dot products $\mathbf{N}\cdot\mathbf{L}_i$ and $\mathbf{N}\cdot\mathbf{H}_i$ are clamped to zero, and the quantities involved are defined as follows.

$\mathcal{D}$ = diffuse reflection color
$\mathcal{S}$ = specular reflection color
m = specular exponent
$\mathcal{A}$ = ambient light color

$\mathcal{E}$ = emission color
$\mathcal{T}$ = texture map color
$\mathcal{G}$ = gloss map color
$\mathcal{M}$ = emission map color
$\mathcal{C}_i$ = color of i-th light at $\mathbf{Q}$
$\mathbf{L}_i$ = direction vector to i-th light
$\mathbf{H}_i$ = halfway vector for i-th light
$\mathbf{N}$ = normal vector

Bump Mapping

The tangent $\mathbf{T}$ and bitangent $\mathbf{B}$ for a triangle whose vertices lie at the points $\mathbf{P}_0$, $\mathbf{P}_1$, and $\mathbf{P}_2$ are calculated using the formula

$$
\begin{bmatrix} T_x & T_y & T_z \\ B_x & B_y & B_z \end{bmatrix} = \frac{1}{s_1 t_2 - s_2 t_1} \begin{bmatrix} t_2 & -t_1 \\ -s_2 & s_1 \end{bmatrix} \begin{bmatrix} (\mathbf{Q}_1)_x & (\mathbf{Q}_1)_y & (\mathbf{Q}_1)_z \\ (\mathbf{Q}_2)_x & (\mathbf{Q}_2)_y & (\mathbf{Q}_2)_z \end{bmatrix},
$$

where $\mathbf{Q}_1 = \mathbf{P}_1 - \mathbf{P}_0$, $\mathbf{Q}_2 = \mathbf{P}_2 - \mathbf{P}_0$, and

$$
\langle s_1, t_1 \rangle = \langle s_1 - s_0, t_1 - t_0 \rangle
$$
$$
\langle s_2, t_2 \rangle = \langle s_2 - s_0, t_2 - t_0 \rangle.
$$

The direction-to-light vector $\mathbf{L}$ and halfway vector $\mathbf{H}$ are transformed from object space to tangent space using the matrix

$$
\begin{bmatrix} T'_x & T'_y & T'_z \\ B'_x & B'_y & B'_z \\ N_x & N_y & N_z \end{bmatrix},
$$

where $\mathbf{T}'$ and $\mathbf{B}'$ are orthogonal to $\mathbf{N}$ and each other.

Bidirectional Reflectance Distribution Functions

The radiance $\mathcal{C}_R$ of the light reflected in the direction $\mathbf{V}$ from a surface illuminated by n lights is given by

$$
\mathcal{C}_R(\mathbf{V}) = \sum_{i=1}^{n} \varrho(\mathbf{V}, \mathbf{L}_i) \mathcal{C}_i(\mathbf{N} \cdot \mathbf{L}_i),
$$

where $\mathcal{C}_i$ is the radiance of the i-th light source. The BRDF ϱ can be divided into diffuse and specular components by writing

$$\varrho(\mathbf{V},\mathbf{L}) = k\mathcal{D} + (1-k)\varrho_s(\mathbf{V},\mathbf{L}),$$

where k is the fraction of light that is reflected diffusely.

Cook-Torrance Illumination

The specular component of the BRDF used in the Cook-Torrance illumination model is given by

$$\varrho_s(\mathbf{V},\mathbf{L}) = \mathcal{F}(\mathbf{V},\mathbf{L})\frac{D(\mathbf{V},\mathbf{L})G(\mathbf{V},\mathbf{L})}{\pi(\mathbf{N}\cdot\mathbf{V})(\mathbf{N}\cdot\mathbf{L})},$$

where $\mathcal{F}$ is the Fresnel factor, D is the microfacet distribution function, and G is the geometrical attenuation factor.

Fresnel Factor

The Fresnel factor for a single color is given by

$$F_\lambda(\mathbf{V},\mathbf{L}) = \frac{1}{2}\frac{(g-\mathbf{L}\cdot\mathbf{H})^2}{(g+\mathbf{L}\cdot\mathbf{H})^2}\left(\frac{[(\mathbf{L}\cdot\mathbf{H})(g+\mathbf{L}\cdot\mathbf{H})-1]^2}{[(\mathbf{L}\cdot\mathbf{H})(g-\mathbf{L}\cdot\mathbf{H})+1]^2}+1\right),$$

where g is defined by

$$g = \sqrt{\eta_\lambda^2 - 1 + (\mathbf{L}\cdot\mathbf{H})^2}.$$

The index of refraction η_λ can be calculated using the Equation

$$\eta_\lambda = \frac{1+\sqrt{S_\lambda}}{1-\sqrt{S_\lambda}},$$

where S is the specular reflection color at normal incidence.

Microfacet Distribution Functions

The microfacet distribution function D_m for isotropic surfaces is given by

$$D_m(\mathbf{V},\mathbf{L}) = \frac{1}{4m^2(\mathbf{N}\cdot\mathbf{H})^4}\exp\left(\frac{(\mathbf{N}\cdot\mathbf{H})^2-1}{m^2(\mathbf{N}\cdot\mathbf{H})^2}\right),$$

where m is the root mean square slope of the microfacets. For anisotropic surfaces, the microfacet distribution function becomes

$$D_{\mathbf{m}}(\mathbf{V},\mathbf{L}) = \frac{1}{4m_x m_y (\mathbf{N}\cdot\mathbf{H})^4} \exp\left[\left(\frac{(\mathbf{T}\cdot\mathbf{P})^2}{m_x^2} + \frac{1-(\mathbf{T}\cdot\mathbf{P})^2}{m_y^2}\right)\frac{(\mathbf{N}\cdot\mathbf{H})^2-1}{(\mathbf{N}\cdot\mathbf{H})^2}\right],$$

where m_x and m_y represent the root mean square slopes parallel and perpendicular to the tangent direction $\mathbf{T}$. The vector $\mathbf{P}$ is the normalized projection of the half-way vector $\mathbf{H}$ onto the tangent plane.

Geometrical Attenuation Factor

The geometrical attenuation factor is given by the formula

$$G(\mathbf{V},\mathbf{L}) = \min\left\{1, \frac{2(\mathbf{N}\cdot\mathbf{H})(\mathbf{N}\cdot\mathbf{V})}{\mathbf{L}\cdot\mathbf{H}}, \frac{2(\mathbf{N}\cdot\mathbf{H})(\mathbf{N}\cdot\mathbf{L})}{\mathbf{L}\cdot\mathbf{H}}\right\}$$

and accounts for the incident or reflected light for a microfacet that is blocked by adjacent microfacets.

Exercises for Chapter 6

1. A point light source has attenuation constants $k_c = 1$, $k_l = 0$, and $k_q = \frac{1}{2}$. At what distance from the light source is the radiant intensity one-fourth that of the intensity at a distance of one meter?

2. A spot light source positioned 10 meters above the origin at the point $\mathbf{P} = \langle 0,0,10\rangle$ and radiating energy in the direction $\mathbf{R} = \langle 0,0,-1\rangle$ is configured so that no distance attenuation takes place by setting $k_c = 1$ and $k_l = k_q = 0$. If the color of the light is white ($C_0 = (1,1,1)$) and the spot exponent is 8, then what is the radius of the circle lying in the x-y plane where the intensity of the light is 50 percent gray ($C = (\frac{1}{2},\frac{1}{2},\frac{1}{2})$)?

3. Describe how it is possible for $\mathbf{N}\cdot\mathbf{H}$ to be a positive number when $\mathbf{N}\cdot\mathbf{L}$ is a negative number, thus necessitating the $(\mathbf{N}\cdot\mathbf{L}>0)$ term in the illumination formula.

4. Let $\mathbf{L}$ be the normalized direction to the light source and $\mathbf{V}$ be the normalized direction to the viewer at a surface point where the unit normal vector is $\mathbf{N}$. Show that

$$(\mathbf{N}\cdot\mathbf{H})^{m} = \left[\frac{(\mathbf{N}\cdot\mathbf{L}+\mathbf{N}\cdot\mathbf{V})^{2}}{2(\mathbf{L}\cdot\mathbf{V}+1)}\right]^{m/2},$$

where **H** is the halfway vector defined by Equation (6.20), and m is an arbitrary specular exponent.

5. Write a program that calculates vertex normals and vertex tangents for an arbitrary triangle mesh. Assume that the triangle mesh is specified such that each of n triangles indexes three entries in an array of m vertices. Each entry in the vertex array contains the position of the vertex and two-dimensional texture-mapping coordinates.

6. Modify Listings 6.2 and 6.3 so that they perform bump mapping as well as isotropic microfacet shading.

7. Implement a simple ray tracer that calculates diffuse and specular reflections using Equations (6.6) and (6.19). The ray tracer should be able to model spheres and should support directional, point, and spot light sources.

8. Extend the ray tracer from Exercise 7 to implement Cook-Torrance microfacet shading.

Chapter 7

Visibility Determination

When it comes to the performance of a real-time 3D engine, the single most important component of the rendering architecture is visibility determination. Given a particular camera position and orientation, every engine must be able to efficiently determine which parts of the world are potentially visible and therefore should be rendered. This problem is usually attacked from the opposite perspective—the engine determines which parts of the world are definitely *not* visible and renders whatever is left over.

Most engines perform visibility determination at multiple levels. The general goal is to determine what world geometry cannot possibly intersect the view frustum. At the smallest scale, 3D hardware performs backface culling to eliminate individual triangles that face away from the camera. At the level above that, bounding volume tests are usually performed to determine whether an object lies completely outside the view frustum. Moderate-size groups of geometry can be culled from the visible set by organizing areas of the world into tree structures such as binary space partitioning (BSP) trees or octrees. At the largest scale, entire regions of world geometry can be eliminated by using a technique known as a portal system.

7.1 Bounding Volume Construction

Bounding volumes are constructed so that they enclose all the vertices belonging to a triangle mesh, thereby ensuring that every triangle in the mesh is also contained in the bounding volume. The bounding volume should be made as small as possible so that it falls completely outside the view frustum as often as possible, thus enabling the object it contains to be culled from the visible set of geometry as often as possible.

Figure 7.1(a) shows a box bounding a set of points that represent the vertices of a triangle mesh. The box is aligned to the coordinate axes, but the vertices are distributed in such a way that the box enclosing them contains a lot of empty space. As Figure 7.1(b) demonstrates, choosing a bounding box that is aligned to the natural axes of the data set can greatly reduce the size of the box. We present a method for determining the natural alignment in the next section.

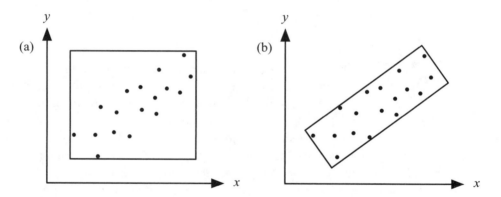

Figure 7.1 A bounding volume aligned to the coordinate axes is usually a poor choice for most vertex distributions.

7.1.1 Principal Component Analysis

We can reduce the size of each of our bounding volumes by determining a coordinate system that is naturally aligned to the set of vertices belonging to each triangle mesh. We can calculate these coordinate axes by using a statistical method called *principal component analysis*. Principal component analysis allows us to find a coordinate space in which a set of data composed of multiple variables, such as the x-, y-, and z-coordinates stored in an array of vertex positions, can be separated into uncorrelated components. The *primary* principal component of the data is represented by the direction in which the data varies the most.

To determine the natural coordinate system for an arbitrary set of N vertices $P_1, P_2, \ldots, P_N$, where $P_i = \langle x_i, y_i, z_i \rangle$, we first calculate the mean (average) position $\mathbf{m}$ using the formula

$$\mathbf{m} = \frac{1}{N} \sum_{i=1}^{N} \mathbf{P}_i. \tag{7.1}$$

We then construct a 3×3 matrix $\mathbf{C}$ called the *covariance matrix* as follows.

$$\mathbf{C} = \frac{1}{N} \sum_{i=1}^{N} (\mathbf{P}_i - \mathbf{m})(\mathbf{P}_i - \mathbf{m})^{\mathrm{T}} \tag{7.2}$$

The covariance matrix is a symmetric matrix made up of the following six unique entries.

$$
\begin{aligned}
C_{11} &= \frac{1}{N} \sum_{i=1}^{N} (x_i - m_x)^2 & C_{12} = C_{21} &= \frac{1}{N} \sum_{i=1}^{N} (x_i - m_x)(y_i - m_y) \\
C_{22} &= \frac{1}{N} \sum_{i=1}^{N} (y_i - m_y)^2 & C_{13} = C_{31} &= \frac{1}{N} \sum_{i=1}^{N} (x_i - m_x)(z_i - m_z) \\
C_{33} &= \frac{1}{N} \sum_{i=1}^{N} (z_i - m_z)^2 & C_{23} = C_{32} &= \frac{1}{N} \sum_{i=1}^{N} (y_i - m_y)(z_i - m_z)
\end{aligned} \tag{7.3}
$$

The entries of the covariance matrix represent the correlation between each pair of the x-, y-, and z-coordinates. An entry of zero indicates no correlation between the two coordinates used to calculate that entry. If $\mathbf{C}$ is a diagonal matrix, then all three coordinates are completely uncorrelated, meaning that the points are distributed evenly about each axis.

We want to find a basis to which we can transform our set of vertices so that the covariance matrix is diagonal. If we apply a transformation matrix $\mathbf{A}$ to each of the points $\{\mathbf{P}_i\}$, then the covariance matrix $\mathbf{C}'$ of the transformed set of points is given by

$$
\begin{aligned}
\mathbf{C}' &= \frac{1}{N} \sum_{i=1}^{N} (\mathbf{A}\mathbf{P}_i - \mathbf{A}\mathbf{m})(\mathbf{A}\mathbf{P}_i - \mathbf{A}\mathbf{m})^{\mathrm{T}} \\
&= \frac{1}{N} \sum_{i=1}^{N} \mathbf{A}(\mathbf{P}_i - \mathbf{m})(\mathbf{P}_i - \mathbf{m})^{\mathrm{T}} \mathbf{A}^{\mathrm{T}} \\
&= \mathbf{A}\mathbf{C}\mathbf{A}^{\mathrm{T}}.
\end{aligned} \tag{7.4}
$$

Thus, we require an orthogonal transformation matrix **A** whose transpose diagonalizes the matrix **C**. Since **C** is a real symmetric matrix, we know by Theorem 2.26 that its eigenvectors are orthogonal. The matrix whose rows consist of the eigenvectors of **C** meets our requirements and maps our vertices into a space where their coordinates are uncorrelated.

We have now turned the problem of finding the natural axes of a set of points into that of calculating the eigenvectors of the covariance matrix. One possible way to do this is to first calculate the eigenvalues given by the roots of the characteristic polynomial, a cubic in the case of the 3×3 covariance matrix. Fortunately, since the covariance matrix is symmetric, it has only real eigenvalues (see Theorem 2.25), and we can therefore use the method presented in Section 5.1.2 to explicitly calculate all of them. Finding the corresponding eigenvectors is then achieved by solving three homogeneous linear systems, as in the following example. Alternatively, a numerical method may be used to calculate the eigenvalues and eigenvectors, as discussed in Section 14.2

Example 7.1. Determine the natural axes for the following set of points.

$$\mathbf{P}_1 = \langle -1, -2, 1 \rangle$$
$$\mathbf{P}_2 = \langle 1, 0, 2 \rangle$$
$$\mathbf{P}_3 = \langle 2, -1, 3 \rangle$$
$$\mathbf{P}_4 = \langle 2, -1, 2 \rangle$$

Solution. We first calculate the average position **m**:

$$\mathbf{m} = \frac{1}{4} \sum_{i=1}^{4} \mathbf{P}_i = \langle 1, -1, 2 \rangle. \tag{7.5}$$

The covariance matrix **C** is then given by

$$\mathbf{C} = \begin{bmatrix} \frac{3}{2} & \frac{1}{2} & \frac{3}{4} \\ \frac{1}{2} & \frac{1}{2} & \frac{1}{4} \\ \frac{3}{4} & \frac{1}{4} & \frac{1}{2} \end{bmatrix}. \tag{7.6}$$

The eigenvalues of the covariance matrix are the roots of the characteristic polynomial:

$$\det(\mathbf{C} - \lambda \mathbf{I}) = \begin{vmatrix} \frac{3}{2} - \lambda & \frac{1}{2} & \frac{3}{4} \\ \frac{1}{2} & \frac{1}{2} - \lambda & \frac{1}{4} \\ \frac{3}{4} & \frac{1}{4} & \frac{1}{2} - \lambda \end{vmatrix}$$

$$= -\lambda^3 + \tfrac{5}{2}\lambda^2 - \tfrac{7}{8}\lambda + \tfrac{1}{16}. \tag{7.7}$$

Explicitly solving for the roots of the characteristic polynomial using the method presented in Section 5.1.2 gives us the following eigenvalues.

$$\lambda_1 = 2.097$$
$$\lambda_2 = 0.3055$$
$$\lambda_3 = 0.09756 \tag{7.8}$$

The eigenvectors, which we call $\mathbf{R}$, $\mathbf{S}$, and $\mathbf{T}$ here, are found by solving the linear systems $(\mathbf{C} - \lambda_i \mathbf{I})\mathbf{V}_i = \mathbf{0}$. Omitting the details of these calculations, the unit-length eigenvectors of the matrix $\mathbf{C}$ are

$$\mathbf{R} = \begin{bmatrix} -0.833 \\ -0.330 \\ -0.443 \end{bmatrix} \quad \mathbf{S} = \begin{bmatrix} -0.257 \\ 0.941 \\ -0.218 \end{bmatrix} \quad \mathbf{T} = \begin{bmatrix} 0.489 \\ -0.0675 \\ -0.870 \end{bmatrix}, \tag{7.9}$$

and these represent the natural axes of the set of vertices $\mathbf{P}_i$. ∎

In the remainder of this chapter, we use the letters $\mathbf{R}$, $\mathbf{S}$, and $\mathbf{T}$ to represent the natural axes of a set of vertices. The direction $\mathbf{R}$ always represents the principal axis, which corresponds to the largest eigenvalue of the covariance matrix. The directions $\mathbf{S}$ and $\mathbf{T}$ represent the axes corresponding to the second largest and the smallest eigenvalues, respectively. That is, if λ_1, λ_2, and λ_3 are the eigenvalues corresponding to the vectors $\mathbf{R}$, $\mathbf{S}$, and $\mathbf{T}$, respectively, then $|\lambda_1| \geq |\lambda_2| \geq |\lambda_3|$.

7.1.2 Bounding Box Construction

Given a set of vertex positions $\mathbf{P}_1, \mathbf{P}_2, \ldots, \mathbf{P}_N$ for a triangle mesh, we can now calculate the directions $\mathbf{R}$, $\mathbf{S}$, and $\mathbf{T}$ corresponding to the natural axes of the object. To construct a bounding box, we need to determine the minimum and maximum extents of the vertex set along these three directions. These extents immediately produce the six planes of the bounding box; other types of bounding volumes require a little more computation.

To find the extents, we simply compute the dot product of each vertex position $\mathbf{P}_i$ with the unit length vectors $\mathbf{R}$, $\mathbf{S}$, and $\mathbf{T}$, and take the minimum and maximum values. The six planes of the bounding box are then given by

$$
\begin{aligned}
&\left\langle \mathbf{R}, -\min_{1 \le i \le N}\{\mathbf{P}_i \cdot \mathbf{R}\} \right\rangle && \left\langle -\mathbf{R}, \max_{1 \le i \le N}\{\mathbf{P}_i \cdot \mathbf{R}\} \right\rangle \\
&\left\langle \mathbf{S}, -\min_{1 \le i \le N}\{\mathbf{P}_i \cdot \mathbf{S}\} \right\rangle && \left\langle -\mathbf{S}, \max_{1 \le i \le N}\{\mathbf{P}_i \cdot \mathbf{S}\} \right\rangle \\
&\left\langle \mathbf{T}, -\min_{1 \le i \le N}\{\mathbf{P}_i \cdot \mathbf{T}\} \right\rangle && \left\langle -\mathbf{T}, \max_{1 \le i \le N}\{\mathbf{P}_i \cdot \mathbf{T}\} \right\rangle.
\end{aligned}
\tag{7.10}
$$

Example 7.2. Calculate the six planes of the naturally aligned bounding box for the set of points given in Example 7.1.

Solution. The natural axes for this set of points are given by Equation (7.9). The dot products of each of the four points with the directions $\mathbf{R}$, $\mathbf{S}$, and $\mathbf{T}$ are listed below.

$$
\begin{aligned}
&\mathbf{P}_1 \cdot \mathbf{R} = 1.05 && \mathbf{P}_1 \cdot \mathbf{S} = -1.84 && \mathbf{P}_1 \cdot \mathbf{T} = -1.22 \\
&\mathbf{P}_2 \cdot \mathbf{R} = -1.72 && \mathbf{P}_2 \cdot \mathbf{S} = -0.693 && \mathbf{P}_2 \cdot \mathbf{T} = -1.25 \\
&\mathbf{P}_3 \cdot \mathbf{R} = -2.67 && \mathbf{P}_3 \cdot \mathbf{S} = -2.11 && \mathbf{P}_3 \cdot \mathbf{T} = -1.56 \\
&\mathbf{P}_4 \cdot \mathbf{R} = -2.22 && \mathbf{P}_4 \cdot \mathbf{S} = -1.89 && \mathbf{P}_4 \cdot \mathbf{T} = -0.695
\end{aligned}
\tag{7.11}
$$

Using the minimum and maximum values of $\mathbf{P}_i \cdot \mathbf{R}$, the two planes perpendicular to the direction $\mathbf{R}$ are given by

$$
\langle \mathbf{R}, 2.67 \rangle \quad \langle -\mathbf{R}, 1.05 \rangle.
\tag{7.12}
$$

Similarly, the planes perpendicular to the $\mathbf{S}$ and $\mathbf{T}$ directions are given by

$$
\begin{aligned}
&\langle \mathbf{S}, 2.11 \rangle && \langle -\mathbf{S}, -0.693 \rangle \\
&\langle \mathbf{T}, 1.56 \rangle && \langle -\mathbf{T}, -0.695 \rangle. \quad \blacksquare
\end{aligned}
\tag{7.13}
$$

The dimensions of the bounding box are given by the differences between the minimum and maximum dot products in each of the directions $\mathbf{R}$, $\mathbf{S}$, and $\mathbf{T}$. The center $\mathbf{Q}$ of the bounding box is the point at which the three planes lying halfway between each pair of opposing faces intersect. We assign to the scalars a, b, and c the average extent in the $\mathbf{R}$, $\mathbf{S}$, and $\mathbf{T}$ directions, respectively, as follows.

$$a = \frac{\min_{1 \le i \le N}\{\mathbf{P}_i \cdot \mathbf{R}\} + \max_{1 \le i \le N}\{\mathbf{P}_i \cdot \mathbf{R}\}}{2}$$

$$b = \frac{\min_{1 \le i \le N}\{\mathbf{P}_i \cdot \mathbf{S}\} + \max_{1 \le i \le N}\{\mathbf{P}_i \cdot \mathbf{S}\}}{2}$$

$$c = \frac{\min_{1 \le i \le N}\{\mathbf{P}_i \cdot \mathbf{T}\} + \max_{1 \le i \le N}\{\mathbf{P}_i \cdot \mathbf{T}\}}{2} \qquad (7.14)$$

The three planes that divide the box in half are given by $\langle \mathbf{R}, -a \rangle$, $\langle \mathbf{S}, -b \rangle$, and $\langle \mathbf{T}, -c \rangle$. Using Equation (4.21) to calculate the point of intersection provides us with the following expression for the center $\mathbf{Q}$.

$$\mathbf{Q} = a\mathbf{R} + b\mathbf{S} + c\mathbf{T}. \qquad (7.15)$$

7.1.3 Bounding Sphere Construction

Bounding spheres are commonly used in tests for object visibility due to the speed with which such a test can be performed. As with all bounding volumes, we should construct bounding spheres that are as tight as possible so as to minimize the occurrence of its intersection with the view frustum. Achieving an absolutely optimal bounding sphere in all cases turns out to be a hard problem that we do not discuss here, but we are able to construct bounding spheres that are acceptably efficient without requiring an excessively complex algorithm.

We begin constructing a bounding sphere for a set of points $\mathbf{P}_1, \mathbf{P}_2, \ldots, \mathbf{P}_N$ by first calculating the principal axis $\mathbf{R}$ and locating the points $\mathbf{P}_k$ and $\mathbf{P}_l$ representing the minimum and maximum extents in that direction (i.e., we locate the points having the least and greatest dot product with $\mathbf{R}$). We then construct a sphere whose center $\mathbf{Q}$ and radius r are given by

$$\mathbf{Q} = \frac{\mathbf{P}_k + \mathbf{P}_l}{2}$$

$$r = \|\mathbf{P}_k - \mathbf{Q}\|. \qquad (7.16)$$

That is, the center of the sphere lies halfway between the points producing the minimum and maximum extents in the $\mathbf{R}$ direction, and the radius is the distance from the center to either of those points.

Although it is a good approximation to the final bounding sphere, the sphere given by Equation (7.16) may not enclose all the points $\mathbf{P}_1, \mathbf{P}_2, \ldots, \mathbf{P}_N$. We must therefore test each of the points $\{\mathbf{P}_i\}$ to make sure they fall inside the sphere. Whenever a point is encountered that lies outside the sphere, we expand the sphere by adjusting the center $\mathbf{Q}$ and radius r to enclose the previous sphere and the exterior point, as shown in Figure 7.2. A point $\mathbf{P}_i$ lies outside the sphere if

$$\|\mathbf{P}_i - \mathbf{Q}\|^2 > r^2. \tag{7.17}$$

We expand the sphere by placing the new center $\mathbf{Q}'$ on the line connecting the previous center $\mathbf{Q}$ and the exterior point $\mathbf{P}_i$. The new sphere is then tangent to the previous sphere at a point $\mathbf{G}$ given by

$$\mathbf{G} = \mathbf{Q} - r\frac{\mathbf{P}_i - \mathbf{Q}}{\|\mathbf{P}_i - \mathbf{Q}\|}, \tag{7.18}$$

which also lies on the line containing $\mathbf{Q}$ and $\mathbf{P}_i$. The new center $\mathbf{Q}'$ is placed halfway between the points $\mathbf{G}$ and $\mathbf{P}_i$, and the new radius r' is the distance from the new center to either of these points:

$$\mathbf{Q}' = \frac{\mathbf{G} + \mathbf{P}_i}{2}$$
$$r' = \|\mathbf{P}_i - \mathbf{Q}'\|. \tag{7.19}$$

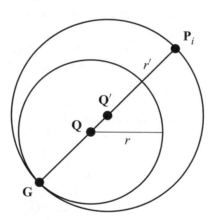

Figure 7.2 The initial bounding sphere determined by the extents of the set of points in the direction of the principal axis is expanded to include any points in the set that lie outside of the sphere.

7.1.4 Bounding Ellipsoid Construction

An ellipsoidal bounding volume may be appropriate for a triangle mesh having an elongated shape. To determine a good bounding ellipsoid for a set of vertices $\mathbf{P}_1, \mathbf{P}_2, \ldots, \mathbf{P}_N$, we need to calculate the lengths of the three semi-axes of the ellipsoid aligned to the natural axes $\mathbf{R}$, $\mathbf{S}$, and $\mathbf{T}$. We can transform the problem into that of finding a bounding sphere by scaling the vertex positions in these directions so that their bounding box becomes a cube. Once the bounding sphere of the scaled set is known, we scale its radius by the reciprocal amount in each direction to derive the semi-axis lengths.

To scale the vertex positions so that they are bounded by a cube, we need to know the distance between the planes representing the minimum and maximum extents in each natural axis direction. These distances are equal to the dimensions of the standard bounding box, which are given by the differences between the minimum and maximum dot products of the points $\mathbf{P}_i$ with the vectors $\mathbf{R}$, $\mathbf{S}$, and $\mathbf{T}$. Calling these distances a, b, and c, respectively, we have

$$a = \max_{1 \le i \le N}\{\mathbf{P}_i \cdot \mathbf{R}\} - \min_{1 \le i \le N}\{\mathbf{P}_i \cdot \mathbf{R}\}$$
$$b = \max_{1 \le i \le N}\{\mathbf{P}_i \cdot \mathbf{S}\} - \min_{1 \le i \le N}\{\mathbf{P}_i \cdot \mathbf{S}\}$$
$$c = \max_{1 \le i \le N}\{\mathbf{P}_i \cdot \mathbf{T}\} - \min_{1 \le i \le N}\{\mathbf{P}_i \cdot \mathbf{T}\}. \tag{7.20}$$

To transform the vertex set into one bounded by a cube, we need to scale their positions by $1/a$ in the $\mathbf{R}$ direction, by $1/b$ in the $\mathbf{S}$ direction, and by $1/c$ in the $\mathbf{T}$ direction. As stated in Equation (3.11), the matrix $\mathbf{M}$ that performs this scale is given by

$$\mathbf{M} = [\mathbf{R} \quad \mathbf{S} \quad \mathbf{T}] \begin{bmatrix} 1/a & 0 & 0 \\ 0 & 1/b & 0 \\ 0 & 0 & 1/c \end{bmatrix} [\mathbf{R} \quad \mathbf{S} \quad \mathbf{T}]^{\mathrm{T}}, \tag{7.21}$$

where we have replaced the inverse operation for the rightmost matrix by a transpose operation since the vectors $\mathbf{R}$, $\mathbf{S}$, and $\mathbf{T}$ are orthonormal.

Once each of the points $\{\mathbf{P}_i\}$ has been transformed by the matrix $\mathbf{M}$, we calculate the bounding sphere for the set of points $\mathbf{M}\mathbf{P}_1, \mathbf{M}\mathbf{P}_2, \ldots, \mathbf{M}\mathbf{P}_N$. Once the center $\mathbf{Q}$ of this sphere is known, we can calculate the center of the bounding ellipsoid of the original set of vertices by transforming $\mathbf{Q}$ back into the unscaled coordinate space. The ellipsoid center is simply given by $\mathbf{M}^{-1}\mathbf{Q}$, where the inverse of $\mathbf{M}$ is

$$\mathbf{M}^{-1} = \begin{bmatrix} \mathbf{R} & \mathbf{S} & \mathbf{T} \end{bmatrix} \begin{bmatrix} a & 0 & 0 \\ 0 & b & 0 \\ 0 & 0 & c \end{bmatrix} \begin{bmatrix} \mathbf{R} & \mathbf{S} & \mathbf{T} \end{bmatrix}^{\mathrm{T}}. \tag{7.22}$$

The lengths of the semi-axes of the bounding ellipsoid are calculated by scaling the radius r of the bounding sphere calculated for the points $\{\mathbf{MP}_i\}$. The semi-axis lengths corresponding to the directions $\mathbf{R}$, $\mathbf{S}$, and $\mathbf{T}$ are given by ar, br, and cr, respectively.

7.1.5 Bounding Cylinder Construction

A cylindrical bounding volume is represented by its radius and the two points corresponding to the centers of its endcaps. The endcaps of a cylinder bounding the set of points $\mathbf{P}_1, \mathbf{P}_2, \ldots, \mathbf{P}_N$ coincide with the planes of the bounding box that are perpendicular to the principal axis $\mathbf{R}$. Most of the calculations involved in determining the bounding cylinder for a triangle mesh lie in finding the circle that bounds the projection of the points $\mathbf{P}_i$ onto the plane containing the natural axes $\mathbf{S}$ and $\mathbf{T}$.

We find the bounding circle in a manner similar to the way we calculate bounding spheres, except that the component of each point $\mathbf{P}_i$ parallel to the $\mathbf{R}$ direction is ignored. Instead of working directly with the points $\{\mathbf{P}_i\}$, we remove the projection of each $\mathbf{P}_i$ onto $\mathbf{R}$ and work with the points $\{\mathbf{H}_i\}$ given by

$$\mathbf{H}_i = \mathbf{P}_i - (\mathbf{P}_i \cdot \mathbf{R})\mathbf{R}. \tag{7.23}$$

We first locate the points $\mathbf{H}_k$ and $\mathbf{H}_l$ that have the least and greatest dot products with the vector $\mathbf{S}$. (Recall that the axis $\mathbf{S}$ corresponds to the second largest eigenvalue of the covariance matrix.) The initial center $\mathbf{Q}$ and radius r of the bounding circle are given by

$$\mathbf{Q} = \frac{\mathbf{H}_k + \mathbf{H}_l}{2}$$
$$r = \|\mathbf{H}_k - \mathbf{Q}\|. \tag{7.24}$$

We then proceed exactly as we would when calculating a bounding sphere. We check each point to make sure it falls inside the bounding circle. When a point $\mathbf{H}_i$ for which

$$\|\mathbf{H}_i - \mathbf{Q}\|^2 > r^2 \tag{7.25}$$

is encountered, we expand the bounding circle so that it has a new center $\mathbf{Q}'$ and new radius r' given by

$$\mathbf{Q}' = \frac{\mathbf{G} + \mathbf{H}_i}{2}$$
$$r' = \|\mathbf{H}_i - \mathbf{Q}'\|, \tag{7.26}$$

where

$$\mathbf{G} = \mathbf{Q} - r\frac{\mathbf{H}_i - \mathbf{Q}}{\|\mathbf{H}_i - \mathbf{Q}\|}. \tag{7.27}$$

The radius of the bounding cylinder is the same as the radius of the circle bounding the set of points $\{\mathbf{H}_i\}$. The center $\mathbf{Q}$ of the bounding circle lies in the plane perpendicular to the direction $\mathbf{R}$ but passing through the origin. The centers of the cylinder's endcaps are found by projecting $\mathbf{Q}$ onto the bounding box planes corresponding to the least and greatest dot products of the points $\{\mathbf{P}_i\}$ with the direction $\mathbf{R}$. Calling the endpoints $\mathbf{Q}_1$ and $\mathbf{Q}_2$, we have

$$\mathbf{Q}_1 = \mathbf{Q} + \min_{1 \le i \le N}\{\mathbf{P}_i \cdot \mathbf{R}\}\mathbf{R}$$
$$\mathbf{Q}_2 = \mathbf{Q} + \max_{1 \le i \le N}\{\mathbf{P}_i \cdot \mathbf{R}\}\mathbf{R}. \tag{7.28}$$

7.2 Bounding Volume Tests

Now that we have seen how to construct a variety of bounding volumes, we turn our attention to the methods used to determine whether each type is visible. All the techniques presented in this section reduce the problem of intersecting a bounding volume with the view frustum to that of intersecting a point or a line segment with a properly modified view frustum. This is accomplished by moving the planes of the view frustum outward by appropriate amounts, which are determined differently for each type of bounding volume.

7.2.1 Bounding Sphere Test

A sphere of radius r intersects the view frustum if its center lies inside the view frustum or lies within a distance r of any of the six sides of the view frustum. The gray region shown in Figure 7.3(a) corresponds to the volume in which the sphere's center must lie whenever it is visible. The boundary of this region, formed by rolling the sphere around the outside edges of the view frustum, is parallel to one of the frustum planes everywhere except at the corners, where it is rounded. As Figure 7.3(b) shows, we can approximate the exact volume of visibility by moving each of the six frustum planes outward by a distance r.

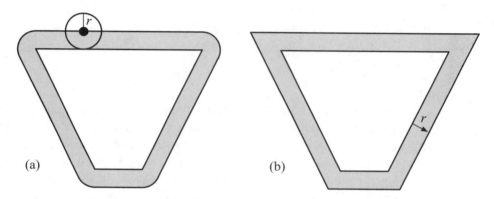

(a)

(b)

Figure 7.3 (a) The gray region corresponds to the volume in which the center of a sphere of radius r must lie whenever it is visible. (b) We can approximate the exact volume of visibility by moving each of the six frustum planes outward by a distance r.

Given a sphere of radius r whose center resides at the point $\mathbf{Q}$ in camera space, we compute the 4D dot products of the homogeneous extension of $\mathbf{Q}$ with the six frustum planes listed in Table 4.1. Since the frustum plane normals point inward, a negative dot product indicates that $\mathbf{Q}$ lies outside the visible volume of space. If any one of the dot products is less than or equal to $-r$, then the sphere does not intersect the view frustum at all, and the object bounded by it should be culled from the visible set of geometry. Otherwise, some part of the sphere probably lies inside all six frustum planes, the exception being the case shown in Figure 7.4. Near the edges of the view frustum, some spheres that are not visible may not be culled because they do not fall far enough outside any single frustum plane. This infrequent occurrence is normally tolerated to preserve the simplicity of the visibility test. We examine a small enhancement that reduces this effect in Section 7.4.2.

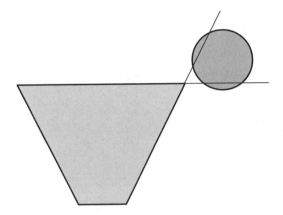

Figure 7.4 Near the edges of the view frustum, some spheres that are not visible are not culled because they do not fall far enough outside any single frustum plane.

7.2.2 Bounding Ellipsoid Test

When testing the visibility of a sphere, we move each of the six frustum planes outward by the radius of the sphere and test whether the sphere's center lies on the positive side of these modified planes. A similar method can be used to test the visibility of an ellipsoid, but since an ellipsoid does not possess the isotropic symmetry that a sphere does, the *effective* radius of the ellipsoid is different for each frustum plane.

Suppose that an object is bounded by an ellipsoid whose semi-axes are given by the mutually perpendicular vectors $\mathbf{R}$, $\mathbf{S}$, and $\mathbf{T}$, as shown in Figure 7.5, where $\mathbf{R}$, $\mathbf{S}$, and $\mathbf{T}$ are parallel to the principal axes of the bounded object but have magnitudes equal to the semi-axis lengths of the ellipsoid. A point $\mathbf{P}$ on the surface of the ellipsoid can be expressed in terms of the three vectors $\mathbf{R}$, $\mathbf{S}$, and $\mathbf{T}$ as follows.

$$\mathbf{P} = \mathbf{R}\cos\theta\sin\varphi + \mathbf{S}\sin\theta\sin\varphi + \mathbf{T}\cos\varphi \tag{7.29}$$

This expression represents a spherical coordinate system aligned to the axes of the ellipsoid. The angle φ represents the angle that the point $\mathbf{P}$ makes with the vector $\mathbf{T}$. The angle θ represents the angle that the projection of $\mathbf{P}$ onto the plane containing the vectors $\mathbf{R}$ and $\mathbf{S}$ makes with the vector $\mathbf{R}$. Over the entire surface of the ellipsoid, φ ranges from 0 to π, and θ ranges from 0 to 2π.

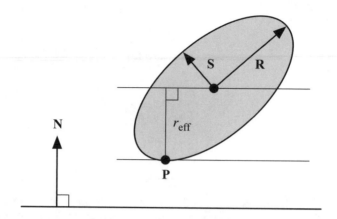

Figure 7.5 A bounding ellipsoid whose semi-axes are given by the mutually perpendicular vectors **R**, **S**, and **T** (where **T** points out of the page). The effective radius of the ellipsoid with respect to a plane is equal to the maximum distance from the ellipsoid's center to any point on the surface projected onto the plane's normal.

Given a unit direction vector **N**, we would like to find the point **P** on the surface of the ellipsoid whose projection onto **N** has the greatest magnitude. This would give us the effective radius r_{eff} of the ellipsoid with respect to a plane whose normal vector is **N**. Since **N** has unit length, the magnitude of the projection of **P** onto **N** is simply given by $\mathbf{P} \cdot \mathbf{N}$. We wish to find the angles φ and θ that maximize this quantity, so we set partial derivatives to zero as follows.

$$\frac{\partial}{\partial \varphi}(\mathbf{P} \cdot \mathbf{N}) = (\mathbf{R} \cdot \mathbf{N})\cos \theta \cos \varphi + (\mathbf{S} \cdot \mathbf{N})\sin \theta \cos \varphi - (\mathbf{T} \cdot \mathbf{N})\sin \varphi = 0 \quad (7.30)$$

$$\frac{\partial}{\partial \theta}(\mathbf{P} \cdot \mathbf{N}) = -(\mathbf{R} \cdot \mathbf{N})\sin \theta \sin \varphi + (\mathbf{S} \cdot \mathbf{N})\cos \theta \sin \varphi = 0 \quad (7.31)$$

In our derivation of an expression for the quantity $\mathbf{P} \cdot \mathbf{N}$, we make use of the trigonometric identity

$$\tan^2 \alpha + 1 = \sec^2 \alpha, \quad (7.32)$$

which can be transformed into the identities

$$\sin \alpha = \frac{\tan \alpha}{\sqrt{\tan^2 \alpha + 1}}$$

$$\cos \alpha = \frac{1}{\sqrt{\tan^2 \alpha + 1}}. \qquad (7.33)$$

Equation (7.31) can be rewritten as

$$(\mathbf{S} \cdot \mathbf{N}) \cos \theta = (\mathbf{R} \cdot \mathbf{N}) \sin \theta, \qquad (7.34)$$

allowing us to express $\tan \theta$ as

$$\tan \theta = \frac{\mathbf{S} \cdot \mathbf{N}}{\mathbf{R} \cdot \mathbf{N}}. \qquad (7.35)$$

Equation (7.30) can be rewritten as

$$(\mathbf{T} \cdot \mathbf{N}) \sin \varphi = (\mathbf{R} \cdot \mathbf{N}) \cos \theta \cos \varphi + (\mathbf{S} \cdot \mathbf{N}) \sin \theta \cos \varphi, \qquad (7.36)$$

allowing us to express $\tan \varphi$ as

$$\begin{aligned}
\tan \varphi &= \frac{\mathbf{R} \cdot \mathbf{N}}{\mathbf{T} \cdot \mathbf{N}} \cos \theta + \frac{\mathbf{S} \cdot \mathbf{N}}{\mathbf{T} \cdot \mathbf{N}} \sin \theta \\
&= \frac{1}{\sqrt{\tan^2 \theta + 1}} \left(\frac{\mathbf{R} \cdot \mathbf{N}}{\mathbf{T} \cdot \mathbf{N}} + \tan \theta \frac{\mathbf{S} \cdot \mathbf{N}}{\mathbf{T} \cdot \mathbf{N}} \right) \\
&= \frac{\mathbf{R} \cdot \mathbf{N}}{\mathbf{T} \cdot \mathbf{N}} \frac{1}{\sqrt{\tan^2 \theta + 1}} \left(1 + \tan^2 \theta \right) \\
&= \frac{\mathbf{R} \cdot \mathbf{N}}{\mathbf{T} \cdot \mathbf{N}} \sqrt{\tan^2 \theta + 1} \\
&= \frac{\mathbf{R} \cdot \mathbf{N}}{\mathbf{T} \cdot \mathbf{N}} \sqrt{\left(\frac{\mathbf{S} \cdot \mathbf{N}}{\mathbf{R} \cdot \mathbf{N}} \right)^2 + 1}, \qquad (7.37)
\end{aligned}$$

where Equation (7.35) has been used in two steps. Using the identities given by Equation (7.33), the value of $\mathbf{P} \cdot \mathbf{N}$ can now be written as

$$\begin{aligned}
\mathbf{P} \cdot \mathbf{N} &= (\mathbf{R} \cdot \mathbf{N}) \cos \theta \sin \varphi + (\mathbf{S} \cdot \mathbf{N}) \sin \theta \sin \varphi + (\mathbf{T} \cdot \mathbf{N}) \cos \varphi \\
&= \frac{1}{\sqrt{\tan^2 \varphi + 1}} \left\{ \frac{\tan \varphi}{\sqrt{\tan^2 \theta + 1}} [\mathbf{R} \cdot \mathbf{N} + (\mathbf{S} \cdot \mathbf{N}) \tan \theta] + \mathbf{T} \cdot \mathbf{N} \right\}. \qquad (7.38)
\end{aligned}$$

Substituting expressions from Equations (7.35) and (7.37) for $\tan\theta$ and $\tan\varphi$ gives us

$$\mathbf{P}\cdot\mathbf{N} = \frac{\dfrac{\mathbf{R}\cdot\mathbf{N}}{\mathbf{T}\cdot\mathbf{N}}\left(\mathbf{R}\cdot\mathbf{N} + \dfrac{(\mathbf{S}\cdot\mathbf{N})^2}{\mathbf{R}\cdot\mathbf{N}}\right) + \mathbf{T}\cdot\mathbf{N}}{\sqrt{\left(\dfrac{\mathbf{R}\cdot\mathbf{N}}{\mathbf{T}\cdot\mathbf{N}}\right)^2\left[\left(\dfrac{\mathbf{S}\cdot\mathbf{N}}{\mathbf{R}\cdot\mathbf{N}}\right)^2 + 1\right] + 1}}$$

$$= \frac{(\mathbf{R}\cdot\mathbf{N})^2 + (\mathbf{S}\cdot\mathbf{N})^2 + (\mathbf{T}\cdot\mathbf{N})^2}{\mathbf{T}\cdot\mathbf{N}\sqrt{\left(\dfrac{\mathbf{R}\cdot\mathbf{N}}{\mathbf{T}\cdot\mathbf{N}}\right)^2\left[\left(\dfrac{\mathbf{S}\cdot\mathbf{N}}{\mathbf{R}\cdot\mathbf{N}}\right)^2 + 1\right] + 1}}$$

$$= \frac{(\mathbf{R}\cdot\mathbf{N})^2 + (\mathbf{S}\cdot\mathbf{N})^2 + (\mathbf{T}\cdot\mathbf{N})^2}{\sqrt{(\mathbf{R}\cdot\mathbf{N})^2 + (\mathbf{S}\cdot\mathbf{N})^2 + (\mathbf{T}\cdot\mathbf{N})^2}}, \tag{7.39}$$

which yields the relatively simple expression

$$r_{\text{eff}} = \mathbf{P}\cdot\mathbf{N} = \sqrt{(\mathbf{R}\cdot\mathbf{N})^2 + (\mathbf{S}\cdot\mathbf{N})^2 + (\mathbf{T}\cdot\mathbf{N})^2}. \tag{7.40}$$

Equation (7.40) provides the effective radius of an arbitrary ellipsoid with respect to a plane having unit normal direction $\mathbf{N}$. Since the near and far planes are parallel, the ellipsoid's effective radius for those two planes is the same. Thus, to test whether an ellipsoid falls outside the view frustum, we need to calculate at most five effective radii. As with the sphere test, we compute the four-dimensional dot products of the ellipsoid's center with each of the frustum plane vectors. If any single dot product is less than or equal to $-r_{\text{eff}}$, then the ellipsoid is not visible. Otherwise, the object bounded by the ellipsoid should be drawn.

7.2.3 Bounding Cylinder Test

We reduced the problem of intersecting a sphere or an ellipsoid with the view frustum to that of testing whether a point fell on the positive side of frustum planes that were offset by the bounding volume's effective radius. To intersect a cylinder with the view frustum, we instead reduce the problem to determining whether a line segment is visible in a properly expanded frustum.

As with the ellipsoid test, we must determine the effective radius of a bounding cylinder with respect to each of the view frustum planes. The effective radius depends on the cylinder's orientation and ranges from zero (when the cylinder is perpendicular to a plane) to the actual radius (when the cylinder is parallel to a plane). Suppose that we are given a cylinder of radius r whose endpoints lie at $\mathbf{Q}_1$

and $\mathbf{Q}_2$. We define the vector $\mathbf{A}$ to be the unit vector parallel to the axis of the cylinder:

$$\mathbf{A} = \frac{\mathbf{Q}_2 - \mathbf{Q}_1}{\|\mathbf{Q}_2 - \mathbf{Q}_1\|}. \tag{7.41}$$

As shown in Figure 7.6, the effective radius r_{eff} of the cylinder with respect to a plane having unit normal direction $\mathbf{N}$ is given by

$$r_{\text{eff}} = r\sin\alpha, \tag{7.42}$$

where α is the angle formed between the vectors $\mathbf{A}$ and $\mathbf{N}$. This can also be written as

$$\begin{aligned} r_{\text{eff}} &= r\sqrt{1 - \cos^2\alpha} \\ &= r\sqrt{1 - (\mathbf{A} \cdot \mathbf{N})^2}. \end{aligned} \tag{7.43}$$

We perform the visibility test by visiting each of the six view frustum planes, beginning with the near and far planes since they are parallel and thus share the same effective radius. For each frustum plane $\mathbf{L}$, we first calculate the 4D dot products $\mathbf{L} \cdot \mathbf{Q}_1$ and $\mathbf{L} \cdot \mathbf{Q}_2$. If *both* dot products are less than or equal to the value $-r_{\text{eff}}$ corresponding to the plane $\mathbf{L}$, then we immediately know that the cylinder is not visible, and the test exits. If both dot products are greater than or equal to $-r_{\text{eff}}$, then we cannot draw any conclusions and simply proceed to the next plane.

In the remaining case that one of the dot products is less than $-r_{\text{eff}}$, and the other dot product is greater than $-r_{\text{eff}}$, we calculate the point $\mathbf{Q}_3$ such that

$$\mathbf{L} \cdot \mathbf{Q}_3 = -r_{\text{eff}} \tag{7.44}$$

and replace the exterior endpoint with it. This effectively chops off the part of the cylinder that is now known to lie outside the view frustum. To find the point $\mathbf{Q}_3$, we use the parametric line equation

$$\mathbf{Q}_3(t) = \mathbf{Q}_1 + t(\mathbf{Q}_2 - \mathbf{Q}_1), \tag{7.45}$$

where the range $0 \le t \le 1$ represents the axis of the cylinder. Substituting the right side of this equation for $\mathbf{Q}_3$ in Equation (7.44) allows us to solve for the value of t:

$$t = \frac{r_{\text{eff}} + \mathbf{L} \cdot \mathbf{Q}_1}{\mathbf{L} \cdot (\mathbf{Q}_1 - \mathbf{Q}_2)}. \tag{7.46}$$

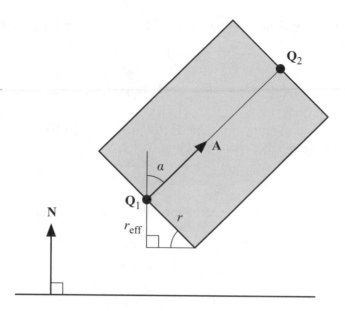

Figure 7.6 The effective radius of a bounding cylinder.

(Note that the difference $\mathbf{Q}_1 - \mathbf{Q}_2$ has a w-coordinate of 0.) Plugging this back into Equation (7.45) gives us our new endpoint $\mathbf{Q}_3$. After replacing the exterior endpoint with it, we continue to the next plane.

If we visit all six planes of the view frustum and never encounter the case that both endpoints produce a dot product less than or equal to $-r_{\text{eff}}$, then the cylinder is probably at least partially visible. Of course, this means that we do not have to replace any endpoints for the last plane that we visit. As soon as we know that at least one endpoint $\mathbf{Q}_i$ satisfies $\mathbf{L} \cdot \mathbf{Q}_i > -r_{\text{eff}}$ for the final plane, we know that part of the cylinder intersects the view frustum.

7.2.4 Bounding Box Test

When determining whether a box intersects the view frustum, we have a choice between reducing the problem to that of testing a point or to that of testing a line segment. If the bounding box extents in the primary axis direction $\mathbf{R}$ are significantly greater than those in the $\mathbf{S}$ and $\mathbf{T}$ directions, then we may choose to test a line segment. For bounding boxes whose dimensions are roughly equal, we favor the point test.

We assume in this section that the magnitudes of the vectors $\mathbf{R}$, $\mathbf{S}$, and $\mathbf{T}$ representing the principal axes of the object bounded by the box are equal to the dimensions of the box itself. To reduce the problem of intersecting a box with the view frustum to that of testing whether its center lies inside the expanded frustum planes, we need a way to determine the box's effective radius. As shown in Figure 7.7, we can calculate the effective radius r_{eff} of a box with respect to a plane having unit normal direction $\mathbf{N}$ using the formula

$$r_{\text{eff}} = \tfrac{1}{2}(|\mathbf{R} \cdot \mathbf{N}| + |\mathbf{S} \cdot \mathbf{N}| + |\mathbf{T} \cdot \mathbf{N}|). \tag{7.47}$$

Once the effective radius is known, we proceed in exactly the same manner as we would to test an ellipsoid. For each frustum plane $\mathbf{L}$, we calculate the 4D dot product between the plane and the center $\mathbf{Q}$ of the bounding box. If for any plane $\mathbf{L} \cdot \mathbf{Q} \le -r_{\text{eff}}$, then the box is not visible.

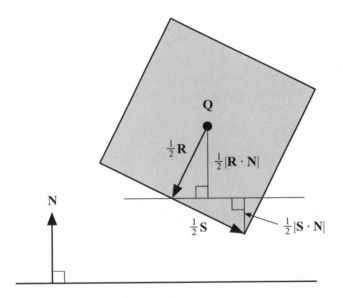

Figure 7.7 Calculating the effective radius of a box.

In the case that the length of $\mathbf{R}$ is much greater than the lengths of $\mathbf{S}$ and $\mathbf{T}$, a box may not be rejected in many situations when it lies far outside the view frustum. An instance of this case is demonstrated in Figure 7.8. To circumvent this problem, we can reduce the box intersection test to a line segment intersection, as is done for cylinders.

In terms of the bounding box center $\mathbf{Q}$ and its primary axis $\mathbf{R}$, we can express the endpoints $\mathbf{Q}_1$ and $\mathbf{Q}_2$ of the line segment representing the box as

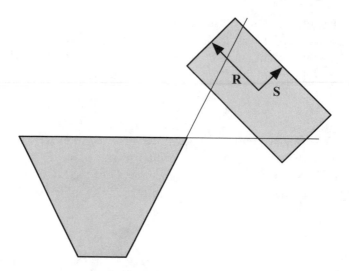

Figure 7.8 This example demonstrates that using the point test for a box having one dimension much larger than the other two can result in the failure to reject a box that lies a significant distance outside the view frustum.

$$\mathbf{Q}_1 = \mathbf{Q} + \tfrac{1}{2}\mathbf{R}$$
$$\mathbf{Q}_2 = \mathbf{Q} - \tfrac{1}{2}\mathbf{R}. \tag{7.48}$$

The effective radius r_{eff} with respect to a plane having unit normal direction $\mathbf{N}$ is given by

$$r_{\text{eff}} = \tfrac{1}{2}(|\mathbf{S} \cdot \mathbf{N}| + |\mathbf{T} \cdot \mathbf{N}|), \tag{7.49}$$

where the $|\mathbf{R} \cdot \mathbf{N}|$ term appearing in Equation (7.47) is now absent since it is represented by the line segment connecting $\mathbf{Q}_1$ and $\mathbf{Q}_2$.

We now proceed in exactly the same manner as we would to test a cylinder. For each frustum plane $\mathbf{L}$, we first calculate the 4D dot products $\mathbf{L} \cdot \mathbf{Q}_1$ and $\mathbf{L} \cdot \mathbf{Q}_2$. If both dot products are less than or equal to the value $-r_{\text{eff}}$ corresponding to the plane $\mathbf{L}$, then we immediately know that the box is not visible, and the test exits. If both dot products are greater than or equal to $-r_{\text{eff}}$, then we cannot draw any conclusions and simply proceed to the next plane. When one of the dot products is less than $-r_{\text{eff}}$ and the other dot product is greater than $-r_{\text{eff}}$, we calculate the point $\mathbf{Q}_3$ such that $\mathbf{L} \cdot \mathbf{Q}_3 = -r_{\text{eff}}$ using Equations (7.45) and (7.46), and replace the exterior endpoint with it. If we are able to visit all six frustum planes without encountering the case that both endpoints produce a dot product less than or equal to $-r_{\text{eff}}$, then the box is probably at least partially visible.

7.3 Spatial Partitioning

It is possible to increase the efficiency for which the visibility of a large number of objects is determined by organizing them into a structure whose properties allow large regions of space to be culled from the visible set of geometry using very simple tests. This practice is called *spatial partitioning* and comes in two popular varieties that we discuss in this section: octrees and binary space partitioning trees. Both methods are usually applied only to static world geometry since computation of the data structures involved is generally too expensive to perform at runtime.

7.3.1 Octrees

Suppose that all the geometry belonging to an entire world or to a particular region of a world is contained within a rectangular box B. An *octree* is a structure that partitions this box into eight smaller, equal-size rectangular boxes called *octants*. These smaller boxes are further subdivided into eight even smaller octants, and the process continues to some maximum number of iterations called the *depth* of the octree. Each octant is linked to the box from which it was partitioned, and each object in the world is linked to the smallest octant that completely contains it (which may be the original box B).

Figure 7.9(a) illustrates the two-dimensional analog of an octree, called a *quadtree*, constructed for an area containing a single object. Figure 7.9(b) shows how the corresponding data structure is organized. Each node in a quadtree structure has at most four subnodes—octrees can have up to eight. As this example demonstrates, if no world geometry intersects a quadrant (or an octant in an octree), then that quadrant is not subdivided. Furthermore, any quadrant that does not completely contain any objects is deleted from the tree. We always assume that any missing quadrants are empty.

Organizing geometry into a tree structure has the benefit that whenever we can determine that a node of the tree is not visible, then we immediately know that every subnode of that node is also not visible and can simultaneously be culled. (Chapter 8 discusses how a similar property of tree structures benefits collision detection.) Visibility determination for the octree begins by testing the box surrounding the root node for intersection with the view frustum. If the camera is known to always lie within the boundary of the octree, then it can be assumed that the root node is always visible. When any node's bounding box is determined to be visible, we consider each object linked to that node by testing its bounding volume for visibility. We then perform the same test for any existing subnodes of the visible node. When a node's bounding box fails the visibility test, we ignore all objects linked to that node and any subnodes belonging to that node.

We can use the fact that the bounding boxes at each level of an octree all have the same orientation to our advantage. For any given camera position and orientation, we transform the axes of the octree into camera space and calculate the five effective radii (one for the near and far planes and four corresponding to the side planes) of the box B bounding the entire structure. If r_{eff} is the effective radius of the box B with respect to a particular view frustum plane, then the effective radius of any box residing one level deeper within the tree is simply $r_{\text{eff}}/2$. This saves us from having to use Equation (7.47) to calculate effective radii for every octant at every level—calculating it once at the beginning is sufficient.

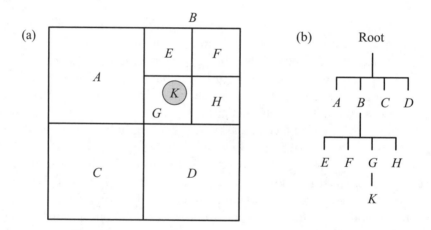

Figure 7.9 (a) A quadtree constructed for an area containing a single object. (b) The data structure representation of the quadtree.

7.3.2 Binary Space Partitioning Trees

A *Binary Space Partitioning (BSP) tree* is a structure that divides space into two regions at each level. Unlike the planes that partition octrees, the planes partitioning a BSP tree can be arbitrarily oriented. A BSP tree is constructed for a set of objects by choosing a partitioning plane, sometimes called a *splitting plane*, and sorting the geometry into two groups: objects lying on the positive side of the plane (also called the positive *halfspace*) and objects lying on the negative side of the plane (the negative halfspace).

Traditionally, the partitioning planes of a BSP tree have been aligned to the polygons that make up the world geometry. Figure 7.10 illustrates a two-dimensional example of a region containing several polygons that determine the structure of the BSP tree. One polygon is chosen to represent the splitting plane at each level, and the remaining polygons are sorted into positive and negative groups. Any polygons intersecting the plane are split into two polygons that lie in the positive and negative halfspaces. The positive and negative groups are then partitioned, and the process continues for each halfspace until no polygons remain.

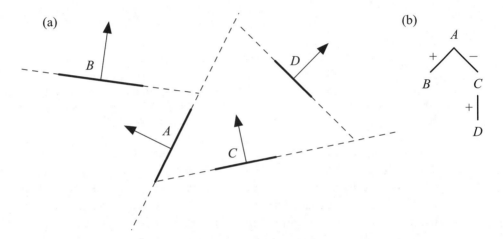

Figure 7.10 (a) A traditional BSP tree and (b) the associated data structure.

The large number of polygons and curved surfaces used in modern 3D engines makes the traditional BSP tree impractical. In a somewhat modified approach, we create one splitting for each *object* instead of each polygon. As shown in Figure 7.11, the splitting plane for an object is aligned so that it is perpendicular to the object's principal axis **T** corresponding to the smallest dimension of its bounding box. This minimizes the distance that the object extends away from the splitting plane. After a splitting plane has been chosen for an object, the other objects are sorted into those that lie completely within the positive halfspace and those that lie completely within the negative halfspace. Any objects that straddle the splitting plane are added to *both* the positive and negative groups. The halfspaces are recursively partitioned until no objects remain.

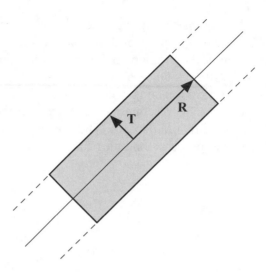

Figure 7.11 An object's splitting plane is aligned so that it is perpendicular to the object's principal axis **T** corresponding to the smallest dimension of its bounding box.

For each splitting plane of a BSP tree, we need to determine the visibility of each halfspace and the visibility of the object associated with the plane. This requires that we have a way to determine whether a plane **K** intersects the view frustum. The simplest approach would be to test the eight vertices of the view frustum in world space against the plane **K** by calculating the 4D dot products and comparing them to zero. If all eight dot products have the same sign (meaning that all eight points lie on the same side of the plane), then the plane does not intersect the view frustum. Fortunately, we can find a better method by transforming the plane **K** into homogeneous clip space and utilizing the cubic symmetry of the view frustum in that space (see Section 4.5.1).

A plane **K** can be transformed from world space to homogeneous clip space using the formula

$$\mathbf{K}' = \left[(\mathbf{PM})^{-1} \right]^{\mathrm{T}} \mathbf{K}, \tag{7.50}$$

where **P** is the projection matrix and **M** is the transformation from world space to camera space. The components of each vertex of the view frustum in clip space are ± 1. The vertex producing the greatest dot product with the plane **K**′ is the one having component signs that match the signs of the x-, y-, and z-components of **K**′. The vertex producing the least dot product with **K**′ is the one having component signs opposite those of the components of **K**′. The greatest dot product $d_{\max}$ and the least dot product $d_{\min}$ are thus given by

$$d_{max} = |K'_x| + |K'_y| + |K'_z| + K'_w$$
$$d_{min} = -|K'_x| - |K'_y| - |K'_z| + K'_w. \qquad (7.51)$$

As shown in Figure 7.12, if $d_{max} \leq 0$, then the view frustum lies entirely on the negative side of the plane **K**. This means that nothing on the *positive* side of the plane is visible. Similarly, if $d_{min} \geq 0$, then the view frustum lies entirely on the positive side of the plane **K**, and thus nothing on the *negative* side of the plane is visible. If neither of the conditions $d_{max} \leq 0$ or $d_{min} \geq 0$ is satisfied, then the plane **K** intersects the view frustum, and we cannot cull either halfspace.

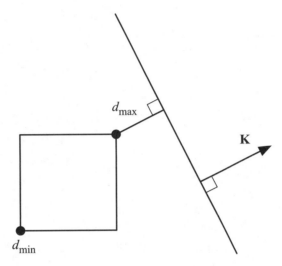

Figure 7.12 Let d_{max} and d_{min} be the greatest dot product and least dot product of any frustum vertex with the plane **K**. If $d_{max} \leq 0$ or $d_{min} \geq 0$, then the view frustum lies completely on one side of **K**, so the other side is not visible.

7.4 Portal Systems

A *portal system* is an extremely powerful technique that can be used to quickly eliminate massive regions of world geometry from the visible set. The general idea is surprisingly simple—the world is divided into many disjoint *zones* that are connected by *portals*. A portal is represented by a convex polygon through which one region can be seen from another. The advantage of a portal system is that any region of space that cannot be seen through a series of portals is never even considered for rendering. When determining what parts of a world are visible, using a portal system allows us to touch only a small fraction of the entire data set because any geometry that lies on the opposite side of an invisible portal is ignored.

Figure 7.13 illustrates how visibility determination is carried out for a portal system. We first locate the zone in which the camera resides—this zone is always considered visible. We then examine each of the portals leading out of the zone containing the camera. For each portal that intersects the view frustum, we consider the zone to which it connects visible. Each portal leading out of the connecting zone, excluding any leading back to the first zone, is then tested for visibility, but this time against a view frustum that has been reduced in size by the boundary of the portal through which we are looking. This technique is applied recursively until no new portals are visible.

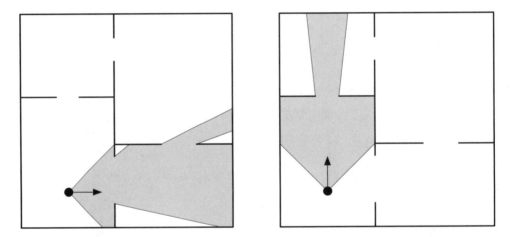

Figure 7.13 Only regions of space that can be seen through a series of portals are considered visible.

The zones connected by portals may be further organized into tree structures, and the objects residing in these regions may still have bounding volumes. The visibility of large regions determined by the portal system is a large-scale culling process that should be supplemented by smaller-scale visibility determination in each zone.

7.4.1 Portal Clipping

Whenever the camera looks through a portal connecting to another zone, we know that the volume of visibility in that zone is smaller than the whole view frustum. Thus, we can reject a larger number of objects during smaller-scale visibility testing by using a smaller view frustum. The near and far planes remain the same, but the side planes of the new view frustum are replaced by a set of planes that represents the intersection of the original view frustum and the sides of any polygonal portals through which we are looking.

As a convention, the plane containing a portal must have a normal direction that points toward the camera, and the vertices of the portal must be wound counterclockwise, as shown in Figure 7.14. Consequently, portals are one-way in the sense that if a portal leads from zone X to zone Y, then the same portal does *not* lead backward from zone Y to zone X. When the camera lies on the negative side of a plane containing a portal, that portal is never considered visible. Two-way visibility between two zones requires that each zone have a portal leading to the other.

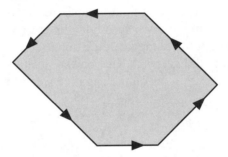

Figure 7.14 The vertices of a portal are wound counterclockwise about the normal of the plane containing them. Here, the normal points out of the page.

Whenever we consider a portal leading out of a zone, we are interested only in the visible area of that portal. The visible area of a portal is equal to the area that intersects the current view frustum, which may be the original view frustum or a reduced view frustum. To determine what area of a portal is visible, we *clip* its polygon against the planes bounding the current view frustum. Clipping a polygon against a plane removes the portion of the polygon lying on the negative side of the plane, resulting in a new polygon whose interior lies completely on the positive side of the plane. Clipping a polygon against every plane of the current view frustum effectively chops off any part lying outside the volume of space that is visible to the camera.

Suppose we need to clip a portal whose vertices lie at the points $V_1, V_2, \ldots, V_n$ and connect to form a convex polygon. When we clip this polygon against a plane L, we produce a new convex polygon having at most $n+1$ vertices. We begin the clipping process by classifying all of the vertices into three categories:

those lying on the positive side of **L**, those lying on the negative side of **L**, and those considered to be lying in the plane **L** itself. A vertex $\mathbf{V}_i$ is classified as lying in the plane if its dot product with **L** satisfies

$$-\varepsilon < \mathbf{L} \cdot \mathbf{V}_i \leq 0 \tag{7.52}$$

for some small constant ε (typically, $\varepsilon \approx 0.001$). This prevents problems associated with round-off error that would otherwise wreak havoc on our visibility tests by destroying the convexity of the view frustum. If no vertices lie on the positive side of the plane **L**, then the portal is not visible, and we do not render anything in the zone to which it connects. If no vertices lie on the *negative* side of the plane **L**, then no clipping is necessary. Otherwise, we visit every pair of neighboring vertices, looking for edges having one positive vertex and one negative vertex. As shown in Figure 7.15, new vertices are added to the polygon where edges intersect the clipping plane, and vertices lying on the negative side of the plane are removed. Vertices lying on the positive side of the clipping plane or lying in the clipping plane itself are not affected.

Suppose that the vertex $\mathbf{V}_i$ lies on the positive side of the clipping plane **L**, and that the vertex $\mathbf{V}_{i+1}$ lies on the negative side of **L**, or equivalently,

$$\mathbf{L} \cdot \mathbf{V}_i > 0$$
$$\mathbf{L} \cdot \mathbf{V}_{i+1} \leq -\varepsilon. \tag{7.53}$$

A point **W** lying on the line segment connecting $\mathbf{V}_i$ and $\mathbf{V}_{i+1}$ can be expressed as

$$\mathbf{W}(t) = \mathbf{V}_i + t(\mathbf{V}_{i+1} - \mathbf{V}_i), \tag{7.54}$$

where the parameter t satisfies $0 \leq t \leq 1$. Solving for the value of t that yields $\mathbf{L} \cdot \mathbf{W}(t) = 0$, we have

$$t = \frac{\mathbf{L} \cdot \mathbf{V}_i}{\mathbf{L} \cdot (\mathbf{V}_i - \mathbf{V}_{i+1})}. \tag{7.55}$$

(Note that the difference $\mathbf{V}_i - \mathbf{V}_{i+1}$ has a w-coordinate of 0.) Substituting this value back into Equation (7.54) gives us our new vertex **W**.

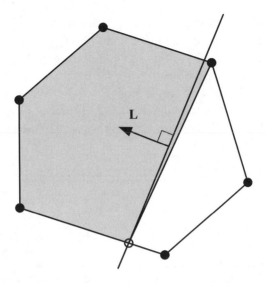

Figure 7.15 When a portal is clipped against a plane, new vertices are added where edges intersect the plane, and vertices lying on the negative side of the plane are removed. Vertices lying on the positive side of the clipping plane or lying in the clipping plane itself are not affected.

7.4.2 Reduced View Frustums

Given a clipped portal, we wish to calculate the planes surrounding the volume of space visible through that portal. This enables us to perform visibility determination against a view frustum that is smaller than the original view frustum, resulting in a greater number of objects being culled. Fortunately, the camera-space plane corresponding to an edge of a portal is simple to calculate. The plane $\mathbf{L}_i$ passing through the origin and the two portal vertices $\mathbf{V}_i$ and $\mathbf{V}_{i+1}$ is given by

$$\mathbf{L}_i = \left\langle \frac{\mathbf{V}_{i+1} \times \mathbf{V}_i}{\|\mathbf{V}_{i+1} \times \mathbf{V}_i\|}, 0 \right\rangle. \tag{7.56}$$

For a portal having n vertices, we use Equation (7.56) to calculate the n side planes of our reduced view frustum. (For the plane $\mathbf{L}_n$, we wrap around by setting $\mathbf{V}_{n+1} = \mathbf{V}_0$.) If the distance between any two portal vertices $\mathbf{V}_i$ and $\mathbf{V}_{i+1}$ is very small, then round-off errors can cause convexity problems, so we discard any plane $\mathbf{L}_i$ for which

$$\|\mathbf{V}_{i+1} - \mathbf{V}_i\|^2 < \varepsilon, \tag{7.57}$$

where ε is a small constant that can be adjusted to produce acceptable results.

The side planes of a reduced view frustum can meet at highly acute angles. As shown in Figure 7.16, this can impact the effectiveness of bounding volume visibility tests because objects lying far from the view frustum still may not lie on the negative side of any single frustum plane. We can eliminate this problem by detecting cases in which adjacent frustum planes meet at a small angle and adding an extra plane to the view frustum whenever such cases occurs.

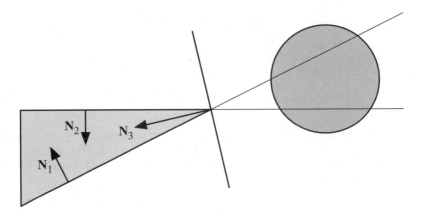

Figure 7.16 Side planes of the reduced view frustum that meet at an acute angle can impact the effectiveness of bounding volume visibility tests. The bounding sphere shown here does not fail the visibility test even though it lies far outside the view frustum.

Figure 7.16 shows a new plane having normal direction $\mathbf{N}_3$ added to the view frustum between two adjacent planes having normal vectors $\mathbf{N}_1$ and $\mathbf{N}_2$. The vector $\mathbf{N}_3$ is constructed by first calculating the average (unnormalized) direction between $\mathbf{N}_1$ and $\mathbf{N}_2$, which is simply given by the sum $\mathbf{N}_1 + \mathbf{N}_2$. We then subtract the projection of this average onto the direction $\mathbf{N}_1 \times \mathbf{N}_2$ to ensure that the new plane contains the line at which the two original planes intersect. This gives us the following expression for $\mathbf{N}_3$.

$$\mathbf{A} = \mathbf{N}_1 + \mathbf{N}_2$$
$$\mathbf{B} = \mathbf{N}_1 \times \mathbf{N}_2$$
$$\mathbf{N}_3 = \frac{\mathbf{A} - (\mathbf{A} \cdot \mathbf{B})\mathbf{B}}{\|\mathbf{A} - (\mathbf{A} \cdot \mathbf{B})\mathbf{B}\|} \tag{7.58}$$

Since it passes through the origin in camera space, the new plane has a *w*-coordinate of 0.

The situation demonstrated in Figure 7.16 can be avoided by constructing an extra plane whenever two adjacent frustum planes having normals $\mathbf{N}_1$ and $\mathbf{N}_2$ satisfy the condition $\mathbf{N}_1 \cdot \mathbf{N}_2 < \alpha$, where α represents an acuteness threshold. The extra planes do not actually contribute to the shape of the view frustum since they are coincident with the lines at which previously existing planes intersect. They should be used only for visibility testing within a single zone and should not participate in the clipping of any portals leading to other zones.

Chapter 7 Summary

Principal Components

The principal axes $\mathbf{R}$, $\mathbf{S}$, and $\mathbf{T}$ of a set of N vertices $\mathbf{P}_1, \mathbf{P}_2, \ldots, \mathbf{P}_N$ are given by the eigenvectors of the covariance matrix $\mathbf{C}$ defined by

$$\mathbf{C} = \frac{1}{N} \sum_{i=1}^{N} (\mathbf{P}_i - \mathbf{m})(\mathbf{P}_i - \mathbf{m})^{\mathrm{T}},$$

where the mean position $\mathbf{m}$ is given by

$$\mathbf{m} = \frac{1}{N} \sum_{i=1}^{N} \mathbf{P}_i.$$

If λ_1, λ_2, and λ_3 are the eigenvalues corresponding to the vectors $\mathbf{R}$, $\mathbf{S}$, and $\mathbf{T}$, respectively, then $|\lambda_1| \geq |\lambda_2| \geq |\lambda_3|$.

Bounding Boxes

The two planes perpendicular to the principal axis $\mathbf{A}$ that bound the set of vertices $\mathbf{P}_1, \mathbf{P}_2, \ldots, \mathbf{P}_N$ are given by

$$\left\langle \mathbf{A}, -\min_{1 \leq i \leq N} \{\mathbf{P}_i \cdot \mathbf{A}\} \right\rangle \quad \left\langle -\mathbf{A}, \max_{1 \leq i \leq N} \{\mathbf{P}_i \cdot \mathbf{A}\} \right\rangle.$$

The center $\mathbf{Q}$ of a bounding box is given by

$$\mathbf{Q} = k_1 \mathbf{A}_1 + k_2 \mathbf{A}_2 + k_3 \mathbf{A}_3,$$

where

$$k_j = \frac{\min_{1 \le i \le N}\{\mathbf{P}_i \cdot \mathbf{A}_j\} + \max_{1 \le i \le N}\{\mathbf{P}_i \cdot \mathbf{A}_j\}}{2},$$

and $\mathbf{A}_1$, $\mathbf{A}_2$, and $\mathbf{A}_3$ are the unit-length principal axes.

The effective radius r_{eff} with respect to a plane having normal direction $\mathbf{N}$ of a bounding box whose dimensions and orientation are described by the vectors $\mathbf{R}$, $\mathbf{S}$, and $\mathbf{T}$ is given by

$$r_{\text{eff}} = \tfrac{1}{2}|\mathbf{R} \cdot \mathbf{N} + \mathbf{S} \cdot \mathbf{N} + \mathbf{T} \cdot \mathbf{N}|.$$

Bounding Spheres

A bounding sphere for the set of vertices $\mathbf{P}_1, \mathbf{P}_2, \ldots, \mathbf{P}_N$ is constructed by locating the points $\mathbf{P}_k$ and $\mathbf{P}_l$ that produce the least and greatest dot products with the primary axis $\mathbf{R}$ and setting the initial center $\mathbf{Q}$ and radius r to

$$\mathbf{Q} = \frac{\mathbf{P}_k + \mathbf{P}_l}{2}$$
$$r = \|\mathbf{P}_k - \mathbf{Q}\|.$$

For any point $\mathbf{P}_i$ satisfying $\|\mathbf{P}_i - \mathbf{Q}\|^2 > r^2$, we replace the center and radius with the values

$$\mathbf{Q}' = \frac{\mathbf{G} + \mathbf{P}_i}{2}$$
$$r' = \|\mathbf{P}_i - \mathbf{Q}'\|,$$

where $\mathbf{G}$ is defined as

$$\mathbf{G} = \mathbf{Q} - r\frac{\mathbf{P}_i - \mathbf{Q}}{\|\mathbf{P}_i - \mathbf{Q}\|}.$$

A bounding sphere having center $\mathbf{Q}$ and radius r is not visible if for any view frustum plane $\mathbf{L}$ we have $\mathbf{L} \cdot \mathbf{Q} \le -r$.

Bounding Ellipsoids

A bounding ellipsoid for the set of vertices $\mathbf{P}_1, \mathbf{P}_2, \ldots, \mathbf{P}_N$ is constructed by transforming into a space in which the box bounding the set is a cube, constructing a bounding sphere in that space, and then performing the reverse transformation to scale the sphere to the original dimensions of the bounding box.

The effective radius r_{eff} with respect to a plane having normal direction $\mathbf{N}$ of a bounding ellipsoid whose semi-axis lengths and orientations are described by the vectors $\mathbf{R}$, $\mathbf{S}$, and $\mathbf{T}$ is given by

$$r_{\text{eff}} = \sqrt{(\mathbf{R} \cdot \mathbf{N})^2 + (\mathbf{S} \cdot \mathbf{N})^2 + (\mathbf{T} \cdot \mathbf{N})^2}.$$

A bounding ellipsoid having center $\mathbf{Q}$ is not visible if for any view frustum plane $\mathbf{L}$ we have $\mathbf{L} \cdot \mathbf{Q} \leq -r_{\text{eff}}$.

Bounding Cylinders

A bounding cylinder for the set of vertices $\mathbf{P}_1, \mathbf{P}_2, \ldots, \mathbf{P}_N$ is constructed by first calculating the points $\{\mathbf{H}_i\}$ using the formula

$$\mathbf{H}_i = \mathbf{P}_i - (\mathbf{P}_i \cdot \mathbf{R})\mathbf{R},$$

where $\mathbf{R}$ is the unit vector parallel to the primary axis. After finding a bounding circle for the points $\{\mathbf{H}_i\}$ having center $\mathbf{Q}$ and radius r, the endpoints $\mathbf{Q}_1$ and $\mathbf{Q}_2$ of the bounding cylinder are given by

$$\mathbf{Q}_1 = \mathbf{Q} + \min_{1 \leq i \leq N} \{\mathbf{P}_i \cdot \mathbf{R}\}\mathbf{R}$$
$$\mathbf{Q}_2 = \mathbf{Q} + \max_{1 \leq i \leq N} \{\mathbf{P}_i \cdot \mathbf{R}\}\mathbf{R}.$$

The effective radius r_{eff} with respect to a plane having normal direction $\mathbf{N}$ of a bounding cylinder is given by

$$r_{\text{eff}} = r\sqrt{1 - (\mathbf{A} \cdot \mathbf{N})^2},$$

where $\mathbf{A}$ is the unit vector parallel to the axis of the cylinder given by

$$\mathbf{A} = \frac{\mathbf{Q}_2 - \mathbf{Q}_1}{\|\mathbf{Q}_2 - \mathbf{Q}_1\|}.$$

A bounding cylinder is not visible if the line segment connecting the endpoints $\mathbf{Q}_1$ and $\mathbf{Q}_2$ is completely clipped away by the view frustum planes.

Binary Space Partitioning (BSP) Trees

We can determine whether a world-space plane $\mathbf{K}$ intersects the view frustum by transforming the plane into homogeneous clip space using the formula

$$\mathbf{K}' = \left[(\mathbf{PM})^{-1}\right]^{\text{T}}\mathbf{K},$$

where $\mathbf{P}$ is the projection matrix and $\mathbf{M}$ is the transformation from world space to camera space. The greatest dot product d_{max} and least dot product d_{min} of any frustum vertex with the plane $\mathbf{K}'$ are given by

$$d_{max} = |K'_x| + |K'_y| + |K'_z| + K'_w$$
$$d_{min} = -|K'_x| - |K'_y| - |K'_z| + K'_w.$$

If $d_{max} \leq 0$ or $d_{min} \geq 0$, then the view frustum lies completely on one side of $\mathbf{K}$, so the other side is not visible.

Portal Systems

When clipping a portal having vertices $\mathbf{V}_1, \mathbf{V}_2, \ldots, \mathbf{V}_n$ against a plane $\mathbf{L}$, we add a new vertex between any two adjacent vertices $\mathbf{V}_i$ and $\mathbf{V}_{i+1}$ lying on opposite sides of $\mathbf{L}$. The new vertex $\mathbf{W}$ is given by

$$\mathbf{W} = \mathbf{V}_i + t(\mathbf{V}_{i+1} - \mathbf{V}_i),$$

where the parameter t is given by

$$t = \frac{\mathbf{L} \cdot \mathbf{V}_i}{\mathbf{L} \cdot (\mathbf{V}_i - \mathbf{V}_{i+1})}.$$

The plane $\mathbf{L}_i$ passing through the origin and the two portal vertices $\mathbf{V}_i$ and $\mathbf{V}_{i+1}$ is given by

$$\mathbf{L}_i = \left\langle \frac{\mathbf{V}_{i+1} \times \mathbf{V}_i}{\|\mathbf{V}_{i+1} \times \mathbf{V}_i\|}, 0 \right\rangle.$$

An extra plane may be added to the view frustum to improve bounding volume visibility determination when planes having normal directions $\mathbf{N}_1$ and $\mathbf{N}_2$ meet at an acute angle. The new plane passes through the origin and has the normal direction $\mathbf{N}_3$ given by

$$\mathbf{A} = \mathbf{N}_1 + \mathbf{N}_2$$
$$\mathbf{B} = \mathbf{N}_1 \times \mathbf{N}_2$$
$$\mathbf{N}_3 = \frac{\mathbf{A} - (\mathbf{A} \cdot \mathbf{B})\mathbf{B}}{\|\mathbf{A} - (\mathbf{A} \cdot \mathbf{B})\mathbf{B}\|}.$$

Exercises for Chapter 7

1. Given two spheres S_1 and S_2 centered at the points $\mathbf{Q}_1$ and $\mathbf{Q}_2$, and having radii r_1 and r_2, respectively, determine the center $\mathbf{Q}$ and radius r of the smallest single sphere that encloses both S_1 and S_2. Account for the cases that the two spheres are disjoint, that the two spheres intersect, and that one of the spheres encloses the other.

2. Determine formulas for the center $\mathbf{Q}$ and radius r of the optimal bounding sphere for a cone whose radius (at the base) is s, whose height is h, and whose base is centered on the origin of the x-y plane as shown in Figure 7.17. Consider the two cases that $s < h$ and $s \geq h$.

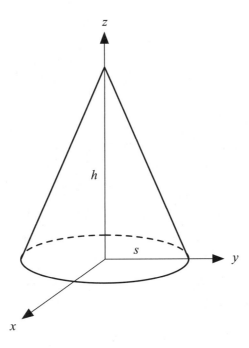

Figure 7.17 The cone used in Exercise 2.

3. Determine the effective radius r_{eff} of a box whose edges are described by the vectors $\mathbf{R} = \langle 2,0,1 \rangle$, $\mathbf{S} = \langle 1,0,-2 \rangle$, and $\mathbf{T} = \langle 0,1,0 \rangle$ with respect to a plane having unit normal direction $\mathbf{N} = \left\langle \frac{\sqrt{3}}{3}, -\frac{\sqrt{3}}{3}, \frac{\sqrt{3}}{3} \right\rangle$.

4. Write programs that construct a bounding box, a bounding sphere, a bounding ellipsoid, and a bounding cylinder given an array of n vertex positions.

5. Implement a portal system that can clip the view frustum to an arbitrary convex polygon and perform visibility tests against the reduced frustum.

Chapter 8

Collision Detection

Every 3D game is filled with the action of moving objects. Except when an object is emitting a force field that affects its surroundings, interaction between two objects generally occurs only when they attempt to occupy the same space at the same time. The process by which game engines determine when such events occur is called *collision detection*. With the exception of those that take place in deep space, most games need to determine when a collision occurs between a moving object and the environment. The complex geometrical shapes that moving objects may possess are usually approximated by simple bounding volumes in order to reduce the cost of collision detection calculations.

Suppose that the position of a moving object is known at the time that a frame is rendered, and that we are able to calculate the position to which the object would move if it is unobstructed before the next frame is rendered. Since the time between frames is usually small, it is commonly assumed that objects travel along straight lines during the time between frames, even if it is known that an object is following a curved path. Thus, the general collision detection problem is determining whether the extrusion of an object's surface along a line segment intersects some part of the environment. Very small moving objects are often treated as points, reducing the collision detection problem to a ray intersection calculation. For larger objects, finding the exact point where the object makes contact with a complex environment can be extremely difficult. For that reason, surfaces of moving objects are often approximated by simpler bounding volumes.

8.1 Plane Collisions

Detecting a collision between a moving object and a single infinite plane amounts to the problem of determining what point on the object would be in contact with the plane at the time of a collision. We can then represent the entire moving object by that point in a ray intersection calculation. Being able to detect collisions with infinite planes is useful in environments that are partitioned in some way (see Section 8.1.3), so we examine the calculations involved in determining when a sphere or box collides with an infinite plane in this section. Later, we discuss the more difficult, but very practical method of determining the collision of a sphere with an arbitrary environment.

8.1.1 Collision of a Sphere and a Plane

As shown in Figure 8.1, when a sphere is in contact with a plane $\mathbf{L}$ (on the positive side), the distance from the center of the sphere $\mathbf{P}$ to the plane is r, so $\mathbf{L} \cdot \mathbf{P} = r$. Writing the plane $\mathbf{L}$ as the 4D vector

$$\mathbf{L} = \langle \mathbf{N}, D \rangle, \tag{8.1}$$

the relationship $\mathbf{L} \cdot \mathbf{P} = r$ can be written as

$$\mathbf{N} \cdot \mathbf{P} + D = r. \tag{8.2}$$

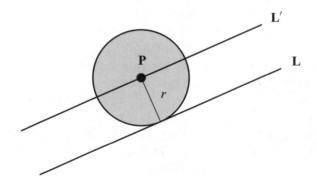

Figure 8.1 A sphere of radius r is in contact with a plane $\mathbf{L}$ when its center lies on the plane $\mathbf{L}'$ that has been shifted by a distance r.

If we move r to the left side of the equation, then this is equivalent to

$$\mathbf{N} \cdot \mathbf{P} + D - r = 0, \tag{8.3}$$

which is the same as stating that the point $\mathbf{P}$ lies on the plane $\mathbf{L}'$ given by

$$\mathbf{L}' = \langle \mathbf{N}, D - r \rangle. \tag{8.4}$$

The plane $\mathbf{L}'$ is parallel to $\mathbf{L}$, but it has been shifted by the distance r in the direction of its normal.

Suppose that the center of a sphere of radius r moves from the point $\mathbf{P}_1$ at time $t = 0$ to the point $\mathbf{P}_2$ at the time $t = 1$, and that we wish to determine whether it collides with a plane $\mathbf{L}$. We assume that the sphere is not initially intersecting the plane and that the starting point $\mathbf{P}_1$ lies on the positive side of a plane since the negative side represents the interior of some structure. Thus, $\mathbf{L} \cdot \mathbf{P}_1 \geq r$. If it is also the case that $\mathbf{L} \cdot \mathbf{P}_2 \geq r$, then the sphere remains on the positive side of the plane during the time interval $0 \leq t < 1$, in which case we know that no collision occurs.

The position $\mathbf{P}(t)$ of the sphere's center at time t is then given by

$$\mathbf{P}(t) = \mathbf{P}_1 + t\mathbf{V}, \tag{8.5}$$

where $\mathbf{V}$ is the velocity of the sphere:

$$\mathbf{V} = \mathbf{P}_2 - \mathbf{P}_1. \tag{8.6}$$

A collision occurs between the sphere and the plane $\mathbf{L} = \langle \mathbf{N}, D \rangle$ if the equation

$$\mathbf{L}' \cdot \mathbf{P}(t) = 0 \tag{8.7}$$

(where $\mathbf{L}'$ is defined by Equation (8.4)) has a solution t such that $0 \leq t < 1$. Substituting the value given by Equation (8.5) for $\mathbf{P}(t)$, we have

$$\mathbf{L}' \cdot \mathbf{P}_1 + t(\mathbf{L}' \cdot \mathbf{V}) = 0. \tag{8.8}$$

Solving for t yields

$$t = -\frac{\mathbf{L}' \cdot \mathbf{P}_1}{\mathbf{L}' \cdot \mathbf{V}}. \tag{8.9}$$

Remember that the vector $\mathbf{V}$ represents a direction and therefore has a w-coordinate of 0, so the denominator is equal to $\mathbf{N} \cdot \mathbf{V}$. If $\mathbf{N} \cdot \mathbf{V} = 0$, then the sphere is moving parallel to the plane, so no intersection occurs. Otherwise, the sphere collides with the plane at the time t given by Equation (8.9). The point $\mathbf{C}$ at which the sphere makes contact with the plane is given by

$$\mathbf{C} = \mathbf{P}(t) - r\mathbf{N} \tag{8.10}$$

since this point lies at a distance r from the sphere's center in the direction opposite that of the plane's normal $\mathbf{N}$.

8.1.2 Collision of a Box and a Plane

Determining whether a moving box collides with a plane can be accomplished using a method similar to that used to determine whether a sphere collides with a plane. The difference is that we must offset the plane by the *effective* radius of the box, introduced in Section 7.2.4. Furthermore, the box can make contact with the plane at more than one point. It is possible that an edge of the box collides with the plane or that the box meets the plane directly parallel to one of its faces.

Suppose that a box has edges whose lengths and orientations are described by the vectors $\mathbf{R}$, $\mathbf{S}$, and $\mathbf{T}$. The effective radius r_{eff} of the box with respect to a plane having normal direction $\mathbf{N}$ is given by

$$r_{\text{eff}} = \tfrac{1}{2}(|\mathbf{R} \cdot \mathbf{N}| + |\mathbf{S} \cdot \mathbf{N}| + |\mathbf{T} \cdot \mathbf{N}|). \tag{8.11}$$

Let $\mathbf{Q}_1$ be the position of the box's center at time $t = 0$, and let $\mathbf{Q}_2$ be its position at time $t = 1$, as shown in Figure 8.2. Then the position $\mathbf{Q}(t)$ of the box is given by

$$\mathbf{Q}(t) = \mathbf{Q}_1 + t\mathbf{V}, \tag{8.12}$$

where $\mathbf{V}$ is the velocity of the box:

$$\mathbf{V} = \mathbf{Q}_2 - \mathbf{Q}_1. \tag{8.13}$$

To find an intersection with the plane $\mathbf{L} = \langle \mathbf{N}, D \rangle$, we calculate

$$t = -\frac{\mathbf{L}' \cdot \mathbf{Q}_1}{\mathbf{L}' \cdot \mathbf{V}}, \tag{8.14}$$

where $\mathbf{L}'$ is the plane parallel to $\mathbf{L}$ that has been offset by a distance r_{eff}:

$$\mathbf{L}' = \langle \mathbf{N}, D - r_{\text{eff}} \rangle. \tag{8.15}$$

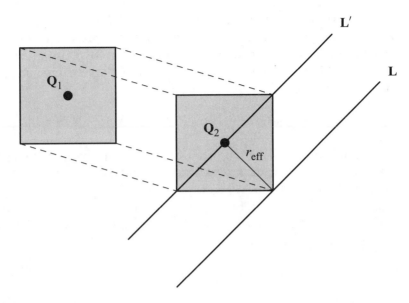

Figure 8.2 Whether a moving box collides with a plane can be determined by shifting the plane by the box's effective radius.

Again, we assume that the box is not initially intersecting the plane and that its center lies on the positive side of $\mathbf{L}'$ at time $t = 0$ (i.e., $\mathbf{L}' \cdot \mathbf{Q}_1 \geq 0$). Therefore, if the condition $\mathbf{L}' \cdot \mathbf{Q}_2 \geq 0$ is also satisfied, then the box remains on the positive side of the plane $\mathbf{L}$, and no collision occurs.

Once we have determined that a collision between the box and the plane has occurred (because the value of t given by Equation (8.14) satisfies $0 \leq t < 1$), we must determine the point or set of points at which contact has been made. If all three of the quantities $|\mathbf{R} \cdot \mathbf{N}|$, $|\mathbf{S} \cdot \mathbf{N}|$, and $|\mathbf{T} \cdot \mathbf{N}|$ are nonzero, then no edge of the box is parallel to the plane $\mathbf{L}$. In this case, the collision must occur at one of the box's vertices. We can find a general formula for the position of the vertex that makes contact with the plane by examining expressions for all eight of the box's vertices. The position $\mathbf{Z}$ of each vertex of the box is given by

$$\mathbf{Z} = \mathbf{Q}(t) \pm \tfrac{1}{2}\mathbf{R} \pm \tfrac{1}{2}\mathbf{S} \pm \tfrac{1}{2}\mathbf{T}. \qquad (8.16)$$

To find the vertex closest to the plane, we choose signs such that the dot product $\mathbf{L} \cdot \mathbf{Z}$ is minimized. This occurs when the quantities $\pm\mathbf{R} \cdot \mathbf{N}$, $\pm\mathbf{S} \cdot \mathbf{N}$, and $\pm\mathbf{T} \cdot \mathbf{N}$ are all negative; so if any one is positive, we choose the corresponding negative sign in Equation (8.16). The point of contact $\mathbf{C}$ is then given by

$$\mathbf{C} = \mathbf{Q}(t) - \tfrac{1}{2}[\text{sgn}(\mathbf{R} \cdot \mathbf{N})\mathbf{R} + \text{sgn}(\mathbf{S} \cdot \mathbf{N})\mathbf{S} + \text{sgn}(\mathbf{T} \cdot \mathbf{N})\mathbf{T}]. \qquad (8.17)$$

In the case that exactly one of the quantities $|\mathbf{R} \cdot \mathbf{N}|$, $|\mathbf{S} \cdot \mathbf{N}|$, and $|\mathbf{T} \cdot \mathbf{N}|$ is zero, the corresponding axis of the box is parallel to the plane, and any collision must occur at an edge. The endpoints $\mathbf{C}_1$ and $\mathbf{C}_2$ of the edge are given by modifying Equation (8.17) so that both signs are chosen for the term containing the zero dot product. For instance, if $|\mathbf{T} \cdot \mathbf{N}| = 0$, then we have

$$\mathbf{C}_{1,2} = \mathbf{Q}(t) - \tfrac{1}{2}[\operatorname{sgn}(\mathbf{R} \cdot \mathbf{N})\mathbf{R} + \operatorname{sgn}(\mathbf{S} \cdot \mathbf{N})\mathbf{S} \pm \mathbf{T}]. \tag{8.18}$$

This modification is taken one step further when two of the quantities $|\mathbf{R} \cdot \mathbf{N}|$, $|\mathbf{S} \cdot \mathbf{N}|$, and $|\mathbf{T} \cdot \mathbf{N}|$ are zero. In this case, the collision occurs at a face of the box whose vertices are given by modifying Equation (8.17) so that both signs are chosen for both of the terms containing zero dot products. For instance, if $|\mathbf{S} \cdot \mathbf{N}| = 0$ and $|\mathbf{T} \cdot \mathbf{N}| = 0$, then the vertices $\mathbf{C}_1$, $\mathbf{C}_2$, $\mathbf{C}_3$, and $\mathbf{C}_4$ of the face in contact with the plane are given by

$$\mathbf{C}_{1,2,3,4} = \mathbf{Q}(t) - \tfrac{1}{2}[\operatorname{sgn}(\mathbf{R} \cdot \mathbf{N})\mathbf{R} \pm \mathbf{S} \pm \mathbf{T}]. \tag{8.19}$$

8.1.3 Spatial Partitioning

Being able to determine whether an object collides with a plane is essential to fast collision detection in a spatially partitioned environment. Since regions of octrees and BSP trees are separated by planes, we can usually tell that a moving object does not collide with large parts of the world without having to perform collision detection tests with the actual geometry in those regions.

Suppose that an object moves from the point $\mathbf{P}_1$ to the point $\mathbf{P}_2$ during a single frame. Let $\mathbf{L} = \langle \mathbf{N}, D \rangle$ represent a plane that partitions the world geometry in some way, and suppose that the moving object has an effective radius of r_{eff} with respect to that plane. We say that the object lies completely on the positive side of the plane $\mathbf{L}$ if its position $\mathbf{P}$ satisfies

$$\mathbf{L} \cdot \mathbf{P} \geq r_{\text{eff}}, \tag{8.20}$$

and we say that the object lies completely on the negative side of the plane $\mathbf{L}$ if its position $\mathbf{P}$ satisfies

$$\mathbf{L} \cdot \mathbf{P} \leq -r_{\text{eff}}. \tag{8.21}$$

If both of the points $\mathbf{P}_1$ and $\mathbf{P}_2$ represent positions of the object for which it lies completely on the positive side of the plane, then we know that no part of the object ever crosses into the negative side of the plane $\mathbf{L}$. Similarly, if both of the points $\mathbf{P}_1$ and $\mathbf{P}_2$ represent positions of the object for which it lies completely on the negative side of the plane, then we know that no part of the object ever crosses into the positive side of the plane **L**. When these cases occur, we can avoid performing collision detection calculations between the moving object and any geometry that lies on the opposite side of the plane **L**.

8.2 General Sphere Collisions

We now study a powerful technique for determining when a moving sphere collides with an arbitrary static environment. The method presented in this section is quite capable of serving as the entire collision detection system for a 3D game engine, so long as it is acceptable to approximate moving objects by their bounding spheres. It can also be employed to detect collisions between a moving sphere and any other arbitrarily complex moving object by subtracting velocities.

The collision detection method is based on the fact that the center of a sphere of radius r in contact with another object lies at exactly the distance r from the surface of the object. If we consider a sphere in contact with a polygonal model, the set of all possible centers forms a surface having three kinds of components. First, the set of centers for which a sphere is in contact with a single face of the model consists of the interior of the face moved outward in the face's normal direction by the radius r. Second, the center of a sphere in contact with a single edge of the model lies on the cylinder of radius r having the edge as its axis. Third, the center of a sphere in contact with a single vertex of the model lies on the sphere of radius r centered at the vertex position. We can determine when a moving sphere collides with the model by determining when the ray representing the motion of the sphere's center intersects the expanded surface of the model, as illustrated in Figure 8.3.

The procedure for determining whether a sphere of radius r collides with a polygonal model is summarized by the following three steps.

A. Determine whether the sphere's center intersects any of the faces of the model after they have been moved outward by the distance r. If it does intersect a face, then skip the next two steps.

B. Determine whether the sphere's center intersects any of the cylinders of radius r corresponding to the expanded edges of the model. If it does intersect an edge, skip the third step.

C. Determine whether the sphere's center intersects any of the spheres of radius r corresponding to the expanded vertices of the model.

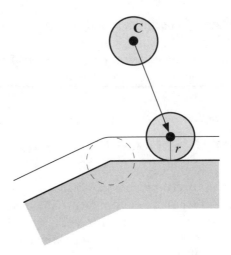

Figure 8.3 A sphere of radius r collides with a polygonal model when its center **C** intersects the expansion of the surface by the distance r.

When performing intersections with the edge cylinders, we do not have to worry about whether the intersection occurs on the exterior surface because an intersection with the interior surface would be preceded along the ray by a face intersection (see Figure 8.4). Likewise, an interior intersection with a vertex sphere would be preceded by either a face intersection or an edge cylinder intersection.

A ray intersection with a triangular face of a model can be accomplished using the method discussed in Section 5.2.1. Each face's plane needs to be offset by the distance r to determine the point of ray intersection. The barycentric coordinates of that point can then be calculated using the original vertex positions of the triangle (see Chapter 5, Exercise 5). A ray intersection with a vertex sphere can be performed using the method discussed in Section 5.2.3 after translating the vertex's position to the origin. Calculating the intersection of a ray and an edge cylinder is slightly more complicated since the cylinder can have an arbitrary orientation.

Suppose we need to determine at what parameter value t the ray given by $\mathbf{P}(t) = \mathbf{S} + t\mathbf{V}$ intersects a cylinder of radius r corresponding to the edge having endpoints $\mathbf{E}_1$ and $\mathbf{E}_2$. It is convenient to translate our coordinate system by $-\mathbf{E}_1$ so that one end of the cylinder is centered at the origin, resulting in the cylinder shown in Figure 8.5. A point $\mathbf{P}$ lies on the lateral surface of the infinite cylinder aligned to the edge if its distance from the axis $\mathbf{A} = \mathbf{E}_2 - \mathbf{E}_1$ is equal to r. Using the distance formula derived in Section 4.1.1, we can describe the set of points on the surface of the infinite cylinder as follows.

$$r^2 = P^2 - \left(\text{proj}_A \, P \right)^2$$

$$= P^2 - \frac{(P \cdot A)^2}{A^2}. \tag{8.22}$$

Replacing P with the translated ray $P(t) - E_1$ gives us

$$r^2 = (S_0 + tV)^2 - \frac{[(S_0 + tV) \cdot A]^2}{A^2}, \tag{8.23}$$

where $S_0 = S - E_1$. Expanding this and collecting terms, we obtain the quadratic equation $at^2 + 2bt + c = 0$, where

$$a = V^2 - \frac{(V \cdot A)^2}{A^2}$$

$$b = S_0 \cdot V - \frac{(S_0 \cdot A)(V \cdot A)}{A^2}$$

$$c = S_0^2 - r^2 - \frac{(S_0 \cdot A)^2}{A^2}. \tag{8.24}$$

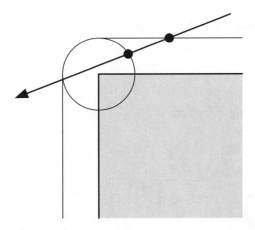

Figure 8.4 A ray intersection with the interior surface of an edge cylinder must be preceded by a face intersection, in which case the cylinder intersection calculation would never have been performed. Thus, cylinder intersections can be assumed to lie on the exterior of the expanded surface. A similar argument applies to vertex spheres.

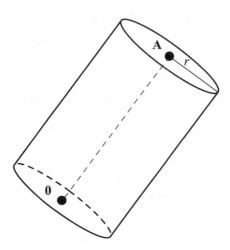

Figure 8.5 A cylinder of radius r corresponding to an edge having endpoints $\mathbf{E}_1$ and $\mathbf{E}_2$. The cylinder has been translated so that the center of one end lies at the origin, and the center $\mathbf{A}$ of the other end lies at $\mathbf{E}_2 - \mathbf{E}_1$.

The discriminant $D/4 = b^2 - ac$ tells us whether the ray intersects the infinite cylinder. If $D/4 > 0$, we must also check that the point of intersection falls within the edge. Since the value of a is always positive, the parameter t corresponding to the first intersection along the path followed by the ray is given by

$$t = \frac{-b - \sqrt{b^2 - ac}}{a}. \tag{8.25}$$

The signed length L of the projection of $\mathbf{P}(t) - \mathbf{E}_1$ onto the vector $\mathbf{A}$ is equal to

$$L = \frac{[\mathbf{P}(t) - \mathbf{E}_1] \cdot \mathbf{A}}{\|\mathbf{A}\|}.$$

The ray intersects the portion of the cylinder corresponding to the edge if L is positive and less than $\|\mathbf{A}\|$, so we simply need to check that

$$0 < [\mathbf{P}(t) - \mathbf{E}_1] \cdot \mathbf{A} < A^2.$$

When determining whether a swept sphere collides with a complex geometrical model, we want to avoid as many ray-triangle, ray-cylinder, and ray-sphere intersects as possible. The first step should always be to determine whether a collision would occur with the model's bounding sphere. For a moving sphere of radius r and a model having a bounding sphere of radius R, we need to intersect a ray with a sphere of radius $R + r$. The point of intersection is irrelevant—we only need to know whether an intersection occurs.

If the bounding sphere test passes, we must determine whether the swept sphere collides with a face, edge, or vertex of the model. To avoid unnecessary intersection tests, these components of a model should be sorted into some kind of hierarchical structure, such as an octree, and stored in an efficiently traversable format ahead of time. Creating separate structures for faces, edges, and vertices helps reduce memory access costs since edge and vertex intersects do not need to be performed if a face intersection is found.

Not all of a model's edges and vertices need to be considered for collision detection. As shown in Figure 8.6, the cylinder surrounding an edge where two faces meet at an exterior angle of less than or equal to 180 degrees lies completely inside the expanded surface. Thus, no part of the cylinder contributes to the collision surface, and the edge can be safely ignored. A similar principle applies to vertices. If a particular vertex is not the endpoint of any eligible edge, then it must also lie completely inside the expanded surface.

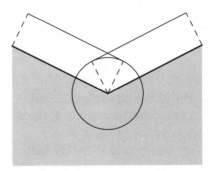

Figure 8.6 When two faces meet at an exterior angle of less than 180 degrees, the cylinder surrounding the shared edge lies completely inside the expanded collision surface. In this case, the cylinder does not need to be considered for collision detection.

To determine whether two faces sharing an edge with endpoints $\mathbf{E}_1$ and $\mathbf{E}_2$ meet at an exterior angle less than or equal to 180 degrees, we need to know for which of the two faces the vertices $\mathbf{E}_1$ and $\mathbf{E}_2$ occur in counterclockwise order. (For each edge structure created by the `BuildEdges` function shown in Listing 10.1, the triangle for which the vertices occur counterclockwise is always listed first.) Let $\mathbf{N}_1$ be the normal to the face for which the vertices $\mathbf{E}_1$ and $\mathbf{E}_2$ occur in counterclockwise order, and let $\mathbf{N}_2$ be the normal to the face for which the vertices $\mathbf{E}_1$ and $\mathbf{E}_2$ occur in clockwise order. The two faces meet at an exterior angle less than or equal to 180 degrees if

$$[\mathbf{N}_1 \times (\mathbf{E}_2 - \mathbf{E}_1)] \cdot \mathbf{N}_2 \geq 0. \qquad (8.26)$$

8.3 Sliding

When a moving object collides with a stationary part of the environment and is not destroyed as a consequence of the collision, most games allow the object to slide along the surface of the geometry that it hit. This is especially useful when the moving object is a character under user control, since sliding avoids the frustration of getting stuck whenever a player runs into something.

The distance by which an object slides over a surface during the single frame that it collides with part of the environment is determined by the angle with which the object struck the surface. As shown in Figure 8.7, a typical sliding implementation may choose to move an object to the point on the surface that is closest to the point at which it would have reached had the surface not been there to obstruct its motion. The difference between this point and the point at which the object hits the surface is perpendicular to the normal direction at the point of collision.

Suppose an object attempts to move from the point $\mathbf{P}_1$ to the point $\mathbf{P}_2$ during a single frame, but collides with the expansion of some surface at the point $\mathbf{Q}$. If the unit normal direction to the surface at the point $\mathbf{Q}$ is $\mathbf{N}$, then we can project the untraveled portion of the object's path onto the direction perpendicular to the surface to find a new destination $\mathbf{P}_3$ by calculating

$$\mathbf{P}_3 = \mathbf{P}_2 - [(\mathbf{P}_2 - \mathbf{Q}) \cdot \mathbf{N}]\mathbf{N}. \qquad (8.27)$$

Of course, we need to consider possible collisions between $\mathbf{Q}$ and $\mathbf{P}_3$, so the process repeats until either no collision occurs or the sliding distance falls below some minimum threshold.

When an object collides with a face of a model at a point $\mathbf{Q}$, one may be tempted to interpolate the vertex normal vectors using the barycentric coordinates of the point $\mathbf{Q}$ to obtain the normal direction there. This should be avoided not only because it creates a discontinuity in the normal direction at the cylindrical edges and spherical vertices, but because it prevents the calculation of an accurate sliding direction. Using a normal vector that is not truly perpendicular to the expanded surface causes the sliding direction to either take the moving object away from the surface or causes it to point inward, in which case another collision occurs immediately when attempting to slide.

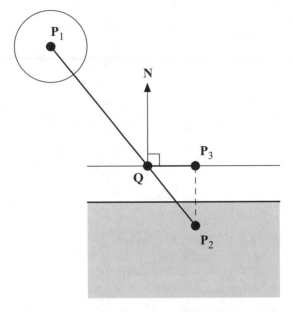

Figure 8.7 The part of the path from P_1 to P_2 that lies beyond the point of collision Q is projected onto the direction perpendicular to the normal vector N to determine how far an object should slide.

8.4 Collision of Two Spheres

Suppose that two spheres are in motion and have a constant linear velocity during a time interval beginning at $t = 0$ and ending at $t = 1$. We assume that the spheres are not already intersecting and that neither sphere contains the other. Let the points P_1 and P_2 represent the initial and final positions of the first sphere's center, and let Q_1 and Q_2 be the initial and final positions of the second sphere's center, as shown in Figure 8.8. We define the velocity vectors V_P and V_Q as

$$V_P = P_2 - P_1$$
$$V_Q = Q_2 - Q_1. \tag{8.28}$$

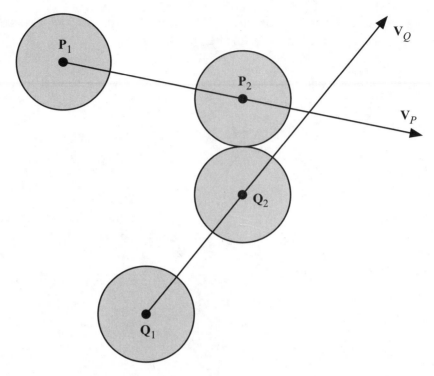

Figure 8.8 Detecting a collision between two moving spheres.

The position $\mathbf{P}(t)$ of the first sphere's center and the position $\mathbf{Q}(t)$ of the second sphere's center are then given by

$$\mathbf{P}(t) = \mathbf{P}_1 + t\mathbf{V}_P$$
$$\mathbf{Q}(t) = \mathbf{Q}_1 + t\mathbf{V}_Q. \tag{8.29}$$

Let r_P and r_Q be the radii of the two spheres. We wish to determine whether the distance d between the centers $\mathbf{P}(t)$ and $\mathbf{Q}(t)$ is ever equal to $r_P + r_Q$ at some time $t \in [0,1)$. If so, then the spheres are tangent to each other at time t, and a collision has taken place. We examine the squared distance between $\mathbf{P}(t)$ and $\mathbf{Q}(t)$ given by

$$d^2 = \|\mathbf{P}(t) - \mathbf{Q}(t)\|^2. \tag{8.30}$$

Substituting the values given by Equation (8.29) for $\mathbf{P}(t)$ and $\mathbf{Q}(t)$, we have

$$d^2 = \|\mathbf{P}_1 + t\mathbf{V}_P - \mathbf{Q}_1 - t\mathbf{V}_Q\|^2. \tag{8.31}$$

For convenience, we define

$$\mathbf{A} = \mathbf{P}_1 - \mathbf{Q}_1$$
$$\mathbf{B} = \mathbf{V}_P - \mathbf{V}_Q \tag{8.32}$$

so that Equation (8.31) can be written as

$$d^2 = \|\mathbf{A} + t\mathbf{B}\|^2$$
$$= A^2 + 2t(\mathbf{A} \cdot \mathbf{B}) + t^2 B^2. \tag{8.33}$$

Using the quadratic formula to solve for t gives us the formulas

$$t_1 = \frac{-(\mathbf{A} \cdot \mathbf{B}) - \sqrt{(\mathbf{A} \cdot \mathbf{B})^2 - B^2 (A^2 - d^2)}}{B^2}$$
$$t_2 = \frac{-(\mathbf{A} \cdot \mathbf{B}) + \sqrt{(\mathbf{A} \cdot \mathbf{B})^2 - B^2 (A^2 - d^2)}}{B^2}. \tag{8.34}$$

Setting $d = r_P + r_Q$ gives us the times t_1 and t_2 when the two spheres are tangent, if ever. It is possible that the value inside the radical is negative, in which case the spheres never collide. It is also possible that $B^2 = 0$, meaning that either both spheres are stationary or that both are traveling in the same direction at the same speed and thus cannot collide.

Since B^2 is not negative, the value of t_1 is always less than or equal to the value of t_2. The time t_1 represents the instant at which the spheres are tangent while they are still approaching each other. The time t_2, however, represents the instant at which the spheres are tangent while they are moving away from each other. Since we assume that the spheres are not intersecting to begin with, we are only interested in the time t_1 when they first collide. Thus, we only need to calculate the following time t to determine when a collision occurs.

$$t = \frac{-(\mathbf{A} \cdot \mathbf{B}) - \sqrt{(\mathbf{A} \cdot \mathbf{B})^2 - B^2 \left[A^2 - (r_P + r_Q)^2 \right]}}{B^2} \tag{8.35}$$

If t does not fall in the range $[0,1)$, then no collision occurs during our time interval of interest.

It is possible to determine that a collision cannot occur without evaluating Equation (8.35). The time t at which the squared distance d^2 is minimized can be found by setting the derivative of the right side of Equation (8.33) to zero as follows.

$$2B^2 t + 2(\mathbf{A} \cdot \mathbf{B}) = 0 \qquad (8.36)$$

Solving for t produces the following time at which the distance between the centers of the spheres is the least.

$$t = -\frac{\mathbf{A} \cdot \mathbf{B}}{B^2} \qquad (8.37)$$

Plugging this time into Equation (8.33) yields the smallest distance ever separating the centers of the two spheres:

$$d^2 = A^2 - \frac{(\mathbf{A} \cdot \mathbf{B})^2}{B^2}. \qquad (8.38)$$

If $d^2 > (r_P + r_Q)^2$, then we know that the two spheres can never collide.

Once we have determined that a collision has occurred at time t, we can calculate the centers $\mathbf{P}(t)$ and $\mathbf{Q}(t)$ of the two spheres at that time by plugging t into Equations (8.29). As shown in Figure 8.9, the point of contact $\mathbf{C}$ lies on the line segment connecting $\mathbf{P}(t)$ and $\mathbf{Q}(t)$ at a distance r_P from $\mathbf{P}(t)$, and is thus given by

$$\mathbf{C} = \mathbf{P}(t) + r_P \mathbf{N}, \qquad (8.39)$$

where $\mathbf{N}$ is the unit length normal vector pointing from $\mathbf{P}(t)$ to $\mathbf{Q}(t)$:

$$\mathbf{N} = \frac{\mathbf{Q}(t) - \mathbf{P}(t)}{\|\mathbf{Q}(t) - \mathbf{P}(t)\|}. \qquad (8.40)$$

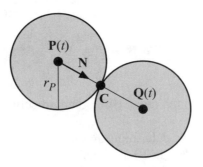

Figure 8.9 The point of contact **C** where two spheres meet lies on the line connecting their centers at the time of the collision.

Chapter 8 Summary

Collision of a Sphere and a Plane

A sphere of radius r whose center moves from the point $\mathbf{P}_1$ at time $t = 0$ to the point $\mathbf{P}_2$ at time $t = 1$ collides with a plane $\mathbf{L} = \langle \mathbf{N}, D \rangle$ at time

$$t = -\frac{\mathbf{L}' \cdot \mathbf{P}_1}{\mathbf{L}' \cdot \mathbf{V}},$$

where $\mathbf{L}' = \langle \mathbf{N}, D - r \rangle$.

Collision of a Box and a Plane

A box described by the vectors $\mathbf{R}$, $\mathbf{S}$, and $\mathbf{T}$ whose center moves from the point $\mathbf{Q}_1$ at time $t = 0$ to the point $\mathbf{Q}_2$ at time $t = 1$ collides with a plane $\mathbf{L} = \langle \mathbf{N}, D \rangle$ at time

$$t = -\frac{\mathbf{L}' \cdot \mathbf{Q}_1}{\mathbf{L}' \cdot \mathbf{V}},$$

where $\mathbf{L}' = \langle \mathbf{N}, D - r_{\text{eff}} \rangle$ and r_{eff} is the effective radius of the box, given by

$$r_{\text{eff}} = \tfrac{1}{2}\left(|\mathbf{R} \cdot \mathbf{N}| + |\mathbf{S} \cdot \mathbf{N}| + |\mathbf{T} \cdot \mathbf{N}|\right).$$

When a box collides with the plane at a point, the position $\mathbf{C}$ of the vertex making contact with the plane is given by

$$\mathbf{C} = \mathbf{Q}(t) - \tfrac{1}{2}\left[\operatorname{sgn}(\mathbf{R} \cdot \mathbf{N})\mathbf{R} + \operatorname{sgn}(\mathbf{S} \cdot \mathbf{N})\mathbf{S} + \operatorname{sgn}(\mathbf{T} \cdot \mathbf{N})\mathbf{T}\right],$$

where $\mathbf{Q}(t) = \mathbf{Q}_1 + t(\mathbf{Q}_2 - \mathbf{Q}_1)$.

General Sphere Collisions

Two faces sharing an edge with endpoints $\mathbf{E}_1$ and $\mathbf{E}_2$ meet at an exterior angle less than or equal to 180 degrees if

$$[\mathbf{N}_1 \times (\mathbf{E}_2 - \mathbf{E}_1)] \cdot \mathbf{N}_2 \geq 0,$$

where $\mathbf{N}_1$ is the normal to the face for which the vertices $\mathbf{E}_1$ and $\mathbf{E}_2$ occur in counterclockwise order, and $\mathbf{N}_2$ is the normal to the face for which the vertices $\mathbf{E}_1$ and $\mathbf{E}_2$ occur in clockwise order.

A ray $\mathbf{P}(t) = \mathbf{S} + t\mathbf{V}$ intersects an infinite cylinder of radius r representing the edge with endpoints $\mathbf{E}_1$ and $\mathbf{E}_2$ at the parameter value

$$t = \frac{-b - \sqrt{b^2 - ac}}{a},$$

where

$$a = V^2 - \frac{(\mathbf{V} \cdot \mathbf{A})^2}{A^2}$$

$$b = \mathbf{S}_0 \cdot \mathbf{V} - \frac{(\mathbf{S}_0 \cdot \mathbf{A})(\mathbf{V} \cdot \mathbf{A})}{A^2}$$

$$c = S_0^2 - r^2 - \frac{(\mathbf{S}_0 \cdot \mathbf{A})^2}{A^2}$$

$$\mathbf{A} = \mathbf{E}_2 - \mathbf{E}_1$$

$$\mathbf{S}_0 = \mathbf{S} - \mathbf{E}_1.$$

The intersection occurs between the edge's endpoints if

$$0 < [\mathbf{P}(t) - \mathbf{E}_1] \cdot \mathbf{A} < A^2.$$

Sliding

If an object traveling from the point $\mathbf{P}_1$ to $\mathbf{P}_2$ collides with a surface at the point $\mathbf{Q}$, then the point $\mathbf{P}_3$ to which it should slide is given by

$$\mathbf{P}_3 = \mathbf{P}_2 - [(\mathbf{P}_2 - \mathbf{Q}) \cdot \mathbf{N}]\mathbf{N},$$

where $\mathbf{N}$ is the unit normal vector at the point $\mathbf{Q}$.

Collision of Two Spheres

A sphere of radius r_P moving from the point $\mathbf{P}_1$ at time $t = 0$ to the point $\mathbf{P}_2$ at time $t = 1$ collides with another sphere of radius r_Q moving from the point $\mathbf{Q}_1$ to the point $\mathbf{Q}_2$ at time

$$t = \frac{-(\mathbf{A} \cdot \mathbf{B}) - \sqrt{(\mathbf{A} \cdot \mathbf{B})^2 - B^2 \left[A^2 - (r_P + r_Q)^2\right]}}{B^2},$$

where

$$A = P_1 - Q_1$$
$$B = (P_2 - P_1) - (Q_2 - Q_1).$$

Exercises for Chapter 8

1. Determine the time t when a sphere having a radius of two meters collides with the plane $x = 10$ m if its center lies at the origin at time $t = 0$ and it moves with a constant velocity of $\langle 2,0,1 \rangle$ m/s.

2. Suppose a collision occurs at the point $\mathbf{Q}$ on the surface of a cylinder of radius r whose ends are centered at the origin and the point $\mathbf{A}$. Find an expression for the unit normal vector $\mathbf{N}$ at the point $\mathbf{Q}$.

3. Write a program that determines whether two spheres collide within a given time interval. The program should take as parameters the initial positions and velocities of the two spheres. If a collision occurs, the program should calculate the point of contact at the time of collision.

Chapter **9**

Polygonal Techniques

T his chapter discusses several techniques that involve the manipulation of polygonal models. A 3D graphics engine often needs to create polygonal models in real-time in addition to working with models that have been preprocessed in some way. We begin this chapter with techniques pertaining to decal construction and billboarding, operations usually performed on the fly. Subsequent sections discuss preprocessing methods such as polygon reduction and triangulation, which are normally performed by a tool that generates structures used for rendering at a later time.

9.1 Depth Value Offset

Many games need to render special effects such as scorch marks on a wall or footprints on the ground that are not an original part of a scene, but are created during gameplay. (A method for creating these is discussed in Section 9.2.) These types of decorative additions are usually decaled onto an existing surface and thus consist of polygons that are coplanar with other polygons in a scene. The problem is that pixels rendered as part of one polygon rarely have exactly the same interpolated depth value as pixels rendered as part of a coplanar polygon.

The result is an undesired pattern in which parts of the original surface show through the decaled polygons.

The goal is to find a way to offset a polygon's depth in a scene without changing its projected screen coordinates or altering its texture-mapping perspective. Most 3D graphics systems contain some kind of polygon offset function to help achieve this goal. However, these solutions generally lack fine control and usually incur a per-vertex performance cost. In this section, we present an alternative method that modifies the projection matrix to achieve the depth offset effect.

9.1.1 Projection Matrix Modification

Let us first examine the effect of the standard OpenGL perspective projection matrix on an eye space point $\mathbf{P} = (P_x, P_y, P_z, 1)$. To simplify the matrix given in Equation (4.52) a bit, we assume that the view frustum is centered about the z-axis so that the left and right planes intersect the near plane at $x = \pm n/e$, and the top and bottom planes intersect the near plane at $y = \pm an/e$, where e is the focal length and a is the aspect ratio. Calling the distance to the near clipping plane n and the distance to the far clipping plane f, we have

$$\begin{bmatrix} e & 0 & 0 & 0 \\ 0 & e/a & 0 & 0 \\ 0 & 0 & -\dfrac{f+n}{f-n} & -\dfrac{2fn}{f-n} \\ 0 & 0 & -1 & 0 \end{bmatrix} \begin{bmatrix} P_x \\ P_y \\ P_z \\ 1 \end{bmatrix} = \begin{bmatrix} eP_x \\ (e/a)P_y \\ -\dfrac{f+n}{f-n}P_z - \dfrac{2fn}{f-n} \\ -P_z \end{bmatrix}. \tag{9.1}$$

To finish the projection, we need to divide this result by its w-coordinate, which has the value $-P_z$. The resulting point $\mathbf{P}'$ is given by

$$\mathbf{P}' = \begin{bmatrix} -\dfrac{eP_x}{P_z} \\ -\dfrac{(e/a)P_y}{P_z} \\ \dfrac{f+n}{f-n} + \dfrac{2fn}{P_z(f-n)} \end{bmatrix}. \tag{9.2}$$

It is clear from Equation (9.2) that preserving the value of $-P_z$ for the w-coordinate will guarantee the preservation of the projected x- and y-coordinates as well. From this point forward, we shall concern ourselves only with the lower-right 2×2 portion of the projection matrix, since this is the only part that affects the z- and w-coordinates.

The projected z-coordinate may be altered without disturbing the w-coordinate by introducing a factor of $1 + \varepsilon$, for some small ε, as follows.

$$
\begin{bmatrix} -(1+\varepsilon)\dfrac{f+n}{f-n} & -\dfrac{2fn}{f-n} \\ -1 & 0 \end{bmatrix} \begin{bmatrix} P_z \\ 1 \end{bmatrix} = \begin{bmatrix} -(1+\varepsilon)\dfrac{f+n}{f-n}P_z - \dfrac{2fn}{f-n} \\ -P_z \end{bmatrix} \tag{9.3}
$$

After dividing by w, we arrive at the following value for the projected z-coordinate.

$$
\begin{aligned}
P_z' &= (1+\varepsilon)\frac{f+n}{f-n} + \frac{2fn}{P_z(f-n)} \\
&= \frac{f+n}{f-n} + \frac{2fn}{P_z(f-n)} + \varepsilon\frac{f+n}{f-n}
\end{aligned} \tag{9.4}
$$

Comparing this to the z-coordinate in Equation (9.2), we see that we have found a way to offset projected depth values by a constant $\varepsilon\frac{f+n}{f-n}$.

9.1.2 Offset Value Selection

Due to the nonlinear nature of the z-buffer, the constant offset given in Equation (9.4) corresponds to a larger difference far from the camera than it does near the camera. Although this constant offset may work well for some applications, there is no single solution that works for every application at all depths. The best we can do is choose an appropriate ε, given a camera-space offset δ and a depth value P_z, that collectively represents the object that we are offsetting. To determine a formula for ε, we examine the result of applying the standard projection matrix from Equation (9.1) to a point whose z-coordinate has been offset by some small δ as follows.

$$
\begin{bmatrix} -\dfrac{f+n}{f-n} & -\dfrac{2fn}{f-n} \\ -1 & 0 \end{bmatrix} \begin{bmatrix} P_z+\delta \\ 1 \end{bmatrix} = \begin{bmatrix} -\dfrac{f+n}{f-n}(P_z+\delta) - \dfrac{2fn}{f-n} \\ -(P_z+\delta) \end{bmatrix} \tag{9.5}
$$

Dividing by w, we have the following value for the projected z-coordinate.

$$P_z' = \frac{f+n}{f-n} + \frac{2fn}{(P_z+\delta)(f-n)}$$

$$= \frac{f+n}{f-n} + \frac{2fn}{P_z(f-n)} + \frac{2fn}{f-n}\left(\frac{1}{P_z+\delta} - \frac{1}{P_z}\right) \qquad (9.6)$$

Equating this result to Equation (9.4) and simplifying a bit, we end up with

$$\varepsilon = -\frac{2fn}{f+n}\left(\frac{\delta}{P_z(P_z+\delta)}\right). \qquad (9.7)$$

A good value of δ for a particular application can be found with a little experimentation. It should be kept in mind that δ is a camera-space offset, and thus becomes less effective as P_z gets larger. For an m-bit integer depth buffer, we want to make sure that

$$|\varepsilon| \geq \frac{1}{2^m - 1}\left(\frac{f-n}{f+n}\right) \qquad (9.8)$$

since smaller values of ε will not yield an offset significant enough to alter the integer depth value. Substituting the right side of Equation (9.7) for ε and solving for δ gives us

$$\delta \geq \frac{kP_z^2}{1 - kP_z} \qquad (9.9)$$

or

$$\delta \leq \frac{-kP_z^2}{1 + kP_z}, \qquad (9.10)$$

where the constant k is given by

$$k = \frac{f-n}{2fn(2^m - 1)}. \qquad (9.11)$$

Equation (9.9) gives us the minimum effective value for δ when offsetting a polygon toward the camera (the usual case), and Equation (9.10) gives us the maximum effective value for δ when offsetting a polygon away from the camera.

9.1.3 Implementation

Listing 9.1 demonstrates how the projection matrix shown in Equation (9.3) may be implemented under OpenGL. The function `LoadOffsetMatrix` takes the same six values that are passed to the OpenGL function `glFrustum()`. It also takes the values for δ and P_z that are used to calculate ε.

Listing 9.1 This code modifies the OpenGL projection matrix so that it offsets depth values by the constant ε given by Equation (9.7).

```
void LoadOffsetMatrix(GLdouble l, GLdouble r,
   GLdouble b, GLdouble t,
   GLdouble n, GLdouble f,
   GLfloat delta, GLfloat pz)
{
   GLfloat    matrix[16];

   // Set up standard perspective projection
   glMatrixMode(GL_PROJECTION);
   glFrustum(l, r, b, t, n, f);

   // Retrieve the projection matrix
   glGetFloatv(GL_PROJECTION_MATRIX, matrix);

   // Calculate epsilon with Equation (9.7)
   GLfloat epsilon = -2.0F * f * n * delta /
      ((f + n) * pz * (pz + delta));

   // Modify entry (3,3) of the projection matrix
   matrix[10] *= 1.0F + epsilon;

   // Send the projection matrix back to OpenGL
   glLoadMatrix(matrix);
}
```

9.2 Decal Application

Effects such as scorch marks on walls or footprints on the ground are commonly implemented by creating a new object, called a *decal*, that coincides with an existing surface and rendering it using a depth offset technique such as that discussed in Section 9.1. Applying a decal to the interior of a planar surface is simple, but difficulties arise when applying decals to the more complex surfaces used in today's games to represent curved objects and terrain patches. In this section, we present a general method for applying a decal to an arbitrarily shaped surface and concurrently clipping the decal to the surface's boundary. An example of the technique we present is shown in Figure 9.1.

Figure 9.1 A scorch mark decal applied to a curved surface.

9.2.1 Decal Mesh Construction

We begin with a point **P** that lies on an existing surface and a unit normal direction **N** that is perpendicular to the surface at that point. The point **P** represents the center of the decal and may be the point at which a projectile has hit the surface or the point where a character's foot has stepped upon the ground. A unit tangent direction **T** must also be chosen to determine the orientation of the decal. This configuration is illustrated in Figure 9.2.

Given the point **P** and the directions **N** and **T**, we have an oriented plane that is tangent to the surface geometry at **P**. We can carve a rectangle out of this plane that represents the area of our decal by constructing four boundary planes that are parallel to the normal direction **N**. Let w and h be the width and height of the decal. Then the 4D vectors corresponding to the four border planes are given by

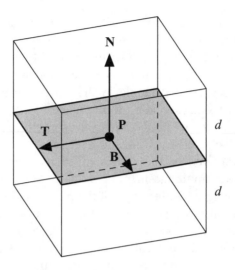

Figure 9.2 The configuration of a decal.

$$left = \left(\mathbf{T}, \frac{w}{2} - \mathbf{T} \cdot \mathbf{P} \right)$$

$$right = \left(-\mathbf{T}, \frac{w}{2} + \mathbf{T} \cdot \mathbf{P} \right)$$

$$bottom = \left(\mathbf{B}, \frac{h}{2} - \mathbf{B} \cdot \mathbf{P} \right)$$

$$top = \left(-\mathbf{B}, \frac{h}{2} + \mathbf{B} \cdot \mathbf{P} \right), \tag{9.12}$$

where $\mathbf{B} = \mathbf{N} \times \mathbf{T}$. We generate a triangle mesh for the decal object by clipping nearby surfaces to the four boundary planes. We also want to clip to front and back planes to avoid bleeding through to parts of the same surface mesh that may be inside the boundary planes but far in front of or behind the point $\mathbf{P}$. The 4D vectors corresponding to the front and back planes are given by

$$front = (-\mathbf{N}, d + \mathbf{N} \cdot \mathbf{P})$$

$$back = (\mathbf{N}, d - \mathbf{N} \cdot \mathbf{P}), \tag{9.13}$$

where d is the maximum distance that any vertex in the decal may be from the tangent plane passing through the point $\mathbf{P}$.

The mesh construction algorithm proceeds as follows. First, we identify which surfaces in the world could potentially be affected by the decal. This may be determined by locating each surface whose bounding volume reaches within a certain distance of the point **P**. For each potentially affected surface, we individually examine every triangle in the surface's mesh. Let **M** denote the unit normal direction corresponding to the plane of a triangle in the mesh. We throw out any triangles for which $\mathbf{N} \cdot \mathbf{M} < \varepsilon$ for some fixed positive value ε since these triangles are facing away from the decal's normal direction **N**. The remaining triangles are clipped to the planes given by Equations (9.12) and (9.13) and stored in a new triangle mesh.

When a triangle overlaps any of the planes and needs to be clipped, we interpolate the normal vectors as well as the vertex positions so that we can later apply coloring to the clipped vertices that reflects the angle between each vertex's normal direction and the decal's normal direction. This has the effect of smoothly fading the decal texture in relation to each triangle's orientation relative to the plane of the decal. We assign an alpha value to each vertex using the equation

$$alpha = \frac{\dfrac{\mathbf{N} \cdot \mathbf{R}}{\|\mathbf{R}\|} - \varepsilon}{1 - \varepsilon}, \tag{9.14}$$

where **R** is the (possibly unnormalized due to interpolation) normal vector corresponding to the vertex. This maps the dot product range $[\varepsilon, 1]$ to the alpha value range $[0, 1]$.

Texture mapping coordinates are applied to the resulting triangle mesh by measuring the distance from each vertex to the planes passing through the point **P** and having normal directions **T** and **B**. Let **Q** be the position of a vertex in the decal's triangle mesh. Then the texture coordinates s and t are given by

$$s = \frac{\mathbf{T} \cdot (\mathbf{Q} - \mathbf{P})}{w} + \frac{1}{2}$$
$$t = \frac{\mathbf{B} \cdot (\mathbf{Q} - \mathbf{P})}{h} + \frac{1}{2}. \tag{9.15}$$

9.2.2 Polygon Clipping

Each triangle belonging to a surface that could potentially be affected by the decal is treated as a convex polygon and clipped to each of the six boundary planes, one at a time. Clipping a convex polygon having n vertices to a plane results in a new convex polygon having at most $n + 1$ vertices. Thus, polygons that have been clipped against all six planes may possess as many as nine vertices. Once the clipping process is complete, each polygon is treated as a triangle fan and added to the decal's triangle mesh.

To clip a convex polygon against an arbitrary plane, we first classify all the vertices belonging to the polygon into two categories: those lying on the negative side of the plane and those lying on the positive side of the plane or in the plane itself. (This differs from the method used to clip portals in Section 7.4.1 in that we do not have a separate classification for vertices lying in the plane.) If all the polygon's vertices lie on the negative side of the plane, then the polygon is discarded. Otherwise, we visit every pair of neighboring vertices in the polygon looking for edges that intersect the clipping plane. As shown in Figure 9.3, new vertices are added to the polygon where such intersections occur, and vertices lying on the negative side of the plane are removed.

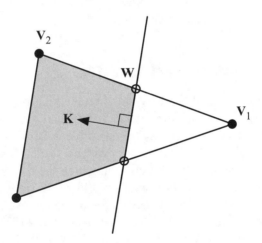

Figure 9.3 When a polygon is clipped against a plane, new vertices are added where edges intersect the plane, and vertices lying on the negative side of the plane are removed.

Suppose that the vertex $\mathbf{V}_1$ lies on the positive side of the clipping plane $\mathbf{K}$ and that the vertex $\mathbf{V}_2$ lies on the negative side of $\mathbf{K}$. A point $\mathbf{W}$ lying on the line segment connecting $\mathbf{V}_1$ and $\mathbf{V}_2$ can be expressed as

$$\mathbf{W}(t) = \mathbf{V}_1 + t(\mathbf{V}_2 - \mathbf{V}_1),\qquad(9.16)$$

where the parameter t satisfies $0 \leq t \leq 1$. The value of t for which $\mathbf{K} \cdot \mathbf{W}(t) = 0$ is given by

$$t = \frac{\mathbf{K} \cdot \mathbf{V}_1}{\mathbf{K} \cdot (\mathbf{V}_1 - \mathbf{V}_2)}. \tag{9.17}$$

(Note that the difference $\mathbf{V}_1 - \mathbf{V}_2$ has a w-coordinate of 0.) Substituting this value of t back into Equation (9.16) gives us our new vertex $\mathbf{W}$.

9.3 Billboarding

Many special effects are implemented by applying a two-dimensional texture map to a flat polygon that is always oriented to face the camera. This technique is called *billboarding* and is an effective way to create the illusion that a flat object has volume. This section examines methods for calculating the vertices of billboard polygons in different situations.

9.3.1 Unconstrained Quads

An unconstrained quad is a four-sided rectangular polygon that is free to rotate in any direction. Unconstrained quads are typically used to create special effects such as particle systems, smoke trails, and lens flare coronas.

We billboard an unconstrained quad by forcing its vertices to lie in a plane that is perpendicular to the direction in which the camera is pointing. Let the vectors $\mathbf{R}$ and $\mathbf{U}$ denote the unit-length world space right direction and up direction of the current camera view. (These correspond to the camera space x- and y-axes, respectively.) The quad that we wish to billboard is defined by the following quantities.

(a) The world space position $\mathbf{P}$ corresponding to the center of the quad.

(b) The width w and height h of the quad. These may be changed over time to produce the effect of an expanding or shrinking billboard.

(c) The angle θ by which the quad should be rotated relative to the camera's orientation. This may be changed over time to produce the effect of a spinning billboard. If θ is constant, then the quad rotates with the camera about the view direction.

Using these quantities, we define the vectors $\mathbf{X}$ and $\mathbf{Y}$ as follows.

$$\mathbf{X} = \left(\frac{w}{2}\cos\theta\right)\mathbf{R} + \left(\frac{w}{2}\sin\theta\right)\mathbf{U}$$

$$\mathbf{Y} = \left(-\frac{h}{2}\sin\theta\right)\mathbf{R} + \left(\frac{h}{2}\cos\theta\right)\mathbf{U} \tag{9.18}$$

The rotation θ is typically quantized to some number of possible angles so that a lookup table may be used for the sine and cosine functions. Of course, if $\theta = 0$, then the expressions for the vectors $\mathbf{X}$ and $\mathbf{Y}$ reduce to

$$\mathbf{X} = \frac{w}{2}\mathbf{R}$$

$$\mathbf{Y} = \frac{h}{2}\mathbf{U}. \tag{9.19}$$

As illustrated in Figure 9.4, the four vertices $\mathbf{Q}_1$, $\mathbf{Q}_2$, $\mathbf{Q}_3$, and $\mathbf{Q}_4$ of the quad are given by

$$\mathbf{Q}_1 = \mathbf{P} + \mathbf{X} + \mathbf{Y} \qquad \mathbf{Q}_2 = \mathbf{P} - \mathbf{X} + \mathbf{Y}$$

$$\mathbf{Q}_3 = \mathbf{P} - \mathbf{X} - \mathbf{Y} \qquad \mathbf{Q}_4 = \mathbf{P} + \mathbf{X} - \mathbf{Y}. \tag{9.20}$$

These vertices are arranged in a counterclockwise winding order so that the front of the quad faces the camera. The corresponding two-dimensional texture mapping coordinates are given by

$$\langle s_1, t_1 \rangle = \langle 1, 1 \rangle \qquad \langle s_2, t_2 \rangle = \langle 0, 1 \rangle$$

$$\langle s_3, t_3 \rangle = \langle 0, 0 \rangle \qquad \langle s_4, t_4 \rangle = \langle 1, 0 \rangle. \tag{9.21}$$

Billboarded quads whose vertices derive from the vectors $\mathbf{X}$ and $\mathbf{Y}$ given by Equation (9.18) are always aligned to the plane of the camera. As Figure 9.5 demonstrates, this alignment can differ significantly from the plane perpendicular to the true direction from the quad's center to the camera position. When hundreds or thousands of small particles are being rendered, one may wish to use Equation (9.18) for efficiency, but large quads may look better if oriented to face the actual camera position instead of the plane of the camera.

We align a quad so that it faces the camera position by presenting a more computationally expensive formulation of the vectors $\mathbf{X}$ and $\mathbf{Y}$. Let the vector $\mathbf{C}$ denote the world space camera position. Assuming that the center $\mathbf{P}$ of the quad does not lie on the line containing $\mathbf{C}$ and running in the direction $\mathbf{U}$, we can calculate

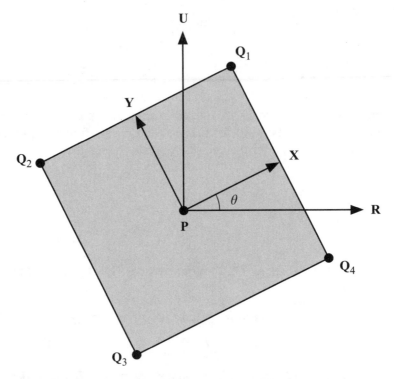

Figure 9.4 Calculating the vertices of an unconstrained billboarded quad.

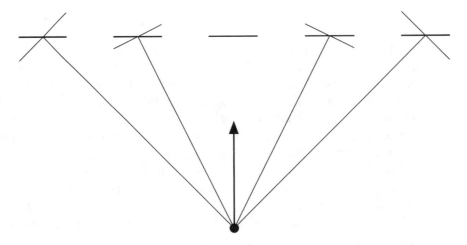

Figure 9.5 A billboarded quad that is aligned to the plane of the camera may differ significantly from a quad that directly faces the camera position.

$$\mathbf{Z} = \frac{\mathbf{C} - \mathbf{P}}{\|\mathbf{C} - \mathbf{P}\|}$$

$$\mathbf{A} = \frac{\mathbf{U} \times \mathbf{Z}}{\|\mathbf{U} \times \mathbf{Z}\|}$$

$$\mathbf{B} = \mathbf{Z} \times \mathbf{A}. \tag{9.22}$$

The vector $\mathbf{Z}$ is the unit vector that points from the quad's center toward the camera position. Calculating the cross product with $\mathbf{U}$ produces orthogonal vector $\mathbf{A}$ lying in the plane of the billboard. If $\mathbf{U} \times \mathbf{Z}$ is close to zero, then we can use the alternate formula

$$\mathbf{B} = \frac{\mathbf{Z} \times \mathbf{R}}{\|\mathbf{Z} \times \mathbf{R}\|}$$

$$\mathbf{A} = \mathbf{B} \times \mathbf{Z}. \tag{9.23}$$

The vectors $\mathbf{A}$ and $\mathbf{B}$ form an orthogonal pair of unit vectors that we can use to express the vectors $\mathbf{X}$ and $\mathbf{Y}$:

$$\mathbf{X} = \left(\frac{w}{2}\cos\theta\right)\mathbf{A} + \left(\frac{w}{2}\sin\theta\right)\mathbf{B}$$

$$\mathbf{Y} = \left(-\frac{h}{2}\sin\theta\right)\mathbf{A} + \left(\frac{h}{2}\cos\theta\right)\mathbf{B}. \tag{9.24}$$

Using these in Equation (9.20) produces the vertices of the billboarded quad.

9.3.2 Constrained Quads

We now consider how to orient a quad that is constrained to rotate only about the z-axis. An example of how such a quad might be used is to render the fire texture for a torch. In this case, the fire is always pointing upward, but the plane of the quad rotates to face the camera. As long as the camera does not view the quad from sharply above or below, this produces the convincing illusion that the fire has volume.

Suppose that the camera resides at the world space point $\mathbf{C}$. For a quad centered at the point $\mathbf{P}$, we define the vector $\mathbf{X}$ as

$$\mathbf{X} = \langle P_y - C_y, C_x - P_x, 0 \rangle. \tag{9.25}$$

As shown in Figure 9.6, this vector is constructed by taking the difference between the camera position and the center of the quad, projecting it onto the x-y plane, and rotating it 90 degrees counterclockwise about the z-axis. If $\|\mathbf{X}\| = 0$, then the camera is either directly above or directly below the quad. In this case, the quad is being viewed on edge and therefore should not be rendered. Otherwise, we calculate the four vertices $\mathbf{Q}_1$, $\mathbf{Q}_2$, $\mathbf{Q}_3$, and $\mathbf{Q}_4$ of the quad as follows.

$$\mathbf{Q}_1 = \mathbf{P} + \frac{w}{2}\frac{\mathbf{X}}{\|\mathbf{X}\|} + \left\langle 0, 0, \frac{h}{2} \right\rangle \qquad \mathbf{Q}_2 = \mathbf{P} - \frac{w}{2}\frac{\mathbf{X}}{\|\mathbf{X}\|} + \left\langle 0, 0, \frac{h}{2} \right\rangle$$

$$\mathbf{Q}_3 = \mathbf{P} - \frac{w}{2}\frac{\mathbf{X}}{\|\mathbf{X}\|} - \left\langle 0, 0, \frac{h}{2} \right\rangle \qquad \mathbf{Q}_4 = \mathbf{P} + \frac{w}{2}\frac{\mathbf{X}}{\|\mathbf{X}\|} - \left\langle 0, 0, \frac{h}{2} \right\rangle \qquad (9.26)$$

The texture mapping coordinates are the same as those for an unconstrained quad given by Equation (9.21).

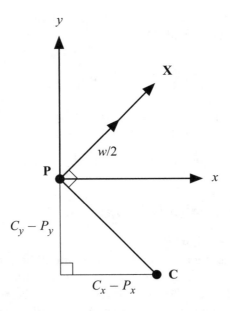

Figure 9.6 Calculating the vertices of a billboarded quad that is constrained to rotate about the z-axis.

9.3.3 Polyline Quadstrips

A polyline defined by a series of N points $\mathbf{P}_1, \mathbf{P}_2, \ldots, \mathbf{P}_N$ can be given some thickness r by constructing a quadstrip that traces the polyline in the manner shown in Figure 9.7. One application of such a quadstrip is to render a lightning bolt whose path is defined by a set of points. Another application is to render a motion-blurred particle for which a number of intermediate positions have been calculated between its position on the previous frame and its current position.

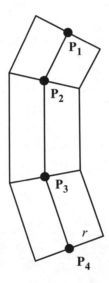

Figure 9.7 A quadstrip of radius r that traces a polyline.

For each point $\mathbf{P}_i$ defining the polyline, we generate two quadstrip vertices lying at a distance r from $\mathbf{P}_i$. The direction of the line on which these vertices and the point $\mathbf{P}_i$ lie should be orthogonal to both the direction to the camera position and the tangent direction of the polyline at $\mathbf{P}_i$. The unit direction $\mathbf{Z}_i$ to the camera is given by

$$\mathbf{Z}_i = \frac{\mathbf{C} - \mathbf{P}_i}{\|\mathbf{C} - \mathbf{P}_i\|}, \tag{9.27}$$

where $\mathbf{C}$ is the camera position. A unit tangent vector $\mathbf{T}_i$ may be calculated for the point $\mathbf{P}_i$ using the formula

$$\mathbf{T}_i = \frac{\mathbf{P}_{i+1} - \mathbf{P}_{i-1}}{\|\mathbf{P}_{i+1} - \mathbf{P}_{i-1}\|}, \tag{9.28}$$

or in the case that $\mathbf{P}_i$ is an endpoint,

$$\mathbf{T}_1 = \frac{\mathbf{P}_2 - \mathbf{P}_1}{\|\mathbf{P}_2 - \mathbf{P}_1\|}$$

$$\mathbf{T}_N = \frac{\mathbf{P}_N - \mathbf{P}_{N-1}}{\|\mathbf{P}_N - \mathbf{P}_{N-1}\|}. \tag{9.29}$$

The two quadstrip vertices $\mathbf{G}_i$ and $\mathbf{H}_i$ corresponding to the point $\mathbf{P}_i$ are then given by

$$\mathbf{G}_i = \mathbf{P}_i + r(\mathbf{T}_i \times \mathbf{Z}_i)$$

$$\mathbf{H}_i = \mathbf{P}_i - r(\mathbf{T}_i \times \mathbf{Z}_i). \tag{9.30}$$

Each edge of the quadstrip constructed using the vertices $\mathbf{G}_1, \mathbf{H}_1, \mathbf{G}_2, \mathbf{H}_2, \ldots, \mathbf{G}_N, \mathbf{H}_N$ is perpendicular to the direction to the camera. Figure 9.8 demonstrates a lightning bolt generated using this technique.

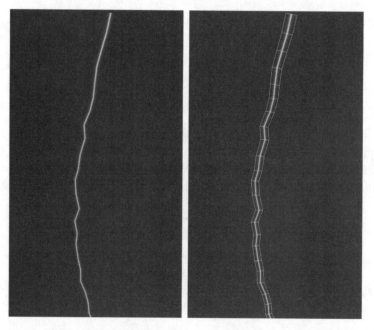

Figure 9.8 A polyline quadstrip used to render a lightning bolt.

9.4 Polygon Reduction

When a model consisting of a large number of triangles is rendered far from the camera, it is likely that many of the triangles make no perceptible contribution to the resulting image. By reducing the number of rendered triangles as the distance from the camera to the model increases, we can reduce the amount of computation needed to process the mesh as well as the amount of data sent to the graphics hardware.

A common method used to reduce the number of triangles in a mesh is the edge collapse technique. This method works by locating edges within a triangle mesh whose removal would not cause a large change in the shape of the model. The process of removing an edge is called an *edge collapse* and is performed by merging the edge's two endpoints. As illustrated in Figure 9.9, one endpoint remains stationary, and the other endpoint is moved to the same location as the first. Thus, there are two ways in which an edge can be collapsed, depending on which endpoint remains stationary. The two triangles sharing the collapsed edge are eliminated, and any triangles using the moved vertex are stretched to fill in the space left behind. Of course, since the two endpoints now occupy the same location, the one that was moved can simply be eliminated. Thus, a single edge collapse results in the removal of two triangles, one edge, and one vertex from the mesh.

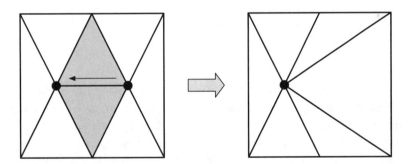

Figure 9.9 An edge collapse merges the two endpoints of the edge and eliminates the triangles that share the edge.

We decide which edges to collapse in a triangle mesh by calculating two *costs* for each edge. A cost is assigned to each endpoint of an edge based on how much the appearance of the triangle mesh would be altered if the edge is collapsed by removing that endpoint. Endpoints having the lowest collapse cost determine which edges are the first to be eliminated. If it is known that an edge should definitely *not* be eliminated, then the collapse costs of its endpoints can be set to some large value to indicate this.

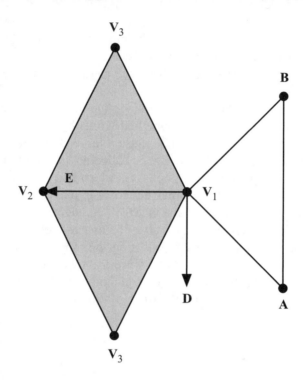

Figure 9.10 Calculating the collapse cost.

There are many possible ways to calculate edge collapse costs. The method presented in this section assigns costs based on a combination of the edge's length and the flatness of the triangle mesh on both sides of the edge around the endpoint being considered for elimination. Suppose that we wish to calculate the cost of eliminating the vertex V_1 in Figure 9.10 by collapsing it into the vertex V_2. We first calculate the normal vector N for the vertex V_1 by averaging the normals of the surrounding triangles (see Section 6.7.1). We then define the vector D to be

$$D = \frac{N \times E}{\|N \times E\|},$$

(9.31)

where E is the direction pointing from V_1 to V_2:

$$\mathbf{E} = \mathbf{V}_2 - \mathbf{V}_1. \tag{9.32}$$

The direction $\mathbf{D}$ is perpendicular to both the normal to the surface at $\mathbf{V}_1$ and the edge that we are considering. It will be used to determine on which side of the edge a point lies.

It should be noted that if *any* of the edges leading away from the vertex $\mathbf{V}_1$ are not shared by two triangles, then $\mathbf{V}_1$ should not be eliminated because doing so would change the shape of the triangle mesh's boundary. If $\mathbf{V}_1$ does lie in the interior of the mesh, then for each of the two triangles sharing the edge that connects $\mathbf{V}_1$ and $\mathbf{V}_2$, we examine the vertex $\mathbf{V}_3$ of the triangle that does not lie on the edge to determine whether the triangle lies on the positive side or negative side of the edge. If the condition

$$\mathbf{D} \cdot (\mathbf{V}_3 - \mathbf{V}_1) \geq 0 \tag{9.33}$$

is satisfied, then the triangle lies on the positive side of the edge; otherwise, it lies on the negative side of the plane. We must have one of each, so if both triangles lie on the positive side or both triangles lie on the negative side, then the edge should not be collapsed.

Let $\mathbf{T}_{pos}$ represent the unit-length normal vector of the triangle lying on the positive side of the edge, and let $\mathbf{T}_{neg}$ represent the unit-length normal vector of the triangle lying on the negative side of the edge. We estimate the flatness of the triangle mesh on either side of the edge being considered for collapse by comparing the normal vectors $\mathbf{T}_{pos}$ and $\mathbf{T}_{neg}$ to those of the other triangles using the vertex $\mathbf{V}_1$. As we examine these triangles, we maintain a value d corresponding to the smallest dot product found between the normal of any triangle occupying space on the positive side of the edge and the vector $\mathbf{T}_{pos}$ and between the normal of any triangle occupying space on the negative side of the edge and the vector $\mathbf{T}_{neg}$. A value of d near one indicates that the mesh is mostly flat on either side of the edge, but a small value of d indicates that large angles exist between triangles sharing the vertex $\mathbf{V}_1$. If d falls below some threshold corresponding to the maximum surface roughness allowed, then the edge connecting $\mathbf{V}_1$ and $\mathbf{V}_2$ should not be collapsed. Otherwise, we assign the cost c to the edge using the formula

$$c = (1 - d) \|\mathbf{E}\|. \tag{9.34}$$

To clarify the procedure for calculating the value of d, suppose that a triangle has vertices $\mathbf{V}_1$, $\mathbf{A}$, and $\mathbf{B}$ (where neither $\mathbf{A}$ nor $\mathbf{B}$ is equal to $\mathbf{V}_2$), and has the unit-length normal vector $\mathbf{T}$. We classify the vertices $\mathbf{A}$ and $\mathbf{B}$ as lying on the positive side of the edge, on the negative side of the edge, or on the edge itself by examining the dot products

$$a = \mathbf{D} \cdot (\mathbf{A} - \mathbf{V}_1)$$
$$b = \mathbf{D} \cdot (\mathbf{B} - \mathbf{V}_1). \tag{9.35}$$

The quantities a and b represent the distances from the plane containing the edge and having normal vector $\mathbf{D}$ to the points $\mathbf{A}$ and $\mathbf{B}$. If $a > \varepsilon$ or $b > \varepsilon$ for some small distance ε, then we consider the corresponding point to lie on the positive side of the edge. Similarly, if $a < -\varepsilon$ or $b < -\varepsilon$, then we consider the corresponding point to lie on the negative side of the edge. Points lying within the distance ε of the edge are considered to be lying on the edge itself. If either $\mathbf{A}$ or $\mathbf{B}$ lies on the positive side of the edge, then we replace the minimum dot product d with the dot product $\mathbf{T} \cdot \mathbf{T}_{\text{pos}}$ if it is smaller:

$$d \leftarrow \min\{d, \mathbf{T} \cdot \mathbf{T}_{\text{pos}}\}. \tag{9.36}$$

If either $\mathbf{A}$ or $\mathbf{B}$ lies on the negative side of the edge, then we replace d with the dot product $\mathbf{T} \cdot \mathbf{T}_{\text{neg}}$ if it is smaller:

$$d \leftarrow \min\{d, \mathbf{T} \cdot \mathbf{T}_{\text{neg}}\}. \tag{9.37}$$

It is possible that both of the operations given by Equations (9.36) and (9.37) are performed for a single triangle.

The edge collapse cost calculation presented in this section allows the collapse of an edge such as that shown in Figure 9.11. As long as the triangle mesh is reasonably flat on both sides of the edge, a collapse may occur along an edge between two triangles having largely differing orientations.

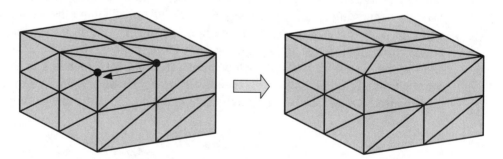

Figure 9.11 The edge collapse cost calculation allows the collapse of an edge between two triangles having largely differing orientations as long as the triangle mesh is reasonably flat on both sides of the edge.

Figure 9.12 shows the original triangle mesh for a character model and the same model after 30 percent of its triangles have been eliminated using the edge collapse technique. Notice how edges in regions of high triangle concentration and regions of relative flatness were the first edges chosen to be removed.

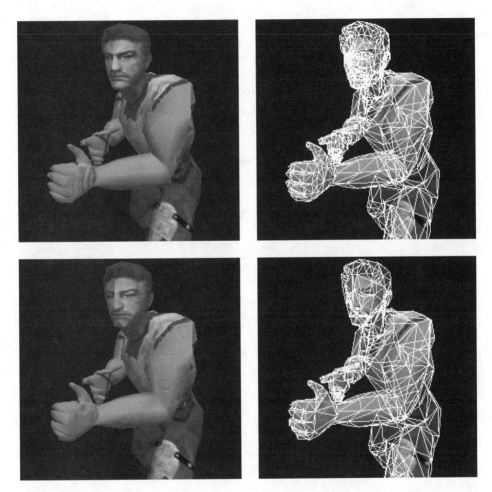

Figure 9.12 The top pair of images show a character model and the wireframe of its triangle mesh. The bottom pair of images shows the same model after 30 percent of its triangles have been eliminated.

9.5 T-Junction Elimination

Suppose that a scene contains two polygons that share a common edge, as shown in Figure 9.13(a). When two such polygons belong to the same model, the vertices representing the endpoints of the common edge are not ordinarily duplicated unless some vertex attribute (such as texture coordinates) is different for the two polygons. Vertices shared by multiple polygons are usually stored once in an array and referenced multiple times by the polygons that use them. Graphics hardware is designed so that when adjacent polygons use *exactly* the same coordinates for the endpoints of shared edges, rasterization produces sets of pixels that are precise complements of each other. Along the shared edge, there is no overlap between the pixels belonging to one polygon and those belonging to the other, and there are no gaps where pixels do not belong to either polygon.

A problem arises when adjacent polygons belong to different objects. Each object has its own copy of the endpoint vertices for the shared edge, and these vertices may differ greatly in each object's local coordinate space. When the vertices are transformed into world space, floating-point round-off error may produce slightly different positions for each object. Since the vertex coordinates are no longer exactly equal, a seam may appear when the polygons are rasterized.

A larger problem occurs when two polygons have edges that fall within the same line in space but do not share the same endpoints, as illustrated in Figure 9.13(b). In such a situation, a vertex belonging to one polygon lies within the interior of an edge belonging to the other polygon. Due to the shape that the edges form, the location at which this occurs is called a *T-junction*. Because the adjacent edges do not share identical endpoints, T-junctions are a major cause of visible seams in any real-time graphics engine that does not take measures to eliminate them.

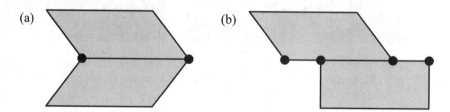

Figure 9.13 (a) Two polygons share an edge and both endpoint vertices. (b) Two polygons share an edge but do not share endpoint vertices. The location where a vertex of one polygon lies on the edge of another polygon is called a T-junction.

In this section, we describe how to detect possible sources of seams in complex 3D scenes and how to modify static geometry so that visible artifacts are avoided. The removal of seams is absolutely necessary in order for graphics engines to employ stencil shadow techniques for global illumination (see Section 10.1). When T-junctions are eliminated, new vertices are added to existing polygons. A method for triangulating arbitrary polygons is described in Section 9.6.

Given an immovable object A in our world, we need to determine whether there exist any other immovable objects possessing a vertex that lies within an edge of object A. We consider only those objects whose bounding volumes intersect the bounding volume of object A. Let object X be an object that lies close enough to object A to possibly have adjacent polygons. We treat both objects as collections of polygons having the greatest possible number of edges. We perform triangulation of these polygons *after* the T-junction elimination process to avoid the creation of superfluous triangles.

Before we locate any T-junctions, we first want to find out if any of object A's vertices lie very close to any of object X's vertices. We must transform the vertices belonging to both objects into some common coordinate space and search for vertices separated by a distance less than some small constant ε. Any vertex $\mathbf{V}_A$ of object A that is this close to a vertex $\mathbf{V}_X$ of object X should be moved so that $\mathbf{V}_A$ and $\mathbf{V}_X$ have the exact same coordinates. This procedure is sometimes called *welding*.

Once existing vertices have been welded, we need to search for vertices of object X that lie within a small distance ε of an edge of object A but do not lie within the distance ε of any vertex of object A. This tells us where T-junctions occur. Let $\mathbf{P}_1$ and $\mathbf{P}_2$ be endpoints of an edge of object A, and let $\mathbf{Q}$ be a vertex of object X. The squared distance d^2 between the point $\mathbf{Q}$ and the line passing through $\mathbf{P}_1$ and $\mathbf{P}_2$ is given by

$$d^2 = (\mathbf{Q} - \mathbf{P}_1)^2 - \frac{[(\mathbf{Q} - \mathbf{P}_1) \cdot (\mathbf{P}_2 - \mathbf{P}_1)]^2}{(\mathbf{P}_2 - \mathbf{P}_1)^2}. \tag{9.38}$$

If $d^2 < \varepsilon^2$, then we know that the point $\mathbf{Q}$ lies close enough to the line containing the edge of object A, but we still need to determine whether $\mathbf{Q}$ actually lies between $\mathbf{P}_1$ and $\mathbf{P}_2$. We can make this determination by measuring the projected length t of the line segment connecting $\mathbf{P}_1$ to $\mathbf{Q}$ onto the edge formed by $\mathbf{P}_1$ and $\mathbf{P}_2$. This length is given by

$$t = \|\mathbf{Q} - \mathbf{P}_1\| \cos \alpha, \tag{9.39}$$

where α is the angle between the line segment and the edge. Using a dot product to compute the cosine, we have

$$t = \frac{(\mathbf{Q} - \mathbf{P}_1) \cdot (\mathbf{P}_2 - \mathbf{P}_1)}{\|\mathbf{P}_2 - \mathbf{P}_1\|}. \tag{9.40}$$

If $t < \varepsilon$ or $t > \|\mathbf{P}_2 - \mathbf{P}_1\| - \varepsilon$, then the point $\mathbf{Q}$ does not lie within the interior of the edge formed by $\mathbf{P}_1$ and $\mathbf{P}_2$. Otherwise, we have found a T-junction, and a new vertex should be added to the polygon of object A between $\mathbf{P}_1$ and $\mathbf{P}_2$ precisely at $\mathbf{Q}$'s location.

9.6 Triangulation

Triangulation is the process by which a polygon is divided into triangles that use the same array of vertices and collectively cover the same area. Polygons must be triangulated before they can be passed to the graphics hardware. A polygon having n vertices is always decomposed into $n - 2$ triangles. Convex polygons are particularly easy to triangulate—we simply choose one vertex and connect edges to every other nonadjacent vertex to form a triangle fan like the one shown in Figure 9.14. Polygons that are not convex or possess three or more collinear vertices cannot generally be triangulated in this way, so we have to employ more complicated algorithms.

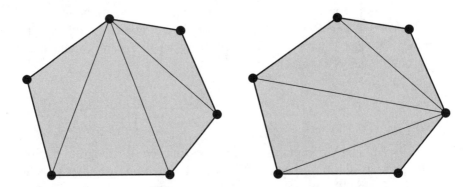

Figure 9.14 A convex polygon is triangulated by connecting edges from one arbitrarily chosen vertex to every other nonadjacent vertex, creating a triangle fan.

A modeling system may produce a list of polygons that might be convex or concave. After static world geometry has been processed by performing welding and T-junction elimination, any polygon may also contain several vertices that are collinear (or at least nearly collinear) with some of its other vertices. This prevents us from using a simple fanning approach that might ordinarily be used to triangulate a convex polygon. We are instead forced to treat the polygon as concave.

The algorithm that we describe takes as input a list of n vertices wound in a counterclockwise direction and produces a list of $n-2$ triangles. At each iteration, we search for a set of three consecutive vertices for which the corresponding triangle is not degenerate, is not wound in the wrong direction, and does not contain any of the polygon's remaining vertices. The triangle formed by such a set of three vertices is called an *ear*. Once an ear is found, a triangle is emitted, and the middle vertex is disqualified from successive iterations. The algorithm repeats until only three vertices remain. This process of reducing the size of the triangulation problem by removing one ear at a time is called *ear clipping*.

In order to determine whether a set of three vertices is wound in a counterclockwise direction, we must know beforehand the normal direction $\mathbf{N}_0$ of the plane containing the polygon being triangulated. Let $\mathbf{P}_1$, $\mathbf{P}_2$, and $\mathbf{P}_3$ represent the positions of the three vertices. If the cross product $(\mathbf{P}_2 - \mathbf{P}_1) \times (\mathbf{P}_3 - \mathbf{P}_1)$ points in the same direction as the normal $\mathbf{N}_0$, then the corresponding triangle is wound counterclockwise. If the cross product is near zero, then the triangle is degenerate. Thus, two of our three requirements for a triangle are satisfied only if

$$(\mathbf{P}_2 - \mathbf{P}_1) \times (\mathbf{P}_3 - \mathbf{P}_1) \cdot \mathbf{N}_0 > \varepsilon \tag{9.41}$$

for some small value ε (typically, $\varepsilon \approx 0.001$).

Our third requirement is that the triangle contains no other vertices belonging to the polygon. We can construct three inward-facing normals $\mathbf{N}_1$, $\mathbf{N}_2$, and $\mathbf{N}_3$ corresponding to the three sides of the triangle, as follows.

$$\mathbf{N}_1 = \mathbf{N}_0 \times (\mathbf{P}_2 - \mathbf{P}_1)$$
$$\mathbf{N}_2 = \mathbf{N}_0 \times (\mathbf{P}_3 - \mathbf{P}_2)$$
$$\mathbf{N}_3 = \mathbf{N}_0 \times (\mathbf{P}_1 - \mathbf{P}_3) \tag{9.42}$$

As shown in Figure 9.15, a point $\mathbf{Q}$ lies inside the triangle formed by $\mathbf{P}_1$, $\mathbf{P}_2$, and $\mathbf{P}_3$ if and only if $\mathbf{N}_i \cdot (\mathbf{Q} - \mathbf{P}_i) > -\varepsilon$ for $i \in \{1,2,3\}$.

Since we have to calculate the normals given by Equation (9.42) for each triangle, we can save a little computation by replacing the condition given by Equation (9.41) with the equivalent expression

$$\mathbf{N}_1 \cdot (\mathbf{P}_3 - \mathbf{P}_1) > \varepsilon. \tag{9.43}$$

This determines whether the point P_3 lies on the positive side of the edge connecting P_1 and P_2.

The implementation shown in Listing 9.2 maintains a working set of *four* consecutive vertices and at each iteration determines whether a valid triangle can be formed using the first three vertices or the last three vertices of that group. If only one of the sets of three vertices forms a valid triangle, then that triangle is emitted, and the algorithm continues to its next iteration. If both sets of three vertices can produce valid triangles, then the code selects the triangle having the larger smallest angle. In the case that neither set of three vertices provides a valid triangle, the working set of four vertices is advanced until a valid triangle can be constructed.

The method presented in Listing 9.2 was chosen so that the output of the algorithm would consist of a series of triangle strips and triangle fans. Such a triangle structure exhibits excellent vertex cache usage on modern graphics processors. The implementation also includes a safety mechanism. If a polygon is passed to it that is degenerate, self-intersecting, or otherwise nontriangulatable, then the algorithm terminates prematurely to avoid becoming stuck in an infinite loop. This happens when the code cannot locate a set of three consecutive vertices that form a valid triangle.

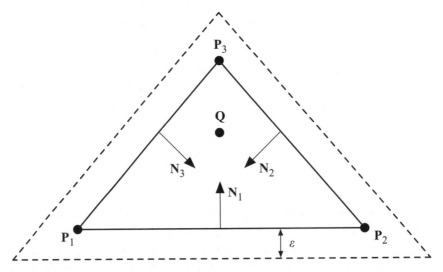

Figure 9.15 A point **Q** lies in the interior of a triangle (or nearly on its boundary) if $N_i \cdot (Q - P_i) > -\varepsilon$ for $i \in \{1, 2, 3\}$.

Listing 9.2 The `TriangulatePolygon` function takes an arbitrary planar polygon having *n* vertices and triangulates it, producing at most *n* − 2 triangles.

Parameters

   `vertexCount`   The number of vertices.

   `vertex`   A pointer to an array of *n* `Point3D` structures representing the polygon's vertices.

   `normal`   The polygon's normal direction.

   `triangle`   A pointer to an array of *n* − 2 `Triangle` structures where the results of the triangulation are stored.

```cpp
const float epsilon = 0.001F;

struct Triangle
{
  unsigned short   index[3];
};

struct Vector3D
{
  float   x, y, z;

  Vector3D() {}
  Vector3D(float r, float s, float t)
  {
    x = r; y = s; z = t;
  }

  float operator *(const Vector3D& v) const
  { // Dot product
    return (x * v.x + y * v.y + z * v.z);
  }

  Vector3D operator %(const Vector3D& v) const
  { // Cross product
    return (Vector3D(y * v.z - z * v.y,
      z * v.x - x * v.z, x * v.y - y * v.x));
  }

  Vector3D& Normalize(void)
  {
    return (*this /= sqrt(x * x + y * y + z * z));
  }
};
```

```cpp
struct Point3D : Vector3D
{
   Point3D() {}
   Point3D(float r, float s, float t) :
      Vector3D(r, s, t) {}

   Vector3D operator -(const Point3D& p) const
   { // Difference between two points is a vector
      return (Vector3D(x - p.x, y - p.y, z - p.z));
   }
};

static long GetNextActive(long x, long vertexCount,
   const bool *active)
{
   for (;;)
   {
      if (++x == vertexCount) x = 0;
      if (active[x]) return (x);
   }
}

static long GetPrevActive(long x, long vertexCount,
   const bool *active)
{
   for (;;)
   {
      if (--x == -1) x = vertexCount - 1;
      if (active[x]) return (x);
   }
}

long TriangulatePolygon(long vertexCount,
   const Point3D *vertex, const Vector3D& normal,
   Triangle *triangle)
{
   bool *active = new bool[vertexCount];
   for (long a = 0; a < vertexCount; a++)
      active[a] = true;

   long triangleCount = 0;
   long start = 0;
   long p1 = 0;
   long p2 = 1;
```

```
long m1 = vertexCount - 1;
long m2 = vertexCount - 2;

bool lastPositive = false;
for (;;)
{
   if (p2 == m2)
   { // Only three vertices remain
      triangle->index[0] = m1;
      triangle->index[1] = p1;
      triangle->index[2] = p2;
      triangleCount++;
      break;
   }

   const Point3D& vp1 = vertex[p1];
   const Point3D& vp2 = vertex[p2];
   const Point3D& vm1 = vertex[m1];
   const Point3D& vm2 = vertex[m2];
   bool positive = false;
   bool negative = false;

   // Determine whether vp1, vp2, and vm1 form
   // a valid triangle
   Vector3D n1 = normal % (vm1 - vp2).Normalize();
   if (n1 * (vp1 - vp2) > epsilon)
   {
      positive = true;
      Vector3D n2 = (normal % (vp1 - vm1).Normalize());
      Vector3D n3 = (normal % (vp2 - vp1).Normalize());

      for (long a = 0; a < vertexCount; a++)
      { // Look for other vertices inside the triangle
         if ((active[a])
            && (a != p1) && (a != p2) && (a != m1))
         {
            const Vector3D& v = vertex[a];
            if ((n1 * (v - vp2).Normalize() > -epsilon)
            && (n2 * (v - vm1).Normalize() > -epsilon)
            && (n3 * (v - vp1).Normalize() > -epsilon))
            {
               positive = false;
               break;
            }
         }
```

```
      }
   }

   // Determine whether vm1, vm2, and vp1 form
   // a valid triangle
   n1 = normal % (vm2 - vp1).Normalize();
   if (n1 * (vm1 - vp1) > epsilon)
   {
      negative = true;
      Vector3D n2 = (normal % (vm1 - vm2).Normalize());
      Vector3D n3 = (normal % (vp1 - vm1).Normalize());

      for (long a = 0; a < vertexCount; a++)
      { // Look for other vertices inside the triangle
         if ((active[a])
            && (a != m1) && (a != m2) && (a != p1))
         {
            const Vector3D& v = vertex[a];
            if ((n1 * (v - vp1).Normalize() > -epsilon)
            && (n2 * (v - vm2).Normalize() > -epsilon)
            && (n3 * (v - vm1).Normalize() > -epsilon))
            {
               negative = false;
               break;
            }
         }
      }
   }

   // If both triangles valid, choose the one
   // having the larger smallest angle
   if ((positive) && (negative))
   {
      float pd = (vp2 - vm1).Normalize() *
         (vm2 - vm1).Normalize();
      float md = (vm2 - vp1).Normalize() *
         (vp2 - vp1).Normalize();

      if (fabs(pd - md) < epsilon)
      {
         if (lastPositive) positive = false;
         else negative = false;
      }
      else
      {
```

```
      if (pd < md) negative = false;
      else positive = false;
    }
  }

  if (positive)
  { // Output the triangle m1, p1, p2
    active[p1] = false;
    triangle->index[0] = m1;
    triangle->index[1] = p1;
    triangle->index[2] = p2;
    triangleCount++;
    triangle++;

    p1 = GetNextActive(p1, vertexCount, active);
    p2 = GetNextActive(p2, vertexCount, active);
    lastPositive = true;
    start = -1;
  }
  else if (negative)
  { // Output the triangle m2, m1, p1
    active[m1] = false;
    triangle->index[0] = m2;
    triangle->index[1] = m1;
    triangle->index[2] = p1;
    triangleCount++;
    triangle++;

    m1 = GetPrevActive(m1, vertexCount, active);
    m2 = GetPrevActive(m2, vertexCount, active);
    lastPositive = false;
    start = -1;
  }
  else
  {
    // Exit if we've gone all the way around the
    // polygon without finding a valid triangle
    if (start == -1) start = p2;
    else if (p2 == start) break;

    // Advance working set of vertices
    m2 = m1;
    m1 = p1;
    p1 = p2;
    p2 = GetNextActive(p2, vertexCount, active);
```

```
        }
    }

    delete[] active;
    return (triangleCount);
}
```

Chapter 9 Summary

Depth Value Offset

To offset the depth of a vertex whose z-coordinate is roughly P_z by a distance δ, the (3,3) entry of the perspective projection matrix should be multiplied by $1 + \varepsilon$, where

$$\varepsilon = -\frac{2fn}{f+n} \left(\frac{\delta}{P_z (P_z + \delta)} \right).$$

Decal Application

A decal of width w and height h centered at the point $\mathbf{P}$, having normal direction $\mathbf{N}$ and tangent direction $\mathbf{T}$, should be clipped to the planes

$$left = \left(\mathbf{T}, \frac{w}{2} - \mathbf{T} \cdot \mathbf{P} \right) \qquad right = \left(-\mathbf{T}, \frac{w}{2} + \mathbf{T} \cdot \mathbf{P} \right)$$

$$bottom = \left(\mathbf{B}, \frac{h}{2} - \mathbf{B} \cdot \mathbf{P} \right) \qquad top = \left(-\mathbf{B}, \frac{h}{2} + \mathbf{B} \cdot \mathbf{P} \right)$$

$$front = (-\mathbf{N}, d + \mathbf{N} \cdot \mathbf{P}) \qquad back = (\mathbf{N}, d - \mathbf{N} \cdot \mathbf{P}),$$

where $\mathbf{B} = \mathbf{N} \times \mathbf{T}$ and d is the maximum distance that any vertex in the decal may be from the tangent plane passing through the point $\mathbf{P}$. The texture coordinates for a decal vertex $\mathbf{Q}$ are given by

$$s = \frac{\mathbf{T} \cdot (\mathbf{Q} - \mathbf{P})}{w} + \frac{1}{2}$$

$$t = \frac{\mathbf{B} \cdot (\mathbf{Q} - \mathbf{P})}{h} + \frac{1}{2}.$$

Billboarding

The vertices of an unconstrained billboarded quad of width w, height h, and orientation θ centered at the point $\mathbf{P}$ may be calculated using

$$\mathbf{Q}_1 = \mathbf{P} + \mathbf{X} + \mathbf{Y} \qquad \mathbf{Q}_2 = \mathbf{P} - \mathbf{X} + \mathbf{Y}$$
$$\mathbf{Q}_3 = \mathbf{P} - \mathbf{X} - \mathbf{Y} \qquad \mathbf{Q}_4 = \mathbf{P} + \mathbf{X} - \mathbf{Y},$$

where

$$\mathbf{X} = \left(\frac{w}{2}\cos\theta\right)\mathbf{R} + \left(\frac{w}{2}\sin\theta\right)\mathbf{U}$$
$$\mathbf{Y} = \left(-\frac{h}{2}\sin\theta\right)\mathbf{R} + \left(\frac{h}{2}\cos\theta\right)\mathbf{U},$$

and the directions $\mathbf{R}$ and $\mathbf{U}$ are the world space right and up directions of the camera view. The vertices of a billboarded quad constrained to rotate only about the z-axis are given by

$$\mathbf{Q}_1 = \mathbf{P} + \frac{w}{2}\frac{\mathbf{X}}{\|\mathbf{X}\|} + \left\langle 0,0,\frac{h}{2}\right\rangle \qquad \mathbf{Q}_2 = \mathbf{P} - \frac{w}{2}\frac{\mathbf{X}}{\|\mathbf{X}\|} + \left\langle 0,0,\frac{h}{2}\right\rangle$$
$$\mathbf{Q}_3 = \mathbf{P} - \frac{w}{2}\frac{\mathbf{X}}{\|\mathbf{X}\|} - \left\langle 0,0,\frac{h}{2}\right\rangle \qquad \mathbf{Q}_4 = \mathbf{P} + \frac{w}{2}\frac{\mathbf{X}}{\|\mathbf{X}\|} - \left\langle 0,0,\frac{h}{2}\right\rangle,$$

where

$$\mathbf{X} = \left\langle P_y - C_y, C_x - P_x, 0\right\rangle,$$

and $\mathbf{C}$ is the world space camera position.

T-Junction Elimination

The squared distance d^2 between the point $\mathbf{Q}$ and the line passing through $\mathbf{P}_1$ and $\mathbf{P}_2$ is given by

$$d^2 = (\mathbf{Q} - \mathbf{P}_1)^2 - \frac{[(\mathbf{Q} - \mathbf{P}_1)\cdot(\mathbf{P}_2 - \mathbf{P}_1)]^2}{(\mathbf{P}_2 - \mathbf{P}_1)^2}.$$

A point $\mathbf{Q}$ satisfying $d^2 < \varepsilon^2$ lies within the interior of the edge formed by $\mathbf{P}_1$ and $\mathbf{P}_2$ if $\varepsilon < t < \|\mathbf{P}_2 - \mathbf{P}_1\| - \varepsilon$, where t is given by

$$t = \frac{(\mathbf{Q} - \mathbf{P}_1) \cdot (\mathbf{P}_2 - \mathbf{P}_1)}{\|\mathbf{P}_2 - \mathbf{P}_1\|}.$$

Triangulation

A point $\mathbf{Q}$ lies inside (or near the boundary of) a triangle defined by the three vertices $\mathbf{P}_1$, $\mathbf{P}_2$, and $\mathbf{P}_3$ belonging to a polygon if and only if $\mathbf{N}_i \cdot (\mathbf{Q} - \mathbf{P}_i) > -\varepsilon$ for $i \in \{1, 2, 3\}$, where

$$\mathbf{N}_1 = \mathbf{N}_0 \times (\mathbf{P}_2 - \mathbf{P}_1)$$
$$\mathbf{N}_2 = \mathbf{N}_0 \times (\mathbf{P}_3 - \mathbf{P}_2)$$
$$\mathbf{N}_3 = \mathbf{N}_0 \times (\mathbf{P}_1 - \mathbf{P}_3),$$

and $\mathbf{N}_0$ is the polygon's normal direction. The triangle is wound counterclockwise and is nondegenerate if

$$\mathbf{N}_1 \cdot (\mathbf{P}_3 - \mathbf{P}_1) > \varepsilon.$$

Exercises for Chapter 9

1. Suppose that the distance to the near plane is $n = 1$, and the distance to the far plane is $f = 100$ for a particular view frustum. Calculate by what value the $(3, 3)$ entry of the projection matrix should be multiplied in order to offset a model centered at a depth of $z = -20$ toward the camera by a distance of 0.2.

2. Calculate the least distance d by which the model in Exercise 1 can be offset toward the camera if a 16-bit depth buffer is used.

3. Write a program that applies a decal to a surface. Assume that the decal is described by its center $\mathbf{P}$, a normal direction $\mathbf{N}$, a tangent direction $\mathbf{T}$, its width w, and its height h. The program should construct a decal object by clipping an arbitrary triangle mesh to the planes bounding the decal and should then calculate texture coordinates for each vertex in the decal object.

4. Implement a particle system for which each particle is rendered as a textured quad centered at the particle's position. Each particle should be described by its position $\mathbf{P}$ in world space, its radius r, its window-space orientation θ, and its velocity $\mathbf{V}$.

Chapter 10

Shadows

S hadows are an essential component of any rendered scene that attempts to depict a realistic environment. Due to hardware limitations, shadow generation in most real-time rendering applications was accompanied by many restrictions for the first several years in which 3D graphics processors were widely available.

One classical shadow-rendering technique, called *light mapping*, precomputes low-resolution texture maps for every immovable surface in an environment. Each sample stored in this *light map* represents the color and intensity of light reaching a particular point on the surface to which it is attached. When rendering a scene, multitexturing is used to modulate the surface's reflection color with the lighting values fetched from the light map. With the help of bilinear filtering, the results are more than adequate visually, but the technique suffered from the inescapable fact that the lighting is baked into the texture maps and cannot be changed in real-time on anything other than small scales. Thus, world geometry cannot be moved without leaving behind a shadow that no longer has a castor.

Greatly more-flexible shadow generation methods are now available and can be implemented for real-time rendering applications. One such method is called *shadow mapping* and is so named because a scene is rendered from the perspective of a light source to generate a *shadow map* that is subsequently used in the ordinary rendering pass from the camera's perspective. Each pixel in the shadow map holds the depth of the associated point in the scene with respect to the light source. During the ordinary rendering pass, vertices are transformed into the light's coordinate space. The light-space depth is interpolated across the face of a polygon and compared to the depth stored in the shadow map at the light-space x- and y-coordinates. If the transformed depth is greater, then the point corresponding to the pixel lies in shadow. Shadow mapping is performed entirely on the graphics hardware using functionality exposed through the OpenGL extensions `GL_ARB_shadow` and `GL_ARB_depth_texture`. Unfortunately, since shadow mapping relies on a rendered image from the light source's location, the technique suffers from significant aliasing problems. There are also limitations on where the light source can reside in a scene, and additional difficulties arise for omnidirectional lights.

In this chapter, we focus exclusively on a technique called *stencil shadows*. The stencil shadow method can be used to render accurate shadows for fully dynamic scenes using any type of light source residing at any location. Unlike shadow mapping, stencil shadows require a significant amount of geometrical computation that must usually be performed by the CPU. The advantage is that the shadows are as accurate as the polygonal representation of the models that cast them, completely avoid aliasing artifacts.

10.1 Algorithm Overview

Using an idea that was first conceived in the 1970s [CROW77], the stencil buffer can be employed to generate extremely accurate shadows in real time. Two decades after the algorithm's invention, 3D graphics hardware finally advanced to the point where stencil shadows became practical, but several unsolved problems still existed that prevented the algorithm from working correctly under various conditions. These problems have now been solved, and stencil shadows can be robustly implemented to handle arbitrarily positioned point lights and infinite directional lights having any desired spatial relationship with the camera.

The basic concept of the stencil shadow algorithm is to use the stencil buffer as a masking mechanism that prevents pixels in shadow from being drawn during the rendering pass for a particular light source. This is accomplished by rendering an invisible shadow volume for each shadow-casting object in a scene using stencil operations that leave nonzero values in the stencil buffer wherever light is blocked. Once the stencil buffer has been filled with the appropriate mask, a lighting pass only illuminates pixels where the value in the stencil buffer is zero.

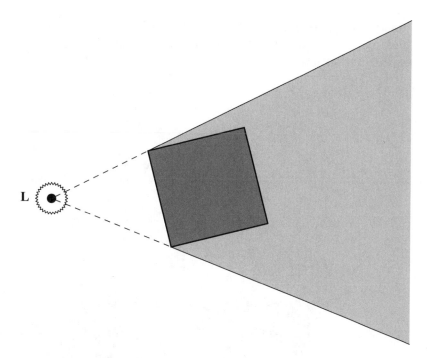

Figure 10.1 An object's shadow volume encloses the region of space for which light emitted by the light source **L** is blocked by the object.

As shown in Figure 10.1, an object's shadow volume encloses the region of space for which light is blocked by the object. This volume is constructed by finding the edges in the object's triangle mesh representing the boundary between lit triangles and unlit triangles and extruding those edges away from the light source. Such a collection of edges is called the object's *silhouette* with respect to the light source. The shadow volume is rendered into the stencil buffer using operations that modify the stencil value at each pixel depending on whether the depth test passes or fails. Of course, this requires that the depth buffer has already been initialized to the correct values by a previous rendering pass. Thus, the scene is first rendered using a shader that applies surface attributes that do not depend on any light source, such as ambient illumination, emission, and environment mapping.

The original stencil algorithm renders the shadow volume in two stages. In the first stage, the front faces of the shadow volume (with respect to the camera) are rendered using a stencil operation that increments the value in the stencil buffer whenever the depth test passes. In the second stage, the back faces of the shadow volume are rendered using a stencil operation that decrements the value in the stencil buffer whenever the depth test passes. As illustrated in Figure 10.2, this technique leaves nonzero values in the stencil buffer wherever the shadow volume intersects any surface in the scene, including the surface of the object casting the shadow.

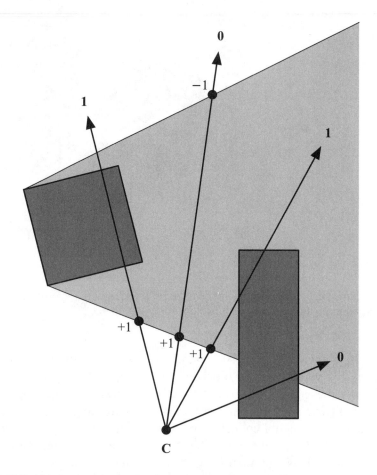

Figure 10.2 Numbers at the ends of rays emanating from the camera position **C** represent the values left in the stencil buffer for a variety of cases. The stencil value is incremented when front faces of the shadow volume pass the depth test, and the stencil value is decremented when back faces of the shadow volume pass the depth test. The stencil value is not changed when the depth test fails.

There are two major problems with the method just described. The first is that no matter what finite distance we extrude an object's silhouette away from a light source, it is still possible that it is not far enough to cast a shadow on every object in the scene that should intersect the shadow volume. The example shown in Figure 10.3 demonstrates how this problem arises when a light source is very close to a shadow-casting object. Fortunately, this problem can be elegantly solved by using a special projection matrix and extruding shadow volumes all the way to infinity.

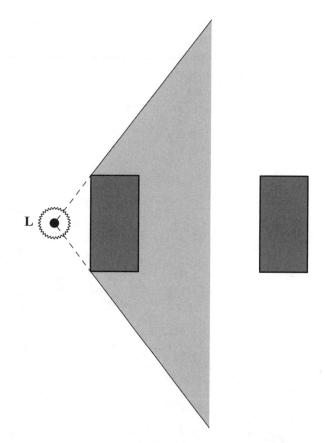

Figure 10.3 No matter what finite distance an object's silhouette is extruded away from a light source **L**, moving the light close enough to the object can result in a shadow volume that cannot reach other objects in the scene.

The second problem shows up when the camera lies inside the shadow volume or the shadow volume is clipped by the near plane. Either of these occurrences can leave incorrect values in the stencil buffer, causing the wrong surfaces to be illuminated. The solution to this problem is to add caps to the shadow volume geometry, making it a closed surface, and using different stencil operations. The two caps added to the shadow volume are derived from the object's triangle mesh as follows. A front cap is constructed using the unmodified vertices of triangles facing toward the light source. A back cap is constructed by projecting the vertices of triangles facing away from the light source to infinity. For the resulting closed shadow volume, we render back faces (with respect to the camera) using a stencil operation that increments the stencil value whenever the depth test fails, and we render front faces using a stencil operation that decrements the stencil value whenever the depth test fails. As shown in Figure 10.4, this technique leaves nonzero values in the stencil buffer for any surface intersecting the shadow volume for arbitrary camera positions. Rendering shadow volumes in this manner is more expensive than using the original technique, but we can determine when it's safe to use the less-costly depth-pass method without having to worry about capping our shadow volumes.

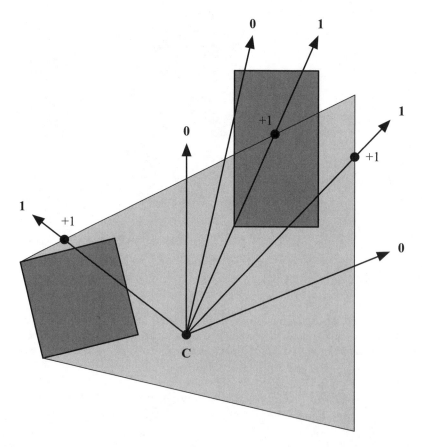

Figure 10.4 Using a capped shadow volume and depth-fail stencil operations allows the camera to be inside the shadow volume. The stencil value is incremented when back faces of the shadow volume fail the depth test, and the stencil value is decremented when front faces of the shadow volume fail the depth test. The stencil value does not change when the depth test passes.

The details of everything just described are discussed throughout the remainder of this section. In summary, the rendering algorithm for a single frame runs through the following steps.

A. Clear the frame buffer and perform an ambient rendering pass. Render the visible scene using any surface shading attribute that does not depend on any particular light source.

B. Choose a light source and determine what objects may cast shadows into the visible region of the world. If this is not the first light to be rendered, clear the stencil buffer.

C. For each object, calculate the silhouette representing the boundary between triangles facing toward the light source and triangles facing away from the light source. Construct a shadow volume by extruding the silhouette away from the light source.

D. Render the shadow volume using specific stencil operations that leave nonzero values in the stencil buffer where surfaces are in shadow.

E. Perform a lighting pass using the stencil test to mask areas that are not illuminated by the light source.

F. Repeat steps B through E for every light source that may illuminate the visible region of the world.

For a scene illuminated by n lights, this algorithm requires at least $n+1$ rendering passes. More than $n+1$ passes may be necessary if surface-shading calculations for a single light source cannot be accomplished in a single pass. To efficiently render a large scene containing many lights, one must be careful during each pass to render only objects that could potentially be illuminated by a particular light source. An additional optimization using the scissor rectangle can also save a significant amount of rasterization work—this optimization is discussed in Section 10.7.

10.2 Infinite View Frustums

To ensure that shadow volumes surround every last bit of space for which light is blocked by an object, we must extrude the object's silhouette to infinity. Using a standard perspective projection matrix would cause such a shadow volume to be clipped by the far plane. To avoid this unwanted effect, we can actually place the far plane at an infinite distance from the camera.

The standard OpenGL perspective projection matrix $\mathbf{M}_{\text{frustum}}$, derived in Section 4.5.1, has the form

$$
\mathbf{M}_{\text{frustum}} =
\begin{bmatrix}
\dfrac{2n}{r-l} & 0 & \dfrac{r+l}{r-l} & 0 \\[2ex]
0 & \dfrac{2n}{t-b} & \dfrac{t+b}{t-b} & 0 \\[2ex]
0 & 0 & -\dfrac{f+n}{f-n} & -\dfrac{2fn}{f-n} \\[2ex]
0 & 0 & -1 & 0
\end{bmatrix},
\tag{10.1}
$$

where n is the distance to the near plane, f is the distance to the far plane, and l, r, b, and t represent the left, right, bottom, and top edges of the rectangle carved out of the near plane by the view frustum. By evaluating the limit as f tends to infinity, we obtain the matrix

$$
\mathbf{M}_{\text{infinite}} = \lim_{f \to \infty} \mathbf{M}_{\text{frustum}} =
\begin{bmatrix}
\dfrac{2n}{r-l} & 0 & \dfrac{r+l}{r-l} & 0 \\[2ex]
0 & \dfrac{2n}{t-b} & \dfrac{t+b}{t-b} & 0 \\[2ex]
0 & 0 & -1 & -2n \\[2ex]
0 & 0 & -1 & 0
\end{bmatrix}.
\tag{10.2}
$$

The matrix $\mathbf{M}_{\text{infinite}}$ transforms a 4D homogeneous eye-space point $\mathbf{P}_{\text{eye}} = \langle x, y, z, w \rangle$ to the clip-space point $\mathbf{P}_{\text{clip}}$ as follows.

$$
\mathbf{P}_{\text{clip}} = \mathbf{M}_{\text{infinite}} \mathbf{P}_{\text{eye}} =
\begin{bmatrix}
\dfrac{2n}{r-l} & 0 & \dfrac{r+l}{r-l} & 0 \\[2ex]
0 & \dfrac{2n}{t-b} & \dfrac{t+b}{t-b} & 0 \\[2ex]
0 & 0 & -1 & -2n \\[2ex]
0 & 0 & -1 & 0
\end{bmatrix}
\begin{bmatrix}
x \\[1ex] y \\[1ex] z \\[1ex] w
\end{bmatrix}
=
\begin{bmatrix}
\dfrac{2n}{r-l}x + \dfrac{r+l}{r-l}z \\[2ex]
\dfrac{2n}{t-b}y + \dfrac{t+b}{t-b}z \\[2ex]
-z - 2nw \\[2ex]
-z
\end{bmatrix}
\tag{10.3}
$$

Assuming $w > 0$ (it is normally the case that $w = 1$), the resulting z-coordinate of $\mathbf{P}_{\text{clip}}$ is always less than the resulting w-coordinate of $\mathbf{P}_{\text{clip}}$, ensuring that projected points are never clipped by the far plane. A point at infinity is represented by a 4D homogeneous vector having a w-coordinate of 0 in eye space. For such a point, $\left(\mathbf{P}_{\text{clip}}\right)_z = \left(\mathbf{P}_{\text{clip}}\right)_w$, and the perspective divide produces a 3D point in normalized device coordinates having the maximal z-value of 1.

In practice, the limitations of hardware precision can produce points having a normalized z-coordinate slightly greater than 1. This causes severe problems when the z-coordinate is converted to an integer value to be used in the depth buffer because the stencil operations that depend on the depth test to render shadow volumes may no longer function correctly. To circumvent this undesirable effect, we can map the z-coordinate of a point at infinity to a value slightly less than 1 in normalized device coordinates. The z-coordinate of a 3D point $\mathbf{D}$ in normalized device coordinates is mapped from a value D_z in the range $[-1,1]$ to a value D_z' in the range $[-1,1-\varepsilon]$, where ε is a small positive constant, using the relation

$$D_z' = (D_z + 1)\frac{2-\varepsilon}{2} - 1. \tag{10.4}$$

We need to find a way to modify the z-coordinate of $\mathbf{P}_{\text{clip}}$ in order to perform this mapping as points are transformed from eye space into clip space. We can rewrite Equation (10.4) as an adjustment to $\left(\mathbf{P}_{\text{clip}}\right)_z$ by replacing D_z with $\left(\mathbf{P}_{\text{clip}}\right)_z / \left(\mathbf{P}_{\text{clip}}\right)_w$ and D_z' with $\left(\mathbf{P}_{\text{clip}}'\right)_z / \left(\mathbf{P}_{\text{clip}}\right)_w$ as follows.

$$\frac{\left(\mathbf{P}_{\text{clip}}'\right)_z}{\left(\mathbf{P}_{\text{clip}}\right)_w} = \left(\frac{\left(\mathbf{P}_{\text{clip}}\right)_z}{\left(\mathbf{P}_{\text{clip}}\right)_w} + 1\right)\frac{2-\varepsilon}{2} - 1 \tag{10.5}$$

Plugging in the values of $\left(\mathbf{P}_{\text{clip}}\right)_z$ and $\left(\mathbf{P}_{\text{clip}}\right)_w$ given by Equation (10.3), we have

$$\frac{\left(\mathbf{P}_{\text{clip}}'\right)_z}{-z} = \left(\frac{-z - 2nw}{-z} + 1\right)\frac{2-\varepsilon}{2} - 1. \tag{10.6}$$

Solving for $\left(\mathbf{P}_{\text{clip}}'\right)_z$ and simplifying yields

$$\left(\mathbf{P}_{\text{clip}}'\right)_z = z(\varepsilon - 1) + nw(\varepsilon - 2). \tag{10.7}$$

We can incorporate this mapping into the projection matrix $\mathbf{M}_{\text{infinite}}$ given by Equation (10.2) as follows to arrive at the slightly tweaked matrix $\mathbf{M}_{\text{infinite}}'$ that we actually use to render a scene.

$$\mathbf{M}'_{\text{infinite}} = \begin{bmatrix} \dfrac{2n}{r-l} & 0 & \dfrac{r+l}{r-l} & 0 \\[2ex] 0 & \dfrac{2n}{t-b} & \dfrac{t+b}{t-b} & 0 \\[2ex] 0 & 0 & \varepsilon-1 & n(\varepsilon-2) \\[2ex] 0 & 0 & -1 & 0 \end{bmatrix} \tag{10.8}$$

For graphics hardware that supports depth clamping, the use of the matrix $\mathbf{M}'_{\text{infinite}}$ given by Equation (10.8) is not necessary. The GL_NV_depth_clamp extension to OpenGL allows a renderer to force depth values in normalized device coordinates to saturate to the range $[-1,1]$, thus curing the precision problem at the infinite far plane. When depth clamping is enabled using the function call

```
glEnable(GL_DEPTH_CLAMP_NV);
```

the projection matrix $\mathbf{M}_{\text{infinite}}$ given by Equation (10.2) can safely be used.

The question of depth buffer precision arises when using an infinite projection matrix. It is true that placing the far plane at infinity reduces the number of discrete depth values that can occur within any finite interval along the z-axis, but in most situations this effect is small. Consider the function $d_{\text{frustum}}(\mathbf{P})$ that uses the matrix $\mathbf{M}_{\text{frustum}}$ given in Equation (10.1) to map an eye-space point $\mathbf{P} = \langle P_x, P_y, P_z, 1 \rangle$ to its corresponding depth in normalized device coordinates:

$$d_{\text{frustum}}(\mathbf{P}) = \frac{(\mathbf{M}_{\text{frustum}}\mathbf{P})_z}{(\mathbf{M}_{\text{frustum}}\mathbf{P})_w} = \frac{f+n}{f-n} + \frac{1}{P_z}\left(\frac{2fn}{f-n}\right). \tag{10.9}$$

We obtain a different function $d_{\text{infinite}}(\mathbf{P})$ by using the matrix $\mathbf{M}_{\text{infinite}}$ given by Equation (10.2) to map an eye-space point $\mathbf{P}$ to its normalized depth:

$$d_{\text{infinite}}(\mathbf{P}) = \frac{(\mathbf{M}_{\text{infinite}}\mathbf{P})_z}{(\mathbf{M}_{\text{infinite}}\mathbf{P})_w} = 1 + \frac{1}{P_z}(2n). \tag{10.10}$$

Given two eye-space points $\mathbf{P}_1$ and $\mathbf{P}_2$, we can compare the differences in depth values produced by the functions d_{frustum} and d_{infinite} as follows.

$$d_{\text{frustum}}(\mathbf{P}_2) - d_{\text{frustum}}(\mathbf{P}_1) = \frac{2fn}{f-n}\left(\frac{1}{(\mathbf{P}_2)_z} - \frac{1}{(\mathbf{P}_1)_z}\right)$$

$$d_{\text{infinite}}\left(\mathbf{P}_2\right) - d_{\text{infinite}}\left(\mathbf{P}_1\right) = 2n\left(\frac{1}{\left(\mathbf{P}_2\right)_z} - \frac{1}{\left(\mathbf{P}_1\right)_z}\right) \qquad (10.11)$$

This demonstrates that the standard projection matrix $\mathbf{M}_{\text{frustum}}$ maps the points $\mathbf{P}_1$ and $\mathbf{P}_2$ to a range that is a factor $f/(f-n)$ larger than the range to which the points are mapped by the infinite projection matrix $\mathbf{M}_{\text{infinite}}$, thus equating to greater precision. For practical values of f and n, where f is much larger than 1 and n is much smaller than 1, $f/(f-n)$ is close to unity, so the loss of precision is not a significant disadvantage.

10.3 Silhouette Determination

The stencil shadow algorithm requires that the models in our world be closed triangle meshes. In mathematical terms, the surface of any object that casts a shadow must be a two-dimensional closed manifold. What this boils down to is that every edge in a mesh must be shared by exactly two triangles, disallowing any holes that would let us see the interior of the mesh.

Edge connectivity information must be precomputed so that we can determine a mesh's silhouette for shadow volume rendering. Suppose that we have an indexed triangle mesh consisting of an array of N vertices $\mathbf{V}_1, \mathbf{V}_2, \ldots, \mathbf{V}_N$ and an array of M triangles $T_1, T_2, \ldots, T_M$. Each triangle simply indicates which three vertices it uses by storing three integer indexes i_1, i_2, and i_3. We say that an index i_p precedes an index i_q if the number p immediately precedes the number q in the cyclic chain $1 \to 2 \to 3 \to 1$. For instance, i_2 precedes i_3 and i_3 precedes i_1, but i_2 does not precede i_1.

The indexes i_1, i_2, and i_3 are ordered such that the positions of the vertices $\mathbf{V}_{i_1}$, $\mathbf{V}_{i_2}$, and $\mathbf{V}_{i_3}$ to which they refer are wound counterclockwise about the triangle's normal vector. Suppose that two triangles share an edge whose endpoints are the vertices $\mathbf{V}_a$ and $\mathbf{V}_b$ as shown in Figure 10.5. The consistent winding rule enforces the property that for one of the triangles, the index referring to $\mathbf{V}_a$ precedes the index referring to $\mathbf{V}_b$, and that for the other triangle, the index referring to $\mathbf{V}_b$ precedes the index referring to $\mathbf{V}_a$.

As demonstrated in Listing 10.1, the edges of a triangle mesh can be identified by making a single pass through the triangle list. For any triangle having vertex indexes i_1, i_2, and i_3, we create an edge record for every instance in which $i_1 < i_2$, $i_2 < i_3$, or $i_3 < i_1$ and store the index of the current triangle in the edge record. This procedure creates exactly one edge for every pair of triangles that share two vertices $\mathbf{V}_a$ and $\mathbf{V}_b$, duplicating any edges that are shared by multiple pairs of triangles.

Once we have identified all the edges, we make a second pass through the triangle list to find the second triangle that shares each edge. This is done by locating triangles for which $i_1 > i_2$, $i_2 > i_3$, or $i_3 > i_1$ and matching it to an edge having the same vertex indexes that has not yet been supplied with a second triangle index.

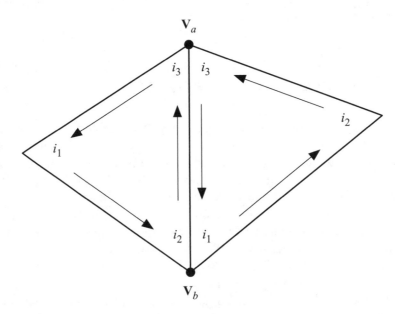

Figure 10.5 When consistent winding is enforced, it is always the case that the indexes referring to the vertices $\mathbf{V}_a$ and $\mathbf{V}_b$ of exactly one of the two triangles sharing an edge satisfies the property that the index referring to $\mathbf{V}_a$ precedes the index referring to $\mathbf{V}_b$.

Armed with the edge list for a triangle mesh, we determine the silhouette by first calculating the dot product between the light position and the plane of each triangle. For a triangle whose vertex indexes are i_1, i_2, and i_3, the (unnormalized) outward-pointing normal direction $\mathbf{N}$ is given by

$$\mathbf{N} = \left(\mathbf{V}_{i_2} - \mathbf{V}_{i_1}\right) \times \left(\mathbf{V}_{i_3} - \mathbf{V}_{i_1}\right) \tag{10.12}$$

since the vertices are assumed to be wound counterclockwise. The 4D plane vector $\mathbf{F}$ corresponding to the triangle is then given by

$$\mathbf{F} = \langle N_x, N_y, N_z, -\mathbf{N} \cdot \mathbf{V}_{i_1} \rangle. \qquad (10.13)$$

Let $\mathbf{L}$ represent the 4D homogeneous position of the light source. For point light sources, $L_w \neq 0$; and for infinite directional light sources, $L_w = 0$. A triangle faces the light source if $\mathbf{F} \cdot \mathbf{L} > 0$. Otherwise, the triangle faces away from the light source. The silhouette is equal to the set of edges shared by one triangle facing the light and one triangle facing away from the light.

Listing 10.1 This code examines an array of indexed triangles and constructs an array of edge records that refer back to the triangles that share them. The return value is the number of edges written to the array `edgeArray`.

Parameters

triangleCount	The number of triangles in the array pointed to by the `triangleArray` parameter.
triangleArray	A pointer to an array of `Triangle` structures describing the polygonal mesh.
edgeArray	A pointer to a location in which a pointer to the edge array is returned.

```
struct Edge
{
    unsigned short    vertexIndex[2];
    unsigned short    triangleIndex[2];
};

struct Triangle
{
    unsigned short    index[3];
};

long BuildEdges(long triangleCount,
    const Triangle *triangleArray, Edge **edgeArray)
{
    // Allocate enough space to hold all edges
    *edgeArray = new Edge[triangleCount * 3];

    long edgeCount = 0;
    Edge *edge = *edgeArray;

    // First pass: find edges
    const Triangle *triangle = triangleArray;
    for (long a = 0; a < triangleCount; a++)
```

```
{
  long i1 = triangle->index[0];
  long i2 = triangle->index[1];
  long i3 = triangle->index[2];

  if (i1 < i2)
  {
    edge->vertexIndex[0] = i1;
    edge->vertexIndex[1] = i2;
    edge->triangleIndex[0] = a;
    edge->triangleIndex[1] = -1;
    edgeCount++;
    edge++;
  }

  if (i2 < i3)
  {
    edge->vertexIndex[0] = i2;
    edge->vertexIndex[1] = i3;
    edge->triangleIndex[0] = a;
    edge->triangleIndex[1] = -1;
    edgeCount++;
    edge++;
  }

  if (i3 < i1)
  {
    edge->vertexIndex[0] = i3;
    edge->vertexIndex[1] = i1;
    edge->triangleIndex[0] = a;
    edge->triangleIndex[1] = -1;
    edgeCount++;
    edge++;
  }

  triangle++;
}

// Second pass: match triangles to edges
triangle = triangleArray;
for (long a = 0; a < triangleCount; a++)
{
  long i1 = triangle->index[0];
  long i2 = triangle->index[1];
  long i3 = triangle->index[2];
```

```
if (i1 > i2)
{
   edge = *edgeArray;
   for (long b = 0; b < edgeCount; b++)
   {
      if ((edge->vertexIndex[0] == i2) &&
         (edge->vertexIndex[1] == i1) &&
         (edge->triangleIndex[1] == -1))
      {
         edge->triangleIndex[1] = a;
         break;
      }

      edge++;
   }
}

if (i2 > i3)
{
   edge = *edgeArray;
   for (long b = 0; b < edgeCount; b++)
   {
      if ((edge->vertexIndex[0] == i3) &&
         (edge->vertexIndex[1] == i2) &&
         (edge->triangleIndex[1] == -1))
      {
         edge->triangleIndex[1] = a;
         break;
      }

      edge++;
   }
}

if (i3 > i1)
{
   edge = *edgeArray;
   for (long b = 0; b < edgeCount; b++)
   {
      if ((edge->vertexIndex[0] == i1) &&
         (edge->vertexIndex[1] == i3) &&
         (edge->triangleIndex[1] == -1))
      {
         edge->triangleIndex[1] = a;
```

```
                break;
            }

            edge++;
        }
    }

    triangle++;
}

return (edgeCount);
}
```

10.4 Shadow Volume Construction

Once the set of an object's silhouette edges has been determined with respect to a light source, we must extrude each edge away from the light's position to form the object's shadow volume. Such an extrusion may be accomplished by making use of widely available vertex programming hardware exposed by the GL_ARB_vertex_program extension to OpenGL.

For a point light source, the extrusion of the silhouette edges consists of a set of quads, each of which has the two unmodified vertices belonging to an edge and two additional vertices corresponding to the extrusion of the same edge to infinity. For an infinite directional light source, all points project to the same point at infinity, so the extrusion of the silhouette edges can be represented by a set of triangles that all share a common vertex. We distinguish between points that should be treated normally and those that should be extruded to infinity by using 4D homogeneous coordinates. A w-coordinate of 1 is assigned to the unmodified vertices and a w-coordinate of 0 is assigned to the extruded vertices. The vertex program performing the extrusion utilizes the information stored in the w-coordinate to perform the appropriate vertex modifications.

Before we examine the extrusion method, we must prepare the appropriate quad list or triangle list (depending on whether we are using a point light or infinite directional light). We need to make sure that the vertices of each extrusion primitive are wound so that the face's normal direction points out of the shadow volume. Suppose that a silhouette edge E has endpoints $\mathbf{A}$ and $\mathbf{B}$. The edge-finding code presented in Listing 10.1 associates the triangle for which the vertices $\mathbf{A}$ and $\mathbf{B}$ occur in counterclockwise order as the first triangle sharing the edge E. Thus, if the first triangle faces toward the light source, then we want the vertices $\mathbf{A}$ and $\mathbf{B}$ to occur in the opposite order for the extruded primitive so that its vertices are wound counterclockwise. If the first triangle faces away from the light source, then we use the vertices **A** and **B** in the same order for the extruded primitive. Table 10.1 lists the vertices of the extrusion of the edge E for point light sources and infinite directional light sources for the cases that the first triangle associated with the edge E faces toward or away from the light source.

Table 10.1 Given a silhouette edge E having endpoints **A** and **B**, this table lists the object-space vertices of the extruded shadow volume face corresponding to E. The first triangle associated with the edge E is the triangle for which the vertices **A** and **B** occur in counterclockwise order.

Facing of First Triangle	Point Light Source (Extrusion is a list of quads)	Infinite Light Source (Extrusion is a list of triangles)
Toward light source	$\mathbf{V}_1 = \langle B_x, B_y, B_z, 1 \rangle$ $\mathbf{V}_2 = \langle A_x, A_y, A_z, 1 \rangle$ $\mathbf{V}_3 = \langle A_x, A_y, A_z, 0 \rangle$ $\mathbf{V}_4 = \langle B_x, B_y, B_z, 0 \rangle$	$\mathbf{V}_1 = \langle B_x, B_y, B_z, 1 \rangle$ $\mathbf{V}_2 = \langle A_x, A_y, A_z, 1 \rangle$ $\mathbf{V}_3 = \langle 0, 0, 0, 0 \rangle$
Away from light source	$\mathbf{V}_1 = \langle A_x, A_y, A_z, 1 \rangle$ $\mathbf{V}_2 = \langle B_x, B_y, B_z, 1 \rangle$ $\mathbf{V}_3 = \langle B_x, B_y, B_z, 0 \rangle$ $\mathbf{V}_4 = \langle A_x, A_y, A_z, 0 \rangle$	$\mathbf{V}_1 = \langle A_x, A_y, A_z, 1 \rangle$ $\mathbf{V}_2 = \langle B_x, B_y, B_z, 1 \rangle$ $\mathbf{V}_3 = \langle 0, 0, 0, 0 \rangle$

Using the `GL_ARB_vertex_program` extension, we can write a couple simple vertex programs to perform edge extrusion and transformation to clip space. In each program, we obtain the product of the projection matrix and model-view matrix from the OpenGL state `state.matrix.mvp`, and we assume that the object-space light position has been stored in program environment register `program.env[0]`.

For a point light source residing at the point **L** in object space (where $L_w = 1$), a vertex **V** from Table 10.1 is unmodified if its w-coordinate is 1 and is extruded to infinity if its w-coordinate is 0 by using the formula

$$\mathbf{V}' = V_w \mathbf{L} + \langle V_x - L_x, V_y - L_y, V_z - L_z, 0 \rangle. \tag{10.14}$$

The vertex program shown in Listing 10.2 applies this formula and then transforms the resulting vertex position **V**' into clip space.

Listing 10.2 This vertex program applies Equation (10.14) to extrude vertices having a *w*-coordinate of 0 away from a point light source whose position is stored in program environment parameter 0. Vertex positions are then transformed into homogeneous clip space.

```
!!ARBvp1.0

PARAM     mvp[4] = {state.matrix.mvp};
PARAM     light  = program.env[0];

TEMP      temp;

ADD       temp, vertex.position, -light;
SWZ       temp, temp, x, y, z, 0;
MAD       temp, vertex.position.w, light, temp;
DP4       result.position.x, mvp[0], temp;
DP4       result.position.y, mvp[1], temp;
DP4       result.position.z, mvp[2], temp;
DP4       result.position.w, mvp[3], temp;
END
```

In the case that shadow volume caps must be rendered (see the next section), a vertex program similar to the one in Listing 10.2 should be used to transform vertices belonging to triangles that face away from the light source. As demonstrated in Listing 10.3, extruded cap vertices can be obtained by simply subtracting the light's position from the vertex's position since such a subtraction always yields a *w*-coordinate of 0.

Listing 10.3 This vertex program extrudes vertices belonging to a shadow volume cap away from a point light source whose position is stored in program environment parameter 0. Vertex positions are then transformed into homogeneous clip space.

```
!!ARBvp1.0

PARAM     mvp[4] = {state.matrix.mvp};
PARAM     light  = program.env[0];

TEMP      temp;

ADD       temp, vertex.position, -light;
DP4       result.position.x, mvp[0], temp;
DP4       result.position.y, mvp[1], temp;
DP4       result.position.z, mvp[2], temp;
DP4       result.position.w, mvp[3], temp;
END
```

For an infinite light source residing at the point **L** in object space (where $L_w = 0$), a vertex **V** is unmodified or extruded by using the formula

$$\mathbf{V}' = V_w (\mathbf{V} + \mathbf{L}) - \mathbf{L}. \qquad (10.15)$$

The vertex program shown in Listing 10.4 applies this formula and then transforms the resulting vertex position **V**′ into clip space. Figure 10.6 shows a cylinder illuminated by an infinite light source and demonstrates how its silhouette is extruded to a point.

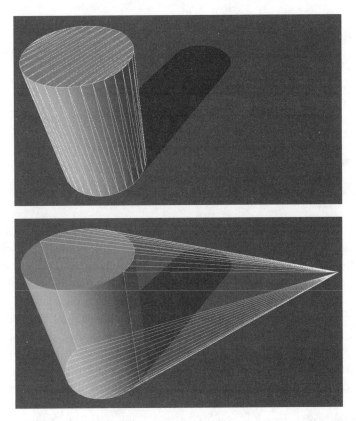

Figure 10.6 A cylinder illuminated by an infinite light source and the shadow volume formed by the extrusion of its silhouette.

Listing 10.4 This vertex program applies Equation (10.15) to extrude vertices having a *w*-coordinate of 0 away from an infinite light source whose position is stored in program environment parameter 0. Vertex positions are then transformed into homogeneous clip space.

```
!!ARBvp1.0

PARAM     mvp[4] = {state.matrix.mvp};
PARAM     light  = program.env[0];

TEMP      temp;

ADD       temp, vertex.position, light;
MAD       temp, vertex.position.w, temp, -light;
DP4       result.position.x, mvp[0], temp;
DP4       result.position.y, mvp[1], temp;
DP4       result.position.z, mvp[2], temp;
DP4       result.position.w, mvp[3], temp;
END
```

10.5 Determining Cap Necessity

As mentioned earlier, a completely closed shadow volume having a front cap and a back cap must be rendered whenever the camera lies inside the shadow volume, or the faces of the silhouette extrusion could potentially be clipped by the near plane. We wish to render this more expensive shadow volume as infrequently as possible, so a test for determining when it is not necessary would be useful.

The *near rectangle* is the rectangle carved out of the near plane by the four side planes of the view frustum. As shown in Figure 10.7, we can devise a test to determine whether the shadow volume might be clipped by the near plane by constructing the set of planes that connect the boundary of the near rectangle to the light source. We call the volume of space bounded by these planes and by the near plane itself the *near-clip volume*. Only a point inside the near-clip volume can have an extrusion away from the light source that intersects the near rectangle. Thus, if an object is known to lie completely outside the near-clip volume, then we do not have to render a capped shadow volume.

When constructing the near-clip volume, we consider three cases: 1) the light source lies in front of the near plane, 2) the light source lies behind the near plane, and 3) the light source is very close to lying in the near plane. Let $\mathbf{W}$ be the transformation matrix that maps eye space to world space, and suppose that our light source lies at the 4D homogeneous point $\mathbf{L}$ in world space. We consider a point light source (for which $L_w = 1$) to be lying in the near plane if its distance to the near plane is at most some small positive value δ. For an infinite directional light source (for which $L_w = 0$), we consider the distance to the near plane to be the length of the projection of the light's normalized direction vector $\langle L_x, L_y, L_z \rangle$ onto the near plane's normal direction. In either case, we can obtain a signed distance d from the light source to the near plane by calculating

$$d = \left(\mathbf{W}^{-1} \mathbf{L} \right) \cdot \langle 0, 0, -1, -n \rangle. \tag{10.16}$$

If $d > \delta$, then the light source lies in front of the near plane; if $d < -\delta$, then the light source lies behind the near plane; otherwise, the light source lies in the near plane.

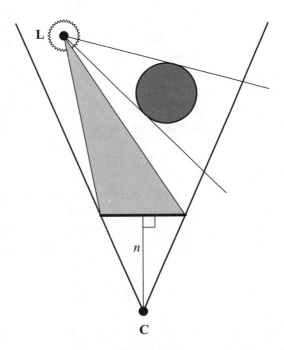

Figure 10.7 The near-clip volume is bounded by the planes connecting the near rectangle to the light position **L**. If an object lies completely outside the near-clip volume, then its shadow volume cannot intersect the near rectangle, so it is safe to render it without caps.

In the case that the light source lies in the near plane, the near-clip volume is defined by the planes $\mathbf{K}_0 = \langle 0,0,-1,-n \rangle$ and $\mathbf{K}_1 = \langle 0,0,1,n \rangle$. These two planes are coincident but have opposite normal directions. This encloses a degenerate near-clip volume, so testing whether an object is outside the volume amounts to determining whether the object intersects the near plane.

If the light source does not lie in the near plane, we need to calculate the vertices of the near rectangle. In eye space, the points $\mathbf{R}_0$, $\mathbf{R}_1$, $\mathbf{R}_2$, and $\mathbf{R}_3$ at the four corners of the near rectangle are given by

$$\begin{aligned}
\mathbf{R}_0 &= \langle n/e, an/e, -n \rangle \\
\mathbf{R}_1 &= \langle -n/e, an/e, -n \rangle \\
\mathbf{R}_2 &= \langle -n/e, -an/e, -n \rangle \\
\mathbf{R}_3 &= \langle n/e, -an/e, -n \rangle,
\end{aligned} \tag{10.17}$$

where n is the distance from the camera to the near plane; a is the aspect ratio of the viewport, equal to its height divided by its width; and e is the camera's focal length, related to the horizontal field-of-view angle α by Equation (4.27). These four points are ordered counterclockwise from the camera's perspective. For a light source lying in front of the near plane, the world-space normal directions $\mathbf{N}_i$, where $0 \le i \le 3$, are given by the cross products

$$\mathbf{N}_i = \left(\mathbf{R}'_i - \mathbf{R}'_{(i-1) \bmod 4} \right) \times \left(\langle L_x, L_y, L_z \rangle - L_w \mathbf{R}'_i \right), \tag{10.18}$$

where each $\mathbf{R}'_i$ is the world-space vertex of the near rectangle given by $\mathbf{R}'_i = \mathbf{W} \mathbf{R}_i$. For a light source lying behind the near plane, the normal directions are simply the negation of those given by Equation (10.18). The corresponding world-space planes $\mathbf{K}_i$ bounding the near-clip volume are given by

$$\mathbf{K}_i = \frac{1}{\|\mathbf{N}_i\|} \langle (\mathbf{N}_i)_x, (\mathbf{N}_i)_y, (\mathbf{N}_i)_z, -\mathbf{N}_i \cdot \mathbf{R}'_i \rangle. \tag{10.19}$$

We close the near-clip volume by adding a fifth plane that is coincident with the near plane and has a normal pointing toward the light source. For a light source lying in front on the near plane, the fifth plane $\mathbf{K}_4$ is given by

$$\mathbf{K}_4 = \left(\mathbf{W}^{-1} \right)^{\mathrm{T}} \langle 0,0,-1,-n \rangle; \tag{10.20}$$

and for a light source lying behind the near plane, the fifth plane is given by the negation of this vector. (Remember that if $\mathbf{W}$ is orthogonal, then $\left(\mathbf{W}^{-1} \right)^{\mathrm{T}} = \mathbf{W}$.)

We determine whether a shadow-casting object lies completely outside the near-clip volume by testing the object's bounding volume against each of the planes $\mathbf{K}_i$. If the bounding volume lies completely on the negative side of any one plane, then the object's shadow volume cannot intersect the near rectangle. In the case that an object is bounded by a sphere having center $\mathbf{C}$ and radius r, we do not need to render a capped shadow volume if $\mathbf{K}_i \cdot \mathbf{C} < -r$ for any i.

Figure 10.8 demonstrates that for point light sources, bounding volumes lying behind the light source from the camera's perspective may often be mistaken for those belonging to objects that might cast shadows through the near rectangle. This happens when the bounding volume lies outside the near-clip volume, but does not fall completely on the negative side of any one plane. We can improve this situation substantially by adding an extra plane to the near-clip volume for point lights. As shown in Figure 10.8, the extra plane contains the light position $\mathbf{L}$ and has a normal direction that points toward the center of the near rectangle. The normal direction $\mathbf{N}_5$ is given by

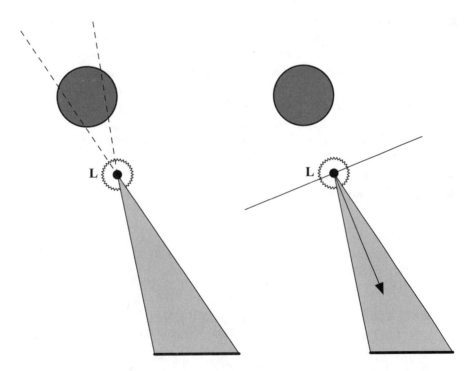

Figure 10.8 Adding an extra plane to the near-clip volume for point light sources enables more objects to be classified as outside the near-clip volume.

$$\mathbf{N}_5 = \left(\mathbf{W}^{-1}\right)^{\mathrm{T}}\langle 0,0,-n,1\rangle - \mathbf{L}, \tag{10.21}$$

and the corresponding plane $\mathbf{K}_5$ is given by

$$\mathbf{K}_5 = \frac{1}{\|\mathbf{N}_5\|}\langle (\mathbf{N}_5)_x,(\mathbf{N}_5)_y,(\mathbf{N}_5)_z,-\mathbf{N}_5\cdot\mathbf{L}\rangle. \tag{10.22}$$

The plane $\mathbf{K}_5$ is added to the near-clip volume boundary for point light sources regardless of whether the light position is in front of, behind, or in the near plane.

10.6 Rendering Shadow Volumes

Now that we can determine an object's silhouette with respect to a light source, construct a shadow volume by extruding the silhouette edges away from the light source, and decide whether front and back caps are necessary, we are finally ready to render the shadow volume into the stencil buffer. We assume that the frame buffer has already been cleared and that an ambient rendering pass has been performed to initialize the depth buffer. This section concentrates on the operations necessary to illuminate the scene using a single light source, and these operations should be repeated for all light sources that can affect the visible region of the world being rendered.

First, we must clear the stencil buffer, configure the stencil test so that it always passes, and configure the depth test so that it passes only when fragment depth values are less than those already in the depth buffer. This can be done in OpenGL using the following function calls.

```
glClear(GL_STENCIL_BUFFER_BIT);
glEnable(GL_STENCIL_TEST);
glStencilFunc(GL_ALWAYS, 0, ~0);
glEnable(GL_DEPTH_TEST);
glDepthFunc(GL_LESS);
```

We are only going to be drawing into the stencil buffer, so we need to disable writes to the color buffer and depth buffer as follows.

```
glColorMask(GL_FALSE, GL_FALSE, GL_FALSE, GL_FALSE);
glDepthMask(GL_FALSE);
```

Shadow volume faces are rendered using different stencil operations depending on whether they face toward or away from the camera, so we need to enable face culling with the following function call.

```
glEnable(GL_CULL_FACE);
```

For a shadow volume that does not require capping because it cannot possibly intersect the near rectangle, we modify the values in the stencil buffer when the depth test passes. The stencil value is incremented for fragments belonging to front-facing polygons and is decremented for fragments belonging to back-facing polygons. These operations are performed by the following function calls, where the function DrawShadowVolume() renders all of the polygons belonging to the shadow volume.

```
glCullFace(GL_BACK);
glStencilOp(GL_KEEP, GL_KEEP, GL_INCR);
DrawShadowVolume();

glCullFace(GL_FRONT);
glStencilOp(GL_KEEP, GL_KEEP, GL_DECR);
DrawShadowVolume();
```

If a shadow volume does require capping, then we modify the values in the stencil buffer when the depth test fails. The stencil value is incremented for fragments belonging to back-facing polygons and is decremented for fragments belonging to front-facing polygons (the opposite of the depth-pass operations). These operations are accomplished using the following function calls. In this case, the DrawShadowVolume() function renders the polygons belonging to the shadow volume's caps as well as its extruded silhouette edges.

```
glCullFace(GL_FRONT);
glStencilOp(GL_KEEP, GL_INCR, GL_KEEP);
DrawShadowVolume();

glCullFace(GL_BACK);
glStencilOp(GL_KEEP, GL_DECR, GL_KEEP);
DrawShadowVolume();
```

Once shadow volumes have been rendered for all objects that could potentially cast shadows into the visible region of the world, we perform a lighting pass that illuminates surfaces wherever the stencil value remains zero. We re-enable writes to the color buffer, change the depth test to pass only when fragment depth values are equal to those in the depth buffer, and configure the stencil test to pass only when the value in the stencil buffer is zero using the following function calls.

```
glColorMask(GL_TRUE, GL_TRUE, GL_TRUE, GL_TRUE);
glDepthFunc(GL_EQUAL);
glStencilFunc(GL_EQUAL, 0, ~0);
glStencilOp(GL_KEEP, GL_KEEP, GL_KEEP);
```

Since the lighting pass adds to the ambient illumination already present in the color buffer, we need to configure the blending equation as follows.

```
glEnable(GL_BLEND);
glBlendFunc(GL_ONE, GL_ONE);
```

We also need to make the function call `glCullFace(GL_BACK)` just in case a depth-pass shadow volume was most recently rendered, leaving the culling state set to `GL_FRONT`. After the lighting pass has been rendered, we clean up by resetting a few rendering states back to those needed by the ambient pass for the next frame using the following function calls.

```
glDepthMask(GL_TRUE);
glDepthFunc(GL_LEQUAL);
glStencilFunc(GL_ALWAYS, 0, ~0);
```

Because we needed to perform different stencil operations for front-facing polygons and back-facing polygons in our shadow volumes, we had to render the shadow volumes twice. Of course, each polygon was culled by the graphics hardware on either the first pass or the second, but the vertices still had to be processed twice. The `GL_EXT_stencil_two_side` extension to OpenGL provides a way to avoid this suboptimal situation by allowing separate stencil state for front faces and back faces to be specified simultaneously. When using this extension, we render both front faces and back faces of the shadow volume at the same time, so face culling should be disabled. We therefore prepare to render shadow volumes by making the following function calls.

```
glEnable(GL_STENCIL_TWO_SIDE_EXT);
glDisable(GL_CULL_FACE);
```

Using the `GL_EXT_stencil_two_side` extension, an uncapped shadow volume is rendered using the following code, which uses depth-pass stencil operations.

```
glActiveStencilFaceEXT(GL_FRONT);
glStencilOp(GL_KEEP, GL_KEEP, GL_INCR_WRAP_EXT);
```

```
glActiveStencilFaceEXT(GL_BACK);
glStencilOp(GL_KEEP, GL_KEEP, GL_DECR_WRAP_EXT);
DrawShadowVolume();
```

A capped shadow volume is rendered using the depth-fail stencil operations shown in the code below.

```
glActiveStencilFaceEXT(GL_FRONT);
glStencilOp(GL_KEEP, GL_DECR_WRAP_EXT, GL_KEEP);
glActiveStencilFaceEXT(GL_BACK);
glStencilOp(GL_KEEP, GL_INCR_WRAP_EXT, GL_KEEP);
DrawShadowVolume();
```

Note the use of the GL_INCR_WRAP_EXT and GL_DECR_WRAP_EXT stencil operations. These are provided by the GL_EXT_stencil_wrap extension to OpenGL and allow stencil values to wrap when they exceed the minimum and maximum stencil values instead of being clamped. These operations are necessary because we do not know in what order the polygons belonging to the shadow volume will be rendered, and we must account for the possibility that the stencil value for a particular pixel could be decremented before it is incremented.

10.7 Scissor Optimization

When using an attenuated light source, it is usually convenient to define a range r beyond which the light source does not contribute any illumination to the world. Although this is not a physically correct model, using an attenuation function that vanishes at a distance r from the light's position allows us to quickly cull any light source whose sphere of illumination does not intersect the view frustum. When a light source's sphere of illumination is visible, the area within the viewport that could possibility be affected by the light source may not be the entire viewport. By projecting the sphere of illumination to the image plane and using the scissor rectangle to limit our drawing to the projected area of influence, we can avoid a significant amount of superfluous rendering of both shadow volumes and illuminated surfaces.

Suppose that we have a point light source whose center lies at the point **L** in eye space and whose range is r, as shown in Figure 10.9. We wish to find four planes, two parallel to the x-axis and two parallel to the y-axis, that pass through the camera position (the origin in eye space) and are also tangent to the light source's bounding sphere. Once these planes have been determined, we can locate their intersections with the image plane to find the rectangular boundary of the projection of the light source's bounding sphere.

We assume that the tangent planes parallel to the y-axis have a unit-length normal vector $\mathbf{N}$ whose y-coordinate is 0. Since the planes pass through the origin, each can be represented by a 4D vector $\mathbf{T} = \langle N_x, 0, N_z, 0 \rangle$. We wish to calculate values of N_x and N_z such that the following conditions are satisfied.

$$\mathbf{T} \cdot \mathbf{L} = r \tag{10.23}$$

$$N_x^2 + N_z^2 = 1 \tag{10.24}$$

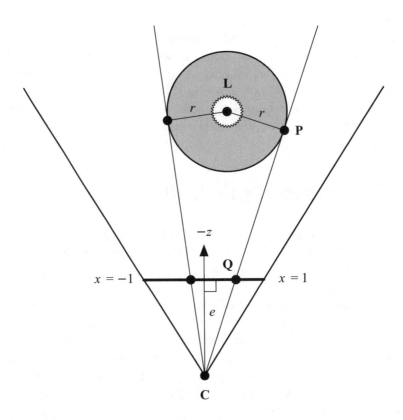

Figure 10.9 For a point light source at the position **L** having range r, we calculate the four planes that pass through the camera position **C** and are tangent to the light's sphere of illumination. By calculating the intersection of each tangent plane with the image plane lying at a distance e from the camera, we can limit our drawing to an area smaller than the full size of the viewport.

By expanding the dot product and rearranging slightly, we can rewrite Equation (10.23) as

$$N_z L_z = r - N_x L_x. \tag{10.25}$$

Squaring both sides of Equation (10.25) and making the substitution $N_z^2 = 1 - N_x^2$, we have

$$\left(1 - N_x^2\right) L_z^2 = r^2 - 2r N_x L_x + N_x^2 L_x^2. \tag{10.26}$$

This can be rewritten as a quadratic equation in N_x as follows.

$$\left(L_x^2 + L_z^2\right) N_x^2 + \left(-2r L_x\right) N_x + r^2 - L_z^2 = 0 \tag{10.27}$$

The discriminant D is given by

$$D = 4 \left[r^2 L_x^2 - \left(L_x^2 + L_z^2\right)\left(r^2 - L_z^2\right) \right]. \tag{10.28}$$

$D \le 0$ precisely when $L_x^2 + L_z^2 \le r^2$ (i.e., when the origin falls within the parallel projection of the sphere onto the x-z plane). When this happens, we know the light source's bounding sphere fills the entire viewport, and we do not continue.

If $D > 0$, then we can solve equation (10.27) using the quadratic formula to obtain

$$\begin{aligned} N_x &= \frac{2r L_x \pm \sqrt{D}}{2\left(L_x^2 + L_z^2\right)} \\ &= \frac{r L_x \pm \sqrt{D/4}}{L_x^2 + L_z^2}. \end{aligned} \tag{10.29}$$

This gives us two values for N_x. The corresponding values for N_z are calculated by making a small adjustment to Equation (10.25):

$$N_z = \frac{r - N_x L_x}{L_z}. \tag{10.30}$$

The point **P** at which the plane **T** is tangent to the sphere is simply given by

$$\begin{aligned} \mathbf{P} &= \mathbf{L} - r\mathbf{N} \\ &= \langle L_x - r N_x, 0, L_z - r N_z, 1 \rangle. \end{aligned} \tag{10.31}$$

We only want to consider planes whose point of tangency with the light source's bounding sphere lies in front of the camera. If $P_z < 0$, then we have found a plane that may allow us to shrink the scissor rectangle. We now need to determine where the tangent plane intersects the image plane.

As shown in Figure 10.9, the image plane is perpendicular to the z-axis and lies at a distance e from the camera. On the image plane, the area of the viewport corresponds to x-coordinates in the range $[-1,1]$ and y-coordinates in the range $[-a,a]$, where a is the aspect ratio given by the height of the viewport divided by its width. Any point $\mathbf{Q}$ lying in the image plane has coordinates $\mathbf{Q} = \langle x, y, -e \rangle$. A point $\mathbf{Q}$ lying in the plane tangent to the light source's bounding sphere satisfies $\mathbf{N} \cdot \mathbf{Q} = 0$, so we can solve for x:

$$x = \frac{N_z e}{N_x}. \tag{10.32}$$

This x-coordinate can be mapped to the viewport coordinate x' using the formula

$$x' = l + \frac{x+1}{2} w, \tag{10.33}$$

where l is the left edge of the viewport and w is the viewport's width, both in pixels.

Given a value x' calculated using Equation (10.33), we need to determine whether it represents a left-side boundary or a right-side boundary. If $P_x < L_x$ (or equivalently, if $N_x > 0$), then x' represents a left-side boundary because the point of tangency falls to the left of the light source. If $P_x > L_x$, then x' represents a right-side boundary. Since the value x' may lie outside the viewport (if $x \notin [-1,1]$), we calculate the left and right edges of the scissor rectangle as follows.

$$\begin{aligned} scissor.left &= \max(x',l) \\ scissor.right &= \min(x',l+w) \end{aligned} \tag{10.34}$$

The two tangent planes parallel to the x-axis are found in an almost identical manner. Each of these planes is represented by a 4D vector $\langle 0, N_y, N_z, 0 \rangle$, whose nonzero components are given by the following formulas.

$$N_y = \frac{rL_y \pm \sqrt{r^2 L_y^2 - (L_y^2 + L_z^2)(r^2 - L_z^2)}}{L_y^2 + L_z^2}$$

$$N_z = \frac{r - N_y L_y}{L_z} \tag{10.35}$$

The point of tangency **P** is given by

$$\mathbf{P} = \langle 0, L_y - rN_y, L_z - rN_z, 1 \rangle. \tag{10.36}$$

If $P_z < 0$, then the y-coordinate where each plane intersects the image plane is given by

$$y = \frac{N_z e}{N_x a}, \tag{10.37}$$

where the viewport's aspect ratio a has been added to the denominator. Finally, the viewport coordinate y' is calculated using the formula

$$y' = b + \frac{y+1}{2} h, \tag{10.38}$$

where b is the bottom edge of the viewport and h is the viewport's height, both in pixels.

If $P_y < L_y$ (or equivalently, if $N_y > 0$), then y' represents a bottom-side boundary. If $P_y > L_y$, then y' represents a top-side boundary. As with the left and right sides, the values of y' should be clamped to the viewport's range as follows.

$$\begin{aligned} scissor.bottom &= \max(y', b) \\ scissor.top &= \min(y', b+h) \end{aligned} \tag{10.39}$$

Using the values given by Equations (10.34) and (10.39), the OpenGL scissor rectangle is enabled and set to the appropriate values using the following function calls.

```
glEnable(GL_SCISSOR_TEST);
glScissor(scissor.left, scissor.bottom,
    scissor.right - scissor.left,
    scissor.top - scissor.bottom);
```

The scissor rectangle affects the clear operation as well, so once rendering has been completed, one should either disable the scissor test or set the scissor rectangle back to the entire viewport rectangle by making the call `glScissor(l, b, w, h)`.

Chapter 10 Summary

Silhouette Determination

An edge shared by two triangles lying in the planes F_1 and F_2 is part of an object's silhouette with respect to the light position L if the dot products $F_1 \cdot L$ and $F_2 \cdot L$ have opposite signs. For point light sources, $L_w \neq 0$, and for infinite directional light sources, $L_w = 0$.

Shadow Volume Construction

The vertices of a silhouette edge E having endpoints A and B are listed in Table 10.1. For a point light source at the position L (where $L_w = 1$), an edge vertex V is extruded using the formula

$$\mathbf{V}' = V_w \mathbf{L} + \langle V_x - L_x, V_y - L_y, V_z - L_z, 0 \rangle.$$

For an infinite light source at the position L (where $L_w = 0$), an edge vertex V is extruded using the formula

$$\mathbf{V}' = V_w (\mathbf{V} + \mathbf{L}) - \mathbf{L}.$$

Determining Cap Necessity

The near-clip volume is bounded by the planes connecting the near rectangle to the world-space light position L. The four world-space normal directions N_i for the near-clip volume are given by

$$\mathbf{N}_i = \left(\mathbf{R}_i' - \mathbf{R}_{(i-1) \bmod 4}' \right) \times \left(\langle L_x, L_y, L_z \rangle - L_w \mathbf{R}_i' \right),$$

where each $\mathbf{R}_i'$ is the world-space vertex of the near rectangle given by $\mathbf{R}_i' = \mathbf{W} \mathbf{R}_i$, $\mathbf{W}$ is the transformation from camera space to world space, and the values of $\mathbf{R}_i$ are given by Equation (10.17). The corresponding world-space planes K_i bounding the near-clip volume are given by

$$\mathbf{K}_i = \frac{1}{\|\mathbf{N}_i\|} \langle (\mathbf{N}_i)_x, (\mathbf{N}_i)_y, (\mathbf{N}_i)_z, -\mathbf{N}_i \cdot \mathbf{R}_i' \rangle.$$

The near-clip volume is closed by adding a fifth plane that is coincident with the near plane and has a normal pointing toward the light source. For a light source lying in front on the near plane, the fifth plane K_4 is given by

$$\mathbf{K}_4 = \left(\mathbf{W}^{-1}\right)^{\mathrm{T}} \langle 0,0,-1,-n \rangle.$$

For an object that is bounded by a sphere having center $\mathbf{C}$ and radius r, we do not need to render a capped shadow volume if $\mathbf{K}_i \cdot \mathbf{C} < -r$ for any i.

Exercises for Chapter 10

1. Use a technique similar to that described in Section 9.1 to derive the $(3,3)$ entry of a projection matrix based on the matrix $\mathbf{M}'_{\text{infinite}}$ given by Equation (10.8) that offsets depth values at a camera-space depth P_z by a small amount δ.

2. Write a program that renders a stencil shadow for a triangle mesh illuminated by a single point light source. Assume that the triangle mesh is specified such that each of n triangles indexes three entries in an array of m vertices. The program should precalculate an edge list, determine the edges belonging to the model's silhouette with respect to the light source, and render the extruded silhouette edges using the stencil buffer operations described in Section 10.6.

Chapter **11**

Linear Physics

Simulating the accurate motion and interaction of dynamic objects adds a pervasive feeling of realism to a game and can usually be achieved without overly complex mathematics. This chapter and Chapter 12 discuss several general topics in classical mechanics that apply to game programming. We begin with an examination of linear motion, which refers to any motion that is not taking place in a rotating environment.

11.1 Position Functions

A *position function* provides the 3D position of an object as a function of time. Time is usually measured relative to some starting point when the position of an object is known. For instance, suppose that an object is traveling in a straight line with a constant velocity $\mathbf{v}_0$. If the position of the object at time $t = 0$ is known to be $\mathbf{x}_0$, then its position $\mathbf{x}(t)$ at any time afterward is given by

$$\mathbf{x}(t) = \mathbf{x}_0 + \mathbf{v}_0 t. \tag{11.1}$$

A *velocity function* describes the 3D velocity of an object as a function of time. The velocity function $\mathbf{v}(t)$ of an object is given by the derivative of the position function with respect to time. The time derivative is commonly denoted by placing a dot above the function being differentiated:

$$\mathbf{v}(t) = \dot{\mathbf{x}}(t) = \frac{d}{dt}\mathbf{x}(t). \tag{11.2}$$

Since the velocity of the object whose position is given by Equation (11.1) is constant, its velocity function $\mathbf{v}(t)$ is simply given by

$$\mathbf{v}(t) = \mathbf{v}_0. \tag{11.3}$$

An object undergoing a constant acceleration $\mathbf{a}_0$ has the velocity function

$$\mathbf{v}(t) = \mathbf{v}_0 + \mathbf{a}_0 t. \tag{11.4}$$

The *acceleration function* $\mathbf{a}(t)$ of an object, which describes the object's 3D acceleration as a function of time, is given by the derivative of the velocity function:

$$\mathbf{a}(t) = \dot{\mathbf{v}}(t) = \ddot{\mathbf{x}}(t) = \frac{d^2}{dt^2}\mathbf{x}(t). \tag{11.5}$$

We can integrate any velocity function to determine the distance d that an object has traveled between times t_1 and t_2 as follows.

$$d = \int_{t_1}^{t_2} \mathbf{v}(t)\,dt \tag{11.6}$$

Integrating Equation (11.4) from time zero to time t, we have

$$d = \int_0^t (\mathbf{v}_0 + \mathbf{a}_0 t)\,dt$$
$$= \mathbf{v}_0 t + \tfrac{1}{2}\mathbf{a}_0 t^2. \tag{11.7}$$

Adding the distance d to an initial position $\mathbf{x}_0$, the position function $\mathbf{x}(t)$ of a uniformly accelerating object is given by

$$\mathbf{x}(t) = \mathbf{x}_0 + \mathbf{v}_0 t + \tfrac{1}{2}\mathbf{a}_0 t^2. \tag{11.8}$$

It is often the case that we are aware of the forces acting on an object, and we want to find a function that predicts the future position of the object. The sum of the forces $\mathbf{F}_1, \mathbf{F}_2, \ldots, \mathbf{F}_N$ acting on an object is equal to the object's mass m times its acceleration $\mathbf{a}(t)$:

$$\sum_{i=1}^{N} \mathbf{F}_i(t) = m\mathbf{a}(t) = m\ddot{\mathbf{x}}(t). \tag{11.9}$$

Each force $\mathbf{F}_i(t)$ may be a constant, a function of the object's position, or a function of the object's velocity. Equation (11.9) is a second-order differential equation whose solution $\mathbf{x}(t)$ is the object's position function. The next section reviews the general solutions to second-order differential equations, and solutions to specific force equations are discussed at various places throughout this chapter and Chapter 12.

11.2 Second-Order Differential Equations

A second-order linear ordinary differential equation in the function $x(t)$ is one of the following form.

$$\frac{d^2}{dt^2}x(t) + a\frac{d}{dt}x(t) + bx(t) = f(t) \tag{11.10}$$

Using prime symbols to denote derivatives, we can write this in a slightly more compact form as

$$x''(t) + ax'(t) + bx(t) = f(t). \tag{11.11}$$

In this chapter, a and b are always constants; but in general, they may be functions of t.

11.2.1 Homogeneous Equations

The function $f(t)$ is identically zero in many situations, in which case the differential equation is called *homogeneous*. Before attempting to find a solution $x(t)$ to the equation

$$x''(t) + ax'(t) + bx(t) = 0, \tag{11.12}$$

we make a couple of important observations. First, suppose that the functions $x_1(t)$ and $x_2(t)$ are solutions to Equation (11.12). Then the functions $Ax_1(t)$ and

$Bx_2(t)$ are also solutions, where A and B are arbitrary constants. Furthermore, the function $Ax_1(t) + Bx_2(t)$ is also a solution to Equation (11.12) since we can write

$$Ax_1''(t) + Bx_2''(t) + a[Ax_1'(t) + Bx_2'(t)] + b[Ax_1(t) + Bx_2(t)]$$
$$= A[x_1''(t) + ax_1'(t) + bx_1(t)] + B[x_2''(t) + ax_2'(t) + bx_2(t)]$$
$$= A \cdot 0 + B \cdot 0 = 0. \tag{11.13}$$

A general solution $x(t)$ to Equation (11.12) becomes evident upon making the substitution

$$x(t) = e^{rt}. \tag{11.14}$$

The first and second derivatives of $x(t)$ are given by

$$x'(t) = re^{rt}$$
$$x''(t) = r^2 e^{rt}, \tag{11.15}$$

and substitution into Equation (11.12) yields

$$r^2 e^{rt} + are^{rt} + be^{rt} = 0. \tag{11.16}$$

Multiplying both sides by e^{-rt} eliminates the exponentials, and we have

$$r^2 + ar + b = 0. \tag{11.17}$$

Equation (11.17) is called the *auxiliary equation* and has the solutions

$$r_1 = -\frac{a}{2} + \frac{1}{2}\sqrt{a^2 - 4b}$$

$$r_2 = -\frac{a}{2} - \frac{1}{2}\sqrt{a^2 - 4b}. \tag{11.18}$$

Unless $r_1 = r_2$, the general solution to Equation (11.12) is thus given by

$$x(t) = Ae^{r_1 t} + Be^{r_2 t}. \tag{11.19}$$

Example 11.1. Solve the differential equation

$$x''(t) - 5x'(t) + 6x(t) = 0. \tag{11.20}$$

Solution. The auxiliary equation is

$$r^2 - 5r + 6 = 0, \tag{11.21}$$

which has the solutions $r_1 = 2$ and $r_2 = 3$. The general solution to Equation (11.20) is therefore given by

$$x(t) = Ae^{2t} + Be^{3t}, \tag{11.22}$$

where A and B are arbitrary constants. ∎

If $r_1 = r_2$, then it must be true that $a^2 = 4b$, so Equation (11.12) can be written as

$$x''(t) + ax'(t) + \frac{a^2}{4}x(t) = 0. \tag{11.23}$$

It is a simple task to verify that the function

$$x(t) = te^{-(a/2)t} \tag{11.24}$$

is a solution to Equation (11.23), so the general solution to Equation (11.12) when $r_1 = r_2$ is given by

$$x(t) = Ae^{rt} + Bte^{rt}, \tag{11.25}$$

where we have set $r = r_1 = r_2$.

If $a^2 - 4b < 0$, then the roots of the auxiliary equation are complex. The solution given by Equation (11.19) is still correct, but it requires the use of complex arithmetic. We can express the solution entirely in terms of real-valued functions by using the formula

$$e^{\alpha + \beta i} = e^{\alpha}(\cos \beta + i \sin \beta) \tag{11.26}$$

(see Appendix A, Section A.4). Assuming that a and b are real numbers, the roots r_1 and r_2 of the auxiliary equation are complex conjugates, so we may write

$$\begin{aligned} r_1 &= \alpha + \beta i \\ r_2 &= \alpha - \beta i, \end{aligned} \tag{11.27}$$

where

$$\alpha = -\frac{a}{2}$$

$$\beta = \frac{1}{2}\sqrt{4b - a^2}. \tag{11.28}$$

The solution given by Equation (11.19) can now be written as

$$x(t) = Ae^{(\alpha+\beta i)t} + Be^{(\alpha-\beta i)t}$$
$$= Ae^{\alpha t}(\cos\beta t + i\sin\beta t) + Be^{\alpha t}(\cos\beta t - i\sin\beta t)$$
$$= e^{\alpha t}[(A+B)\cos\beta t + (A-B)i\sin\beta t]. \tag{11.29}$$

This solution can be expressed using two real constants C_1 and C_2 by setting

$$A = \tfrac{1}{2}(C_1 + C_2 i)$$
$$B = \tfrac{1}{2}(C_1 - C_2 i). \tag{11.30}$$

Plugging these values into Equation (11.29) yields

$$x(t) = e^{\alpha t}(C_1 \cos\beta t + C_2 \sin\beta t). \tag{11.31}$$

Example 11.2. Solve the differential equation

$$x''(t) + 4x(t) = 0. \tag{11.32}$$

Solution. The auxiliary equation is

$$r^2 + 4 = 0, \tag{11.33}$$

which has the solutions $r_1 = 2i$ and $r_2 = -2i$. The solution to Equation (11.32) given by

$$x(t) = Ae^{2it} + Be^{-2it} \tag{11.34}$$

is valid, but we can also express the solution entirely in terms of real-valued functions by using Equation (11.31) with $\alpha = 0$ and $\beta = 2$ as

$$x(t) = C_1 \cos 2t + C_2 \sin 2t, \tag{11.35}$$

where C_1 and C_2 are arbitrary constants. ∎

Equation (11.31) can be transformed into an alternate solution involving only a single trigonometric function by introducing the constant $D = \left(C_1^2 + C_2^2 \right)^{1/2}$ and writing

$$x(t) = De^{\alpha t} \left(\frac{C_1}{D} \cos \beta t + \frac{C_2}{D} \sin \beta t \right). \qquad (11.36)$$

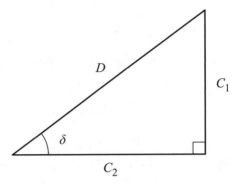

Figure 11.1 In this triangle, $\sin \delta = C_1/D$ and $\cos \delta = C_2/D$. This enables us to write Equation (11.36) in the form given by Equation (11.39).

Suppose that C_1 and C_2 are the lengths of the legs of a right triangle and that δ is the angle opposite the side of length C_1 (see Figure 11.1). Then D is the length of the hypotenuse, so

$$\frac{C_1}{D} = \sin \delta$$

$$\frac{C_2}{D} = \cos \delta. \qquad (11.37)$$

Plugging these into Equation (11.36) yields

$$x(t) = De^{\alpha t} \left(\cos \beta t \sin \delta + \sin \beta t \cos \delta \right). \qquad (11.38)$$

Using an angle sum identity (see Appendix B, Section B.4), this is equivalent to

$$x(t) = De^{\alpha t} \sin \left(\beta t + \delta \right). \qquad (11.39)$$

11.2.2 Nonhomogeneous Equations

Differential equations of the form

$$x''(t) + ax'(t) + bx(t) = f(t) \qquad (11.40)$$

for which the function $f(t)$ is not identically zero are called *nonhomogeneous*. The solution to a nonhomogeneous differential equation has the form

$$x(t) = g(t) + p(t), \qquad (11.41)$$

where the function $g(t)$ is the general solution to the corresponding homogeneous equation

$$x''(t) + ax'(t) + bx(t) = 0. \qquad (11.42)$$

The function $p(t)$ is called a *particular solution* to the nonhomogeneous equation and satisfies

$$p''(t) + ap'(t) + bp(t) = f(t). \qquad (11.43)$$

To see that $g(t) + p(t)$ is in fact a solution to Equation (11.40), we simply plug it in:

$$\begin{aligned}
g''(t) + p''(t) &+ a[g'(t) + p'(t)] + b[g(t) + p(t)] \\
&= g''(t) + ag'(t) + bg(t) + p''(t) + ap'(t) + bp(t) \\
&= 0 + f(t) = f(t). \qquad (11.44)
\end{aligned}$$

There are several methods for finding the particular solution to a nonhomogeneous differential equation. The method that we present in this section is called the method of *undetermined coefficients* and is sufficient for the nonhomogeneous equations encountered later in this chapter. The general idea upon which the method of undetermined coefficients is based is to guess at the form of the particular solution $p(t)$ using the knowledge that we possess about the form of the function $f(t)$. It is usually effective to choose $p(t)$ to be a sum of terms that have the same form as $f(t)$ or whose derivatives have the same form as $f(t)$. Each term is multiplied by an unknown coefficient for which we attempt to find a solution by plugging $p(t)$ into the nonhomogeneous equation. If coefficients can be determined for which $p(t)$ satisfies Equation (11.40), then a particular solution has been found. The following examples illustrate this technique in detail.

Example 11.3. Solve the differential equation

$$x''(t) - 5x'(t) + 6x(t) = 12t - 4. \tag{11.45}$$

Solution. We have already found the general solution $g(t)$ to the homogeneous equation in Example 11.1:

$$g(t) = Ae^{2t} + Be^{3t}. \tag{11.46}$$

The nonhomogeneous portion of Equation (11.45) is a linear polynomial, so we presume that the particular solution has the form

$$p(t) = Dt^2 + Et + F, \tag{11.47}$$

where the coefficients D, E, and F need to be determined. Plugging $p(t)$ into Equation (11.45) produces

$$\begin{aligned} 12t - 4 &= 2D - 5(2Dt + E) + 6(Dt^2 + Et + F) \\ &= 6Dt^2 + (-10D + 6E)t + 2D - 5E + 6F. \end{aligned} \tag{11.48}$$

Equating the coefficients of like terms from each side, we find that

$$D = 0, \; E = 2, \text{ and } F = 1. \tag{11.49}$$

Thus, the function $p(t) = 2t + 1$ is a particular solution to Equation (11.45). The complete solution is given by

$$\begin{aligned} x(t) &= g(t) + p(t) \\ &= Ae^{2t} + Be^{3t} + 2t + 1, \end{aligned} \tag{11.50}$$

where A and B are arbitrary constants. ■

Example 11.4. Solve the differential equation

$$x''(t) + 4x(t) = 12\sin t. \tag{11.51}$$

Solution. We have already found the general solution $g(t)$ to the homogeneous equation in Example 11.2:

$$g(t) = A\cos 2t + B\sin 2t. \tag{11.52}$$

Equivalently, we could write $g(t)$ in the form

$$g(t) = C\sin(2t + \delta). \tag{11.53}$$

Since the nonhomogeneous portion of Equation (11.51) is a sine function, we presume that the particular solution has the form

$$p(t) = D\sin t + E\cos t, \tag{11.54}$$

where the coefficients D and E need to be determined. Plugging $p(t)$ into Equation (11.51) produces

$$12\sin t = -D\sin t - E\cos t + 4(D\sin t + E\cos t)$$
$$= 3D\sin t + 3E\cos t. \tag{11.55}$$

Equating the coefficients of the sine and cosine terms from each side, we find that

$$D = 4 \text{ and } E = 0. \tag{11.56}$$

Thus, the function $p(t) = 4\sin t$ is a particular solution to Equation (11.51). The complete solution is given by

$$x(t) = A\cos 2t + B\sin 2t + 4\sin t \tag{11.57}$$

or, equivalently,

$$x(t) = C\sin(2t + \delta) + 4\sin t, \tag{11.58}$$

where A, B, C, and δ are arbitrary constants. ∎

11.2.3 Initial Conditions

In every solution to a second-order differential equation presented so far, there have been two arbitrary constants. These constants allow for the specification of certain *initial conditions* that dictate the values of $x(t)$ and $x'(t)$ when $t = 0$. Suppose that the initial value of $x(t)$ is required to be x_0 and the initial value of $x'(t)$ is required to be v_0. Then the arbitrary constants appearing in the function $x(t)$ can be determined by examining the following system of equations.

$$x(0) = x_0$$
$$x'(0) = v_0 \tag{11.59}$$

This is demonstrated in the following examples.

Example 11.5. Solve the differential equation

$$x''(t) - 5x'(t) + 6x(t) = 0 \tag{11.60}$$

subject to the initial conditions

$$x(0) = 3$$
$$x'(0) = 0. \tag{11.61}$$

Solution. The general solution to the differential equation has already been found in Example 11.1:

$$x(t) = Ae^{2t} + Be^{3t}. \tag{11.62}$$

The derivative of $x(t)$ is given by

$$x'(t) = 2Ae^{2t} + 3Be^{3t}. \tag{11.63}$$

Imposing the initial conditions given by Equation (11.61), we have

$$x(0) = A + B = 3$$
$$x'(0) = 2A + 3B = 0. \tag{11.64}$$

Solving this linear system yields

$$A = 9 \text{ and } B = -6. \tag{11.65}$$

Thus, the solution to the differential equation that satisfies the initial conditions is given by

$$x(t) = 9e^{2t} - 6e^{3t}. \ \blacksquare \tag{11.66}$$

Example 11.6. Solve the differential equation

$$x''(t) + 4x(t) = 12\sin t \tag{11.67}$$

subject to the initial conditions

$$x(0) = 0$$
$$x'(0) = 6. \tag{11.68}$$

Solution. The general solution to the differential equation has already been found in Example 11.4:

$$x(t) = A\cos 2t + B\sin 2t + 4\sin t. \tag{11.69}$$

The derivative of $x(t)$ is given by

$$x'(t) = -2A\sin 2t + 2B\cos 2t + 4\cos t. \tag{11.70}$$

Imposing the initial conditions given by Equation (11.68), we have

$$
\begin{aligned}
x(0) &= A = 0 \\
x'(0) &= 2B + 4 = 6,
\end{aligned}
\tag{11.71}
$$

from which we immediately deduce that $B = 1$. Thus, the solution to the differential equation that satisfies the initial conditions is given by the simplified function

$$x(t) = \sin 2t + 4\sin t. \; \blacksquare \tag{11.72}$$

11.3 Projectile Motion

In this section, we examine the motion of objects that are influenced only by the force of gravity. The convention used in this chapter is that the z-axis points upward in world space, so the downward acceleration of gravity $\mathbf{g}$ is the vector

$$\mathbf{g} = \langle 0, 0, -g \rangle, \tag{11.73}$$

where the scalar g is approximately 9.8 m/s^2 on the surface of the earth. An object in a gravitational field experiences a downward force of $m\mathbf{g}$.

The position $\mathbf{x}(t)$ of a projectile having initial position $\mathbf{x}_0$ and initial velocity $\mathbf{v}_0$ at time $t = 0$ is given by

$$\mathbf{x}(t) = \mathbf{x}_0 + \mathbf{v}_0 t + \tfrac{1}{2}\mathbf{g}t^2. \tag{11.74}$$

Since the x- and y-components of $\mathbf{g}$ are 0, only the z-component of Equation (11.74) is quadratic. Using $x(t)$, $y(t)$, and $z(t)$ to represent the components of $\mathbf{x}(t)$, we have

$$x(t) = x_0 + v_x t$$
$$y(t) = y_0 + v_y t$$
$$z(t) = z_0 + v_z t - \tfrac{1}{2} g t^2, \tag{11.75}$$

where x_0, y_0, and z_0 are the components of the initial position and v_x, v_y, and v_z are the components of the initial velocity.

When a projectile attains its maximum height, its vertical velocity is zero. We can determine the time t at which this occurs by solving the equation

$$\dot{z}(t) = v_z - gt = 0. \tag{11.76}$$

Thus, a projectile reaches its maximum height at time

$$t = \frac{v_z}{g}. \tag{11.77}$$

Plugging this time into the function $z(t)$ gives us the following expression for the maximum height h attained by a projectile.

$$h = z_0 + \frac{v_z^2}{2g} \tag{11.78}$$

Example 11.7. A projectile is launched from a platform 10 meters above the ground with an initial speed of 50 m/s in a direction forming an angle of 70 degrees with the horizontal plane (see Figure 11.2). What is the maximum height above the ground attained by the projectile?

Solution. The projectile's initial height z_0 and initial upward velocity v_z are given by

$$z_0 = 10 \, \text{m}$$
$$v_z = 50 \sin 70° \approx 47.0 \, \text{m/s}. \tag{11.79}$$

Plugging these values into Equation (11.78) and using the value 9.8 m/s^2 for g, we have $h \approx 123$ m. ■

The horizontal distance that a projectile travels before returning to the height from which it was launched is called the projectile's range. If a projectile is launched from a horizontal plane at $z_0 = 0$, then the time t at which it lands is given by the solution to the equation

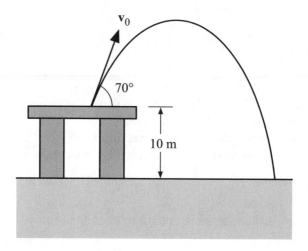

Figure 11.2 The projectile used in Example 11.7.

$$v_z t - \tfrac{1}{2} g t^2 = 0. \tag{11.80}$$

One solution to this equation is $t = 0$, corresponding to the time when the projectile was launched. The other solution is

$$t = \frac{2v_z}{g}, \tag{11.81}$$

and as we would expect, this is twice as long as it takes for the projectile to reach its maximum height. If we assume that the projectile follows a path lying in the x-z plane, then plugging this time into the function $x(t)$ and subtracting the initial x-coordinate x_0 gives us the following expression for the range r of a projectile.

$$r = \frac{2v_x v_z}{g} \tag{11.82}$$

Example 11.8. A projectile is launched with an initial speed of 30 m/s in a direction forming an angle of 40 degrees with the ground (see Figure 11.3). Assuming the ground is flat down range, how far does the projectile travel before landing?

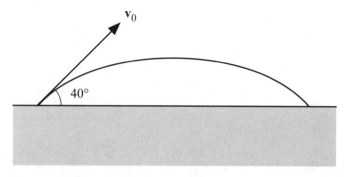

Figure 11.3 The projectile used in Example 11.8.

Solution. We assume that the projectile is launched from the origin and that the path of the projectile lies in the x-z plane. The v_x and v_z components of the initial velocity are given by

$$v_x = 30\cos 40° \approx 23.0 \, \text{m/s}$$
$$v_z = 30\sin 40° \approx 19.3 \, \text{m/s}. \tag{11.83}$$

Plugging these values into Equation (11.82) and using the value $9.8 \, \text{m/s}^2$ for g, the range of the projectile is 90.4 meters. ∎

Given an initial speed s at which a projectile is launched, we can determine at what angle the initial velocity vector should point in order for the projectile to reach a particular maximum height or to have a particular range. For motion in the x-z plane, the components of the initial velocity are given by

$$v_x = s\cos\alpha$$
$$v_z = s\sin\alpha, \tag{11.84}$$

where α is the angle formed between the initial trajectory and the horizontal plane. Given a desired maximum height h, we can plug the value of v_z into Equation (11.78) and solve for α to obtain

$$\alpha = \sin^{-1}\left(\frac{1}{s}\sqrt{2g(h - z_0)}\right). \tag{11.85}$$

Given a desired range r, we can plug the values of v_x and v_z into Equation (11.82) as follows.

$$r = \frac{2s^2}{g} \sin \alpha \cos \alpha = \frac{s^2}{g} \sin 2\alpha \qquad (11.86)$$

Solving for α gives us

$$\alpha = \frac{1}{2} \sin^{-1} \frac{rg}{s^2}. \qquad (11.87)$$

Since $\sin(\pi - \alpha) = \sin \alpha$, there are two angles that produce the range r in Equation (11.86): the angle α given by Equation (11.87) and its complementary angle $\pi/2 - \alpha$. If the values inside the inverse sine functions in Equations (11.85) and (11.87) are greater than 1, then the initial speed s is not great enough to achieve the desired maximum height or range.

Example 11.9. A projectile is launched from the ground with an initial speed of 65 m/s (see Figure 11.4). Assuming that the ground is flat, at what angle α should the projectile be launched so that it lands 400 meters down range?

Solution. Plugging the values $s = 65$ and $r = 400$ into Equation (11.87), we have $\alpha \approx 34°$. The complementary angle $\beta = 56°$ would also result in the projectile traveling a distance of 400 m. If we use the angle α, then the initial velocity is given by

$$v_x = 65 \cos 34° \approx 53.9 \text{ m/s}$$
$$v_z = 65 \sin 34° \approx 36.3 \text{ m/s}. \ \blacksquare \qquad (11.88)$$

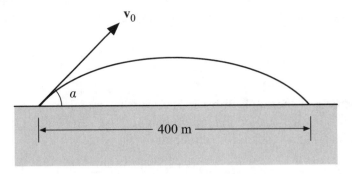

Figure 11.4 The projectile used in Example 11.9.

11.4 Resisted Motion

In the previous section, we neglected any kind of resistance to the motion of an object. In reality, an object's velocity is slowed by the medium through which it is moving, whether it be air, water, or some other substance. A precise physical formulation of resisted motion is complicated, but a decent approximation is achieved by assuming that resistance produces a force that acts in the direction opposite that in which an object is moving and is proportional to the magnitude of the object's velocity.

The force equation for an object of mass m influenced by gravity and experiencing resistance from the surrounding medium is given by

$$m\mathbf{g} - mk\dot{\mathbf{x}}(t) = m\ddot{\mathbf{x}}(t), \tag{11.89}$$

where mk is a constant describing the strength of the resistance. This can be rewritten as the following second-order nonhomogeneous differential equation.

$$\ddot{\mathbf{x}}(t) + k\dot{\mathbf{x}}(t) = \mathbf{g} \tag{11.90}$$

The method of undetermined coefficients provides the following particular solution to Equation (11.90).

$$\mathbf{x}(t) = \frac{\mathbf{g}}{k} t \tag{11.91}$$

Adding the general solution to the homogeneous differential equation, we have

$$\mathbf{x}(t) = \mathbf{A} + \mathbf{B}e^{-kt} + \frac{\mathbf{g}}{k} t, \tag{11.92}$$

where the vectors $\mathbf{A}$ and $\mathbf{B}$ are arbitrary constants that can be determined by establishing initial conditions. Specifying the initial position $\mathbf{x}_0$ and initial velocity $\mathbf{v}_0$, we have

$$\mathbf{x}(0) = \mathbf{x}_0$$
$$\dot{\mathbf{x}}(0) = \mathbf{v}_0. \tag{11.93}$$

Setting these equal to the values given by the functions $\mathbf{x}(t)$ and $\dot{\mathbf{x}}(t)$ at time $t = 0$ gives us the system

$$\mathbf{A} + \mathbf{B} = \mathbf{x}_0$$

$$-k\mathbf{B} + \frac{\mathbf{g}}{k} = \mathbf{v}_0, \tag{11.94}$$

from which we can derive the following expressions for **A** and **B**.

$$\mathbf{A} = \mathbf{x}_0 - \frac{\mathbf{g}}{k^2} + \frac{\mathbf{v}_0}{k}$$

$$\mathbf{B} = \frac{\mathbf{g}}{k^2} - \frac{\mathbf{v}_0}{k} \tag{11.95}$$

The position function $\mathbf{x}(t)$ for an object moving through a resistive medium is given by

$$\mathbf{x}(t) = \mathbf{x}_0 + \frac{\mathbf{g}}{k}t + \frac{k\mathbf{v}_0 - \mathbf{g}}{k^2}\left(1 - e^{-kt}\right). \tag{11.96}$$

The velocity function $\mathbf{v}(t)$ is given by the derivative of $\mathbf{x}(t)$:

$$\mathbf{v}(t) = \dot{\mathbf{x}}(t) = \frac{\mathbf{g}}{k} + \left(\mathbf{v}_0 - \frac{\mathbf{g}}{k}\right)e^{-kt}. \tag{11.97}$$

Over time, the velocity of an object whose motion is being resisted approaches a constant called the *terminal velocity*. The terminal velocity $\mathbf{v}_T$ is given by the limit of the velocity function $\mathbf{v}(t)$ as t tends to infinity:

$$\mathbf{v}_T = \lim_{t \to \infty} \mathbf{v}(t) = \frac{\mathbf{g}}{k}. \tag{11.98}$$

Although it is not apparent from Equation (11.96), the position function for an object moving through a resistive medium does converge to the familiar Equation (11.74) as the constant k approaches zero. This can be seen by evaluating the limit

$$\mathbf{x}(t) = \lim_{k \to 0}\left[\mathbf{x}_0 + \frac{\mathbf{g}}{k}t + \frac{k\mathbf{v}_0 - \mathbf{g}}{k^2}\left(1 - e^{-kt}\right)\right]. \tag{11.99}$$

Replacing the exponential function with its power series (see Appendix D, Equation (D.11)), we have

$$\mathbf{x}(t) = \lim_{k \to 0} \left[\mathbf{x}_0 + \frac{\mathbf{g}}{k} t + \frac{k\mathbf{v}_0 - \mathbf{g}}{k^2} \left(kt - \frac{k^2 t^2}{2!} + \frac{k^3 t^3}{3!} - \frac{k^4 t^4}{4!} + - \cdots \right) \right]$$

$$= \lim_{k \to 0} \left[\mathbf{x}_0 + \frac{\mathbf{g}}{k} t + (k\mathbf{v}_0 - \mathbf{g}) \left(\frac{t}{k} - \frac{t^2}{2!} + \frac{k t^3}{3!} - \frac{k^2 t^4}{4!} + - \cdots \right) \right]$$

$$= \lim_{k \to 0} \left[\mathbf{x}_0 + \mathbf{v}_0 t - \tfrac{1}{2} k \mathbf{v}_0 t^2 + \tfrac{1}{2} \mathbf{g} t^2 + (k\mathbf{v}_0 - \mathbf{g}) \left(\frac{k t^3}{3!} - \frac{k^2 t^4}{4!} + - \cdots \right) \right]$$

$$= \mathbf{x}_0 + \mathbf{v}_0 t + \tfrac{1}{2} \mathbf{g} t^2 . \tag{11.100}$$

11.5 Friction

Friction is the well-known force that arises when two surfaces are in contact. We discuss two types of friction in this section: kinetic friction and static friction. Kinetic friction occurs between two surfaces that are in motion relative to each other and has the effect of resisting that motion. Static friction refers to the force that holds a stationary object in place when it is in contact with another surface.

The forces resisting the motion of one object sliding across the surface of another object are very complex, but it turns out that the net kinetic frictional force F_K can usually be approximated quite accurately using the simple formula

$$F_K = -\mu_K N, \tag{11.101}$$

where N is the normal component of the force by which the object is bound to the surface (usually gravity), and μ_K is called the *coefficient of kinetic friction*. The minus sign appears in Equation (11.101) because the kinetic friction force always acts in the direction opposite that in which an object is moving across a surface. The coefficient of kinetic friction μ_K is a positive constant that depends on the types of the surfaces in contact with each other. Typical values of μ_K for various surfaces are listed in Table 11.1 at the end of this section.

Example 11.10. Suppose that a 10-kg block is sliding down a plane that is inclined at an angle of 30 degrees. If the coefficient of kinetic friction is $\mu_K = 0.5$, determine the block's acceleration.

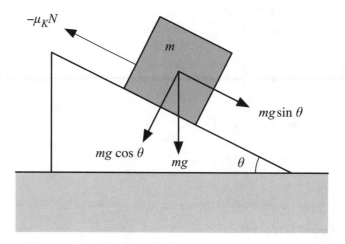

Figure 11.5 The block used in Example 11.10.

Solution. Let m be the mass of the block, and let θ be the angle by which the plane is inclined. As shown in Figure 11.5, the block is acted on by a gravitational force and a resisting force due to friction. The gravitational force can be divided into components that are parallel to the plane and perpendicular to the plane. The parallel component F_G is given by

$$F_G = mg\sin\theta \tag{11.102}$$

and pulls the block across the plane. The perpendicular component produces the force holding the block to the plane:

$$N = mg\cos\theta. \tag{11.103}$$

The force F_K due to kinetic friction is given by

$$F_K = -\mu_K N = -\mu_K mg\cos\theta \tag{11.104}$$

and acts in the direction opposite that of F_G. The acceleration a of the block is equal to the net force acting on it divided by its mass:

$$a = \frac{F_G + F_K}{m} = g\sin\theta - \mu_K g\cos\theta. \tag{11.105}$$

Plugging in the angle of inclination and coefficient of kinetic friction, we obtain the result

$$a = \left(9.8 \text{ m/s}^2\right) \cdot \frac{1}{2} - 0.5 \cdot \left(9.8 \text{ m/s}^2\right) \cdot \frac{\sqrt{3}}{2} \approx 0.656 \text{ m/s}^2. \qquad (11.106)$$

Notice that the mass of the block is inconsequential. ∎

The static friction force prevents an object on a surface from moving by opposing any tangential force that may be acting on it. The maximum force F_S that can be exerted due to static friction is given by

$$F_S = -\mu_S N, \qquad (11.107)$$

where N is the normal force and μ_S is called the *coefficient of static friction*. Again, we use a minus sign to indicate that the force acts in the direction opposite that of any force trying to move the object. Typical values of μ_S for various surfaces are listed in Table 11.1.

Table 11.1 Typical values of the coefficient of kinetic friction μ_K and coefficient of static friction μ_S.

Surfaces	μ_K	μ_S
Aluminum on aluminum	1.40	1.10
Aluminum on steel	0.47	0.61
Copper on steel	0.36	0.53
Steel on steel	0.57	0.74
Nickel on nickel	0.53	1.10
Glass on glass	0.40	0.94
Copper on glass	0.53	0.68
Oak on oak (parallel to grain)	0.48	0.62
Oak on oak (perpendicular to grain)	0.32	0.54
Rubber on concrete (dry)	0.90	1.00
Rubber on concrete (wet)	0.25	0.30

As soon as a force on an object exceeds the maximum value of F_S given by Equation (11.107), the object begins to move, and the static friction force is replaced by the kinetic friction force F_K. It is often the case that $F_K < F_S$, so less force is required to move an object once it has been set in motion than was required to initiate the motion.

Example 11.11. A block is resting on a horizontal plane for which the coefficient of static friction is given by $\mu_S = 0.5$. Determine by what angle the plane needs to be inclined before the block begins sliding under the influence of gravity.

Solution. We need to determine when the component of the gravitation force that is parallel to the plane exceeds the static friction force. This occurs when

$$mg \sin\theta = \mu_S N = \mu_S mg \cos\theta, \tag{11.108}$$

where θ is the angle of inclination. Solving for θ, we have

$$\theta = \tan^{-1}\mu_S \approx 26.6°. \; \blacksquare \tag{11.109}$$

Chapter 11 Summary

Force Equation

The acceleration $\mathbf{a}(t)$ of an object multiplied by its mass m is equal to the sum of the forces acting on it:

$$\sum_{i=1}^{N}\mathbf{F}_i(t) = m\mathbf{a}(t) = m\ddot{\mathbf{x}}(t).$$

Second-Order Differential Equations

The general solution to the homogeneous second-order differential equation

$$x''(t) + ax'(t) + bx(t) = 0$$

is given by

$$x(t) = Ae^{r_1 t} + Be^{r_2 t},$$

where

$$r_1 = -\frac{a}{2} + \frac{1}{2}\sqrt{a^2 - 4b}$$

$$r_2 = -\frac{a}{2} - \frac{1}{2}\sqrt{a^2 - 4b}.$$

If $r_1 = r_2 = r$, then the general solution is given by

$$x(t) = Ae^{rt} + Bte^{rt}.$$

If r_1 and r_2 are complex numbers, then the general solution can also be written as

$$x(t) = e^{\alpha t}\left(C_1 \cos \beta t + C_2 \sin \beta t\right),$$

where

$$\alpha = -\frac{a}{2}$$

$$\beta = \frac{1}{2}\sqrt{4b - a^2}.$$

This is equivalent to the solution

$$x(t) = D\sin\left(\beta t + \delta\right),$$

where

$$D = \sqrt{C_1^2 + C_2^2}$$

$$\delta = \sin^{-1}\frac{C_1}{D}.$$

Projectile Motion

The position $\mathbf{x}(t)$ of a projectile is given by the function

$$\mathbf{x}(t) = \mathbf{x}_0 + \mathbf{v}_0 t + \tfrac{1}{2}\mathbf{g}t^2,$$

where $\mathbf{x}_0$ is the initial position, $\mathbf{v}_0$ is the initial velocity, and $\mathbf{g} = \langle 0,0,-g \rangle$ is the acceleration of gravity. The maximum height h attained by the projectile is given by

$$h = z_0 + \frac{v_z^2}{2g},$$

and the range r of the projectile is given by

$$r = \frac{2v_x v_y}{g}.$$

Resisted Motion

The position function $\mathbf{x}(t)$ for an object moving through a resistive medium is given by

$$\mathbf{x}(t) = \mathbf{x}_0 + \frac{\mathbf{g}}{k}t + \frac{k\mathbf{v}_0 - \mathbf{g}}{k^2}\left(1 - e^{-kt}\right),$$

where k represents the intensity of the damping force. The terminal velocity $\mathbf{v}_T$ is given by

$$\mathbf{v}_T = \frac{\mathbf{g}}{k}.$$

Friction

The force of kinetic friction F_K is given by

$$F_K = -\mu_K N,$$

where μ_K is the coefficient of kinetic friction. The kinetic friction force acts in the direction opposite that of the motion.

The maximum force of static friction F_S is given by

$$F_S = -\mu_S N,$$

where μ_S is the coefficient of static friction. The static friction force acts in the direction opposite that of any tangential force trying to move an object.

Exercises for Chapter 11

1. Solve the differential equation

    $$x''(t) - 6x'(t) + 9x(t) = 9t + 3.$$

2. Solve the differential equation

    $$x''(t) + 16x(t) = 0$$

    subject to the initial conditions $x(0) = 3$ and $x'(0) = 1$.

3. A projectile is launched from a platform 20 meters above the ground with an initial speed of 20 m/s in a direction forming an angle of 45 degrees with the horizontal plane. What is the maximum height above the ground attained by the projectile? Assume that the acceleration of gravity has magnitude g.

4. For what period of time does the projectile in Exercise 3 travel before it lands on the ground?

5. Suppose a projectile is launched from the origin and travels toward a point **P** in the x-z plane as shown in Figure 11.6. Assuming an acceleration of gravity $\mathbf{g} = \langle 0,0,-g \rangle$, at what initial velocity $\mathbf{v}_0$ would the projectile have to be launched so that it strikes the point **P** under the constraint that its path attains a maximum vertical difference h with the straight line connecting the origin and the point **P**?

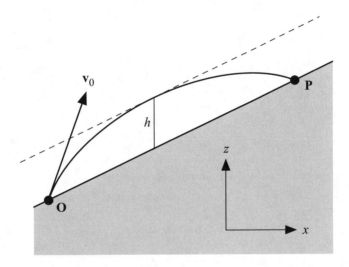

Figure 11.6 The projectile launched in Exercise 5.

6. A rock is dropped from rest at 50 meters above the ground and allowed to fall straight down through a resistive medium. Suppose that $k = 1\,\text{s}^{-1}$, and use Newton's method (see Section 5.1.4) to approximate the time t when the rock hits the ground.

7. An object of mass M is hanging from a rope that runs over a frictionless pulley and connects to another object of mass m lying on an inclined plane that forms an angle θ with the horizontal (see Figure 11.7). The coefficient of

kinetic friction on the incline is μ_K. Assuming that M is much larger than m, determine the downward acceleration a of the hanging object. [*Hint.* Both masses are being accelerated, so the sum of the forces acting on the system should be set equal to $(M + m)a$.]

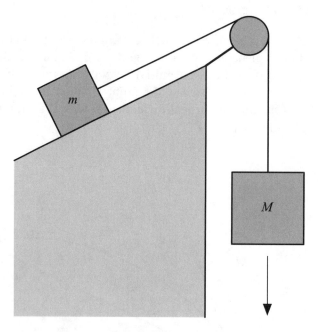

Figure 11.7 The system used in Exercise 7.

Chapter **12**

Rotational Physics

This chapter continues the survey of physics that begins in Chapter 11. We now enter the domain of rotational mechanics to examine the behavior of rotating objects and the forces experienced in a rotating environment. Rotational physics has a wide range of applications in game programming, from interaction between players and objects in the environment to space combat simulations. Virtually any object that is flying through the air or otherwise not resting on a surface is probably rotating, and thus would benefit from an accurate simulation of its motion.

12.1 Rotating Environments

This section discusses the physics that apply to an object in a rotating environment. A rotating environment refers to any frame of reference that is rotating about some axis and includes everything from a merry-go-round to the planet Earth. We begin with the introduction of angular velocity, and then we investigate the forces experienced by an object in the rotating reference frame.

12.1.1 Angular Velocity

Suppose that a particle of mass m is rotating about an axis parallel to the unit vector $\mathbf{A}$ because it is attached to the axis by a string of length r (see Figure 12.1). Let the vectors $\mathbf{X}$ and $\mathbf{Y}$ be unit vectors lying in the plane perpendicular to $\mathbf{A}$ such that the axes $\mathbf{X}$, $\mathbf{Y}$, and $\mathbf{A}$ form a right-handed coordinate system (i.e., $\mathbf{X} \times \mathbf{Y} = \mathbf{A}$). Let $\theta(t)$ represent the counterclockwise angle that the projection of the string onto the $\mathbf{X}$-$\mathbf{Y}$ plane makes with the vector $\mathbf{X}$ at time t. The *angular velocity* of the particle is defined to be the rate at which this angle is changing, and is usually denoted by ω.

$$\omega(t) = \dot{\theta}(t) = \frac{d}{dt}\theta(t). \tag{12.1}$$

The angular velocity is often written as a vector that is parallel to the axis of rotation $\mathbf{A}$ and has the magnitude $|\omega(t)|$. The vector angular velocity $\boldsymbol{\omega}(t)$ is defined as

$$\boldsymbol{\omega}(t) = \omega(t)\mathbf{A} = \dot{\theta}(t)\mathbf{A}. \tag{12.2}$$

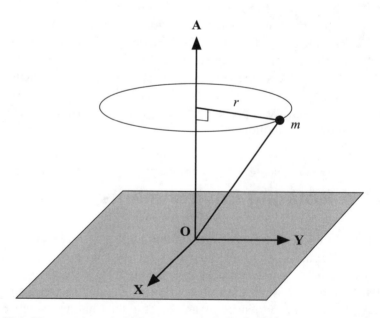

Figure 12.1 The angular velocity of a particle is a vector that is parallel to the axis of rotation **A** and whose magnitude is equal to the rate of change of the angle formed in the plane perpendicular to the axis.

The speed at which a rotating particle moves through space is calculated by multiplying the particle's angular velocity by its distance from the axis of rotation. For the particle shown in Figure 12.1, the speed $v(t)$ is given by

$$v(t) = |\omega(t)r|. \tag{12.3}$$

However, this tells us nothing about what direction the particle is moving. Let the vector function $\mathbf{r}(t)$ represent the position of the particle relative to a fixed origin lying on the axis of rotation. As illustrated in Figure 12.2, the linear velocity vector $\mathbf{v}(t)$ of the particle is given by

$$\mathbf{v}(t) = \boldsymbol{\omega}(t) \times \mathbf{r}(t) \tag{12.4}$$

since the distance from the particle to the axis of rotation is equal to $\|\mathbf{r}(t)\| \sin \alpha$, and the velocity $\mathbf{v}(t)$ is always perpendicular to the direction pointing toward the axis.

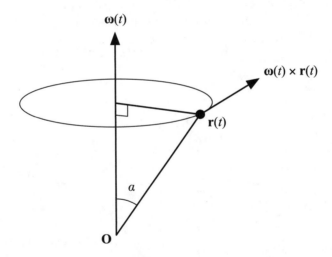

Figure 12.2 The linear velocity $\mathbf{v}(t)$ is equal to the cross product of the angular velocity $\boldsymbol{\omega}(t)$ and the position $\mathbf{r}(t)$.

12.1.2 The Centrifugal Force

We continue to consider the example in which a particle is fastened by a string to the axis about which it is rotating. The linear acceleration $\mathbf{a}(t)$ of the particle is equal to the derivative of its linear velocity with respect to time. Taking the time derivative of the function $\mathbf{v}(t)$ given by Equation (12.4), we have

$$\mathbf{a}(t) = \dot{\mathbf{v}}(t) = \dot{\boldsymbol{\omega}}(t) \times \mathbf{r}(t) + \boldsymbol{\omega}(t) \times \dot{\mathbf{r}}(t). \qquad (12.5)$$

Since $\dot{\mathbf{r}}(t)$ is equal to the linear velocity $\mathbf{v}(t)$ of the particle, we can write

$$\mathbf{a}(t) = \dot{\boldsymbol{\omega}}(t) \times \mathbf{r}(t) + \boldsymbol{\omega}(t) \times [\boldsymbol{\omega}(t) \times \mathbf{r}(t)]. \qquad (12.6)$$

If the angular velocity is constant, then the $\dot{\boldsymbol{\omega}}(t) \times \mathbf{r}(t)$ term of the acceleration is zero. The $\boldsymbol{\omega}(t) \times [\boldsymbol{\omega}(t) \times \mathbf{r}(t)]$ term, however, is always present and points in the direction from the particle toward the axis of rotation (see Figure 12.3). This part of the acceleration arises from the tension in the string connecting the particle to the axis of rotation. The particle itself experiences an equal but opposite force known as the *centrifugal force*. The centrifugal force, given by

$$\mathbf{F}_{\text{centrifugal}} = -m(\boldsymbol{\omega}(t) \times [\boldsymbol{\omega}(t) \times \mathbf{r}(t)]), \qquad (12.7)$$

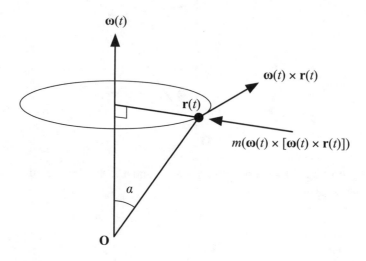

Figure 12.3 The centrifugal force.

is responsible for the well-known effect that causes objects in a rotating system to move away from the axis of rotation. In the case that $\mathbf{r}(t)$ and $\boldsymbol{\omega}(t)$ are perpendicular, the centrifugal force can be expressed as the scalar

$$F_{\text{centrifugal}} = m\omega^2 r = \frac{mv^2}{r}, \tag{12.8}$$

where r is the radial distance from the particle to the axis of rotation.

12.1.3 The Coriolis Force

We now consider a somewhat more complicated situation in which a particle is moving on the surface of a rotating object. Suppose that a particle of mass m is rotating about some axis with angular velocity $\boldsymbol{\omega}(t)$. Further suppose that the particle is also moving *relative* to the rotating system with a velocity $\mathbf{v}_r(t)$. Then the velocity $\mathbf{v}(t)$ of the particle for a stationary observer outside the system is given by

$$\mathbf{v}(t) = \boldsymbol{\omega}(t) \times \mathbf{r}(t) + \mathbf{v}_r(t), \tag{12.9}$$

where $\mathbf{r}(t)$ is the position of the particle relative to some origin lying on the axis of rotation. Since the velocity $\mathbf{v}_r(t)$ is rotating with the system, a stationary observer sees the particle accelerating with respect to a fixed coordinate system according to the function

$$\mathbf{a}_f(t) = \boldsymbol{\omega}(t) \times \mathbf{v}_r(t) + \mathbf{a}_r(t), \tag{12.10}$$

where $\mathbf{a}_r(t) = \dot{\mathbf{v}}_r(t)$ is the acceleration of the particle in the rotating reference frame. The total linear acceleration $\mathbf{a}(t)$ of the particle is thus given by

$$\begin{aligned}
\mathbf{a}(t) = \dot{\mathbf{v}}(t) &= \dot{\boldsymbol{\omega}}(t) \times \mathbf{r}(t) + \boldsymbol{\omega}(t) \times \dot{\mathbf{r}}(t) + \mathbf{a}_f(t) \\
&= \dot{\boldsymbol{\omega}}(t) \times \mathbf{r}(t) + \boldsymbol{\omega}(t) \times \dot{\mathbf{r}}(t) + \boldsymbol{\omega}(t) \times \mathbf{v}_r(t) + \mathbf{a}_r(t).
\end{aligned} \tag{12.11}$$

Since $\dot{\mathbf{r}}(t)$ is equal to the linear velocity $\mathbf{v}(t)$ of the particle, we can write

$$\mathbf{a}(t) = \dot{\boldsymbol{\omega}}(t) \times \mathbf{r}(t) + \boldsymbol{\omega}(t) \times [\boldsymbol{\omega}(t) \times \mathbf{r}(t)] + 2\boldsymbol{\omega}(t) \times \mathbf{v}_r(t) + \mathbf{a}_r(t). \tag{12.12}$$

The force $\mathbf{F}(t)$ experienced by the particle is therefore

$$\begin{aligned}
\mathbf{F}(t) = m\mathbf{a}(t) &= m\dot{\boldsymbol{\omega}}(t) \times \mathbf{r}(t) + m\boldsymbol{\omega}(t) \times [\boldsymbol{\omega}(t) \times \mathbf{r}(t)] \\
&\quad + 2m\boldsymbol{\omega}(t) \times \mathbf{v}_r(t) + m\mathbf{a}_r(t).
\end{aligned} \tag{12.13}$$

In the reference frame of the rotating system, the force $\mathbf{F}_r(t)$ on the object appears to be the following.

$$\mathbf{F}_r(t) = m\mathbf{a}_r(t) = \mathbf{F}(t) - m\dot{\boldsymbol{\omega}}(t) \times \mathbf{r}(t) - m\boldsymbol{\omega}(t) \times [\boldsymbol{\omega}(t) \times \mathbf{r}(t)]$$
$$- 2m\boldsymbol{\omega}(t) \times \mathbf{v}_r(t) \tag{12.14}$$

As expected, the centrifugal force shows up again, but there is also a new term called the *Coriolis force* that acts on the particle in a direction perpendicular to its velocity in the rotating reference frame (see Figure 12.4). The Coriolis force, given by

$$\mathbf{F}_{\text{Coriolis}} = -2m\boldsymbol{\omega}(t) \times \mathbf{v}_r(t), \tag{12.15}$$

arises only when the particle is moving within the rotating system. It is this force that is responsible for the large-scale cyclonic motion of certain weather phenomena. For instance, hurricanes rotate counterclockwise in the northern hemisphere and clockwise in the southern hemisphere because the cross product in Equation (12.15) changes sign at the equator.

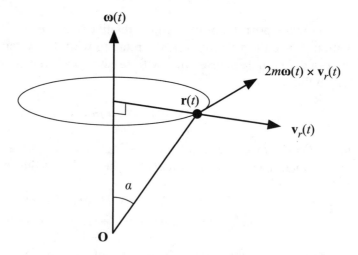

Figure 12.4 The Coriolis force.

12.2 Rigid Body Motion

We define a *rigid body* to be a system of particles that are absolutely fixed with respect to each other and thus share the same angular velocity. A solid object can be thought of as a collection of an infinite number of particles, each having an infinitesimal mass. Since the particles composing a rigid body do not move with respect to each other, the centrifugal and Coriolis forces do not apply when the object is rotating. The only motions that a rigid body may undergo are the linear motion associated with the path along which it travels through space and the angular motion that it experiences because it is rotating about some axis. In this section, we investigate the rotational properties of a rigid body and the effects of external forces on this rotation.

12.2.1 Center of Mass

When a rigid body rotates freely in the absence of any external forces, it does so about an axis that passes through the body's center of mass. The center of mass is the point within the rigid body at which a force could be applied in any direction without causing any net torque when that point is considered the origin.

Suppose that a rigid body is composed of some number of particles whose position and mass are known. The total mass M of the system of particles is given by

$$M = \sum_{\alpha} m_{\alpha},\qquad(12.16)$$

where m_{α} is the mass of the α-th particle, and the summation is taken over all of the particles belonging to the system. Let $\mathbf{r}_{\alpha}$ denote the position of the α-th particle. The center of mass $\mathbf{C}$ of the system is defined to be

$$\mathbf{C} = \frac{1}{M} \sum_{\alpha} m_{\alpha} \mathbf{r}_{\alpha}.\qquad(12.17)$$

For a solid object, we compute the total mass of a continuous volume using the integral

$$M = \int_{V} dm(\mathbf{r}),\qquad(12.18)$$

where $dm(\mathbf{r})$ represents the differential mass at the position $\mathbf{r}$, and V is the volume occupied by the object. If the density at the position $\mathbf{r}$ is described by the function $\rho(\mathbf{r})$, then this integral can be written as

$$M = \int_V \rho(\mathbf{r})\,dV. \qquad (12.19)$$

The center of mass for a solid object is then computed using the integral

$$\mathbf{C} = \frac{1}{M}\int_V \mathbf{r}\rho(\mathbf{r})\,dV. \qquad (12.20)$$

Example 12.1. Calculate the center of mass of a cone of radius R, height h, and constant density ρ, whose base is centered at the origin on the x-y plane (see Figure 12.5).

Solution. We use cylindrical coordinates. The radius $r(z)$ of a cross section of the cone at a height z above the x-y plane is given by

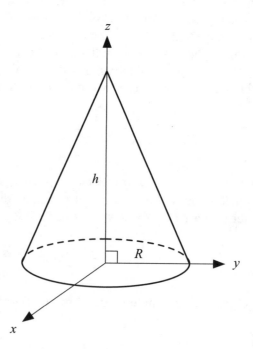

Figure 12.5 The cone used in Example 12.1.

$$r(z) = (h - z)\frac{R}{h}. \tag{12.21}$$

We calculate the total mass of the cone using Equation (12.19) to integrate over the volume it occupies. The differential volume dV in cylindrical coordinates is given by

$$dV = r\,dr\,d\theta\,dz, \tag{12.22}$$

so the integral that we need to evaluate is

$$M = \int_0^h \rho\pi[r(z)]^2\,dz, \tag{12.23}$$

where the integrand represents the differential mass of a disk at height z above the x-y plane. Replacing $r(z)$ with the value given by Equation (12.21), we have

$$M = \rho\pi\frac{R^2}{h^2}\int_0^h (h - z)^2\,dz$$

$$= \tfrac{1}{3}\rho\pi R^2 h. \tag{12.24}$$

Due to the cylindrical symmetry of the cone, the x- and y-components of the center of mass are clearly zero. The z-component of the center of mass is found by applying Equation (12.20):

$$C_z = \frac{1}{M}\int_0^h \int_0^{2\pi} \int_0^{r(z)} \rho z r\,dr\,d\theta\,dz. \tag{12.25}$$

Evaluating the integral over θ leaves us with

$$C_z = \frac{2\rho\pi}{M}\int_0^h \int_0^{r(z)} z r\,dr\,dz. \tag{12.26}$$

We next integrate over r and replace $r(z)$ with the value given by Equation (12.21):

$$C_z = \frac{\rho\pi R^2}{Mh^2}\int_0^h z(h - z)^2\,dz$$

$$= \frac{\rho \pi R^2}{Mh^2} \int_0^h \left(h^2 z - 2hz^2 + z^3 \right) dz. \tag{12.27}$$

Finally, integrating over z, we obtain

$$C_z = \frac{\rho \pi R^2 h^2}{12M} = \frac{h}{4}. \tag{12.28}$$

Thus, the center of mass of the cone is given by $\mathbf{C} = \langle 0, 0, h/4 \rangle$. ∎

12.2.2 Angular Momentum and Torque

Recall that the linear momentum $\mathbf{p}$ of a particle having mass m moving at a velocity $\mathbf{v}$ is given by $\mathbf{p} = m\mathbf{v}$. Just as angular velocity is the rotational analog of linear velocity, there exists a quantity called angular momentum that serves as the rotational analog of linear momentum.

Suppose that a particle of mass m is rotating about some axis with an angular velocity of $\boldsymbol{\omega}(t)$ and that the position of the particle is given by the function $\mathbf{r}(t)$. The *angular momentum* $\mathbf{L}(t)$ of the particle is defined to be

$$\mathbf{L}(t) = \mathbf{r}(t) \times \mathbf{p}(t), \tag{12.29}$$

where $\mathbf{p}(t) = m\mathbf{v}(t)$ is the linear momentum of the particle.

Differentiating both sides of Equation (12.29) gives us

$$\dot{\mathbf{L}}(t) = \dot{\mathbf{r}}(t) \times \mathbf{p}(t) + \mathbf{r}(t) \times \dot{\mathbf{p}}(t). \tag{12.30}$$

Since $\dot{\mathbf{r}}(t) = \mathbf{v}(t)$, the vectors $\dot{\mathbf{r}}(t)$ and $\mathbf{p}(t)$ point in the same direction, so the cross product $\dot{\mathbf{r}}(t) \times \mathbf{p}(t)$ is zero. Thus,

$$\dot{\mathbf{L}}(t) = \mathbf{r}(t) \times \dot{\mathbf{p}}(t) = \mathbf{r}(t) \times m\dot{\mathbf{v}}(t). \tag{12.31}$$

The vector $m\dot{\mathbf{v}}(t)$ is equal to the net force $\mathbf{F}(t)$ acting on the particle, so we can write

$$\dot{\mathbf{L}}(t) = \mathbf{r}(t) \times \mathbf{F}(t). \tag{12.32}$$

The quantity on the right side of Equation (12.32) is called the *torque* $\boldsymbol{\tau}(t)$ being applied to the particle:

$$\boldsymbol{\tau}(t) = \mathbf{r}(t) \times \mathbf{F}(t). \tag{12.33}$$

Torque is the rotational analog to linear force and induces an angular acceleration. If the net torque acting on a particle is zero, then the angular momentum
remains constant because

$$\dot{\mathbf{L}}(t) = \boldsymbol{\tau}(t).$$ (12.34)

12.2.3 The Inertia Tensor

Angular momentum is related to angular velocity in a much more complicated
way than linear momentum is related to linear velocity. In fact, the angular momentum vector and the associated angular velocity vector do not necessarily
point in the same direction. The relationship between these two quantities is the
topic of this section.

The angular momentum of a rigid body composed of a set of particles is
equal to the sum

$$\mathbf{L}(t) = \sum_{\alpha} \mathbf{r}_{\alpha}(t) \times \mathbf{p}_{\alpha}(t),$$ (12.35)

where $\mathbf{r}_{\alpha}(t)$ represents the position of the α-th particle, $\mathbf{p}_{\alpha}(t)$ represents the momentum of the α-th particle, and the summation is taken over all the particles
belonging to the system. Since the linear momentum $\mathbf{p}_{\alpha}(t)$ can be written as

$$\mathbf{p}_{\alpha}(t) = m_{\alpha}\mathbf{v}_{\alpha}(t) = m_{\alpha}\boldsymbol{\omega}(t) \times \mathbf{r}_{\alpha}(t),$$ (12.36)

the angular momentum becomes

$$\mathbf{L}(t) = \sum_{\alpha} m_{\alpha}\mathbf{r}_{\alpha}(t) \times [\boldsymbol{\omega}(t) \times \mathbf{r}_{\alpha}(t)].$$ (12.37)

Using the vector identity given by Theorem 1.9(f),

$$\mathbf{P} \times (\mathbf{Q} \times \mathbf{P}) = \mathbf{P} \times \mathbf{Q} \times \mathbf{P} = P^2\mathbf{Q} - (\mathbf{P} \cdot \mathbf{Q})\mathbf{P},$$ (12.38)

the angular momentum can also be written as

$$\mathbf{L}(t) = \sum_{\alpha} m_{\alpha}\left(r_{\alpha}^2(t)\boldsymbol{\omega}(t) - [\mathbf{r}_{\alpha}(t) \cdot \boldsymbol{\omega}(t)]\mathbf{r}_{\alpha}(t)\right).$$ (12.39)

Dropping the function-of-t notation for the moment, we can express the i-th component of $\mathbf{L}$ by

$$L_i = \sum_\alpha m_\alpha \left[r_\alpha^2 \omega_i - (\mathbf{r}_\alpha)_i \sum_{j=1}^{3} (\mathbf{r}_\alpha)_j \omega_j \right]. \tag{12.40}$$

We can express the quantity ω_i as

$$\omega_i = \sum_{j=1}^{3} \omega_j \delta_{ij}, \tag{12.41}$$

where δ_{ij} is the Kronecker delta defined by Equation (1.42). This substitution allows us to write L_i as

$$L_i = \sum_\alpha m_\alpha \sum_{j=1}^{3} \left[r_\alpha^2 \omega_j \delta_{ij} - (\mathbf{r}_\alpha)_i (\mathbf{r}_\alpha)_j \omega_j \right]$$

$$= \sum_{j=1}^{3} \omega_j \sum_\alpha m_\alpha \left[\delta_{ij} r_\alpha^2 - (\mathbf{r}_\alpha)_i (\mathbf{r}_\alpha)_j \right]. \tag{12.42}$$

The sum over α can be interpreted as the (i, j) entry of a 3×3 matrix $\mathcal{I}$:

$$\mathcal{I}_{ij} = \sum_\alpha m_\alpha \left[\delta_{ij} r_\alpha^2 - (\mathbf{r}_\alpha)_i (\mathbf{r}_\alpha)_j \right]. \tag{12.43}$$

This allows us to express L_i as

$$L_i = \sum_{j=1}^{3} \omega_j \mathcal{I}_{ij}, \tag{12.44}$$

and thus the angular momentum $\mathbf{L}(t)$ can be written as

$$\mathbf{L}(t) = \mathcal{I}\boldsymbol{\omega}(t). \tag{12.45}$$

The entity $\mathcal{I}$ is called the *inertia tensor* and relates the angular velocity of a rigid body to its angular momentum. The inertia tensor also relates the torque $\boldsymbol{\tau}(t)$ acting on a rigid body to the body's angular acceleration $\boldsymbol{\alpha}(t) = \dot{\boldsymbol{\omega}}(t)$. Differentiating both sides of Equation (12.45) gives us

$$\dot{\mathbf{L}}(t) = \boldsymbol{\tau}(t) = \mathcal{I}\boldsymbol{\alpha}(t). \tag{12.46}$$

Written as a 3×3 matrix, the inertia tensor is given by

$$\mathcal{I} = \begin{bmatrix} \sum_\alpha m_\alpha \left(r_\alpha^2 - x_\alpha^2 \right) & -\sum_\alpha m_\alpha x_\alpha y_\alpha & -\sum_\alpha m_\alpha x_\alpha z_\alpha \\ -\sum_\alpha m_\alpha x_\alpha y_\alpha & \sum_\alpha m_\alpha \left(r_\alpha^2 - y_\alpha^2 \right) & -\sum_\alpha m_\alpha y_\alpha z_\alpha \\ -\sum_\alpha m_\alpha x_\alpha z_\alpha & -\sum_\alpha m_\alpha y_\alpha z_\alpha & \sum_\alpha m_\alpha \left(r_\alpha^2 - z_\alpha^2 \right) \end{bmatrix}, \qquad (12.47)$$

where $x_\alpha = (\mathbf{r}_\alpha)_1$, $y_\alpha = (\mathbf{r}_\alpha)_2$, and $z_\alpha = (\mathbf{r}_\alpha)_3$. Clearly, $\mathcal{I}$ is a symmetric matrix. The diagonal entries $\mathcal{I}_{11}$, $\mathcal{I}_{22}$, and $\mathcal{I}_{33}$ are called the *moments of inertia* with respect to the x-, y-, and z-axes, respectively. The off-diagonal entries are called the *products of inertia*.

For a continuous mass distribution, Equation (12.43) is formulated as the integral

$$\mathcal{I}_{ij} = \int_V \left(\delta_{ij} r^2 - r_i r_j \right) dm(\mathbf{r}), \qquad (12.48)$$

where $dm(\mathbf{r})$ represents the differential mass at the position $\mathbf{r}$, and V is the volume occupied by the rigid body. If the density at the position $\mathbf{r}$ is described by the function $\rho(\mathbf{r})$, then this integral can be written as

$$\mathcal{I}_{ij} = \int_V \left(\delta_{ij} r^2 - r_i r_j \right) \rho(\mathbf{r}) dV. \qquad (12.49)$$

Example 12.2. Calculate the moment of inertia about the z-axis of a solid sphere of radius R that is centered at the origin and has a uniform density ρ.

Solution. The moment of inertia about the z-axis is equal to the $(3,3)$ entry of the inertia tensor $\mathcal{I}$. We need to evaluate the integral

$$\mathcal{I}_{33} = \int_V \left(r^2 - z^2 \right) \rho \, dV. \qquad (12.50)$$

The quantity $r^2 - z^2$ is equal to the squared distance from the z-axis, which in spherical coordinates is equal to $r^2 \sin^2 \varphi$, where φ is the polar angle. The differential volume dV in spherical coordinates is given by

$$dV = r^2 \sin \varphi \, dr \, d\theta \, d\varphi, \qquad (12.51)$$

so Equation (12.50) becomes

$$\mathcal{I}_{33} = \int_0^\pi \int_0^{2\pi} \int_0^R \left(r^2 \sin^2 \varphi\right) \rho r^2 \sin \varphi \, dr \, d\theta \, d\varphi$$

$$= \rho \int_0^\pi \int_0^{2\pi} \int_0^R r^4 \sin^3 \varphi \, dr \, d\theta \, d\varphi. \tag{12.52}$$

Evaluating the integrals over r and θ, we have

$$\mathcal{I}_{33} = \tfrac{2}{5}\pi\rho R^5 \int_0^\pi \sin^3 \varphi \, d\varphi = \tfrac{2}{5}\pi\rho R^5 \int_0^\pi \left(1 - \cos^2 \varphi\right) \sin \varphi \, d\varphi. \tag{12.53}$$

By making the substitutions $u = -\cos\varphi$ and $du = \sin\varphi \, d\varphi$, we can evaluate the remaining integral as follows.

$$\mathcal{I}_{33} = \tfrac{2}{5}\pi\rho R^5 \int_{-1}^1 \left(1 - u^2\right) du$$

$$= \tfrac{8}{15}\pi\rho R^5 \tag{12.54}$$

The volume of the sphere is given by $V = \tfrac{4}{3}\pi R^3$, so we can write the moment of inertia as

$$\mathcal{I}_{33} = \tfrac{2}{5}\rho V R^2 = \tfrac{2}{5} m R^2, \tag{12.55}$$

where $m = \rho V$ is the mass of the sphere. ■

Due to the symmetry of the sphere, its moments of inertia about the x- and y-axes are also equal to $\tfrac{2}{5}mR^2$. Furthermore, the products of inertia are zero, so the inertia tensor $\mathcal{I}$ of a sphere has the form

$$\mathcal{I} = \begin{bmatrix} \tfrac{2}{5}mR^2 & 0 & 0 \\ 0 & \tfrac{2}{5}mR^2 & 0 \\ 0 & 0 & \tfrac{2}{5}mR^2 \end{bmatrix}. \tag{12.56}$$

Consequently, the angular momentum of a rotating sphere may be written in terms of a scalar moment of inertia $I = \tfrac{2}{5}mR^2$:

$$\mathbf{L}(t) = I\boldsymbol{\omega}(t). \tag{12.57}$$

Example 12.3. Calculate the inertia tensor of a solid cylinder of radius R and height h that is aligned to the z-axis, centered at the origin, and has a uniform density ρ (see Figure 12.6).

Solution. We first calculate the moment of inertia about the z-axis using cylindrical coordinates to evaluate the integral

$$\mathcal{I}_{33} = \int_V \left(s^2 - z^2 \right) \rho \, dV. \tag{12.58}$$

(We have used s^2 to represent the squared distance from the origin to avoid confusion with the radial distance r in cylindrical coordinates). The quantity $s^2 - z^2$ is equal to the squared distance from the z-axis, which in cylindrical coordinates is simply r^2. The differential volume dV in cylindrical coordinates is given by

$$dV = r \, dr \, d\theta \, dz, \tag{12.59}$$

so Equation (12.58) becomes

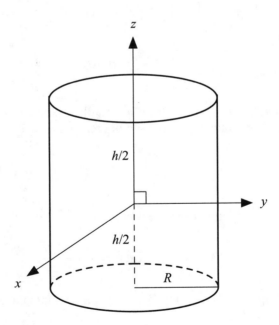

Figure 12.6 The cylinder used in Example 12.3.

$$\mathcal{I}_{33} = \rho \int_{-h/2}^{h/2} \int_0^{2\pi} \int_0^R r^3 \, dr \, d\theta \, dz$$

$$= \tfrac{1}{2} \pi \rho h R^4 . \tag{12.60}$$

The volume of the cylinder is given by $V = \pi h R^2$, so we can write the moment of inertia as

$$\mathcal{I}_{33} = \tfrac{1}{2} \rho V R^2 = \tfrac{1}{2} m R^2 , \tag{12.61}$$

where $m = \rho V$ is the mass of the cylinder. Since a cylinder is symmetric about the z-axis, we must have $\mathcal{I}_{11} = \mathcal{I}_{22}$. We can calculate the moment of inertia about the x-axis by evaluating the integral

$$\mathcal{I}_{11} = \int_V \left(s^2 - x^2 \right) \rho \, dV . \tag{12.62}$$

Making the substitutions $s^2 = r^2 + z^2$ and $x^2 = r^2 \cos^2 \theta$, we have

$$\mathcal{I}_{11} = \rho \int_{-h/2}^{h/2} \int_0^{2\pi} \int_0^R (r^2 + z^2 - r^2 \cos^2 \theta) r \, dr \, d\theta \, dz$$

$$= \rho \int_{-h/2}^{h/2} \int_0^{2\pi} \int_0^R r^3 \sin^2 \theta \, dr \, d\theta \, dz + \rho \int_{-h/2}^{h/2} \int_0^{2\pi} \int_0^R z^2 r \, dr \, d\theta \, dz . \tag{12.63}$$

Evaluating the integrals for the variables r and z in the first term, and evaluating all three integrals in the second term gives us

$$\mathcal{I}_{11} = \tfrac{1}{4} \rho h R^4 \int_0^{2\pi} \sin^2 \theta \, d\theta + \tfrac{1}{12} \pi \rho h^3 R^2 . \tag{12.64}$$

Using the trigonometric identity

$$\sin^2 \theta = \frac{1 - \cos 2\theta}{2} \tag{12.65}$$

(see Appendix B, Section B.4), we can evaluate the remaining integral:

$$\int_0^{2\pi} \sin^2 \theta \, d\theta = \int_0^{2\pi} \left(\tfrac{1}{2} - \tfrac{1}{2} \cos 2\theta \right) d\theta$$

$$= \tfrac{1}{2}\theta - \tfrac{1}{4}\sin 2\theta\big]_0^{2\pi}$$

$$= \pi. \tag{12.66}$$

The moment of inertia about the x- and y-axes is therefore given by

$$\mathcal{I}_{11} = \mathcal{I}_{22} = \tfrac{1}{4}\pi\rho h R^4 + \tfrac{1}{12}\pi\rho h^3 R^2$$
$$= \tfrac{1}{4}mR^2 + \tfrac{1}{12}mh^2. \tag{12.67}$$

The product of inertia $\mathcal{I}_{12}$ is equal to the integral

$$\mathcal{I}_{12} = \int_V -xy\rho\,dV = -\rho \int_{-h/2}^{h/2}\int_0^{2\pi}\int_0^R r^3 \sin\theta\cos\theta\,dr\,d\theta\,dz. \tag{12.68}$$

Since

$$\int_0^{2\pi} \sin\theta\cos\theta\,d\theta = 0, \tag{12.69}$$

it is the case that $\mathcal{I}_{12} = \mathcal{I}_{21} = 0$. It can also be shown that all of the other products of inertia are equal to zero, so the inertia tensor $\mathcal{I}$ of a cylinder has the form

$$\mathcal{I} = \begin{bmatrix} \tfrac{1}{4}mR^2 + \tfrac{1}{12}mh^2 & 0 & 0 \\ 0 & \tfrac{1}{4}mR^2 + \tfrac{1}{12}mh^2 & 0 \\ 0 & 0 & \tfrac{1}{2}mR^2 \end{bmatrix}, \tag{12.70}$$

where $m = \rho V$ is the mass of the cylinder. ■

Nonzero products of inertia arise when we consider a solid box that rotates about an axis passing through one of its vertices. The significance of an inertia tensor that is not diagonal is discussed in Section 12.2.4.

Example 12.4. Calculate the inertia tensor of a solid box having dimensions a, b, and c that is aligned to the coordinate axes, has one vertex at the origin, and has a uniform density ρ (see Figure 12.7).

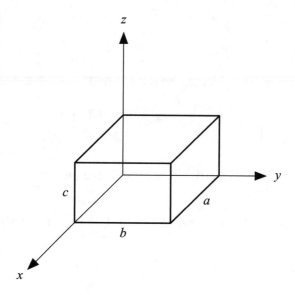

Figure 12.7 The box used in Example 12.4.

Solution. The moment of inertia about the x-axis $\mathcal{I}_{11}$ is given by the integral

$$\mathcal{I}_{11} = \int_V \left(r^2 - x^2\right)\rho\,dV$$

$$= \rho \int_0^c \int_0^b \int_0^a \left(y^2 + z^2\right) dx\,dy\,dz$$

$$= \rho a c \int_0^b y^2\,dy + \rho a b \int_0^c z^2\,dz$$

$$= \tfrac{1}{3}\rho a b^3 c + \tfrac{1}{3}\rho a b c^3$$

$$= \tfrac{1}{3}\rho a b c \left(b^2 + c^2\right). \tag{12.71}$$

The volume of the box is given by $V = abc$, so we can write the moment of inertia as

$$\mathcal{I}_{11} = \tfrac{1}{3}m\left(b^2 + c^2\right), \tag{12.72}$$

where $m = \rho V$ is the mass of the box. Similar calculations yield the moments of inertia about the y- and z-axes:

$$I_{22} = \tfrac{1}{3}m\left(a^2 + c^2\right)$$

$$I_{33} = \tfrac{1}{3}m\left(a^2 + b^2\right). \qquad (12.73)$$

The product of inertia I_{12} is given by the integral

$$I_{12} = -\int_V xy\rho\, dV$$

$$= -\rho \int_0^c \int_0^b \int_0^a xy\, dx\, dy\, dz$$

$$= -\rho c \int_0^b \int_0^a xy\, dx\, dy$$

$$= -\tfrac{1}{4}\rho a^2 b^2 c = -\tfrac{1}{4}mab. \qquad (12.74)$$

Similar calculations yield the remaining two unique products of inertia:

$$I_{13} = -\tfrac{1}{4}mac$$

$$I_{23} = -\tfrac{1}{4}mbc. \qquad (12.75)$$

The inertia tensor I of a box is therefore given by

$$I = \begin{bmatrix} \tfrac{1}{3}m\left(b^2 + c^2\right) & -\tfrac{1}{4}mab & -\tfrac{1}{4}mac \\ -\tfrac{1}{4}mab & \tfrac{1}{3}m\left(a^2 + c^2\right) & -\tfrac{1}{4}mbc \\ -\tfrac{1}{4}mac & -\tfrac{1}{4}mbc & \tfrac{1}{3}m\left(a^2 + b^2\right) \end{bmatrix}, \qquad (12.76)$$

where $m = \rho V$ is the mass of the box. ∎

12.2.4 Principal Axes of Inertia

Because the angular momentum $\mathbf{L}(t)$ and angular velocity $\boldsymbol{\omega}(t)$ are related by the equation

$$\mathbf{L}(t) = I\boldsymbol{\omega}(t), \qquad (12.77)$$

the two vectors are parallel precisely when $\boldsymbol{\omega}(t)$ is an eigenvector of the inertia tensor I. Since the inertia tensor is a symmetric matrix, it has three real eigenvalues, and the associated eigenvectors are orthogonal (see Section 2.5). The eigenvalues of the inertia tensor are called the *principal moments of inertia*, and the associated eigenvectors are called the *principal axes of inertia*. If a rigid body is rotating about one of its principal axes of inertia, then its angular momentum is given by

$$\mathbf{L}(t) = I\boldsymbol{\omega}(t), \tag{12.78}$$

where I is the principal moment of inertia associated with the principal axis.

If the inertia tensor is a diagonal matrix, as it is for a sphere and a cylinder, then the principal moments of inertia are the same as the diagonal entries, and the principal axes of inertia are simply the x-, y-, and z-axes. If the inertia tensor is not a diagonal matrix, then we must calculate its eigenvalues and eigenvectors to determine the principal axes, as demonstrated in the following example.

Example 12.5. Determine the principal axes of inertia for a solid cube having side length a that is aligned to the coordinate axes and has one vertex at the origin.

Solution. The inertia tensor $\mathcal{I}$ for a box is given by Equation (12.76). Setting the lengths in all three dimensions equal to each other produces the inertia tensor for a cube:

$$\mathcal{I} = \begin{bmatrix} \frac{2}{3}ma^2 & -\frac{1}{4}ma^2 & -\frac{1}{4}ma^2 \\ -\frac{1}{4}ma^2 & \frac{2}{3}ma^2 & -\frac{1}{4}ma^2 \\ -\frac{1}{4}ma^2 & -\frac{1}{4}ma^2 & \frac{2}{3}ma^2 \end{bmatrix}. \tag{12.79}$$

The determinant

$$\begin{vmatrix} \frac{2}{3}ma^2 - I & -\frac{1}{4}ma^2 & -\frac{1}{4}ma^2 \\ -\frac{1}{4}ma^2 & \frac{2}{3}ma^2 - I & -\frac{1}{4}ma^2 \\ -\frac{1}{4}ma^2 & -\frac{1}{4}ma^2 & \frac{2}{3}ma^2 - I \end{vmatrix} = 0, \tag{12.80}$$

yields the characteristic polynomial whose roots are the eigenvalues of $\mathcal{I}$. Since the determinant is not affected by adding a multiple of one row to another row, we can subtract the first row from the second row to simplify our calculations:

$$
\begin{vmatrix}
\frac{2}{3}ma^2 - I & -\frac{1}{4}ma^2 & -\frac{1}{4}ma^2 \\
-\frac{11}{12}ma^2 + I & \frac{11}{12}ma^2 - I & 0 \\
-\frac{1}{4}ma^2 & -\frac{1}{4}ma^2 & \frac{2}{3}ma^2 - I
\end{vmatrix} = 0. \tag{12.81}
$$

Factoring $\frac{11}{12}ma^2 - I$ out of the second row and setting $b = \frac{1}{4}ma^2$ gives us

$$
\left(\tfrac{11}{3}b - I\right)
\begin{vmatrix}
\frac{8}{3}b - I & -b & -b \\
-1 & 1 & 0 \\
-b & -b & \frac{8}{3}b - I
\end{vmatrix} = 0. \tag{12.82}
$$

Evaluating the resulting determinant, we have

$$
\begin{aligned}
0 &= \left(\tfrac{11}{3}b - I\right)\left[\left(\tfrac{8}{3}b - I\right)^2 - b\left(\tfrac{8}{3}b - I\right) - 2b^2\right] \\
&= \left(\tfrac{11}{3}b - I\right)\left(I^2 - \tfrac{13}{3}bI + \tfrac{22}{9}b^2\right) \\
&= \left(\tfrac{11}{3}b - I\right)\left(\tfrac{11}{3}b - I\right)\left(\tfrac{2}{3}b - I\right).
\end{aligned} \tag{12.83}
$$

The principal moments of inertia I_1, I_2, and I_3 are thus given by

$$
\begin{aligned}
I_1 &= \tfrac{11}{3}b = \tfrac{11}{12}ma^2 \\
I_2 &= \tfrac{11}{3}b = \tfrac{11}{12}ma^2 \\
I_3 &= \tfrac{2}{3}b = \tfrac{1}{6}ma^2.
\end{aligned} \tag{12.84}
$$

To find the principal axis of inertia corresponding to the eigenvalue I_3, we need to solve the homogeneous linear system

$$
\begin{bmatrix}
\frac{2}{3}ma^2 - I_3 & -\frac{1}{4}ma^2 & -\frac{1}{4}ma^2 \\
-\frac{1}{4}ma^2 & \frac{2}{3}ma^2 - I_3 & -\frac{1}{4}ma^2 \\
-\frac{1}{4}ma^2 & -\frac{1}{4}ma^2 & \frac{2}{3}ma^2 - I_3
\end{bmatrix}
\begin{bmatrix}
x \\
y \\
z
\end{bmatrix} = \mathbf{0}. \tag{12.85}
$$

Again using the constant $b = \frac{1}{4}ma^2$ and substituting the value $I_3 = \frac{2}{3}b$, we have

$$\begin{bmatrix} 2b & -b & -b \\ -b & 2b & -b \\ -b & -b & 2b \end{bmatrix} \begin{bmatrix} x \\ y \\ z \end{bmatrix} = \mathbf{0}. \tag{12.86}$$

The reduced form of this system is

$$\begin{bmatrix} 1 & 0 & -1 \\ 0 & 1 & -1 \\ 0 & 0 & 0 \end{bmatrix} \begin{bmatrix} x \\ y \\ z \end{bmatrix} = \mathbf{0}, \tag{12.87}$$

and thus $x = y = z$. This tells us that the vector $\langle 1,1,1 \rangle$, a diagonal of the cube, represents the principal axis corresponding to the principal moment of inertia I_3. The principal axes corresponding to the eigenvalues I_1 and I_2 are found by solving the system

$$\begin{bmatrix} \frac{8}{3}b - I_1 & -b & -b \\ -b & \frac{8}{3}b - I_1 & -b \\ -b & -b & \frac{8}{3}b - I_1 \end{bmatrix} \begin{bmatrix} x \\ y \\ z \end{bmatrix} = \mathbf{0}. \tag{12.88}$$

Every entry of this matrix is the same, so the reduced form of the system is

$$\begin{bmatrix} 1 & 1 & 1 \\ 0 & 0 & 0 \\ 0 & 0 & 0 \end{bmatrix} \begin{bmatrix} x \\ y \\ z \end{bmatrix} = \mathbf{0}. \tag{12.89}$$

Therefore, the y- and z-components of each principal axis may be chosen arbitrarily (but not such that both are zero). The value of x is then given by $x = -y - z$. Any vector of the form $\langle -y - z, y, z \rangle$ is perpendicular to the vector $\langle 1,1,1 \rangle$, so the principal axes corresponding to the principal moments of inertia given by I_1 and I_2 can be any orthogonal pair in the plane perpendicular to the cube's diagonal. ∎

If a rigid body is not rotating about one of its principal axes, then the angular velocity vector $\boldsymbol{\omega}(t)$ and the angular momentum vector $\mathbf{L}(t)$ are not parallel. In this situation, the vector $\mathbf{L}(t)$ rotates about the axis $\boldsymbol{\omega}(t)$ at the rate

$$\dot{\mathbf{L}}(t) = \boldsymbol{\omega}(t) \times \mathbf{L}(t) \neq 0. \tag{12.90}$$

An angular acceleration results that changes the axis of rotation, an effect called *precession*. Since $\dot{\mathbf{L}}(t) = \mathcal{I}\boldsymbol{\alpha}(t)$, the angular acceleration $\boldsymbol{\alpha}(t)$ is given by

$$\boldsymbol{\alpha}(t) = \mathcal{I}^{-1}\dot{\mathbf{L}}(t) = \mathcal{I}^{-1}\left[\boldsymbol{\omega}(t) \times \mathbf{L}(t)\right]. \tag{12.91}$$

To counter this angular acceleration and prevent the axis of rotation from changing, a torque equal in magnitude to $\boldsymbol{\omega}(t) \times \mathbf{L}(t)$ must be applied in the opposite direction. Therefore, the motion of a rotating rigid body can be described by the equation

$$\sum_{i=1}^{N} \boldsymbol{\tau}_i(t) - \boldsymbol{\omega}(t) \times \mathbf{L}(t) = \mathcal{I}\boldsymbol{\alpha}(t) = \mathcal{I}\ddot{\boldsymbol{\theta}}(t), \tag{12.92}$$

where $\boldsymbol{\tau}_1, \boldsymbol{\tau}_2, \ldots, \boldsymbol{\tau}_N$ represent the external torques acting on the body. Equation (12.92) is the rotational analog of Equation (11.9).

12.3 Oscillatory Motion

The motion of an object is *oscillatory* if it repeats over a period of time by moving back and forth through the same region of space. Such behavior is often caused by a restoring force that may be constant or may act on a object with greater magnitude as the object moves further away from some equilibrium position. We examine oscillatory motion in this chapter because it shares some characteristics with rotational motion, such as angular velocity. The motion of a pendulum, discussed in Section 12.3.2, is an example of an object that rotates about a point with an oscillatory nature.

12.3.1 Spring Motion

Oscillatory motion is exhibited by an object having mass m that is attached to the end of a spring whose natural length is d (see Figure 12.8). Suppose that the spring is aligned to the z-axis and that one end is attached to an immovable object at $z = d$. Let the mass be attached to the other end, which coincides with the origin. Ignoring gravity for the moment, when the spring is stretched or compressed so that its length is greater than or less than d, a restoring force is exerted by the spring that is proportional to the displacement of the mass from its natural resting position. If the position of the mass along the z-axis is z, then the restoring force F in that direction is given by

$$F = -kz. \tag{12.93}$$

This formula is known as *Hooke's law*. The constant k is a property of the spring corresponding to its stiffness. A larger value of k means that more work is required to move the mass attached to the end of the spring.

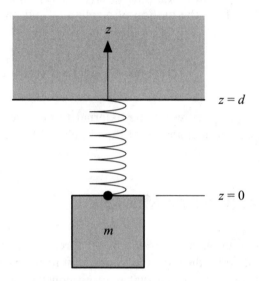

Figure 12.8 A mass attached to the end of a spring.

The position of a mass attached to the end of a spring can be determined as a function of time by examining the differential equation

$$m\ddot{z}(t) = -kz(t). \tag{12.94}$$

The general solution to this equation is

$$z(t) = A\sin \omega t + B\cos \omega t, \tag{12.95}$$

where $\omega = \sqrt{k/m}$ is called the *angular frequency* of the oscillations, measured in radians per unit time. The frequency f corresponding to the number of oscillations per unit time, measured in hertz (Hz) when the unit of time is the second, is related to the angular frequency by the equation

$$f = \frac{\omega}{2\pi}. \tag{12.96}$$

The period P of the oscillations is equal to the time that passes between each repetition of the motion and is given by the reciprocal of the frequency:

$$P = \frac{2\pi}{\omega} = 2\pi\sqrt{\frac{m}{k}}. \tag{12.97}$$

The constants A and B in Equation (12.95) must be determined by imposing initial conditions. Suppose that the initial position of the mass is z_0 and the initial velocity of the mass is v_0. Since

$$z(0) = B$$
$$\dot{z}(0) = A\omega, \tag{12.98}$$

we can easily deduce

$$A = \frac{v_0}{\omega}$$
$$B = z_0. \tag{12.99}$$

As discussed in Section 11.2.1, we may express Equation (12.95) in the form

$$z(t) = C\sin(\omega t + \delta), \tag{12.100}$$

where

$$C = \sqrt{\frac{v_0^2}{\omega^2} + z_0^2}$$
$$\delta = \sin^{-1}\frac{z_0}{C}. \tag{12.101}$$

The constant C represents the *amplitude* of the oscillations and corresponds to the largest distance that the mass is ever displaced from its equilibrium position. The constant δ represents the *phase* of the oscillations and corresponds to the initial position of the mass.

Example 12.6. Determine the frequency and amplitude of a 2-kg mass attached to a spring having a restoring constant of $k = 3\,\text{kg/s}^2$. Suppose that the mass was previously being pulled downward and that it is released at time $t = 0$ with an initial displacement of $z_0 = -4$ m and an initial velocity of $v_0 = -1$ m/s.

Solution. The angular frequency ω is given by

$$\omega = \sqrt{\frac{k}{m}} = \frac{\sqrt{6}}{2} \text{ rad/s}. \tag{12.102}$$

Dividing by 2π radians gives us the frequency f in oscillations per second:

$$f = \frac{\omega}{2\pi} = \frac{\sqrt{6}}{4\pi} \approx 0.195 \text{ Hz}. \tag{12.103}$$

The amplitude C of the oscillations can be found by using Equation (12.101):

$$C = \sqrt{\frac{v_0^2}{\omega^2} + z_0^2} = \frac{5\sqrt{6}}{3} \approx 4.08 \text{ m. } \blacksquare \tag{12.104}$$

Suppose that a mass m attached to the end of a vertical spring is now acted upon by gravity. Adding the constant downward gravitational force $-mg$ to Equation (12.94) gives us

$$m\ddot{z}(t) = -kz(t) - mg. \tag{12.105}$$

The restoring force of the spring and the gravitational force are balanced when they are equal in magnitude and act in opposite directions. Thus, the mass experiences no net force when

$$-kz(t) = mg. \tag{12.106}$$

Solving for $z(t)$ gives us the equilibrium position of the hanging mass:

$$z(t) = -\frac{mg}{k}. \tag{12.107}$$

If the mass lies at the position $z = -mg/k$ and has no velocity, then it will never move.

Equation (12.107) is in fact a particular solution to Equation (12.105). Adding this to the general solution to the homogeneous problem given by Equation (12.95), we have

$$z(t) = A\sin \omega t + B\cos \omega t - \frac{mg}{k}. \tag{12.108}$$

Imposing the same initial conditions as before, $z(0) = z_0$ and $\dot{z}(0) = v_0$, produces the same value for A but a different value for B:

$$A = \frac{v_0}{\omega}$$

$$B = z_0 + \frac{mg}{k}. \tag{12.109}$$

When we write Equation (12.108) in the form

$$z(t) = C\sin(\omega t + \delta) - \frac{mg}{k}, \tag{12.110}$$

the amplitude C and phase δ are given by Equation (12.101) with the modification that z_0 is replaced by $z_0 + mg/k$. The influence of gravity has the effect of increasing the oscillation amplitude and advancing the phase angle corresponding to the initial displacement.

12.3.2 Pendulum Motion

Suppose that an object of mass m under the influence of gravity is attached to a massless rod of length L hanging from a fixed point coinciding with the origin as shown in Figure 12.9. We assume that the rod is able to pivot freely about its fixed end and that the mass is able to move in the x-z plane. Let I be the moment of inertia of the object with respect to the y-axis (about which the mass rotates). If all of the mass is concentrated at a single point, then $I = mL^2$.

Let $\mathbf{r}(t)$ represent the position of the object. Gravity pulls downward on the object with the force $m\mathbf{g}$, exerting a torque $\boldsymbol{\tau}(t)$ given by

$$\boldsymbol{\tau}(t) = \mathbf{r}(t) \times m\mathbf{g}. \tag{12.111}$$

The resulting angular acceleration $\boldsymbol{\alpha}(t)$ is

$$\boldsymbol{\alpha}(t) = \frac{\boldsymbol{\tau}(t)}{I} = \frac{\mathbf{r}(t) \times m\mathbf{g}}{I}. \tag{12.112}$$

Since $\boldsymbol{\tau}(t)$ and $\boldsymbol{\alpha}(t)$ are always perpendicular to the x-z plane in which the pendulum rotates, we can write them as scalar quantities $\tau(t)$ and $\alpha(t)$. Equation (12.112) can then be written as

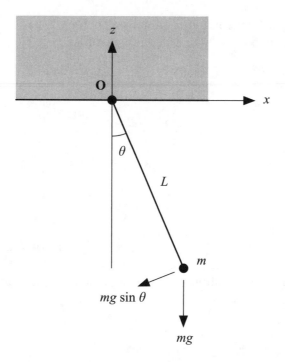

Figure 12.9 The plane pendulum.

$$\alpha(t) = \ddot{\theta}(t) = -\frac{mgL}{I}\sin\theta(t), \qquad (12.113)$$

where $\theta(t)$ is the counterclockwise angle between the pendulum and the negative z-axis.

Equation (12.113) cannot be solved analytically for the function $\theta(t)$ due to the presence of the sine function. We can, however, transform the equation into a form that can be solved by replacing $\sin\theta(t)$ with the first term of its power series:

$$\ddot{\theta}(t) = -\frac{mgL}{I}\theta(t). \qquad (12.114)$$

Equation (12.114) approximates the motion of a pendulum for which the angle $\theta(t)$ is always small. The solution to Equation (12.114) is given by

$$\theta(t) = A\sin(\omega t + \delta), \qquad (12.115)$$

where the angular frequency ω is

$$\omega = \sqrt{\frac{mgL}{I}}, \tag{12.116}$$

and the constants A and δ are determined by initial conditions. The period P of the oscillations is given by

$$P = \frac{2\pi}{\omega} = 2\pi\sqrt{\frac{I}{mgL}}. \tag{12.117}$$

For a point mass, we have

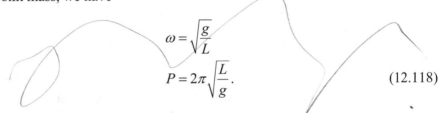

$$\omega = \sqrt{\frac{g}{L}}$$

$$P = 2\pi\sqrt{\frac{L}{g}}. \tag{12.118}$$

Chapter 12 Summary

Centrifugal Force

The centrifugal force experienced by an object in a rotating environment is given by

$$\mathbf{F}_{\text{centrifugal}} = -m\big(\boldsymbol{\omega}(t)\times[\boldsymbol{\omega}(t)\times\mathbf{r}(t)]\big),$$

where $\boldsymbol{\omega}(t)$ is the angular velocity and $\mathbf{r}(t)$ is the position of the object relative to an origin through which the axis of rotation passes. In the case that $\boldsymbol{\omega}(t)$ and $\mathbf{r}(t)$ are perpendicular, the centrifugal force can be expressed as the scalar

$$F_{\text{centrifugal}} = m\omega^2 r = \frac{mv^2}{r}.$$

Coriolis Force

The Coriolis force experienced by an object in a rotating environment is given by

$$\mathbf{F}_{\text{Coriolis}} = -2m\boldsymbol{\omega}(t)\times\mathbf{v}_r(t),$$

where $\mathbf{v}_r(t)$ is the velocity of the object relative to the rotating reference frame.

Center of Mass

The center of mass $\mathbf{C}$ of a solid object whose density at the point $\mathbf{r}$ is $\rho(\mathbf{r})$ is given by

$$\mathbf{C} = \frac{1}{M} \int_V \mathbf{r}\rho(\mathbf{r})\,dV,$$

where M is the total mass of the object.

Angular Momentum

The angular momentum $\mathbf{L}(t)$ of a particle is given by

$$\mathbf{L}(t) = \mathbf{r}(t) \times \mathbf{p}(t),$$

where $\mathbf{r}(t)$ is the position of the object relative to an origin through which the axis of rotation passes, and $\mathbf{p}(t) = m\mathbf{v}(t)$ is the linear momentum of the particle.

Torque

The torque $\boldsymbol{\tau}(t)$ acting on a particle is given by

$$\boldsymbol{\tau}(t) = \mathbf{r}(t) \times \mathbf{F}(t),$$

where $\mathbf{F}(t)$ is the force applied at the position $\mathbf{r}(t)$. The net torque acting on a particle is equal to the time rate of change of its angular momentum:

$$\dot{\mathbf{L}}(t) = \boldsymbol{\tau}(t).$$

Inertia Tensor

The (i, j) entry of the inertia tensor $\mathcal{I}$ of a rigid body is given by

$$\mathcal{I}_{ij} = \int_V \left(\delta_{ij}r^2 - r_i r_j\right)\rho(\mathbf{r})\,dV,$$

where $\rho(\mathbf{r})$ is the density at the point $\mathbf{r}$.

The inertia tensor relates the angular velocity to the angular momentum and the angular acceleration to the torque:

$$\mathbf{L}(t) = \mathcal{I}\boldsymbol{\omega}(t)$$
$$\boldsymbol{\tau}(t) = \mathcal{I}\boldsymbol{\alpha}(t).$$

Spring Motion

The position $z(t)$ of a mass m attached to oscillating spring having restoration constant k is given by

$$z(t) = C\sin(\omega t + \delta),$$

where

$$C = \sqrt{\frac{mv_0^2}{k} + z_0^2}$$

$$\delta = \sin^{-1}\frac{z_0}{C},$$

z_0 is the initial position, and v_0 is the initial velocity.

Pendulum Motion

A pendulum consisting of a mass m suspended from a rod of length L obeys the equation of motion

$$\alpha(t) = \ddot{\theta}(t) = -\frac{mgL}{I}\sin\theta(t),$$

where $\theta(t)$ is the angle formed with the vertical direction, and I is the moment of inertia of the mass. Small oscillations of the pendulum have an angular frequency ω given by

$$\omega = \sqrt{\frac{mgL}{I}}.$$

Exercises for Chapter 12

1. An ant is walking radially outward with a velocity v on the surface of a disk rotating counterclockwise with an angular velocity ω. At a distance r from the center of the disk, what is the total magnitude F of the forces experienced by the ant?

2. Suppose that a block of mass m is resting on the surface of a rotating disk at a distance r from the axis of rotation. If the coefficient of static friction at

the surface is μ_S, determine the angular velocity at which the disk must rotate to cause the block to begin sliding outward.

3. Calculate the center of mass $\mathbf{C}$ of a cylinder of radius R and height h whose base is resting at the origin on the x-y plane if the density is given by $\rho(\mathbf{r}) = 1 + r_z / h$.

4. Calculate the moment of inertia about the z-axis for the annular cylinder of inner radius R_1, outer radius R_2, and height h shown in Figure 12.10. Let m be the mass of the cylinder, and assume a uniform density ρ.

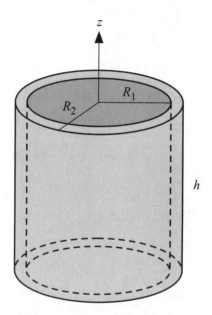

Figure 12.10 The annular cylinder used in Exercise 4.

5. Calculate the inertia tensor about the center of mass of a box having dimensions a, b, and c in the x-, y-, and z-directions. Let m be the mass of the box and assume a uniform density ρ.

6. Suppose that an object of mass m is hanging from a rope of negligible mass that is wrapped around a cylindrical spool many times (see Figure 12.11). If the cylinder has mass M and radius R, determine at what rate a the object accelerates downward under the influence of gravity. Assume that the rope does not slip as it unwinds from the spool. [*Hint.* As gravity pulls on the ob-

ject, it creates a tension T in the rope that is counteracted by the cylinder, so the force equation is $ma = mg - T$. The tension T exerts a torque on the cylinder that induces an angular acceleration α. Use the fact that $a = R\alpha$.]

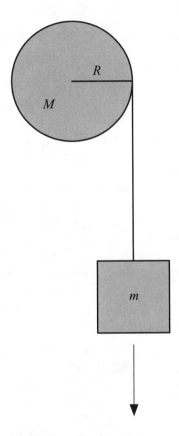

Figure 12.11 The system used in Exercise 6.

7. A spherical ball of mass m and radius R is placed on an incline that forms an angle θ with the ground (see Figure 12.12). The coefficient of static friction at the surface is μ_s. If the ball rolls down the incline under the influence of gravity without slipping, determine its acceleration a. [*Hint.* Two forces are acting on the ball, gravity and the frictional force, whose sum is equal to ma. The frictional force also exerts torque on the ball, inducing an angular acceleration α. Use the fact that $a = R\alpha$ as the ball rolls down the incline.]

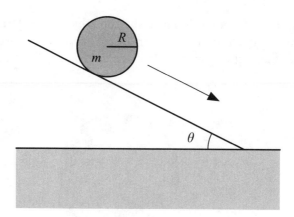

Figure 12.12 The ball used in Exercise 7.

8. Suppose that a box of uniform density having mass m is resting on the ground where the coefficient of static friction is μ_S (see Figure 12.13). The box has a square base of length and width d, and the box's height is h. Determine the minimum height z at which a force $F < \mu_S mg$ applied directly to the horizontal center of a side of the box would cause the box to begin toppling over. [*Hint.* Equate the torques induced by the pull of gravity on the center of mass and the force F about the bottom edge on the side opposite that where the force is applied.]

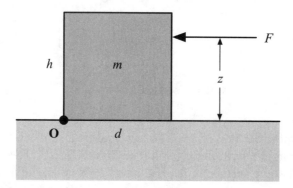

Figure 12.13 The box used in Exercise 8.

Chapter 13

Fluid Simulation

The worlds presented by many games contain regions covered by a fluid surface. Whether it be a pool of water, a vat of deadly acid, or a pit of molten lava, we would like the fluid surface to behave in a physically realistic manner. To accomplish this, we need to be able to model the way in which disturbances propagate through the fluid as waves. In this chapter, we introduce the well-known wave equation and apply it to real-time simulation of fluid surfaces.

13.1 The Wave Equation

The wave equation is a partial differential equation that describes the motion of each point on a one-dimensional string or a two-dimensional surface experiencing a constant tension. We can derive the one-dimensional wave equation by considering a flexible elastic string that is tightly bound between two fixed endpoints lying on the x-axis (see Figure 13.1). We assume that the string has a constant linear density (mass per unit length) ρ and experiences a constant tension T that acts in the tangential direction.

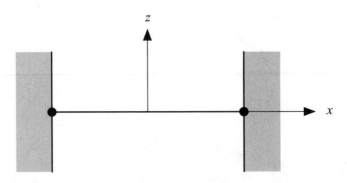

Figure 13.1 A string having linear density ρ is tightly bound between two endpoints and experiences a constant tension T.

Let the function $z(x,t)$ represent the vertical displacement of the string at the horizontal position x and at time t. When the string is displaced in the z direction, the tension produces a force at each point along the string that results in an acceleration. Newton's second law dictates that the net force $\mathbf{F}(x,t)$ experienced by a small segment of the string lying between $x = s$ and $x = s + \Delta x$ at any time t is equal to the product of its mass and its acceleration $\mathbf{a}(x,t)$. Since the linear density of the string is ρ, the mass of the segment is equal to $\rho \Delta x$, and we have

$$\mathbf{a}(x,t) = \frac{\mathbf{F}(x,t)}{\rho \Delta x}. \tag{13.1}$$

As shown in Figure 13.2, we can divide the force experienced by each endpoint of the segment lying between $x = s$ and $x = s + \Delta x$ into horizontal and vertical components $H(x,t)$ and $V(x,t)$. Let θ represent the angle between the tangent to the string and the x-axis at the endpoint where $x = s$. Since the tension T acts in the tangential direction, the horizontal component $H(s,t)$ and vertical component $V(s,t)$ are given by

$$H(s,t) = T \cos \theta$$
$$V(s,t) = T \sin \theta. \tag{13.2}$$

Let $\theta + \Delta \theta$ represent the angle between the tangent to the string and the x-axis at the endpoint where $x = s + \Delta x$. The horizontal component $H(s + \Delta x, t)$ and vertical component $V(s + \Delta x, t)$ of the tension experienced at this endpoint are given by

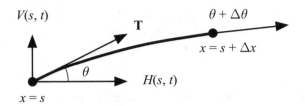

Figure 13.2 The forces experienced at each endpoint of the segment lying between $x = s$ and $x = s + \Delta x$ can be divided into horizontal and vertical components.

$$H(s + \Delta x, t) = T\cos(\theta + \Delta\theta)$$
$$V(s + \Delta x, t) = T\sin(\theta + \Delta\theta). \tag{13.3}$$

For small motions, we assume that the net horizontal force is zero so that the segment accelerates only in the vertical direction. Thus, for the segment lying between $x = s$ and $x = s + \Delta x$, we require that

$$H(s + \Delta x, t) - H(s, t) = 0. \tag{13.4}$$

Consequently, the function H is independent of x, so we can write $H(t)$ instead of $H(x, t)$.

The net vertical force acting on the segment lying between $x = s$ and $x = s + \Delta x$ produces an acceleration that is given by the z-component of Equation (13.1). Since the vertical acceleration is equal to the second derivative of the position function $z(x, t)$, we have

$$a_z(s, t) = \frac{\partial^2}{\partial t^2} z(s, t) = \frac{V(s + \Delta x, t) - V(s, t)}{\rho \Delta x}. \tag{13.5}$$

Multiplying both sides by the density ρ and taking the limit as Δx approaches zero gives us

$$\rho \frac{\partial^2}{\partial t^2} z(s, t) = \lim_{\Delta x \to 0} \frac{V(s + \Delta x, t) - V(s, t)}{\Delta x}. \tag{13.6}$$

The right side of Equation (13.6) is equal to the definition of the partial derivative of V with respect to x evaluated at s, so we can rewrite it as

$$\rho \frac{\partial^2}{\partial t^2} z(s, t) = \frac{\partial}{\partial x} V(s, t). \tag{13.7}$$

Using the values of $H(t)$ and $V(s,t)$ given by Equation (13.2), we can express $V(s,t)$ in terms of $H(t)$ as follows.

$$V(s,t) = H(t)\tan\theta \tag{13.8}$$

Since θ is the angle formed between the tangent to the string and the x-axis, $\tan\theta$ is equal to the slope of the function $z(x,t)$ at s. Therefore,

$$V(s,t) = H(t)\frac{\partial}{\partial x}z(s,t), \tag{13.9}$$

and Equation (13.7) becomes

$$\rho\frac{\partial^2}{\partial t^2}z(s,t) = \frac{\partial}{\partial x}\left[H(t)\frac{\partial}{\partial x}z(s,t)\right]. \tag{13.10}$$

Since $H(t)$ does not depend on x, we can write

$$\rho\frac{\partial^2}{\partial t^2}z(s,t) = H(t)\frac{\partial^2}{\partial x^2}z(s,t). \tag{13.11}$$

For small motions, $\cos\theta$ is close to 1, so we approximate $H(t)$ with the tension T. Letting $c^2 = T/\rho$, we now arrive at the one-dimensional wave equation:

$$\frac{\partial^2 z}{\partial t^2} = c^2\frac{\partial^2 z}{\partial x^2}. \tag{13.12}$$

The two-dimensional wave equation is obtained by adding a second spatial term to Equation (13.12) as follows.

$$\frac{\partial^2 z}{\partial t^2} = c^2\left(\frac{\partial^2 z}{\partial x^2} + \frac{\partial^2 z}{\partial y^2}\right) \tag{13.13}$$

The constant c has dimensions of distance per unit time and thus represents a velocity. A fact that we do not prove here is that c is actually the velocity at which waves propagate along a string or through a surface. This makes sense since the wave speed increases with tension experienced by the medium and decreases with the density of the medium.

Equation (13.13) does not account for any forces other than the surface tension. Thus, the average amplitude of the waves on the surface never diminishes as it does for a real-world fluid. We can add a viscous damping force to the equation by introducing a force that acts in the direction opposite that of the velocity of a point on the surface to obtain

$$\frac{\partial^2 z}{\partial t^2} = c^2 \left(\frac{\partial^2 z}{\partial x^2} + \frac{\partial^2 z}{\partial y^2} \right) - \mu \frac{\partial z}{\partial t}, \tag{13.14}$$

where the nonnegative constant μ represents the viscosity of the fluid. The value of μ generally controls how long it takes for waves on a surface to calm down. A small value of μ allows waves to exist for a long time, as with water, but a large value of μ causes waves to diminish rapidly, as for a thick oil.

13.2 Approximating Derivatives

The two-dimensional wave equation with viscous damping given by Equation (13.14) can be solved analytically using separation of variables. The solution, however, is quite complex and would require a significant amount of computation for a real-time simulation. We instead choose to use a numerical technique to model the propagation of waves over a fluid surface.

Suppose that our fluid surface is represented by a triangle mesh whose vertices are arranged on an $n \times m$ regular grid as shown in Figure 13.3. Let d be the distance between adjacent vertices in both the x- and y-directions, and let t be the time interval between consecutive calculations of the fluid's state. We denote the displacement of a vertex in the mesh by $z(i, j, k)$, where i and j are integers satisfying $0 \le i < n$ and $0 \le j < m$ that represent the spatial coordinates, and k is a nonnegative integer that represents the temporal coordinate. That is, $z(i, j, k)$ is equal to the displacement of the vertex lying at the point $\langle id, jd \rangle$ at the time kt.

We impose the boundary condition that the vertices lying on the edge of the surface are fixed at a displacement of zero. The displacement of the interior points can be calculated by using Equation (13.14) and approximating the derivatives using the differences in the displacements of adjacent vertices. As illustrated in Figure 13.4, we can approximate the x-axis–aligned tangent to the surface at a vertex having coordinates (i, j) by calculating the average ratio of Δz to Δx between that vertex and its immediate neighbors in the x direction. Using this technique and the fact that $\Delta x = d$, we define the derivative $\partial z / \partial x$ as follows.

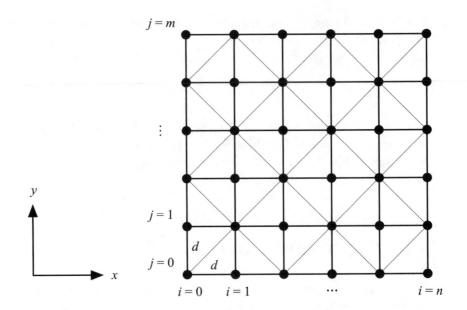

Figure 13.3 A fluid surface is represented by a triangle mesh whose vertices are arranged on an $n \times m$ regular grid.

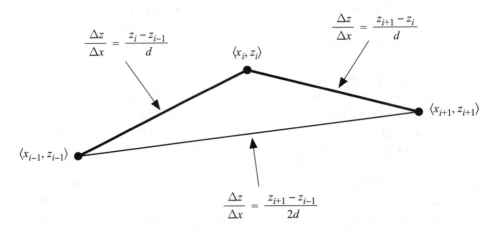

Figure 13.4 The x-axis aligned tangent to the surface can be approximated by calculating the average ratio of Δz to Δx between that vertex and its immediate neighbors.

$$\frac{\partial}{\partial x}z(i,j,k) = \frac{\dfrac{z(i,j,k)-z(i-1,j,k)}{d} + \dfrac{z(i+1,j,k)-z(i,j,k)}{d}}{2}$$

$$= \frac{z(i+1,j,k)-z(i-1,j,k)}{2d} \tag{13.15}$$

We define the derivative $\partial z/\partial y$ at the vertex having coordinates (i,j) in a similar manner by calculating the average ratio of Δz to Δy between that vertex and its immediate neighbors in the y-direction. As with the x-direction, $\Delta y = d$, so we have

$$\frac{\partial}{\partial y}z(i,j,k) = \frac{z(i,j+1,k)-z(i,j-1,k)}{2d}. \tag{13.16}$$

We can define the temporal derivative $\partial z/\partial t$ by calculating the average difference in the displacement of a vertex between the current time and the previous and succeeding times at which the displacement is evaluated. The time between evaluations is t, so the average ratio of Δz to Δt is given by

$$\frac{\partial}{\partial t}z(i,j,k) = \frac{z(i,j,k+1)-z(i,j,k-1)}{2t}. \tag{13.17}$$

Second derivatives can be approximated by employing the same method used to approximate the first derivatives. This is done by calculating the average ratios of the differences between the first derivatives to one of the spatial or temporal coordinates. To illustrate, we consider the second derivative at the vertex having coordinates (i,j) with respect to x. The average difference $\Delta(\partial z/\partial x)$ between first derivatives at this vertex is given by

$$\Delta\left[\frac{\partial}{\partial x}z(i,j,k)\right] = \frac{\dfrac{\partial}{\partial x}z(i+1,j,k)-\dfrac{\partial}{\partial x}z(i-1,j,k)}{2}. \tag{13.18}$$

Substituting the value given by Equation (13.15) for the derivatives with respect to x, we have the following.

$$\Delta\left[\frac{\partial}{\partial x}z(i,j,k)\right] = \frac{\dfrac{z(i+2,j,k)-z(i,j,k)}{2d} - \dfrac{z(i,j,k)-z(i-2,j,k)}{2d}}{2}$$

$$= \frac{z(i+2,j,k)-2z(i,j,k)+z(i-2,j,k)}{4d} \tag{13.19}$$

Dividing by d gives us the ratio of $\Delta(\partial z / \partial x)$ to Δx, which we use to define the second derivative:

$$\frac{\partial^2}{\partial x^2} z(i,j,k) = \frac{z(i+2,j,k) - 2z(i,j,k) + z(i-2,j,k)}{4d^2}. \qquad (13.20)$$

This formula requires that we use the displacements of neighbors lying two vertices away from the vertex where we wish to calculate the second derivative. Fortunately, the adjacent neighbors are not used, so we can scale the coordinate system about the vertex lying at (i,j) by one-half. Using the nearest neighbors and cutting the distance Δx in half, we obtain the following equivalent formula for the second derivative with respect to x.

$$\frac{\partial^2}{\partial x^2} z(i,j,k) = \frac{z(i+1,j,k) - 2z(i,j,k) + z(i-1,j,k)}{d^2} \qquad (13.21)$$

The following similar formulas give the second derivatives with respect to the spatial coordinate y and the temporal coordinate t.

$$\frac{\partial^2}{\partial y^2} z(i,j,k) = \frac{z(i,j+1,k) - 2z(i,j,k) + z(i,j-1,k)}{d^2} \qquad (13.22)$$

$$\frac{\partial^2}{\partial t^2} z(i,j,k) = \frac{z(i,j,k+1) - 2z(i,j,k) + z(i,j,k-1)}{t^2} \qquad (13.23)$$

13.3 Evaluating Surface Displacement

Using the first derivative with respect to t given by Equation (13.17) and the second derivatives given by Equations (13.21), (13.22), and (13.23), the two-dimensional wave equation with viscous damping given by Equation (13.14) can be written as follows for the vertex having coordinates (i,j).

$$\frac{z(i,j,k+1)-2z(i,j,k)+z(i,j,k-1)}{t^2} =$$

$$c^2 \frac{z(i+1,j,k)-2z(i,j,k)+z(i-1,j,k)}{d^2}$$

$$+c^2 \frac{z(i,j+1,k)-2z(i,j,k)+z(i,j-1,k)}{d^2}$$

$$-\mu \frac{z(i,j,k+1)-z(i,j,k-1)}{2t} \tag{13.24}$$

We would like to be able to determine the future displacement $z(i,j,k+1)$ occurring after the time interval t has passed, given that we already know the current displacement $z(i,j,k)$ and the previous displacement $z(i,j,k-1)$. Solving Equation (13.24) for $z(i,j,k+1)$ yields

$$z(i,j,k+1) = \frac{4-8c^2t^2/d^2}{\mu t + 2} z(i,j,k) + \frac{\mu t - 2}{\mu t + 2} z(i,j,k-1)$$

$$+\frac{2c^2t^2/d^2}{\mu t + 2}[z(i+1,j,k)+z(i-1,j,k)+z(i,j+1,k)+z(i,j-1,k)], \tag{13.25}$$

which provides exactly what we need. The constants preceding each term can be precomputed, leaving only three multiplications and four additions to be calculated at each vertex in the mesh.

If the wave velocity c is too fast, or the time interval t is too long, then successive iterations of Equation (13.25) cause the displacements to diverge toward infinity. To keep the displacements finite, we need to determine the exact conditions under which Equation (13.25) is stable. These conditions are revealed when we impose the requirement that any vertex displaced and held away from an otherwise flat surface should move toward the surface when released.

Suppose that we have an $n \times m$ array of vertices for which $z(i,j,0)=0$ and $z(i,j,1)=0$ for every vertex except the one having coordinates (i_0,j_0). Let the vertex at (i_0,j_0) be held in place such that $z(i_0,j_0,0)=h$ and $z(i_0,j_0,1)=h$, where h is a nonzero displacement. Now suppose that the vertex at (i_0,j_0) is released at time $2t$. When $z(i_0,j_0,2)$ is evaluated, the third term of Equation (13.25) is zero, so we have

$$z(i_0,j_0,2) = \frac{4-8c^2t^2/d^2}{\mu t + 2} z(i_0,j_0,1) + \frac{\mu t - 2}{\mu t + 2} z(i_0,j_0,0)$$

$$= \frac{2-8c^2t^2/d^2 + \mu t}{\mu t + 2} h. \tag{13.26}$$

For the vertex to move toward the surrounding flat surface, its displacement must be smaller at time $2t$ than it was at time t. Thus, we must require that

$$|z(i_0, j_0, 2)| < |z(i_0, j_0, 1)| = |h|. \tag{13.27}$$

Plugging in the value given by Equation (13.26) for $z(i_0, j_0, 2)$, we have

$$\left| \frac{2 - 8c^2 t^2 / d^2 + \mu t}{\mu t + 2} \right| |h| < |h|. \tag{13.28}$$

Thus,

$$-1 < \frac{2 - 8c^2 t^2 / d^2 + \mu t}{\mu t + 2} < 1. \tag{13.29}$$

Solving for c, we find

$$0 < c < \frac{d}{2t} \sqrt{\mu t + 2}. \tag{13.30}$$

This tells us that for any given distance d between adjacent vertices and any time interval t between consecutive iterations of Equation (13.25), the wave velocity c must be less than the maximum value imposed by Equation (13.30).

Alternatively, we may calculate a maximum time interval t given the distance d and the wave velocity c. Multiplying both sides of Equation (13.29) by $-(\mu t + 2)$ and simplifying yields

$$0 < \frac{4c^2}{d^2} t^2 < \mu t + 2. \tag{13.31}$$

The left inequality simply requires that $t > 0$, a condition that we would naturally impose in any case. The right inequality yields the quadratic expression

$$\frac{4c^2}{d^2} t^2 - \mu t - 2 < 0. \tag{13.32}$$

Using the quadratic equation, the roots of the polynomial are given by

$$t = \frac{\mu \pm \sqrt{\mu^2 + 32c^2 / d^2}}{8c^2 / d^2}. \tag{13.33}$$

Since the coefficient of the quadratic term in Equation (13.32) is positive, the corresponding parabola is concave upward, and the polynomial is therefore negative when t lies in between the two roots. The value under the radical in Equation (13.33) is larger than μ, so the lesser of the two roots is negative and can be discarded. We can now express the restriction on the time interval t as

$$0 < t < \frac{\mu + \sqrt{\mu^2 + 32c^2/d^2}}{8c^2/d^2}. \tag{13.34}$$

Using a value for the wave velocity c falling outside the range given by Equation (13.30) or a value for the time interval t falling outside the range given by Equation (13.34) results in an exponential explosion of the vertex displacements.

13.4 Implementation

An implementation of Equation (13.25) for a fluid surface requires that we store two buffers, each containing an $n \times m$ array of vertex positions. At each frame, one of the buffers contains the current vertex positions, and the other buffer contains the previous vertex positions. When we evaluate new displacements, we replace each vertex in the buffer containing the previous vertex positions with the new vertex position. The buffer containing the current vertex positions then becomes the buffer containing the previous vertex positions, so we actually alternate which buffer is used to render each frame.

To perform lighting calculations, we need to know the correct normal vector at each vertex and possibly the correct tangent vector at each vertex. At the vertex having coordinates (i, j), the (unnormalized) x-axis–aligned tangent vector $\mathbf{T}$ and y-axis–aligned tangent vector $\mathbf{B}$ are given by

$$\mathbf{T} = \left\langle 1, 0, \frac{\partial}{\partial x} z(i, j, k) \right\rangle$$

$$\mathbf{B} = \left\langle 0, 1, \frac{\partial}{\partial y} z(i, j, k) \right\rangle. \tag{13.35}$$

Substituting the formulas for the partial derivatives given by Equations (13.15) and (13.16), we have

$$\mathbf{T} = \left\langle 1, 0, \frac{z(i+1, j, k) - z(i-1, j, k)}{2d} \right\rangle$$

$$\mathbf{B} = \left\langle 0, 1, \frac{z(i, j+1, k) - z(i, j-1, k)}{2d} \right\rangle. \qquad (13.36)$$

The (also unnormalized) normal vector $\mathbf{N}$ is then simply given by $\mathbf{N} = \mathbf{T} \times \mathbf{B}$, which can be expressed as follows.

$$\mathbf{N} = \begin{vmatrix} \mathbf{i} & \mathbf{j} & \mathbf{k} \\ 1 & 0 & \dfrac{z(i+1, j, k) - z(i-1, j, k)}{2d} \\ 0 & 1 & \dfrac{z(i, j+1, k) - z(i, j-1, k)}{2d} \end{vmatrix}$$

$$= \left\langle -\frac{z(i+1, j, k) - z(i-1, j, k)}{2d}, -\frac{z(i, j+1, k) - z(i, j-1, k)}{2d}, 1 \right\rangle \qquad (13.37)$$

Multiplying the vectors $\mathbf{T}$, $\mathbf{B}$, and $\mathbf{N}$ by $2d$ does not change the direction in which they point but does eliminate the divisions, yielding the following formulas.

$$\mathbf{T} = \langle 2d, 0, z(i+1, j, k) - z(i-1, j, k) \rangle$$
$$\mathbf{B} = \langle 0, 2d, z(i, j+1, k) - z(i, j-1, k) \rangle$$
$$\mathbf{N} = \langle z(i-1, j, k) - z(i+1, j, k), z(i, j-1, k) - z(i, j+1, k), 2d \rangle \qquad (13.38)$$

Listing 13.1 demonstrates how a fluid surface simulation might be implemented. It is important to realize that the time interval between evaluations of the fluid displacement must be constant. The frame rate for most games varies considerably, so some mechanism should be used to ensure that the position of the surface is updated only after enough time has passed in situations when the frame rate is high.

When an object interacts with the fluid surface (e.g., a rock is thrown into it), it should cause a disturbance. The surface can be displaced by explicitly modifying the current and previous positions of the vertices surrounding the point where the interaction takes place. Displacing the vertex nearest to the point of impact and, by a lesser amount, the eight nearest neighbors generally produces pleasing results.

Listing 13.1 This code implements a two-buffer surface displacement algorithm. The constructor of the `Fluid` class takes the size of the vertex array, the distance *d* between adjacent vertices, the time interval *t*, the wave velocity *c*, and the viscosity *μ*. The `renderBuffer` member variable indicates which buffer should be rendered for the current frame—it alternates between 0 and 1 during each call to the `Fluid::Evaluate` function.

```
struct Vector3D
{
   float   x, y, z;

   Vector3D& Set(float r, float s, float t)
   {
      x = r;
      y = s;
      z = t;
      return (*this);
   }
};

class Fluid
{
   private:

      long     width;
      long     height;

      Vector3D *buffer[2];
      long     renderBuffer;

      Vector3D *normal;
      Vector3D *tangent;

      float    k1, k2, k3;

   public:

      Fluid(long n, long m, float d, float t,
         float c, float mu);
      ~Fluid();

      void Evaluate(void);
};
```

```
Fluid::Fluid(long n, long m, float d, float t,
   float c, float mu)
{
   width = n;
   height = m;
   long count = n * m;

   buffer[0] = new Vector3D[count];
   buffer[1] = new Vector3D[count];
   renderBuffer = 0;

   normal = new Vector3D[count];
   tangent = new Vector3D[count];

   // Precompute constants for Equation (13.25)
   float f1 = c * c * t * t / (d * d);
   float f2 = 1.0F / (mu * t + 2);
   k1 = (4.0F - 8.0F * f1) * f2;
   k2 = (mu * t - 2) * f2;
   k3 = 2.0F * f1 * f2;

   // Initialize buffers
   long a = 0;
   for (long j = 0; j < m; j++)
   {
      float y = d * j;
      for (long i = 0; i < n; i++)
      {
         buffer[0][a].Set(d * i, y, 0.0F);
         buffer[1][a] = buffer[0][a];
         normal[a].Set(0.0F, 0.0F, 2.0F * d);
         tangent[a].Set(2.0F * d, 0.0F, 0.0F);
         a++;
      }
   }
}

Fluid::~Fluid()
{
   delete[] tangent;
   delete[] normal;
   delete[] buffer[1];
   delete[] buffer[0];
}
```

```
void Fluid::Evaluate(void)
{
   // Apply Equation (13.25)
   for (long j = 1; j < height - 1; j++)
   {
      const Vector3D *crnt = buffer[renderBuffer] +
         j * width;
      Vector3D *prev = buffer[1 - renderBuffer] +
         j * width;
      for (long i = 1; i < width - 1; i++)
      {
         prev[i].z = k1 * crnt[i].z + k2 * prev[i].z +
            k3 * (crnt[i + 1].z + crnt[i - 1].z +
            crnt[i + width].z + crnt[i - width].z);
      }
   }

   // Swap buffers
   renderBuffer = 1 - renderBuffer;

   // Calculate normals and tangents
   for (long j = 1; j < height - 1; j++)
   {
      const Vector3D *next = buffer[renderBuffer] +
         j * width;
      Vector3D *nrml = normal + j * width;
      Vector3D *tang = tangent + j * width;
      for (long i = 1; i < width - 1; i++)
      {
         nrml[i].x = next[i - 1].z - next[i + 1].z;
         nrml[i].y = next[i - width].z -
            next[i + width].z;
         tang[i].z = next[i + 1].z - next[i - 1].z;
      }
   }
}
```

Chapter 13 Summary

The Wave Equation

The two-dimensional wave equation for a surface experiencing a viscous damping force is

$$\frac{\partial^2 z}{\partial t^2} = c^2\left(\frac{\partial^2 z}{\partial x^2} + \frac{\partial^2 z}{\partial y^2}\right) - \mu \frac{\partial z}{\partial t}.$$

The constant c is the speed at which waves propagate through the medium, and the constant μ represents the viscosity of the medium.

Approximating Derivatives

The first derivative of a function $z(x)$ can be approximated by the formula

$$\frac{d}{dx}z(x) \approx \frac{z(x+d) - z(x-d)}{2d},$$

where d represents some constant step size. The second derivative of $z(x)$ can be approximated by the formula

$$\frac{d^2}{dx^2}z(x) \approx \frac{z(x+d) - 2z(x) + z(x-d)}{d^2}.$$

Evaluating Surface Displacement

The future displacement $z(i, j, k+1)$ of a point on the surface of a fluid after a time t has passed is calculated using the equation

$$z(i,j,k+1) = \frac{4 - 8c^2t^2/d^2}{\mu t + 2}z(i,j,k) + \frac{\mu t - 2}{\mu t + 2}z(i,j,k-1)$$
$$+ \frac{2c^2t^2/d^2}{\mu t + 2}\left[z(i+1,j,k) + z(i-1,j,k) + z(i,j+1,k) + z(i,j-1,k)\right],$$

where d is the distance between neighboring vertices in the triangle mesh.

Stability of Numerical Method

Given a constant time step t, the wave speed c must satisfy

$$0 < c < \frac{d}{2t}\sqrt{\mu t + 2}.$$

Given a constant wave speed c, the time step t must satisfy

$$0 < t < \frac{\mu + \sqrt{\mu^2 + 32c^2/d^2}}{8c^2/d^2}.$$

Exercises for Chapter 13

1. Suppose that the surface displacement of each vertex in a triangle mesh is evaluated 20 times per second. If the distance between neighboring vertices is $0.1\,\text{m}$ and the viscous damping constant is $\mu = 1\,\text{s}^{-1}$, what is the maximum wave speed for which Equation (13.25) is numerically stable?

2. Suppose that the distance between neighboring vertices of a surface mesh is $0.1\,\text{m}$ and the viscous damping constant is $\mu = 1\,\text{s}^{-1}$, as in the previous exercise. What is the maximum time interval between consecutive evaluations that allows a stable wave speed of $2\,\text{m/s}$?

Chapter **14**

Numerical Methods

Du.during the course of 3D graphics development, problems often arise that require us to numerically calculate the solution to some kind of mathematical model. In this chapter, we discuss numerical methods for solving three classes of problems. First, we discuss techniques for solving arbitrary linear systems and linear systems having a special form. Second, we examine methods for finding the eigenvalues and eigenvectors of a symmetric matrix. Lastly, we introduce classical procedures for approximating the solutions to ordinary differential equations.

14.1 Linear Systems

In Chapter 2, we discussed a method for solving linear systems by transforming the augmented coefficient matrix to reduced form. In this section, we more closely investigate the problem of solving nonhomogeneous linear systems and pay particular attention to implementation details. The general problem that we examine is written $\mathbf{Mx} = \mathbf{r}$, where $\mathbf{M}$ is an $n \times n$ invertible matrix representing the coefficients of a set of linear equations, and $\mathbf{r}$ is an $n \times 1$ vector of constants. Our goal is to find the $n \times 1$ vector $\mathbf{x}$ for which the equation $\mathbf{Mx} = \mathbf{r}$ is satisfied.

14.1.1 Triangular Systems

A triangular system is one for which the coefficient matrix is either lower triangular or upper triangular, as defined by the following.

> **Definition 14.1.** A *lower triangular* matrix **L** is a square matrix for which $L_{ij} = 0$ when $i < j$. That is, a lower triangular matrix has nonzero entries only on and below the main diagonal.

> **Definition 14.2.** An *upper triangular* matrix **U** is a square matrix for which $U_{ij} = 0$ when $i > j$. That is, an upper triangular matrix has nonzero entries only on and above the main diagonal.

Triangular systems can be solved quite easily using direct substitution. In the case of the linear system $\mathbf{Lx} = \mathbf{r}$, where **L** is an $n \times n$ lower triangular matrix, we can write

$$\begin{bmatrix} L_{11} & 0 & \cdots & 0 \\ L_{21} & L_{22} & \cdots & 0 \\ \vdots & \vdots & \ddots & \vdots \\ L_{n1} & L_{n2} & \cdots & L_{nn} \end{bmatrix} \begin{bmatrix} x_1 \\ x_2 \\ \vdots \\ x_n \end{bmatrix} = \begin{bmatrix} r_1 \\ r_2 \\ \vdots \\ r_n \end{bmatrix}. \tag{14.1}$$

From the first row in the coefficient matrix, we can immediately see that

$$x_1 = \frac{r_1}{L_{11}}. \tag{14.2}$$

If we solve the equation represented by the second row of the coefficient matrix for x_2, we have

$$x_2 = \frac{1}{L_{22}}(r_2 - L_{21}x_1). \tag{14.3}$$

We already know the value of x_1, so it can be substituted into Equation (14.3) to obtain the value of x_2. Continuing this process, we observe the general formula

$$x_i = \frac{1}{L_{ii}}\left(r_i - \sum_{k=1}^{i-1} L_{ik}r_k\right). \tag{14.4}$$

This process is called *forward substitution*. For an $n \times n$ upper triangular matrix **U**, a similar process, called *backward substitution*, allows us to solve the linear system **Ux** = **r**. In this case, we can write

$$
\begin{bmatrix}
U_{11} & U_{12} & \cdots & U_{1n} \\
0 & U_{22} & \cdots & U_{2n} \\
\vdots & \vdots & \ddots & \vdots \\
0 & 0 & \cdots & U_{nn}
\end{bmatrix}
\begin{bmatrix}
x_1 \\
x_2 \\
\vdots \\
x_n
\end{bmatrix}
=
\begin{bmatrix}
r_1 \\
r_2 \\
\vdots \\
r_n
\end{bmatrix}.
\tag{14.5}
$$

The last row of the coefficient matrix tells us that

$$
x_n = \frac{r_n}{U_{nn}}.
\tag{14.6}
$$

By substituting into preceding rows, we obtain the general backward substitution formula

$$
x_i = \frac{1}{U_{ii}} \left(r_i - \sum_{k=i+1}^{n} U_{ik} r_k \right).
\tag{14.7}
$$

In the remainder of this section, we examine two methods for solving general linear systems. Each method transforms the problem into one in which triangular systems appear. Forward and backward substitution can then be used to obtain a solution.

14.1.2 Gaussian Elimination

Suppose we have a nonhomogeneous linear system of n equations having n unknowns $x_1, x_2, \ldots, x_n$ that can be written as **Mx** = **r**. By performing elementary row operations (see Definition 2.3) on the coefficient matrix **M**, we can reduce the linear system to

$$
\mathbf{Ux} = \mathbf{r'},
\tag{14.8}
$$

where **U** is an upper triangular matrix, and the new constant vector **r'** is the result of performing the same row operations on **r**. The values of x_i are then calculated using the backward substitution formula given by Equation (14.7).

The process of transforming the linear system **Mx** = **r** into the linear system **Ux** = **r'** is known as *Gaussian elimination*. For each column $j = 1, 2, \ldots, n$, we eliminate the entries M_{ij} below the main diagonal by adding row j multiplied by $-M_{ij}/M_{jj}$ to row i for each $i > j$. If $M_{jj} = 0$, we must exchange row j with another row below it before performing the eliminations in column j. It is generally true that the best numerical stability is achieved by exchanging rows so that the absolute value of M_{jj} is maximized, so we search for the largest entry on or below the main diagonal as we process each column. As mentioned in Chapter 2, this is called *pivoting*.

Since multiplying any row of the matrix **M** and the corresponding entry of the vector **r** by a nonzero scalar does not alter the solution to the linear system, we can normalize each row of **M** so that its largest coefficient is ±1. This improves numerical stability by placing all of the rows on equal ground, avoiding the possibility that one row dominates the others during pivoting because it has been scaled by a large value. Normalizing the rows for this reason is called *implicit pivoting*.

The SolveLinearSystem function shown in Listing 14.1 solves a linear system of the form **Mx** = **r** using Gaussian elimination and implicit pivoting. A disadvantage of Gaussian elimination is that the constant vector **r** must be known at the time that the coefficient matrix is transformed into an upper triangular matrix. If the solution to the system is desired for multiple values of **r** (e.g., to calculate the inverse of **M**), then the entire elimination process must be redone. This limitation is circumvented by LU decomposition, which is discussed in the next section.

Listing 14.1 The SolveLinearSystem function solves the linear system **Mx** = **r** using Gaussian elimination. The return value is false of the matrix **M** is singular and true otherwise.

Parameters

n	The size of the matrix **M**.
m	A pointer to the entries of the matrix **M**. The entries must be stored in column-major order. This matrix is transformed into the matrix **U** appearing in Equation (14.8).
r	A pointer to the constant vector **r**. The solution vector **x** is returned in this array.

```
bool SolveLinearSystem(int n, float *m, float *r)
{
    float *rowNormalizer = new float[n];
    bool result = false;

    // Calculate a normalizer for each row
    for (int i = 0; i < n; i++)
```

```
{
  const float *entry = m + i;
  float maxvalue = 0.0F;

  for (int j = 0; j < n; j++)
  {
    float value = fabs(*entry);
    if (value > maxvalue) maxvalue = value;
    entry += n;
  }

  if (maxvalue == 0.0F) goto exit; // Singular
  rowNormalizer[i] = 1.0F / maxvalue;
}

// Perform elimination one column at a time
for (int j = 0; j < n - 1; j++)
{
  // Find pivot element
  int pivotRow = -1;
  float maxvalue = 0.0F;
  for (int i = j; i < n; i++)
  {
    float p = fabs(m[j * n + i]) * rowNormalizer[i];
    if (p > maxvalue)
    {
      maxvalue = p;
      pivotRow = i;
    }
  }

  if (pivotRow != j)
  {
    if (pivotRow == -1) goto exit; // Singular

    // Exchange rows
    for (int k = 0; k < n; k++)
    {
      float temp = m[k * n + j];
      m[k * n + j] = m[k * n + pivotRow];
      m[k * n + pivotRow] = temp;
    }

    float temp = r[j];
    r[j] = r[pivotRow];
```

```
            r[pivotRow] = temp;

            rowNormalizer[pivotRow] = rowNormalizer[j];
        }

        float denom = 1.0F / m[j * n + j];
        for (int i = j + 1; i < n; i++)
        {
            float factor = m[j * n + i] * denom;
            r[i] -= r[j] * factor;
            for (int k = 0; k < n; k++)
                m[k * n + i] -= m[k * n + j] * factor;
        }
    }

    // Perform backward substitution
    for (int i = n - 1; i >= 0; i--)
    {
        float sum = r[i];
        for (int k = i + 1; k < n; k++)
            sum -= m[k * n + i] * r[k];
        r[i] = sum / m[i * n + i];
    }

    result = true;

exit:
    delete[] rowNormalizer;
    return (result);
}
```

14.1.3 LU Decomposition

Suppose again that we have a linear system of n equations that can be written as $\mathbf{Mx} = \mathbf{r}$. If we can find two matrices $\mathbf{L}$ and $\mathbf{U}$, where $\mathbf{L}$ is a lower triangular matrix and $\mathbf{U}$ is an upper triangular matrix, such that $\mathbf{LU} = \mathbf{M}$, then the linear system $\mathbf{Mx} = \mathbf{r}$ can be written as

$$\mathbf{L}(\mathbf{Ux}) = \mathbf{r}. \tag{14.9}$$

This transforms the problem of solving the system $\mathbf{Mx} = \mathbf{r}$ into the problems of solving the system $\mathbf{Ly} = \mathbf{r}$ and then solving the system $\mathbf{Ux} = \mathbf{y}$. The solutions to both of these systems is easily calculated using forward substitution (for $\mathbf{Ly}=\mathbf{r}$) and backward substitution (for $\mathbf{Ux}=\mathbf{y}$).

The pair of triangular matrices $\mathbf{L}$ and $\mathbf{U}$ whose product yields $\mathbf{M}$ is called the *LU decomposition* of $\mathbf{M}$. Once determined, the LU decomposition of a matrix can be repeatedly used to solve linear systems having the same coefficient matrix $\mathbf{M}$ and different constant vectors $\mathbf{r}$. In particular, we can calculate the j-th column of $\mathbf{M}^{-1}$ by setting $r_i = \delta_{ij}$, where δ is the Kronecker delta symbol.

We need an algorithm that determines the matrices $\mathbf{L}$ and $\mathbf{U}$ such that

$$
\begin{bmatrix}
L_{11} & 0 & \cdots & 0 \\
L_{21} & L_{22} & \cdots & 0 \\
\vdots & \vdots & \ddots & \vdots \\
L_{n1} & L_{n2} & \cdots & L_{nn}
\end{bmatrix}
\begin{bmatrix}
U_{11} & U_{12} & \cdots & U_{1n} \\
0 & U_{22} & \cdots & U_{2n} \\
\vdots & \vdots & \ddots & \vdots \\
0 & 0 & \cdots & U_{nn}
\end{bmatrix}
=
\begin{bmatrix}
M_{11} & M_{12} & \cdots & M_{1n} \\
M_{21} & M_{22} & \cdots & M_{2n} \\
\vdots & \vdots & \ddots & \vdots \\
M_{n1} & M_{n2} & \cdots & M_{nn}
\end{bmatrix}. \quad (14.10)
$$

When examining how the matrix product $\mathbf{LU}$ produces each entry of the matrix $\mathbf{M}$, we observe the following two summations.

$$
M_{ij} = \sum_{k=1}^{i} L_{ik} U_{kj}, \quad \text{if } i \le j \quad (14.11)
$$

$$
M_{ij} = \sum_{k=1}^{j} L_{ik} U_{kj}, \quad \text{if } i \ge j \quad (14.12)
$$

(Both equations are valid for $i = j$.) The nonzero entries of $\mathbf{L}$ and $\mathbf{U}$ represent $n^2 + n$ unknown values, and Equations (14.11) and (14.12) give a total of n^2 equations relating those unknowns. We therefore expect that n of the unknowns may be arbitrarily chosen, and we can then solve for the remaining n^2 unknowns. For the method that we present here, known as *Doolittle's method*, we set all of the diagonal elements of $\mathbf{L}$ to unity. That is,

$$
L_{ii} \equiv 1, \quad i = 1, 2, \ldots, n. \quad (14.13)
$$

(A similar method in which the diagonal elements of $\mathbf{U}$ are set to unity is known as *Crout's method*.) To make efficient usage of storage space, we write the values of the remaining nonzero entries of $\mathbf{L}$ and $\mathbf{U}$ in a single matrix $\mathbf{D}$ as follows.

$$\mathbf{D} = \begin{bmatrix} U_{11} & U_{12} & U_{13} & \cdots & U_{1n} \\ L_{21} & U_{22} & U_{23} & \cdots & U_{2n} \\ L_{31} & L_{32} & U_{33} & \cdots & U_{3n} \\ \vdots & \vdots & \vdots & \ddots & \vdots \\ L_{n1} & L_{n2} & L_{n3} & \cdots & U_{nn} \end{bmatrix} \tag{14.14}$$

Doolittle's method determines the (i,j) entry of the matrix $\mathbf{D}$ using only the (i,j) entry of the matrix $\mathbf{M}$ and entries of $\mathbf{D}$ in the same column above D_{ij} and in the same row to the left of D_{ij}. Solving Equation (14.11) for U_{ij} and applying Equation (14.13) gives us

$$U_{1j} = M_{1j};$$
$$U_{ij} = M_{ij} - \sum_{k=1}^{i-1} L_{ik} U_{kj}, \quad \text{if } i > 1. \tag{14.15}$$

The calculation of U_{ij} requires the entries of $\mathbf{U}$ in the j-th column above row i and the entries of $\mathbf{L}$ in the i-th row to the left of the main diagonal. Similarly, solving Equation (14.12) for L_{ij} gives us

$$L_{i1} = \frac{M_{i1}}{U_{11}};$$
$$L_{ij} = \frac{1}{U_{jj}} \left(M_{ij} - \sum_{k=1}^{j-1} L_{ik} U_{kj} \right), \quad \text{if } j > 1. \tag{14.16}$$

The calculation of L_{ij} requires the entries of $\mathbf{L}$ in the i-th row to the left of column j and the entries of $\mathbf{U}$ in the j-th column above and on the main diagonal.

The general procedure for producing the matrix $\mathbf{D}$ is to calculate the columns from left to right. For each column j, we first use Equation (14.15) to calculate U_{ij} for $1 \le i \le j$. These values are subsequently used in Equation (14.16) to calculate L_{ij} for $j+1 \le i \le n$. It is possible to store each value U_{ij} or L_{ij} at the location that M_{ij} originally occupied since M_{ij} is only used in the calculation for the (i,j) entry of the matrix $\mathbf{D}$.

The division in Equation (14.16) requires that we pivot when performing LU decomposition. We do so for each column j by choosing the largest possible divisor from the candidates P_{ij} given by

$$P_{ij} = M_{ij} - \sum_{k=1}^{j-1} L_{ik} U_{kj} \qquad (14.17)$$

for $i \geq j$. When $i = j$, Equation (14.17) yields U_{jj} given by Equation (14.15); and when $i > j$, Equation (14.17) yields L_{ij} given by Equation (14.16), except that the division is not performed. Once the value of P_{ij} having the largest absolute value has been identified, we exchange the row in which it appears with row j to move P_{ij} to the main diagonal where it becomes U_{jj}. All of the other entries P_{ij} in column j below the main diagonal are then divided by U_{jj} to obtain L_{ij}. All of this produces the LU decomposition of a matrix $\mathbf{M}$ that is actually the LU decomposition of a permutation of the rows of $\mathbf{M}$. We must keep track of the row exchanges so that they can be accounted for when using the matrix $\mathbf{D}$ to solve a linear system.

The `LUDecompose` function shown in Listing 14.2 performs in-place LU decomposition of a given $n \times n$ matrix $\mathbf{M}$. Pivoting is performed using the normalized rows of $\mathbf{M}$ in a manner similar to that used in Gaussian elimination. In addition to returning the decomposed matrix $\mathbf{D}$ given by Equation (14.14), the function returns an array of indexes that indicate how the rows were permuted during the decomposition. All of this information is subsequently passed to the `LUBacksubstitute` function shown in Listing 14.3 to solve a linear system.

After a matrix $\mathbf{M}$ has been decomposed into the product $\mathbf{LU}$, its determinant can be calculated using the equation

$$\det \mathbf{M} = \pm \det \mathbf{L} \det \mathbf{U}. \qquad (14.18)$$

Since the diagonal entries of $\mathbf{L}$ are all unity, $\det \mathbf{L} = 1$, and the right side reduces to $\pm \det \mathbf{U}$. Which sign we choose depends on the number of row exchanges performed during the decomposition. The `LUDecompose` function returns a parity $p = \pm 1$ in the `detSign` parameter indicating whether the number of row exchanges performed was even or odd. Since each row exchange negates the determinant (see Theorem 2.17), this value enables us to calculate the determinant of $\mathbf{M}$ using the formula

$$\det \mathbf{M} = p \det \mathbf{U} = p \sum_{i=1}^{n} U_{ii}. \qquad (14.19)$$

Listing 14.2 The `LUDecompose` function performs the LU decomposition of an $n \times n$ matrix **M**. The decomposition is performed in place—the matrix **D** given by Equation (14.14) is returned in the space occupied by **M**. This function also returns an array of indexes that indicate how the rows were permuted during the decomposition process. The matrix **D** and the permutation array are passed to the `LUBacksubstitute` function (see Listing 14.3) to solve linear systems. The `LUDecompose` function returns `false` if the matrix **M** is singular and `true` otherwise.

Parameters

n   The size of the matrix **M**.

m   A pointer to the entries of the matrix **M**. The entries must be stored in column-major order.

index   A pointer to an array of size *n* where the row permutation information can be stored.

detSign   A pointer to a location where the parity of the row exchanges can be stored. This may be `NULL` if this information is not needed.

```
bool LUDecompose(int n, float *m,
   unsigned short *index, float *detSign)
{
   float *rowNormalizer = new float[n];
   float exchangeParity = 1.0F;
   bool result = false;

   // Calculate a normalizer for each row
   for (int i = 0; i < n; i++)
   {
      const float *entry = m + i;
      float maxvalue = 0.0F;

      for (int j = 0; j < n; j++)
      {
         float value = fabs(*entry);
         if (value > maxvalue) maxvalue = value;
         entry += n;
      }

      if (maxvalue == 0.0F) goto exit; // Singular
      rowNormalizer[i] = 1.0F / maxvalue;
      index[i] = i;
   }

   // Perform decomposition
   for (int j = 0; j < n; j++)
```

```
{
  for (int i = 1; i < j; i++)
  {
    // Evaluate Equation (14.15)
    float sum = m[j * n + i];
    for (int k = 0; k < i; k++)
      sum -= m[k * n + i] * m[j * n + k];
    m[j * n + i] = sum;
  }

  // Find pivot element
  int pivotRow = -1;
  float maxvalue = 0.0F;
  for (int i = j; i < n; i++)
  {
    // Evaluate Equation (14.17)
    float sum = m[j * n + i];
    for (int k = 0; k < j; k++)
      sum -= m[k * n + i] * m[j * n + k];
    m[j * n + i] = sum;

    sum = fabs(sum) * rowNormalizer[i];
    if (sum > maxvalue)
    {
      maxvalue = sum;
      pivotRow = i;
    }
  }

  if (pivotRow != j)
  {
    if (pivotRow == -1) goto exit; // Singular

    // Exchange rows
    for (int k = 0; k < n; k++)
    {
      float temp = m[k * n + j];
      m[k * n + j] = m[k * n + pivotRow];
      m[k * n + pivotRow] = temp;
    }

    unsigned short temp = index[j];
    index[j] = index[pivotRow];
    index[pivotRow] = temp;
```

```
        rowNormalizer[pivotRow] = rowNormalizer[j];
        exchangeParity = -exchangeParity;
    }

    // Divide by pivot element
    if (j != n - 1)
    {
        float denom = 1.0F / m[j * n + j];
        for (int i = j + 1; i < n; i++)
            m[j * n + i] *= denom;
    }
}

if (detSign) *detSign = exchangeParity;
result = true;

exit:
delete[] rowNormalizer;
return (result);
}
```

Listing 14.3 The LUBacksubstitute function takes the LU-decomposed matrix **D** and permutation array returned by the LUDecompose function (see Listing 14.2) and uses them to solve a linear system of *n* equations **Mx** = **r**. First, the system **Ly** = **r** is solved using Equation (14.4), and then the system **Ux** = **y** is solved using Equation (14.7).

Parameters

n   The size of the matrix **D**.

d   A pointer to the entries of the matrix **D**. This should be the same pointer that was passed to the m parameter of the LUDecompose function.

index   A pointer to the array of row permutation indexes returned by the LUDecompose function.

r   A pointer to an array of *n* constant values representing the vector **r** for which the linear system **Mx** = **r** is to be solved.

x   A pointer to the array in which the *n* solutions representing the vector **x** are to be returned.

```
void LUBacksubstitute(int n, const float *d,
    const unsigned short *index, const float *r, float *x)
{
    for (int i = 0; i < n; i++) x[i] = r[index[i]];
```

```
// Perform forward substitution for Ly = r
for (int i = 0; i < n; i++)
{
    float sum = x[i];
    for (int k = 0; k < i; k++)
        sum -= d[k * n + i] * x[k];
    x[i] = sum;
}

// Perform backward substitution for Ux = y
for (int i = n - 1; i >= 0; i--)
{
    float sum = x[i];
    for (int k = i + 1; k < n; k++)
        sum -= d[k * n + i] * x[k];
    x[i] = sum / d[i * n + i];
}
}
```

14.1.4 Error Reduction

Suppose that we have solved a linear system $\mathbf{Mx} = \mathbf{r}$ and obtained the solution $\mathbf{x} = \mathbf{x}_0$. Due to round-off error, it is usually the case that $\mathbf{x}_0$ is slightly different from the true solution to the system, and thus $\mathbf{Mx}_0 = \mathbf{r}_0$, where $\mathbf{r}_0$ is slightly different from the original constant vector $\mathbf{r}$. Calling the true solution to the system $\mathbf{x}$, we can write

$$\mathbf{M}(\mathbf{x} + \Delta\mathbf{x}) = \mathbf{r} + \Delta\mathbf{r}, \tag{14.20}$$

where $\Delta\mathbf{x} = \mathbf{x}_0 - \mathbf{x}$ and $\Delta\mathbf{r} = \mathbf{r}_0 - \mathbf{r}$. Subtracting the original system $\mathbf{Mx} = \mathbf{r}$ from this equation gives us

$$\mathbf{M}\Delta\mathbf{x} = \Delta\mathbf{r}. \tag{14.21}$$

If we solve Equation (14.20) for $\Delta\mathbf{r}$ and plug it into Equation (14.21), then we arrive at the following linear system.

$$\mathbf{M}\Delta\mathbf{x} = \mathbf{Mx}_0 - \mathbf{r} \tag{14.22}$$

The entire right side of this equation is known, so we can solve for the error vector $\Delta\mathbf{x}$ and subtract from our original solution $\mathbf{x}_0$ to obtain a better answer.

The `LURefineSolution` function shown in Listing 14.4 solves the system given by Equation (14.22) using the same LU decomposition needed to solve the original system $\mathbf{Mx} = \mathbf{r}$. The result is then used to improve the original solution $\mathbf{x}_0$. The right side of Equation (14.22) is evaluated in double precision since its value may become very small during its computation. We need both the original coefficient matrix $\mathbf{M}$ and the LU-decomposed matrix $\mathbf{D}$ given by Equation (14.14). The code assumes that the matrix $\mathbf{M}$ has already been copied and decomposed into the matrix $\mathbf{D}$ using the `LUDecompose` function shown in Listing 14.2.

Listing 14.4 The `LURefineSolution` function uses Equation (14.22) to improve the solution **x** to the linear system **Mx** = **r**.

Parameters

n	The size of the matrix **M**.
m	A pointer to the entries of the matrix **M**. The entries must be stored in column-major order.
d	A pointer to the entries of the matrix **D**. This should be the same pointer that was passed to the m parameter of the `LUDecompose` function.
index	A pointer to the array of row permutation indexes returned by the `LUDecompose` function.
r	A pointer to an array of *n* constant values representing the vector **r** for which the linear system **Mx** = **r** was originally solved.
x	A pointer to the array containing the *n* solutions representing the vector **x**. This function refines these solutions.

```
void LURefineSolution(int n, const float *m,
    const float *d, const unsigned short *index,
    const float *r, float *x)
{
    float *t = new float[n];

    for (int i = 0; i < n; i++)
    {
        double q = -r[i];
        for (int k = 0; k < n; k++)
            q += m[k * n + i] * x[k];
        t[i] = (float) q;
    }

    LUBacksubstitute(n, d, index, t, t);
```

```
    for (int i = 0; i < n; i++) x[i] -= t[i];

    delete[] t;
}
```

14.1.5 Tridiagonal Systems

A particular type of linear system $\mathbf{Mx} = \mathbf{r}$ frequently arises in which each equation has only three nonzero coefficients and those coefficients are centered on the main diagonal of $\mathbf{M}$. This special form of the coefficient matrix is given the following name.

> **Definition 14.3.** A square matrix $\mathbf{M}$ is *tridiagonal* if $M_{ij} = 0$ whenever $|i - j| > 1$. That is, a tridiagonal matrix has nonzero entries only on the main diagonal and immediately above and below the main diagonal.

A tridiagonal matrix having the property that its diagonal elements are larger than the sum of the remaining elements in their rows is described using the following term.

> **Definition 14.4.** Let $\mathbf{M}$ be the tridiagonal matrix
>
> $$\mathbf{M} = \begin{bmatrix} b_1 & c_1 & 0 & 0 & 0 & \cdots \\ a_2 & b_2 & c_2 & 0 & 0 & \\ 0 & a_3 & b_3 & c_3 & 0 & \\ \vdots & & \ddots & \ddots & \ddots & \end{bmatrix}. \tag{14.23}$$
>
> $\mathbf{M}$ is *diagonally dominant* if $|b_i| > |a_i| + |c_i|$ for all i, where we assume $a_1 \equiv 0$ and $c_n \equiv 0$.

Suppose we have a linear system $\mathbf{Mx} = \mathbf{r}$ of n equations, where $\mathbf{M}$ is a tridiagonal matrix. It turns out that such a linear system can be solved very efficiently. Furthermore, if $\mathbf{M}$ is diagonally dominant, then we can prove that a solution to the linear system must exist.

Expanding the equation $\mathbf{Mx} = \mathbf{r}$, we can write

$$\begin{bmatrix} b_1 & c_1 & 0 & \cdots & 0 & 0 & 0 \\ a_2 & b_2 & c_2 & & 0 & 0 & 0 \\ & & \ddots & & & & \\ 0 & 0 & 0 & & a_{n-1} & b_{n-1} & c_{n-1} \\ 0 & 0 & 0 & \cdots & 0 & a_n & b_n \end{bmatrix} \begin{bmatrix} x_1 \\ x_2 \\ \vdots \\ x_{n-1} \\ x_n \end{bmatrix} = \begin{bmatrix} r_1 \\ r_2 \\ \vdots \\ r_{n-1} \\ r_n \end{bmatrix}. \tag{14.24}$$

The first two rows of the matrix $\mathbf{M}$ represent the equations

$$b_1 x_1 + c_1 x_2 = r_1 \tag{14.25}$$

and

$$a_2 x_1 + b_2 x_2 + c_2 x_3 = r_2. \tag{14.26}$$

We can solve Equation (14.25) for x_1 and substitute the result into Equation (14.26) to obtain

$$\left(b_2 - a_2 \frac{c_1}{b_1} \right) x_2 + c_2 x_3 = r_2 - a_2 \frac{r_1}{b_1}, \tag{14.27}$$

which now contains only two unknowns instead of three. Continuing this process, we can write each of the equations as

$$\beta_i x_i + c_i x_{i+1} = \rho_i, \tag{14.28}$$

where β_i and ρ_i are constants given by the recurrence formulas

$$\beta_i = b_i - a_i \frac{c_{i-1}}{\beta_{i-1}}$$

$$\rho_i = r_i - a_i \frac{\rho_{i-1}}{\beta_{i-1}}. \tag{14.29}$$

The equation corresponding to the last row of the matrix $\mathbf{M}$ becomes $\beta_n x_n = \rho_n$, giving us the value of x_n:

$$x_n = \frac{\rho_n}{\beta_n}. \tag{14.30}$$

Plugging this value back into Equation (14.28) for $i = n-1$ gives us the value of x_{n-1}, and in general,

$$x_i = \frac{\rho_i}{\beta_i} - \frac{c_i}{\beta_i} x_{i+1}.$$ (14.31)

An implementation of this algorithm is shown in Listing 14.5. The algorithm is begun with $\beta_1 = b_1$ and $\rho_1 = r_1$. Each value of c_i / β_i calculated with Equation (14.29) is saved for later use in Equation (14.31). This implementation assumes that β_i is never zero, which is guaranteed to be true if the matrix $\mathbf{M}$ is diagonally dominant. The fact that a diagonally dominant matrix is always invertible is summarized by the following theorem.

Theorem 14.5. Let $\mathbf{M}$ be an $n \times n$ diagonally dominant tridiagonal matrix. Then the linear system $\mathbf{Mx} = \mathbf{r}$ is always solvable, and as a corollary, the matrix $\mathbf{M}$ is invertible.

Proof. Let the entries of $\mathbf{M}$ be named as shown in Equation (14.23). Since $\mathbf{M}$ is diagonally dominant, $|b_i| > |a_i| + |c_i|$ for all i. We will show that the value of β_i given by Equation (14.29) always satisfies $|\beta_i| > |c_i|$ and is therefore never zero. For $i = 1$, this is trivially true since $|\beta_1| = |b_1| > |c_1|$. Now assume that for any $i > 1$ that $|\beta_{i-1}| > |c_{i-1}|$. For $|\beta_i|$, we have

$$|\beta_i| = \left| b_i - a_i \frac{c_{i-1}}{\beta_{i-1}} \right|$$

$$\geq |b_i| - |a_i| \left| \frac{c_{i-1}}{\beta_{i-1}} \right|$$

$$> |a_i| + |c_i| - |a_i| \left| \frac{c_{i-1}}{\beta_{i-1}} \right|$$

$$= |c_i| + |a_i| \left(1 - \left| \frac{c_{i-1}}{\beta_{i-1}} \right| \right).$$ (14.32)

Since $|\beta_{i-1}| > |c_{i-1}|$, the quantity $1 - |c_{i-1}/\beta_{i-1}|$ is positive, and thus $|\beta_i| > |c_i|$. By induction, this shows that $|\beta_i| > |c_i|$ for all i. Consequently, the value of each x_i can always be calculated using Equation (14.31). The inverse of the matrix $\mathbf{M}$ can be found by solving the system n times, producing the columns of $\mathbf{M}^{-1}$ one at a time. The j-th column of $\mathbf{M}^{-1}$ is found by setting $r_i = \delta_{ij}$. ∎

Listing 14.5 The `SolveTridiagonalSystem` function solves a tridiagonal system of n equations having the form $\mathbf{Mx} = \mathbf{r}$ given by Equation (14.24).

Parameters

n	The size of the tridiagonal matrix **M**.
a, b, c	Pointers to arrays containing the coefficients a_i, b_i, and c_i, where $1 \leq i \leq n$. (These arrays are accessed using zero-based indexes, so $b[0] = b_1$.) The coefficients $a[0]$ and $c[n-1]$ do not exist and are never accessed.
r	A pointer to an array of n constant values representing the vector **r** for which the linear system $\mathbf{Mx} = \mathbf{r}$ is to be solved.
x	A pointer to the array in which the n solutions representing the vector **x** are to be returned.

```cpp
void SolveTridiagonalSystem(int n,
    const float *a, const float *b, const float *c,
    const float *r, float *x)
{
    // Allocate temporary storage for c[i]/beta[i]
    float *t = new float[n - 1];

    float recipBeta = 1.0F / b[0];
    x[0] = r[0] * recipBeta;

    for (int i = 1; i < n; i++)
    {
        t[i - 1] = c[i - 1] * recipBeta;

        recipBeta = 1.0F / (b[i] - a[i] * t[i - 1]);
        x[i] = (r[i] - a[i] * x[i - 1]) * recipBeta;
    }

    for (int i = n - 2; i >= 0; i--)
        x[i] -= t[i] * x[i + 1];

    delete t;
}
```

14.2 Eigenvalues and Eigenvectors

Eigenvalues and eigenvectors were introduced in Section 2.5. We have studied how they are important for performing principal component analysis (see Section 7.1.1) and for determining principal axes of inertia (see Section 12.2.4). Both of these problems required calculating the eigenvalues and eigenvectors of a 3×3 symmetric matrix, and we restrict our discussion to that particular problem in this section. For a treatment of larger and nonsymmetric matrices, the reader is encouraged to see [PRES88].

Recall from Section 2.6 that a symmetric matrix $\mathbf{M}$ can be written as

$$\mathbf{M} = \mathbf{A}^{\mathrm{T}} \mathbf{D} \mathbf{A}, \tag{14.33}$$

where $\mathbf{D}$ is a diagonal matrix whose entries are the eigenvalues of $\mathbf{M}$, and $\mathbf{A}$ is an orthogonal matrix whose columns are the eigenvectors of $\mathbf{M}$. Our strategy in this section is to apply a series of transformations to a given symmetric matrix $\mathbf{M}_0$ of the form

$$\mathbf{M}_k = \mathbf{R}_k^{\mathrm{T}} \mathbf{M}_{k-1} \mathbf{R}_k, \tag{14.34}$$

where $\mathbf{R}_k$ is an orthogonal matrix, in such a way that each iteration moves the matrix $\mathbf{M}_k$ closer to being diagonal. Once the off-diagonal entries have been made sufficiently small (perhaps even zero to machine precision), we are left with the following.

$$\mathbf{M}_m = \mathbf{R}_m^{\mathrm{T}} \mathbf{R}_{m-1}^{\mathrm{T}} \cdots \mathbf{R}_1^{\mathrm{T}} \mathbf{M}_0 \mathbf{R}_1 \mathbf{R}_2 \cdots \mathbf{R}_m \tag{14.35}$$

After m iterations, the diagonal entries of the matrix $\mathbf{M}_m$ are the eigenvalues of $\mathbf{M}_0$ and the columns of the product $\mathbf{R}_1 \mathbf{R}_2 \cdots \mathbf{R}_m$ are the corresponding eigenvectors.

We choose each matrix $\mathbf{R}_k$ to be a rotation matrix that annihilates one of the three distinct off-diagonal entries of $\mathbf{M}_{k-1}$ when Equation (14.34) is evaluated. The use of this process to diagonalize the matrix $\mathbf{M}_0$ is known as the *Jacobi method*. Each iteration sets a symmetric pair of off-diagonal entries to zero, but also undoes previous annihilations. We will show, however, that the off-diagonal entries become smaller in magnitude as a group and eventually vanish.

For a 3×3 matrix $\mathbf{M}_0$, the rotation matrix $\mathbf{R}_k$ may assume one of the following three forms, where s and c represent the sine and cosine of some rotation angle θ.

$$\mathbf{R}^{(12)} = \begin{bmatrix} c & s & 0 \\ -s & c & 0 \\ 0 & 0 & 1 \end{bmatrix}, \quad \mathbf{R}^{(13)} = \begin{bmatrix} c & 0 & s \\ 0 & 1 & 0 \\ -s & 0 & c \end{bmatrix}, \quad \mathbf{R}^{(23)} = \begin{bmatrix} 1 & 0 & 0 \\ 0 & c & s \\ 0 & -s & c \end{bmatrix} \quad (14.36)$$

Suppose that we use one of the matrices $\mathbf{R}^{(pq)}$ to transform the matrix $\mathbf{M}$ into the matrix $\mathbf{M}'$ through the formula $\mathbf{M}' = \mathbf{R}^{(pq)\text{T}}\mathbf{M}\mathbf{R}^{(pq)}$. By explicitly calculating the entries of $\mathbf{M}'$, we obtain the following relationships.

$$\left.\begin{aligned} M'_{ii} &= M_{ii} \\ M'_{ip,pi} &= cM_{ip} - sM_{iq} \\ M'_{iq,qi} &= sM_{ip} + cM_{iq} \end{aligned}\right\} \quad \text{if } i \neq p \text{ and } i \neq q; \quad (14.37)$$

$$M'_{pp} = c^2 M_{pp} + s^2 M_{qq} - 2scM_{pq} \quad (14.38)$$

$$M'_{qq} = s^2 M_{pp} + c^2 M_{qq} + 2scM_{pq} \quad (14.39)$$

$$M'_{pq,qp} = sc\left(M_{pp} - M_{qq}\right) + \left(c^2 - s^2\right)M_{pq} \quad (14.40)$$

We use the rotation matrix $\mathbf{R}^{(pq)}$ to annihilate the (p,q) entry of $\mathbf{M}$ and therefore need to choose the angle θ so that $M'_{pq} = 0$. Equation (14.40) thus becomes

$$\frac{c^2 - s^2}{sc} = \frac{M_{pp} - M_{qq}}{M_{pq}}. \quad (14.41)$$

Using the trigonometric identities

$$\sin 2\alpha = 2\sin\alpha\cos\alpha$$
$$\cos 2\alpha = \cos^2\alpha - \sin^2\alpha \quad (14.42)$$

(see Appendix B, Section B.4), we define u as

$$u = \frac{1}{\tan 2\theta} = \frac{c^2 - s^2}{2sc} = \frac{M_{pp} - M_{qq}}{2M_{pq}}. \quad (14.43)$$

We could now determine the angle θ by calculating $\frac{1}{2}\tan^{-1}\frac{1}{u}$. However, c and s can be found much more efficiently by observing that

$$t^2 + 2ut - 1 = 0, \tag{14.44}$$

where $t = s/c = \tan\theta$. Applying the quadratic formula, we have

$$t = -u \pm \sqrt{u^2 + 1}. \tag{14.45}$$

For best numerical stability, we want to choose the smaller of the two angles of rotation represented by this equation. The smaller value of t is given by

$$t = \operatorname{sgn}(u)\left(\sqrt{u^2 + 1} - |u|\right). \tag{14.46}$$

(In this case, we need $\operatorname{sgn}(0) = 1$ so that $t = 1$ when $u = 0$.) If u is so large that u^2 produces a floating-point infinity (possible when $\theta \approx 0$), we assign $t = 1/(2u)$ because

$$\operatorname{sgn}(u)\left(\sqrt{u^2 + 1} - |u|\right)\frac{\sqrt{u^2 + 1} + |u|}{\sqrt{u^2 + 1} + |u|} = \frac{\operatorname{sgn}(u)}{\sqrt{u^2 + 1} + |u|} \tag{14.47}$$

and

$$\lim_{u \to \infty} \frac{\sqrt{u^2 + 1}}{|u|} = 1. \tag{14.48}$$

Using the identity $t^2 + 1 = 1/c^2$ (see Appendix B, Section B.3), we can now compute the values of c and s as follows.

$$c = \frac{1}{\sqrt{t^2 + 1}}$$
$$s = ct \tag{14.49}$$

When calculating the entries of $\mathbf{M}'$, we simply assume that $M'_{pq} = 0$. We can then solve Equation (14.40) for M_{pp} and M_{qq}:

$$M_{pp} = M_{qq} + \frac{s^2 - c^2}{sc} M_{pq}$$
$$M_{qq} = M_{pp} - \frac{s^2 - c^2}{sc} M_{pq}. \tag{14.50}$$

Plugging this value of M_{qq} into Equation (14.38) and this value of M_{pp} into Equation (14.39) gives us the much simpler expressions

$$M'_{pp} = c^2 M_{pp} + s^2 \left(M_{pp} - \frac{s^2 - c^2}{sc} M_{pq} \right) - 2sc M_{pq}$$

$$= M_{pp} - t M_{pq} \tag{14.51}$$

and

$$M'_{qq} = s^2 \left(M_{qq} + \frac{s^2 - c^2}{sc} M_{pq} \right) + c^2 M_{qq} + 2sc M_{pq}$$

$$= M_{qq} + t M_{pq}. \tag{14.52}$$

To see that the Jacobi method converges to a diagonal matrix, we examine the sum of the squares of the distinct off-diagonal entries. For the matrix $\mathbf{M}$, the sum S of these three entries is

$$S = M_{ip}^2 + M_{iq}^2 + M_{pq}^2, \tag{14.53}$$

where $i \neq p,q$. Using Equation (14.37) to calculate the same sum S' for the matrix $\mathbf{M}'$ gives us

$$S' = \left(c M_{ip} - s M_{iq} \right)^2 + \left(s M_{ip} + c M_{iq} \right)^2 + \left(M'_{pq} \right)^2$$

$$= M_{ip}^2 + M_{iq}^2. \tag{14.54}$$

Thus, choosing a nonzero entry to serve as M_{pq} guarantees that the sum of the squares of the off-diagonal entries decreases by M_{pq}^2. Over many iterations, the sequence of sums decreases monotonically and has a lower bound of zero, so it must converge to zero.

The `CalculateEigensystem` function shown in Listing 14.6 implements the Jacobi method for finding the eigenvalues and eigenvectors of a 3×3 symmetric matrix $\mathbf{M}$. It annihilates the $(1,2)$ entry of $\mathbf{M}$, then the $(1,3)$ entry, and finally the $(2,3)$ entry. This process of cycling through the off-diagonal entries, each iteration of which is called a *sweep*, is repeated until the total size of the off-diagonal entries falls below a small positive threshold or a maximum number of sweeps have been executed.

Listing 14.6 The `CalculateEigensystem` function calculates the eigenvalues and eigenvectors of a 3×3 symmetric matrix.

Parameters

m   The 3×3 matrix for which eigenvalues and eigenvectors are to be calculated. This matrix must be symmetric.

lambda   A pointer to an array where the three eigenvalues are to be returned.

r   A 3×3 matrix whose columns contain the eigenvectors upon return. The *i*-th column corresponds to the *i*-th eigenvalue returned in the `lambda` array.

```cpp
const float epsilon = 1.0e-10F;
const int maxSweeps = 32;

struct Matrix3D
{
   float n[3][3];

   float& operator()(int i, int j)
   {
      return (n[j][i]);
   }

   const float& operator()(int i, int j) const
   {
      return (n[j][i]);
   }

   void SetIdentity(void)
   {
      n[0][0] = n[1][1] = n[2][2] = 1.0F;
      n[0][1] = n[0][2] = n[1][0] = n[1][2] =
         n[2][0] = n[2][1] = 0.0F;
   }
};

void CalculateEigensystem(const Matrix3D& m,
   float *lambda, Matrix3D& r)
{
   float m11 = m(0,0);
   float m12 = m(0,1);
   float m13 = m(0,2);
   float m22 = m(1,1);
   float m23 = m(1,2);
```

```
float m33 = m(2,2);

r.SetIdentity();
for (int a = 0; a < maxSweeps; a++)
{
    // Exit if off-diagonal entries small enough
    if ((Fabs(m12) < epsilon) && (Fabs(m13) < epsilon) &&
        (Fabs(m23) < epsilon)) break;

    // Annihilate (1,2) entry
    if (m12 != 0.0F)
    {
        float u = (m22 - m11) * 0.5F / m12;
        float u2 = u * u;
        float u2p1 = u2 + 1.0F;
        float t = (u2p1 != u2) ?
            ((u<0.0F) ? -1.0F : 1.0F) * (sqrt(u2p1) - fabs(u))
            : 0.5F / u;
        float c = 1.0F / sqrt(t * t + 1.0F);
        float s = c * t;

        m11 -= t * m12;
        m22 += t * m12;
        m12 = 0.0F;

        float temp = c * m13 - s * m23;
        m23 = s * m13 + c * m23;
        m13 = temp;

        for (int i = 0; i < 3; i++)
        {
            float temp = c * r(i,0) - s * r(i,1);
            r(i,1) = s * r(i,0) + c * r(i,1);
            r(i,0) = temp;
        }
    }

    // Annihilate (1,3) entry
    if (m13 != 0.0F)
    {
        float u = (m33 - m11) * 0.5F / m13;
        float u2 = u * u;
        float u2p1 = u2 + 1.0F;
        float t = (u2p1 != u2) ?
            ((u<0.0F) ? -1.0F : 1.0F) * (sqrt(u2p1) - fabs(u))
```

```
             : 0.5F / u;
      float c = 1.0F / sqrt(t * t + 1.0F);
      float s = c * t;

      m11 -= t * m13;
      m33 += t * m13;
      m13 = 0.0F;

      float temp = c * m12 - s * m23;
      m23 = s * m12 + c * m23;
      m12 = temp;

      for (int i = 0; i < 3; i++)
      {
         float temp = c * r(i,0) - s * r(i,2);
         r(i,2) = s * r(i,0) + c * r(i,2);
         r(i,0) = temp;
      }
   }

   // Annihilate (2,3) entry
   if (m23 != 0.0F)
   {
      float u = (m33 - m22) * 0.5F / m23;
      float u2 = u * u;
      float u2p1 = u2 + 1.0F;
      float t = (u2p1 != u2) ?
         ((u<0.0F) ? -1.0F : 1.0F) * (sqrt(u2p1) - fabs(u))
         : 0.5F / u;
      float c = 1.0F / sqrt(t * t + 1.0F);
      float s = c * t;

      m22 -= t * m23;
      m33 += t * m23;
      m23 = 0.0F;

      float temp = c * m12 - s * m13;
      m13 = s * m12 + c * m13;
      m12 = temp;

      for (int i = 0; i < 3; i++)
      {
         float temp = c * r(i,1) - s * r(i,2);
         r(i,2) = s * r(i,1) + c * r(i,2);
         r(i,1) = temp;
```

```
            }
        }
    }

    lambda[0] = m11;
    lambda[1] = m22;
    lambda[2] = m33;
}
```

14.3 Ordinary Differential Equations

In this section, we study methods for numerically solving first-order ordinary differential equations. We can always write such equations in the form

$$y'(x) = f(x, y),$$ (14.55)

where f is a function that we are able to evaluate for any given values of x and y. Most differential equations encountered in a physical simulation are second-order or higher, but we will be able to show that the ability to solve first-order equations also gives us the ability to solve equations of any order by writing them as a system of first-order equations.

14.3.1 Euler's Method

Euler's method is an extremely simple technique for approximating values of the solution $y(x)$ to the differential equation given by Equation (14.55). Coupled with this simplicity is low accuracy, so we describe Euler's method now only as an introduction to later discussions of more effective methods.

Suppose that we know an initial state $y(x_0) = y_0$, and we wish to approximate the value of the function y at $x = x_0 + h$, where h is some small step size. Writing the derivative $y'(x_0)$ as a finite difference, Equation (14.55) becomes

$$\frac{y(x_0 + h) - y_0}{h} = f(x, y).$$ (14.56)

Solving for $y(x_0 + h)$, we have

$$y(x_0 + h) = y_0 + hf(x, y).$$ (14.57)

This gives us the state $(x_1, y_1) = (x_0 + h, y(x_0 + h))$ from which the process can be repeated. The general formula for Euler's method is thus

$$x_{i+1} = x_i + h$$
$$y_{i+1} = y_i + hf(x_i, y_i). \tag{14.58}$$

Let us consider as an example a projectile moving under the influence of gravity. Its equation of motion is

$$y'(t) = v_0 - gt, \tag{14.59}$$

where t is time, y represents the height of the projectile, v_0 is the initial vertical velocity, and g is the (positive) acceleration of gravity. (We assume the horizontal velocity is constant.) We can use Euler's method to move from the point (t_i, y_i) to the point (t_{i+1}, y_{i+1}) by evaluating the equation

$$y_{i+1} = y_i + h(v_0 - gt). \tag{14.60}$$

Figure 14.1 shows the exact solution to Equation (14.59) for $v_0 = 6\,\text{m/s}$ and $y(0) = 0$, which we know to be $y(t) = v_0 t - \frac{1}{2} gt^2$, and the approximation to the projectile's position calculated using Euler's method with a step size of $h = 0.1\,\text{s}$. The minimal accuracy of Euler's method is clearly demonstrated by the divergence of the two curves. We could improve the situation by decreasing the step size h, but doing so requires more evaluations of Equation (14.58).

14.3.2 Taylor Series Method

Any method for approximating the solution to a differential equation by taking one step at a time assumes the form

$$y(x_i + h) = y(x_i) + hF(x_i, y_i), \tag{14.61}$$

where the function F is some function that produces an approximation to the derivative of y over the interval $[x_i, x_i + h]$. For Euler's method, the function F is simply the function f. To find a function F that achieves greater accuracy than that provided by Euler's method, we consider the Taylor series (see Appendix D) of $y(x_i + h)$:

$$y(x_i + h) = y(x_i) + hy'(x_i) + \frac{h^2}{2!} y''(x_i) + \frac{h^3}{3!} y^{(3)}(x_i) + \cdots. \tag{14.62}$$

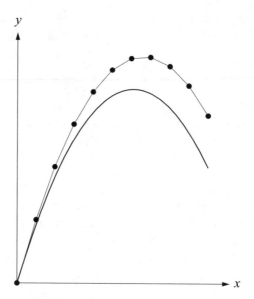

Figure 14.1 The solution to the differential equation $y'(t) = v_0 - gt$ with $y(0) = 0$, $v_0 = 6\,\text{m/s}$, and $g = 9.8\,\text{m/s}^2$. The piecewise curve is the approximation calculated using Euler's method with a step size of $h = 0.1\,\text{s}$.

For a differential equation written in the form of Equation (14.55), the derivatives of $y(x)$ can all be calculated using the relationship

$$y^{(n)}(x) = f^{(n-1)}(x, y). \qquad (14.63)$$

By taking $k - 1$ derivatives, we can calculate the Taylor series approximation of $y(x_i + h)$ to k-th order in the step size h, yielding

$$y(x_i + h) \approx y_i + hf(x_i, y_i) + \frac{h^2}{2!}f'(x_i, y_i) + \cdots + \frac{h^k}{k!}f^{(k-1)}(x_i, y_i), \qquad (14.64)$$

where $y_i = y(x_i)$. When $k = 1$, this reduces to Euler's method. Writing Equation (14.64) in the form of Equation (14.61), we have

$$y(x_i + h) = y(x_i) + hT_k(x_i, y_i), \qquad (14.65)$$

where $T_k(x_i, y_i)$ is defined as

$$T_k(x_i, y_i) = f(x_i, y_i) + \frac{h^2}{2!}f'(x_i, y_i) + \cdots + \frac{h^{k-1}}{k!}f^{(k-1)}(x_i, y_i). \qquad (14.66)$$

This is known as the *k-th order Taylor series method*.

Since y is a function of x, we must be careful to evaluate the total derivatives of $f(x, y)$ in the Taylor series. The first derivative is

$$f'(x, y) = \frac{\partial}{\partial x} f(x, y) + \frac{\partial}{\partial y} f(x, y) \frac{dy}{dx}. \tag{14.67}$$

Since $dy/dx = f(x, y)$, this becomes

$$f'(x, y) = \frac{\partial}{\partial x} f(x, y) + f(x, y) \frac{\partial}{\partial y} f(x, y). \tag{14.68}$$

Higher derivatives of $f(x, y)$ quickly become very messy, but we could theoretically compute them to construct the k-th order Taylor series approximation. The function f may have a form that enables easy calculation of its derivatives.

14.3.3 Runge-Kutta Method

Because of the necessity of calculating derivatives, the Taylor series method is not commonly used. Everything that we have examined so far in this section has served as a prelude to our discussion of the *Runge-Kutta method*, a reliable and accurate technique for numerically solving most differential equations that arise in physical simulations appearing in a 3D graphics application.

The Runge-Kutta method determines how to step from y_i to y_{i+1} by choosing the function F in Equation (14.61) to be one that evaluates $f(x, y)$ at multiple points and takes a weighted average to approximate the derivative of y. In general, the function F has the form

$$F(x_i, y_i) = \sum_{j=1}^{m} w_j f(u_j, v_j), \tag{14.69}$$

where m is the number of points at which $f(x, y)$ is evaluated, each point (u_j, v_j) lies near the point (x_i, y_i), and w_j is the weight associated with the j-th point. The points and weights are chosen so that $F(x_i, y_i)$ matches a k-th order Taylor series function $T_k(x_i, y_i)$ given by Equation (14.66). This is accomplished without having to evaluate derivatives of f.

The value of m is called the number of *stages* of the method. We first consider a two-stage Runge-Kutta method in which the function F has the form

$$F(x_i, y_i) = w_1 f(x_i, y_i) + w_2 f(x_i + ah, y_i + ahf(x_i, y_i)). \tag{14.70}$$

We would like to choose w_1, w_2, and a so that this function matches the second order Taylor series function $T_2(x_i, y_i)$ as closely as possible. To achieve this goal, we expand $f(x_i + ah, y_i + ahf(x_i, y_i))$ in a Taylor series as follows.

$$f(x_i + ah, y_i + ahf(x_i, y_i))$$
$$= f(x_i, y_i) + ah\left[\frac{\partial}{\partial x}f(x_i, y_i) + f(x_i, y_i)\frac{\partial}{\partial y}f(x_i, y_i)\right] + R \quad (14.71)$$

The remainder term R involves only higher powers of ah. Using this expansion, the function F can be written as

$$F(x_i, y_i) = (w_1 + w_2)f(x_i, y_i) +$$
$$w_2 ah\left[\frac{\partial}{\partial x}f(x_i, y_i) + f(x_i, y_i)\frac{\partial}{\partial y}f(x_i, y_i)\right] + w_2 R. \quad (14.72)$$

The Taylor series function $T_2(x_i, y_i)$ is given by

$$T_2(x_i, y_i) = f(x_i, y_i) + \frac{h}{2}\left[\frac{\partial}{\partial x}f(x, y) + f(x, y)\frac{\partial}{\partial y}f(x, y)\right]. \quad (14.73)$$

Equating like terms in Equations (14.72) and (14.73) (ignoring the term containing R), we see that the weights w_1 and w_2 must satisfy

$$w_1 + w_2 = 1$$
$$aw_2 = \tfrac{1}{2}. \quad (14.74)$$

Thus, $w_2 = 1/(2a)$ and $w_1 = 1 - 1/(2a)$. The value of a is unrestricted, but we should use a quantity that keeps the second point sampled in Equation (14.70) in the neighborhood of the point (x_i, y_i).

Choosing $a = \tfrac{1}{2}$ forces $w_1 = 0$ and produces the following step after plugging $F(x_i, y_i)$ into Equation (14.61).

$$y_{i+1} = y_i + hf\left(x_i + \frac{h}{2}, y_i + \frac{h}{2}f(x_i, y_i)\right) \quad (14.75)$$

Equation (14.75) is called the *modified Euler's method*. If we instead choose $a = 1$, then the weights are equal, and we have

$$y_{i+1} = y_i + \frac{h}{2}[f(x_i, y_i) + f(x_i + h, y_i + hf(x_i, y_i))]. \quad (14.76)$$

Equation (14.76) is called the *improved Euler's method* and is also known as *Heun's method*.

Runge-Kutta methods having a greater number of stages are derived in a manner similar to that used to derive the two-stage method, except that higher-order Taylor series expansions are equated. Without concerning ourselves with the details of the long and uninteresting derivation, we state a popular four-stage Runge-Kutta method, often called the *RK4 method*, as follows.

$$y_{i+1} = y_i + \frac{h}{6}[K_1(x_i,y_i) + 2K_2(x_i,y_i) + 2K_3(x_i,y_i) + K_4(x_i,y_i)] \quad (14.77)$$

$$
\begin{aligned}
K_1(x_i,y_i) &= f(x_i,y_i) \\
K_2(x_i,y_i) &= f\left(x_i + \frac{h}{2}, y_i + \frac{h}{2}K_1(x_i,y_i)\right) \\
K_3(x_i,y_i) &= f\left(x_i + \frac{h}{2}, y_i + \frac{h}{2}K_2(x_i,y_i)\right) \\
K_4(x_i,y_i) &= f(x_i + h, y_i + hK_3(x_i,y_i))
\end{aligned}
\quad (14.78)
$$

The RK4 method is usually more than adequate for the types of real-time simulations encountered in a 3D game application. The calculation of Equation (14.77) is very straightforward and also rather efficient for the accuracy that the RK4 method provides.

14.3.4 Higher-Order Differential Equations

We mentioned earlier that a higher-order differential equation could be transformed into a system of first-order differential equations, allowing us to solve it numerically using the methods already presented. First, let us consider a second-order differential equation

$$y''(x) = f(x,y,y'). \quad (14.79)$$

This can be expressed as the following pair of first-order equations.

$$
\begin{aligned}
y'(x) &= z(x) \\
z'(x) &= f(x,y,z)
\end{aligned}
\quad (14.80)
$$

Given initial conditions $y(x_0) = y_0$ and $z(x_0) = z_0$, we can solve this system using Euler's method by applying the following step formula.

$$x_{i+1} = x_i + h$$
$$y_{i+1} = y_i + hz_i$$
$$z_{i+1} = z_i + hf(x_i, y_i, z_i) \qquad (14.81)$$

In general, an n-th order differential equation $y^{(n)}(x) = f(x, y, y', \ldots, y^{(n-1)})$ can be written as the system of n first-order equations

$$z_1'(x) = z_2(x)$$
$$z_2'(x) = z_3(x)$$
$$\vdots$$
$$z_n'(x) = f(x, z_1, z_2, \ldots, z_n), \qquad (14.82)$$

where $z_1(x) = y(x)$, $z_2(x) = y'(x)$, and so on to $z_n(x) = y^{(n-1)}(x)$. We can express this as the vector first-order differential equation

$$\mathbf{z}'(x) = \mathbf{f}(x, \mathbf{z}), \qquad (14.83)$$

where $\mathbf{z}(x) = \langle z_1(x), z_2(x), \ldots, z_n(x) \rangle$ and

$$\mathbf{f}(x, \mathbf{z}) = \begin{bmatrix} z_2(x) \\ z_3(x) \\ \vdots \\ f(x, z_1, z_2, \ldots, z_n) \end{bmatrix}. \qquad (14.84)$$

The vector analog of Equation (14.61) is

$$\mathbf{z}(x_i + h) = \mathbf{z}(x_i) + h\mathbf{F}(x_i, \mathbf{z}_i), \qquad (14.85)$$

where $\mathbf{F}(x_i, \mathbf{z}_i)$ is a vector function representing an Euler method, Taylor series method, or Runge-Kutta method that is simply calculated componentwise.

Chapter 14 Summary

Linear Systems

The solution to a linear system $\mathbf{Lx} = \mathbf{r}$, where $\mathbf{L}$ is an $n \times n$ lower triangular matrix, can be found by forward substitution:

$$x_i = \frac{1}{L_{ii}}\left(r_i - \sum_{k=1}^{i-1} L_{ik} r_k\right).$$

The solution to a linear system $\mathbf{U}\mathbf{x} = \mathbf{r}$, where $\mathbf{U}$ is an $n \times n$ upper triangular matrix, can be found by backward substitution:

$$x_i = \frac{1}{U_{ii}}\left(r_i - \sum_{k=i+1}^{n} U_{ik} r_k\right).$$

A matrix $\mathbf{M}$ can be decomposed into the product $\mathbf{L}\mathbf{U}$, where $\mathbf{L}$ is lower triangular and $\mathbf{U}$ is upper triangular, using Doolittle's method. The linear system $\mathbf{M}\mathbf{x} = \mathbf{r}$ then becomes $\mathbf{L}(\mathbf{U}\mathbf{x}) = \mathbf{r}$, which can be solved in two stages by first using forward substitution to solve $\mathbf{L}\mathbf{y} = \mathbf{r}$ and then backward substitution to solve $\mathbf{U}\mathbf{x} = \mathbf{y}$.

Eigenvalues and Eigenvectors

The eigenvalues and eigenvectors of a 3×3 symmetric matrix $\mathbf{M}$ can be numerically calculated by applying the Jacobi method to diagonalize $\mathbf{M}$. When $\mathbf{M}$ is transformed by one of the rotation matrices $\mathbf{R}^{(pq)}$ given by Equation (14.36), the new entries of $\mathbf{M}$ are given by

$$\left.\begin{aligned} M'_{ii} &= M_{ii} \\ M'_{ip,pi} &= cM_{ip} - sM_{iq} \\ M'_{iq,qi} &= sM_{ip} + cM_{iq} \end{aligned}\right\} \quad \text{if } i \neq p \text{ and } i \neq q;$$

$$\begin{aligned} M'_{pp} &= M_{pp} - tM_{pq} \\ M'_{qq} &= M_{qq} + tM_{pq} \\ M'_{pq,qp} &= 0, \end{aligned}$$

where $t = s/c$.

Ordinary Differential Equations

The first-order ordinary differential equation $y'(x) = f(x,y)$ can be approximated using Euler's method as follows.

$$y_{i+1} = y_i + hf(x_i, y_i)$$

The improved Euler's method, also known as Heun's method, uses the step formula

$$y_{i+1} = y_i + \frac{h}{2}[f(x_i, y_i) + f(x_i + h, y_i + hf(x_i, y_i))].$$

The RK4 method has the following formulation.

$$y_{i+1} = y_i + \frac{h}{6}[K_1(x_i, y_i) + 2K_2(x_i, y_i) + 2K_3(x_i, y_i) + K_4(x_i, y_i)]$$

$$K_1(x_i, y_i) = f(x_i, y_i)$$

$$K_2(x_i, y_i) = f\left(x_i + \frac{h}{2}, y_i + \frac{h}{2}K_1(x_i, y_i)\right)$$

$$K_3(x_i, y_i) = f\left(x_i + \frac{h}{2}, y_i + \frac{h}{2}K_2(x_i, y_i)\right)$$

$$K_4(x_i, y_i) = f(x_i + h, y_i + hK_3(x_i, y_i))$$

Exercises for Chapter 14

1. Extend the Jacobi method to find eigenvalues and eigenvectors for an $n \times n$ symmetric matrix $\mathbf{M}$. Modify Listing 14.6 so that it cycles through all of the off-diagonal entries, annihilating them one at a time.

2. Calculate the second total derivative of $f(x, y(x))$ necessary to implement the third-order Taylor series method.

3. Implement the improved Euler's method (Heun's method) and apply it to the case of a projectile under the influence of gravity. Show that this method gives the exact solution to the equation $y'(t) = v_0 - gt$ no matter what step size is used.

4. Implement the RK4 method for first-order differential equations.

5. Implement the vector form of the RK4 method and apply it to the exact equation of motion for a pendulum given by Equation (12.113).

Chapter **15**

Curves and Surfaces

Curved geometry has become commonplace in 3D graphics engines due to modern hardware's ability to render the high number of vertices and faces needed to convincingly render smoothly varying surfaces. In addition to geometrical modeling, curves may be employed as paths along which certain objects travel. This chapter examines several classes of three-dimensional cubic curves and then discusses how they can be used to produce bicubic parametric surfaces.

15.1 Cubic Curves

Due to the balance that they possess between simplicity and flexibility, curves defined by cubic polynomials have earned widespread use by computer graphics applications. In the sections that follow, we examine several classes of cubic curves and compare their properties.

The fundamental form of a cubic curve is given by the parametric representation

$$\mathbf{Q}(t) = \mathbf{a} + \mathbf{b}t + \mathbf{c}t^2 + \mathbf{d}t^3, \qquad (15.1)$$

where **a**, **b**, **c**, and **d** are constant vectors, and $\mathbf{Q}(t)$ is the point on the curve corresponding to the parameter value t. Writing the components of $\mathbf{Q}(t)$ separately, we have

$$Q_x(t) = a_x + b_x t + c_x t^2 + d_x t^3$$
$$Q_y(t) = a_y + b_y t + c_y t^2 + d_y t^3$$
$$Q_z(t) = a_z + b_z t + c_z t^2 + d_z t^3. \tag{15.2}$$

It is convenient for us to write this as the following matrix product.

$$\mathbf{Q}(t) = \begin{bmatrix} a_x & b_x & c_x & d_x \\ a_y & b_y & c_y & d_y \\ a_z & b_z & c_z & d_z \end{bmatrix} \begin{bmatrix} 1 \\ t \\ t^2 \\ t^3 \end{bmatrix} \tag{15.3}$$

Using a more compact notation, we can write

$$\mathbf{Q}(t) = \mathbf{CT}(t), \tag{15.4}$$

where **C** represents the matrix of coefficients and $\mathbf{T}(t) \equiv \langle 1, t, t^2, t^3 \rangle$. The derivative of $\mathbf{Q}(t)$, which gives the tangent direction to the curve at t, is easy to calculate in this form since the matrix **C** is constant. Thus, we can write

$$\mathbf{Q}'(t) = \mathbf{C}\frac{d}{dt}\mathbf{T}(t) = \mathbf{C} \begin{bmatrix} 0 \\ 1 \\ 2t \\ 3t^2 \end{bmatrix}. \tag{15.5}$$

A long, curving path is generally composed of several smaller cubic "pieces" that are connected together at their endpoints. At the points where two adjacent pieces of a curve join together, there are the notions of *parametric continuity* and *geometric continuity*. The symbol C^n is used to represent n-th order parametric continuity, and the symbol G^n is used to represent n-th order geometric continuity. The two curves are said to have C^1 continuity if their tangent vectors are equal in both magnitude and direction at the join point. If the tangent vectors point in the same direction but have different magnitudes, then the curves have G^1 continuity. In general, two curves meet with C^n continuity if their n-th derivatives are equal, and two curves meet with G^n continuity if their n-th derivatives are nonzero and point in the same direction but do not have the same magnitude. C^n continuity implies G^n continuity unless the n-th derivatives are zero. C^0 and G^0 continuity are equivalent and simply mean that the curves share a common endpoint.

The classes of cubic curves that we examine in this chapter are defined in terms of certain geometrical constraints such as the endpoint positions (i.e., the values of $Q(t)$ at $t = 0$ and $t = 1$) or endpoint tangent directions (i.e., the values of $Q'(t)$ at $t = 0$ and $t = 1$). Since an arbitrary cubic curve has four coefficients, we need four constraints in order to define a particular curve. Calling these constraints g_1, g_2, g_3, and g_4, we can express the curve $Q(t)$ as

$$\begin{aligned} Q(t) = &\left(a_1 + b_1 t + c_1 t^2 + d_1 t^3\right)g_1 \\ &+ \left(a_2 + b_2 t + c_2 t^2 + d_2 t^3\right)g_2 \\ &+ \left(a_3 + b_3 t + c_3 t^2 + d_3 t^3\right)g_3 \\ &+ \left(a_4 + b_4 t + c_4 t^2 + d_4 t^3\right)g_4. \end{aligned} \tag{15.6}$$

This is simply a weighted sum of the four geometrical constraints. The polynomials $a_i + b_i t + c_i t^2 + d_i t^3$ are called the *blending functions*. Equation (15.6) can be written in matrix form as

$$Q(t) = \begin{bmatrix} g_1 & g_2 & g_3 & g_4 \end{bmatrix} \begin{bmatrix} a_1 & b_1 & c_1 & d_1 \\ a_2 & b_2 & c_2 & d_2 \\ a_3 & b_3 & c_3 & d_3 \\ a_4 & b_4 & c_4 & d_4 \end{bmatrix} \begin{bmatrix} 1 \\ t \\ t^2 \\ t^3 \end{bmatrix}. \tag{15.7}$$

We can write this more compactly as

$$Q(t) = GMT(t), \tag{15.8}$$

where the matrix G defined by

$$G = \begin{bmatrix} g_1 & g_2 & g_3 & g_4 \end{bmatrix} = \begin{bmatrix} \left(g_1\right)_x & \left(g_2\right)_x & \left(g_3\right)_x & \left(g_4\right)_x \\ \left(g_1\right)_y & \left(g_2\right)_y & \left(g_3\right)_y & \left(g_4\right)_y \\ \left(g_1\right)_z & \left(g_2\right)_z & \left(g_3\right)_z & \left(g_4\right)_z \end{bmatrix} \tag{15.9}$$

is called the *geometry matrix*, and the 4×4 matrix M defined by

$$\mathbf{M} = \begin{bmatrix} a_1 & b_1 & c_1 & d_1 \\ a_2 & b_2 & c_2 & d_2 \\ a_3 & b_3 & c_3 & d_3 \\ a_4 & b_4 & c_4 & d_4 \end{bmatrix} \tag{15.10}$$

is called the *basis matrix*. In most of the discussions that follow, there is a constant basis matrix $\mathbf{M}$ pertaining to each class of cubic curve, and the shapes of particular curves in each class are determined solely by the geometry matrix $\mathbf{G}$.

15.2 Hermite Curves

A cubic Hermite curve is defined by two endpoints $\mathbf{P}_1$ and $\mathbf{P}_2$, and the tangent directions $\mathbf{T}_1$ and $\mathbf{T}_2$ at those endpoints. Using these four quantities to define the geometry matrix, we can express a Hermite curve $\mathbf{H}(t)$ as

$$\mathbf{H}(t) = [\mathbf{P}_1 \quad \mathbf{P}_2 \quad \mathbf{T}_1 \quad \mathbf{T}_2] \mathbf{M}_H \begin{bmatrix} 1 \\ t \\ t^2 \\ t^3 \end{bmatrix}, \tag{15.11}$$

where $\mathbf{M}_H$ is a 4×4 basis matrix that we need to determine. The geometry matrix is $\mathbf{G}_H = [\mathbf{P}_1 \quad \mathbf{P}_2 \quad \mathbf{T}_1 \quad \mathbf{T}_2]$. By imposing the geometrical constraints, we obtain the four equations

$$\begin{aligned} \mathbf{H}(0) &= [\mathbf{P}_1 \quad \mathbf{P}_2 \quad \mathbf{T}_1 \quad \mathbf{T}_2] \mathbf{M}_H \langle 1,0,0,0 \rangle = \mathbf{P}_1 \\ \mathbf{H}(1) &= [\mathbf{P}_1 \quad \mathbf{P}_2 \quad \mathbf{T}_1 \quad \mathbf{T}_2] \mathbf{M}_H \langle 1,1,1,1 \rangle = \mathbf{P}_2 \\ \mathbf{H}'(0) &= [\mathbf{P}_1 \quad \mathbf{P}_2 \quad \mathbf{T}_1 \quad \mathbf{T}_2] \mathbf{M}_H \langle 0,1,0,0 \rangle = \mathbf{T}_1 \\ \mathbf{H}'(1) &= [\mathbf{P}_1 \quad \mathbf{P}_2 \quad \mathbf{T}_1 \quad \mathbf{T}_2] \mathbf{M}_H \langle 0,1,2,3 \rangle = \mathbf{T}_2. \end{aligned} \tag{15.12}$$

Writing this as the single equation

$$[\mathbf{P}_1 \quad \mathbf{P}_2 \quad \mathbf{T}_1 \quad \mathbf{T}_2]\mathbf{M}_H \begin{bmatrix} 1 & 1 & 0 & 0 \\ 0 & 1 & 1 & 1 \\ 0 & 1 & 0 & 2 \\ 0 & 1 & 0 & 3 \end{bmatrix} = [\mathbf{P}_1 \quad \mathbf{P}_2 \quad \mathbf{T}_1 \quad \mathbf{T}_2], \qquad (15.13)$$

we deduce that $\mathbf{M}_H$ must be given by

$$\mathbf{M}_H = \begin{bmatrix} 1 & 1 & 0 & 0 \\ 0 & 1 & 1 & 1 \\ 0 & 1 & 0 & 2 \\ 0 & 1 & 0 & 3 \end{bmatrix}^{-1} = \begin{bmatrix} 1 & 0 & -3 & 2 \\ 0 & 0 & 3 & -2 \\ 0 & 1 & -2 & 1 \\ 0 & 0 & -1 & 1 \end{bmatrix}. \qquad (15.14)$$

The basis matrix $\mathbf{M}_H$ provides the coefficients of the blending functions, allowing us to write the Hermite curve as the weighted sum of the geometrical constraints $\mathbf{P}_1$, $\mathbf{P}_2$, $\mathbf{T}_1$, and $\mathbf{T}_2$:

$$\mathbf{H}(t) = \left(1 - 3t^2 + 2t^3\right)\mathbf{P}_1 + t^2\left(3 - 2t\right)\mathbf{P}_2 + t(t-1)^2\mathbf{T}_1 + t^2(t-1)\mathbf{T}_2. \qquad (15.15)$$

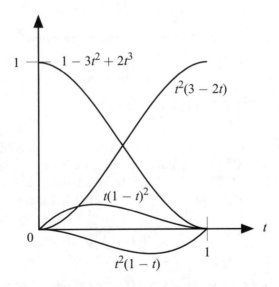

Figure 15.1 Blending functions for the Hermite class of cubic curves.

The blending functions are shown in Figure 15.1. As expected, only the weight corresponding to $\mathbf{P}_1$ is nonzero at $t = 0$, and only the weight corresponding to $\mathbf{P}_2$ is nonzero at $t = 1$.

Figure 15.2 shows two Hermite curves $\mathbf{H}_1(t)$ and $\mathbf{H}_2(t)$ that share a common endpoint. If the geometry matrix corresponding to the curve $\mathbf{H}_1(t)$ is given by $[\mathbf{P}_1 \quad \mathbf{P}_2 \quad \mathbf{T}_1 \quad \mathbf{T}_2]$, then G^1 continuity is achieved if the geometry matrix for the curve $\mathbf{H}_2(t)$ is equal to $[\mathbf{P}_2 \quad \mathbf{P}_3 \quad u\mathbf{T}_2 \quad \mathbf{T}_3]$ with $u > 0$, and C^1 continuity is achieved if $u = 1$.

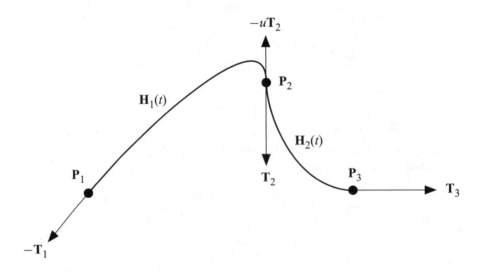

Figure 15.2 Two Hermite curves sharing the endpoint $\mathbf{P}_2$.

15.3 Bézier Curves

Although we shall limit ourselves to studying the cubic variety, a Bézier (pronounced BAY-ZEE-AY) curve can be defined for any polynomial degree n. Given $n+1$ points $\mathbf{P}_0, \mathbf{P}_1, \ldots, \mathbf{P}_n$, called the *control points* of the curve, the degree n Bézier curve $\mathbf{B}(t)$ is given by the parametric function

$$\mathbf{B}(t) = \sum_{k=0}^{n} B_{n,k}(t) \mathbf{P}_k , \tag{15.16}$$

where the blending functions $B_{n,k}(t)$ are the *Bernstein polynomials* defined by

$$B_{n,k} = \binom{n}{k} t^k (1-t)^{n-k} \qquad (15.17)$$

with the binomial coefficient

$$\binom{n}{k} = \frac{n!}{k!(n-k)!}. \qquad (15.18)$$

The first and last control points, $\mathbf{P}_0$ and $\mathbf{P}_n$, are interpolated by the curve, and the interior control points $\mathbf{P}_1, \mathbf{P}_2, \ldots, \mathbf{P}_{n-1}$ are approximated by the curve. The Bernstein polynomials can be generated by the recurrence relation

$$B_{n,k}(t) = (1-t) B_{n-1,k-1} + t B_{n-1,k}, \qquad (15.19)$$

where $B_{0,0} = 1$, and $B_{n,k} = 0$ whenever $k < 0$ or $k > n$. As shown in Figure 15.3, this recurrence resembles Pascal's triangle, but with the modification that each value is the weighted average of the two closest values above it instead of the sum.

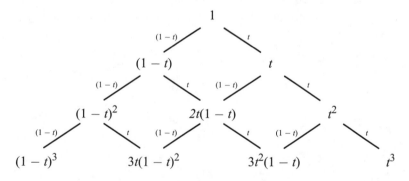

Figure 15.3 The Bernstein polynomials, generated by the recurrence relation given in Equation (15.19), can be calculated using a method similar to that used to calculate binomial coefficients in Pascal's triangle. Each value is the weighted average of the two closest values above it, where the weights are t and $1-t$. (For values on the left and right edges of the triangle, the missing value above it is assumed to be zero.)

15.3.1 Cubic Bézier Curves

The cubic Bézier curve has four control points whose positions are blended together by evaluating Equation (15.16) for $n = 3$:

$$\mathbf{B}(t) = \sum_{k=0}^{3} B_{3,k}(t)\mathbf{P}_k$$

$$= (1-t)^3 \mathbf{P}_0 + 3t(1-t)^2 \mathbf{P}_1 + 3t^2(1-t)\mathbf{P}_2 + t^3\mathbf{P}_3. \qquad (15.20)$$

The geometry matrix for a cubic Bézier curve is $\mathbf{G}_B = \begin{bmatrix} \mathbf{P}_0 & \mathbf{P}_1 & \mathbf{P}_2 & \mathbf{P}_3 \end{bmatrix}$. From Equation (15.20), we can derive the basis matrix $\mathbf{M}_B$ for the cubic Bézier curve and write $\mathbf{B}(t)$ as follows.

$$\mathbf{B}(t) = \begin{bmatrix} \mathbf{P}_0 & \mathbf{P}_1 & \mathbf{P}_2 & \mathbf{P}_3 \end{bmatrix} \begin{bmatrix} 1 & -3 & 3 & -1 \\ 0 & 3 & -6 & 3 \\ 0 & 0 & 3 & -3 \\ 0 & 0 & 0 & 1 \end{bmatrix} \begin{bmatrix} 1 \\ t \\ t^2 \\ t^3 \end{bmatrix} \qquad (15.21)$$

The four Bernstein polynomials appearing in Equation (15.20) are shown in Figure 15.4. Since the Bézier curve interpolates the endpoints $\mathbf{P}_0$ and $\mathbf{P}_3$, we must have

$$B_{3,k}(0) = \begin{cases} 1, & \text{if } k = 0; \\ 0, & \text{if } k = 1,2,3; \end{cases} \qquad (15.22)$$

and

$$B_{3,k}(1) = \begin{cases} 0, & \text{if } k = 0,1,2; \\ 1, & \text{if } k = 3. \end{cases} \qquad (15.23)$$

An additional property of the Bernstein polynomials is that they sum to unity for all values of t:

$$\sum_{k=0}^{3} B_{3,k}(t) = 1. \qquad (15.24)$$

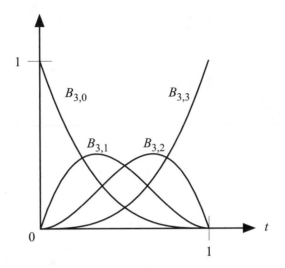

Figure 15.4 The blending functions for the cubic Bézier curve. The functions $B_{3,k}$ are the degree 3 Bernstein polynomials.

Figure 15.5 shows some of the shapes that a Bézier curve may assume. A useful property of the Bézier curve is that it is entirely contained within the convex hull of its control points. That is, the smallest polyhedron containing all four control points of a Bézier curve $\mathbf{B}(t)$ also contains every point on the curve between $t = 0$ and $t = 1$. This is a consequence of the fact that the Bernstein polynomials are nonnegative on the interval $[0,1]$ and that they sum to unity.

The derivative of a Bézier curve $\mathbf{B}(t)$, giving the tangent direction to the curve, can be expressed as

$$\mathbf{B}'(t) = \begin{bmatrix} \mathbf{P}_0 & \mathbf{P}_1 & \mathbf{P}_2 & \mathbf{P}_3 \end{bmatrix} \begin{bmatrix} -3 & 6 & -3 \\ 3 & -12 & 9 \\ 0 & 6 & -9 \\ 0 & 0 & 3 \end{bmatrix} \begin{bmatrix} 1 \\ t \\ t^2 \end{bmatrix}. \tag{15.25}$$

Examining the derivative at $t = 0$ and $t = 1$, we find

$$\mathbf{B}'(0) = 3(\mathbf{P}_1 - \mathbf{P}_0)$$
$$\mathbf{B}'(1) = 3(\mathbf{P}_3 - \mathbf{P}_2). \tag{15.26}$$

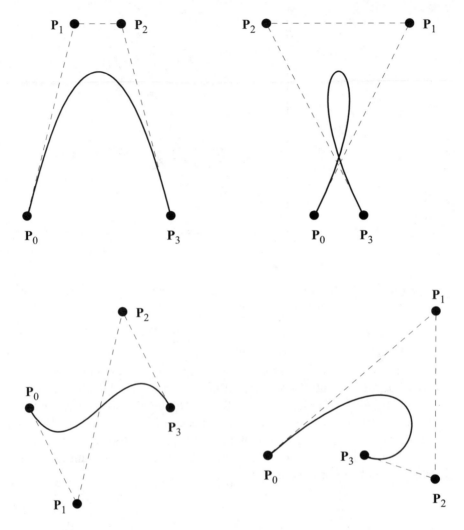

Figure 15.5 A variety of Bézier curves having control points P_0, P_1, P_2, and P_3.

This reveals that the tangent directions at the endpoints are multiples of the differences between the endpoints and the adjacent interior control points. This provides us with a mechanism for easily translating between the Bézier form and Hermite form of a cubic curve. To translate from Bézier to Hermite (where we are now calling the endpoints of the Hermite curve P_0 and P_3), we simply use the values given by Equation (15.26) as the tangents T_1 and T_2 corresponding to the endpoints P_0 and P_3, respectively. To translate from Hermite to Bézier, we solve Equation (15.26) for the interior control points as follows.

$$\mathbf{P}_1 = \mathbf{P}_0 + \frac{\mathbf{T}_1}{3}$$

$$\mathbf{P}_2 = \mathbf{P}_3 - \frac{\mathbf{T}_2}{3} \tag{15.27}$$

15.3.2 Bézier Curve Truncation

Equation (15.27) is also useful for calculating the interior controls points for a Bézier curve that exactly matches another Bézier curve on an interval $[t_0, t_1]$. This process is called *truncation* and is illustrated in Figure 15.6. Suppose we wish to truncate a Bézier curve $\mathbf{B}_P(t)$ having the control points $\mathbf{P}_0$, $\mathbf{P}_1$, $\mathbf{P}_2$, and $\mathbf{P}_3$ to the interval $[t_0, t_1]$ by creating a new Bézier curve $\mathbf{B}_Q(u)$ having the control points $\mathbf{Q}_0$, $\mathbf{Q}_1$, $\mathbf{Q}_2$, and $\mathbf{Q}_3$. The new parameter u is related to the parameter t by the function

$$t(u) = t_0 + (t_1 - t_0)u. \tag{15.28}$$

The endpoints $\mathbf{Q}_0$ and $\mathbf{Q}_3$ of the new Bézier curve are simply

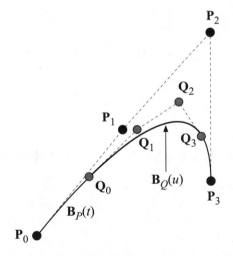

Figure 15.6 A Bézier curve $\mathbf{B}_P(t)$ having the control points $\mathbf{P}_0$, $\mathbf{P}_1$, $\mathbf{P}_2$, and $\mathbf{P}_3$ is truncated to the interval $[t_0, t_1]$ to create a new Bézier curve $\mathbf{B}_Q(u)$ having the control points $\mathbf{Q}_0$, $\mathbf{Q}_1$, $\mathbf{Q}_2$, and $\mathbf{Q}_3$.

$$\mathbf{Q}_0 = \mathbf{B}_P(t_0)$$
$$\mathbf{Q}_3 = \mathbf{B}_P(t_1). \tag{15.29}$$

The interior control points $\mathbf{Q}_1$ and $\mathbf{Q}_2$ are obtained using Equation (15.27), but we must be careful to calculate the tangents with respect to the parameter u. Since the curves $\mathbf{B}_P(t)$ and $\mathbf{B}_Q(u)$ are coincident,

$$\mathbf{B}_Q(u) = \mathbf{B}_P(t(u)).$$

Thus, applying the chain rule, we have

$$\frac{d}{du}\mathbf{B}_Q(u) = \frac{d}{dt}\mathbf{B}_P(t(u))\frac{d}{du}t(u)$$
$$= (t_1 - t_0)\mathbf{B}'_P(t_0 + (t_1 - t_0)u). \tag{15.30}$$

The tangents $\mathbf{T}_0$ and $\mathbf{T}_3$ to the curve $\mathbf{B}_Q(u)$ at $u = 0$ and $u = 1$ are given by

$$\mathbf{T}_0 = \mathbf{B}'_Q(0) = (t_1 - t_0)\mathbf{B}'_P(t_0)$$
$$\mathbf{T}_3 = \mathbf{B}'_Q(1) = (t_1 - t_0)\mathbf{B}'_P(t_1), \tag{15.31}$$

and the control points $\mathbf{Q}_1$ and $\mathbf{Q}_2$ are therefore

$$\mathbf{Q}_1 = \mathbf{Q}_0 + \frac{\mathbf{T}_0}{3} = \mathbf{Q}_0 + \frac{(t_1 - t_0)}{3}\mathbf{B}'_P(t_0)$$
$$\mathbf{Q}_2 = \mathbf{Q}_3 - \frac{\mathbf{T}_3}{3} = \mathbf{Q}_3 - \frac{(t_1 - t_0)}{3}\mathbf{B}'_P(t_1). \tag{15.32}$$

15.3.3 The de Casteljau Algorithm

The de Casteljau algorithm provides a geometrical construction by which we can subdivide a Bézier curve into two parts at an arbitrary parameter value $t \in [0,1]$. During the construction, we obtain the four control points corresponding to both components of the subdivided curve.

Suppose that we split a Bézier curve $\mathbf{B}_P(t)$ having the controls points $\mathbf{P}_0$, $\mathbf{P}_1$, $\mathbf{P}_2$, and $\mathbf{P}_3$ at the parameter value $t = s$ to create two new Bézier curves $\mathbf{B}_Q(u)$ and $\mathbf{B}_R(v)$ coinciding with the original curve on the intervals $[0,s]$ and $[s,1]$, respectively. Equations (15.29) and (15.32) provide the control points $\mathbf{Q}_0$, $\mathbf{Q}_1$, $\mathbf{Q}_2$, and $\mathbf{Q}_3$ of the curve $\mathbf{B}_Q(u)$:

$$\mathbf{Q}_0 = \mathbf{B}_P(0) = \mathbf{P}_0$$

$$\mathbf{Q}_1 = \mathbf{B}_P(0) + \frac{s}{3}\mathbf{B}'_P(0)$$

$$\mathbf{Q}_2 = \mathbf{B}_P(s) - \frac{s}{3}\mathbf{B}'_P(s)$$

$$\mathbf{Q}_3 = \mathbf{B}_P(s). \tag{15.33}$$

Evaluating the functions $\mathbf{B}_P$ and $\mathbf{B}'_P$ for $\mathbf{Q}_1$ and $\mathbf{Q}_2$ gives us the following formulas for the interior control points of $\mathbf{B}_Q(u)$.

$$\mathbf{Q}_1 = (1-s)\mathbf{P}_0 + s\mathbf{P}_1$$
$$= (1-s)\mathbf{Q}_0 + s\mathbf{P}_1 \tag{15.34}$$

$$\mathbf{Q}_2 = (1-s)[(1-s)\mathbf{P}_0 + s\mathbf{P}_1] + s[(1-s)\mathbf{P}_1 + s\mathbf{P}_2]$$
$$= (1-s)\mathbf{Q}_1 + s[(1-s)\mathbf{P}_1 + s\mathbf{P}_2] \tag{15.35}$$

We repeat a similar procedure for the control points $\mathbf{R}_0$, $\mathbf{R}_1$, $\mathbf{R}_2$, and $\mathbf{R}_3$ of the curve $\mathbf{B}_R(v)$:

$$\mathbf{R}_0 = \mathbf{B}_P(s)$$

$$\mathbf{R}_1 = \mathbf{B}_P(s) + \frac{1-s}{3}\mathbf{B}'_P(s)$$

$$\mathbf{R}_2 = \mathbf{B}_P(1) - \frac{1-s}{3}\mathbf{B}'_P(1)$$

$$\mathbf{R}_3 = \mathbf{B}_P(1) = \mathbf{P}_3. \tag{15.36}$$

Formulas for the interior control points of $\mathbf{B}_R(v)$ are found by evaluating the functions $\mathbf{B}_P$ and $\mathbf{B}'_P$ as follows.

$$\mathbf{R}_2 = (1-s)\mathbf{P}_2 + s\mathbf{P}_3$$
$$= (1-s)\mathbf{P}_2 + s\mathbf{R}_3 \tag{15.37}$$

$$\mathbf{R}_1 = (1-s)[(1-s)\mathbf{P}_1 + s\mathbf{P}_2] + s[(1-s)\mathbf{P}_2 + s\mathbf{P}_3]$$
$$= (1-s)[(1-s)\mathbf{P}_1 + s\mathbf{P}_2] + s\mathbf{R}_2 \tag{15.38}$$

Finally, we take a look at the value of $\mathbf{Q}_3 = \mathbf{R}_0$. This is the point where the line segment connecting $\mathbf{Q}_2$ and $\mathbf{R}_1$ is tangent to the curve $\mathbf{B}_P(t)$. If we evaluate $\mathbf{B}_P(s)$ and compare it to Equations (15.35) and (15.38), we see that

$$\mathbf{B}_P(s) = (1-s)\mathbf{Q}_2 + s\mathbf{R}_1. \tag{15.39}$$

The entire procedure that we just went through leads us to the formulation of the de Casteljau algorithm. As illustrated in Figure 15.7, we begin by connecting adjacent pairs of the four control points $\mathbf{P}_0$, $\mathbf{P}_1$, $\mathbf{P}_2$, and $\mathbf{P}_3$, creating three line segments. We then construct the points $\mathbf{P}_0^{(1)}$, $\mathbf{P}_1^{(1)}$, and $\mathbf{P}_2^{(1)}$ by linearly interpolating the endpoints of each of the line segments using the parameter value s as follows.

$$\mathbf{P}_i^{(1)} = (1-s)\mathbf{P}_i + s\mathbf{P}_{i+1} \tag{15.40}$$

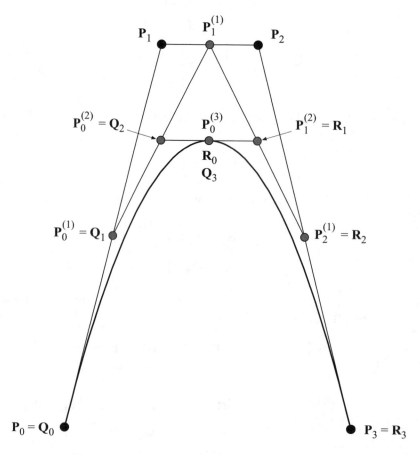

Figure 15.7 A Bézier curve is subdivided into two components at the parameter value $s = 1/2$. The gray points are those constructed by the de Casteljau algorithm.

This process recurs by connecting these new points and interpolating at the parameter value s until we are left with only one point $\mathbf{P}_0^{(3)}$. In general, we have the recurrence formula

$$\mathbf{P}_i^{(k)} = (1-s)\mathbf{P}_i^{(k-1)} + s\mathbf{P}_{i+1}^{(k-1)}, \tag{15.41}$$

where we have equated $\mathbf{P}_i^{(0)} \equiv \mathbf{P}_i$. The control points of the two components of the subdivided Bézier curve are given by

$$\begin{aligned} \mathbf{Q}_i &= \mathbf{P}_0^{(i)} \\ \mathbf{R}_i &= \mathbf{P}_i^{(3-i)}. \end{aligned} \tag{15.42}$$

15.4 Catmull-Rom Splines

Given a set of $n+1$ points $\{\mathbf{P}_0, \mathbf{P}_1, \ldots, \mathbf{P}_n\}$ with $n \geq 3$, a Catmull-Rom spline interpolates the points $\{\mathbf{P}_1, \mathbf{P}_2, \ldots, \mathbf{P}_{n-1}\}$ using a piecewise cubic curve. The tangent direction $\mathbf{T}_i$ at each point $\mathbf{P}_i$ is given by

$$\mathbf{T}_i = \frac{1}{2}(\mathbf{P}_{i+1} - \mathbf{P}_{i-1}). \tag{15.43}$$

We can express each piece $\mathbf{C}_i(t)$ of the spline, where $1 \leq i \leq n-2$, as a Hermite curve having the endpoints $\mathbf{P}_i$ and $\mathbf{P}_{i+1}$ and the tangents $\mathbf{T}_i$ and $\mathbf{T}_{i+1}$:

$$\mathbf{C}_i(t) = \begin{bmatrix} \mathbf{P}_i & \mathbf{P}_{i+1} & \mathbf{T}_i & \mathbf{T}_{i+1} \end{bmatrix} \mathbf{M}_H \begin{bmatrix} 1 \\ t \\ t^2 \\ t^3 \end{bmatrix}. \tag{15.44}$$

We would like to find a basis matrix $\mathbf{M}_{CR}$ that allows us to express the geometry matrix $\mathbf{G}_{CR}$ as four points, so we observe the following.

$$
\begin{bmatrix} \mathbf{P}_i & \mathbf{P}_{i+1} & \mathbf{T}_i & \mathbf{T}_{i+1} \end{bmatrix} = \begin{bmatrix} \mathbf{P}_{i-1} & \mathbf{P}_i & \mathbf{P}_{i+1} & \mathbf{P}_{i+2} \end{bmatrix} \begin{bmatrix} 0 & 0 & -\frac{1}{2} & 0 \\ 1 & 0 & 0 & -\frac{1}{2} \\ 0 & 1 & \frac{1}{2} & 0 \\ 0 & 0 & 0 & \frac{1}{2} \end{bmatrix} \tag{15.45}
$$

Substituting this into Equation (15.44) shows us that the basis matrix $\mathbf{M}_{CR}$ must be the product of the rightmost matrix in Equation (15.45) and the Hermite basis matrix $\mathbf{M}_H$. Thus,

$$
\mathbf{M}_{CR} = \frac{1}{2} \begin{bmatrix} 0 & 0 & -1 & 0 \\ 2 & 0 & 0 & -1 \\ 0 & 2 & 1 & 0 \\ 0 & 0 & 0 & 1 \end{bmatrix} \begin{bmatrix} 1 & 0 & -3 & 2 \\ 0 & 0 & 3 & -2 \\ 0 & 1 & -2 & 1 \\ 0 & 0 & -1 & 1 \end{bmatrix} = \frac{1}{2} \begin{bmatrix} 0 & -1 & 2 & -1 \\ 2 & 0 & -5 & 3 \\ 0 & 1 & 4 & -3 \\ 0 & 0 & -1 & 1 \end{bmatrix}, \tag{15.46}
$$

and we can express the pieces of the Catmull-Rom spline as

$$
\mathbf{C}_i(t) = \begin{bmatrix} \mathbf{P}_{i-1} & \mathbf{P}_i & \mathbf{P}_{i+1} & \mathbf{P}_{i+2} \end{bmatrix} \mathbf{M}_{CR} \begin{bmatrix} 1 \\ t \\ t^2 \\ t^3 \end{bmatrix}, \tag{15.47}
$$

where the geometry matrix is $\mathbf{G}_{CR} = \begin{bmatrix} \mathbf{P}_{i-1} & \mathbf{P}_i & \mathbf{P}_{i+1} & \mathbf{P}_{i+2} \end{bmatrix}$. Figure 15.8 shows an example of a Catmull-Rom spline and illustrates how the tangent at each point is parallel to the line segment connecting the two neighboring points.

15.5 Cubic Splines

The piecewise cubic curves that we have examined up to this point exhibit *local control*, meaning that if the geometrical constraints are modified for one of the cubic functions composing the curve, then only that piece of the curve and its immediate neighbors can be affected. We now examine a different kind of curve called a *cubic spline*. Cubic splines exhibit *global control* through the fact that moving one of the control points affects the entire curve.

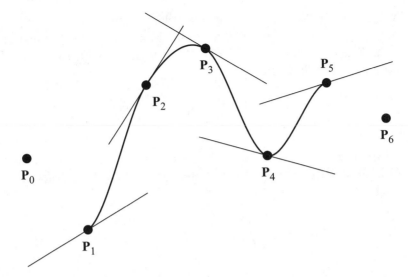

Figure 15.8 A Catmull-Rom spline interpolates a set of points in such a way that the tangent direction at each point is parallel to the line segment connecting the two neighboring points.

A cubic spline is a set of piecewise cubic polynomials that interpolate a given set of points and maintain C^2 continuity everywhere. Cubic splines require no geometrical constraints, such as tangent directions or control points, in addition to the points that they interpolate. We derive the cubic spline as a set of scalar functions $S_i(x)$. This can be extended to a parametric interpolation of a set of 3D points by constructing cubic splines for each coordinate independently.

Suppose we have a set of $n+1$ points $\{\langle x_0, y_0 \rangle, \langle x_1, y_1 \rangle, \ldots, \langle x_n, y_n \rangle\}$ where $x_i < x_{i+1}$ for $0 \le i \le n-1$. We wish to find a set of n cubic polynomial functions $\{S_0(x), S_1(x), \ldots, S_{n-1}(x)\}$ where each function $S_i(x)$ is defined on the interval $[x_i, x_{i+1}]$.

$$S_i(x_{i+1}) = S_{i+1}(x_{i+1}) \tag{15.48}$$

$$S_i'(x_{i+1}) = S_{i+1}'(x_{i+1}) \tag{15.49}$$

$$S_i''(x_{i+1}) = S_{i+1}''(x_{i+1}) \tag{15.50}$$

We define the constants h_i and k_i as follows for $0 \le i \le n-1$.

$$\begin{aligned} h_i &= x_{i+1} - x_i \\ k_i &= y_{i+1} - y_i \end{aligned} \tag{15.51}$$

We construct the cubic spline interpolating the points $\{\langle x_i, y_i \rangle\}_{i=0}^{n}$ by choosing values for the second derivatives of the functions $\{S_i(x)\}_{i=0}^{n-1}$ that cause the conditions listed in Equations (15.48), (15.49), and (15.50) to be satisfied. We begin with the set of functions

$$S_i''(x) = \frac{y_i''}{h_i}(x_{i+1} - x) + \frac{y_{i+1}''}{h_i}(x - x_i), \tag{15.52}$$

where the constants $y_0'', y_1'', \ldots y_n''$ have not yet been determined, but Equation (15.50) is satisfied regardless of their eventual values. Integrating $S_i''(x)$ twice, we have

$$S_i(x) = \frac{y_i''}{6h_i}(x_{i+1} - x)^3 + \frac{y_{i+1}''}{6h_i}(x - x_i)^3 + C_i x + D_i, \tag{15.53}$$

where C_i and D_i are the constants of integration. For later convenience, we replace the arbitrary linear polynomial $C_i x + D_i$ with a different linear polynomial,

$$A_i(x_{i+1} - x) + B_i(x - x_i), \tag{15.54}$$

to obtain

$$S_i(x) = \frac{y_i''}{6h_i}(x_{i+1} - x)^3 + \frac{y_{i+1}''}{6h_i}(x - x_i)^3 + A_i(x_{i+1} - x) + B_i(x - x_i). \tag{15.55}$$

Applying the requirements that $S_i(x_i) = y_i$ and $S_i(x_{i+1}) = y_{i+1}$ allows us to write the pair of equations

$$y_i = \frac{y_i''}{6}h_i^2 + A_i h_i$$

$$y_{i+1} = \frac{y_{i+1}''}{6}h_i^2 + B_i h_i, \tag{15.56}$$

from which we can deduce the following values of A_i and B_i.

$$A_i = \frac{y_i}{h_i} - \frac{y_i'' h_i}{6}$$

$$B_i = \frac{y_{i+1}}{h_i} - \frac{y_{i+1}'' h_i}{6} \tag{15.57}$$

Plugging these values into Equation (15.55) gives us

$$S_i(x) = \frac{y_i''}{6h_i}(x_{i+1} - x)^3 + \frac{y_{i+1}''}{6h_i}(x - x_i)^3$$

$$+ \left(\frac{y_i}{h_i} - \frac{y_i''h_i}{6}\right)(x_{i+1} - x) + \left(\frac{y_{i+1}}{h_i} - \frac{y_{i+1}''h_i}{6}\right)(x - x_i). \qquad (15.58)$$

Differentiating, we have

$$S_i'(x) = -\frac{y_i''}{2h_i}(x_{i+1} - x)^2 + \frac{y_{i+1}''}{2h_i}(x - x_i)^2 + \frac{k_i}{h_i} + \frac{h_i}{6}(y_i'' - y_{i+1}''). \qquad (15.59)$$

By applying the requirement that $S_i'(x_{i+1}) = S_{i+1}'(x_{i+1})$, we arrive at the following system of $n-1$ equations.

$$h_i y_i'' + 2(h_i + h_{i+1}) y_{i+1}'' + h_{i+1} y_{i+2}'' = 6\left(\frac{k_{i+1}}{h_{i+1}} - \frac{k_i}{h_i}\right); \qquad 0 \le i \le n-2 \qquad (15.60)$$

Since there are $n+1$ unknowns $y_0'', y_1'', \ldots, y_n''$, the solution set to the system given by Equation (15.60) is a two-dimensional space. We can reduce this to a single solution by choosing any values we like for the second derivatives y_0'' and y_n'' at the endpoints and moving the terms in which they appear to the right side of Equation (15.60) for $i = 0$ and $i = n-2$. The resulting system of $n-1$ equations having $n-1$ unknowns is written in matrix form as

$$\begin{bmatrix} m_0 & h_1 & 0 & \cdots & 0 & 0 & 0 \\ h_1 & m_1 & h_2 & \cdots & 0 & 0 & 0 \\ \vdots & & \ddots & & & & \vdots \\ 0 & 0 & 0 & \cdots & h_{n-3} & m_{n-3} & h_{n-2} \\ 0 & 0 & 0 & \cdots & 0 & h_{n-2} & m_{n-2} \end{bmatrix} \begin{bmatrix} y_1'' \\ y_2'' \\ \vdots \\ y_{n-2}'' \\ y_{n-1}'' \end{bmatrix} = \begin{bmatrix} p_0 - h_0 y_0'' \\ p_1 \\ \vdots \\ p_{n-3} \\ p_{n-2} - h_{n-1} y_n'' \end{bmatrix}, \qquad (15.61)$$

where

$$m_i = 2(h_i + h_{i+1})$$

$$p_i = 6\left(\frac{k_{i+1}}{h_{i+1}} - \frac{k_i}{h_i}\right). \qquad (15.62)$$

The matrix appearing in Equation (15.61) is tridiagonal and diagonally dominant, so the values $\{y_i''\}_{i=1}^{n-1}$ can easily be found using the method described in Section 14.1.5.

Plugging the values $\{y_i''\}_{i=0}^{n}$ into Equation (15.58) gives us the pieces of the cubic spline. The second derivatives y_0'' and y_n'' at the ends of the curve may be arbitrarily chosen and are usually set to zero. When $y_0'' = y_n'' = 0$, the curve is called a *natural cubic spline*. An example of a natural cubic spline is shown in Figure 15.9.

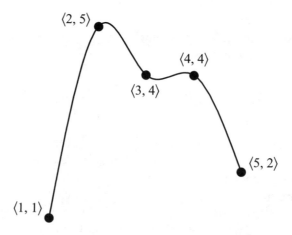

Figure 15.9 A natural cubic spline interpolates a set of points with C^2 continuity.

15.6 B-Splines

The Catmull-Rom spline and the natural cubic spline both interpolate a set of points without requiring any information in excess of the points themselves. The Catmull-Rom spline exhibits the local control property and provides C^1 continuity. The natural cubic spline provides C^2 continuity, but at the cost of local control since moving one point changes the entire curve. We now examine the *B-spline*, a curve that possesses the local control property and provides C^2 continuity everywhere. The trade-off is that a B-spline does not generally interpolate a set of points, but only approximates their positions.

15.6.1 Uniform B-Splines

Like Hermite and Bézier curves, each piece of a B-spline can be expressed as a cubic curve in terms of a basis matrix and geometry matrix. The letter "B" in B-spline stands for "basis" and distinguishes the curve from the natural cubic spline, which does not use the basis and geometry matrix formulation. The geometry matrix $\mathbf{G}_{BS}$ used by the B-spline is the same as that used by the Catmull-Rom spline:

$$\mathbf{G}_{BS} = \begin{bmatrix} \mathbf{P}_{i-1} & \mathbf{P}_i & \mathbf{P}_{i+1} & \mathbf{P}_{i+2} \end{bmatrix}. \tag{15.63}$$

Given a set of $n+1$ control points $\{\mathbf{P}_0, \mathbf{P}_1, \ldots, \mathbf{P}_n\}$, a B-spline is composed of $n-2$ cubic curves $\mathbf{Q}_i(t)$ corresponding to the pair of points $\mathbf{P}_i$ and $\mathbf{P}_{i+1}$. Each of these pieces is expressed as the weighted sum

$$\mathbf{Q}_i(t) = \sum_{k=0}^{3} B_k(t) \mathbf{P}_{i+k-1}, \tag{15.64}$$

where the blending functions $B_k(t)$ are determined by imposing the constraint that the entire curve possess C^2 continuity.

The set of points $\{\mathbf{Q}_2(0), \mathbf{Q}_3(0), \ldots, \mathbf{Q}_{n-2}(0)\}$ where the pieces of the B-spline join together are called *knots*. We also classify as knots the endpoints of the curve, $\mathbf{Q}_1(0)$ and $\mathbf{Q}_{n-2}(1)$, and thus a curve having $n+1$ controls points possesses $n-1$ knots. A B-spline is called *uniform* if the knots are spaced at equal parameter values along the entire curve. At this point, we are only considering the case that each piece $\mathbf{Q}_i(t)$ of the curve corresponds to a parameter range of $[0,1]$, so we are dealing with uniform B-splines. Nonuniform B-splines, in which the knots may not be equally spaced with respect to the parameterization, are discussed in Section 15.6.3. Figure 15.10 shows the six knots belonging to a B-spline curve having eight control points and thus five cubic pieces.

The blending functions $B_k(t)$ are found by requiring C^2 continuity at each knot, leading to the following equations.

$$\mathbf{Q}_i(1) = \mathbf{Q}_{i+1}(0)$$
$$\mathbf{Q}_i'(1) = \mathbf{Q}_{i+1}'(0)$$
$$\mathbf{Q}_i''(1) = \mathbf{Q}_{i+1}''(0) \tag{15.65}$$

Expanding the first of these requirements with Equation (15.64), we have

$$B_0(1)\mathbf{P}_{i-1} + B_1(1)\mathbf{P}_i + B_2(1)\mathbf{P}_{i+1} + B_3(1)\mathbf{P}_{i+2}$$
$$= B_0(0)\mathbf{P}_i + B_1(0)\mathbf{P}_{i+1} + B_2(0)\mathbf{P}_{i+2} + B_3(0)\mathbf{P}_{i+3}. \tag{15.66}$$

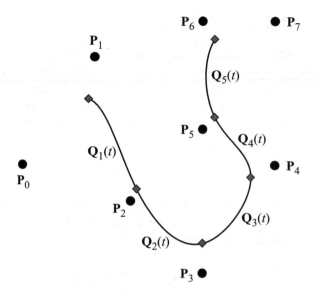

Figure 15.10 A B-spline curve constructed using the eight control points P_i. The gray diamonds indicate the positions of the six knots corresponding to the values of $Q_i(0)$ and $Q_i(1)$.

Since this equation must be satisfied for arbitrary choices of the control points P_i, the coefficients of each point in the equation must be equal on both the left and right sides. Three points appear on both sides of Equation (15.66) and two more appear only on one side, so we obtain the following five equalities.

$$
\begin{aligned}
B_0(1) &= 0 \\
B_1(1) - B_0(0) &= 0 \\
B_2(1) - B_1(0) &= 0 \\
B_3(1) - B_2(0) &= 0 \\
-B_3(0) &= 0
\end{aligned}
\tag{15.67}
$$

Applying the same procedure to the first and second derivatives, we also have

$$
\begin{aligned}
B_0'(1) &= 0 \\
B_1'(1) - B_0'(0) &= 0 \\
B_2'(1) - B_1'(0) &= 0 \\
B_3'(1) - B_2'(0) &= 0 \\
-B_3'(0) &= 0
\end{aligned}
\tag{15.68}
$$

and

$$B_0''(1) \qquad\quad = 0$$
$$B_1''(1) \; -B_0''(0) = 0$$
$$B_2''(1) \; -B_1''(0) = 0$$
$$B_3''(1) \; -B_2''(0) = 0$$
$$\qquad\qquad -B_3''(0) = 0. \qquad\qquad (15.69)$$

This gives us 15 equations, but the coefficients of $B_0(t)$, $B_1(t)$, $B_2(t)$, and $B_3(t)$ amount to 16 unknowns. We remedy this deficiency by forcing the blending functions to sum to unity at $t = 0$, giving us the final equation

$$B_0(0) + B_1(0) + B_2(0) + B_3(0) = 1. \qquad\qquad (15.70)$$

By solving the linear system represented by Equations (15.67), (15.68), (15.69), and (15.70), we obtain the following blending functions for the uniform B-spline.

$$B_0(t) = \frac{(1-t)^3}{6}$$

$$B_1(t) = \frac{4 - 6t^2 + 3t^3}{6}$$

$$B_2(t) = \frac{1 + 3t + 3t^2 - 3t^3}{6}$$

$$B_3(t) = \frac{t^3}{6} \qquad\qquad (15.71)$$

The basis matrix $\mathbf{M}_{BS}$ is thus

$$\mathbf{M}_{BS} = \frac{1}{6}\begin{bmatrix} 1 & -3 & 3 & 1 \\ 4 & 0 & -6 & 3 \\ 1 & 3 & 3 & -3 \\ 0 & 0 & 0 & 1 \end{bmatrix}. \qquad\qquad (15.72)$$

The blending functions $B_0(t)$, $B_1(t)$, $B_2(t)$, and $B_3(t)$ are shown in Figure 15.11. A major difference between these blending functions and those for Hermite curves, Bézier curves, and Catmull-Rom splines is that more than one function is nonzero at both endpoints. The fact that the control points are not interpolated, but only approximated by the knots, is a consequence of this property of the blending functions.

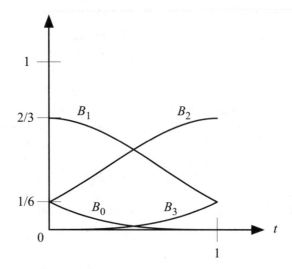

Figure 15.11 The blending functions for the uniform B-spline.

Control points may be replicated, but doing so incurs the cost of one degree of continuity each time the same control point appears consecutively along a B-spline curve. The benefit is that more control over where the curve goes is acquired. One location at which control point replication is particularly useful is at the endpoints. Consider the case in which the first control point is replicated three times so that $P_0 = P_1 = P_2$. The first component $Q_1(t)$ of the B-spline curve is then given by

$$Q_1(t) = B_0(t)P_0 + B_1(t)P_1 = B_2(t)P_2 + B_3(t)P_3$$
$$= [B_0(t) + B_1(t) + B_2(t)]P_0 + B_3(t)P_3. \qquad (15.73)$$

This is a linear interpolation between the two points P_0 and P_3. Plugging in the values $t = 0$ and $t = 1$, we see that $Q_1(0) = P_0$ and $Q_1(1) = \frac{5}{6}P_0 + \frac{1}{6}P_3$. The curve $Q_1(t)$ traces out the first sixth of the straight line running from P_0 to P_3. Similarly, replicating the last control point P_n of a B-spline curve three times results in the final component $Q_{n-2}(t)$ tracing out the last sixth of the straight line running from P_{n-3} to P_n. Figure 15.12 shows the same B-spline shown in Figure 15.10 with its first and last control points both replicated three times.

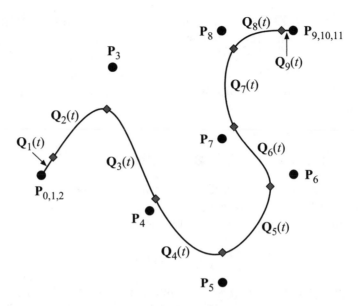

Figure 15.12 The same B-spline shown in Figure 15.10 with its first and last control points replicated three times each. The gray diamonds represent the knots. The components $\mathbf{Q}_1(t)$ and $\mathbf{Q}_9(t)$ are straight lines.

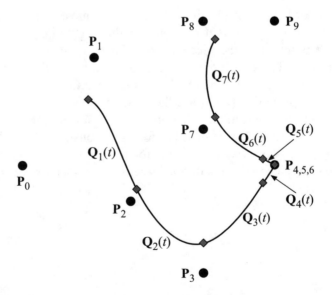

Figure 15.13 The same B-spline shown in Figure 15.10 with one of its interior control points replicated three times. The gray diamonds represent the knots.

Figure 15.13 shows the same B-spline curve again, but this time with one of its interior points replicated three times. The curve interpolates the replicated control point, but only exhibits C^0 continuity at that point. This is equivalent to two separate B-spline curves for which the last control point of the first curve is equal to the first control point of the second curve and each is replicated three times.

15.6.2 B-Spline Globalization

Each piece $\mathbf{Q}_i(t)$ of a uniform B-spline is defined over the range of parameter values $t \in [0,1)$. For a curve having $n+1$ control points, we can define each piece in terms of a global parameter u by assigning $t_i = i$ and writing

$$\tilde{\mathbf{Q}}_i(u) = \mathbf{Q}_i(u - t_i). \tag{15.74}$$

The pieces $\tilde{\mathbf{Q}}_i(u)$ compose the same curve using the range of parameter values $u \in [1, n-1)$. We can write Equation (15.74) in terms of the B-spline basis functions as follows.

$$\tilde{\mathbf{Q}}_i(u) = \sum_{k=0}^{3} B_k(u - t_i) \mathbf{P}_{i+k-1} \tag{15.75}$$

Any one of the control points $\mathbf{P}_i$ affects at most four pieces of the curve, and fewer than four only if it occurs near the beginning or end of the sequence of control points. For the piece $\tilde{\mathbf{Q}}_i(u)$, the point $\mathbf{P}_i$ is weighted by the blending function B_1. The same point is weighted by the blending function B_0 for the piece $\tilde{\mathbf{Q}}_{i+1}(u)$, the blending function B_2 for the piece $\tilde{\mathbf{Q}}_{i-1}(u)$, and the blending function B_3 for the piece $\tilde{\mathbf{Q}}_{i-2}(u)$. Since the point $\mathbf{P}_i$ does not contribute to any other piece of the curve, we can say that its weight is zero for any piece $\tilde{\mathbf{Q}}_j(u)$ where $j < i-2$ or $j > i+1$. It is possible for us to construct a weighting function $N_i(u)$ that is always used as the weight for the point $\mathbf{P}_i$ for every piece of the curve. Since each piece $\tilde{\mathbf{Q}}_i(u)$ is defined over the parameter range $u \in [t_i, t_{i+1})$, we define $N_i(u)$ as

$$N_i(u) = \begin{cases} B_0(u - t_{i+1}), & \text{if } u \in [t_{i+1}, t_{i+2}); \\ B_1(u - t_i), & \text{if } u \in [t_i, t_{i+1}); \\ B_2(u - t_{i-1}), & \text{if } u \in [t_{i-1}, t_i); \\ B_3(u - t_{i-2}), & \text{if } u \in [t_{i-2}, t_{i-1}); \\ 0, & \text{otherwise.} \end{cases} \qquad (15.76)$$

This allows us to express the entire curve as the following weighted sum of *all* of the $n+1$ control points.

$$\tilde{\mathbf{Q}}(u) = \sum_{k=0}^{n} N_k(u) \mathbf{P}_k \qquad (15.77)$$

Of course, any single piece $\tilde{\mathbf{Q}}_i(u)$ is still only affected by four control points, so we can write

$$\tilde{\mathbf{Q}}_i(u) = \sum_{k=0}^{3} N_{i+k-1} \mathbf{P}_{i+k-1}. \qquad (15.78)$$

The shape of the blending function $N_i(u)$ is shown in Figure 15.14. Since it is composed of shifted versions of the four blending functions shown in Figure 15.11, the function $N_i(u)$ possesses C^2 continuity.

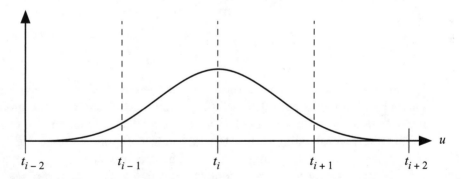

Figure 15.14 The global blending function $N_i(u)$ given by Equation (15.76). Each of the four components is a shifted version of one of the uniform B-spline blending functions shown in Figure 15.11.

The values t_i are called *knot values* since they correspond to the global parameter value at each of the curve's knots. The collection of knot values $\{t_0, t_1, \ldots, t_n\}$ is called the *knot vector*. The uniformity of the B-spline corresponds to the fact that the difference $t_{i+1} - t_i$ is the same for any choice of i. This limitation is removed for nonuniform B-splines—the only restriction is that the difference between consecutive knot values be nonnegative.

15.6.3 Nonuniform B-Splines

A *nonuniform B-spline* is a generalization of the uniform B-spline in which the knot values are not required to be equally spaced. As with uniform B-splines, a nonuniform B-spline defined by a set of $n+1$ control points $\{P_0, P_1, \ldots, P_n\}$ is composed of $n-2$ cubic curves $Q_i(u)$ where $1 \leq i \leq n-2$. The only restriction on the knot value t_i corresponding to the control point P_i is that it is not less than the preceding knot value t_{i-1}. Each piece $Q_i(u)$ of the spline is expressed as the weighted sum

$$Q_i(u) = \sum_{k=0}^{3} N_{i+k-1,3}(u) P_{i+k-1}, \qquad (15.79)$$

where the per-control-point blending functions $N_{i,3}(u)$ are given by the following recursive formula, known as the Cox-de Boor algorithm.

$$N_{i,0}(u) = \begin{cases} 1, & \text{if } u \in [t_{i-2}, t_{i-1}) \\ 0, & \text{otherwise} \end{cases}$$

$$N_{i,k}(u) = (u - t_{i-2}) \frac{N_{i,k-1}(u)}{t_{i+k-2} - t_{i-2}} + (t_{i+k-1} - u) \frac{N_{i+1,k-1}(u)}{t_{i+k-1} - t_{i-1}} \qquad (15.80)$$

It is allowable for consecutive knot values to be equal, so the convention that division by zero yields zero is used in Equation (15.80). As with the global blending function $N_i(u)$ given by Equation (15.76), the function $N_{i,3}(u)$ used to weight the control point P_i has four separate components covering the ranges $[t_{i-2}, t_{i-1})$, $[t_{i-1}, t_i)$, $[t_i, t_{i+1})$, and $[t_{i+1}, t_{i+2})$. These components can be precomputed for a particular knot vector and control point index. Outside the range (t_{i-2}, t_{i+2}), the function $N_{i,3}(u)$ is zero. The blending functions $N_{i,3}(u)$ are always nonnegative and always sum to unity, so a nonuniform B-spline is contained within the convex hull determined by its control points.

Maintaining consistency with globally-parameterized uniform B-splines, a piece $Q_i(u)$ of a nonuniform B-spline depends only on the control points P_{i-1}

through $\mathbf{P}_{i+2}$ and is defined only over the range $u \in [t_i, t_{i+1})$. However, the four blending functions corresponding to $\mathbf{Q}_i(u)$ collectively require the eight knot values t_{i-3} through t_{i+4}. The first piece $\mathbf{Q}_1(u)$ depends on the knot values t_{-2} through t_5, and the last piece $\mathbf{Q}_{n-2}(u)$ depends on the knot values t_{n-5} through t_{n+2}. Thus, a nonuniform B-spline having $n+1$ control points requires $n+5$ knot values. We begin the knot vector at the index -2 so that the piece $\mathbf{Q}_i(u)$ conveniently begins at t_i.

Although it is by no means a necessity, the first four and last four knot values are usually set to t_1 and t_{n-1}, respectively. This guarantees the nice property that the first and last knots are coincident with the first and last control points, as shown in Figure 15.15. We recover the uniform B-spline by assigning $t_i = i$ for every i. We may modify this so that the spline interpolates its first and last control points by setting

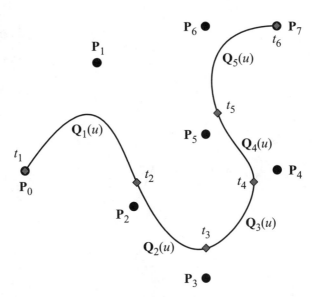

Figure 15.15 A nonuniform B-spline possessing the 8 control points $\mathbf{P}_0$ through $\mathbf{P}_7$ and using the knot vector $\{0,0,0,0,1,2,3,4,5,5,5,5\}$ representing knot values t_{-2} through t_9. These are the same control points used by the uniform B-spline shown in Figure 15.10, but the curve has now been modified so that it interpolates its first and last control points. The gray diamonds represent the knots corresponding to the knot values shown next to them.

$$t_i = \begin{cases} 1, & \text{if } -2 \le i \le 1; \\ i, & \text{if } 2 \le i \le n-2; \\ n-1, & \text{if } n-1 \le i \le n+2. \end{cases} \qquad (15.81)$$

A knot value that is repeated m times is said to have *multiplicity m*. As the difference between knot values t_i and t_{i+1} decreases, the length of the piece $\mathbf{Q}_i(u)$ becomes shorter. When $t_i = t_{i+1}$, the piece $\mathbf{Q}_i(u)$ is reduced to a single point. Every time a knot value is repeated, a degree of continuity is lost at the corresponding knot. As shown in Figure 15.16, if the knot value t_i has multiplicity 3 (so that $t_i = t_{i+1} = t_{i+2}$), then the control point $\mathbf{P}_{i+1}$ is interpolated by the curve, but there is only C^0 continuity at that point. If the multiplicity is increased to 4, as shown in Figure 15.17, then the curve actually breaks at $\mathbf{P}_{i+1}$.

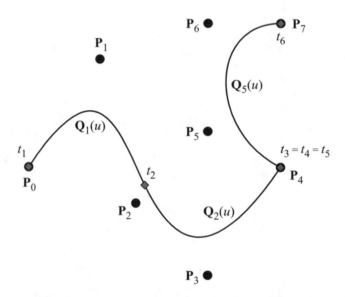

Figure 15.16 A nonuniform B-spline having an interior knot value of multiplicity 3. The knot vector is $\{0,0,0,0,1,2,2,2,3,3,3,3\}$. The curve interpolates the control point $\mathbf{P}_4$, but only with C^0 continuity.

For the knot vector $\{0,0,0,0,1,1,1,1\}$, the blending functions $N_{i,3}$ given by the Cox-de Boor algorithm are equivalent to the Bernstein polynomials $B_{i,3}$. Thus, a curve having this knot vector is a Bézier curve. The two separate components of the curve shown in Figure 15.17 are both Bézier curves since the multiplicities of the knot values at their endpoints are 4.

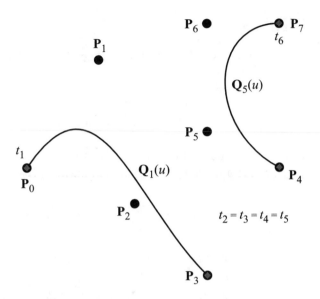

Figure 15.17 A nonuniform B-spline having an interior knot value of multiplicity 4. The knot vector is $\{0,0,0,0,1,1,1,1,2,2,2,2\}$. There is a discontinuity at $u = t_2$.

A major advantage that nonuniform B-splines have over uniform B-splines is that it is possible to insert a control point corresponding to a new knot value without changing the shape of the curve. Suppose that we have a knot vector $\{t_{-2},\ldots,t_{n+2}\}$ and control points P_0 through P_n. To add a new knot value $t' \in (t_j, t_{j+1}]$, we must find a new set of control points P_0' through P_{n+1}' such that the curves determined by the original control points and the new control points are coincident. The new control points are given by the following formulas, a process known as Böhm subdivision.

$$
P_i' = \begin{cases} P_i, & \text{if } i \leq j-1 \\[2mm] \left(1 - \dfrac{t' - t_{i-2}}{t_{i+1} - t_{i-2}}\right)P_{i-1} + \dfrac{t' - t_{i-2}}{t_{i+1} - t_{i-2}}P_i, & \text{if } j \leq i \leq j+2 \\[2mm] P_{i-1}, & \text{if } i \geq j+3 \end{cases} \qquad (15.82)
$$

(We again use the convention that division by zero yields zero.) This process replaces two original control points with three new control points and leaves the rest alone. Böhm subdivision can be used to increment the multiplicity of a knot by setting $t' = t_{j+1}$.

15.6.4 NURBS

Nonuniform B-splines can be made even more flexible by extending them to homogeneous coordinates. A weight w_i is assigned to each control point $\mathbf{P}_i$, and we express each control point as

$$\mathbf{P}_i = \langle w_i x_i, w_i y_i, w_i z_i, w_i \rangle. \tag{15.83}$$

As usual, the control point's position in 3D space is obtained by dividing by the w-coordinate. Since a piece $\mathbf{Q}_i(u)$ of the nonuniform B-spline is expressed as

$$\mathbf{Q}_i(u) = \sum_{k=0}^{3} N_{i+k-1,3}(u)\mathbf{P}_{i+k-1}, \tag{15.84}$$

the w-coordinate at some point along the curve is given by

$$[\mathbf{Q}_i(u)]_w = \sum_{k=0}^{3} N_{i+k-1,3}(u)w_{i+k-1}. \tag{15.85}$$

The 3D position $\tilde{\mathbf{Q}}_i(u)$ at the parameter value u is therefore

$$\tilde{\mathbf{Q}}_i(u) = \frac{\displaystyle\sum_{k=0}^{3} N_{i+k-1,3}(u)w_{i+k-1}\langle x_{i+k-1}, y_{i+k-1}, z_{i+k-1}\rangle}{\displaystyle\sum_{k=0}^{3} N_{i+k-1,3}(u)w_{i+k-1}}. \tag{15.86}$$

This can also we written as

$$\tilde{\mathbf{Q}}_i(u) = \sum_{k=0}^{3} R_{i+k-1}(u)\langle x_{i+k-1}, y_{i+k-1}, z_{i+k-1}\rangle, \tag{15.87}$$

where

$$R_{i+k-1}(u) = \frac{N_{i+k-1,3}(u)w_{i+k-1}}{\displaystyle\sum_{l=0}^{3} N_{i+l-1,3}(u)w_{i+l-1}}. \tag{15.88}$$

Since points on the curve are expressed as a ratio of two polynomials, these curves are called nonuniform rational B-splines, or *NURBS*.

The weights affect how strongly the associated control points influence the shape of the curve. As shown in Figure 15.18, a larger weight w_i causes the curve to be pulled toward the control point $\mathbf{P}_i$, and a smaller weight causes the curve to move away from control point. Like the control points, the weights only affect at most four pieces of the entire curve, so the influence of a single weight is isolated to a local portion of the entire curve.

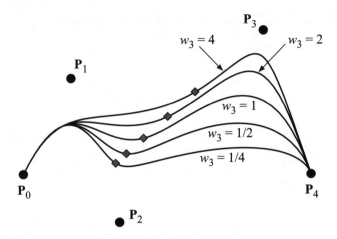

Figure 15.18 A nonuniform rational B-spline. The different curves show what happens as the weight corresponding to the control point $\mathbf{P}_3$ changes.

All of the curves described in this chapter are invariant with respect to any translation, rotation, or scaling transformation. That is, transforming the geometrical constraints (e.g., the control points) and generating the curve produces the same results as generating the curve using the untransformed geometrical constraints and then transforming the result. NURBS are also invariant with respect to a homogeneous projection transformation. The curve generated by the homogeneous control points after projection is the same as the projection of the curve generated using the unprojected control points. This property can be gained by a nonuniform B-spline by promoting it to a NURBS curve in which every weight has been assigned a value of 1.

NURBS have been widely adopted by computer modeling systems because of their generality. NURBS can represent any of the other types of curves discussed in this chapter, and unlike nonrational curves, can represent conic sections exactly. The interested reader is referred to [ROGE90].

15.7 Bicubic Surfaces

Our knowledge of cubic curves can be readily extended to bicubic surfaces. Whereas a single component $\mathbf{Q}_i(t)$ of a cubic curve required four geometrical constraints $\mathbf{G}_i$ through $\mathbf{G}_{i+3}$, a single component $\mathbf{Q}_{ij}(s,t)$ of a bicubic surface, called a *patch*, requires 16 geometrical constraints $\mathbf{G}_{i,j}$ through $\mathbf{G}_{i+3,j+3}$. The general parametric representation of a surface patch is given by

$$\mathbf{Q}_{ij}(s,t) = \sum_{k=0}^{3}\sum_{l=0}^{3} B_k(s) B_l(t) \mathbf{G}_{i+k,j+l}, \qquad (15.89)$$

where the parameters s and t range from 0 to 1, and the functions B_0, B_1, B_2, and B_3 are the blending functions for the type of cubic curve on which the surface patch is based. Calling the basis matrix corresponding to the blending functions $\mathbf{M}$, we can write Equation (15.89) in the form

$$Q_{ij}^r(s,t) = \mathbf{S}^{\mathrm{T}}(s)\mathbf{M}^{\mathrm{T}} \begin{bmatrix} G_{i,j}^r & G_{i,j+1}^r & G_{i,j+2}^r & G_{i,j+3}^r \\ G_{i+1,j}^r & G_{i+1,j+1}^r & G_{i+1,j+2}^r & G_{i+1,j+3}^r \\ G_{i+2,j}^r & G_{i+2,j+1}^r & G_{i+2,j+2}^r & G_{i+2,j+3}^r \\ G_{i+3,j}^r & G_{i+3,j+1}^r & G_{i+3,j+2}^r & G_{i+3,j+3}^r \end{bmatrix} \mathbf{M}\mathbf{T}(t), \qquad (15.90)$$

where $\mathbf{S}(s) \equiv \langle 1,s,s^2,s^3 \rangle$, $\mathbf{T}(t) \equiv \langle 1,t,t^2,t^3 \rangle$, and the index r represents one of the x-, y-, or z-coordinates of $\mathbf{Q}_{ij}(s,t)$. The geometrical constraint matrix $\mathbf{G}$ for a bicubic surface patch is a $4 \times 4 \times 3$ array of coordinates.

A bicubic Bézier surface patch is defined by 16 control points. The surface passes through 12 of these points around the boundary of the patch, and the remaining four control points influence the shape of the interior of the patch. A simple example is shown in Figure 15.19. Two adjacent Bézier patches have C^0 continuity at the edge where they meet whenever they share the same four control points along that edge. They have G^1 continuity across the edge if the adjacent control points on either side of the edge are collinear with the control points on the edge, and C^1 is achieved if the distances to the control points on either side of the edge are equal, ensuring that the tangent vectors have equal magnitude. When four Bézier patches meet at a single point $\mathbf{P}$, C^1 continuity at that point requires that each pair of adjacent patches meet with C^1 continuity and that the eight nearest control points are coplanar with $\mathbf{P}$.

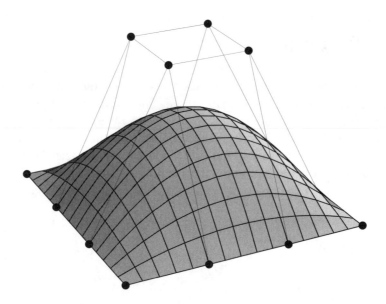

Figure 15.19 A Bézier surface patch is defined by 16 control points. The surface passes through the 12 control points lying on the boundary of the patch. The remaining four control points determine the shape of the patch's interior.

The normal vector at a point on a bicubic surface patch $\mathbf{Q}_{ij}(s,t)$ is obtained by finding two tangent vectors and then calculating their cross product. The tangent vectors are found by taking the derivatives of $\mathbf{Q}_{ij}(s,t)$ with respect to s and t. Using Equation (15.90), we can write the derivatives as

$$\frac{\partial}{\partial s}Q_{ij}^{r}(s,t)=\left[\frac{d}{ds}\mathbf{S}^{\mathrm{T}}(s)\right]\mathbf{M}^{\mathrm{T}}\mathbf{G}^{r}\mathbf{M}\mathbf{T}(t)$$

$$\frac{\partial}{\partial t}Q_{ij}^{r}(s,t)=\mathbf{S}^{\mathrm{T}}(s)\mathbf{M}^{\mathrm{T}}\mathbf{G}^{r}\mathbf{M}\left[\frac{d}{dt}\mathbf{T}(t)\right], \tag{15.91}$$

where r again represents one of the x-, y-, or z-coordinates. The normal vector $\mathbf{N}_{ij}(s,t)$ is then given by

$$\mathbf{N}_{ij}(s,t)=\frac{\partial}{\partial s}\mathbf{Q}_{ij}(s,t)\times\frac{\partial}{\partial t}\mathbf{Q}_{ij}(s,t). \tag{15.92}$$

15.8 Curvature and Torsion

In this section, we investigate quantities that characterize the amounts by which an arbitrary path through space curves and twists. In the process, we are able to construct an orthogonal coordinate system at each point along a curving path such that one axis is parallel to the tangent direction.

Let $\mathbf{P}(t)$ represent a twice-differentiable parametric curve. The *curvature* $\kappa(t)$ of $\mathbf{P}(t)$ is defined to be the magnitude of the rate at which the unit tangent direction $\hat{\mathbf{T}}(t)$ changes with respect to distance s traveled along the curve. That is,

$$\kappa(t) = \left\| \frac{d}{ds}\hat{\mathbf{T}}(t) \right\| = \frac{\left\| \dfrac{d}{dt}\hat{\mathbf{T}}(t) \right\|}{\dfrac{ds}{dt}}, \tag{15.93}$$

where ds is the differential length given by

$$ds = \left\| \frac{d}{dt}\mathbf{P}(t) \right\| dt, \tag{15.94}$$

and the unit tangent vector $\hat{\mathbf{T}}(t)$ can be expressed as

$$\hat{\mathbf{T}}(t) = \frac{\mathbf{T}(t)}{\|\mathbf{T}(t)\|} = \frac{\dfrac{d}{dt}\mathbf{P}(t)}{\left\| \dfrac{d}{dt}\mathbf{P}(t) \right\|} = \frac{\dfrac{d}{dt}\mathbf{P}(t)}{\dfrac{ds}{dt}}. \tag{15.95}$$

Intuitively, the curvature $\kappa(t)$ quantifies how much a curve bends at the point $\mathbf{P}(t)$. For a straight line, whose tangent vector always points in the same direction, the curvature is zero as would be expected.

Rearranging Equation (15.95), we can write the first derivative of $\mathbf{P}(t)$ as

$$\frac{d}{dt}\mathbf{P}(t) = \frac{ds}{dt}\hat{\mathbf{T}}(t). \tag{15.96}$$

Since the curvature depends on the derivative of the tangent direction, we would like to see how it relates to the second derivative of $\mathbf{P}(t)$. The derivative of the unit tangent vector $\hat{\mathbf{T}}(t)$ points in a direction $\mathbf{N}(t)$ that is orthogonal to the tangent vector itself (assuming that the derivative is not zero). This can be seen by first observing that $\hat{\mathbf{T}}(t) \cdot \hat{\mathbf{T}}(t) \equiv 1$ and then calculating

$$0 = \frac{d}{dt}\left(\hat{\mathbf{T}}(t) \cdot \hat{\mathbf{T}}(t)\right) = 2\hat{\mathbf{T}}(t) \cdot \frac{d}{dt}\hat{\mathbf{T}}(t). \tag{15.97}$$

The direction $\mathbf{N}(t)$ can be thought of as a normal direction to the curve $\mathbf{P}(t)$. It always points inward with respect to the direction in which the curve is bending.

Evaluating the derivative of $\hat{\mathbf{T}}(t)$, we have

$$\frac{d}{dt}\hat{\mathbf{T}}(t) = \frac{\dfrac{ds}{dt}\dfrac{d^2}{dt^2}\mathbf{P}(t) - \dfrac{d^2 s}{dt^2}\dfrac{d}{dt}\mathbf{P}(t)}{\left(\dfrac{ds}{dt}\right)^2}. \tag{15.98}$$

Using Equation (15.96) to replace the first derivative of $\mathbf{P}(t)$ gives us

$$\frac{d}{dt}\hat{\mathbf{T}}(t) = \frac{\dfrac{d^2}{dt^2}\mathbf{P}(t) - \dfrac{d^2 s}{dt^2}\hat{\mathbf{T}}(t)}{\dfrac{ds}{dt}}. \tag{15.99}$$

Solving for the second derivative of $\mathbf{P}(t)$ yields

$$\frac{d^2}{dt^2}\mathbf{P}(t) = \frac{d^2 s}{dt^2}\hat{\mathbf{T}}(t) + \frac{ds}{dt}\frac{d}{dt}\hat{\mathbf{T}}(t). \tag{15.100}$$

Since the derivative of $\hat{\mathbf{T}}(t)$ points in the direction $\mathbf{N}(t)$, we can write

$$\frac{d}{dt}\hat{\mathbf{T}}(t) = \left\|\frac{d}{dt}\hat{\mathbf{T}}(t)\right\|\hat{\mathbf{N}}(t), \tag{15.101}$$

where $\hat{\mathbf{N}}(t)$ has unit length. Using the definition of $\kappa(t)$ given by Equation (15.93), we rewrite Equation (15.100) as

$$\frac{d^2}{dt^2}\mathbf{P}(t) = \frac{d^2 s}{dt^2}\hat{\mathbf{T}}(t) + \kappa(t)\left(\frac{ds}{dt}\right)^2\hat{\mathbf{N}}(t). \tag{15.102}$$

If we take the cross product of the first and second derivatives of $\mathbf{P}(t)$ given by Equations (15.96) and (15.102), we obtain

$$\frac{d}{dt}\mathbf{P}(t)\times\frac{d^2}{dt^2}\mathbf{P}(t)=\frac{ds}{dt}\hat{\mathbf{T}}(t)\times\left[\frac{d^2s}{dt^2}\hat{\mathbf{T}}(t)+\kappa(t)\left(\frac{ds}{dt}\right)^2\hat{\mathbf{N}}(t)\right]$$

$$=\kappa(t)\left(\frac{ds}{dt}\right)^3\left[\hat{\mathbf{T}}(t)\times\hat{\mathbf{N}}(t)\right]. \tag{15.103}$$

Since $\hat{\mathbf{T}}(t)$ and $\hat{\mathbf{N}}(t)$ are both unit vectors, the magnitude of their cross product is unity. Thus, upon using Equation (15.94) to replace the quantity ds/dt, we arrive at the following expression for $\kappa(t)$.

$$\kappa(t)=\frac{\|\mathbf{P}'(t)\times\mathbf{P}''(t)\|}{\|\mathbf{P}'(t)\|^3} \tag{15.104}$$

Let us consider the curvature of a circle of radius ρ. Such a circle lying in the x-y plane can be expressed parametrically as

$$\mathbf{P}(t)=\langle\rho\cos t,\rho\sin t,0\rangle. \tag{15.105}$$

Applying Equation (15.104), we see that the curvature is

$$\kappa(t)=\frac{\langle-\rho\sin t,\rho\cos t,0\rangle\times\langle-\rho\cos t,-\rho\sin t,0\rangle}{\|\langle-\rho\sin t,\rho\cos t,0\rangle\|^3}=\frac{1}{\rho}, \tag{15.106}$$

or simply the reciprocal of the radius of the circle. For a general curve, we call the quantity $\rho(t)=1/\kappa(t)$ the *radius of curvature*. As shown in Figure 15.20, the radius of curvature at a point $\mathbf{P}(t)$ corresponds to the radius of a circle that is tangent to the curve at $\mathbf{P}(t)$ and lies in the plane determined by the directions $\hat{\mathbf{T}}(t)$ and $\hat{\mathbf{N}}(t)$. This plane is called the *osculating plane*, and the circle is called the *osculating circle*.

The second derivative of the position vector $\mathbf{P}(t)$ gives the acceleration of a particle following the path at time t. Examining Equation (15.102) more closely, we observe

$$\mathbf{a}(t)=\frac{d^2}{dt^2}\mathbf{P}(t)=\frac{d}{dt}v(t)\hat{\mathbf{T}}(t)+\frac{[v(t)]^2}{\rho(t)}\hat{\mathbf{N}}(t), \tag{15.107}$$

where $v(t)=ds/dt$ is the scalar speed at time t. The coefficients a_T and a_N defined by

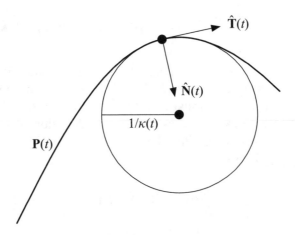

Figure 15.20 The osculating circle lies in the plane determined by the tangent direction $\hat{\mathbf{T}}(t)$ and the normal direction $\hat{\mathbf{N}}(t)$. The radius of the osculating circle is the reciprocal of the curvature $\kappa(t)$.

$$a_T = \frac{d}{dt}v(t)$$

$$a_N = \frac{[v(t)]^2}{\rho(t)} \tag{15.108}$$

are called the *tangential* and *centrifugal* components of the acceleration, respectively. The centrifugal component agrees with the acceleration corresponding to the centrifugal force given by Equation (12.8).

We can complete a three-dimensional orthonormal basis at a point $\mathbf{P}(t)$ by defining the unit *binormal* $\hat{\mathbf{B}}(t)$ as

$$\hat{\mathbf{B}}(t) = \hat{\mathbf{T}}(t) \times \hat{\mathbf{N}}(t). \tag{15.109}$$

The coordinate system having the axes $\hat{\mathbf{T}}(t)$, $\hat{\mathbf{N}}(t)$, and $\hat{\mathbf{B}}(t)$ is called the *Frenet frame*. The derivatives of the axes with respect to the distance s along a path can be written in terms of the axes themselves. For the tangent direction $\hat{\mathbf{T}}(t)$, we have

$$\frac{d}{ds}\hat{\mathbf{T}}(t) = \left\|\frac{d}{ds}\hat{\mathbf{T}}(t)\right\|\hat{\mathbf{N}}(t) = \kappa(t)\hat{\mathbf{N}}(t). \tag{15.110}$$

The derivative of the binormal can be written as

$$\frac{d}{ds}\hat{\mathbf{B}}(t) = \frac{d}{ds}\hat{\mathbf{T}}(t) \times \hat{\mathbf{N}}(t) + \hat{\mathbf{T}}(t) \times \frac{d}{ds}\hat{\mathbf{N}}(t). \tag{15.111}$$

Since the derivative of the tangent direction is parallel to the normal direction, the first cross product is zero. The derivative of the normal direction must be perpendicular to the normal direction itself (because it has constant length) and can therefore be expressed as a linear combination of the tangent and binormal directions. Thus, using the functions $\alpha(t)$ and $\tau(t)$, we simplify Equation (15.111) as follows.

$$\frac{d}{ds}\hat{\mathbf{B}}(t) = \hat{\mathbf{T}}(t) \times \left[\alpha(t)\hat{\mathbf{T}}(t) + \tau(t)\hat{\mathbf{B}}(t) \right]$$
$$= -\tau(t)\hat{\mathbf{N}}(t) \tag{15.112}$$

Finally, the derivative of the normal direction yields

$$\frac{d}{ds}\hat{\mathbf{N}}(t) = \frac{d}{ds}\left[\hat{\mathbf{B}}(t) \times \hat{\mathbf{T}}(t) \right]$$
$$= \frac{d}{ds}\hat{\mathbf{B}}(t) \times \hat{\mathbf{T}}(t) + \hat{\mathbf{B}}(t) \times \frac{d}{ds}\hat{\mathbf{T}}(t)$$
$$= -\tau(t)\hat{\mathbf{N}}(t) \times \hat{\mathbf{T}}(t) + \hat{\mathbf{B}}(t) \times \kappa(t)\hat{\mathbf{N}}(t)$$
$$= \tau(t)\hat{\mathbf{B}}(t) - \kappa(t)\hat{\mathbf{T}}(t). \tag{15.113}$$

(This shows that the value of $\alpha(t)$ in Equation (15.112) is $-\kappa(t)$.) Taken together, the three relations

$$\frac{d}{ds}\hat{\mathbf{T}}(t) = \kappa(t)\hat{\mathbf{N}}(t)$$

$$\frac{d}{ds}\hat{\mathbf{N}}(t) = \tau(t)\hat{\mathbf{B}}(t) - \kappa(t)\hat{\mathbf{T}}(t)$$

$$\frac{d}{ds}\hat{\mathbf{B}}(t) = -\tau(t)\hat{\mathbf{N}}(t) \tag{15.114}$$

are called the *Frenet formulas*.

The quantity $\tau(t)$ is called the *torsion* of the curve and pertains to the amount by which the Frenet frame twists about the tangent direction as it travels along a path. By taking the dot product of both sides of Equation (15.112) with $\hat{\mathbf{N}}(t)$, we obtain the following explicit formula for the torsion.

$$\tau(t) = -\hat{\mathbf{N}}(t) \cdot \frac{d}{ds}\hat{\mathbf{B}}(t) \tag{15.115}$$

For a planar curve, the vectors $\hat{\mathbf{T}}(t)$ and $\hat{\mathbf{N}}(t)$ always lie in the plane containing the curve, so $\hat{\mathbf{B}}(t)$ is constant except for discontinuities that occur when $\kappa(t) = 0$. Thus, the torsion of planar curves is zero everywhere.

Chapter 15 Summary

Cubic Curves

Several classes of cubic curves can be expressed in the form

$$\mathbf{Q}(t) = \mathbf{GMT}(t),$$

where $\mathbf{G}$ is the geometrical constraint matrix associated with the class of cubic curve, $\mathbf{M}$ is the constant basis matrix, and $\mathbf{T}(t) \equiv \langle 1, t, t^2, t^3 \rangle$. Table 15.1 summarizes the geometrical constraint matrices and basis matrices discussed in this chapter.

Nonuniform B-Splines

A nonuniform B-spline having the $n+1$ control points $\{\mathbf{P}_0, \mathbf{P}_1, \ldots, \mathbf{P}_n\}$ and the knot vector $\{t_{-2}, t_{-1}, t_0, \ldots, t_{n+2}\}$ is composed of $n-2$ cubic curves $\mathbf{Q}_i(u)$, where $1 \le i \le n-2$. Each piece $\mathbf{Q}_i(u)$ is defined as

$$\mathbf{Q}_i(u) = \sum_{k=0}^{3} N_{i+k-1,3}(u) \mathbf{P}_{i+k-1},$$

where the blending functions $N_{i,3}(u)$ are given by the Cox-de Boor algorithm:

$$N_{i,0}(u) = \begin{cases} 1, & \text{if } u \in [t_{i-2}, t_{i-1}) \\ 0, & \text{otherwise} \end{cases}$$

$$N_{i,k}(u) = (u - t_{i-2})\frac{N_{i,k-1}(u)}{t_{i+k-2} - t_{i-2}} + (t_{i+k-1} - u)\frac{N_{i+1,k-1}(u)}{t_{i+k-1} - t_{i-1}}.$$

NURBS

For a set of control points $\{\mathbf{P}_i = \langle w_i x_i, w_i y_i, w_i z_i, w_i \rangle\}$, a nonuniform rational B-spline is defined as

$$\tilde{Q}_i(u) = \sum_{k=0}^{3} R_{i+k-1}(u)\langle x_{i+k-1}, y_{i+k-1}, z_{i+k-1}\rangle,$$

where

$$R_{i+k-1}(u) = \frac{N_{i+k-1,3}(u)w_{i+k-1}}{\sum_{l=0}^{3} N_{i+l-1,3}(u)w_{i+l-1}}.$$

Table 15.1 Geometrical constraint matrices and basis matrices for various classes of parametric cubic curves.

Class	Geometrical Constraint Matrix G	Basis Matrix M
Hermite	$[\mathbf{P}_1 \quad \mathbf{P}_2 \quad \mathbf{T}_1 \quad \mathbf{T}_2]$	$\begin{bmatrix} 1 & 0 & -3 & 2 \\ 0 & 0 & 3 & -2 \\ 0 & 1 & -2 & 1 \\ 0 & 0 & -1 & 1 \end{bmatrix}$
Bézier	$[\mathbf{P}_0 \quad \mathbf{P}_1 \quad \mathbf{P}_2 \quad \mathbf{P}_3]$	$\begin{bmatrix} 1 & -3 & 3 & -1 \\ 0 & 3 & -6 & 3 \\ 0 & 0 & 3 & -3 \\ 0 & 0 & 0 & 1 \end{bmatrix}$
Catmull-Rom	$[\mathbf{P}_{i-1} \quad \mathbf{P}_i \quad \mathbf{P}_{i+1} \quad \mathbf{P}_{i+2}]$	$\frac{1}{2}\begin{bmatrix} 0 & -1 & 2 & -1 \\ 2 & 0 & -5 & 3 \\ 0 & 1 & 4 & -3 \\ 0 & 0 & -1 & 1 \end{bmatrix}$
Uniform B-spline	$[\mathbf{P}_{i-1} \quad \mathbf{P}_i \quad \mathbf{P}_{i+1} \quad \mathbf{P}_{i+2}]$	$\frac{1}{6}\begin{bmatrix} 1 & -3 & 3 & 1 \\ 4 & 0 & -6 & 3 \\ 1 & 3 & 3 & -3 \\ 0 & 0 & 0 & 1 \end{bmatrix}$

Bicubic Surfaces

A bicubic surface patch is defined as

$$Q_{ij}^r(s,t) = \mathbf{S}^{\mathrm{T}}(s)\mathbf{M}^{\mathrm{T}}\mathbf{G}^r\mathbf{M}\mathbf{T}(t),$$

where $\mathbf{S}(s) \equiv \langle 1,s,s^2,s^3 \rangle$, $\mathbf{T}(t) \equiv \langle 1,t,t^2,t^3 \rangle$, $\mathbf{M}$ is the 4×4 basis matrix corresponding to the class of cubic curve on which the patch is based, and r represents one of the x-, y-, or z-coordinates of $\mathbf{Q}_{ij}(s,t)$. $\mathbf{G}$ is the $4 \times 4 \times 3$ array of control point coordinates.

The normal vector $\mathbf{N}_{ij}(s,t)$ to the surface of a bicubic patch $\mathbf{Q}_{ij}(s,t)$ is given by

$$\mathbf{N}_{ij}(s,t) = \frac{\partial}{\partial s}\mathbf{Q}_{ij}(s,t) \times \frac{\partial}{\partial t}\mathbf{Q}_{ij}(s,t).$$

Curvature and Torsion

The curvature $\kappa(t)$ of a curve $\mathbf{P}(t)$ is given by

$$\kappa(t) = \frac{\|\mathbf{P}'(t) \times \mathbf{P}''(t)\|}{\|\mathbf{P}'(t)\|^3}.$$

The radius of curvature is $\rho(t) = 1/\kappa(t)$.

The torsion $\tau(t)$ is defined as

$$\tau(t) = -\hat{\mathbf{N}}(t) \cdot \frac{d}{ds}\hat{\mathbf{B}}(t),$$

where $\hat{\mathbf{N}}(t)$ is the unit normal vector given by the normalized derivative of the unit tangent direction $\hat{\mathbf{T}}(t)$, and $\hat{\mathbf{B}}(t) = \hat{\mathbf{T}}(t) \times \hat{\mathbf{N}}(t)$.

Exercises for Chapter 15

1. Suppose that $\mathbf{B}_2(t)$ is a quadratic Bézier curve having the three control points $\mathbf{P}_0$, $\mathbf{P}_1$, and $\mathbf{P}_2$. That is,

    $$\mathbf{B}_2(t) = (1-t)^2 \mathbf{P}_0 + 2t(1-t)\mathbf{P}_1 + t^2 \mathbf{P}_2.$$

    Determine the four control points $\mathbf{P}_0'$ through $\mathbf{P}_3'$ such that the cubic Bézier curve

    $$\mathbf{B}_3(t) = (1-t)^3 \mathbf{P}_0' + 3t(1-t)^2 \mathbf{P}_1' + 3t^2(1-t)\mathbf{P}_2' + t^3 \mathbf{P}_3'$$

    is exactly coincident with the quadratic Bézier curve $\mathbf{B}_2(t)$. (This process is called *degree elevation*.)

2. Suppose that the de Casteljau algorithm is used to split a Bézier curve having the control points $\mathbf{P}_0$, $\mathbf{P}_1$, $\mathbf{P}_2$, and $\mathbf{P}_3$ at the parameter value $t = \frac{1}{2}$. Find the matrix $\mathbf{M}_Q$ that transforms the control points of the original curve into the control points $\mathbf{Q}_0$, $\mathbf{Q}_1$, $\mathbf{Q}_2$, and $\mathbf{Q}_3$ for the curve coinciding with the interval $[0, \frac{1}{2}]$, and find the matrix $\mathbf{M}_R$ that transforms the control points of the original curve into the control points $\mathbf{R}_0$, $\mathbf{R}_1$, $\mathbf{R}_2$, and $\mathbf{R}_3$ for the curve coinciding with the interval $[\frac{1}{2},1]$. That is, find matrices $\mathbf{M}_Q$ and $\mathbf{M}_R$ such that

    $$[\mathbf{Q}_0 \quad \mathbf{Q}_1 \quad \mathbf{Q}_2 \quad \mathbf{Q}_3] = [\mathbf{P}_0 \quad \mathbf{P}_1 \quad \mathbf{P}_2 \quad \mathbf{P}_3]\mathbf{M}_Q$$

    and

    $$[\mathbf{R}_0 \quad \mathbf{R}_1 \quad \mathbf{R}_2 \quad \mathbf{R}_3] = [\mathbf{P}_0 \quad \mathbf{P}_1 \quad \mathbf{P}_2 \quad \mathbf{P}_3]\mathbf{M}_R.$$

3. A *Kochanek-Bartels spline* extends the formulation of the Catmull-Rom spline by allowing three parameters, tension τ_i, continuity γ_i, and bias β_i, to be specified at each control point $\mathbf{P}_i$. (Hence, Kochanek-Bartels splines are sometimes called *TCB splines*.) For a cubic curve interpolating the points $\mathbf{P}_i$ and $\mathbf{P}_{i+1}$, the tangent direction $\mathbf{T}_{i,1}$ corresponding to $\mathbf{P}_i$ and the tangent direction $\mathbf{T}_{i,2}$ corresponding to the point $\mathbf{P}_{i+1}$ are given by

$$T_{i,1} = \frac{(1-\tau_i)(1+\gamma_i)(1+\beta_i)}{2}(P_i - P_{i-1})$$

$$+ \frac{(1-\tau_i)(1-\gamma_i)(1-\beta_i)}{2}(P_{i+1} - P_i)$$

$$T_{i,2} = \frac{(1-\tau_{i+1})(1-\gamma_{i+1})(1+\beta_{i+1})}{2}(P_{i+1} - P_i)$$

$$+ \frac{(1-\tau_{i+1})(1+\gamma_{i+1})(1-\beta_{i+1})}{2}(P_{i+2} - P_{i+1}).$$

(Note that the tangent direction used at a point P_i is not necessarily the same for both of the curves for which P_i is an endpoint.)

(a) For what values of τ_i, γ_i, and β_i does the Kochanek-Bartels spline reduce to the Catmull-Rom spline?

(b) Under what conditions does the tangent direction $T_{i,2}$ for the curve interpolating P_i and P_{i+1} match the tangent direction $T_{i+1,1}$ for the curve interpolating P_{i+1} and P_{i+2}?

(c) Find the basis matrix M_{KB} corresponding to the curve interpolating P_i and P_{i+1} that describes the Kochanek-Bartels blending functions. Assume that the geometry matrix is $G_{KB} = [P_{i-1} \quad P_i \quad P_{i+1} \quad P_{i+2}]$. [*Hint.* Use a method similar to that which produces the Catmull-Rom basis matrix in Equation (15.46).]

4. Let $Q(u)$ be a nonuniform B-spline lying in the x-y plane having control points $P_0 = \langle 0,0 \rangle$, $P_1 = \langle 1,2 \rangle$, $P_2 = \langle 2,2 \rangle$, and $P_3 = \langle 3,0 \rangle$. Suppose the knot vector is $\{0,0,0,0,1,1,1,1\}$. Use Böhm subdivision to insert a new knot at $t' = \frac{1}{2}$ and determine the new control points P_0' through P_4'.

5. Calculate the curvature $\kappa(t)$ and the torsion $\tau(t)$ of the helix given by

$$P(t) = \langle r\cos t, r\sin t, ct \rangle.$$

6. Given a path $P(t)$ having C^3 continuity, show that

$$\frac{d}{ds}P(t) \cdot \left[\frac{d^2}{ds^2}P(t) \times \frac{d^3}{ds^3}P(t) \right] = [\kappa(t)]^2 \tau(t),$$

where $\kappa(t)$ is the curvature of the path and $\tau(t)$ is the torsion of the path.

Appendix A

Complex Numbers

A.1 Definition

The set of complex numbers $\mathbb{C}$ is a field containing the set of real numbers $\mathbb{R}$ and the 'imaginary' number i. The number i is defined to be the square root of -1:

$$i = \sqrt{-1}. \tag{A.1}$$

Thus, the square root of any negative number $-n$ can be written as

$$\sqrt{-n} = i\sqrt{n}. \tag{A.2}$$

A *complex number z* is one of the form

$$z = a + bi, \tag{A.3}$$

where a and b are real numbers. The number a is called the *real part* of z, denoted by $\mathrm{Re}(z)$, and the number b is called the *imaginary part* of z, denoted by $\mathrm{Im}(z)$. If $b = 0$, then the number z is purely real. If $a = 0$, then the number z is purely imaginary.

A.2 Addition and Multiplication

The sum of two complex numbers $a + bi$ and $c + di$ is given by

$$(a + bi) + (c + di) = (a + c) + (b + d)i. \tag{A.4}$$

The product of two complex numbers can be calculated by using the distributive property and the fact that $i^2 = -1$. The product of $a + bi$ and $c + di$ is given by

$$(a + bi)(c + di) = (ac - bd) + (ad + bc)i. \tag{A.5}$$

Addition and multiplication of complex numbers are both commutative and associative. This means that for any three complex numbers z_1, z_2, and z_3, the following properties hold.

(a) $z_1 + z_2 = z_2 + z_1$

(b) $(z_1 + z_2) + z_3 = z_1 + (z_2 + z_3)$

(c) $z_1 z_2 = z_2 z_1$

(d) $(z_1 z_2) z_3 = z_1 (z_2 z_3)$

A.3 Conjugates and Inverses

The *conjugate* of a complex number $z = a + bi$ is denoted by $\bar{z}$ and is defined as

$$\bar{z} = a - bi. \tag{A.6}$$

The conjugate of z has the same components as the number z itself, except that the imaginary part is negated. Taking the product of z and its conjugate $\bar{z}$ yields

$$z\bar{z} = (a + bi)(a - bi) = a^2 + b^2. \tag{A.7}$$

Thus, the product $z\bar{z}$ is a real number that reflects the magnitude of the number z. We use this to define the absolute value of a complex number, which is sometimes called the *modulus*. The modulus of a complex number $z = a + bi$ is denoted by $|z|$ and is defined as

$$|z| = \sqrt{z\overline{z}} = \sqrt{a^2 + b^2}. \tag{A.8}$$

If z is purely real, then this definition reduces to that of the ordinary absolute value for a real number.

Let $z_1 = a + bi$ and $z_2 = c + di$ be complex numbers such that $z_2 \neq 0$. We can determine the value of the quotient z_1/z_2 by multiplying the numerator and denominator by the conjugate of z_2. This gives us

$$\frac{z_1}{z_2} = \frac{a+bi}{c+di} = \frac{a+bi}{c+di} \cdot \frac{c-di}{c-di} = \frac{(a+bi)(c-di)}{c^2+d^2} = z_1 \frac{\overline{z_2}}{|z_2|^2}. \tag{A.9}$$

We now have a way to define the inverse of a nonzero complex number z, which we denote by z^{-1}, as follows.

$$z^{-1} = \frac{\overline{z}}{|z|^2} \tag{A.10}$$

As shown below, the product of a complex number z and its inverse is 1.

$$zz^{-1} = \frac{z\overline{z}}{|z|^2} = \frac{z\overline{z}}{z\overline{z}} = 1 \tag{A.11}$$

A.4 The Euler Formula

A fascinating property of complex numbers ties exponential and trigonometric functions together. For any real number x representing a radian angle of measure, we have the following identity.

$$e^{ix} = \cos x + i \sin x \tag{A.12}$$

This equation is known as the *Euler formula* and can be used to derive a multitude of trigonometric identities (see Appendix B, Section B.4). The formula can be verified by expanding the function e^{ix} into its power series and collecting real and imaginary terms, as shown in Appendix D, Section D.3.

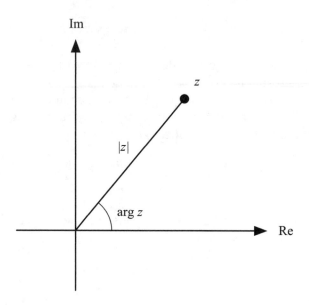

Figure A.1 A complex number z can be expressed in terms of its distance $|z|$ from the origin and the angle $\arg z$ that it forms with the real axis in the complex plane.

The *complex plane* is a 2D coordinate system having a real axis and an imaginary axis that are perpendicular to each other. As shown in Figure A.1, a complex number z can be uniquely identified by its absolute value and the angle that it forms with the real axis in the complex plane. This angle is called the *argument* of a complex number and is denoted by $\arg z$. One possible value of the argument of $z = a + bi$ is given by

$$\arg z = \begin{cases} \tan^{-1}\dfrac{b}{a}, & \text{if } a > 0; \\[2mm] \operatorname{sgn}(b)\dfrac{\pi}{2}, & \text{if } a = 0; \\[2mm] \tan^{-1}\dfrac{b}{a} + \operatorname{sgn}(b)\pi, & \text{if } a < 0. \end{cases} \qquad (A.13)$$

Any angle differing from the value given by Equation (A.13) by a multiple of 2π is also correct.

We can now express any complex number z as

$$z = re^{i\theta}, \qquad (A.14)$$

where $r = |z|$ and $\theta = \arg z$. Since the sine and cosine functions have a period of 2π, we know that

$$e^{i\theta} = e^{i(\theta + 2\pi k)} \tag{A.15}$$

for any integer k.

The Euler formula is useful for raising a complex number to a power. The quantity z^n can be written as

$$z^n = r^n e^{in\theta} = r^n \left(\cos n\theta + i \sin n\theta \right). \tag{A.16}$$

In particular, we can calculate the n-th roots of a complex number z by writing

$$z^{1/n} = \left(r e^{i(\theta + 2\pi k)} \right)^{1/n} = \sqrt[n]{r} \left(\cos \frac{\theta + 2\pi k}{n} + i \sin \frac{\theta + 2\pi k}{n} \right), \tag{A.17}$$

where k is an integer. Choosing $k = 0, 1, \ldots, n-1$ produces all n roots of the number z. A root ρ is called *primitive* if the smallest positive power m yielding $\rho^m = z$ is $m = n$.

The n-th roots of unity can be calculated using the formula

$$e^{2\pi k i / n} = \cos \frac{2\pi k}{n} + i \sin \frac{2\pi k}{n} \tag{A.18}$$

since $r = 1$ and $\theta = 0$ in this case. For example, the three cube roots of unity ρ_0, ρ_1, and ρ_2 are given by

$$\rho_0 = 1$$
$$\rho_1 = \cos \frac{2\pi}{3} + i \sin \frac{2\pi}{3} = -\frac{1}{2} + i \frac{\sqrt{3}}{2}$$
$$\rho_2 = \cos \frac{4\pi}{3} + i \sin \frac{4\pi}{3} = -\frac{1}{2} - i \frac{\sqrt{3}}{2}. \tag{A.19}$$

Note that ρ_1 and ρ_2 are both primitive roots of unity, and that $\rho_1^2 = \rho_2$ and $\rho_2^2 = \rho_1$. In general, a primitive n-th root of unity generates all the n-th roots of unity when raised to the powers $1, 2, \ldots, n$.

Appendix B

Trigonometry Reference

B.1 Function Definitions

For the angle α shown in Figure B.1, the trigonometric functions are defined as follows.

$$\sin \alpha = \frac{y}{r} \qquad \cos \alpha = \frac{x}{r}$$

$$\tan \alpha = \frac{y}{x} \qquad \cot \alpha = \frac{x}{y}$$

$$\sec \alpha = \frac{r}{x} \qquad \csc \alpha = \frac{r}{y} \qquad \text{(B.1)}$$

The relationships among the trigonometric functions listed below follow immediately from the definitions.

$$\tan \alpha = \frac{\sin \alpha}{\cos \alpha} \qquad \cot \alpha = \frac{1}{\tan \alpha}$$

$$\sec \alpha = \frac{1}{\cos \alpha} \qquad \csc \alpha = \frac{1}{\sin \alpha} \qquad \text{(B.2)}$$

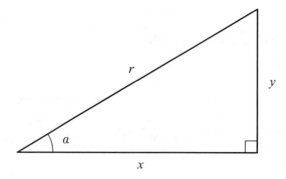

Figure B.1 Equation (B.1) defines the trigonometric functions in terms of the angle α shown in this triangle.

B.2 Symmetry and Phase Shifts

The cosine function is an *even* function, meaning that it is symmetric about the y-axis. The sine and tangent functions are *odd* functions, meaning that they are symmetric about the origin. We thus have the following identities.

$$\sin(-\alpha) = -\sin \alpha$$
$$\cos(-\alpha) = \cos \alpha$$
$$\tan(-\alpha) = -\tan \alpha \qquad \text{(B.3)}$$

The cosine function produces the same value at an angle α that the sine function does at the angle $\alpha + \pi/2$. That is, the graph of the cosine function is identical to the graph of the sine function shifted to the left by $\pi/2$ radians. We can thus formulate the following phase shift identities.

$$\sin(\alpha + \pi/2) = \cos\alpha$$
$$\cos(\alpha + \pi/2) = -\sin\alpha$$
$$\tan(\alpha + \pi/2) = -\cot\alpha \qquad \text{(B.4)}$$

Using the symmetry properties given by Equation (B.3), we can also state

$$\sin(\pi/2 - \alpha) = \cos\alpha$$
$$\cos(\pi/2 - \alpha) = \sin\alpha$$
$$\tan(\pi/2 - \alpha) = \cot\alpha. \qquad \text{(B.5)}$$

Shifting the sine or cosine function by a value of π simply negates the values of the function. This gives us

$$\sin(\alpha + \pi) = -\sin\alpha$$
$$\cos(\alpha + \pi) = -\cos\alpha$$
$$\tan(\alpha + \pi) = \tan\alpha. \qquad \text{(B.6)}$$

Again using the symmetry properties of the functions, we can also state

$$\sin(\pi - \alpha) = \sin\alpha$$
$$\cos(\pi - \alpha) = -\cos\alpha$$
$$\tan(\pi - \alpha) = -\tan\alpha. \qquad \text{(B.7)}$$

B.3 Pythagorean Identities

The following identities arise directly from the definitions given in Equation (B.1) and the fact that $x^2 + y^2 = r^2$.

$$\sin^2\alpha + \cos^2\alpha = 1$$
$$\tan^2\alpha + 1 = \sec^2\alpha$$
$$\cot^2\alpha + 1 = \csc^2\alpha \qquad \text{(B.8)}$$

If the angle α satisfies $0 \le \alpha \le \pi/2$, then we can write

$$\sin \alpha = \sqrt{1 - \cos^2 \alpha} = \frac{1}{\sqrt{\cot^2 \alpha + 1}}$$

$$\cos \alpha = \sqrt{1 - \sin^2 \alpha} = \frac{1}{\sqrt{\tan^2 \alpha + 1}}. \tag{B.9}$$

B.4 Exponential Identities

The Euler formula states

$$e^{\alpha i} = \cos \alpha + i \sin \alpha. \tag{B.10}$$

This relationship can be used to derive several trigonometric identities simply by applying the laws of exponents. The angle sum and difference identities are given by the equation

$$e^{(\alpha + \beta)i} = e^{\alpha i} e^{\beta i}. \tag{B.11}$$

Expanding this using Equation (B.10) yields

$$\cos(\alpha + \beta) + i \sin(\alpha + \beta) = (\cos \alpha + i \sin \alpha)(\cos \beta + i \sin \beta). \tag{B.12}$$

By equating the real and imaginary components of one side to those of the other, we can infer the following.

$$\sin(\alpha + \beta) = \sin \alpha \cos \beta + \cos \alpha \sin \beta$$
$$\cos(\alpha + \beta) = \cos \alpha \cos \beta - \sin \alpha \sin \beta \tag{B.13}$$

The angle difference identities are derived by negating β as follows.

$$\sin(\alpha - \beta) = \sin \alpha \cos \beta - \cos \alpha \sin \beta$$
$$\cos(\alpha - \beta) = \cos \alpha \cos \beta + \sin \alpha \sin \beta \tag{B.14}$$

When the angles α and β are the same, the angle sum identities become

$$\sin 2\alpha = 2 \sin \alpha \cos \alpha$$
$$\cos 2\alpha = \cos^2 \alpha - \sin^2 \alpha. \tag{B.15}$$

Using the fact that $\sin^2 \alpha + \cos^2 \alpha = 1$, we can rewrite $\cos 2\alpha$ in the following ways.

$$\cos 2\alpha = 1 - 2\sin^2 \alpha$$
$$\cos 2\alpha = 2\cos^2 \alpha - 1 \qquad\qquad\text{(B.16)}$$

Solving these for $\sin^2 \alpha$ and $\cos^2 \alpha$ gives us

$$\sin^2 \alpha = \frac{1 - \cos 2\alpha}{2}$$

$$\cos^2 \alpha = \frac{1 + \cos 2\alpha}{2}. \qquad\qquad\text{(B.17)}$$

B.5 Inverse Functions

The inverse $f^{-1}(x)$ of a trigonometric function $f(\alpha)$ returns the angle α for which $f(\alpha) = x$. The domains and ranges of the inverse trigonometric functions are listed in Table B.1.

Table B.1 Domains and ranges of inverse trigonometric functions.

Function	Domain	Range
$\sin^{-1} x$	$[-1,1]$	$[-\pi/2, \pi/2]$
$\cos^{-1} x$	$[-1,1]$	$[0, \pi]$
$\tan^{-1} x$	$\mathbb{R}$	$[-\pi/2, \pi/2]$

As shown in Figure B.2, the inverse sine of x is equal to the acute angle α in a triangle having an opposite side of length x and a hypotenuse of length 1. Since we know that the third side of the triangle has length $\sqrt{1 - x^2}$, we can derive the values of the other trigonometric functions at the angle $\sin^{-1} x$ as follows.

$$\cos\left(\sin^{-1} x\right) = \sqrt{1 - x^2}$$

$$\tan\left(\sin^{-1} x\right) = \frac{x}{\sqrt{1 - x^2}} \qquad\qquad\text{(B.18)}$$

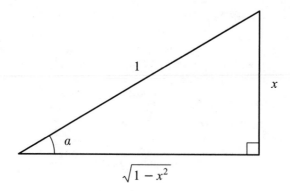

Figure B.2. A triangle representing the inverse sine function.

Applying the same technique for the inverse cosine and inverse tangent functions, we have the following.

$$\sin\left(\cos^{-1}x\right)=\sqrt{1-x^2}$$

$$\tan\left(\cos^{-1}x\right)=\frac{\sqrt{1-x^2}}{x}$$

$$\sin\left(\tan^{-1}x\right)=\frac{x}{\sqrt{x^2+1}}$$

$$\cos\left(\tan^{-1}x\right)=\frac{1}{\sqrt{x^2+1}} \tag{B.19}$$

B.6 Laws of Sines and Cosines

Consider the triangle shown in Figure B.3 and observe the following.

$$\sin\alpha=\frac{z}{c}$$

$$\sin\beta=\frac{y}{c} \tag{B.20}$$

Solving these for c allows us to form the equality

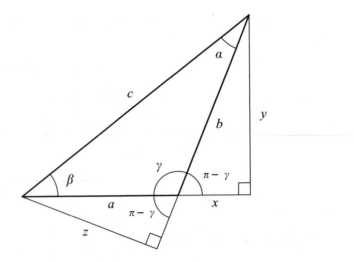

Figure B.3 For the triangle having side lengths a, b, and c, and angles α, β, and γ, the law of sines is given by Equation (B.24), and the law of cosines is given by Equation (B.29).

$$\frac{z}{\sin \alpha} = \frac{y}{\sin \beta}.$$

(B.21)

The following observations may also be made.

$$\sin(\pi - \gamma) = \frac{z}{a}$$

$$\sin(\pi - \gamma) = \frac{y}{b}$$

(B.22)

Thus, $z/a = y/b$. Multiplying the left side of Equation (B.21) by a/z and the right side of Equation (B.21) by b/y yields the *law of sines*:

$$\frac{a}{\sin \alpha} = \frac{b}{\sin \beta}.$$

(B.23)

The same relationship can be derived for the pair of angles α and γ or the pair of angles β and γ, so we can write

$$\frac{a}{\sin \alpha} = \frac{b}{\sin \beta} = \frac{c}{\sin \gamma}.$$

(B.24)

Now observe the following Pythagorean relationships in the triangle shown in Figure B.3.

$$x^2 + y^2 = b^2$$
$$(a+x)^2 + y^2 = c^2 \tag{B.25}$$

Solving the first equation for y^2 and substituting into the second equation gives us

$$c^2 = (a+x)^2 + b^2 - x^2$$
$$= a^2 + b^2 + 2ax. \tag{B.26}$$

The value of x can be replaced by observing

$$\cos(\pi - \gamma) = \frac{x}{b}. \tag{B.27}$$

Since $\cos(\pi - \gamma) = -\cos\gamma$, we have

$$x = -b\cos\gamma. \tag{B.28}$$

Plugging this into Equation (B.26) produces the *law of cosines*:

$$c^2 = a^2 + b^2 - 2ab\cos\gamma. \tag{B.29}$$

Of course, this reduces to the Pythagorean theorem when γ is a right angle since $\cos\pi/2 = 0$.

Appendix C

Coordinate Systems

C.1 Cartesian Coordinates

A Cartesian coordinate system is characterized by three mutually perpendicular axes, usually named x, y, and z. As shown in Figure C.1, a point $\mathbf{P}$ can be expressed as

$$\mathbf{P} = x\mathbf{i} + y\mathbf{j} + z\mathbf{k}, \tag{C.1}$$

where $\mathbf{i}$, $\mathbf{j}$, and $\mathbf{k}$ are unit vectors parallel to the three axes. The scalars x, y, and z are the Cartesian coordinates of the point $\mathbf{P}$.

The gradient operator ∇ has the following form in Cartesian coordinates.

$$\nabla \equiv \mathbf{i}\frac{\partial}{\partial x} + \mathbf{j}\frac{\partial}{\partial y} + \mathbf{k}\frac{\partial}{\partial z} \tag{C.2}$$

In other coordinate systems in which a point $\mathbf{P}$ has coordinates u, v, and w, where we can write $u = u(x,y,z)$, $v = v(x,y,z)$, and $w = w(x,y,z)$, the gradient operator follows the chain rule to become

$$\nabla' = \nabla u\frac{\partial}{\partial u} + \nabla v\frac{\partial}{\partial v} + \nabla w\frac{\partial}{\partial w}. \tag{C.3}$$

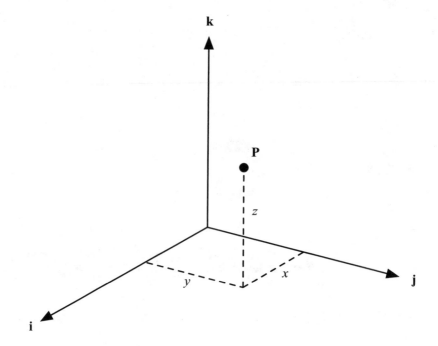

Figure C.1 Cartesian coordinates.

C.2 Cylindrical Coordinates

A point P is represented by the quantities r, θ, and z in cylindrical coordinates. As shown in Figure C.2, r is equal to the radial distance between P and the z-axis. The angle θ is called the *azimuthal angle*, or simply the *azimuth*, and is equal to the counterclockwise angle formed between the x-axis and the line connecting the projection of P onto the x-y plane to the origin. The z-coordinate has the same meaning as it does in Cartesian coordinates.

The x and y Cartesian coordinates corresponding to a point having cylindrical coordinates $\langle r, \theta, z \rangle$ are given by

$$x = r\cos\theta$$
$$y = r\sin\theta. \tag{C.4}$$

The cylindrical coordinates r and θ can be written in terms of the Cartesian coordinates x and y as follows.

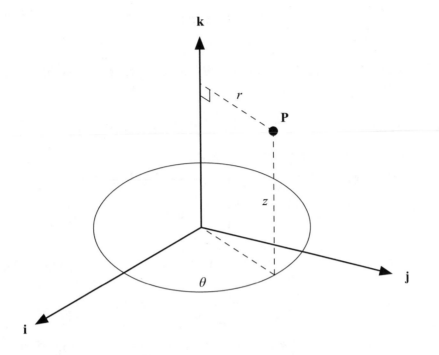

Figure C.2 Cylindrical coordinates.

$$r(x,y,z) = \sqrt{x^2 + y^2}$$

$$\theta(x,y,z) = \operatorname{sgn}(y)\cos^{-1}\frac{x}{\sqrt{x^2 + y^2}} \qquad \text{(C.5)}$$

The azimuthal angle θ can also be expressed as

$$\theta(x,y,z) = \begin{cases} \tan^{-1}\dfrac{y}{x}, & \text{if } x > 0; \\[2ex] \operatorname{sgn}(y)\dfrac{\pi}{2}, & \text{if } x = 0; \\[2ex] \tan^{-1}\dfrac{y}{x} + \operatorname{sgn}(y)\pi, & \text{if } x < 0. \end{cases} \qquad \text{(C.6)}$$

(In both Equations (C.5) and (C.6), the value of θ satisfies $-\pi \le \theta \le \pi$.)

A point **P** having cylindrical coordinates $\langle r, \theta, z \rangle$ is written in terms of the Cartesian basis vectors **i**, **j**, and **k** as follows.

$$\mathbf{P} = (r\cos\theta)\mathbf{i} + (r\sin\theta)\mathbf{j} + z\mathbf{k} \tag{C.7}$$

Taking partial derivatives with respect to the coordinates r, θ, and z, and normalizing gives us the unit vectors $\hat{\mathbf{r}}$, $\hat{\boldsymbol{\theta}}$, and $\hat{\mathbf{z}}$ at the point $\mathbf{P}$ in the cylindrical coordinate system:

$$\hat{\mathbf{r}} = \frac{\partial\mathbf{P}/\partial r}{\|\partial\mathbf{P}/\partial r\|} = (\cos\theta)\mathbf{i} + (\sin\theta)\mathbf{j}$$

$$\hat{\boldsymbol{\theta}} = \frac{\partial\mathbf{P}/\partial\theta}{\|\partial\mathbf{P}/\partial\theta\|} = (-\sin\theta)\mathbf{i} + (\cos\theta)\mathbf{j}$$

$$\hat{\mathbf{z}} = \frac{\partial\mathbf{P}/\partial z}{\|\partial\mathbf{P}/\partial z\|} = \mathbf{k}. \tag{C.8}$$

The gradient operator in cylindrical coordinates is given by

$$\nabla' = \nabla r(x,y,z)\frac{\partial}{\partial r} + \nabla\theta(x,y,z)\frac{\partial}{\partial\theta} + \hat{\mathbf{z}}\frac{\partial}{\partial z}. \tag{C.9}$$

Using the definitions given in Equation (C.5) for $r(x,y,z)$ and $\theta(x,y,z)$, we obtain the following for the gradients $\nabla r(x,y,z)$ and $\nabla\theta(x,y,z)$.

$$\nabla r(x,y,z) = \mathbf{i}\frac{\partial r}{\partial x} + \mathbf{j}\frac{\partial r}{\partial y} + \mathbf{k}\frac{\partial r}{\partial z}$$

$$= \mathbf{i}\frac{x}{\sqrt{x^2+y^2}} + \mathbf{j}\frac{y}{\sqrt{x^2+y^2}}$$

$$= \mathbf{i}\cos\theta + \mathbf{j}\sin\theta$$

$$= \hat{\mathbf{r}} \tag{C.10}$$

$$\nabla\theta(x,y,z) = \mathbf{i}\frac{\partial\theta}{\partial x} + \mathbf{j}\frac{\partial\theta}{\partial y} + \mathbf{k}\frac{\partial\theta}{\partial z}$$

$$= \mathbf{i}\frac{-y}{x^2+y^2} + \mathbf{j}\frac{x}{x^2+y^2}$$

$$= \mathbf{i}\left(-\frac{\sin\theta}{r}\right) + \mathbf{j}\left(\frac{\cos\theta}{r}\right)$$

$$= \frac{1}{r}\hat{\boldsymbol{\theta}} \tag{C.11}$$

Thus, the gradient operator can be written as

$$\nabla' = \hat{\mathbf{r}}\frac{\partial}{\partial r} + \frac{1}{r}\hat{\boldsymbol{\theta}}\frac{\partial}{\partial \theta} + \hat{\mathbf{z}}\frac{\partial}{\partial z}. \tag{C.12}$$

C.3 Spherical Coordinates

A point **P** is represented by the quantities r, θ, and φ in spherical coordinates. As shown in Figure C.3, r is equal to the distance from the origin to the point **P**. The angle θ is the azimuth representing the angle formed between the x-axis and the line connecting the projection of **P** onto the x-y plane to the origin (just as in cylindrical coordinates). The angle φ is called the *polar angle* and represents the angle formed between the z-axis and the line connecting **P** to the origin. The polar angle φ always satisfies $0 \leq \varphi \leq \pi$.

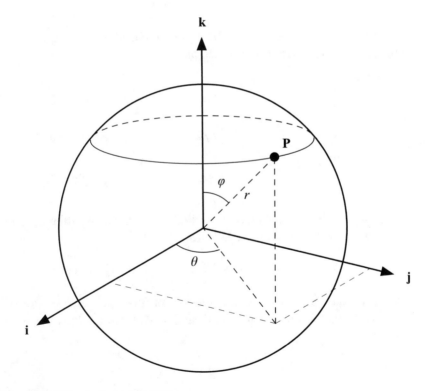

Figure C.3 Spherical coordinates.

The Cartesian coordinates $\langle x, y, z \rangle$ corresponding to a point having spherical coordinates $\langle r, \theta, \varphi \rangle$ are given by

$$x = r \sin \varphi \cos \theta$$
$$y = r \sin \varphi \sin \theta$$
$$z = r \cos \varphi. \tag{C.13}$$

The spherical coordinates $\langle r, \theta, \varphi \rangle$ can be written in terms of the Cartesian coordinates $\langle x, y, z \rangle$ as follows.

$$r(x, y, z) = \sqrt{x^2 + y^2 + z^2}$$

$$\theta(x, y, z) = \mathrm{sgn}(y) \cos^{-1} \frac{x}{\sqrt{x^2 + y^2}}$$

$$\varphi(x, y, z) = \cos^{-1} \frac{z}{\sqrt{x^2 + y^2 + z^2}} \tag{C.14}$$

The azimuthal angle θ can also be expressed as shown in Equation (C.6), and the polar angle φ can also be expressed as

$$\varphi(x, y, z) = \begin{cases} \tan^{-1} \dfrac{\sqrt{x^2 + y^2}}{z}, & \text{if } z > 0; \\[2mm] \pi/2, & \text{if } z = 0; \\[2mm] \tan^{-1} \dfrac{\sqrt{x^2 + y^2}}{z} + \pi, & \text{if } z < 0. \end{cases} \tag{C.15}$$

A point $\mathbf{P}$ having spherical coordinates $\langle r, \theta, \varphi \rangle$ is written in terms of the Cartesian basis vectors $\mathbf{i}$, $\mathbf{j}$, and $\mathbf{k}$ as follows.

$$\mathbf{P} = (r \sin \varphi \cos \theta) \mathbf{i} + (r \sin \varphi \sin \theta) \mathbf{j} + (r \cos \varphi) \mathbf{k} \tag{C.16}$$

Taking partial derivatives with respect to the coordinates r, θ, and φ, and normalizing gives us the unit vectors $\hat{\mathbf{r}}$, $\hat{\boldsymbol{\theta}}$, and $\hat{\boldsymbol{\varphi}}$ at the point $\mathbf{P}$ in the spherical coordinate system:

$$\hat{\mathbf{r}} = \frac{\partial \mathbf{P}/\partial r}{\|\partial \mathbf{P}/\partial r\|} = (\sin\varphi\cos\theta)\mathbf{i} + (\sin\varphi\sin\theta)\mathbf{j} + (\cos\varphi)\mathbf{k}$$

$$\hat{\boldsymbol{\theta}} = \frac{\partial \mathbf{P}/\partial \theta}{\|\partial \mathbf{P}/\partial \theta\|} = (-\sin\theta)\mathbf{i} + (\cos\theta)\mathbf{j}$$

$$\hat{\boldsymbol{\varphi}} = \frac{\partial \mathbf{P}/\partial \varphi}{\|\partial \mathbf{P}/\partial \varphi\|} = (\cos\varphi\cos\theta)\mathbf{i} + (\cos\varphi\sin\theta)\mathbf{j} + (-\sin\varphi)\mathbf{k}. \qquad \text{(C.17)}$$

The gradient operator in spherical coordinates is given by

$$\nabla' = \nabla r(x,y,z)\frac{\partial}{\partial r} + \nabla\theta(x,y,z)\frac{\partial}{\partial\theta} + \nabla\varphi(x,y,z)\frac{\partial}{\partial\varphi}. \qquad \text{(C.18)}$$

Using the definitions given in Equation (C.14) for $r(x,y,z)$, $\theta(x,y,z)$ and $\varphi(x,y,z)$, we obtain the following for the gradients $\nabla r(x,y,z)$, $\nabla\theta(x,y,z)$, and $\nabla\varphi(x,y,z)$.

$$\nabla r(x,y,z) = \mathbf{i}\frac{\partial r}{\partial x} + \mathbf{j}\frac{\partial r}{\partial y} + \mathbf{k}\frac{\partial r}{\partial z}$$

$$= \mathbf{i}\frac{x}{\sqrt{x^2+y^2+z^2}} + \mathbf{j}\frac{y}{\sqrt{x^2+y^2+z^2}} + \mathbf{k}\frac{z}{\sqrt{x^2+y^2+z^2}}$$

$$= \mathbf{i}\sin\varphi\cos\theta + \mathbf{j}\sin\varphi\sin\theta + \mathbf{k}\cos\varphi$$

$$= \hat{\mathbf{r}} \qquad \text{(C.19)}$$

$$\nabla\theta(x,y,z) = \mathbf{i}\frac{\partial\theta}{\partial x} + \mathbf{j}\frac{\partial\theta}{\partial y} + \mathbf{k}\frac{\partial\theta}{\partial z}$$

$$= \mathbf{i}\frac{-y}{x^2+y^2} + \mathbf{j}\frac{x}{x^2+y^2}$$

$$= \mathbf{i}\left(-\frac{\sin\theta}{r\sin\varphi}\right) + \mathbf{j}\left(\frac{\cos\theta}{r\sin\varphi}\right)$$

$$= \frac{1}{r\sin\varphi}\hat{\boldsymbol{\theta}} \qquad \text{(C.20)}$$

$$\nabla \varphi(x,y,z) = \mathbf{i}\frac{\partial \varphi}{\partial x} + \mathbf{j}\frac{\partial \varphi}{\partial y} + \mathbf{k}\frac{\partial \varphi}{\partial z}$$

$$= \mathbf{i}\frac{xz}{\left(x^2 + y^2 + z^2\right)\sqrt{x^2 + y^2}} + \mathbf{j}\frac{yz}{\left(x^2 + y^2 + z^2\right)\sqrt{x^2 + y^2}}$$

$$+ \mathbf{k}\frac{-\sqrt{x^2 + y^2}}{x^2 + y^2 + z^2}$$

$$= \mathbf{i}\frac{\cos\varphi\cos\theta}{r} + \mathbf{j}\frac{\cos\varphi\sin\theta}{r} + \mathbf{k}\frac{-\sin\varphi}{r}$$

$$= \frac{1}{r}\hat{\boldsymbol{\varphi}} \tag{C.21}$$

Thus, the gradient operator can be written as

$$\nabla' = \hat{\mathbf{r}}\frac{\partial}{\partial r} + \frac{1}{r\sin\varphi}\hat{\boldsymbol{\theta}}\frac{\partial}{\partial \theta} + \frac{1}{r}\hat{\boldsymbol{\varphi}}\frac{\partial}{\partial \varphi}. \tag{C.22}$$

C.4 Generalized Coordinates

Let S be a coordinate system in which points are described by three coordinates u_1, u_2, and u_3, and let $x(u_1,u_2,u_3)$, $y(u_1,u_2,u_3)$, and $z(u_1,u_2,u_3)$ be functions that transform coordinates in S to the corresponding Cartesian coordinates x, y, and z. Then a point $\mathbf{P}$ having coordinates u_1, u_2, and u_3 in S can be written as

$$\mathbf{P} = x(u_1,u_2,u_3)\mathbf{i} + y(u_1,u_2,u_3)\mathbf{j} + z(u_1,u_2,u_3)\mathbf{k}. \tag{C.23}$$

The contravariant basis vectors $\mathbf{e}_1$, $\mathbf{e}_2$, and $\mathbf{e}_3$ for the coordinate system S are given by the partial derivatives of $\mathbf{P}$ with respect to the coordinates u_1, u_2, and u_3 as follows.

$$\mathbf{e}_1 = \frac{\partial \mathbf{P}}{\partial u} = \frac{\partial}{\partial u}x(u_1,u_2,u_3)\mathbf{i} + \frac{\partial}{\partial u}y(u_1,u_2,u_3)\mathbf{j} + \frac{\partial}{\partial u}z(u_1,u_2,u_3)\mathbf{k}$$

$$\mathbf{e}_2 = \frac{\partial \mathbf{P}}{\partial v} = \frac{\partial}{\partial v}x(u_1,u_2,u_3)\mathbf{i} + \frac{\partial}{\partial v}y(u_1,u_2,u_3)\mathbf{j} + \frac{\partial}{\partial v}z(u_1,u_2,u_3)\mathbf{k}$$

$$\mathbf{e}_3 = \frac{\partial \mathbf{P}}{\partial w} = \frac{\partial}{\partial w}x(u_1,u_2,u_3)\mathbf{i} + \frac{\partial}{\partial w}y(u_1,u_2,u_3)\mathbf{j} + \frac{\partial}{\partial w}z(u_1,u_2,u_3)\mathbf{k} \tag{C.24}$$

The scalar quantities g_{ij} defined by

$$g_{ij} \equiv \mathbf{e}_i \cdot \mathbf{e}_j \qquad\qquad (C.25)$$

constitute the nine components of the *metric tensor*, at most six of which are distinct since $g_{ij} = g_{ji}$. The metric tensors corresponding to Cartesian coordinates, cylindrical coordinates, and spherical coordinates are displayed in Table C.1.

Table C.1 Metric tensors.

Coordinate System	Metric Tensor
Cartesian coordinates	$\left[g_{ij}\right] = \begin{bmatrix} 1 & 0 & 0 \\ 0 & 1 & 0 \\ 0 & 0 & 1 \end{bmatrix}$
Cylindrical coordinates	$\left[g_{ij}\right] = \begin{bmatrix} 1 & 0 & 0 \\ 0 & r^2 & 0 \\ 0 & 0 & 1 \end{bmatrix}$
Spherical coordinates	$\left[g_{ij}\right] = \begin{bmatrix} 1 & 0 & 0 \\ 0 & r^2 \sin^2 \varphi & 0 \\ 0 & 0 & r^2 \end{bmatrix}$

The metric tensor is used in the generalized formula for the dot product between two vectors in an arbitrary coordinate system. The dot product between two vectors $\mathbf{a}$ and $\mathbf{b}$ having coordinates in S is given by

$$\mathbf{a} \cdot \mathbf{b} = \sum_{i=1}^{3} \sum_{j=1}^{3} g_{ij} a_i b_j. \qquad\qquad (C.26)$$

The squared magnitude of a vector $\mathbf{v}$ is given by its dot product with itself, so we have

$$\|\mathbf{v}\| = \sqrt{\mathbf{v} \cdot \mathbf{v}} = \sqrt{\sum_{i=1}^{3} \sum_{j=1}^{3} g_{ij} v_i v_j}. \qquad\qquad (C.27)$$

This establishes a metric in the coordinate system S and reveals the source of the metric tensor's name. If the vector $\mathbf{v}$ represents the coordinate difference between two points, then the metric tensor is used in Equation (C.27) to obtain a (not generally Euclidean) measure of distance between the two points.

To calculate the Euclidean distance between two points, we integrate differential distances along a straight-line path. Straight lines are not generally given by linear functions of the coordinates, so we consider an arbitrary parametric path $\mathbf{u}(t)$ in the coordinate system S. The length L of the path over the interval in which $t \in [a,b]$ is given by

$$L = \int_a^b \left\| \frac{d\mathbf{u}}{dt} \right\| dt = \int_a^b \left(\frac{d\mathbf{u}}{dt} \cdot \frac{d\mathbf{u}}{dt} \right)^{1/2} dt$$

$$= \int_a^b \left(\sum_{i=1}^{3} \sum_{j=1}^{3} g_{ij} \frac{du_i}{dt} \frac{du_j}{dt} \right)^{1/2} dt. \tag{C.28}$$

The quantity

$$ds^2 = \sum_{i=1}^{3} \sum_{j=1}^{3} g_{ij} \, du_i \, du_j \tag{C.29}$$

is called the *line element* and characterizes the differential unit of length in the coordinate system S. The line element is a generalization of the Pythagorean theorem, of which the familiar form $ds^2 = \sum_{i=1}^{3} dx_i^2$ of Equation (C.29) in Cartesian coordinates is a special case.

In an orthogonal coordinate system (in which the basis vectors are always mutually perpendicular), we have

$$\mathbf{e}_i \cdot \mathbf{e}_j = g_{ij} \delta_{ij}, \tag{C.30}$$

where δ_{ij} is the Kronecker delta. In such a coordinate system, the metric tensor is diagonal, and we define the *scale factors* h_i as

$$h_i \equiv \sqrt{g_{ii}}. \tag{C.31}$$

The line element reduces to

$$ds^2 = \sum_{i=1}^{3} h_i^2 \, du_i^2. \tag{C.32}$$

The *volume element dV* in an orthogonal coordinate system is defined as

$$dV = \prod_{i=1}^{3} h_i \, du_i \tag{C.33}$$

and characterizes the differential unit of volume. The volume V of space bounded by the intervals $u_1 \in [a_1, b_1]$, $u_2 \in [a_2, b_2]$, and $u_3 \in [a_3, b_3]$ is given by

$$V = \int_{a_3}^{b_3} \int_{a_2}^{b_2} \int_{a_1}^{b_1} dV = \int_{a_3}^{b_3} \int_{a_2}^{b_2} \int_{a_1}^{b_1} h_1 h_2 h_3 \, du_1 \, du_2 \, du_3 . \tag{C.34}$$

The line elements and volume elements corresponding to Cartesian coordinates, cylindrical coordinates, and spherical coordinates are listed in Table C.2.

Table C.2 Line elements and volume elements.

Coordinate System	Line Element	Volume Element
Cartesian coordinates	$dx^2 + dy^2 + dz^2$	$dx\,dy\,dz$
Cylindrical coordinates	$dr^2 + r^2 d\theta^2 + dz^2$	$r\,dr\,d\theta\,dz$
Spherical coordinates	$dr^2 + r^2 \sin^2 \varphi \, d\theta^2 + r^2 d\varphi^2$	$r^2 \sin\varphi \, dr\,d\theta\,d\varphi$

Appendix D

Taylor Series

D.1 Derivation

Let $f(x)$ be a function whose first n derivatives exist on some interval I. Suppose that we wish to approximate $f(x)$ near the value $x = c$ in I using a degree n polynomial $p_n(x)$ so that

$$p_n(x) = a_0 + a_1(x - c) + a_2(x - c)^2 + \cdots + a_n(x - c)^n \approx f(x) \qquad \text{(D.1)}$$

whenever x is small. The derivatives of $p_n(x)$ evaluated at $x = c$ are the following.

$$p_n'(c) = a_1$$
$$p_n''(c) = 2a_2$$
$$\vdots$$
$$p_n^{(n)}(c) = n!a_n \qquad \text{(D.2)}$$

We can determine the coefficients a_i by requiring that

$$p_n(c) = f(c)$$
$$p_n'(c) = f'(c)$$
$$p_n''(c) = f''(c)$$
$$\vdots$$
$$p_n^{(n)}(c) = f^{(n)}(c). \tag{D.3}$$

The polynomial $p_n(x)$ is thus given by

$$p_n(x) = f(c) + f'(c)(x-c) + \frac{f''(c)}{2!}(x-c)^2 + \cdots + \frac{f^{(n)}(c)}{n!}(x-c)^n. \tag{D.4}$$

We define the error term $r_n(x)$ to be the difference between the approximation $p_n(x)$ and the actual function value $f(x)$ so that

$$f(x) = f(c) + f'(c)(x-c) + \frac{f''(c)}{2!}(x-c)^2 + \cdots$$
$$+ \frac{f^{(n)}(c)}{n!}(x-c)^n + r_n(x). \tag{D.5}$$

Let $g(z)$ be the function defined by

$$g(z) = f(x) - f(z) - f'(z)(x-z) - \frac{f''(z)}{2!}(x-z)^2 - \cdots$$
$$- \frac{f^{(n)}(z)}{n!}(x-z)^n - \frac{(x-z)^{n+1}}{(x-c)^{n+1}} r_n(x). \tag{D.6}$$

It is easily verified that $g(x) = 0$ and, using Equation (D.5), that $g(c) = 0$. The derivative of $g(z)$ simplifies significantly to the following.

$$g'(z) = -\frac{f^{(n+1)}(z)}{n!}(x-z)^n + (n+1)\frac{(x-z)^n}{(x-c)^{n+1}} r_n(x) \tag{D.7}$$

By Rolle's theorem, there exists a z_0 between x and c such that $g'(z_0) = 0$. Evaluating $g'(z_0)$ and solving for $r_n(x)$ yields

$$r_n(x) = \frac{f^{(n+1)}(z_0)}{(n+1)!}(x-c)^{n+1}. \tag{D.8}$$

If a function $f(x)$ is infinitely differentiable, then we may state

$$\lim_{n \to \infty} r_n(x) = 0. \tag{D.9}$$

We can therefore express any such function $f(x)$ as the infinite series

$$f(x) = f(c) + f'(c)(x-c) + \frac{f''(c)}{2!}(x-c)^2 + \frac{f'''(c)}{3!}(x-c)^3 + \cdots$$

$$= \sum_{k=0}^{\infty} \frac{f^{(k)}(c)}{k!}(x-c)^k. \tag{D.10}$$

This is known as the *Taylor series* expansion of the function $f(x)$.

D.2 Power Series

Equation (D.10) can be used to derive power series expansions for common functions by using $c = 0$. Because the exponential function e^x is equal to its own derivative and $e^0 = 1$, its power series is given by

$$e^x = 1 + x + \frac{x^2}{2!} + \frac{x^3}{3!} + \frac{x^4}{4!} + \cdots$$

$$= \sum_{k=0}^{\infty} \frac{x^k}{k!}. \tag{D.11}$$

For the sine function, we first observe the following.

$$f(x) = \sin x \qquad f(0) = 0$$

$$f'(x) = \cos x \qquad f'(0) = 1$$

$$f''(x) = -\sin x \qquad f''(0) = 0 \tag{D.12}$$

$$f'''(x) = -\cos x \qquad f'''(0) = -1$$

The power series for the sine function is thus given by

$$\sin x = x - \frac{x^3}{3!} + \frac{x^5}{5!} - \frac{x^7}{7!} + -\cdots$$

$$= \sum_{k=0}^{\infty} \frac{(-1)^k x^{2k+1}}{(2k+1)!}. \tag{D.13}$$

Similarly, the power series for the cosine function is given by

$$\cos x = 1 - \frac{x^2}{2!} + \frac{x^4}{4!} - \frac{x^6}{6!} + - \cdots$$

$$= \sum_{k=0}^{\infty} \frac{(-1)^k x^{2k}}{(2k)!}.$$

(D.14)

Another interesting function is

$$f(x) = \frac{1}{1+x}$$

(D.15)

because it is the derivative of $\ln(1+x)$ on the interval $(-1,\infty)$. The first few derivatives of $f(x)$ are the following.

$$f'(x) = \frac{-1}{(1+x)^2}$$

$$f''(x) = \frac{2}{(1+x)^3}$$

$$f'''(x) = \frac{-6}{(1+x)^4}$$

(D.16)

In general, the k-th derivative of $f(x)$ is given by

$$f^{(k)}(x) = \frac{(-1)^k k!}{(1+x)^{k+1}},$$

(D.17)

which when evaluated at $x=0$ produces $f^{(k)}(0) = (-1)^k k!$. Thus, the power series for the function $f(x)$ is given by

$$\frac{1}{1+x} = 1 - x + x^2 - x^3 + - \cdots$$

$$= \sum_{k=0}^{\infty} (-1)^k x^k.$$

(D.18)

This series converges on the interval $(-1,1)$. Integrating both sides, we arrive at the following power series for the natural logarithm of $1+x$ on the same interval.

$$\ln(1+x) = x - \frac{x^2}{2} + \frac{x^3}{3} - \frac{x^4}{4} + -\cdots$$

$$= \sum_{k=0}^{\infty} \frac{(-1)^k x^{k+1}}{k+1} \qquad \text{(D.19)}$$

D.3 The Euler Formula

The Euler formula expresses the following relationship between the exponential function and the sine and cosine functions.

$$e^{ix} = \cos x + i \sin x \qquad \text{(D.20)}$$

This can be verified by examining the power series of the function e^{ix}:

$$e^{ix} = \sum_{k=0}^{\infty} \frac{i^k x^k}{k!}. \qquad \text{(D.21)}$$

Using the fact that $i^2 = -1$, $i^3 = -i$, and $i^4 = 1$, we can collect the real and imaginary terms of this series as follows.

$$e^{ix} = \sum_{k=0}^{\infty} \frac{(-1)^k x^{2k}}{(2k)!} + i \sum_{k=0}^{\infty} \frac{(-1)^k x^{2k+1}}{(2k+1)!} \qquad \text{(D.22)}$$

Comparing this to Equations (D.13) and (D.14) confirms the result.

Appendix E

Answers to Exercises

Chapter 1

1. (a) -2 (b) $\langle 2,1,-6 \rangle$ (c) $\left\langle -\frac{4}{9}, -\frac{4}{9}, -\frac{2}{9} \right\rangle$

2. $\mathbf{e}_1' = \mathbf{e}_1$, $\mathbf{e}_2' = \mathbf{e}_2$, $\mathbf{e}_3' = \langle 1, -1, -2 \rangle$

3. 17.5

Chapter 2

1. (a) 22 (b) -1 (c) 1 (d) 0

2. (a) $\begin{bmatrix} \frac{1}{2} & 0 & 0 \\ 0 & \frac{1}{3} & 0 \\ 0 & 0 & \frac{1}{4} \end{bmatrix}$ (b) $\begin{bmatrix} 1 & 0 & 0 \\ \frac{3}{8} & \frac{1}{2} & -\frac{1}{8} \\ -\frac{3}{8} & 0 & \frac{1}{8} \end{bmatrix}$

$$\text{(c)} \begin{bmatrix} \cos\theta & 0 & \sin\theta \\ 0 & 1 & 0 \\ -\sin\theta & 0 & \cos\theta \end{bmatrix} \quad \text{(d)} \begin{bmatrix} 1 & 0 & 0 & -4 \\ 0 & 1 & 0 & -3 \\ 0 & 0 & 1 & -7 \\ 0 & 0 & 0 & 1 \end{bmatrix}$$

3. $\begin{bmatrix} x \\ y \\ z \end{bmatrix} = a \begin{bmatrix} 1 \\ -2 \\ 1 \end{bmatrix}$

4. $\lambda_1 = -1,\ \lambda_2 = 2,\ \lambda_3 = 5$

Chapter 3

1. $\mathbf{R}_x = \begin{bmatrix} 1 & 0 & 0 \\ 0 & \frac{\sqrt{3}}{2} & -\frac{1}{2} \\ 0 & \frac{1}{2} & \frac{\sqrt{3}}{2} \end{bmatrix},\ \mathbf{R}_y = \begin{bmatrix} \frac{\sqrt{3}}{2} & 0 & \frac{1}{2} \\ 0 & 1 & 0 \\ -\frac{1}{2} & 0 & \frac{\sqrt{3}}{2} \end{bmatrix},\ \mathbf{R}_z = \begin{bmatrix} \frac{\sqrt{3}}{2} & -\frac{1}{2} & 0 \\ \frac{1}{2} & \frac{\sqrt{3}}{2} & 0 \\ 0 & 0 & 1 \end{bmatrix}$

2. $\mathbf{q} = \pm\left(\frac{\sqrt{3}}{2} + \left\langle 0, \frac{3}{10}, \frac{2}{5} \right\rangle\right)$

Chapter 4

1. Any scalar multiple of $\langle 2,1,0,-4 \rangle$

2. $t = \dfrac{(\mathbf{Q}-\mathbf{S})\cdot\mathbf{V}}{V^2}$

4. 63.1 degrees

5. Left: $\left\langle \frac{\sqrt{2}}{2}, 0, -\frac{\sqrt{2}}{2}, 0 \right\rangle$; Right: $\left\langle -\frac{\sqrt{2}}{2}, 0, -\frac{\sqrt{2}}{2}, 0 \right\rangle$;

Bottom: $\langle 0,\frac{4}{5},-\frac{3}{5},0\rangle$; Top: $\langle 0,-\frac{4}{5},-\frac{3}{5},0\rangle$

6.
$$\begin{bmatrix} \dfrac{2n}{r-l} & 0 & \dfrac{r+l}{r-l} & 0 \\[2ex] 0 & \dfrac{2n}{t-b} & \dfrac{t+b}{t-b} & 0 \\[2ex] 0 & 0 & -\dfrac{f}{f-n} & -\dfrac{nf}{f-n} \\[2ex] 0 & 0 & -1 & 0 \end{bmatrix}$$

Chapter 5

2. 5.3271783

3. $x_{n+1} = \dfrac{1}{p}x_n\left(p+1-rx^p\right)$

7. $\left(V_x^2 + V_y^2 - \dfrac{r^2}{h^2}V_z^2\right)t^2 + 2\left[S_xV_x + S_yV_y + \dfrac{r}{h}V_z\left(r - \dfrac{r}{h}S_z\right)\right]t$
$\qquad + S_x^2 + S_y^2 + \dfrac{r}{h}S_z\left(2r - \dfrac{r}{h}S_z\right) - r^2 = 0$

6. $\langle -0.315, 0.946, -0.0788\rangle$

8. 49 degrees

Chapter 6

1. 3.16 meters

2. 4.35 meters

Chapter 7

1. If neither sphere encloses the other, $r = \frac{1}{2}(d + r_1 + r_2)$ and

   $$\mathbf{Q} = \mathbf{Q}_1 + \frac{r - r_1}{d}(\mathbf{Q}_2 - \mathbf{Q}_1), \text{ where } d = \|\mathbf{Q}_2 - \mathbf{Q}_1\|.$$

2. If $s < h$, $r = \dfrac{s^2 + h^2}{2h}$ and $\mathbf{Q} = \langle 0, 0, h - r \rangle$.

   If $s \geq h$, $r = s$ and $\mathbf{Q} = \langle 0, 0, 0 \rangle$.

3. $r_{\text{eff}} = \dfrac{5\sqrt{3}}{6} \approx 1.443$

Chapter 8

1. $t = 4\,\text{s}$

2. $\mathbf{N} = \dfrac{1}{r}\left(\mathbf{Q} - \dfrac{\mathbf{Q} \cdot \mathbf{A}}{A^2}\mathbf{A}\right)$

Chapter 9

1. 1.001

2. 0.003

Chapter 10

1. $(\varepsilon - 1)\left(\dfrac{\delta}{P_z(P_z + \delta)}\right)$

Chapter 11

1. $x(t) = Ae^{3t} + Bte^{3t} + t + 1$

2. $x(t) = 3\cos 4t + \sin 4t$

3. 30.2 m

4. 3.93 s

5. $\mathbf{v}_0 = \sqrt{\dfrac{g}{8h}} \langle P_x, 0, P_z + 4h \rangle$

6. $t \approx 6.1\,\mathrm{s}$

7. $a = \dfrac{g}{M+m} [M - m(\sin\theta + \mu_K \cos\theta)]$

Chapter 12

1. $F = m\omega\sqrt{\omega^2 r^2 + 4v^2}$

2. $\omega = \sqrt{\dfrac{\mu_S g}{r}}$

3. $\mathbf{C} = \langle 0, 0, \tfrac{5}{9}h \rangle$

4. $I = \tfrac{1}{2}m(R_1^2 + R_2^2)$

5. $\mathcal{I} = \begin{bmatrix} \tfrac{1}{12}m(b^2 + c^2) & 0 & 0 \\ 0 & \tfrac{1}{12}m(a^2 + c^2) & 0 \\ 0 & 0 & \tfrac{1}{12}m(a^2 + b^2) \end{bmatrix}$

6. $a = \dfrac{g}{1 + I/mR^2} = \dfrac{g}{1 + M/2m}$

7. $a = \dfrac{g\sin\theta}{1 + I/mR^2} = \dfrac{5}{7} g\sin\theta$

8. $z = \dfrac{d}{2\mu_S}$

Chapter 13

1. $1.43\ \mathrm{m/s}$

2. $0.0357\ \mathrm{s}$

Chapter 14

2. $\dfrac{\partial^2}{\partial x^2} f(x,y) + 2 f(x,y) \dfrac{\partial^2}{\partial x\, \partial y} f(x,y) + [f(x,y)]^2 \dfrac{\partial^2}{\partial y^2} f(x,y)$

   $+ \dfrac{\partial}{\partial x} f(x,y) \dfrac{\partial}{\partial y} f(x,y) + f(x,y) \left[\dfrac{\partial}{\partial y} f(x,y) \right]^2$

Chapter 15

1. $\mathbf{P}_0' = \mathbf{P}_0$, $\mathbf{P}_1' = \frac{1}{3}\mathbf{P}_0 + \frac{2}{3}\mathbf{P}_1$, $\mathbf{P}_2' = \frac{2}{3}\mathbf{P}_1 + \frac{1}{3}\mathbf{P}_2$, $\mathbf{P}_3' = \mathbf{P}_2$

2. $\mathbf{M}_Q = \dfrac{1}{8}\begin{bmatrix} 8 & 4 & 2 & 1 \\ 0 & 4 & 4 & 3 \\ 0 & 0 & 2 & 3 \\ 0 & 0 & 0 & 1 \end{bmatrix}$ and $\mathbf{M}_R = \dfrac{1}{8}\begin{bmatrix} 1 & 0 & 0 & 0 \\ 3 & 2 & 0 & 0 \\ 3 & 4 & 4 & 0 \\ 1 & 2 & 4 & 8 \end{bmatrix}$

3. (a) $\tau_i = \gamma_i = \beta_i = 0$

   (b) $\gamma_{i+1} = 0$

   (c) $\mathbf{M}_{KB} = \dfrac{1}{2}\begin{bmatrix} 0 & -\alpha_i^{00} & 2\alpha_i^{00} & -\alpha_i^{00} \\ 2 & \alpha_i^{00} - \alpha_i^{11} & 2(\alpha_i^{00} - \alpha_i^{11}) + \alpha_{i+1}^{10} - 6 & \alpha_i^{00} - \alpha_i^{11} - \alpha_{i+1}^{10} + 4 \\ 0 & \alpha_i^{11} & \alpha_{i+1}^{01} - \alpha_{i+1}^{10} - 2\alpha_i^{11} + 6 & \alpha_{i+1}^{10} - \alpha_{i+1}^{01} + \alpha_i^{11} - 4 \\ 0 & 0 & -\alpha_{i+1}^{01} & \alpha_{i+1}^{01} \end{bmatrix}$,

   where $\alpha_i^{jk} = (1 - \tau_i)\left[1 + (-1)^j \gamma_i\right]\left[1 + (-1)^k \beta_i\right]$.

4. $\mathbf{P}_0' = \langle 0,0 \rangle$, $\mathbf{P}_1' = \langle \tfrac{1}{2},1 \rangle$, $\mathbf{P}_2' = \langle \tfrac{3}{2},2 \rangle$, $\mathbf{P}_3' = \langle \tfrac{5}{2},1 \rangle$, $\mathbf{P}_4' = \langle 3,0 \rangle$

5. $\kappa(t) = \dfrac{r}{r^2 + c^2}$, $\tau(t) = \dfrac{c}{r^2 + c^2}$

Bibliography

BECK63   Petr Beckmann and André Spizzichino, *The Scattering of Electromagnetic Waves from Rough Surfaces*, Macmillan, 1963.

BLIN96   Jim Blinn, *Jim Blinn's Corner: A Trip Down the Graphics Pipeline*, Morgan-Kaufmann, 1996.

BLIN98   Jim Blinn, *Jim Blinn's Corner: Dirty Pixels*, Morgan-Kaufmann, 1998.

BOYC86   William E. Boyce and Richard C. DiPrima, *Elementary Differential Equations and Boundary Value Problems*, 4th ed., Wiley, 1986.

COOK82   Robert L. Cook and Kenneth E. Torrance, "A Reflectance Model for Computer Graphics," *ACM Transactions on Graphics*, Vol. 1, No. 1 (January 1982), pp. 7–24.

CROW77   Frank Crow, "Shadow Algorithms for Computer Graphics," *Proceedings of SIGGRAPH*, 1977, pp. 242–248.

DUMM91   David S. Dummit and Richard M. Foote, *Abstract Algebra*, Prentice-Hall, 1991.

EVER02   Cass Everitt and Mark J. Kilgard, "Practical and Robust Stenciled Shadow Volumes for Hardware-Accelerated Rendering," *Nvidia*, 2002.

FOLE90   James D. Foley, et al., *Computer Graphics: Principles and Practice*, 2nd ed., Addison-Wesley, 1990.

GOME00   Miguel Gomez, "Interactive Simulation of Water Surfaces," *Game Programming Gems*, Charles River Media, 2000.

GONZ92   Rafael C. Gonzalez and Richard E. Woods, *Digital Image Processing*, Addison-Wesley, 1992.

HE91   Xiao D. He, et al., "A Comprehensive Physical Model for Light Reflection," *SIGGRAPH '91, Computer Graphics*, Vol. 25, No. 4 (July 1991), pp. 175–186.

JOHN82   Lee W. Johnson and R. Dean Riess, *Numerical Analysis*, 2nd ed., Addison-Wesley, 1982.

JOHN98   Richard A. Johnson and Dean W. Wichern, *Applied Multivariate Statistical Analysis*, 4th ed., Prentice-Hall, 1998.

KAUT01a   Jan Kautz, et al., "Achieving Real-Time Realistic Reflections, Part 1," *Game Developer*, Vol. 8, No. 1 (January 2001), pp. 32–37.

KAUT01b   Jan Kautz, et al., "Achieving Real-Time Realistic Reflections, Part 2," *Game Developer*, Vol. 8, No. 2 (February 2001), pp. 38–44.

LAND99   Jeff Lander, "The Trials and Tribulations of Tribology," *Game Developer*, Vol. 6, No 8 (August 1999), pp. 19–24.

LENG02   Eric Lengyel, "Mechanics of Robust Stencil Shadows," *Gamasutra.com*, October 11, 2002.

LENG03   Eric Lengyel, *The OpenGL Extensions Guide*, Charles River Media, 2003.

MARI88   Jerry B. Marion and Stephen T. Thornton, *Classical Dynamics of Particles & Systems*, 3rd ed., Harcourt Brace Jovanovich, 1988.

MOLL99 Tomas Möller and Eric Haines, *Real-Time Rendering*, AK Peters, 1999.

ONEI91 Peter V. O'Neil, *Advanced Engineering Mathematics*, 3rd ed., PWS, 1991.

OPEN99a OpenGL Architecture Review Board, *OpenGL Programming Guide*, 3rd ed., Addison-Wesley, 1999.

OPEN99b OpenGL Architecture Review Board, *OpenGL Reference Manual*, 3rd ed., Addison-Wesley, 1999.

PRES88 William H. Press, et al., *Numerical Recipes in C*, Cambridge, 1988.

REIT93 John R. Reitz, Frederick J. Milford, and Robert W. Christy, *Foundations of Electromagnetic Theory*, 4th ed., Addison-Wesley, 1993.

ROGE90 David F. Rogers and J. Alan Adams, *Mathematical Elements for Computer Graphics*, 2nd ed., McGraw-Hill, 1990.

SCHL94 Christophe Schlick, "An Inexpensive BRDF Model for Physically-Based Rendering," *Proc. Eurographics '94, Computer Graphics Forum*, Vol. 13, No. 3, pp. 233–246.

SCHW90 Jochen Schwarze, "Cubic and Quartic Roots," *Graphics Gems*, Academic Press, 1990.

SEAR87 Francis W. Sears, Mark W. Zemansky, and Hugh D. Young, *University Physics*, 7th ed., Addison-Wesley, 1987.

SILL94 François X. Sillion and Claude Puech, *Radiosity and Global Illumination*, Morgan Kaufmann, 1994.

WARD92 Gregory J. Ward, "Measuring and Modeling Anisotropic Reflection," *SIGGRAPH '92, Computer Graphics*, Vol. 26, No. 2 (July 1992), pp. 265–272.

WU92 Xiaolin Wu, "A Linear-Time Simple Bounding Volume Algorithm," *Graphics Gems III*, Academic Press, 1992.

Index